QUALITATIVE RESEARCH METHODS FOR PSYCHOLOGISTS

Introduction through Empirical Studies

QUALITATIVE RESEARCH METHODS FOR PSYCHOLOGISTS

Introduction through Empirical Studies

CONSTANCE T. FISCHER

AMSTERDAM • BOSTON • HEIDELBERG • LONDON
NEW YORK • OXFORD • PARIS • SAN DIEGO
SAN FRANCISCO • SINGAPORE • SYDNEY • TOKYO

Academic Press is an imprint of Elsevier

Academic Press is an imprint of Elsevier
30 Corporate Drive, Suite 400, Burlington, MA 01803, USA
525 B Street, Suite 1900, San Diego, California 92101-4495, USA
84 Theobald's Road, London WC1X 8RR, UK

This book is printed on acid-free paper. ∞

Library of Congress Cataloging-in-Publication Data
Qualitative research methods for psychologists: introduction to empirical
    studies / [edited] by Constance T. Fischer.
        p. cm.
    Includes bibliographical references and index.
    ISBN 0-12-088470-4 (hardcover: alk. paper)
    1. Psychology–Research–Methodology.   2. Qualitative research.
    I. Fischer, Constance T., 1938-
    BF76.5.Q35 2005
    150′.72–dc22

2005024188

British Library Cataloguing in Publication Data
A catalogue record for this book is available from the British Library

ISBN 13: 978-0-12-088470-4
ISBN 10: 0-12-088470-4

For all information on all Academic Press publications
visit our Web site at www.books.elsevier.com

Printed in the United States of America
05 06 07 08 09 10   9 8 7 6 5 4 3 2 1

Working together to grow
libraries in developing countries

www.elsevier.com | www.bookaid.org | www.sabre.org

ELSEVIER   BOOK AID International   Sabre Foundation

To Michael

Contents

Part I

Clinical Practices

PART II

AFFECTIVE AND COGNITIVE PROCESSES

PART III

LIFE SITUATIONS

CONTRIBUTORS

Numbers in parentheses indicate the chapter to which the author has contributed.

Rosemarie Anderson (11), Boulder Creek, CA 95006

Scott D. Churchill (4), Department of Psychology, University of Dallas, Dallas, TX 75062-4799

Arne Collen (12), Walnut Creek, CA 94597

Joseph deRivera (8), Psychology Department, Clark University, Worster, MA 01610

Constance T. Fischer (Questions and Responses), Department of Psychology, Duquesne University, Pittsburgh, PA 15282

Jessie Goicoechea (5), Psychology Clinic, Duquesne University, Pittsburgh, PA 15282

Rhonda Goldman (1), Illinois School of Professional Psychology, Argosy University, Schaumburg, IL 60173

Leslie S. Greenberg (1), Department of Psychology, York University, Toronto, ONT, Canada

Steen Halling (9), Psychology Department, Seattle University, Seattle, WA 98122-4340

Vipassana Esbjörn-Hargens (11), Institute of Transpersonal Psychology, Sebastopol, CA 95472

Michael G. Leifer (9), Redmond, WA 98053

Lisa Lopez Levers (13), School of Education, Duquesne University, Pittsburgh, PA

Anna Madill (2), Psychology Department, Leeds University, Leeds, LS2 9JT, UK

Susan L. Morrow (6), Department of Educational Psychology, University of Utah, Salt Lake City, UT 84112-9255

Howard R. Pollio (10), Psychology Department, University of Tennessee, Knoxville, TN 37996-0900

David Rennie (3), Psychology Department, York University, North York, ONT, M3J IP3, Canada

Brent D. Robbins (7), Buffalo, NY 14223

Jan O. Rowe (9), Psychology Department, College of Arts and Sciences, Seattle University, Seattle, WA 98122-4340

William B. Stiles (1), Department of Psychology, Miami University, Oxford, OH 45056

Michael J. Ursiak (10), University of Tennessee, Knoxville, TN 37996-0900

Lara Honos-Webb (1), Department of Counseling Psychology, Santa Clara University, Santa Clara, CA 95053

PREFACE

This edited volume is written particularly for students, but is appropriate for all levels of social scientists who are interested in qualitative research: advanced undergraduates, graduate students, faculty members, and professionals who are interested in learning more about qualitative research. It also is appropriate for experienced qualitative researchers who are looking for ways to help newcomers. The research topics and methods are diverse, helping the reader to imagine different ways, and combinations of ways, to gain access to his or her own research phenomenon. Variations of many established qualitative research methods are represented, but the selection is not comprehensive.

The entire volume is intended to be a teaching textbook. After defining, illustrating, and characterizing qualitative research, the introductory chapter helps readers to link traditional and qualitative research as it addresses a range of practical matters, such as deciding whether to undertake a qualitative study, zeroing in on a topic, dealing with a dissertation committee, deciding how much of one's personal interest in a topic one should acknowledge, analyzing data, documenting the analysis, representing findings, writing to publish, and evaluating one's own and others' research.

The authors of chapters are specific about their philosophical assumptions, especially those relating to the nature of human knowing (epistemology). But unlike all edited volumes on qualitative research that I know of, this one goes beyond talking about, justifying, and excerpting, to present a range of full case demonstrations. An introduction to each chapter highlights contributions and unique features, and the author's biography concludes the chapter. Authors take the reader along on their research journeys, describing decisions, surprises, and regroupings, as well as the steps of gathering and analyzing data. In short, each chapter is indeed a case demonstration.

A final section is composed entirely of frequently asked questions and responses to them. A reader-friendly glossary defines terms used in this volume as well as additional terms that may be encountered in other qualitative research literature.

Although newcomers to qualitative research will want to acquire a mentor and/or a supportive research team before undertaking a project, they will have a good sense of how to go about qualitative research from the commonalities of method across the diverse topics and approaches presented in this volume.

This book will be useful for the social sciences, counseling, health professions, education, and human services in general. The main title, *Qualitative Research Methods for Psychologists*, emphasizes psychology for two reasons. First, the research methods presented here are all particularly suited for accessing the meanings of situations for individuals, and it is psychology that traditionally has addressed individuals and their experience, thought, perception, affect, and action, albeit usually not holistically. Second, among the social sciences, especially in North America, psychology has been slowest to veer from its natural science model to explore events as lived rather than as measured. Hence this volume is particularly useful to the discipline of psychology as it begins to explore alternative means of researching those phenomena that do not lend themselves to experimental methods.

I have had the good fortune to work in the psychology department of Duquesne University since the 1960s, among faculty and graduate students all developing a human science approach to psychology, including empirical phenomenological research foundations and practices. In alphabetical order, Duquesne and visiting faculty and graduates who have most contributed to my work include Scott Churchill, William Fischer, Amedeo Giorgi, Steiner Kvale, Paul Richer, Rolf vonEckartsburg, and Frederick Wertz. Department Chairpersons whose service across several terms of office have contributed fundamentally to a creative department are Amedeo Giorgi, David Smith, and Russell Walsh.

I appreciate the combination of patience and firmness with which Elsevier Executive Editor J. Scott Bentley, PhD, assisted with the production of this volume from start to finish.

INTRODUCTION

This volume is written as an introduction for students as well as for psychologists who have been trained in traditional psychological research approaches. The chapter authors and I are fairly sophisticated about qualitative psychological research in that we all have practiced and taught it for decades or have been trained in departments that have. We have tried to write so that newcomers' questions are addressed, and for the most part have not engaged in the advanced arguments and excursions through which a discipline grows. My own background and that of many of the authors has been with Duquesne University's psychology department; hence, there is an emphasis on phenomenological psychological research and research compatible with that approach. However, many approaches are represented, including innovative and combined forms. Our goal is to help you, the reader, that discover you can develop your own qualitative studies, probably with consultation, crafting your method to suit your subject matter. Reading the variety of case demonstrations will aid you in developing an understanding of practices through their variation. My own interest in bridging traditional and qualitative research will be evident from time to time.

This introduction defines and characterizes qualitative research, and then addresses a series of concrete, practical issues that are shared to varying degrees with all research, but that are of particular concern to the person attempting to conduct qualitative research. I encourage you to read for an overview of those issues, and of the issues addressed in the closing portion of the book, which is composed entirely of frequently asked questions and responses to them. A look at the glossary may also help you to know when to go there for clarification while reading anywhere in the book.

I write in the first person in this introduction and in Questions and Responses both to encourage you to get into a conversational relation with the material and to remind you that I am not speaking for all qualitative researchers, even though I try not to mischaracterize.

Some of you, as you encounter each case demonstration, may want to read the findings first, and then go back to appreciate better the method and procedures that led to those findings.

DEFINITION, ILLUSTRATION, AND CHARACTERIZATION OF QUALITATIVE RESEARCH

DEFINITION

Qualitative psychological research investigates the quality—the distinctive, essential characteristics—of experience and action as lived by persons. Qualitative research is a reflective, interpretive, descriptive, and usually reflexive effort to *describe and understand* actual instances of human action and experience from the perspective of the participants who are living through a particular situation. Some qualitative research seeks to identify and describe people's interactive ways of gaining or maintaining influence. The term *qualitative* came into general use to contrast this research endeavor to the long-established quantitative methods that psychology adapted from the natural sciences. Both endeavors are empirical in that observable events or reports serve as data (which qualitative researchers sometimes call *text*), and interested persons can read the steps that were taken to come to the study's findings and try them out for themselves.

Both statistical and qualitative research involve researchers' subjectivity in the sense that the projects were designed out of the researchers' interests and hopes, and out of their comprehensions and anticipations. Both kinds of research are developed within the inspirations and constraints of the researchers' cultures, subcultures, and times. For qualitative research, however, subjectivity is, in a sense, both its subject matter and its access to that subject matter. That is, qualitative research methods were devised to study those aspects of being human for which experimental and statistical methods are ill suited—namely, lived world actions and meanings. Our access to the lived world is through our own subjectivity—our being subjects: beings who take action, reflect, experience, plan, hope, and so on.

Experimental or statistical research is the appropriate approach when we want to know about the frequency and magnitude with which something happens in different externally determined circumstances. I sometimes refer to this approach as *categorical* research, meaning that researchers design studies to measure categories and their relations to other categories (for example, the relation of birth order to college grades, or problem-solving efficiency under different types of stress). Similarly, statistical methods are in order when we want to examine large amounts of categorical data that we cannot hold in mind at once.

Qualitative research is the appropriate approach when we want to understand and characterize an experience or interaction in its own right, rather than explaining it in terms of independent variables (whether natural or experimental). Qualitative research asks what something *is* in terms of how it is lived (for example, being criminally victimized, becoming angry, or the manner in which a therapist and client come to mutually agreed-upon interpretations). Instead of asking, Why? We address what, when, and how.

VALIDITY

For qualitative research, validity is not established through properly following experimental design and procedures, nor through statistically significant findings (which are appropriate for natural science models of research). Rather, the soundness of a study is achieved through appropriate selection of participants and inquiries, and scrupulous faithfulness to the data in the analysis and in the representation of the findings. I think of five interrelated kinds of validity, although they can be described in other ways:

1. *Witness validity*—Do readers of data and findings, following the researcher's method, come to basically the similar impressions?
2. *Touchpoint validity*—Do the findings connect with theory and with other studies in a productive way? Are previous understandings affirmed, reconciled, "nuanced," corrected, and/or expanded?
3. *Efficacy validity*—Are the findings useful? Do they make a difference for theory and/or practices?
4. *Resonance validity* (named in this volume by Anderson)—Do the data and findings resonate with readers' lives, both as familiar and as holding personal implication?
5. *Revisionary validity*—Do the findings aid readers to revise, to re-vision, prior understandings, either academic and/or personal? This revision may be a sense of greater affirmation or, more usually, a change in conception or depth of understanding.

ILLUSTRATIONS FROM QUALITATIVE RESEARCH

The following excerpts from an empirical phenomenological study of being criminally victimized (Fischer and Wertz, 1979, 2002) illustrate what qualitative research findings can look like. The case demonstration chapters present still other examples, and this introduction's Suggested Sources

Section includes still other approaches and ways to present findings. The criminal victimization study was unique in that it presented concrete procedural steps for six different forms of findings from analyzing 50 descriptions.

Our original report included an example of how we numbered "meaning units (MUs)" for each transcription, collated those with shared meaning, and synopsized what the victim said, staying very close to his or her wording. Later we combined themes into a "general condensation." Here is an example of MU analysis:

> "I got everything back, I was very fortunate." (12)
> "... except my money, yes." (13)
> "So I got all my keys back, I think the only thing I was out was my money and my driver's license." (18)
> "But I was very fortunate." (19)
> "So I felt very good that I got everything back." (42)
> Synopsis: S felt good, fortunate, that she got her keys back and had lost only her money and driver's license. (Fischer and Wertz, 2002, p. 287)

Here is what we called "a general condensation," which was based on synopses of individual cases:

> Being criminally victimized is a disruption of daily routine. It is a disruption that compels one, despite personal resistance, to face one's fellow as predator and oneself as prey, even though all the while anticipating consequences, planning, acting, and looking to others for assistance. These efforts to little avail, once experiences vulnerability, separateness, and helplessness in the face of the callous, insensitive, often anonymous enemy. Shock and disbelief give way to puzzlement, strangeness, and then to a sense of the crime as perverse, unfair, undeserved. Whether or not expressed immediately, the victim experiences a general inner protest, anger or rage, and a readiness for retaliation, for revenge against the violator.
>
> As life goes on, the victim finds him/herself pervasively attuned to the possibility of victimization—through a continued sense of reduced agency, of the other as predatory, and of community as inadequately supportive. More particularly, one continues to live the victimization through recollections of the crime, imagination of even worse outcomes, vigilant suspiciousness of others, sensitivity to news of disorder and crime, criticalness of justice system agents, and desires to make sense of it all.
>
> But these reminders of vulnerability are simultaneously efforts toward recovery of independence, safety, trust, order, and sense. One begins to get back on top of the situation through considering or taking precautions against crime, usually by restricting one's range of activities so as not to fall prey again. During this process, the victim tries to understand not only how a criminal could have done and could again do such a thing, but also how or she (the victim) may have contributed to the criminal's action. Also, one's intermittent readiness for retaliation provides a glimpse of one's own potential for outrageous violence. The victim thus is confronted with the paradoxical and ambiguous character of social existence: the reversible possibilities we all share, such as being agent or object, same or different, disciplined or disruptive, predator or prey. One may move from this encounter to a more circumspect attitude toward personal responsibility.
>
> However, the person's efforts toward such an integration of the victimization are not sufficient. The environment must, over time, demonstrate that the victim's

extreme vigilance is no longer necessary. And other persons must respond with concern and respect for the victim's full plight, including his or her efforts toward sense making. All three components are necessary for recovery of one's prior life as well as for development of a fuller sense of responsibility, reciprocity, and community. But no component is guaranteed. The absence of any of them eventuates in a deepened victimization of isolation, despair, bitterness, and resignation. (Fischer and Wertz, 2002, pp. 292–293).

This form of results was relatively compact and told the story as a whole. Frederick Wertz also provided what we called a "general psychological structure," in which he drew out previously implicit horizons and structural relations within a respondent's description. See Wertz (1985) for another account of our victimization study and a full presentation of the general psychological structure.

Our joint report (Fischer and Wertz, 1979, 2002) as another form of our findings also presented excerpts from what we called an "illustrated narrative," originally a 19-page handout for panelists and audience at public forums we held to explore the human values aspects of public policy. The experience of being criminally victimized was presented under five headings: Living Routinely, Being Disrupted, Being Violated, Reintegrating, and Going On. Under each heading a general finding was printed in bold print, followed by representative quotations from different participants in brackets. An example follows:

[From Living Routinely] **But unless personal experience has already proven otherwise, he/she nevertheless feels that the defended against crime could never happen to him/her.** ["You think of it; you know nothing like this would have happened to you. That's just the truth"; "I said, 'nah, you've got to be kidding'"; "I always thought it happened to everybody else"; "... that it just happened on television."]

[From Being Disrupted] **Even as the person copes with the threatening or discovered crime, he/she scans imaginatively and perceptually for a still worse outcome.** ["I think that night I was more concerned about my house keys. I thought if those kids still had the purse, and my address was in the wallet ..."; "I told them [her own children] to stop, to come back, 'cause I didn't know what these kids would do if [my] kids got too close"; "You imagine the worst when it's happening ... I just kept thinking my baby's upstairs and I might never see her again"; "By the time I would have got it out, I would have had my head mashed in or shot." (Fischer and Wertz, 2002, pp. 288–289).

See Fischer (1984) for the full illustrated narrative.

This book's case demonstration chapters present other approaches to text analysis and presentation of findings. The annotated Suggested Sources at the end of this introduction contain many other methods, discussions, and some analyses. You will find that researchers choose precedents or develop variations depending on their subject matter, particular interest in that subject matter, issues to which they want to speak, to and the publication outlets and readerships for which they are hoping.

HISTORICAL NOTE

Historically, despite many wonderful, reflective, interpretive studies by psychologists like Gordon Allport, Kurt Lewin, and William James, our discipline's effort to prove itself as a science led to the adoption of philosophical underpinnings that left no room for uniquely human characteristics like relating, reflecting, meaning seeking, and so on. Our research assumed that researchers did not influence what they studied; that findings were of a real world separate from people examining it; that nature was material, measurable, and "knowable" through our experimental operations and deductive logic (realism, materialism, operationalism, logical positivism). Whatever could not be counted did not count! Textbooks published in the 1960s and 1970s defined psychology as the science that predicted and controlled behavior. By now, with psychology having been established as a rigorous empirical discipline, most psychologists no longer accept the "control and predict" definition and no longer cite logical positivism and related philosophical foundations, but often do count on accepted experimental procedures and statistical analysis as adequate to continue building a body of knowledge. Psychology textbooks most often define psychology as the study of human and animal behavior.

Most psychologists respect the power and helpfulness of categorical and experimental psychology, which I refer to as *traditional*, but by now many psychologists also have acknowledged traditional psychology's limits and are becoming open to qualitative methods. For its part, qualitative research in North America is emerging from an era of arguing against reductive practices (reducing human phenomena to biological, causal, or mathematical features). It now is becoming very sophisticated about alternative philosophies of knowledge (epistemologies) and about the nature of being and beings (ontology). Qualitative researchers are establishing assorted research methods, such as grounded theory, ethnography, and empirical phenomenology. We are entering a new stage of qualitative research, one in which we are doing it instead of talking about it, establishing our own journals and publishing our work in many standard journals. A minority but growing body of psychologists regard themselves, in assorted terms and with various emphases, as human–science psychologists—ones who respect psychology as being an empirical discipline but who regard our knowledge as inevitably co-constituted by us as humans. This epistemological perspective is sometimes called *postmodern*—past the era when we believed that humans could know truth directly, somehow without our circumstances and ways of shaping what we know.

Human science psychologists choose their method of research depending upon what they want to understand, whether it is categorical relationships or understandings of situations. In the meantime, many traditional psychological researchers no longer accept realism and positivism, but instead explore relations among outcomes and circumstances, identifying patterns rather than asserting causal explanations. And qualitative researchers now combine interpretive methods to address their subject matter best and their own personal style.

FURTHER CHARACTERIZATION OF QUALITATIVE RESEARCH

Qualitative research is time intensive, requiring dwelling with text, tracking insights, revisiting the texts again and again in light of changing appreciation of its depth and implications. We look again and again, re-searching, as our insight evolves. Hence, single-researcher studies, like dissertations, typically are restricted to one to five to ten participants' protocols. However, in the criminal victimization study, we did use 50 descriptions provided by citizens who had reported crimes to their police department. I had obtained a grant and worked with Frederick Wertz and three other graduate students (Fischer and Wertz, 1979, 2002).

Our findings are local, pertaining to the particular set of participants' reports. We do not claim generalizability. Indeed, in that both researchers and providers of data (our participants) find themselves in changing situations, as do all people, we anticipate that there will be some difference with other participant samples and settings. Sometimes, as in program evaluation studies, our interest is primarily local, as in trying to understand what is going on or not going on for first-year college students who drop out after one semester. Nevertheless, we have learned that careful qualitative reading ("analysis") usually speaks way beyond its few respondents. Still, it is always an empirical matter how well one study's findings will fit with those from another group of respondents. As is the case for traditional studies, reports end with suggestions for follow-up research (for example, varying the researcher's questions addressed to the data, requests of participants, and comparative or extended participant groups).

Speaking of commonalities with traditional research, there are many that typically go unmentioned. Both enterprises are much more complex, demanding, and frustrating than research reports imply. Both typically involve false starts and regrouping until a productive avenue to the subject matter is found. Both are inductive in designing their studies and in gathering data. Both can be imaginative in designing research and in understanding implications of findings. Both utilize insight gained from outside the formal study. Both seek to be rigorous and open to examination from other researchers. Both require efforts to guard against researcher bias in design and interpretation.

But of course there are numerous differences. Colleagues from the natural sciences often ask how analysis of a handful of reports can be called scientific. I respond that the field of empirical research is broader than the field of hard sciences. I explain that our work is scientific in that it examines empirical data, shows others how they could examine the same data to check the study's findings, and contributes to a systematic body of understanding. We do not usually refer to a "body of knowledge," because the latter implies an accumulation of truth that had been awaiting discovery, truth with a full nature that is independent of its describers. I emphasize to colleagues that we strive to understand from within persons' worlds, rather than to explain in terms of determinants. In a sense, though, a coherent descriptive account with no gaps is an explanation.

I also suggest that qualitative research is akin to investigative journalism. The investigative journalist explores in depth a local social situation such as bullying in our schools, the lives of the homeless, or prison conditions. He, she, or a team, interviews, observes, and, after much reviewing of notes, double-checking of data, reflecting, and conferring with editors, writes a descriptive report that evokes how all parties experience and participate in the situation. For example, we might see how police officers, judges and court personnel, parole officers, wards and prison personnel, attorneys, and legislators, as well as prisoners and their families all shape and are shaped by their ways of taking up and perpetuating or changing circumstances. Early on, the report describes the investigator's initial interest in the subject, refers to other reports, and lays out methods, sources, and limitations. The report does not attempt to identify a single under-lying cause, but readers comprehend the overall picture. They come to that understanding through reported instances and illustrations. They can see many points of possible intervention, each of which could contribute to a shift in the structural whole (the "system"). When the journalist has done solid, disciplined work, readers respect the legitimacy of the findings, while recognizing that another investigative reporter would come up with additional and somewhat differing accounts. Readers also understand that although the report pertains to a local situation, many of its aspects probably pertain to other locales as well.

Readers of this book will find that, like investigative journalists, our researchers have disclosed a personal interest in the subject matter; have been disciplined in efforts to represent data and contexts faith-fully, have continuously reworked their understandings in light of ongoing encounters with new data, theories, and contexts; and have repeatedly undertaken self-examination for what may be personal points of access or personal bias.

Colleagues from our natural science traditions of psychological research sometimes also have said that after reading a qualitative research method section that they still would not know how to carry out the study themselves. I can readily empathize, and explain that a shift in project is necessary. The project is not to apply the method in a mechanical manner, ensuring sameness of procedure and of product; rather, the project is more akin to following a tour guide to get to where the author has been, and being in an appreciative mode while viewing the sights (data and interpretive descriptions). The researcher and tour guide serve somewhat like interpretive portraitists. Yes, the qualitative researcher makes use of self in apprehending, appreciating, and portraying his or her impressions. Although this project is necessarily somewhat creative and artistic, it also is rigorous in its faithfulness to the data, in specifying the perspectives from which an analysis was conducted and in the care with which findings are presented. Other viewers too must be able to see what the researcher reports, even though it might not have been visible to the new viewer before. And the new viewer may add to, correct, or refine the reporter's description.

Also, even though qualitative research method sections typically specify that concluding understandings evolved through continual revisiting of current understanding in light of a recent impression, newcomers to qualitative research often assume that there is some single operation leading to results. I do think that we qualitative researchers should emphasize more pointedly that our procedural steps were not always chronological and certainly not linear. Once immersed in data, some of the researcher's insights may come while driving to work, awaking from a dream, or reading a novel or article. The researcher does return to the steps to see that they all have been carried out before concluding the study. For example, although the steps do not instruct one to do so, one revises the wording of an earlier identified theme in light of insight from a newspaper interview with a crime victim, but one does, in the end, check every theme against every participant report, and reread every sentence of that report to be sure that nothing having to do with the researched topic has been left out or distorted. The steps serve as a guide and a check, not as steps that are followed mechanically to qualitative findings. The researcher also discusses nuances to the steps of the analysis that emerged once the study was underway. Procedural steps also serve as a guide for readers of findings, allowing them to experience and to amend the first researcher's findings.

CONCLUDING COMMENTS

Our natural science tradition in psychology has been responsible for psychology not being a branch of philosophy, but psychology is now well enough established as an empirical discipline to revisit our philosophical assumptions and to examine, refine, and broaden them. It seems to me that it is time to develop psychology as a discipline systematically that appreciates humans from a holistic perspective, including the neurobiological, environmental, behavioral, interpersonal, experiential, and spiritual aspects of being human. Qualitative researchers' philosophical discussions, development of methods of investigation, and presentation of findings are part of that growth of psychology.

PRACTICAL MATTERS

DECIDING WHETHER TO UNDERTAKE A QUALITATIVE STUDY

First, do not aim for a qualitative study to avoid an experimental or otherwise statistical research project. Both are demanding! Even if you choose to pursue a qualitative study, you should be familiar with traditional forms of rigor and research design, both to adopt what is pertinent and to know how to present your qualitative work to persons familiar only with statistical designs. Be aware that your personal accountability is much more evident in qualitative studies than when, in the words of one of my statistics professors, "you crank out" the statistical results after entering measurements approved by your committee or consultants. Qualitative research requires acceptance of ambiguity, keeping the whole in mind while working with detail, flexibility, insight, language skill, creative discipline, and rigor.

Positive reasons for undertaking a qualitative study include (1) wanting to gain experience with this approach, along with experimental and other statistical approaches; (2) wanting to understand (versus to explain), especially holistically, an experience, phenomenon, or situation in terms of "what it is like," or to describe the implicit dynamics of human interactions; and (3) when traditional research has reached its limits, and the perspective of persons living a particular situation likely will advance our understanding.

You also may want to have an advisor, co-researchers, or consultants available, just as traditional researchers do.

ZEROING IN ON A TOPIC

As with most of what I am saying in this section on practical matters, choosing a workable topic is the same process as in any research. If one has a choice, of course it's wise to choose a topic in which one has an interest and has been reading for some time. However, regardless of whether there is prior interest, sometimes one chances upon a timely and workable topic. An advisor may provide a project, you may encounter a study that "begs" to be conducted again with this or that variation or focus, or your work setting may urge you to undertake a practical study of an immediately salient topic, like how clients are experiencing their intake interviews and why so many fail to return to the clinic, or what is there about a day center that seems to be working when earlier efforts did not.

If a particular study has not offered itself, and you have identified a general area of interest, the task becomes one of "zeroing in" on a "doable" project. Do not aim, in a first study, for a grand, revolutionary project; that could be a life project, not a single research study. So, for example, instead of choosing "What is empathy?" you could choose to study empathic relating in a particular situation. In choice of the situation and the participants would depend on what is not yet clear in the literature. What study would mesh nicely with current literature and issues? For example, what is the quality of empathic moments between a "juvenile delinquent" and his or her counselor? What is the experience of each party during those moments? Further decisions might involve availability of participants. Gaps and anomalies in the research literature might suggest particular samples: age and gender of the juveniles, types of runins with the law, and so on. Sometimes particular samples and requests for descriptions are chosen with the intent of speaking to prevailing assumptions or theory. For example, if it seems that delinquents are thought to "have character disorders" that preclude empathy with victims, it might be fruitful to choose youngsters who have committed interpersonal crimes (e.g., robbery, mugging). This choice would serve two purposes: First, you could explore the nature of the youngster's perception of the other person and of the adjudicated crime. Second, you could explore the presence and qualities of what might be empathic. Both kinds of findings are likely to be useful. Generally, topics of current interest in professional journals or newspapers have a greater chance of being published.

But choosing a topic must be followed by decisions about what kind of data to collect. If you wish to interview delinquents, for example, then what requests for descriptions should be made? I urge beginning researchers to try out different requests or interview formats with a range of participants before beginning formal research.

If you are interested in a particular population, like male delinquents' experience of their victims, then you should have comparative participants (females, in this case) or it will not be known whether the findings are of males or of delinquents in general. Before going too far with your project, however, other practical questions should be asked, like "Can I find time to do this right?" and "Can I find co-investigators or an advisor willing to work with me?"

Students often make the mistake of wanting to choose a topic that does not seem to have been studied, so they can make an original contribution and not be held accountable for knowing previous studies. The mistake is that, in actuality, you are more likely to have a workable study and to make a contribution via dialogue with other literature. After a while, you may find that the "original" topic has lots of related literature that should be explored. Suppose you choose to do a case study of a circus performer's fear of falling. Even if you have access to such performers, questions need to be asked about how your findings relate to literature on fear, performing, motivation, personality, and on and on.

DECIDING ON A TITLE

Compared with traditional reports, qualitative reports are often longer by virtue of including the name of the method. Traditional studies are assumed to be experimental or otherwise categorical and statistical; hence, that information is not included in a title. However, titles should be informative to prospective readers of the report, and should not be unduly esoteric. That is, titles should be reader friendly to a span of potential readers. In general, you should state the subject matter first, with the method following a colon. For example: Becoming angry: An empirical phenomenological study. When pertinent, situations and participants may also be specified: Becoming angry: An empirical phenomenological study with male residents of a juvenile justice facility. I think that just saying "A qualitative study" as a qualifier does not adequately inform a reader, because that phrase could point to everything from observer notes to questionnaires to formal conversation analysis.

Do avoid pretentious titles, which are off-putting and could embarrass you in later years. For example, "An intentional hermeneutic variation of empirical phenomenological method in an investigation of emotional displays in incarcerated male juvenile offenders" sounds like the author is trying to be ever so sophisticated, but the title suggested earlier is more mature, informative, and respectful of readers. Also, avoid phrases that are uninformative until the full report has been read. For example: "The red rover phenomenon: An empirical phenomenological study of anger in adjudicated teenagers" sounds catchy, but is not helpful. Titles cannot say everything; perhaps the abstract could describe the "red rover" finding (which, by the way, probably is not a *phenomenon* in phenomenology's sense).

Crafting a title is not as simple as you might think. Most qualitative researchers explore a series of working titles, and gain clearer focus along the way. This process also helps authors as they write their proposals and their reports; the resulting documents are to the point, section by section.

WORKING WITH A DISSERTATION COMMITTEE

First, decide on a probable topic and then ask a faculty member with whom you have worked well if he or she would be willing to chair/direct your dissertation. Be prepared to present preliminary thoughts about the relevance of the topic and ideas about the research design. Your chair will be of most help throughout the dissertation process if he or she already is knowledgeable about the topic and is familiar with qualitative methods.

Do *not* choose a chair just because he or she is friendly with you or powerful in the department; choose to ensure knowledgeable, collaborative guidance.

After you have obtained at least tentative agreement to chair your research, and perhaps some suggestions for your design, present your chair with a brief written outline of your proposal, including a "statement of the problem" (a description of the topic and your study's hoped-for contribution toward resolving gaps, anomalies, and/or controversies in the literature, as well as any policy or practice implications). Also include a brief description of how you hope to acquire participants (subjects), how you will acquire data from them, and how you plan to analyze the data. Getting feedback on this early brief document saves you a lot of effort later.

Then think of which faculty members might be most helpful with regard to methodological and subject matter expertise, and ask your chair if you should ask these persons if they would join the committee. Your chair may have other suggestions from knowing colleagues' past helpfulness, timeliness, and actual expertise. Most departments allow experts from outside the department and university to serve as a regular or additional committee member. These experts, often from the community, know different literature than university-based readers, have constructive ideas about obtaining participants/subjects, and see practical implications of findings that the rest of us may miss. After you and your chair are agreed about potential readers (committee members), take your (probably already revised) brief proposal to them and ask them if they would get back to you about serving as readers. You will likely acquire additional good suggestions during this process, and can incorporate them into your full draft of your formal proposal.

Indeed, be prepared for suggested changes at every step of the way. Just as you find big and small things you want to change as you work on your drafts, so too will your committee members note different points that could profit from change each time they read a different version. Most often, changes make new observations possible. It is the naive student who complains, "But you didn't say to change this the last time you saw it." On the other hand, be sure you understand what is being asked of you, and present a rationale for what might be your contrary opinion. Be sure to double-check regarding any communications that you find you do not fully understand. Especially at your defense, and later if you present or write papers on your work, the work should be your own, no matter how much guidance has been provided.

In most departments, after the proposal has been approved, usually with assorted modifications, you will work primarily with your chair, consulting with readers only for expertise that neither you nor your chair has. When you have drafted your actual dissertation research report, your chair will suggest revisions. You will then share the dissertation draft with the rest of the committee, and meet with the full committee at some sort of formal gathering, at which further suggestions are made and the draft is approved, pending the changes. In many, if not most, departments, the defense of the dissertation, now with a larger audience, no longer holds the possibility of failure, after all the changes from committee review have been made. You can now confidently, if nervously, share your work as the person most familiar with it! Piantanida and Garman (1999) have written an especially helpful book describing experiences along the way to "the qualitative dissertation."

APPLYING FOR RESEARCH GRANTS

In the United States, federal granting agencies are almost exclusively neurobiologically and behaviorally oriented. Nevertheless, in recent years some applicants have been instructed to conduct ethnographic studies prior to finalizing their research plans. The Social Services and Humanities Research Council of Canada has long supported carefully designed qualitative studies that are calculated to be relevant to Canada's social policies. In both countries, funding is more likely to be granted from any agency when the investigators include multiple forms of data ("triangulation"), including statistical measures, and when the utility of related qualitative studies can be cited.

DECIDING HOW MUCH OF YOUR PERSONAL INTEREST IN A TOPIC YOU SHOULD ACKNOWLEDGE

First, acknowledge to *yourself*, as fully as you can, during many reflexive and reflective explorations, what your multiple motives are for studying a topic that holds a strong personal relevance. For example, if your research area is "discovering that you are adopted" or "discovering you were one never loved by your spouse," are you wanting to use the research study to demonstrate to the world how you have suffered, or what you have overcome? Are you seeking mastery or resolution through your research project? Are you wanting to prove that you were right all along about some aspect of your personal experience? Any of these sorts of involvement may indicate that you will run the risk of being distracted, biased, or somewhat closed to discovery—that is, adequate distance from which to see freshly may be difficult to achieve. You might do well either to choose another topic or finds ways to shift your motives to use better your personal expertise as access to the topic.

Whatever the complexities of your personal interests in a topic, exploring those interests allows you to specify them and then to check regularly if they are biasing your view. Sharing your biographical interest with an advisor/consultant or with co-researchers allows those persons to invite you to reexamine some of your interpretations and to broaden your perspective. When writing a report of your research, sharing your biographically grounded personal interest in a topic helps readers understand the perspective from which your findings took form. Such sharing should be part of all research. However, you may be wise to protect your future self and your future privacy by toning down your personal interest, while at the same time "owning" something of your involvement. For example, rather than saying "I, myself, was an emotionally abused child," your might say, "I have had a longstanding interest in emotionally abused children and have worked for an agency that serves such youngsters."

ATTENDING TO ETHICAL ISSUES

In all psychological research, we are in a power relation with the persons who provide us with data, in that these people follow our instructions and in that they typically do not know how their data will be used (consent forms notwithstanding). Hence, participant well-being is involved and ethical considerations come into play. Beyond the concern for participants that is occasioned by power and by data use, qualitative researchers also are aware that well-being may be related to participants being directly observed in everyday life or to their providing descriptions of concrete personal experiences. These instances are holistically embedded in the person's sense of his or her life and self, and they are more intimate than the person imagines when agreeing to be a participant. Especially during interviews that follow up on earlier descriptions, many respondents (in one way or another) say that they have been somberly in touch with core aspects of their lives. I think that this frequent occurrence is related to the fact that qualitative research often deals with topics that are inaccessible to natural science methods, topics that involve reflection on personal experience and meanings.

Even readers of qualitative research reports—such as ones on being impatient, being criminally victimized, waiting for biopsy results, and so on—have been moved to tears because the report reverberates with their own lives. Other participants and readers have described finding themselves liberated by new understandings.

So how shall we protect our participants? First, by being mindful that participants may be deeply touched by providing protocols for us. We should allow our appreciation of the person's sharing with us to be explicit and clearly authentic. We want to avoid the person being surprised by the experience or feeling used. Sometimes a postinterview interpersonal discussion of the person's participation helps him or her to acknowledge and integrate the experience. With some topics, like deciding whether to have an abortion, or the experience of (pathological) self-cutting, researchers typically make advance arrangements for emergency counseling to be available in case it becomes advisable. Yes, our responsibilities as qualitative researchers go beyond our standard debriefing with participants after an experiment.

PREPARING TO GATHER DATA

First, develop a working flowchart showing all the steps you plan to take to gather your data (along with steps of analysis and presentation of findings). You likely will revise your chart several times (hence the term *working*—it is your starting place, something concrete that you revise in light of initial efforts, discovery of related research, or in efforts toward obtaining increased clarity for readers). The flowchart will help you to stay on track and to make corrections when you recognize nuances in what you are doing.

Next, if appropriate, visit your prospective participants' settings (e.g., hospital ward, kindergarten classroom). Even if there is not a special setting, talk with persons like those who will be your participants (e.g., persons who have experienced joy, being victimized) to find out what they can tell you directly and to try out different forms of requests for descriptions to determine which request results in appropriate, rich descriptions. You may want to try out requests with a range of persons (e.g., sixth, seventh, and eighth graders; heroin, cocaine, and amphetamine addicts) to determine which groups are most informative or speak most directly to your research concerns—such as gaps or conflicts in the literature—and to determine whether contrast groups might be desirable. If you are conducting a conversation or discourse analysis, similar planning is necessary, such as acquiring permissions to use existing recordings or to record particular interactions. In the United States, because you do not yet have institutional review Board (IRB) permission to gather data that can be used in research reports, you cannot publish material collected at this point. However, do now prepare ways to code data without participants' names or other identifying data and to store it securely.

Prepare requests for volunteers to participate in your research. They may be worded differently for gatekeepers and for readers of bulletin boards and other media. Appeals to potential participants typically are most successful when you explain their contributions (besides helping you, if you are a student completing a research requirement). For example, "Help parents and teachers to understand what it is like to be known as the slowest kid on the team" or "Help us to understand what it is like to be homeless, so we can help city council members and agencies to know what it is like." You may want to try out your requests with potential participants and redraft as they suggest. You also may want to ask agency representatives for feedback on your drafts of consent and assent (children) forms before your formal submission to both your IRB and to the agency.

Your requests for volunteers should include details, succinctly presented, about the amount of time required of participants and what they will be asked to do, who they can contact for more information, and so on. This same information will go into your consent forms, along with contact information for institutional representatives and yourself, and guarantees that participation is indeed voluntary and that participants may quit and take their data with them at any juncture. It is critical that you explain the project in nontechnical language so that potential participants truly understand what they are getting into and what their rights are.

At this point, if you are conducting the research in a United States institution, prepare your IRB proposal. Determine whether your study qualifies for expedited review by a committee or whether it requires full IRB review (mostly when participants are vulnerable [children, patients, prisoners, the elderly]). In the United States, if your participants are patients, you also are required to apply for clearance from your institution's HIPAA representative (Health Information and Portability Accountability Act). Completion of these documents at your own institution will help you to gain approval from any agencies from which you hope to acquire participants. If you have already been in touch with potential participants and agencies as you formulate your flowchart and documents, you will save yourself a lot of later effort.

If your study involves asking for a description of an event or situation, be sure that your participants understand that you do not want hypotheses or explanations, but concrete, life-world descriptions. For example, "Please describe an incident in which you found yourself resenting someone. Please say what was going on before that, what the incident was like, and what happened after that. Please write in enough detail so I will know what it was like to be *you* in that situation." Most researchers find that the richest descriptions are provided when respondents have several days to mull over possible incidents to report, and then write a description. Pondering gradually brings back details and context; writing helps the person to organize, temporalize, and fill in information for the reader. For respondents who may be intimidated by the request to provide a report in written form, it is still productive to ask the person to be thinking about actual incidents and to explain that you will tape-record and later type what the person tells you.

In your request for participants, explain that you will study each person's description, and then will return to ask them to elaborate and clarify any sections that you are not sure you have understood. It is usually a good idea to provide participants with a typed version of their description, ask for a particular section to be read out loud, and then ask, "Could you tell me more about that?" Most researchers see nothing negative about asking direct questions at the end of this procedure. For example, "Could you tell me what your relation with Uncle Bert was like before he moved out of your house?" Or "Can you think of any situations in which you have been resentful of a stranger, someone with whom you had not had direct contact?"

If you tell participants that you will provide them with brief versions of the research findings, be sure to determine in advance a way of reaching them. Let participants know that it may be a year (or whatever) before your research will be ready to share. Write a nontechnical, brief report, and be sure to live up to your promise of providing it to participants.

The number of participants you will want to be part of your study will depend on whether you have co-researchers and the time frame of your study. At Duquesne University, we have found that for our empirical phenomenological studies, at about six or seven sets of data we reach redundancy. Moreover, more than that number is very difficult to keep in mind. I have recommended using only four or five sets of data for thorough analysis, and then comparing those findings with data from additional, adjunctive participants whose data were not formally analyzed. This approach has been efficient and effective.

ANALYZING DATA

First, read and study several different research reports that describe and illustrate the method you plan to use. Be clear about the philosophical approach underlying that method (e.g., that participants co-create their situations or that conversations place participants in positions from which only some responses are possible). Indicate the name of the basic methods you will use and describe any variations you plan to make. Be sure to write these descriptions in your own words. If you just copy other authors' method sections, you may become confused when you start your analysis. As you proceed with your analysis and become more aware of just what is involved in one step or another, describe in a research journal what you have learned about what you are doing (see the section *Documenting the Analysis Steps and Findings*). For example, you might note that, contrary to what your method section in your dissertation proposal says, you find yourself working on reports from several participants at once, instead of one by one. You might note that your analysis is taking place not just when you are staring at participant reports (or other texts), but while you are driving, reading a novel, or falling asleep. You might note that you found yourself making notes on probable general findings even as you were just reading through text for the purpose of familiarizing yourself with the participants' accounts. Later, your research report should spell out these events as not being essential to the findings, but understandings do not emerge just from studying text. Revise your method section to fit what you, in fact, did with regard to formal steps. These revised method sections will be of significant help to other researchers.

Let's get back to approaching the texts. First, read through all the participant reports or records several times to become thoroughly familiar with them. My dissertation students say that when they have typed transcriptions themselves, they find that they are much more attuned to the nuances and flow of an account.

This book of case demonstrations illustrates a range of approaches to data, all of which have worked. Most qualitative researchers first mark the text into workable units, usually defined by shifts in the story line. These units can be numbered and later identified by the participant's pseudonym and the unit number. When I find that more is going on in the unit than I anticipated, I subdivide the unit. Just do what works, keeping track of what you are doing, and do it consistently.

Second, with my background in empirical phenomenological research, my predilection is to ask each unit what is being said there about how the participant is living the event (e.g., becoming angry, awaiting a diagnosis). Dwelling with the text empathically is arduous but rewarding. Periodically I ask whether I have missed anything about how past and future as well as present appear to the person, and I check to determine whether I have missed what is being said about his or her relation to self, world, and others. I stay very close to what the participant said, being faithful to what I see as that person's lived meaning. I write at a level that anyone else likely would agree with me; there are no interpretive leaps. For example, on a sheet next to the data unit number, for a segment that said, "John had promised that this time for sure he would call ahead at the restaurant for a reservation, but once again he just forgot—didn't care enough," I wrote, "Once again John didn't care enough, despite promises." I prefer to continue through the text at this level so that I will not leap ahead to more abstract notions prematurely. Some researchers continue through all participants' texts at this level and then write a summary account from the unit wordings for each participant. I prefer to do that too, for perhaps a half dozen accounts. Then I may characterize themes for my analyzed accounts and check the remaining accounts for fit with those themes, repeatedly revising themes identified earlier in light of new examples. I find that this approach keeps me closer to the psychological phenomenon and keeps me from rushing into something akin to content analysis.

Like other phenomenological researchers, I prefer to present my final analysis with themes integrated into one narrative that preserves the relations among identified aspects of the phenomenon. Other researchers prefer to present a list of themes as the findings. Sometimes less complex data lend themselves to theme identification and listing rather than meaning analysis and narratives.

Some researchers prefer to begin naming themes earlier, as they identify them, like "early trust broken," or "other seen as not caring enough," depending on context, themes already identified, and other text. My procedure requires less revising of themes and more assurance of having stayed close to the data. Naming and revising themes as you go requires less effort line by line and allows you to move more quickly to general, abstract, and conceptual levels. Either way, ultimately you must be able to point back to the text for every theme. This is a rigorous, demanding process, but usually, at least at times, an exciting one.

When the researcher is doing interactional analysis, as in discourse analysis, similar strategies may be taken even though one is looking at interaction units rather than narrative units. I do think that attention to lived worlds assists in interactional studies too.

Yes, different researchers will describe what they see differently, and that is alright, as long as readers can see what is being referred to and as long as descriptions are faithful to reports. Natural sciences, too, struggle with naming. I remember being surprised reading original reports of factor analyses of intelligence test items and realizing that I would have named some factors quite differently. Speaking of surprise, many researchers are surprised when conducting their first projects, whether qualitative or experimental, to find that when the studies are designed thoughtfully and carried out carefully, the methods work!

GETTING BACK FROM BEING LOST

Once you have immersed yourself in protocol descriptions (typed descriptions of an experience or situation provided by your research participants, or typed records of interactions of participants), and you are thoroughly familiar with what it was like for the participants, you are likely to find yourself lost for a while. "Lost" in any of several senses:

1. You feel that anything you write in an effort to describe is a false start. Either it does not seem true to the complexity of the whole or its linear form seems artificial.
2. Because you have no predetermined categories to count on, and you must come up with your own descriptors, you feel arbitrary, like you're making up things to say.
3. Everything you start to write seems utterly obvious and you feel like your work is fake, that your research undertaking is a fraud, or that you are too dull or dim to pull meaning from your protocols.

This getting lost occurs both when noting and naming themes, and again when writing the findings.

If you do experience yourself as lost in these ways, you might smile at something that those of us who pursue empirical phenomenological research say: "Phenomenology is the method that makes the apparent obvious." Remind yourself that the goal is to *comprehend* everyday life affairs, to grasp them (*prehend*) fully (*com*) on their own terms. Hence our comprehensions, our findings, often will indeed seem quite mundane. Often our findings are of the "Oh, I knew that" variety. But in fact, before our research, we did not comprehend them in a full way nor in a way that was useful for other people. The findings, for example, that addicts' experience of dropping out of treatment included not having bus fare, being confused in the absence of signage in the clinic, and not having a vivid sense of a future without drugs, are mundane, but extremely important for revising the program. Similarly, a holistic account (description) of a phenomenon, presenting what is essential to all gathered instances, is powerful and useful in its wholeness and its everydayness. I am reminded of responses from the professional community that I receive to my graduate students' individualized, descriptive psychological assessment reports, which often is a variation of: "Wow, this is wonderful. I can picture the client. I recognize the similarity of how he was in the assessment sessions with how I've seen him. Now he hangs together better for me—I understand him and I know just how to work more effectively with him. Your students will be really great when they learn psychology." Actually, of course, the students knew a great deal about personality, pathology, testing, and intervention, but leaving out jargon and describing the person's actions and interactions and experience in everyday language rendered the report commonsensical (which is not all that common with psychological reports or research!).

Ways to get back to working with more confidence, then, include knowing that your findings should *not* be full of jargon or overly technical. You are doing just fine when your Aunt Matty can understand your findings! It also helps to track (record) formally the various uses that can be made of your findings as you go. This helps you to be sure that your comprehension was not obvious in advance, and it helps you to write your section on contributions. It also is a good idea to track formally surprises, revisions, and discoveries of your misassumptions as you go. This record reminds you that you are not making up what you find, and it provides examples for readers of your empirical dealings with the data. Be sure that your analysis procedures include marking examples from each protocol of each theme. This expected process can go a long way toward reminding you that you're not making up findings.

Finally, yes, you do have to let your original enthusiasm for your subject matter loose and creatively evoke for the reader what your analysis got you in touch with. Although this effort must be highly disciplined, it can be the most rewarding part of the research.

DOCUMENTING THE ANALYSIS STEPS AND FINDINGS

I think of documenting as serving two purposes: (1) tracking to help the researcher stay oriented and to recover later one's pathways to findings and (2) creating records from which to illustrate the research process to readers. Thinking of documentation in this way, rather than as efforts to prove one thing or another, allows the researcher to think creatively rather than defensively.

For my own tracking, beyond my notes on analysis of each set of formal data, I keep a sort of journal, a notebook with numbered pages. I develop a table of contents as I go, for example, "annotated references, p. 1"; "related phenomena (frustration, rage, etc.), p. 3"; "the pause, p. 37"; and so on. As my references go past page 1 and its backside (p. 2), I add, for example, "p. 15" after the page 1 entry in my evolving table of contents and continue entering annotated references on p. 15. I regularly enter notes from bits of paper from occasions when my notebook was not handy. My journal helps me to maintain discipline in keeping track; otherwise, what I am sure I could not forget indeed gets forgotten. Later I am also grateful that even though many entries seem to have repeated similar earlier entries, my review of small changes in language helps me to develop richer under-standings. Eventually I add a page for "examples of insight, shifts." There I may record that it was while brushing my teeth and pondering a dream that it occured to me that even "small" instances of being criminally victimized are similar to the experience of being raped. These concrete examples may later help me to illustrate the analysis process, showing that it is not one of simple induction and deduction.

Similarly, sometime along my way I enter a beginning page for "dis-covered assumptions." For example, in my research on becoming angry, I realized at some point that my attunement to a person's pause before becoming openly angry was based on an incident when I was conducting a psychological assessment with a prisoner. His account of instantaneously checking the placement of police officers before he "blew up" and slugged the one nearest him had become a touch point for me. I then went back to examine numerous written accounts, and found that my notes and inter-pretations still were accurate, but that many people were not as calculating in their pauses. Such examples of discovered assumptions provide the researcher with illustrations of method, of corrections en route, and of points of view that one might retain but now make explicit (such as my valuing "community" in the study of being criminally victimized). Readers are often reassured about the trustworthiness of a study when they see these examples of rigor.

Many researchers maintain a similar journal, or log, in their computers. They regularly make backups (an advantage over my method), and find that later they can copy and paste from different areas of their notes to new documents (another advantage over my method). An advantage for me of my method is that I do not have to lug my laptop computer around with me (although the availability of handheld devices is eroding this advantage).

At any rate, maintaining some kind of record of resources, reflections, illustrations, and so on, not only serves memory later, but also encourages you to find language for present impressions, to "get it down now" for later use.

PRESENTING FINDINGS, REPRESENTING FINDINGS

How best to represent what was found? Presenting findings requires creativity—finding ways to reach different readerships while contending with space (page) limitations. Most researchers find that presenting a general narrative, with illustrations from all participants, best conveys both the general character of the topic and its individual variations. This manner of representation serves as evidence as well as illustration. Sometimes a couple of illustrations, with participants identified, are given in brackets within the general presentation. Then tables can be used to present illustrations of every theme from every participant. This form of presentation works well for dissertations, for which length usually is not an issue. But even in dissertations, for the sake of flow in presenting the findings, sometimes the full illustrations are placed in the appendix.

When presenting findings in articles or chapters, particular readerships are taken into account. When writing to fellow researchers, you might emphasize findings that became available through a variation in method or participants. Technical terms might be used more frequently, although I favor defining terms even in specialized journals. When writing for a popular audience, you might begin with one participant's account to gain reader interest and to concretize the subject matter. When writing for specialists in the subject matter, you might summarize the findings in a general (more abstract, conceptual, brief) manner and then say that findings that throw light on specified issues in the field will be emphasized. Especially if this tack is taken, you should indicate where the fuller findings may be found (in another publication, in the on-line dissertation, by contacting the author). Sometimes I "language" some themes differently for different readerships because the relevance of findings differs. Sometimes different metaphors become appropriate for sharing findings with different audiences or readers. Sometimes the invention of new words best conveys a finding. If so, the meaning should be clear in its usage or the meaning should be clarified in the text or in a footnote.

I think that presentation of traditional research also is most effective when the author is creative in taking account of different readerships. Respect for readers is helpful in all research presentations.

Whatever the format for presenting findings, it should be written and illustrated so that findings evoke the subject matter for the reader, so that the reader's life experience reverberates with the descriptions. In this way, the reader's life as well as intellect provides access to the findings.

WRITING TO PUBLISH

First, decide on several journals that typically address your subject matter, your research topic. Note which organization sponsors the journal. Take notes on maximum length of articles, format, and publishing manual style.

Do not try to write a summary of your entire study, especially if it's a dissertation. Instead, away from your study, choose a particular audience (that journal's readers) and outline one slice of your findings to share. Outline as though you were going to present a 20-minute in-service talk, then fill out with greater detail. Then go back to your data and formal findings and see if you have left out anything critical (you probably have not!).

Consider the editor, who will read through your submission to decide whether its content is appropriate for the journal and, if so, whether the manuscript appears to be well enough crafted to send to reviewers. Be aware that editors are allotted only so many pages per year, so they value succinct articles of clear value to their readers. Unlike commercial publishers of books, journals should be submitted to serially, not several at once. Journal editors are paid only a "smallish" stipend, and reviewers typically are not paid at all and are doing this work as a service to their discipline, on top of their full-time work obligations. So ask colleagues to edit your best draft and then rewrite accordingly. Put the paper aside for a week or more, so that you can read it freshly for continuity and clarity. Submit the best version you are capable of. Journal editors will find still more points for you to clarify, but to be taken seriously and to get the best feedback from reviewers, submit your best work.

So far my suggestions apply to submissions in general, not just qualitative research. The following points likewise are broadly applicable. Follow APA style (or another style designated by the journal) carefully. Write succinctly, pruning any nonessential verbiage; write in the active voice. Explain any technical terms. Be sure that the manuscript flows, with each section being linked to earlier ones. Use the traditional headings: statement of the topic as you are situating it and the relevance of the study; procedures for gathering protocols; procedures for analyzing that data; your findings, with illustrative excerpts; a summary of contributions of your findings and of their limitations; and suggestions for further research.

Now, let me offer some advice for writing qualitative research reports in particular. Bear in mind that reviewers and later readers may not be familiar with qualitative research. Help them understand why you chose to approach your phenomenon qualitatively. As usual, review the literature and then say how a qualitative approach could throw light on identified issues. Acknowledge the limitations of a small number of protocols/participants. Perhaps say that your study could be thought of as a set of case studies. Do not attack traditional research; just say what your qualitative study offers that is not accessible by experimental methods. Be collegial. Explain terms as you go; for example, "By *lived world*, I mean how one experiences and navigates one's daily situations, influencing and being influenced en route." Answer probable criticisms in advance. For example, acknowledge that your (specified) interest in the topic has shaped your findings, that you can't be sure, without further studies of other various respondents whether such findings might be similar to or somewhat different from yours, that other researchers might word the findings somewhat differently and even more felicitously. (See Fischer, 1999, for a chapter on writing qualitative research for publication.)

EVALUATING YOUR OWN AND OTHERS' RESEARCH

An article by Elliott, Fischer, and Rennie (1999), "Evolving guidelines for publication of qualitative research studies in psychology and related fields," describes the criteria shared by quantitative and qualitative researchers, and goes on to discuss the guidelines for qualitative research. The following characterizations include and expand on the guidelines presented in the article. The shared set of guidelines includes specification of scientific context and purpose, detailed description of appropriate methods, respect for participants, clarity of presentation, meaningful discussion of findings and of limitations, and circumspect contribution to knowledge. These guidelines can be used to assess your own research projects as well as those found in publications. For qualitative research practices, the article includes helpful examples of poor practice and of good practice.

Guidelines for qualitative research reports include the following.

1. Researchers specify their theoretical orientations, personal interests in the study, and assumptions and anticipations—both those known in advance and those discovered during the research.

2. In addition to participant characteristics being reported, participants' life circumstances are described to aid readers in judging the range of persons and situations to which the findings might be relevant. Means of procuring participants are reported. Specification of realms of possible relevance of the findings, rather than achieving generalizability, is a standard for qualitative research.

3. Authors provide examples of both analytical procedures and of data so that readers can understand how findings were developed and so that they can appraise the fit between the examples and the claims made. The illustrations also allow readers to consider alternative interpretations and wording.

4. The researcher reports consensus checks. For example, participants may be asked to review parts of the analysis for fidelity of their accounts. Colleagues may be asked to review the analysis. Statistical

coefficients of agreement among reviewers may be calculated for matching themes to text.

5. The findings are coherent. The presented understanding preserves nuances while also integrating the discerned aspects. There are no gaps or contradictions. The findings do not incorporate constructs, but remain directly reflective of the data.

6. The findings resonate with the readers' own exposure to the data and with their own life experiences.

7. Discussion reveals touch points with other explorations reported in the literature. The study contributes, by whatever degree, to our evolving body of understandings.

THE CASE DEMONSTRATIONS

Each demonstration of qualitative research in this book begins with an introduction written by the editor, and the chapter concludes with the author's biographical background. Although certainly not including all established qualitative research methods, this selection presents a broad range of methods, combinations of methods, and methodological innovations, as well as a broad range of topics. You likely will become familiar with *Qualitative Research Methods for Psychologists* by recognizing similarities across chapters as well as by reading the introductory and closing material.

Some readers prefer first to read the findings in each case demonstration and then go back and read the introductory and method sections, thereby better appreciating how issues and method led to those findings.

REFERENCES

Elliott, R., C. T. Fischer, and D. L. Rennie. (1999). Evolving guidelines for publication of qualitative research studies in psychology and related fields. *British Journal of Clinical Psychology*, *38*, 215–229.

Fischer, C. T. (1984). Being criminally victimized: An illustrated structure. *American Behavioral Scientist*, *27*, 723–738.

Fischer, C. T. (1999). Designing qualitative research reports for publication. In Kopala, M., and L. Suzuki. (Eds.). *Using qualitative research methods in psychology* (pp. 105–129). Thousand Oaks, CA: Sage.

Fischer, C. T., and F. J. Wertz. (1979). Empirical phenomenological analyses of being criminally victimized. In Giorgi, A., R. Knowles, and D. Smith. (Eds.). *Duquesne studies in phenomenological psychology*. (Vol. 3, pp. 135–158). Pittsburgh: Duquesne University Press.

Fischer, C. T., and F. J. Wertz. (2002). Empirical phenomenological analyses of being criminally victimized. In Huberman, M., and M. B. Miles. (Eds.). *The qualitative researcher's companion* (pp. 275–304). Thousand Oaks: Sage.

Piantanida, M., and N. B. Garman. (1999). *The qualitative dissertation: A guide for students and faculty.* Thousand Oaks: Corwin Press.

Wertz, F. J. (1985). Method and findings in a phenomenological psychological study of being criminally victimized: Study of a complex life-event: Being criminally victimized. In Giorgi, A. (Ed.). *Phenomenology and psychological research* (pp. 155–216). Pittsburgh: Duquesne University Press.

SUGGESTED SOURCES

Braud, W., and R. Anderson. (Eds.). (1998). *Transpersonal research methods for the social sciences: Honoring human experience.* Thousand Oaks, CA: Sage.

"...introduces transpersonal research methods to the study of the transformative or spiritual dimensions of human experience. Although these new approaches can also be applied to more traditional topics of inquiry, the methods are intended primarily for studying extraordinary or ultimate human experiences such as unitive consciousness, peak experiences, transcendence, bliss, wonder, group synergy, and extrasensory and interspecies awareness" (p. ix). Nonesoteric, helpful; many contributions by the editors' students.

Camic, M. C., J. E. Rhodes, and L. Yardley. (Eds.). (2003). *Qualitative research in psychology: Expanding perspectives in methodology and design.* Washington, DC: American Psychological Association.

One of the best contemporary books on qualitative research in psychology. Geared for professionals and graduate student readership. Several chapters on innovative methods.

Denzin, N. K., and Y. S. Lincoln, (Eds.). (2000). *Handbook of qualitative research.* 2nd ed. Thousand Oaks, CA: Sage.

A classic compendium, the authors of which include many pioneers. Heavy reading for the newcomer. Some emphasis on qualitative research within the discipline of sociology, where much of qualitative research had its beginnings (1065 pp!).

Finlay, L., and Gough. (Eds.). (2003). *Reflexivity: A practical guide for researchers in health and social sciences.* Oxford: Blackwell.

Fifteen authors each characterize and illustrate their qualitative research projects, emphasizing multiple roles of reflexivity throughout the research process. Demystifies and encourages reflexivity.

Giorgi, A. (Ed.). (1985). *Phenomenology and psychological research.* Pittsburgh: Duquesne University Press.

Four experienced phenomenological psychology researchers (C. Anstoos, W. Fischer, A. Giorgi, and F. Wertz) present their own chapters on philosophical foundations, research method, and findings (on thinking in chess, self-deception, verbal learning, and being the victim of attempted rape). Still the best compilation on this approach.

Huberman, M., and M. B. Miles. (Eds.). (2002). *The qualitative researcher's companion.* Thousand Oaks, CA: Sage.

Contributions by accomplished scholar–researchers from a range of disciplines. Strongly theoretical, but accessible. Originally the title was to refer to "classic and contemporary" qualitative research; the collection was published posthumously with regard to both accomplished editors.

Kopala, M., and L. Suzuki. (Eds.). (1999). *Using qualitative research methods in psychology.* Thousand Oaks, CA: Sage.

A brief, helpful introduction.

Kvale, S. (1996). *Interviewing: An introduction to qualitative research interviewing.* Thousand Oaks, CA: Sage.

A sophisticated but concrete, readable, helpful discussion of the complexities of qualitative research interviewing.

Merriam, S. B. (Ed.). (2002). *Qualitative research methods in practice: Examples for discussion and analysis.* San Francisco: Jossey-Bass.
Authors comment on their personal experience doing qualitative research. Wide-ranging topics, but mostly from the area of education.

Patton, M. Q. (2001). *Qualitative research and evaluation methods* (3rd ed.). Thousand Oaks, CA: Sage.
A classic guide. One of the first to address program evaluation. Conversational, helpful.

Piantanida, M., and N. B. Garman. (1999). *The qualitative dissertation: A guide for students and faculty.* Thousand Oaks, CA: Corwin Press.
Highly readable guide primarily for education dissertations, but useful for all disciplines. Lots of descriptions by graduate students of their journeys at various points, as well as descriptions by the authors of their own journeys through several decades of guiding doctoral students. Connections are made between research practice and current philosophical issues within qualitative research.

Smith, J. A. (Ed.). (2003). *Qualitative psychology: A practical guide to research methods.* London: Sage.
Readable, short book at introductory level. Clarifies established methods, with helplful illustrations.

Van Manen, M. (1990). *Researching lived experience: Human science for an action sensitive pedagogy.* New York: State University of New York Press.
Education oriented, but a fine introduction to how caring, action-oriented research can be carried out. Many readers have found this small volume (202 pp.) to be inspirational. Difficult to locate now; out of print.

Wertz, F. W. (1985). Method and findings in a phenomenological psychological study of a complex life-event: Being criminally victimized. In Giorgi, A. (Ed.). *Phenomenology and psychological research* (pp. 155–216). Pittsburgh: Duquesne University Press.
The most detailed and sophisticated account of the psychological/philosophical frame with which to open up a written text (victim of attempted rape).

About the Editor

Constance T. Fischer, PhD, ABPP, is a professor at Duquesne University, where she has taught since 1966. After obtaining an undergraduate degree in political science at the University of Oklahoma, she began graduate studies at the University of Kentucky, with a primary interest in social psychology that then included the Kurt Lewin tradition of field observation and field experiment—close to life. However, she did not want to work in academia, so she opted for a clinical concentration. Because clinical psychology at the time was pretty much restricted to mental hospitals and child clinics, her goal instead was to pursue preventative psychology in the community (which later came into being under President Kennedy as community psychology). Ironically, she became a professor of clinical psychology.

At Duquesne, the department was devoted to establishing philosophical and research foundations as well as practices for psychology conceived as a human science, then primarily based in European phenomenology, and now more broadly hermeneutic. In addition to joining in the department's development of empirical phenomenological research methods, Dr. Fischer initiated a similar approach to psychological assessment in which clients collaborate to develop individualized understandings of their situations, comportment, and options. She published *Individualizing Psychological Assessment* (Erlbaum, 1994/1985) in addition to about 70 other publications on this approach, and about 40 publications on other topics, mostly about human science psychology and qualitative psychology, along with some traditional experimental studies. She has directed 25 dissertations based on qualitative research. Her published qualitative studies include ones on being criminally victimized, being in privacy, being intimate, three styles of living with back pain (with M. A. Murphy), and becoming angry.

Dr. Fischer has been active with professional organizations, having served as the President of two APA Divisions (Philosophical and Theoretical, and Humanistic), and of the Pennsylvania Psychological Association (PPA). She served on both the PPA's and the Society of Personality Assessment's (SPA) Board of Directors for 10 years. Awards received emphasize combining philosophical foundations with practice and service (SPA's Mayman award for contributions to assessment literature, the Humanistic Division's Carl Rogers' award, PPA's awards for service and for contributions to the science and profession of psychology, and Duquesne University's award for professional service). Duquesne also appointed Dr. Fischer to its Noble J. Dick endowed chair of community outreach.

PART

I

—————

CLINICAL PRACTICES

—————

1

AN ASSIMILATION
ANALYSIS OF
PSYCHOTHERAPY:
RESPONSIBILITY FOR
"BEING THERE"

LARA HONOS–WEBB, WILLIAM B. STILES,
LESLIE S. GREENBERG, AND RHONDA GOLDMAN

*Qualitative Research
Methods for Psychologists*

3

EDITOR'S INTRODUCTION

With regard to psychotherapy, assimilation is the process of a client coming to acknowledge previously incompatible and thereby problematic experiences. The issues presented at intake resolve as the person integrates these experiences into his or her sense of self. From qualitative studies of psychodynamic, cognitive–behavioral, and process–experiential therapies, Dr. Honos–Webb, along with others, developed the Assimilation of Problematic Experiences Scale (APES) of seven stages of assimilation. In their studies of assimilation with the APES, researchers typically use transcripts of total or substantial segments of a client's therapy. Dr. Honos–Webb describes the steps of becoming familiar with and indexing the transcripts, and of then identifying themes, extracting relevant passages, and finally assigning ratings of assimilation. As we see in "Lisa's" case, the evolution of a theme is often the most theoretically and practically intriguing contribution of the analysis.

Two thirds of the chapter is devoted to an assimilation analysis with regard to Lisa's theme of responsibility. Her presenting issue was depression in the face of life with her gambling-addicted husband. Readers see Lisa gradually coming to terms with her assumed responsibility for her husband's alcoholism and what she comes to recognize as her choice to remain in the marriage. We witness her coming to own her complexity. Other themes from Lisa's psychotherapy have been published elsewhere.

Dr. Honos–Webb points out that this qualitative study first relied on quantitative data (aggregated beginning and ending scores on five measures of depression) to select from a database a clearly successful therapy case, which was correctly thought to be most likely to reveal assimilation processes. Moreover, in turn, the qualitative analysis allowed understanding of apparently anomalous changes in some of her depression scale (Beck Depression Inventory [BDI]) responses. In addition, assimilation analysis of the responsibility theme led to an appreciation of Lisa's seemingly paradoxical increase *and* decrease in her sense of responsibility for her situation as she significantly resolved her depression. The analysis also led to an appreciation of how two theories of depression (Beck's self blame and Seligman's learned helplessness) were both salient, but in more complex ways than usually described. Readers will take away a respect for the complexity of the therapy process. Practicing clinicians note the promise for their work of assimilation analysis, whether formal or informal.

BACKGROUND

The assimilation model describes clients' incremental assimilation of problematic experiences as they make progress in therapy

(Honos–Webb et al., 1998). Assimilation analysis is a qualitative research method for analyzing tapes or transcripts of psychotherapy cases. In this chapter we present a brief explication of the assimilation model and our method of assimilation analysis. We then describe the case of Lisa (a pseudonym), a 27-year-old woman whose psychotherapy was analyzed. Lisa was treated using an emotion-focused treatment guided by a treatment manual written by Greenberg et al. (1993). Using assimilation analysis, we tracked the theme of responsibility across Lisa's sessions. Elsewhere, we have reported our tracking of another theme in this case (Honos–Webb et al., 1998). The current results illustrate how Lisa's depression and its relationship to responsibility were more complex and paradoxical than might be expected from abstract theoretical formulations. Because assimilation analyses are rooted in the client's immediate experience, the study uncovered contradictions within Lisa's experience that a more abstract theoretical formulation might have missed.

THE ASSIMILATION MODEL

We approached the case of Lisa using the assimilation model (Honos–Webb et al., 2003; Honos–Webb and Stiles, 2002)—a stage model of change that has been examined in treatments from varied theoretical orientations, including integrative approaches (Honos–Webb and Stiles, 2002). The word *assimilation* refers to a client's incorporating and integrating a problematic experience into the self. According to this model, clients resolve symptoms in psychotherapy by incrementally assimilating previously unwanted problematic experiences that may be memories of traumatic events, ego-dystonic thoughts or impulses, or uncomfortable feelings. Assimilation has been studied by examining session-to-session changes in clients' ability to articulate and tolerate awareness of the problematic experience. These qualitative studies of psychodynamic, cognitive–behavioral, and process–experiential therapies have refined a hypothesized sequence of stages, summarized in the Assimilation of Problematic Experiences Scale (APES; Honos–Webb et al., 1998, 1999, 2003). These studies have also supported the association of assimilation with positive outcomes in therapy. For example, in a comparison between a successful and an unsuccessful case (Honos–Webb et al., 1998), the unsuccessful client showed some progress in assimilation, but treatment ended because the research project limited the number of sessions. Because the client had made some progress in gaining awareness of his difficult emotions, he ended therapy with greater awareness of his emotional pain, which he had previously masked. Although he made progress in increasing his awareness, it is not surprising that no improvement in symptom intensity (as determined by self-report measures) occurred. The unsuccessful client made a more authentic connection with his emotional life during therapy than before he entered therapy, but subjectively this did not make him feel better. In contrast, the successful client entered therapy with high levels of awareness of her emotional pain and was able to work through her pain to a sense of emotional resolution. She experienced alleviation of her depressive symptoms that was maintained at follow-up.

The APES stages range from warded off (stage 0) to mastery (stage 7). At APES stage 0 (warded off), the problematic experience is inaccessible. The uncomfortable and previously warded off material intrudes into awareness and is actively avoided at stage 1 (unwanted thoughts) and emerges more clearly at stage 2 (vague awareness/emergence). Stages 1 and 2 are characterized by negative affect with little understanding. At stage 3 (problem statement/clarification), the experience is more focal in awareness and the client is able to state the problem in words. Movement to stage 4 (understanding/insight) is characterized by "aha" types of experiences and a clearer description of the problematic experience, with a mixture of positive and negative affect. At stage 5 (application/working through), clients report more positive affect and efforts at solving specific problems. During stage 6 (problem solution), the client achieves a successful solution to a specific problem. During the final stage, stage 7 (mastery), affect is more neutral and the client is less likely to focus on the problematic experience because he or she has incorporated the change into daily living.

The progression of problematic experiences across stages has been described theoretically in terms of a self that is considered as a community of voices, rather than a monolithic unity (Honos–Webb and Stiles, 2002; Honos–Webb et al., 1999). Voices are thoughts, feelings, or memories. They encompass what have been called *objects* in object relations theory, *automatic thoughts* in cognitive–behavioral therapies, and *top dog* and *underdog* in gestalt approaches. The community of voices refers to an inherently multiple self that is multivoiced with smooth and comfortable transitions among voices (rather than fragmentation among voices, as in dissociation). The dominant community of voices represents accepted experiences. Theoretically, voices of unproblematic experiences are easily assimilated into the community, but voices representing trauma, disturbed primary relationships, and other problematic experiences may be avoided, and are therefore nondominant voices. The assimilation model proposes a developmental sequence in which, through psychotherapy, an initially warded-off or unwanted problematic voice finds expression and gains strength until it challenges the dominant community. The sequence of assimilation stages (the APES) represents a changing relationship between these two voices. In successful cases, this leads to mutual accommodation; both the nondominant and the community voices change as they develop an understanding between each other. The formerly nondominant voice joins (is assimilated into) the community and becomes an accepted aspect of one's experience of oneself. Thus, the client moves from experiencing the self as a stable unitary self (e.g., "I am strong") to experiencing the self as flexible and complex (e.g., "I am strong and needy").

ASSIMILATION ANALYSIS

Psychotherapeutic assimilation has been studied using a qualitative analytic method that we have come to call *assimilation analysis*. It is a systematic way to approach the course of whole therapies, or substantial parts of therapies, or other change-oriented discourse.

Although, in principle, assimilation analysis can be applied to any longitudinal sample of a person's discourse, it has most often been applied to verbatim transcripts or tapes of all (or almost all) of a psychotherapy client's sessions. Clients' spontaneous statements as well as responses to the therapist can be rated. The procedure can be considered in four steps.

STEP 1: FAMILIARIZATION AND INDEXING

The goal of this step is to become fully familiar with what is in the transcription and to construct systematic notes (an index) that make it possible to locate passages later concerning particular topics of interest.

In the case of Lisa, transcripts of her 15-session treatment were read and reread, and each *topic* was listed in sequence, with its session, page, and paragraph numbers to facilitate returning to that passage. Following Stiles et al. (1991), a topic was defined as an *attitude* expressed toward an *object*, where "an *attitude* generally has two aspects—a belief (cognitive aspect) and a feeling or evaluation (affective aspect)—although one or the other of these may be more prominent. An *object* is the person, thing, event, or situation toward which the attitude is held. An object may be concrete or abstract; simple or compound" (p. 198). An example might be "has given up on" (attitude), "husband" (object), "session 1, 11, 14" (session, page, paragraph).

STEP 2: IDENTIFYING AND CHOOSING A THEME

The goal of this step is to select a theme for analysis. In this context, "theme" refers to some topic that was important or was referred to repeatedly during the therapy. Themes in therapy are presumed likely to represent the client's work on particular problematic experiences.

In the case of Lisa, we focused on new understandings, or insights (i.e., events in which a problematic experience reaches level 4 on the APES), as a way of finding problematic experiences to track through therapy. Insights are points in therapy when the client understands something in a new way, suggesting that a problematic experience has been assimilated to a changed schema. "Insight events are affectively charged, and this feature helps to make them salient in the transcript. Often they are marked by process comments, such as 'I've never thought of that before' or 'Now this all makes sense'" (Stiles et al., 1992, p. 85). One advantage of starting with new understandings is that they often include a clear, explicit statement by the client of the newly understood problematic experience. Using such clear statements, researchers can track salient new understandings backward and forward through the transcripts.

STEP 3: EXTRACTING PASSAGES

The goal of this step is to collect a set of passages dealing with a particular problematic experience. One way to do this is to search the index produced in step 1 for key words related to the new understandings or objects selected in step 2.

In Lisa's case, the index was used to locate passages indexed by key words related to the selected new understandings. For example, a significant new understanding event occurred within the context of unfinished business to resolve her anger toward her husband, and "anger" was used as a key word. All passages indexed by the key words were read and reread in context (Honos–Webb et al., 1998). As the theme is understood, it may be helpful to narrow the focus to a particular psychological conflict or problematic experience within the broader theme. For example, in Lisa's case, a conflict between expressing anger and wanting to forgive appeared as a narrower, more specific theme within those passages indexed by "anger." The index was used to locate all passages related to these narrower themes, and they were excerpted and listed for use in step 4.

STEP 4: ASSIGNING RATINGS OF ASSIMILATION

The investigator assigns an assimilation rating to each passage using a scale ranging from 0 to 7 points, guided by an understanding of the problematic experience and knowledge of the passage's context.

More important, although the APES assessments may be expressed in numbers as well as in words, during a qualitative assimilation analysis they need not be considered as objective ratings corresponding to an independently existing state. Instead, they represent attempts to express the investigators' perceptions of the level of assimilation precisely. The assessments are guided by a developing understanding of the problematic experience and are made with knowledge of the passage's context and temporal location within therapy.

Steps 2 to 4 can be repeated any number of times, once for each theme or subtheme that seemed important in each transcription.

GOOD PRACTICE IN QUALITATIVE RESEARCH
AND ASSIMILATION ANALYSIS

Assimilation analysis need not be understood as an attempt to prove that the assimilation model is the only explanation for the outcome in a case. Instead, it can be seen as part of a process of cycling between theory and data meant to refine the model. "It might be argued that this type of theory-guided observation contaminates the data, and that the observations are not 'pure.' ... Data out of context of theory are meaningless, however, and there are no 'pure' observations" (Safran et al., 1988, p. 7).

Like all qualitative research, assimilation analysis is subject to biases, but because it aims to deepen understanding rather than to predict or control, noninvolvement is not necessarily an appropriate standard. "Replacing objectivity is a concept that may be called permeability, the capacity of theories or interpretations or understandings to be changed by encounters with observations" (Stiles, 1993, p. 602). To reduce bias and encourage permeability, our assimilation analysis of Lisa's therapy sought to incorporate principles of good practice, including (1) revealing the investigators' preconceptions and expectations before the research (particularly our understanding of the assimilation model), "meant as orientation for the reader and as an initial anchor point, not as hypotheses to be tested" (Stiles, 1993, p. 600); (2) intensive engagement with the material; (3) iterative cycling between theory and data; and (4) grounding of interpretations in observations.

Iteration is conceived as "an extended 'dialogue' with ... texts (tapes, transcripts), which includes reading, conceptualizing, rereading, and reconceptualizing. ... Interpretations change and evolve as they become infused with the observations" (Stiles, 1993, p. 605). Such engagement promotes the much-called-for contextual understanding of the psychotherapeutic process. "Unlike drugs, psychotherapeutic interventions concern meaning, and hence depend on the active, conscious participation of both patient and therapist, with their idiosyncratic meaning systems.... Psychotherapeutic techniques have no meaning apart from their interpersonal (social–symbolic) context" (Stiles and Shapiro, 1989, p. 524).

Reporting the results of any qualitative analysis demands thorough grounding—linking interpretations to specific observations, such as excerpts from the transcripts, to convey the basis for the interpretations (Guba and Lincoln, 1989; Packer and Addison, 1989; Stiles, 1993). To ground our interpretations in the case of Lisa, we present (later) some of the main passages of the therapy on which our interpretations were based. Thus, to some degree, readers can judge for themselves the "validity" of our conclusions.

Unlike traditional case studies, assimilation analyses are grounded in the client's own words during therapy, rather than in the researcher's abstract formulation of the case. Especially during the earlier stages of assimilation, when a client is still struggling to clarify the nature of the problem, there may be a considerable discrepancy between the topics being tracked for assimilation and the themes deemed central by a case formulation. Although a clinical case emphasizes inferences based on a theory of the etiology of pathology, an assimilation analysis is rooted in the transcripts themselves, and therefore ultimately in the client's self-understandings.

LISA AND RESPONSIBILITY

BACKGROUND

Lisa was a 27-year-old woman who was married and had two school-age children. Her socioeconomic status was working class. She was not working at the beginning of treatment and found part-time employment before the end of treatment. Lisa was given a diagnosis of major depressive episode. At the onset of treatment, Lisa attributed her depression primarily to her husband's addiction to gambling.

Lisa presented with depression and a desire to understand why she felt the way she did. She described herself as isolated, trapped, feeling frozen, and "not wanting to move on." She also described moodiness, which she related to her husband's gambling, and helplessness because she could not control his behavior. She was involved in a support group for individuals whose spouses were addicted to gambling, which attempted to apply a 12-step program designed to overcome codependency (Alcoholics Anonymous, 2002). Lisa often described her attempts to follow the first step of this program—to admit her powerlessness and acknowledge that she could not control her husband.

Lisa participated in a research project studying the process of change in process–experiential psychotherapy (PEP; Greenberg et al., 1993) and client-centered therapy at an urban university (Greenberg and Watson, 1998). Lisa was randomly assigned to PEP and was seen for 15 sessions. Her therapist was a female doctoral student in clinical psychology. Periodic measurement on the Barrett–Lennard Perceived Empathy Scale (Barrett–Lennard, 1986) and the Working Alliance Inventory (Horvath and Greenberg, 1986) indicated that Lisa maintained a positive alliance throughout treatment (Honos–Webb et al., 1998).

PEP is a hybrid therapy that synthesizes elements of client-centered therapy and gestalt therapy, attempting to balance therapist responsiveness and empathic attunement with therapist direction of process (Greenberg et al., 1993). The foundation of PEP is a therapeutic relationship fostered

Table 1-1   Lisa's Assessment Scores

	Occasion of Assessment			
Measure	Pretreatment	Mid treatment	Posttreatment	6-Month follow-up
BDI	25	5	3	0
SCL-90 total score	1.94	0.54	0.22	0.01
SCL-90 depression	2.75	1.23	1.46	0
IIP	1.97	0.91	0.52	0.05
RSE	20	31	33	31

Lower scores indicate less symptom intensity on the BDI, SCL-90, and IIP; higher scores indicate greater self-esteem on the RSE. BDI, Beck Depression Inventory; SCL-90, Symptom Checklist 90; IIP, Inventory of Interpersonal Problems; RSE, Rosenberg Self-Esteem Scale.

by empathy, nonjudgmentalness, and genuineness (Rogers, 1957). PEP assumes that emotional understanding of one's problems is necessary to long-lasting change, and, at appropriate times, the therapist initiates tasks designed to enhance awareness of the client's current emotional experience. For example, rather than focusing on a dreaded event in the future, the therapist guides the client to pay attention to the current experience of anxiety. Similarly, rather than talking about past relationship problems (indicating unfinished business), the therapist directs the client to engage in a dialogue with the unforgiven other (empty-chair work) in an attempt to make the emotions come alive in the present. Such in-session facilitation of emotional experiencing is posited to help change the emotional schemes that underlie the presenting problems.

At the end of her 15 sessions of PEP, assessment measures showed large improvements in Lisa's depression (Table 1-1). Lisa's case was selected for assimilation analysis from among other PEP clients in the Greenberg and Watson (1998) project for having demonstrated the greatest improvement from intake to end of treatment on four of five standard measures of symptom intensity used in the project: the BDI (Beck et al., 1961), the Symptom Check List-90-Revised (SCL-90-R; Derogatis, 1983), the Inventory for Interpersonal Problems (IIP; Horowitz et al., 1988), and the Rosenberg Self-Esteem Scale (RSE; Rosenberg, 1965). In addition, Lisa reported feeling much stronger, more independent, in control, and "helped" by therapy. However, Lisa said she was still in pain and that her home situation had not improved. Thus, it was a puzzle how such dramatic psychological changes had occurred despite the intractability of what she perceived as the source of her problems—her husband's gambling.

ANALYTICAL PROCEDURE

All of Lisa's sessions were audio recorded for use in research, with Lisa's written permission. Transcripts of 14 of 15 of Lisa's sessions (one was omitted because of technical problems) were made by professional transcribers, who omitted identifying details (e.g., names of people and places).

The primary qualitative analysis was carried out by the first author, when I was a graduate student in clinical psychology. I followed the four-step assimilation analysis procedure described earlier. I consulted regularly with the second author, who was my research supervisor. Throughout the period of analysis, I kept a progressive subjectivity journal (Guba and Lincoln, 1989), which included personal reactions to the case and the research, evolving formulations of the case and major themes, and preliminary interpretations of patterns and levels of assimilation. The supervisor served as an auditor who reviewed transcripts and other case materials, and assessed my APES ratings and interpretations. Differences in ratings were discussed and, in some instances, changed. Subsequently, the transcripts and other case materials were reviewed by the third and fourth authors, who tended to view the material through the lens of PEP, and their understandings were incorporated into the interpretations presented here. Differences in interpretations were discussed among investigators and were resolved by consensus or by compromises acceptable to all.

Three recurring themes identified in the assimilation analysis included (1) Lisa's conflict between her anger and her desire to forgive, (2) her growing sense of herself as a separate individual, and (3) her responsibility in her life predicament. In this chapter we present the analysis of the third theme. An analysis of the first theme has been presented in Honos–Webb et al. (1998).

In the following section we present the passages representing the responsibility theme in stanza form, following principles suggested by Gee (1986, 1991; McLeod and Balamoutsou, 1996). Breaking speech into lines and stanzas is meant to convey better our understanding of its rhythm and feeling and to give emphasis to emotional high points and psychologically important thought units. We have identified passages by session number, page number, and paragraph number, based on the printed transcripts, to convey some idea of when the passage occurred. For example, "session 8, 15.9–16.6" means that the passage occurred during session 8, running from paragraph 9 on page 15 to paragraph 6 on page 16. Lisa's session transcripts averaged about 22 pages long with about 19 paragraphs per page. A line of ellipses (. . .) indicates material omitted to save space.

OVERVIEW OF THE RESPONSIBILITY THEME

Responsibility was a recurring theme throughout Lisa's therapy, and we believe she achieved a substantially new understanding of it. It was difficult to say precisely when the new understanding occurred, because Lisa shifted from an early preoccupation with her responsibility for others' behavior (particularly her husband's) to a recognition of her responsibility for her own behavior. This shift was unexpected because it had seemed that her central task would be to relinquish responsibility for her husband's gambling and to overcome her codependency (although this term was never used).

Lisa spoke frequently about the support she got from her 12-step group at church. She entered therapy reciting the principle of admitting lack of control, as advocated by 12-step groups (Alcoholics Anonymous, 2002): "I understand the disease and the character in him ... (session 1, 8.13), and "I-I think I've given up in that sense; I've just kind of let God take over" (session 1, 9.15), and "it's the disease that, that controls him" (session 1, 11.2), and "Yeah, I can do it. I turn to God and that's about it" (session 2, 15.18). During the assimilation analysis, it became apparent that these beliefs, for her, were a dysfunctional schema. She did feel a strong sense of responsibility for her husband's behavior, and this feeling was a problematic experience that was incompatible with the 12-step principles of giving up attempts to control her husband and relinquishing responsibility for his gambling. As the problematic feeling of responsibility emerged into awareness, she clarified her predicament: If she was powerless and he would not change, then she was hopeless.

TRACKING THE THEME

Lisa's intensely painful but vague awareness of her feeling of responsibility was apparent in session 1.

Lisa: Whether it's giving up—I've given up on him—or just-just let it be.

Th: Uh huh.

Lisa: I can't change him.

Th: Uh huh.

Lisa: What's the point? But then-then inside, it-it still hurts me, um.

Th: Uh huh.

Lisa: Which doesn't make sense.

Th: Well, it's not necessarily a rational thing, right?

Lisa: Yeah. No.

Th: But, but, I guess it's like, you're sort of continuing to feel this pain.

Lisa: Yeah, yeah. It's-it's always been there.

Th: Yeah, and it's like it's not going away.

Lisa: No. No matter how much I believe. It is an illness and, you know, it's his character.

Th: It's almost as if you know that and understand that you can't talk yourself into feeling differently about it. (session 1, 11.14–12.1)

Lisa lacked a clear definition of the problem, as is characteristic of vague awareness/emergence (APES level 2), but she experienced a discrepancy between her actual reaction and her view of an appropriate reaction ("doesn't make sense"; a problematic reaction point [Greenberg et al., 1993]). Because she believed gambling was a disease, she thought she should not have taken it personally and yet she was still hurt by his behavior. Her feeling of responsibility emerged more explicitly later in the session:

> **Lisa:** It's almost like, I feel like it's my fault (crying).
>
> **Th:** Uh huh. And that's what sort of feels really painful about this.
>
> **Lisa:** Yeah.
>
> **Th:** So much that it rests on you, like.
>
> **Lisa:** Yeah, And it shouldn't. I'm not responsible for his actions (crying). (session 1, 20.12–14)

In this passage, the problematic feeling of responsibility appeared intermediate between APES levels 2 and 3 (say, 2.5). Lisa approached a statement of the problem, in that she recognized the schema to be changed ("I'm not responsible for his actions") in conjunction with the emerging problematic experience ("I feel like it's my fault"). It was not yet at the level of problem clarification, however, insofar as Lisa was still siding with the dysfunctional schema and was still tentative about the problematic experience ("it's almost like").

In session 6 she arrived at a clear statement of the problem (APES level 3). The problematic experience and the schema were both experienced as having merit, bringing to the fore the intensity of the conflict.

> **Lisa:** Yes, as much as I understand, you know, it's, he's got to make the change too. I don't, I guess I get back into the, the depression." (session 6, 2.7)

Her comment suggests that she identified her belief in her inability to control his behavior as significant in causing her depression. Her words "as much as I understand . . ." were indicative of greater weight being given to her feeling of responsibility. Her problem statement became more explicit during the following passage also from session 6:

> **Lisa:** Um, well, his gambling. That's part of it. It's always been there in my mind. Like it's something I can't control. And I guess I, not that. I don't feel responsible for it anymore, but it, it's there, [I] can't really do anything about it.
>
> **Th:** So it kind of leaves you feeling that. Hopeless.
>
> **Lisa:** Yeah. Hopeless. Um, yes, and I-I-I can't reach out to him anymore. I tried, but I've given up. I feel I've given up on him. (session 6, 11.3–5)

This passage conveyed a sense of being stuck that is characteristic of stage 3, as exemplified by her comment, "I can't really do anything about it." If she was not responsible for her husband, this led to feelings of helplessness. She described her feeling of helplessness using the metaphor of feeling caged in: "These bars that are down and I, I just can't get out of them" (session 6, 12.14). Her sense of helplessness became even more poignant during the following passage, which occurred later in the session:

> **Lisa:** What if he just never does [change]? You know, that's his way. And he's entitled to his way and I'm not going to hold myself responsible anymore.
>
> **Th:** Yeah and so that's s-sort of difference now is that, it's not your fault.
>
> **Lisa:** No. He has a choice, a choice like we all do. Um, and I don't want to control him or be responsible." (session 6, 16.12–14)

Lisa's questioning about her husband clarified the dilemma she was placed in by her beliefs derived from her 12-step group. If she could not control his behavior and he would not change, she had no hope. Similar to stage 3 in the other themes that were assimilated, this stage was characterized by an insolubility. This conflict set the stage for an insight that would synthesize these opposing tendencies by an accommodation in the schema that allowed for the assimilation of the problematic experience.

In session 8, Lisa achieved a shift in focus that represented an accommodation in her "I am not responsible" schema (a new understanding—APES level 4). In the context of an unfinished business exercise with her husband, the following exchange occurred:

> **Lisa:** I want to face it. I think it's time that I face it all, and (sigh) it's not easy. It's painful.
>
> **Th:** Tell him [husband, in the empty chair]. About the painful part, about facing it.
>
> **Lisa:** Um, facing it is scary. It's putting the blame on myself too. I know I'm responsible for a certain amount of it, um, I want to deny it. I want to be me. I want to, I want to enjoy life for what it is. Not—I'm tired of hiding. And I'm not going to hide for you [husband] anymore. I'm going to see it the way it really is." (session 8, 14.14–16)

With this new understanding, Lisa seemed to recognize that her belief that she was not responsible may have been maladaptive. Becoming a separate individual required that she accept responsibility for herself. Lisa underlined this point later in the same session:

> **Lisa:** It feels like I have, I have my life to live. I deserve that, um. I'm responsible for myself. I'm responsible." (session 8, 19.14)

Recognizing the dysfunctional nature of her "I am not responsible" schema opened the way to assimilating the previously problematic experience. Lisa eventually resolved her dilemma by shifting from concern with responsibility for her husband's behavior to concern with responsibility for her own behavior. Her new understanding was that if she was responsible for herself, then she had hope, even if she did not attempt to control her husband. By accepting responsibility for her own life, Lisa resolved the sense of helplessness and hopelessness. The content of her responsibility was clarified in the following passages from her final session:

> **Lisa:** I'm still sad, but (crying) I guess that's, um, my choice. My choice of, um, just being. Being there in this marriage.
>
> **Th:** Hmm, You're saying that even though it's a very hard place to be—
>
> **Lisa:** Yeah.
>
> **Th:** And it is hard, that somehow you feel responsible for it.
>
> **Lisa:** Um, not for all of it. No.
>
> **Th:** No.
>
> **Lisa:** But for being in it. And, um, I guess, the commitment I feel. Maybe that's where I feel responsible.
>
> **Th:** That you feel responsible to your commitment.
>
> **Lisa:** Right, right, you know, as a wife and as a mother . . . .That's why I say, it'd be my choice to be there. (session 15, 22.1–9)

Thus, in Lisa's reframing, she realized that although she may not have been responsible for the source of the pain (her husband's gambling) she was responsible for her choice to stay in the painful situation (the marriage). This ability to differentiate which aspects of her pain she was responsible for and which aspects she was not appeared to be the helpful new understanding (APES level 4).

DISCUSSION

Lisa's objective circumstances changed little during her treatment, yet her depression lifted (Table 1-1). Her husband did not stop gambling, but his problems lost some of their power to control her emotional state. At the end of treatment, Lisa marriage remained painful, but the pain was no longer compounded by depression. Thus, a client's not making bold life changes (e.g., Lisa's not leaving her husband) need not indicate therapeutic failure. Subtle processes, perhaps involving assimilation of problematic experiences and shifts in perspective, may yield dramatic improvements on measures of symptom intensity.

Of course, as in any study of a single case, we cannot be certain that Lisa's therapy in general or her changed schema for responsibility in particular was a cause of her improvement. The responsibility theme was only one of several major themes in Lisa's therapy (cf. Honos–Webb et al., 1998), and the therapy was only one aspect of her life. The case for the contribution of her reframing of her responsibility rests on theoretical and narrative coherence.

The theme of responsibility is central to the etiology of depression in some theories of depression. According to Beck's (1967) cognitive theory, a primary feature of depression is self-blame—feeling overly responsible for negative events. According to Seligman's (1975) learned helplessness theory, people become depressed when repeated attempts to control the painful events in their lives fail, and they learn that they are helpless—failing to accept responsibility for events in their lives. Abramson and Sackeim (1977) pointed out that, conjointly, these theories yield a paradox: The merging of Beck's model and Seligman's model of depression would result in the paradoxical situation of individuals blaming themselves for outcomes that they believe they neither caused nor controlled (p. 843).

In Lisa's case, this paradox was not merely theoretical. These contradictory stances toward responsibility appeared to exist simultaneously within her: "I feel like it's my fault (crying) ... and it shouldn't. I'm not responsible for his actions (crying)" (session 1, 20.12–14). She felt both responsible for her husband's gambling and helpless to control it.

Abramson and Sackeim (1977) suggested that "conceptual willingness to assume responsibility and to castigate the self for events beyond personal control signifies a belief in omnipotence" (p. 849). Lisa's case suggested an alternative account. These two paradoxical aspects of depression appeared to reflect a negation of the self, illustrated by Lisa's descriptions of herself as "attached to his belly button," "I was like a twin," "inside his body," and "glued to him." Feeling psychologically fused with her husband, she assumed responsibility and therefore blame for his behavior. Yet she was helpless. Her attempts to stop his gambling repeatedly failed.

Lisa resolved this paradox by differentiating which domains she was responsible for and which struggles she was not responsible for. She both accepted responsibility and learned to hold others responsible. She came to consider herself in control of her life by realizing she had chosen to stay in the marriage. Consistent with learned helplessness theory, although she was still sad, her perception that she was in control of her situation may have alleviated the sense of helplessness and hence the depression.

An abstract theoretical formulation of the "cause and cure" of Lisa's depression using either of these theories alone would have missed the contradictory and intrinsically paradoxical nature of her sense of responsibility and the relationship of that theme to her depression. She both accepted too much responsibility (for her husband's gambling) and she didn't accept enough responsibility (for her choice to stay in the marriage). Her overcoming depression seemed to involve both giving up responsibility and accepting more responsibility.

In addition to illustrating the use of assimilation analysis as a qualitative research method, the case of Lisa illustrates how quantitative data may be useful in a qualitative research project. This case was drawn from a randomized comparison of the effectiveness of PEP and client-centered therapy (Greenberg and Watson, 1998). In this larger study, the outcome measures were aggregated within each condition to yield an effect size to assess the "effectiveness" of each form of therapy, to permit generalizations about the therapy's effectiveness across individuals.

Our assimilation analysis used the quantitative data differently, to explicate the context more clearly for the intensive analysis of a single case. The aggregate data located Lisa relative to other cases, allowing us to identify Lisa as the most successful of the PEP clients in terms of reduction in symptom intensity. We chose to study the case of Lisa because we felt that a person who experienced large reductions in symptom intensity would be particularly likely to exemplify successful assimilation. Quantitative data need not be restricted to making abstract generalizations in which the individual is lost.

Conversely, idiographic data from a qualitative analysis can contribute to an understanding of clients' responses on standard nomothetic measures. As an illustration, we close by considering, speculatively, how Lisa's responses to an item on the BDI changed across treatment in relation to the responsibility theme. On each of the BDI's 21 items, the respondent endorses one of four statements, each scored from 0 to 3 points to indicate degree of depression.

Lisa's responses to BDI item 8, which concerns self-criticism and self-blame, illustrated the complexity of her responsibility theme. During the pretreatment assessment, she endorsed, "I am critical of myself for my weaknesses or mistakes" (score of 1 point). During Mid treatment, she endorsed, "I don't feel I am any worse than anybody else" (score of 0 points). This improvement may have been attributable to a strengthening of her belief that she was not responsible for others' behavior. However, post-treatment she again endorsed, "I am critical of myself for my weaknesses or mistakes" (1 point). This was the only BDI item on which she regressed. We speculate that, once she assumed responsibility for her own behavior, she could be critical of her actions. During the final session, referring to her choice to remain in her marriage, she said, "If I decide to go that route it's okay, and I can, if I make a mistake, then it's only my fault and nobody else's" (session 15, 13.13). Although Beck's (1967) cognitive theory might consider this as a regression to self-blame, Seligman's (1975) learned helplessness theory could view it as an improvement. Even if she made a poor choice, her perception of control might paradoxically be an improvement over her previous feelings of helplessness and hopelessness. Thus, this pattern of changes on BDI item 8 converges with our interpretation that Lisa's assimilation of her problematic experience included both a decrease and a paradoxical increase in her sense of responsibility for her position in life.

REFERENCES

Abramson, L. Y., and H. A. Sackeim. (1977). A paradox in depression: Uncontrollability and self-blame. *Psychological Bulletin, 84*, 838–851.

Anonymous (2002). *Alcoholics anonymous* (4th ed.). New York: Hogelden.

Barrett–Lennard, G. T. (1986). The Relationship Inventory now: Issues and advances in theory, method and use. In Greenberg, L. S., and W. M. Pinsof. (Eds.). *The psychotherapeutic process: A research handbook* (pp. 439–476). New York: Guilford Press.

Beck, A. T. (1967). *Depression: Clinical, experimental, and theoretical aspects.* New York: Harper & Row.

Beck, A. T., C. H. Ward, M. Mendelson, J. Mock, and J. Erbaugh. (1961). An inventory for measuring depression. *Archives of General Psychiatry, 4*, 561–571.

Derogatis, L. R. (1983). *SCL-90-R administration, scoring and interpretation manual—II.* Towson, MD: Clinical Psychometric Research.

Gee, J. P. (1986). Units in the production of narrative discourse. *Discourse Processes, 9*, 391–422.

Gee, J. P. (1991). A linguistic approach to narrative. *Journal of Narrative and Life History, 1*, 15–39.

Greenberg, L. S., L. N. Rice, and R. Elliott. (1993). *Facilitating emotional change: The moment-by-moment process.* New York: Guilford Press.

Greenberg, L. S., and J. Watson. (1998). Experiential therapy of depression: Differential effects of client-centered relationship conditions and active experiential interventions. *Psychotherapy Research, 8*, 210–224.

Guba, E. G., and Y. S. Lincoln. (1989). *Fourth-generation evaluation.* Newbury Park, CA: Sage.

Honos–Webb, L. and W. B. Stiles (2002). Assimilative integration and responsive use of the assimilation model. *Journal of Psychotherapy Integration, 12*, 406–420.

Honos–Webb, L., W. B. Stiles, L. S. Greenberg, and R. Goldman. (1998). Assimilation analysis of process–experiential psychotherapy: A comparison of two cases. *Psychotherapy Research, 8*, 264–286.

Honos–Webb, L., W. B. Stiles, and L. S. Greenberg. (2003). A method of rating assimilation in psychotherapy based on markers of change. *Journal of Counseling Psychology, 50*, 189–198.

Honos–Webb, L., M. Surko, W. B. Stiles, and L. S. Greenberg, (1999). Assimilation of voices in psychotherapy: The case of Jan. *Journal of Counseling Psychology, 46*, 448–460.

Horowitz, L. M., S. E. Rosenberg, B. A. Baer, G. Ureno, and V. S. Villasenor. (1988). Inventory of interpersonal problems: Psychometric properties and clinical applications. *Journal of Consulting and Clinical Psychology, 56*, 885–892.

Horvath, A., and L. S. Greenberg. (1986). Development of the Working Alliance Inventory. In Greenberg, L. S., and W. M. Pinsof. (Eds.). *The psychotherapeutic process: A research handbook* (pp. 529–556). New York: Guilford Press.

McLeod, J., and S. Balamoutsou. (1996). Representing narrative process in therapy: Qualitative analysis of a single case. *Counselling Psychology Quarterly, 9*, 61–76.

Packer, M. J., and R. B. Addison. (1989). Evaluating an interpretive account. In Packer, M. J., and R. B. Addison. (Eds.). *Entering the circle: Hermeneutic investigation in psychology* (pp. 275–292). Albany, NY: State University of New York Press.

Rogers, C. R. (1957). The necessary and sufficient conditions of therapeutic personality change. *Journal of Consulting Psychology, 21*, 95–103.

Rosenberg, M. (1965). *Society and the adolescent self-image.* Princeton, NJ: Princeton University Press.

Safran, J. D., L. S. Greenberg, and L. N. Rice. (1988). Integrating psychotherapy research and practice: Modeling the change process. *Psychotherapy, 25*, 1–17.

Seligman, M. E. P. (1975). *Helplessness: On depression, development and death.* San Francisco: Freeman.

Stiles, W. B. (1993). Quality control in qualitative research. *Clinical Psychology Review, 13,* 593–618.

Stiles, W. B., C. M. Meshot, T. M. Anderson, and W. W. Sloan Jr. (1992). Assimilation of problematic experiences: The case of John Jones. *Psychotherapy Research, 2,* 81–101.

Stiles, W. B., L. A. Morrison, S. K. Haw, H. Harper, D. A. Shapiro, and J. Firth–Cozens. (1991). Longitudinal study of assimilation in exploratory psychotherapy. *Psychotherapy, 28,* 195–206.

Stiles, W. B., and D. A. Shapiro. (1989). Abuse of the drug metaphor in psychotherapy process–outcome research. *Clinical Psychology Review, 9,* 521–543.

BIOGRAPHICAL BACKGROUNDS

LARA HONOS–WEBB, PhD, is an author/speaker and licensed psychologist. Her first book, *The Gift of ADHD: Transforming Your Child's Problems into Strengths,* was published in 2005 (New Harbinger). Her second book, *The Gift of Depression,* is to be published by New Harbinger in 2006.

Honos–Webb completed a two-year postdoctoral research fellowship supported by the National Institutes of Health at the University of California, San Francisco. She has written more than 25 publications on various topics relevant to psychotherapy outcome and humanistic assessment. She lives in the San Francisco Bay area with her husband and two children. You can learn more about her work at www.visionarysoul.com.

WILLIAM B. STILES, PhD, is a professor of clinical psychology at Miami University in Oxford, Ohio. He received his PhD from UCLA in 1972. He taught previously at the University of North Carolina at Chapel Hill, and he has held visiting positions at the Universities of Sheffield and Leeds in England, at Massey University in New Zealand, and at the University of Joensuu in Finland. He is the author of *Describing Talk: A Taxonomy of Verbal Response Modes.* He has been president of the Society for Psychotherapy Research and North American editor of *Psychotherapy Research,* and he is currently co-editor of *Person-Centered and Experiential Psychotherapies.*

LESLIE GREENBERG, PhD, is a professor of psychology at York University in Toronto and director of the York University Psychotherapy Research Clinic. He has authored the major texts on emotion-focused approaches to treatment. His latest authored book is *Emotion-focused therapy: Coaching clients to work through emotion.* Greenberg is a founding member of the Society of the Exploration of Psychotherapy Integration and a past president of the Society for Psychotherapy Research (SPR). He recently received the SPR Distinguished Research Career award. Greenberg conducts a private practice for individuals and couples and offers training in emotion-focused approaches.

RHONDA GOLDMAN, PhD, is an associate professor at the Illinois School of Professional Psychology at Argosy University and a staff therapist at the Family Institute at Northwestern University. She treats individual adults and couples. She has published many articles and book chapters in the area of emotion-focused therapies, exploring topics such as case formulation, depression, and the relationship between emotional processing in therapy and change. She recently co-authored a book entitled *Learning emotion-focused therapy: A process–experiential approach to change* and co-edited a book entitled *Client-centered and experiential psychotherapies at the millennium.*

2

Exploring Psychotherapy with Discourse Analysis: Chipping away at the Mortar

Anna Madill

Editor's Introduction

Background

What Is Discourse Analysis?

What Are the Basic Epistemological Premises of Discourse Analysis?

What Is the Goal of Discourse Analysis?

What Are the Roots of Discourse Analysis?

What Is the Method of Data Collection in Discourse Analysis?

What Is the Method of Data Analysis in Discourse Analysis?

What Are the Validity Criteria for Discourse Analytical Research?

Discourse Analysis and Psychotherapy

Discourse Analysis of a Theme in One Successful Case of Brief Psychodynamic–Interpersonal Psychotherapy

    Method

    Analysis

    Discussion

EDITOR'S INTRODUCTION

Dr. Madill is from England, where discourse analysis and other qualitative methods have a much longer track record than in America, especially in psychology. Madill speaks of being transformed as an undergraduate through participating in discourse studies and then continuing with graduate and postdoctoral discourse research. Only in recent years have we in America pursued discourse analysis, which is the study of how discussion in specialized settings not only expresses, but forms, views of reality. This chapter illustrates how one's research accounts are social action as well as description. Madill has published her overall findings from the current study elsewhere. Here she illustrates with some findings from just one side of psychotherapy interactions, that of the client.

I asked Madill if she would write a special chapter that would emphasize the philosophy behind qualitative method (in this instance, of discourse analysis) and take us by the hand through some of the steps, commenting on the concrete process and its reasons and complications. Newcomers might want to overview the entire chapter and then come back to study various parts of it. Seasoned researchers will appreciate her careful spelling out of rationales and procedures as well as her presentation of contemporary arguments among discourse analysts. The latter contribution reminds us that even established methods are not monolithic and, instead, are always evolving as new subject matter is addressed and as the research community becomes less concerned with defensive documentation.

This chapter dispels any notions that qualitative research is casual or easy. We see its scholarly development as Madill presents a continuous dialogue with the many assumptions of both traditional and qualitative research. As she systematically addresses the usual expectations of researchers coming from experimental traditions, we find ourselves reflecting on our own preconceptions and philosophical assumptions.

BACKGROUND

Like many other undergraduate psychology students, the prospect of having to select a final-year project seemed utterly daunting. Animal or child studies brought visions of laboratory chaos. Questionnaires needed a good response rate. Experimental research required lots of willing participants. And, anyway, nothing had really grabbed me. However, my luck was in. A new lecturer, Dr. Sue Widdicombe (e.g., McVittie et al., 2003), joined the department, bringing with her an approach called *discourse analysis*. Ideas for projects went up on the notice board: "How has the construction of the self in Western culture changed over the last four centuries? An historical study analyzing descriptions of characters in novels." This sounded intriguing. Could my own identity, then, be studied merely as a form of linguistic description? Involvement in this project (Madill, 1990) challenged my whole way of understanding myself and the world in which I live.

The world I entered is inhabited by shifting texts. Some discourse analysts view this as a world without depth. There are no real selves hidden behind appearances (e.g., Potter, 1996b). Others argue for retaining some distinction between the real world and our descriptions of it (e.g., Parker, 1994). Either way, the discourse analyst focuses on descriptions and the implications that different descriptions have for ways of living. So, a world of shifting texts is not a world of hollow ghosts. Descriptions are never "mere." Descriptions award meaning, or take it away. Descriptions can mean the difference between life and death. The world was the same and yet it had irrevocably changed.

I have continued to be intrigued by the perspective offered by discourse analysis and used the approach in my doctoral thesis on the topic of psychotherapy (Madill, 1995). This chapter illustrates the way in which I used discourse analysis to explore the psychotherapeutic process. I present two extracts from a larger study (Madill and Barkham, 1997) along with a detailed explanation of how the discourse analysis was conducted. Let's start with an explanation of discourse analysis.

WHAT IS DISCOURSE ANALYSIS?

Discourse analysis is an umbrella term that encompasses a number of different strands of work (see Potter and Wetherell, 1994). However, a principal that all discourse analytic approaches have in common is that texts, particularly linguistic texts, are regarded as the primary resource for research. In this context, the word *text* refers to a tissue of meaning on which one can place an interpretative gloss, such as words, actions, symbols, and pictures (Parker, 1992).

The strand of discourse analysis on which I have based my analyses is that developed by Potter and Wetherell (1987; Potter et al., 1993), so, from now on, when I use the term, this is the strand to which I am referring. I say I based my analyses on Potter and Wetherell's approach. This is an important point. First, the literature does offer advice on how to conduct a discourse analytic study (e.g., Potter and Wetherell, 1987, 1994; Parker, 1990a); however, these are guidelines only and are unlikely to be appropriate for all forms of projects. Discourse analysis cannot be molded into a set of procedures. It is more appropriate to consider discourse analysis as an approach stemming from the application of a social constructionist and functional perspective on language. (These terms are explicated in the following few paragraphs.) Second, the discourse analyses I have done are influenced by conversation analysis and thus are more microanalytical, explicating the detail of sequences, than more thematic studies drawing on Potter and Wetherell's idea of the "interpretative repertoire" (e.g., Seymour–Smith et al., 2002).

WHAT ARE THE BASIC EPISTEMOLOGICAL PREMISES OF DISCOURSE ANALYSIS?

Discourse analysis is social constructionist and thus relativist in its epistemological stance (see Edwards et al., 1995). Social construction-ism regards human understanding as an artifact of sociocultural dis-courses rather than a product of direct experience of ourselves and the world (Gergen, 1985). For example, the experience of being a man or a woman would be understood as delimited by available descriptions that have evolved over time and that are linked to social, political, or even economic conditions (e.g., Westkott, 1986). This is a relativist epistemology in that there is considered to be no objective truths, only plausible and useful accounts (see Madillet et al., 2000).

WHAT IS THE GOAL OF DISCOURSE ANALYSIS?

Potter (1988) describes discourse analysis as "fundamentally an inter-pretative exercise which offers up readings of texts for scrutiny" (p. 51). Thus, the goal of analysis is to reach an understanding of the text and present it in such a way that the audience can assess the interpretation. This involves the production of theories to account for patterns and ambiguities in the text. In doing so, one must go some way beyond describing the data, while providing evidence and a rationale for one's interpretation. To this end, analytic claims are linked to specific extracts along with a detailed analysis as to why such claims are being made. The audience is, therefore, not asked to take the analyst's conclusions on trust.

WHAT ARE THE ROOTS OF DISCOURSE ANALYSIS?

Discourse analysis has roots in a variety of theoretical perspectives and subdisciplines with longer and more established histories. These are listed here, specifying a primary feature of the approach that has contributed to the development of discourse analysis:

1. Wittgenstein's (e.g., 1953) later philosophy of language: that the meaning of a word is related to its context of use
2. Austin's (1962) speech act theory: that language is used to *do* things (i.e., is functional). An example would be how a promise establishes an obligation.
3. Poststructuralism (e.g., Foucault, 1971): that forms of knowledge are constituted in and through discursive formulations. For example, scientific knowledge would be understood as the production of a particular kind of account or description of the world.
4. Ethogenics (e.g., Harré, 1979): identification of the rules and conventions people used to generate their behavior
5. Rhetoric (e.g., Billig, 1987): focus on the way in which accounts are implicitly organized to be persuasive and to undermine alternative explanations that may have been offered
6. Ethnomethodology (e.g., Garfinkel, 1967): concern with the ordinary, everyday procedures people use to make sense of their social world
7. Conversation analysis (e.g., Sacks, 1972): explication of the methods and strategies by which conversations are managed and function as an integral part of social life

WHAT IS THE METHOD OF DATA COLLECTION IN DISCOURSE ANALYSIS?

Discourse analysis can be used to examine any phenomenon that is written or spoken about. Beloff (1994) also indicates that forms of discourse analysis can be used to study visual information, such as photographs, and there has been interest in exploring such a possibility (e.g., Finn, 1997; Hamilton, 2005). This makes sense if we understand discourse analysis to involve all forms of text. Even though analysis has been conducted on research interviews (e.g., Wetherell and Potter, 1992), it is considered important to try and study naturally occurring data. This is so because discourse analysis is concerned with the ordinary, everyday ways in which texts offer versions of reality linked to particular contexts of use. Research topics have included gender (e.g., Dixon and Wetherell, 2004), attitudes (e.g., Wiggins and Potter, 2003), and education (e.g., Coll and Edwards, 1997). Discourse analysts have also made use of a variety of resources including interviews (e.g., Edley and Wetherell, 2001), literature (Potter et al., 1984), newspapers (e.g., Potter and Reicher, 1987), television documentary (e.g., Abell et al., 2000), grand jury cross-examination (Locke and Edwards, 2003), and counselling sessions (e.g., Edwards, 1995).

WHAT IS THE METHOD OF DATA ANALYSIS IN DISCOURSE ANALYSIS?

There are three main components to discourse analysis as a research approach.

1. Text as social practice: The discourse analyst is interested in how texts are constructed so as to produce meaning. However, the questions addressed are not linguistic, but social (e.g., How is racism legitimated in talk?; Wetherall and Potter, 1992). The focus is, therefore, on accounts as social actions. That is, discourse analysts explicate the ways in which descriptions produce consequences, for example, in how we interact with others.

2. Threefold concern with construction, variability, and function: The discourse analyst focuses on the way in which language is used to construct versions of reality. In detailed analysis of text, descriptions of events, persons, and circumstances are demonstrated to be variable and often inconsistent. Such inconsistency is regarded as a natural feature of accounts and is used in analysis as a means of assessing the function of any particular account within the context in which it was offered. That is, an analysis would seek to explicate how a particular version of the world was presented and what that version implies about reality (e.g., the allocation or mitigation of responsibility and blame).

3. Rhetorical or argumentative organization of text: Facticity ("telling it as it is") is understood to be a convention of account construction. This contrasts viewing "factual" accounts as essentially unproblematic. For example, a benefit of a "factual" account is that it implicitly undermines other possible understandings of the world through presenting as the one true version. With this in mind, a discursive analysis might explicate the strategies by which facticity, and all other forms of persuasiveness, are produced and contested (see Potter and Edwards, 1990).

In general, discourse analysis requires that one stop reading a text merely for the information it contains and begin to analyze how that information was put together. This entails looking for inconsistencies in description, the assumptions underlying an account's rationale, and articulating the implications a particular account makes available. In this way, the version (or versions) of reality a text offers is opened to critical inspection.

WHAT ARE THE VALIDITY CRITERIA FOR DISCOURSE ANALYTICAL RESEARCH?

Validity criteria have been developed specifically for discourse analytic research. These are (1) coherence, (2) participants' orientation, (3) new problems, and (4) fruitfulness (Potter and Wetherell, 1987).

First, coherence of interpretation can be judge through how well analysis explains both broad patterns in, and microsequences of, a text. Second, participants' orientation refers to the way in which participants themselves respond to the ongoing processes as they happen within the dialogue (if this is what is being analyzed). As a validity check, participants' orientation allows an evaluation of whether the analyst's interpretation is compatible with the participants' own developing understanding of the matter at hand as demonstrated within their conversation. Third, the linguistic resources used to construct versions of the world help participants achieve things within conversations (e.g., a blaming). They, however, can also create new problems with which the participants have to deal (e.g., giving offense). The way in which participants react to such incidents can be used to judge the validity of the analyst's interpretation. Fourth, fruitfulness refers to the power of an analysis to produce novel findings, provide a new way of looking, or in some other way increase understanding of the subject matter.

As a developing approach, Potter (1996a) suggested three more quality criteria that may be applied to different kinds of discourse analytic studies. So, fifth, studies aiming to show some regularity in a discursive phenomenon (e.g., clients' deference to their therapist) might analyze deviant instances in which this pattern is not followed. Deviant case analysis may disconfirm the pattern or demonstrate its genuiness through showing how a break in the pattern is attended to by the interactants. Sixth, the validity of earlier studies can be gauged from their ability to inform later research, because this suggests they are demonstrating something useful about the phenomenon. And seventh, in presenting the extracts that are analyzed (i.e., the "raw data"), discourse analytical research is more open than most approaches to audience evaluation.

DISCOURSE ANALYSIS AND PSYCHOTHERAPY

Psychotherapy appealed to me as a topic for discursive research for several reasons. First, psychotherapy has often been characterized as the "talking cure." This description captures an essential feature of the treatment: verbal communication. As such, discursive analysis of therapy transcripts offered a way of investigating an important process occurring between client and therapist.

Second, another element of psychotherapy that fascinated me was the way in which a topic was likely to focus on "problems." As a discourse analyst, I wanted to understand how descriptions of self, others, or life events were presented as constituting problems. Moreover, in successful therapy, how did these problem descriptions change so as to cease to be problematic?

Third, critical perspectives (e.g., Parker et al., 1995) have drawn attention to psychotherapy as a normalizing and controlling practice. For example, does "getting better" translate to conforming? Changing oneself rather than rallying against the system? Studying psychotherapy conversations would allow me to identify some of the strategies invoked by therapists in practice and to explore the wider implications of them.

DISCOURSE ANALYSIS OF A
THEME IN ONE SUCCESSFUL CASE OF BRIEF
PSYCHODYNAMIC–INTERPERSONAL PSYCHOTHERAPY

To illustrate the use of discourse analysis I will use sections of a published study (Madill and Barkham, 1997). The following method section is based on what appears in the original publication. I present sections of my methodology as published (in italics) interspersed with commentaries. In the commentaries I discuss some of the issues raised in molding the research method into the format traditional for empirical psychology reports. I then present the analysis of two extracts from the theme chosen from the case of therapy that appeared in the original study. This, again, has commentaries that offer an expanded explanation of how the analysis was conducted.

METHOD

Participants

The Case

The case was a successful therapy of a female client who completed eight one-hour weekly sessions of psychodynamic–interpersonal psychotherapy. This therapy was drawn from a pool of 117 cases constituting the Second Sheffield Psychotherapy Project (Shapiro et al., 1990), which compared two durations

(8 or 16 weekly sessions) of two treatments (psychodynamic–interpersonal therapy or cognitive–behavioral therapy).

In this section I was aware that labeling the therapy definitively success-ful was a simplification. Remember, discursive research is interested in descriptions. "Success" as a description is open to investigation. For example, How is success defined? Whose interests does this definition serve? Was the therapy successful in all respects? These are big questions; however, they are not the questions I wanted to investigate in this particular study. Rather, the research focused on understanding some of the processes of therapy in relation to whether particular cases would have been considered successful in a traditional clinical setting.

The Client

The client was a 42-year-old white woman in full-time, white-collar employment. She was living with her husband and elderly mother, whom she described as suffering from senile dementia, and who was in and out of the hospital during the time the client was attending therapy. Written informed consent to use audiotapes of this therapy for research purposes was obtained from the client at the posttherapy assessment. Hence, the client released the audiotapes for research purposes knowing the content of the therapy.

The Therapist

The therapist was a white 36-year-old man with 2 years' postqualification experience. He had received training within the project prior to seeing project clients as well as with an external supervisor. Weekly peer group supervision was the norm. The treatment method was a variant of psychodynamic–interpersonal therapy based on Hobson's (1985) conversational model.

It is useful, and perhaps unavoidable, to offer a brief description of research participants. However, discursive psychology points to an essential ingredient of descriptions; they are never neutral accounts of states of affairs. In describing research participants, the author has to select which features of the participants are relevant to the study and the way in which such features are reported. The issue is that if we do this outside the anal-ysis, our descriptions appear factual, simple, and unproblematic. A way of addressing this issue might be to reflect on the construction of participant identity within the analysis or, perhaps, if appropriate, as it occurred during the interaction between participant and researcher while conducting the study (see Wilkinson and Kitzinger, 1996b; see also Madill, 1996).

Measures

Outcome Measure

During the intake assessment, the client was interviewed by a trained assessor and obtained a diagnosis of major depressive episode as defined in the third edition of the Diagnostic and Statistical Manual of Mental Disorders *(DSM-III; American Psychiatric Association, 1980). The case was selected on the basis of the client's change scores on the BDI (Beck et al., 1961), which was the criterion outcome measure for the study. The BDI was administered on six occasions. The three pretherapy assessments yielded the following scores: 29 points at initial screening, 25 points at intake assessment, and 27 points immediately prior to the first session. Hence, there was little evidence of pretreatment improvement. The three posttreatment scores were as follows: 2 points at 2 weeks after completing therapy, 4 points at 3 months' follow-up, and 5 points at 1 year of follow-up.*

Session Impact

In a subsequent part of the intake assessment, the client was presented with a list of individualized problems derived from the content of the initial interview that summarized the client's presenting problems (e.g., "my difficulty in making decisions"). The client was asked to select a total of ten items, two from each of five categories: symptoms, mood, self-esteem, relationships, and specific performance. These ten items then comprised the client's Personal Questionnaire (PQ; Barkham et al., 1993; Mulhall, 1976). All ten personal statements were rated by the client each week immediately prior to the therapy session. The task required the client to rate how much each problem statement had bothered her during the week on a 7-point scale with anchor points of 1 point (not at all) to 7 points (extremely).

Procedures

Theme Selection

The problem chosen for detailed analysis was drawn from the ten items comprising the client's PQ and concerned the client's difficulties with respect to her mother. This theme was specified by the client in the two relationship problem statements: "Difficulties looking after my dementing mother" and "Feeling I'm being blamed for keeping my mother at home." The ratings for the two selected statements across the eight sessions were as follows: "Difficulties looking after my dementing mother": 7,7,4 —, 5,2,1,1; and "Feeling I'm being blamed for keeping my mother at home": 2,2,2 —, 3,1,1,1. Data from session 4 were missing. Thus, both these problems were resolved by the end of therapy based on the criterion of the client's PQ ratings of problem severity.

Both case and theme selection were made with regard to numerical, self-report data gathered from the client. This study, therefore, uses quantitative tools to contextualize the client and her problems. That is, first, the client is situated within the general population with regard to her level of depression as measured by the BDI. Second, the changing severity of the problematic theme selected for study is available from her weekly ratings.

Quantitative data are an unusual appendage in discourse analytical research. Quantitative data did prove useful, however, in that it provided a rationale for case and theme selection. Both were generally successful. This meant that I could address the question: How was therapeutic change achieved in this successfully resolved, client-specified problematic theme? However, even the use of numerical data is not unproblematic and was by no means essential. From a discourse analytical perspective, both diagnostic categories such as depression and outcome definitions like that provided by the BDI can be regarded as artifacts constructing the phenomenon they aim to evaluate (e.g., Gaines, 1992; see also Puchta and Potter, 2002). For example, it might be pertinent to ask what assumptions about depression have informed a measurement device such as the BDI? Furthermore, client problem statements, like those of the PQ, could be considered to constrain artificially the variable ways clients define aspects of their problems throughout therapy.

An alternative way of investigating the therapeutic process might have been to trace sequences of dialogue that, from a discursive perspective, had interesting interactional features (e.g., Edwards, 1995). In fact, this is what I did when working with the selected text. It is important to stress this to avoid the implication that numerical data somehow provide a prima facie grounding of qualitative research in "the known."

Selection of Dialogue for Analysis

Sessions 1, 3, 5, and 7 were identified as reflecting a range of therapeutic impacts from "no change" to "high change" while covering the range of severity scores for the selected theme. Extracts were therefore selected only from these four sessions. This procedure was accomplished in two stages. First, two raters independently selected extracts relating to the client's difficulties with her mother from audiotapes of these sessions. Both raters were psychology graduates in their mid 20s and white; one was female and one was male. Raters were asked to identify extracts and code the confidence with which they felt the extract addressed the topic. If both confidently agreed that a passage was relevant, it was transcribed and divided into therapist–client adjacency pairs that were defined as a client speaking turn accompanied by the preceding therapist speaking turn. The transcription conventions adopted in this study are a modified version of those developed by Jefferson (Atkinson and Heritage, 1984):

(0)	*Pauses timed in seconds*
(.)	*An untimed short pause*
word	*Stress on word by speaker*
C:	*Client turn*
T:	*Therapist turn*
T: (mm)	*Overlapping utterance*
.	*End of turn*

...	*Extract started or finished mid turn*
(son's name)	*Names excluded*
(whispered)	*Tonal information*
[...]	*Excluded text*

Second, adjacency pairs were then judged for the meaningfulness of the content when considered in isolation. The purpose was to ensure that the client's relationship with her mother was identifiably a central topic of focus of the adjacency pair. Judgments were made on a 3-point scale: yes, no, or ambiguous. This process yielded 24 adjacent pairs: two from session 1, three from session 3, nine from session 5, and ten from session 7. For extended details of the case, theme, and extract selection, see Field et al. (1994).

This study utilized data that had been selected and transcribed as part of an earlier project (Field et al., 1994). This former project was a quantitative study assessing client change in terms of a consecutive, stage model (the assimilation model [Stiles et al., 1990]). Most of the procedures reported here were conducted for this earlier study. The utilization of the data for my own research was purely pragmatic. In subsequent studies, in which I was not using preselected material, I simplified selection procedures. For example, the use of multiple raters suggests that objectivity was a guiding principle in the former study (Field et al., 1994). In contrast, the relativistic stance of discourse analysis undermines the notion of objectivity while stressing quality criteria such as coherence and comprehensiveness.

To demonstrate how selection of material was simplified, I describe the procedure carried out in the subsequent studies. First, I selected a problematic theme from those specified by the client prior to therapy, Second, I listened to all eight hours of therapy, taking note of the session and counter numbers of sections I considered relevant to the theme selected for study. Because there are no absolute criteria by which material could be judged relevant or irrelevant, I would regard careful listening and selection by one person sufficient. However, I was persuaded to obtain a second opinion on the material, so I included a third stage. I wrote a short, inclusive description of the theme selected for study and had a psychology postgraduate student listen to the same tapes and select material on the basis of this definition. I then only used material we had both selected in common. This third stage was a compromise, with the idea of reaching a more objective selection procedure. However, I do not regard it as a necessary step, and the function of the preliminary selection procedure was merely to narrow the body of material while providing a rationale for the selection.

Analysis

The first stage of analysis involved listening to audiotapes of the complete eight-hour therapy to contextualize the extracts obtained for study. During the second stage, all selected extracts were subjected to a close reading to select the text to be analyzed in detail. This involved paying attention to content (the meaning conveyed) and form (how this meaning was constructed or "put together"). Detailed notes examining how the extracts appeared to make sense were written from this close reading of the text, and patterns of consistency and variability in descriptions were identified. When focusing on change processes, particular attention was directed to points during which the client's account appeared to change significantly. Hence, key sections of text were identified at this stage.

Analysis proper was then conducted on these identified key samples of text, linking analytic claims to specific extracts. At this intensive analytic stage, the three main components of discourse analysis were used: construction, variability, and function. Accordingly, analytic procedures focus on the way in which language is used to construct versions of the world and how such versions imply certain things about that reality (e.g., responsibility, blame, obligation). Detailed analysis of text tends to reveal inconsistencies in descriptions. Such inconsistencies allow the researcher to speculate on what "job" a particular account is doing within its interaction context (i.e., how it functions).

From a traditional perspective, a procedure section should allow another researcher to conduct the same study and, if correct, replicate the results. This is problematic for discursive research. Discourse analytical procedures can be specified in general, yet in any study the application of the approach depends on the particulars of the study and the skill of the researcher. This does not mean that discourse analytical studies say nothing beyond the perspective of the individual researcher. Quality criteria include the "test of time." Skillful, rigorously conducted studies should offer insights into phenomena that are of use to other researchers and inform the direction of the field. Moreover, the researchers must justify their understanding of the data through linking analytic claims with extracts of text. On the other hand, differing perspectives are not regarded as inherently problematic. The idea is not that there is one correct way to understand material, but that the production of different perspectives honors the complexities and ambiguities of the data.

The Analyst

The analyst was Anna Madill, who is white, age 29, and female, and has four years of experience in discourse analysis. The analysis carried out on this case was subject to an ongoing audit that comprised three components. First, analyses were passed to the case therapist for comment. Second, the analyst was part of an ongoing weekly discourse analysis group that provided a means of checking procedures. Third, and most important, drafts of the analyses were sent to other discursive psychologists. An early draft was commented on by Jonathan Potter (e.g., Potter and Wetherell, 1987), and later drafts by Geoffrey Beattie (e.g., Beattie and Doherty, 1995) and Kathy Doherty (e.g., Madill and Doherty, 1994). These researchers enabled the development of the analysis through carefully reading drafts and challenging any parts of the analysis insufficiently justified by the text. We believe these procedures protected against undue bias during the analysis.

Much of this section was written to assure readers of the rigor of discursive research through highlighting some elements that fit a hypothetical–deductive viewpoint. The problem addressed is, of course, that of the subjectivity of the analysis or "undue bias." Bias, as a problem, implies the possibility of objectivity and truth. I would, however, argue that subjectivity is unavoidable in all forms of research. Researchers decide the topic, methodology, type of analysis, and how to frame that study and its results in a completed report. These are all selective and constructive procedures. What is problematic, however, is when the discourse analyst has provided an interpretation that is insufficiently justified by the text.

The checks conducted during this study were primarily to gain the perspectives of other discourse analysts. It can take a long time to become proficient in the approach, and it is easy to miss important features of the text. Having other discourse analysts read drafts was, therefore, an invaluable procedure. In fact, when possible, drafts of analysis should be considered by another discourse analyst or, if one is unavailable, an experienced researcher who is willing to consider the analysis from a discursive perspective. The process of analysis does make one keenly aware that one's own basic assumptions about the nature of reality are by no means universal.

ANALYSIS

Subject Position

Before presenting the extracts, it is important to explain the concept of *subject position,* which informs this analysis. Subject position is a concept drawn from perspectives viewing subjectivity and identity as linguistic constructions (e.g., Althusser, 1971; Davies and Harré, 1990). Identity is therefore conceptualized as a contextually variable description that draws on traditional cultural meanings. However, this is not to imply that an experience or expression of individual identity is in some way unreal. It is to suggest that the kind of person one can "be" is bounded by the acceptable descriptions available at a particular historical–cultural juncture.

As an analytic tool, the concept of subject position offered the possibility of a case study tracing the effect of the client's characterization of herself and her mother within the therapy dialogue without being sidetracked into a debate about the accuracy of her descriptions. Moreover, in viewing such characterization as drawing on recognized cultural meanings, the process of psychotherapy is immediately set within its wider social context.

In the complete analysis, three subject positions were abstracted from the client's narrative: the client as dutiful daughter, the client as damaged child, and the client's mother as the bad mother. I found these three subject positions to typify the client's account, and they proved useful in understanding her dilemma and the way in which it was resolved. I detail some of the intricacies of this process in the larger study. However, in this chapter I concentrate on demonstrating how the discourse analysis was carried out through focusing on two of the originally presented 15 extracts. These are the two extracts from which I draw evidence for my abstraction of the "damaged child" as a subject position implicit in the client's narrative.

Selected Extracts

I have selected the following two extracts to illustrate the process of discourse analysis for several reasons. First, the extracts clearly demonstrate the use of inconsistency in description as an analyst's tool. Inconsistency can be problematic from a hypothetical–deductive perspective. It may be characterized as "error variance," "noise," or an issue interfering with the reliability of measures. Discourse analysts, on the other hand, expect people's accounts to be ambiguous, complex, and often inconsistent. Inconsistency is then used as a means of speculating on the way in which a particular description or account is being used. That is, inconsistency can let the researcher come to a conclusion about the function or functions of an account within its immediate interactional context.

Second, the following extracts illustrate how subject positioning is often achieved in a subtle way through implication. I have found *implication* to be an incredibly important aspect of my own analyses. That is, I am continually asking: What implications can be drawn from what has been said? When one views texts as functional constructions, it becomes evident that recipients—the consumers of the text—are very much part of the constructive process. Hence, the discourse analyst is not trying to find out what a text means, but what it may be taken to mean. That is, descriptions make implications available. Little may be directly specified (e.g., the speaker does not directly accuse) for the account to suggest a particular conclusion (e.g., allocation of blame). The following extracts demonstrate how the subject position of the damaged child does not have to be made explicit for it to be available as an implication and to carry a negative message about the client's mother.

Third, the following extracts incidentally contain material pertinent to a discursive understanding of remembering. Memory has almost exclusively been the field of cognitive psychologists. Discourse analysis, however, is radically noncognitive in that the approach eschews intrapsychic explanations and, in fact, offers a reconceptualization of many cognitive topics, such as social representations and attitudes (e.g., Edwards, 1996; Potter, 2003). This provides an opportunity to explore the usefulness of a discursive conception of memory in an actual analysis (see Edwards et al., 1992).

The Damaged Child

The subject position of the damaged child can be identified through contrasting two accounts the client offers of her ability to remember her childhood. These accounts appear in sessions 3 and 7 of this eight-session therapy. The subject position of the damaged child is explicated through analysis of an extract from each of these two sessions. The published analysis of these two extracts is printed in italics. This is interspersed with commentary offering further explication on how the analysis was conducted, which will give you some insight into the evolution of the analysis. So, first consider this extract from session 3 (Extract numbers do not correspond to those in the former publication from which the extracts are drawn [Madill and Barkham, 1997]; T = therapist, C = client):

Extract 1, Session 3

```
1    C:    No (.) I can't go back past um (.) past
2          meeting (husband's name) really (.)
3    T:    (right)
4    C:    I can't go back (.) um (.) I remember
5          basic things (.) I remember (.) um (3)
6          (laughs) where I lived (.) I mean that
7          sounds silly (.) but you know what I mean
8          (.) I remember that sort of thing (.) but I
9          really (.) when people talk about their
10         childhood it bothers me sometimes (.)
11         because it's like amnesia (.) I really cannot
12         remember (.) I do not remember it (.) I can't
13         remember being five years old (.) I can't
14         remember being ten years old ...
```

In this extract the client describes how "when people talk about their childhood it bothers me sometimes (.) because it's like amnesia" (lines 9–11). A contrast is therefore drawn between other people's ability to talk about, and so by implication remember, their childhood and her own inability to do so. Now consider the following extract from session 7, in which the client and therapist discuss the events from the client's life covered during therapy:

Extract 2, Session 7

```
1    C:    ... I've talked about them all (.) from
2          childhood adolescence right through 'til now
3          (.) and let them go.
4    T:    Mm (.) even though they're (.) even though
5          they're so vivid?
6    C:    Yeah (.) and they are (.) um (.) I don't (.)
7          I suppose because I've kept them (.) and I
```

8   suppose I'll always be able to <u>remember</u>
9   them (.) but they're not <u>important</u> any more (.)
10   um for whatever reason if I was to think of
11   one of the incidents (.) like when I was
12   molested (.) <u>then</u> I would even <u>feel</u> (.) feel
13   afraid (.) just thinking about (.) on my <u>own</u>
14   (.) and I would try to stop meself from
15   thinking about it (.) from recalling it
16   (.) from being able to remember it (.) I
17   would try and force it away …

I had listened to the therapy tapes and read the transcript of selected passages several times. During this process my attention was drawn to these two extracts, because the client appeared to contradict herself. In session 3 she indicates her lack of childhood memories. In session 7, however, she refers to have spoken about many childhood memories during therapy. Here was a puzzle. As a discourse analyst, I did not expect the client's account to be completely consistent. This was not the result of any failure on her part, but because discursive research has shown accounts often to be inconsistent, complex, and ambiguous when examined in detail.

Part of the discipline of discourse analytical research is that one builds an interpretation or argument carefully, step-by-step. Therefore, the first thing I had to do was to demonstrate how I came to the understanding that the client had contradicted herself. I did this through pointing to features of the client's accounts that led me to this conclusion. In this way readers can decide whether they concur with my understanding or perhaps see alternative possibilities. So, immediately after presenting the first extract, I drew the readers' attention to a salient feature of it: the client's inability to remember her childhood. Let me repeat this here:

In this extract the client describes how "when people <u>talk</u> about their childhood it <u>bothers</u> me sometimes (.) because it's like amnesia" (lines 9–11). A contrast is therefore drawn between other people's ability to talk about, and so by implication remember, their childhood and her own inability to do so.

In the first extract the client states very clearly that "I <u>can't remember</u> being five years old (.) I <u>can't remember</u> being <u>ten</u> years old" (lines 12–14). It would have been easy just to quote this as evidence regarding the client's account of being unable to remember her childhood during the third session. What I decided to do, however, was to take this opportunity to point out an interesting device the client uses to build this picture. She uses a contrast structure in which she highlights her own inability to remember through comparison with other people's ability to talk about their childhood. This, though, is not a straightforward contrast structure; it includes an unstated implication. That is, the contrast only makes sense if we follow through the implication that other people talking about their childhood strongly suggests that they must be able to remember it.

I then present the second extract and provide evidence for my understanding that the client has contradicted herself through pointing to four features of this latter passage.

1. *Ability to articulate. In this seventh session the client recounts how she has discussed many events from her life including those "from childhood" (lines 1–2). So, in having "talked about them" (line 1), it is indicated that she must have had some memory of the incidents.*

2. *Length of time. She also states, in relation to such events, that she has now "let them go" (line 3). It is therefore implied that she had previously "held on to" and thus remembered them for a significant time.*

3. *Vividness. Moreover, the client agrees with the therapist that these events are "vivid" (line 5), stating that this might be "because I've kept them" (line 7) and that she presumes she will "always be able to remember them" (lines 8–9). So, in having "kept" something "vivid," it is suggested that some clear memories of childhood events have remained available to her throughout her life.*

4. *Significance. As well as suggesting that she has always had some memory of her childhood, another interesting feature of this extract is the description of the types of events to which these memories relate. They are described as things that are "not important any more" (line 9). By implication, though, they must have been of significance to her in the past. Moreover, the client offers an example of one of the incidents— "when I was molested" (lines 11–12)—thus indicating a traumatic event.*

It is only at this point that I could suggest a conclusion warranted by these observations: an inconsistency in the client's account. This has to be spelled out, though, through making a comparison with what the client actually said in the earlier session:

Thus, there appears an inconsistency in the client's account of her childhood memories between sessions 3 and 7. That is, although the indication that the client remembers some events from childhood appears consistent with her earlier statement that she only remembers "basic things" (extract 1, line 5), like where she lived (extract 1, line 6), the implication that she remembers significant and traumatic events does not.

I want to highlight two aspects of the analysis so far. First, note how I continually quote from the actual text during analysis. This is important for two reasons. It means that your reader does not have to go searching for the relevant statements, which may interrupt the flow of your argument. Furthermore, it makes you, as the analyst, very careful to use what was actually said, and to base arguments and understandings only on these words. Second, notice the continual articulation of implications and suggestions made available by the text. When articulating implications, you are going beyond description and into analysis. It is always possible that the reader or another analyst will perceive other implications arising or disagree with your interpretation. Your job is to make as clear an argument as possible for your reading of the text while grounding this argument in examples.

Now that I am reasonably assured that I have gathered evidence and articulated my argument for understanding the client's accounts as inconsistent, I can raise this as an issue worthy of investigation: *How might this inconsistency in the client's description of her childhood memories be understood?*

Possible Explanations

Texts are open to many interpretations. The next stage of analysis, then, was to suggest and examine possible explanations for the inconsistency in the client's account of her childhood memories. In producing possible explanations I drew on my "knowledge as a member." That is, as a person I am used to making sense of textual material in my everyday life (conversations, TV, books). Producing possible explanations within a discourse analysis is, therefore, an articulation of a sense-making process most of us are involved in every day of our lives. I (with help) came up with three possible explanations for why the client produced such contrasting accounts of her ability to remember her childhood.

The first possible explanation is *reasonable exaggeration. In the seventh session (extract 2), the client does suggest that remembering some childhood incidents offered particular difficulties. For example, in relation to being molested she states, "I would try to stop meself from thinking about it (.) from recalling it (.) from being able to remember it (.) I would try and force it away" (lines 14–17). So, the client reports "trying" not to remember this event. Conceivably, such an attempt may be described as "memory loss" early in therapy.*

The idea is, therefore, that not being able to remember could be considered a reasonable exaggeration. It is understandable in human interaction that exaggeration may be used to capture the spirit of an experience. However, having suggested this way of understanding the client's account, I go on to present an argument why this understanding is flawed in this particular case. I do this through pointing to certain features of the sequences: *However, describing "not remembering" as both a struggle and as only an attempt, the implication remains that these memories were available to trouble her and so could not be "like amnesia" (extract 1, line 11).*

Hence, I point to the client's use of the simile "like amnesia" and argue that this stretches the credibility of understanding the difference in the accounts as reasonable exaggeration.

A second possible explanation is that it is *a device that relieves the client from talking. A more plausible explanation is that the client's report of memory loss during the third session might be understood as a device relieving her from talking about particularly distressing things early in therapy.*

I am indebted to Jonathan Potter for suggesting this in some comments on a draft of the analysis. The idea here is that the client may have preferred to present herself as unable to remember much from childhood early in therapy to avoid discussing traumatic events with the therapist at this point. Here it is important to note that the suggestion stems from an understanding of the context in which the client was speaking. Context can be extremely useful in helping the researcher make sense of texts. However, it is important not to assume your understanding of the context is the same as that of your participants. Therefore, if you are using contextualizing information within an analysis, always be tentative and consider carefully whether your speculation is at least consistent with the text.

The third possible explanation is that it is *a functionally contextual account. However, a third explanation is to regard inconsistency as an inherent feature of accounts. For example, from a discursive perspective, inconsistency is regarded as an indication of an account's contextually <u>functional</u> nature. Thus, it is suggested that the client's reported memory loss can be understood as an account oriented to the interactional context of its telling (see Edwards et al., 1992)—a context that has changed between sessions 3 and 7.*

The first two possible explanations that I suggest might account for the client's inconsistency draw on commonsense understandings of the way in which people interact. They may exaggerate to express the spirit of an experience or try to avoid a painful topic. The third possibility I suggest is a bit more technical in that it draws on a functional perspective of language use.

Remember the discourse analyst approaches accounts as social actions rather than as neutral descriptions of states of affairs. The same event, person, or situation can be described in a variety of different ways. Therefore, in producing a description, one constructs a particular version. Recipients also coconstruct the account through ordinary, sense-making procedures. For example, sense-making may be achieved through conversational interaction (e.g., asking questions, adding information, disputing) or merely through drawing conclusions from the descriptions offered (e.g., accountability). Descriptions offered are likely affected by the context in which the account is given (e.g., to whom one is talking, what effect one is trying to achieve, or what action might be taken in light of one's account). That is, accounts are understood to be constructed versions of reality oriented toward the context of production. Accounts regarding what one can remember are no different.

Utilizing this discursive perspective, I suggest that the inconsistency in the client's report of her memory is a normal consequence of orienting to the context of the telling. The context of therapy is likely to have changed between sessions 3 and 7. The client and therapist have a longer history of interaction. That is, the client's account of her ability to remember her childhood may be doing a different "job" in each session. Hence, the next stage of analysis is to persuade the reader that this functional perspective provides a useful understanding of the process of therapy. This is done through asking: What implications are made available by the client's account of childhood memory loss? In other words, what conclusions does this account lead the recipient to make about the client and her situation?

Exploring this discursive perspective further, it might be fruitful to speculate on the function or functions the client's third-session report of having little memory of childhood might serve. To achieve this, it is necessary to examine the implications made available by this particular account (see extract 1).

Working through draft after draft of analysis, it became apparent that three aspects of the client's third-session account of memory loss were of particular relevance in leading a recipient to draw conclusions about the client and her situation.

The first is *importance. So, first, it is interesting to note the strength of the client's claims: "I really cannot remember (.) I do not remember it" (lines 11–12), and that it is "like amnesia" (line 11). If, as suggested earlier, the client merely did not want to discuss her childhood early during therapy, she might have been expected to have either stated her wishes, or avoided or at least deemphasized the topic. However, rather, she draws attention to the issue through stressing her memory failure and, by implication, to suggest its inherent importance.*

Again, "lay" knowledge of interaction is used here. As people involved in interacting with others, we know that there are strategies that can be used to avoid talking about something. I note some of them here, for example, simply stating one's wishes. However, I point out that rather than try to avoid the topic, the client actually stresses it. There are two uses of this analysis. First, by pointing out that the client stresses, rather than avoids, the topic of memory loss, I undermine the possible explanation that the client's account was a device for relieving her from talking about her childhood early during therapy. Second, the analysis provides evidence that a recipient is likely to conclude that the client's memory loss is an important matter.

The second aspect is *abnormality. Second, likening her memory loss to "amnesia" (line 11) suggests that she ought to be able to remember what she cannot. It is therefore implied that her experience is abnormal.*

When exploring the implications raised by descriptions, it is often useful to comment on the connotations invoked by the use of particular words. In such instances it may be helpful to consult a dictionary. This is not to find the "real" meaning of the word, but to clarify some of the different ways in which the word may be used and hence some of the connotations that may be heard. Here I draw attention to the client's use of the simile "like amnesia." The word *amnesia* indicates an abnormal state characterized by the inability to remember chunks of the past that should be available to memory. Thus, although the client does not make a strong claim to being amnesic, the simile has the consequence of construing her memory loss as outside the bounds of normality.

The third aspect is *problematic. Third, she states that the loss "bothers" (line 10) her. So, furthermore, it is indicated to be disturbing and thus problematic.*

Again, I point to the use of a particular word. This time it is to indicate that by describing the memory loss as "bothering" her, the experience is construed as problematic.

Other Possible Descriptions

An important feature of discursive analysis is the idea that phenomena can be described in many different ways. Once one realizes this, it opens up a way of exploring texts, to ask: Why this description and not another? The analysis continues by drawing attention to this feature of descriptions:

Thus, the client's third-session account makes the implications available that her memory loss is important, abnormal, and problematic. Such an account can be seen to contrast other possible descriptions that may have been offered. For example, normalizing accounts could have been offered in which the memory loss was accounted for in terms of fading over time or to her childhood having been particularly uneventful.

I emphasize the idea that accounts and descriptions can usefully be regarded as constructed versions of reality through suggesting some alternative ways in which the client could have presented her memory loss. For example, her memory loss could have been presented as normal but fading over time. The point of this move is to persuade the reader that the actual account offered by the client is functional. That is, it is a constructed version of reality that does a particular job within its interactional context. This step in the analysis highlights the use of the idea of the rhetorical or argumentative organization of text. For example, it might be difficult to suggest to the client that her memory loss is in fact normal, fading over time, following this account because she has already used several rhetorical devices to construct the loss as abnormal: use of the simile "like amnesia" and contrasting her experience with that of other people. Thus, if the client could have offered different descriptions of her memory loss, it is pertinent to ask what job that account was performing. This can be done through exploring the possible consequences of the description offered.

Repressed Childhood Trauma

In contrast, presenting the loss as important, abnormal, and problematic suggests the existence of disordered psychological processes. An obvious implication, particularly in psychodynamic psychotherapy, is, therefore, that the loss might be the result of repressed childhood trauma.

The client has presented her memory loss as abnormal and problematic. An obvious conclusion that may be drawn from such a description is that something has caused this to happen. A commonsense understanding of amnesia is that it may be caused by physical or emotional trauma—a bang on the head or a psychological defense. Moreover, the memory loss has been implied to be important. Within a session of therapy, it may be concluded that this has relevance to understanding the client's problems. Such implications allow me to speculate that the client's account can be heard as suggesting the existence of some childhood trauma in her past, and hence the subject position of the damaged child.

These analytical steps take us some way beyond the data. What I have done is to follow through some of the implications of the client's description, bearing in mind the context in which it was offered. As such, the analysis is speculative but grounded in the data. However, before I was satisfied that the analysis was persuasive, I had to deal with one final issue. For my analysis to work, I was assuming that both participants were working with a psychodynamic understanding of subjectivity. That is, I had to assume that the loss of childhood memories invoked the idea of repression in the form of trauma-induced amnesia. I do this by making a case for the appropriateness of this assumption through reference to the literature:

As psychodynamic concepts like that of the defense mechanisms have been suggested to permeate contemporary Western culture (Moscovici, 1976), allusion to these mechanisms by laypersons in description of events and experiences may not be unusual (Hoffman, 1992; Walker, 1988). Thus, the subject position of the damaged child is implicitly invoked in the client's account.

DISCUSSION

I have now, as it were, talked you through the logic of my analysis of two extracts from a problem theme in one case of therapy. These two extracts have been taken from a larger study that addressed the question: How was therapeutic change achieved in this successfully resolved, client-specified problem? Detailed analysis, like the one demonstrated here, is conducted to provide a carefully argued case for a particular reading of a text. As such, all presented extracts and their analysis should contribute to this aim and together provide a coherent argument. So, how did these extracts help provide an understanding of the processes of change in the selected theme?

Remember at the beginning of the analysis section I stated that three subject positions were found to typify the client's account: the client as dutiful daughter, the client as damaged child, and the client's mother as the bad mother. The first section of the full analysis carefully sets forth the evidence for this conceptualization of the material. The subject positions were an important part of the analysis in two ways. First, the pattern of subject positioning in the theme studied offered a means of understanding variations in description identified across some of the sequences. That is, identification of the "dutiful daughter" helped explain the observation that the client's self-positioning as damaged child and her mother as the bad mother was alluded to obliquely during early sessions, but more directly later in therapy. It was suggested that such positionings might have undermined the client's dutifulness toward her mother had they been articulated before this had been fully established during the interaction (i.e., implicitly accepted, or at least not questioned, by the therapist).

Second, a section of the larger analysis examined the client's understanding of her recovery from depression as articulated within the therapy. This analysis suggested the importance to the client, herself, of understanding her past in terms of the "bad mother" and "damaged child." Hence, the analysis of individual extracts comes together as a coherent argument about some of the processes of change occurring throughout the selected theme.

HOW DOES THIS STUDY CONTRIBUTE TO MAINSTREAM RESEARCH ON PSYCHOTHERAPY?

Psychotherapy research has, since the early 1980s, been relatively open to qualitative methods. In a key publication heralding a new postpositivist paradigm, Elliott (1983) suggested that practitioners, disillusioned with the use of average group data, considered qualitative analyses that focus on the microprocess of actual therapy to have greater practical application to their work with clients. By the early 21st century, the quantity of qualitative research on psychotherapy was such that McLeod (2000) produced a contextualizing primer "to help researchers find their way through the range of methodologies and techniques available to them" (as quoted from the book jacket).

Even so, discourse analysis can sit uneasily with mainstream psychotherapy research as, contrary to most psychotherapeutic theory, it refuses to situate explanations in an intrapsychic world. However, post-Freudian theory (e.g., Winnicott, 1960) has turned its attention to the relational aspects of psychopathology, and psychotherapeutic approaches such as that of White and Epston (1990) have been influenced by narrative and discourse theory. Moreover, the popular and mainstream conceptualization of the psychotherapeutic process as an *alliance* (e.g., Catty, 2004) attempts to capture the mutual influence of client and therapist on each other. Discourse analytical studies, such as the one drawn upon in this chapter, can demonstrate some of the linguistic strategies clients (and therapists) bring to the therapeutic encounter as a way of expounding, for example, how a therapeutic alliance can be developed (or ruptured). So, although the epistemology and ontology of discourse analysis may counter that of mainstream psychotherapeutic research, in practical terms discourse analytical studies can further understanding of reasonably, well-accepted relational aspects of the therapeutic process.

Evaluation criteria for discourse analytic research includes the ability to inform later research, and I have been involved in a series of discourse analytical studies that build on each other. A second study from my doctoral thesis, focusing on the conversation analytical elements of the analysis, continued to identify ways in which problem formulation can be achieved within therapy (Madill et al., 2001). A further study, which I supervised, drew on an expanded concept of subject positioning to identify possible session 1 indicators of end-of-treatment psychotherapy outcome (Madill et al., in press). So, although it is, perhaps, unlikely that discourse analysis itself will become mainstream in psychotherapy research, these studies show how the approach can be utilized to address pragmatic questions of potential utility to counselors and psychotherapists.

QUIRKS OF THIS PARTICULAR STUDY

In the introduction I mentioned that discourse analysis is an approach rather than a methodology. Here I would like to point out some of the features of the presented analysis that are particular to this example but do not necessarily typify discursive research.

First, in the larger analysis, and as demonstrated by the extracts selected for study here, the focus was on the client's account of her situation. This was so because I was particularly concerned with illustrating the work done by descriptions. I have made extensive use of the therapist's input in ongoing research (Madill et al., 2001). Hence, discursive research utilizing conversational material may focus more on interaction than has been illustrated here.

Second, my research has been rather influenced by conversation analysis. Hence, I focus on the fine detail of sequences of text. Discursive work can be much more thematic (e.g., Wetherell and Potter, 1992).

Third, I use a modified version of transcription conventions developed by Jefferson (Atkinson and Heritage, 1984). I selected several basic transcription conventions that I find helpful in communicating important features of speech. For example, I include stress on words (underlining) because this can affect the meaning conveyed. Potter (personal communication) argues for the use of more detailed notation as used by conversation analysts (see Edwards [1995]). I appreciate the detail such transcripts offer; however, I am not myself convinced of the effectiveness of this move. First, although my analysis is detailed, I do not draw on features of the interaction that are not represented by my transcription within my analysis. Second, I want to make my analyses as user friendly as possible. Heavily annotated transcripts are tricky to read. Finally, on a purely pragmatic level, the time taken to do a detailed transcription must be balanced against other demands on one's resources. Thus, my own conclusion is to make sure the transcript is accurate at the level of content with the main, interactional features specified and then spend time making the analysis as thorough as possible.

COMMON MISUNDERSTANDING

It can take a while to get into the "mind-set" of discourse analysis. This is probably because, in many ways, it is counter to a commonsense understanding of psychology. The most fundamental of these is the idea that discourse analyst's are claiming that people don't think. This stems from the fact that discourse analysis is radically noncognitive and does not reduce talk and text back to notions of personal attitudes or opinions of an author. Rather, the focus of interest is in (1) how texts are a kaleidoscope of publicly available formulas (discourses) and (2) how texts are constructed in orientation to an audience (i.e., are functional). Thus, a common misunderstanding is that discourse analysts are claiming that nothing goes on inside people's heads. This is not the case. The discursive position does not deny the existence of internal, mental events. However, thoughts are understood to echo the publicly developed language of interaction and, in the main, follow the well-worn ruts of practiced, public debate (Billig, 1987). Moreover, our understanding of mental events is understood to be discursively constructed; that is, informed by linguistic conventions. Discourse analysis is a truly social perspective.

MISAPPLICATIONS

Discourse analysis is not an approach that can be used to answer any question on any topic (for discussion of the matching of research question and research approach see, Elliott [1995]). For example, discourse analysis would not be the approach of choice for projects asking "how many" questions. My own experience is that discourse analysis is also unsuitable for asking "why" questions. This is so because "why" questions can involve the exploration of motives and search for causalities. These are topics that the discourse analyst is likely to deconstruct as functional descriptions rather than invoke as having explanatory power. On the other hand, discourse analysis is excellent for investigating "how" questions. For example, how is group identity negotiated (Widdicombe and Woofitt, 1995)? How do men account for feminists (Edley and Wetherell, 2001)? How is male rape accounted for in conversation (Doherty and Anderson, 2004)?

Discourse analysis, moreover, is unlikely to complement many other research approaches as part of a larger project. The reason for this is that discourse analysis is a social constructionist perspective and thus can jar with positivist or humanist assumptions about the nature of knowledge and the investigative enterprise (Madill et al., 2000).

The Discourse and Rhetoric Group at Loughborough University, UK, have produced an analysis of shortcomings common to discourse analytical research. These are explained under the headings of underanalysis through summary, underanalysis through taking sides, underanalysis through over-quotation or through isolated quotation, the circular identification of discourses and mental constructs, false survey, and analysis that consists of simply spotting features (Antaki et al., 2003). This online publication contains really useful information from some of the most experienced discourse analysts around, so it is well worth studying.

CONTEMPORARY ISSUES

As with many specialist areas, the field can appear cohesive from the outside whereas within there are tensions and disputes. This can be understood as a productive state of affairs. Debate necessitates exploration and clarification of positions, thus moving the field forward. In this section I would like to touch upon three of the current debates in the field of discursive psychology.

The first involves the tension between poststructuralist (e.g., Parker, 1990a,b) and ethnomethodological discourse analysis (e.g., Potter et al., 1990), which (given the examples cited) overlaps with critical realist and relativist discursive analysis. To simplify, an aspect of this tension is one of level of analysis—macro or micro—and the problems associated with each. Poststructural discourse analysts explore how texts are produced within the constraints of overarching, cultural ideologies (e.g., individualism). The ethnomethodologists argue that such analysis is in danger of awarding undue status to such ideologies—that is, of reifying them. They argue that analysis should be sensitive to variation; to the ways in which overarching ideologies may be challenged, "ironicized," undermined, or sustained in particular interactions. Such analysis, though, may imply that research findings emerge directly from the data, thus undermining their own social constructionist stance. Parker's (1990a, b) response has been to maintain a delicate balance between using cultural discourses as resource (e.g., using psychoanalysis to understand a text) while not awarding such discourses truth status (discussed later).

A second conundrum involves the issue of subjectivity and the grounding of analysis. Unlike traditional psychologists, discourse analysts do not speculate on the motivations or intentions of speakers. Hence, they do not ground research in subjects as the original cause. What is of interest is how speakers themselves produce understandings through, for example, invoking motivations and intentions. Parker (1994) has referred to this in a critique as *blank subjectivity* (for commentary, see Wetherell [1994]). Treating the speaking subject as a "blank" has proved an effective way of focusing on the functionality of language and on the social construction of subjectivity. However, some discursive researchers have found this unsatisfactory. For example, Hollway (1989) argues that it is crucial to theorize an agentic and motivated subject separable from the discourses in which subjectivity is constructed to understand why an individual constructs his or her own identity in particular ways (Hollway, 1989; Madill and Doherty, 1994). Hollway has developed this understanding into a particular strand of psychoanalytic discourse analysis based on Kleinian theory (Hollway and Jefferson, 2000). Parker has also turned to psychoanalytical theory, this time a Lacanian variety, to produce an understanding of subjectivity in discursive analysis. He has, however, criticized Hollway and Jefferson (2000) for risking reifying psychoanalytical discourses as truth and has developed a form of critical discursive psychology about which he states, "I write about psychoanalysis as a form of narrative in a way that locates me inside it that *externalizes* it rather than treating it as something inside me" (italics in original; Parker, 2003; p. 303).

A third, more global, area of debate concerns the criteria used to evaluate qualitative research, including forms of discourse analysis. I have already pointed to those suggested by Potter specifically for discursive research (Potter and Wetherell, 1987; Potter, 1996a). With the aim of setting a standard for the field of qualitative research, some authors have produced general recommendations for quality criteria (e.g., Elliott et al., 1999). Others, including myself, have argued that qualitative research is diverse and that the criteria used to evaluate any particular study should be commensurate with the epistemological stance within which it was conducted (Madill et al., 2000; Reicher, 2000). Parker (2004) has expanded this debate arguing that "criteria of any kind risk legitimating certain varieties of qualitative research, marginalizing others, and so stifling new methodological developments" (pp. 95–96). In response, he suggests some flexible guidelines designed for supervisors of qualitative research projects and their students that he suggests are closed enough to be useful and open enough to allow innovative approaches to research: (1) situating the work in the research literature, (2) producing a coherent argument throughout the study (with exceptions; see Curt [1994]) and, (3) making the work accessible through "clearly accounting for the conceptual background, research process and new perspectives" (p. 101). Parker (2004) also defines three core principles characterizing the best research with respect to both content and form: (1) apprenticeship (learning to "speak the language" of a research discipline), (2) scholarship (sophisticated familiarity with the relevant debates), and (3) innovation (which produces something new and "transforms the coordinates by which a problem is usually understood" [p. 104]).

SUGGESTED READING

I limit my suggestions for further reading to books (and some book chapters) as they include large reference sections that will allow you to follow up topics of interest. However, a glance through the *Journal of Language and Social Psychology, Discourse and Society*, or the *British Journal of Social Psychology* may also turn up some interesting articles.

The strand of discourse analysis on which I have based my analysis was introduced formally by Potter and Wetherell (1987). This is a readable and comprehensive account of discourse analysis as a research approach. Edwards and Potter (1992) represent the development of this approach from a truly ethnomethodological perspective, and Potter (1996b) is an account aimed specifically at an undergraduate audience. The most contemporary chapter outlining discourse analysis by Potter is in the prestigious American Psychological Association text *Qualitative Research in Psychology: Expanding Perspectives in Methodology and Design* (Potter, 2003). These sources will give you a solid grounding in this approach.

Several "classic" discursive works have now appeared on various, specialized topics. Wetherell and Potter (1992) explored racism in interviews with New Zealanders about the Maoris. Wetherell has co-authored a book on the topic of masculinity (Edley and Wetherell, 1995) and has written extensively on identities and groups (e.g., Wetherell, 1996). For those interested in women's studies, Wilkinson and Kitzinger (1996a) have edited a collection that has been described as a groundbreaking text dealing with discourse analysis from a feminist psychological perspective (Hepburn, 1996). Widdicombe and Woofitt (1995) offer an examination of group identity from a discursive perspective using material gathered from various youth subcultures. As touched on in this example analysis, discourse analysis offers an alternative conceptualization of phenomena often considered the field of cognitive psychology. Edwards (1996) explores this in detail and has co-edited a collection on classroom discourse (Coll and Edwards, 1997). For those with an interest in poststructuralism and/or psychoanalysis, I must also mention Parker (1992). This is an introduction to critical discourse analysis that usefully demonstrates some of the limitations to the more ethnomethodological strand. The most up-to-date expositions of Parker's position can be found in Parker (2002, 2005). For an alternative discursive approach to psychoanalytic subjectivity, particularly that of unconscious processes, see Billig (2001). Those interested in a more humanistic angle will find Harré and Gillett (1994) more palatable.

When approaching a text to perform a discursive analysis you can never tell where you will end up. Reading and rereading the text, you begin to create minitheories. Next you try some more detailed analysis of extracts that appear to illustrate some process of interest. From this you identify other sections of text that create problems for your theory that then must be modified. Other extracts become interesting and necessitate detailed analysis. The amazing thing is that by the time you have got into the analysis, you can no longer understand how the text had all made perfect sense when you first read it! People are experts in the discursive art of construction. Words build pictures of the world so skillfully that it takes practice and effort to stop focusing on the beauty of the finished product and to start pulling apart the seams and chipping away at the mortar.

I am still fascinated by the potential of approaching human subjectivity as, at least in part, a linguistic construction. I hope something here might have captured your imagination too!

REFERENCES

Abell, J., E. H. Stokoe, and M. Billig. (2000). Narrative and the discursive (re)construction of events. In: Andrews, M., S. D. Sclater, C. Squire, and A. Treacher. (Eds.). *Lines of narrative: Psychosocial perspectives* (pp. 180–192). London: Routledge.

Althusser, L. (1971). *Lenin and philosophy and other essays.* London: New Left Books.

American Psychiatric Association. (1980). *Diagnostic and statistical manual of mental disorders.* 3rd ed. Washington, DC: Author.

Antaki, C., M. Billig, D. Edwards, and J. Potter. (2003). Discourse analysis means doing analysis: A critique of six analytic shortcomings. *Discourse Analysis Online, 1.* Available at www.shu.ac.uk/daol/previous/v1/n1/index.htm.

Atkinson, J. M., and J. Heritage. (Eds.). (1984). *Structures of social action.* Cambridge, UK: Cambridge University Press.

Austin, J. L. (1962). *How to do things with words.* Oxford, UK: Clarendon Press.

Barkham, M., W. B. Stiles, and D. A. Shapiro. (1993). The shape of change in psychotherapy: Longitudinal assessment of personal problems. *Journal of Consulting and Clinical Psychology, 61,* 667–677.

Beattie, G., and K. Doherty. (1995). "I saw what really happened": The discursive construction of victims and villains in firsthand accounts of paramilitary violence in Northern Ireland. *Journal of Language and Social Psychology, 14,* 408–433.

Beck, A. T., C. H. Ward, M. Mendelson, J. Mock, and J. Erbaugh. (1961). An inventory for measuring depression. *Archives of General Psychiatry, 4,* 561–571.

Beloff, H. (1994). Reading visual rhetoric. *The Psychologist, 7,* 495–499.

Billig, M. (1987). *Arguing and thinking: A rhetorical approach to social psychology.* London: University of Cambridge Press.

Billig, M. (2001). Discursive approaches to studying conscious and unconscious thoughts. In Tolman, D. L., and M. Brydon–Miller. (Eds.). *From subjects to subjectivities: A handbook* of interpretive and participatory methods. *Qualitative studies in psychology* (pp. 290–303). New York: New York University Press.

Catty, J. (2004). "The vehicle of success": Theoretical and empirical perspectives on the therapeutic alliance in psychotherapy and psychiatry. *Psychology and Psychotherapy: Theory, Research and Practice, 77*, 255–272.

Coll, C., and D. Edwards. (Eds.). (1997). *Teaching, learning and classroom discourse: Approaches to the study of education discourse.* Madrid, Spain: Fundacion Infancia y Aprendizaje.

Curt, B. C. (1994). *Textuality and tectonics: Troubling social and psychological science.* Buckingham, UK: Open University Press.

Davies, B., and R. Harré. (1990). Positioning: The discursive production of selves. *Journal for the Theory of Social Behaviour, 20*, 43–63.

Dixon, J., and M. Wetherell. (2004). On discourse and dirty nappies: Gender, the division of household labour and the social psychology of distributive justice. *Theory & Psychology, 14*, 167–189.

Doherty, K., and I. Anderson. (2004). Making sense of male rape: Constructions of gender, sexuality and experience of rape victims. *Journal of Community and Applied Social Psychology, 14*, 85–103.

Edley, N., and M. Wetherell. (1995). *Men in perspective: Practice, power and identity.* London: Harvester Wheatsheaf.

Edley, N., and M. Wetherell. (2001). Jekyll and Hyde: Men's constructions of feminism and feminists. *Feminism & Psychology, 11*, 439–457.

Edwards, D. (1995). Two to tango: Script formulations, dispositions and rhetorical symmetry in relationship troubles talk. *Research on Language and Social Interaction, 28*, 319–350.

Edwards, D. (1996). *Discourse and cognition.* London: Sage.

Edwards, D., M. Ashmore, and J. Potter. (1995). Death and furniture: The rhetoric, politics and theology of bottom line arguments against relativism. *History of the Human Sciences, 8*, 25–49.

Edwards, D., and J. Potter. (1992). *Discursive psychology.* London: Sage.

Edwards, D., J. Potter, and D. Middleton. (1992). Toward a discursive psychology of remembering. *The Psychologist, 5*, 439–455.

Elliott, R. (1983). Fitting process research to the practicing psychotherapist. *Psychotherapy: Theory, Research and Practice, 20*, 47–55.

Elliott, R. (1995). Therapy process research and clinical practice: Practical strategies. In Aveline, M., and D. A. Shapiro. (Eds.). *Research foundations for psychotherapy practice* (pp. 49–72). Chichester, UK: Wiley.

Elliott, R., C. T. Fischer, and D. L. Rennie. (1999). Evolving guidelines for publication of qualitative research studies in psychology and related fields. *British Journal of Clinical Psychology, 38*, 215–229.

Field, S. D., M. Barkham, D. A. Shapiro, and W. B. Stiles. (1994). Assessment of assimilation in psychotherapy: A quantitative case study of problematic experiences with a significant other. *Journal of Counseling Psychology, 41*, 397–406.

Finn, G. P. T. (1997). Qualitative analysis of murals in Northern Ireland: Paramilitary justifications for political violence. In Hayes, N. (Ed.). *Doing qualitative analysis in psychology* (pp. 143–178). Hove, UK: Psychology Press.

Foucault, M. (1971). *Madness and civilisation: A history of sanity in the age of reason.* London: Tavistock.

Gaines, A. D. (1992). From DSM-I to III-R: Voices of self, mastery and the other: A cultural constructivist reading of US psychiatric classification. *Social Science and Medicine, 35*, 3–24.

Garfinkel, H. (1967). *Studies in ethnomethodology.* Englewood Cliffs: Prentice Hall.

Gergen, K. J. (1985). The social constructionist movement in modern psychology. *American Psychologist, 40*, 266–275.

Hamilton, P. (Ed.). (2005). *Visual research methods.* London: Sage.

Harré, R. (1979). *Social being: A theory for social psychology.* Oxford: Blackwell.

Harré, R., and G. Gillett. (1994). *The discursive mind.* London: Sage.

Hepburn, A. (1996). Feminists doing discursive psychology. *The Psychologist, 12,* 557–558.

Hobson, R. F. (1985). *Forms of feeling: The heart of psychotherapy.* London: Tavistock Publications.

Hoffman, L. (1992). A reflexive stance for family therapy. In McNamee, S., and K. J. Gergen. (Eds.). *Therapy as social construction* (pp. 7–24). London: Sage.

Hollway, W. (1989). *Subjectivity and method: Gender, meaning and science.* London: Sage.

Hollway, W., and T. Jefferson. (2000). *Doing qualitative research differently: Free association, narrative and the interview method.* London: Sage.

Locke, A., and D. Edwards. (2003). Bill and Monica: Memory, emotion and normativity in Clinton's grand jury testimony. *British Journal of Social Psychology, 42,* 239–256.

Madill, A. (1990). *An historical study of the construction of the self in literature.* Master's Thesis. University of Edinburgh.

Madill, A. (1995). *Developing a discourse analytic approach to change processes in psychodynamic–interpersonal psychotherapy.* Doctoral thesis. University of Sheffield.

Madill, A. (1996). "Some of this seems to me straight *feminist* stuff ": Representing the other in discursive psychotherapy research. In Wilkinson, S., and C. Kitzinger. (Eds.). *Representing the other: A feminism and psychology reader* (pp. 159–164). London: Sage.

Madill, A., and M. Barkham. (1997). Discourse analysis of a theme in one successful case of brief psychodynamic–interpersonal psychotherapy. *Journal of Counseling Psychology, 44,* 232–244.

Madill, A., and K. Doherty. (1994). "So you did what you wanted then": Discourse analysis, personal agency, and psychotherapy. *Journal of Community and Applied Social Psychology, 4,* 261–273.

Madill, A., A. Jordan, and C. Shirley. (2000). Objectivity and reliability in qualitative analysis: Realist, contextualist, and radical constructionist epistemologies. *British Journal of Psychology, 91,* 1–20.

Madill, A., C. Sermpezis, and M. Barkham. (in press). Interactional positioning and narrative self-construction in the first session of psychodynamic–interpersonal psychotherapy. *Psychotherapy Research.*

Madill, A., S. Widdicombe, and M. Barkham. (2001). The potential of conversation analysis for psychotherapy research. *The Counseling Psychologist, 29,* 413–434.

McLeod, J. (2000). *Qualitative research in counselling and psychotherapy.* London: Sage.

McVittie, C., A. McKinlay, and S. Widdicombe. (2003). Committed to (un)equal opportunities?: 'New ageism' and the older worker. *British Journal of Social Psychology, 42,* 595–612.

Moscovici, S. (1976). *La psychanalyse, son image et son public* (rev. ed.). Paris: Presses Universitaires de France.

Mulhall, D. (1976). Systematic self-assessment by PQRST. *Psychological Medicine, 6,* 591–597.

Parker, I. (1990a). Discourse: Definitions and contradictions. *Philosophical Psychology, 3,* 189–204.

Parker, I. (1990b). Real things: Discourse, context and practice. *Philosophical Psychology, 3,* 227–233.

Parker, I. (1992). *Discourse dynamics: Critical analysis for social and individual psychology.* London: Routledge.

Parker, I. (1994). Reflexive research and the grounding of analysis: Social psychology and the psy-complex. *Journal of Community and Applied Social Psychology, 4,* 239–252.

Parker, I. (2002). *Critical discursive psychology.* New York: Palgrave Macmillan.

Parker, I. (2003). Psychoanalytic narratives: Writing the self into contemporary cultural phenomena. *Narrative Inquiry, 13,* 301–315.

Parker, I. (2004). Criteria for qualitative research in psychology. *Qualitative Research in Psychology, 1*, 95–106.

Parker, I. (2005). *Qualitative psychology: Introducing radical research.* Buckingham, UK: Open University Press.

Parker, I., E. Georgaca, D. Harper, T. McLaughlin, and M. Stowell–Smith. (1995). *Deconstructing psychopathology.* London: Sage.

Potter, J. (1988). What is reflexive about discourse analysis? The case of reading readings. In Woolgar, S. (Ed.). *Knowledge and reflexivity: New frontiers in the sociology of knowledge* (pp. 37–52). London: Sage.

Potter, J. (1996a). Discourse analysis and constructionist approaches: Theoretical background. In J. T. E. (Ed.). *Handbook of qualitative research methods for psychology and the social sciences* (pp. 125–140). Leicester, UK: British Psychological Society.

Potter, J. (1996b). *Representing reality: Discourse, rhetoric and social construction.* London: Sage.

Potter, J. (2003). Discourse analysis and discursive psychology. In: Camic, P. M., J. E. Rhodes, and L. Yardley. (Eds.). *Qualitative research in psychology: Expanding perspectives in methodology and design* (pp. 73–940). Washington, DC: American Psychological Association.

Potter, J., and D. Edwards. (1990). Nigel Lawson's tent: Discourse analysis, attribution theory and the social psychology of fact. *European Journal of Social Psychology, 20*, 405–424.

Potter, J., D. Edwards, and M. Wetherell. (1993). A model of discourse in action. *American Behavioral Scientist, 36*, 383–401.

Potter, J., and S. Reicher. (1987). Discourse of community and conflict: The organisation of social categories in accounts of a "riot." *British Journal of Social Psychology, 26*, 25–40.

Potter, J., P. Stringer, and M. Wetherell. (1984). *Social texts and contexts: Literature and social psychology.* London: Routledge.

Potter, J., and M. Wetherell. (1987). *Discourse and social psychology: Beyond attitudes and behaviour.* London: Sage.

Potter, J., and M. Wetherell. (1994). Analysing discourse. In Bryman, A., and R. G. Burgess. (Eds.). *Analysing qualitative data* (pp. 47–56). London: Routledge.

Potter, J., M. Wetherell, R. Gill, and E. Edwards. (1990). Discourse: Noun, verb or social practice? *Philosophical Psychology, 3*, 205–217.

Puchta, C., and J. Potter. (2002). Manufacturing individual opinions: Market research focus groups and the discursive psychology of evaluation. *British Journal of Social Psychology, 41*, 345–363.

Reicher, S. (2000). Against methodolatry: Some comments on Elliott, Fischer, and Rennie. *British Journal of Clinical Psychology, 39*, 1–6.

Sacks, H. (1972). An initial investigation of the usability of conversational data for doing sociology. In Sudnow, D. (Ed.). *Studies in social interaction* (pp. 31–74). New York: Free Press.

Seymour–Smith, S., M. Wetherell, and A. Phoenix. (2002). "My wife ordered me to come!": A discursive analysis of doctors' and nurses' accounts of men's use of general practitioners. *Journal of Health Psychology, 7*, 253–267.

Shapiro, D. A., M. Barkham, G. E. Hardy, and L. A. Morrison. (1990). The second Sheffield psychotherapy project: Rationale, design and preliminary outcome data. *British Journal of Medical Psychology, 63*, 97–108.

Stiles, W. B., R. Elliott, S. P. Llewelyn, J. A. Firth–Cozens, F. R. Margison, D. A. Shapiro, and G. E. Hardy. (1990). Assimilation of problematic experiences by clients in psychotherapy. *Psychotherapy, 27*, 411–420.

Walker, T. (1988). Whose discourse? In Woolgar, S. (Ed.). *Knowledge and reflexivity: New frontiers in the sociology of knowledge* (pp. 55–80). London: Sage.

Westkott, M. (1986). Historical and developmental roots of female dependency. *Psychotherapy*, *23*, 213–220.

Wetherell, M. (1994). Commentary: The knots of power and negotiation, blank and complex subjectivities. *Journal of Community and Applied and Social Psychology*, *4*, 305–308.

Wetherell, M. (Ed.). (1996). *Identities, groups and social issues*. Buckingham, UK: Sage.

Wetherell, M., and J. Potter. (1992). *Mapping the language of racism: Discourse and the legitimation of exploitation*. London: Harvester.

White, M., and D. Epston. (1990). *Narrative means to therapeutic ends*. London: W. W. Norton.

Widdicombe, S., and R. Woofitt. (1995). *The language of youth sub-cultures: Social identity in action*. London: Harvester Wheatsheaf.

Wiggins, S., and J. Potter. (2003). Attitudes and evaluative practices: Category vs. item and subjective vs. objective constructions in everyday food assessments. *British Journal of Social Psychology*, *42*, 513–531.

Wilkinson, S., and C. Kitzinger. (Eds.). (1996a). *Feminism and discourse: Psychological perspectives*. London: Sage.

Wilkinson, S., and C. Kitzinger. (Eds.). (1996b). *Representing the other: A feminism and psychology reader*. London: Sage.

Winnicott, D. (1960). The theory of the patience–infant relationship. In *The maturational process and the facilitating environment*. New York: International Universities Press.

Wittgenstein, L. (1953). *Philosophical investigations*. Oxford: Blackwell.

BIOGRAPHICAL BACKGROUND

ANNA MADILL, PhD, is a senior lecturer in the Institute of Psychological Sciences, University of Leeds, UK, where she has taught since 1995. Inspired by teaching on discourse analysis during her undergraduate degree at the University of Edinburgh, she used this approach to analyze psychotherapy interaction under the supervision of Profs. Michael Barkham and David A. Shapiro at the University of Sheffield.

Since taking up her academic post at the University of Leeds, Madill supervised one of the first qualitative doctorates in clinical psychology at this institution, has developed a master program in qualitative methods, and worked with colleagues to found a strong qualitative research group that promotes qualitative teaching in the Institute. This group obtained a grant from the Learning and Teaching Support Network and has developed guidelines for the supervision of undergraduate qualitative research in psychology published in *The Psychologist*. Along with colleague Dr. Zazie Todd, Madill has organized the development of a new British Psychological Society section dedicated to qualitative research in psychology that is currently in its final stage of inauguration. She also organized and chaired the qualitative psychology conference "Emerging complexity in conducting qualitative research in psychology" (University of Leeds, UK; April 10–11, 2003). Madill is associate editor of the *British Journal of Clinical Psychology*, book review editor of *Qualitative Research in Psychology*, and member of a review panel for *Discourse Analysis Online*.

Madill has aimed to become familiar with a number of different qualitative approaches and has published research using discourse analysis, conversation analysis, grounded theory, and repertory grids. She also supervises research using psychoanalytically informed discourse analysis. Madill has been drawn to research questions that explore people's subjective experience and, although increasingly focusing on health issues, continues to be involved in research on diverse topics and to explore the wider implications of qualitative methodology. She is currently editing the second edition of the *Handbook of Qualitative Research Methods for Psychology and the Social Sciences* (BPS/Blackwell) with Todd.

Anna Madill was supported by a Medical Research Council training award. She would like to thank Michael Barkham, Psychological Therapies Research Centre, University of Leeds, UK, for giving the study on which this chapter is based his professional sheen. She also thanks Susan Field for allowing her to use extracts selected and transcribed as part of her doctoral research. Moreover, she is most indebted to the client for allowing her to conduct research on her psychotherapy and to the Psychological Therapies Research Centre, University of Leeds, UK, for providing the archive from which this case was drawn.

3

THE GROUNDED THEORY METHOD: APPLICATION OF A VARIANT OF ITS PROCEDURE OF CONSTANT COMPARATIVE ANALYSIS TO PSYCHOTHERAPY RESEARCH

DAVID L. RENNIE

Editors's Introduction

Background

Overview of the Approach to Studying the Client's Experience of an Hour of Psychotherapy

Illustration of a Moment of Experience

The Grounded Theory Method

A Note on Methodology

Constant Comparative Analysis

Return to the Example

Summary of My Understanding Derived from the Study

My Horizon of Understanding

The Main Understanding Derived from the Study

The Current Controversy over the Grounded Theory Method

References

Biographical Background

EDITOR'S INTRODUCTION

Dr. Rennie has conducted a large study of 14 psychotherapy clients' moment-by-moment experiences of the entire hour of a therapy session. His participants were engaged in therapy at the time of the study. He interviewed them about their recall of moments in a therapy session from which they had just emerged, with the recollections having been stimulated by a replay of a tape of the session. He was thus given access to their inner worlds of what it was like to be a client. In this chapter he focuses on the grounded theory method (GTM) and his modifications of it.

This method was originated by sociologists Glaser and Strauss and is among the first rigorous qualitative research methods to be widely practiced. The name refers to the grounding of research in life-world data and to the development of a theory of the subject matter from analysis of those data. In the traditional method, the theory arises from developing codes for the data through a "constant comparative" procedure in which each line of data is compared with identified (coded) content, and either receives an earlier code or is assigned a new one. Categories are similarly developed from the codes, and then a core category is named to hold all the others. Rennie describes the constant comparative procedure originally suggested by Glaser and Strauss, and contrasts it with a variation that he and his students developed. This variation involves breaking transcripts into units of meaning and inter-preting the meanings of each meaning unit. Categorizing is done immediately, from one meaning unit to the next, rather than through the intervening step of developing codes and then categorizing them. He illustrates the variation with a case drawn from his study and gives an overview of the returns from his study as a whole. The chapter closes with a constructive view of the implications, for those wishing to adopt the method at the current time, of a rift that developed between Glaser and Strauss on how to do constant comparative analysis.

BACKGROUND

The GTM (Glaser, 1978, 1992; Glaser and Strauss, 1967; Strauss, 1987; Strauss and Corbin, 1990, 1994) was developed in protest against a perceived prevailing, rational approach to theorizing in their discipline of sociology. Glaser brought to this development a background in descriptive quantitative sociology whereas Strauss was influenced by symbolic interactionism (Blumer, 1969). In the method, theory is developed in a bottom-up, inductive way, in which preconceptions about the topic of interest are put aside as much as possible, so that the resulting under-standing or theory is closely tied to the data from which it is derived, or *grounded*. Since its inception, the GTM has come to be recognized widely as an important member of the family of qualitative approaches to inquiry in the social and health sciences.

My engagement with the method began with my application of it to a study of the client's experience of an hour of psychotherapy. In its use, my research group and I altered a key feature of the method—namely, a procedure having to do with what Glaser and Strauss have described as *constant comparative analysis*, in turn having to do with the conceptualization of categories representing the meaning of phenomena. More recently, as well, I have dwelt on the theory of the method, or its methodology. What I have not done at any time, however, is to spell out in a way that is easy for readers to grasp how the modification of the constant comparative analytical procedure is to be carried out. Even my own students have complained that they could not understand depic-tions of it in my writings without being guided by me personally in its conduct. The goal of this chapter is to make the procedure more transparent.

In achieving this objective, however, it is necessary to attend to the overall method, which in turn must be embedded in my view of its method-ology (i.e., theory of the method). Accordingly, in laying an appropriate context for the presentation of the procedure within the framework of my psychotherapy study, I provide an overview of both method and methodology. It is important to point out that I make this excursion without attempting to get into my position on several issues that have been raised about the GTM—namely, the matters of validity and generalization (see Rennie, 1999, 2000; Rennie et al., 1988), and reliability (Rennie, 1994a, 1995b; Rennie and Frommer, 2001) of the method. To attempt to review my position on these issues would deflect from the focus of the chapter, given the space allowed for it.

I begin with an overview of the psychotherapy study, including an illustration of the kind of report that the participants in the psychotherapy study provided. This section is followed by a general description of the GTM and my position on its methodology, preliminary to the elucidation of the alternative way of doing constant comparative analysis. A case study is used to illustrate the procedure. I then summarize the main under-standings I derived from my study and close the chapter with reference to an emergent difference of opinion between Glaser and Strauss on the proper conduct of the part of the method that has to do with the constant comparative procedure.

I begin, then, with an overview of the phenomenon in which I was interested, and how I went about studying it.

OVERVIEW OF THE APPROACH TO STUDYING THE CLIENT'S EXPERIENCE OF AN HOUR OF PSYCHOTHERAPY

Being interested in their moment-to-moment experience of being in an hour of therapy, I interviewed clients about their recollections of what went on in a therapy interview that they had just completed and that had been either audio- or videotaped. I arranged for clients actively in therapy to replay the therapy tape in my presence, where I invited them to stop the replay and report their recollections of what had been experienced in that particular moment in the therapy session. This interview procedure thus applied Kagan's (1984) technique of *interpersonal process recall* (IPR; cf. Elliott, 1986). The IPR interview was tape-recorded. Both interviews were transcribed. My main focus was on the transcript of the IPR interview, although the transcript of the therapy session itself was necessary, of course, to provide the context for the participant's comments.

The requests for referrals of participants were paced by the speed with which I was able to analyze the IPR transcripts. By the end, six men and eight women had participated—among them, two of my own clients. Two of the participants were interviewed about two separate therapy sessions, resulting in a total of 16 IPR interviews (for details on how I approached the interviews, in terms of both ethics and the issue of the extent to which the research interviewer should lead as opposed to follow the participant's lead, see Rennie, 1995b). The participants ranged in age from mid 20s to mid 40s, had been in therapy for a period of six weeks to more than two years, and were currently engaged in therapy. All were white. Three were with a private practitioner; the others were receiving therapy in the student-counseling center of either of two large Ontario universities (two participants were my own clients seen through the auspices of such a center, who were interviewed about their therapy with me by colleagues). My impression was that none of the participants was psychotic at the time of the interviews; one dropped by my office three years after her research interview, disclosing that she had, in the interim, been hospitalized for a while with what had been diagnosed as bipolar disorder.

The participants' therapists were six women and six men. Eight were psychologists with a doctorate, two were graduate students in clinical psychology, and two were social workers with a master's degree. All had at least five years of experience. Collectively they represented the person-centered, gestalt, transactional analytical, rational–behavioral, rational–emotive, and eclectic approaches to counseling and psychotherapy.

With the exception of one participant, the IPR interviews were conducted within two hours of the therapy session. In five IPR interviews, videotape was replayed; whereas in the others, audiotape replay was used. (More information was given by video recording, but it was easier to get audiotaped interviews than videotaped ones.) The interview format was open ended, with the participant being given primary control over when the tape was stopped for comment. Each interview generally lasted about two hours. In two cases it went to four hours and, for one of these participants, it stretched over two days.

ILLUSTRATION OF A MOMENT OF EXPERIENCE

An illustration of what participants reported in the IPR interviews is given by a participant about his sixth session with his therapist. He had begun that session with a fairly lengthy story about emotional issues residual from his relationship with his ex-wife. Eventually, his therapist had attempted to summarize this material and to relate it to other themes that had emerged in previous sessions, with the following remark:

> So, there's this terrible feeling that you've been kept in the dark all this time and had no sense of control over it. And part of you, you know—we've talked about it before in different ways—[a part of you] really needs, wants to be in control. And part of your head, you know—this activity in your head is all designed for control, to give you a kind of security, you know? I think this ties back also—I mean I'm going to make a broad generalization, but it ties back to, to loss, you know, when you suddenly lose somebody you, you have a sudden disaster. I mean you begin to orient your life to control the world so, so that it will never happen again. I mean, we all do this in a sort of variety of ways. I think your control, the need to be in control is a sort of desire to, to avoid disaster's befall on you, to feel secure.

During the IPR interview, the participant stopped the replay of the therapy tape where the therapist said, "I mean, we all ..." (in the second to last sentence of the excerpt), and commented:

> I couldn't understand what [the therapist] was saying at that point. I *really* couldn't understand at all. I mean, I had a sense that something valuable was being said but I couldn't relate to it, and I was probably in my mind—I mean, I *know* I was impatient because I couldn't make it work in my mind. It wasn't coming in. I couldn't see the meaning. Because it pulled too many events in my life together in some fairly—I mean, I sometimes do get impatient when [the therapist] is talking because I want to get on to something that I can relate to and feel. I, I knew it was right, what he was saying, somehow, without actually seeing the way it was relevant. I couldn't see how he could pull all these things together.

The client had revealed none of this confusion to his therapist, however. Instead, at the end of the therapist's statement ("felt secure"), he had smoothly gone with what the therapist had said, with the reply:

> You can't control the disasters, can you? It's the control of the reactions to the disaster if it ever occurs.

This reply was enthusiastically endorsed by the therapist. Thus, the client's attempt to support the therapist had worked, with the consequence that any possibility of addressing his confusion about what the therapist had said was lost completely, at least in this moment of interaction. All other participants reported such covert management of disjunctive moments in their interactions with their therapists.

It was to this kind of material that I applied the GTM.

THE GROUNDED THEORY METHOD

Grounded theorists are interested mainly in the meaning of persons' experiences and conduct and attempt to understand them by both listening to what people say and observing how they behave. Usually fresh material is acquired through field research. Nevertheless, published descriptions of relevant experience and action may be used as well, especially during the later stages of an inquiry. Glaser and Strauss (1967) recommend that the conceptualization of material should be taken through two main steps. The first is to conceptualize *codes*. These are conceptualizations that stay close to the literal meaning of the passage of text under study (see Charmaz [1995] for a nice depiction of this phase of the analysis). At times the literal text is used as a code, when a representation of experience given by a respondent seems apt (described by Glaser and Strauss as an *in vivo code*). The analyst proceeds to conceptualize *categories* in terms of the relations among codes. Categories are thus generally more abstract than codes. The conceptualization of relations among units of text to produce codes, among codes to produce categories, and among categories to produce higher order categories is referred to as *constant comparative analysis* (elaboration to follow). An important feature of the GTM is that the given unit of text is assigned to however many meanings are seen in it. In the main, this feature of the method distinguishes it from content analysis. Typically, in content analysis a given unit of analysis is assigned only to one category so that statistics can be applied to the frequencies of assignments of units to categories; in the GTM, statistics play no role. Nevertheless, in the GTM, the frequency of assignment of units of analysis to categories may be used as an indicator of the generality of a given category among the participants under study (e.g., Rennie, 1992).

Categories subsumed by higher order ones are called *properties* of the latter. The result is a hierarchical structure of categories, with each level gathering together the categories in the level below it. Eventually a *core* category is conceptualized that is interpreted to subsume all other categories. Thus, the initial categories are grounded in the text, and higher order categories are grounded in those they subsume. This structure applies to phenomena that appear relatively stable over time. Alternatively, if the phenomenon of interest is a process, then the categories and the relations among them should represent the process.

Data gathering and analysis proceed concurrently and are interactive, the activities being guided by considerations of the phenomenon of interest. In this regard, there are three other important aspects of the method. First, throughout the study, the activity of seeking sources of information governed by the topic of interest and by the emergent understanding of it as the analysis proceeds is described as *theoretical sampling* (Glaser and Strauss, 1967). Second, grounded theorists use the technical term *saturation* to describe the state of the inquiry and analysis when new data appear to add little to the understanding of the phenomenon, at least in terms of how it applies to the material investigated. Depending on the uniformity of the phenomenon among its sources of information applied to it, saturation may occur in as few as six or so sources. Meanwhile, third, both before and during the inquiry and analysis, the analyst writes what Glaser and Strauss describe as *theoretical memos*. These entries in a research journal record the analyst's preconceptions and hunches about the phenomenon, sense of the relations among codes and categories, sense of what might be the core category, and so on, at all stages of the inquiry. The theoretical memos are used extensively in the final formulation of the understanding and in the write-up of the study.

A NOTE ON METHODOLOGY

When they put forward the method, the main position on its methodology advanced by Glaser and Strauss (1967) was that it is an inductive way of generating theory. The emphasis was on theory generation more than on theory validation. Validation was to come about subsequent to theory development, in the way of normal science (see Rennie, 1998b). They also maintained that the role of the researcher's perspective is so great that different analysts working with the same data could develop alternative theories, which is acceptable as long as all theories developed are grounded in the data, each in its own way. In my view, in making this observation, Glaser and Strauss failed adequately to take into account the epistemological implications of this operating from a perspective. It may be supposed that, if indeed the researcher's perspective is involved, the method entails interpretation in a major way. In his more recent writings, Strauss (1987; Strauss and Corbin, 1990, 1994), perhaps because of his background in symbolic interactionism (Blumer, 1969) with its kinship with cultural anthropology, explicitly paid heed to the role played by interpretation in the method. This stance was not taken by Glaser, however, who adhered to the position on the matter implicit in the original 1967 presentation of the method (see Glaser, 1992).

With student colleagues, I (Rennie et al., 1988) have concluded that as an interpretive approach, the method involves the application of method to the interpretation of text, or hermeneutics, and so may be thought of as methodical hermeneutics (Rennie, 1998b, 1999, 2000; Rennie and Frommer, 2001). I believe that thinking of it as a form of hermeneutics provides a coherent framework for explaining how it is that the method opens up the space between realism and relativism. Putting this notion another way, the method takes into account both the objectivity of what is being addressed and the subjectivity involved in addressing it. I see this space as being especially pertinent to the human sciences (cf. Fischer, 1977; Giorgi, 1970; Rennie, 1995a; Taylor, 1971).

Having provided this background, we are now in a position to get to the main focus of the chapter. Along the way, my group and I do constant comparative analysis.

CONSTANT COMPARATIVE ANALYSIS

As indicated, Glaser and Strauss distinguish between codes and categories, with the latter being derived from the former. Codes tend to be descriptive whereas categories tend to be more abstract. When we took on the method, my group and I concluded that even the development of codes involves interpretation and that, correspondingly, they are basically low-level categories. Thus, we dispensed with the distinction between codes and categories, representing all conceptualizations of meaning as categories (Rennie et al., 1988).

In Glaser and Strauss's (1967) procedure, it is recommended that the researcher analyze text line by line. Each code is recorded as a note in the margin of the text, such as the transcript of an interview, or perhaps on an index card. Within the framework of the perceived context of the study as a whole, the analyst begins by taking two codes and comparing them, asking: Are they similar in some way, or different? Why? (With, again, both questions being asked within the sociocultural context in which the phenomenon is perceived to be framed.) If judged to be similar, then they are put together. If different, they are kept separate. The third code is compared with the other two. If the first two were kept separate, and the third is similar to one of the two, then it is placed with that code. If the first two are combined, then the third is added to them, creating a single cluster of three codes. Alternatively, if the meaning of the third code is different than that of the other two, then it is kept separate, and so on. The result of this constant comparison is a number of clusters of codes. The overall meaning of the cluster is conceptualized, and this conceptualization is declared a category. After all the codes are sorted in this way, then the analyst scrambles the codes and starts again, choosing a code at random from the set of codes, and repeats the analysis (a *resorting* of the codes). This repetition is done under the assumption that resorting the codes could result in new categories. The resorting is repeated until no new categories seem necessary.

My group developed an alternative way to do the constant comparative procedure (Rennie et al., 1988). In this procedure, the text (in our case, a transcript of an interview) is broken into passages, or *meaning units* (MUs; cf. Giorgi, 1970). In deciding what constitutes an MU, the analyst is alert to the main point or theme of a given passage. We have found that when people are interviewed, they wish to make a point and that, when they have made it, they move on to something else. There's a shift of main meaning. It is as if a given passage is enclosed in what we sense to be an "envelope" of meaning. We declare the material enclosed by the envelope to be an MU. This parsing may be done either prior to the analysis of the MUs or as the analysis proceeds. The MU is studied carefully, and every meaning that we interpret is represented by a category. Categorizing in this way, we found, allows for the meaning of the text to "hang together" in terms of themes and their properties. We also found that the procedure provided the additional advantage of making the analysis less tedious than doing it line by line.

Once conceptualized, the category is indexed (discussion to follow) and the analyst proceeds to the next MU (cf. Turner [1981], who, unknown to us at the time, similarly proposed analyzing text progressively rather than resorting codes). If the meanings of this MU overlap with the meanings of previous MUs, then the new MU is assigned to the categories already formulated. Alternatively, there may be new meanings in this MU, calling for the conceptualization of one or more new categories. New categories are indexed, after which the analyst proceeds to the next MU, repeating the process. As the analysis proceeds, there is a decreasing need to conceptualize new categories because the meaning of the new MU is already accounted for by existing categories.

At times, a word or phrase in the MU seems apt as a category that, analogous to Glaser and Strauss's *in vivo codes* (mentioned earlier), we refer to as an *in vivo category*. For example, in my study, participants sometimes remarked that they were "on track" or "off track" in their discourse with the therapist. Thus I conceptualized the category *Client's Track*. Most often, however, the language used differs from the language of the MU, while containing its meaning. During the analysis, one's sense of each category is best left fluid in the early going. The density of the meaning of the category increases as more MUs are assigned to it. This is so because each MU has a different shade of the same basic meaning (illustration to follow). Eventually, it is possible to define the category in terms of this density—to raise it up by its bootstraps.

It is necessary to develop a filing system to manage the analysis. The system may be either physical or electronic (i.e., a database program). In the physical approach, we list the emerging categories alphabetically on a sheet of paper that we keep at hand when analyzing text. We also use filing cards for two purposes.

The first purpose is create what we refer to as *meaning unit cards*. We print two copies of each transcript. One transcript is kept intact, for our archive. The other is used to isolate and record the MUs. We cut the MUs from this second printout and paste them on index cards. Each MU is given an identifying code that connects it to its source. For example, in my study, I identified each MU in terms of (1) the accumulation of MUs studied in the analysis as a whole, up to the point of this particular MU; (2) the author of the MU; and (3) the placement of the MU in the transcript from which it was extracted. Thus, having decided that the participant's previous response indicating confusion about what the therapist had said was an MU, I gave it identifier 1165K9. This identifier means that it was the 1165th MU among all transcripts studied to that point, that this particular transcript came from the IPR interview with participant K, and that this was the ninth MU parsed out of his transcript. In addition, the categories to which the MU is assigned are entered at the top of the MU card (or at the top of the first card in the set, if more than one card is necessary to handle the size of the MU).

The second use of index cards is as follows: When one is engaged in analysis, it quickly becomes evident that the accumulation of MU cards will become voluminous. To reduce cognitive overload, we reduce the contents of an MU into key words, often abbreviated. We attempt to get the reduction into a single line, producing what we came to call a *one-liner*. It is crucial to emphasize that the "key-worded" summaries are never used in the conceptualization of categories. That activity is applied to the full MU in the context of the transcript as a whole. We have found that, because we are so familiar with the MUs, having worked with them closely and repetitively during the constant comparison analysis, seeing the key words signifying the text of an MU restores our memory of the meanings in the MU. For each category, then, we created what we came to call a *category card*. The one-liners, suitably coded to connect them to the MUs from which they are derived, are entered on the category card. Hence, in the case of my study, at the end of my analysis, when I had settled on 51 categories, I had 51 sets of category cards (for those categories, see Rennie, 1992).

While scanning the one-liners on a category card, the analyst is given a compact representation of the meaning of the respondents' accounts as they pertained to that category. A further advantage of this technique is that the analyst can lay category cards side by side, enabling a comparison of the compacted meaning of a given category with other categories. Indeed, we have found that, when writing up the returns from our analyses, we usually need to work only with the category cards because, as indicated, they are sufficient to remind us of the contents of the full texts. If we want to illustrate a category, we scan the one-liners, choose the best one, and retrieve and use the MU from which the one-liner was derived.

Our approach and the one described by Glaser and Strauss, in essence, are different routes to Rome. Both approaches stay close to the meaning of the text and both eventuate in a hierarchical structure of categories, with lower order categories serving as properties of the higher order ones. Both engage the writing of theoretical memos. In both, the extent to which passages of text are relevant to a given category is an important criterion of whether the category should be kept as is or, alternatively, either modified, pooled into another category, or discarded. Finally, although our procedure entails moving progressively through text, it also calls upon the analyst to backtrack, thus covering the same ground covered by the resorting of codes. When a category is conceptualized for the first time after the analyst has already gone through a number of MUs, he or she refers to earlier MUs to determine whether the category was missed in any of them. Thus, with our procedure, the applicability of categories is addressed comprehensively, just as in the Glaser and Strauss procedure.

RETURN TO THE EXAMPLE

As an illustration of how the procedure works, I focus on the MU mentioned earlier, about the failure to understand what the therapist meant. After reading and rereading the 58-page double-spaced transcript, this was the ninth MU that I parsed out of it. As described, I cut the MU out of the second copy of the transcript and pasted it onto an index card. With the list of categories by my side, I deliberated on the meaning of this MU, and assigned it to four categories: *Client Understanding Therapist's Frame of Reference, Therapist Interpretation, Therapist Accurate Response*, and *Client's Track*. All four categories were on the list, and so I did not conceptualize any new ones for this MU.

This judgment was made possible because I allowed a broad range of meaning to be covered by categories. Hence, I allowed *Therapist Accurate Response* to accommodate inaccurate responding as well as accurate responding. Similarly, I allowed *Client Understanding Therapist's Frame of Reference* to take into account misunderstanding as well as understanding.

I did this because I reasoned that a category about understanding can accommodate whether the client understood. I even allowed this category to accommodate instances when, as in the case of this MU, the client sensed that the therapist was correct without knowing why. I allowed such broad meanings to keep the number of categories within manageable limits. A bonus is that allowing several related meanings to be subsumed by the same category increases its density, its richness, in keeping with the goals of the method.

Continuing with the analysis of this MU, the four categories were indicated on the MU card, whereupon I reduced the meaning to the one-liner that, in some cases, spilled over into two lines:

1165K9   Cldnt undrstd T; sensed T was right; impatient; wntd to get onto smtg that he cld relate to and feel

This reduction was then typed onto the category card for each of the four categories. Thus, the *Client Understanding Therapist's Frame of Reference* category card contains, among others, the following entries which were derived from the transcripts of multiple participants:

1165K9   Clndn't undrstd T; sensd T was right; impatient; wantd to get onto smtg that he cld relate to and feel
177C5   C thinks T thinks it would be easier for C to admit things if T asks for them
469F22   C tried to rembr apprch T usd in intrptng dream
470F22   C wntd his rspns to be in right cntxt; save time
471F23   C wtd to spk same langg as T so T wldnt waste time interpreting
657J1   C ddnt knw wht T meant by "For sake of accuracy;" lost
739J83   C ddnt knw what T was getting at; question whethr the reinfrcng of acdmc work should be up to C
881Su115   C ddnt know if T knew he wntd reassurance; however, he did good
1023S104   Big questn for C: is T's head clear?

This example of a category card illustrates how the summaries give the nuances of various meanings represented by the category. Most of my students are using software to assist the analysis; it saves time to have to type a one-liner only once and then use the computer to enter the reduction into files equivalent to the category cards. We have found that the *N-Vivo* (see Richards, 1999) program seems best equipped to handle both MUs and one-liners. An important caveat in this regard, however, is that any program should be used only to organize the text. The user should not lapse into the belief that use of the program will constitute the analysis itself. The instrument of the analysis is the analyst, not the program. It is easy for analysts to fall into this belief, especially when using a data-based program such as *N-Vivo*, which was designed especially for the GTM. These programs are designed such that the analyst is made to work with "tree" structures, which can easily and inappropriately force the data. Indeed, my students have often found that they have to combine computer analysis with the use of physical tools such as index cards to avoid this peril.

Nevertheless, used in the right way, a database program markedly cuts down the time required for analysis, by virtue of what they offer in the management of text.

SUMMARY OF MY UNDERSTANDING DERIVED FROM THE STUDY

MY HORIZON OF UNDERSTANDING

The matter of perspective has received a lot of attention by phenomenologists (e.g., Husserl, 1931) and hermeneuticists (e.g., Gadamer, 1992), in terms of what they refer to as the *horizon of understanding*. During the promotion of the discovery of something new, it is important to take into account conceptions, intuitions, hunches, hypotheses, and so on, brought into a grounded theory study so that an effort can be made to put them aside. Indeed, in their early works especially, Glaser and Strauss suggested that inquirers into a phenomenon should avoid reading about it prior to inquiry and analysis to minimize the imposition of prejudices (see also Charmaz, 1995). This attempt to put prejudice aside is described by phenomenologists as *bracketing* (e.g., see Zaner, 1970).

Of course, some predisposing assumptions are so deeply ingrained that the researcher is unaware of them, which makes bracketing of them impossible. Nevertheless, every researcher is aware of many of his or her assumptions, and it is these that can be addressed in this way. When a researcher informs the reader about the perspective brought to the study of the phenomenon, it helps the reader to understand the researcher's understanding. This stance goes to the heart of the epistemology entailed in the method. Radical constructionists (see Rosenau, 1992) take the skeptical position that because we can never get to the bottom of the lingual and cultural influences on how we think, there is no point in trying. Alternatively, positivists operate on the principle that it is possible to keep subjectivity out of the picture by focusing on what is evident empirically. Again, I am among those who are attempting to work out an epistemological position between these two extremes by encouraging the communication of prejudices of which we are aware (cf. Charmaz, 1995; Kvale, 2001; Madill et al., 2000).

My approach to counseling and psychotherapy, entitled *experiential person-centered counseling* (Rennie, 1998c, 2004), combines the Rogerian person-centered approach and the experiential approach promoted by Greenberg et al. (1998). Thus, at the time of the study (as now), I saw the client as a person who is engaged in action (as opposed, say, to being primarily under the control of environmental contingencies or, alternatively, of unconscious motivations). I had also come to believe that the client should be helped to engage in action more effectively.

THE MAIN UNDERSTANDING DERIVED FROM THE STUDY

Throughout the analysis, what impressed me consistently was how active, inwardly, the participants had been in the role of client (cf. Bohart and Tallman, 1996, 1999). Although they had often responded in a straightforward manner to the therapist's interventions, they also often had deliberated on their responses, weighing alternatives in deciding whether they would respond at all and, if so, how.

Furthermore, they reported having done a lot of evaluating of the therapist. Moreover, this evaluation was often made within their awareness of their awareness of themselves. This activity, which was reported to me in the IPR inquiry, had often been covert in the interaction with the therapist. In my interpretation, it was the most pervasive activity indicated by their reports. Thus, I eventually concluded that, as a representation of the pervasiveness and the quality of this activity, the core category was *Client's Reflexivity*, which I defined as self-awareness and agency within that self-awareness (Rennie, 1992). Moreover, the kind of reflexivity involved is what Taylor (1989) has called *radical reflexivity*—that is, awareness of being self-aware, a capability that seemingly is limited to humans.

The results of the study have been given in a series of reports (e.g., Rennie, 1994a, b; for a summary, see Rennie, 2002). In what follows, I summarize the understanding represented by the 51 categories subsumed by *Client's Reflexivity* (see Rennie, 1992). To make the presentation less cumbersome, I make no attempt to indicate the actual categories supporting each claim to understanding; that connection is given in previous writings.

Clients are aware of being self-aware while being aware of the therapist. They listen to what the therapist has to say, integrating it into their experience. They may agree with the therapist, or not. They may voice their agreement, or not. Regardless, they think about what the therapist has said, has not said, or should say. They are aware of the therapist's presence, manner, and style, being alert to what the therapist seems to think about them and whether the therapist likes them, cares for them, respects them. At times, their talking is at one with their thinking; at other times, they deliberate on what they say, thinking more thoughts than they utter, evaluating them, choosing what to say, and how, and when. Throughout this activity, they are aware of their feelings. These feelings surround their thoughts, influence their thoughts, or perhaps are the subject of their thoughts, even dominating their thoughts.

They are persons, in relationship with themselves and with this other person, who happens to be a therapist. This is a special relationship. It is a relationship meant for them; it is about their hurts, fears, and concerns. They are in therapy to feel better; they may also be in it to become different in some way. They may intend to get at their feelings, to penetrate the mists of occluded awareness that prevent them from breaking through whatever it is that is in the way of their feeling and being different than they are, in becoming better. Or they may intend, either consciously or semiconsciously, to manage the threat posed by the therapist and/or the threat posed by the way they are.

When desiring to penetrate their experience, they are pulled in a particular direction, on a track, a train of thought. The pull is captivating, compelling. In its grip, clients flow in it, unheedingly, not aware that they are either thinking or talking; instead, they are just doing it (cf. Searle, 1983). In such moments, their experience is not reflexive; instead, they are caught up in it. The intention girding the pursuit of meaning is sustained until it reaches its completion or until it is disturbed. When completed, clients talk about something else. When disturbed, the disturbance may either arise from within or from their experience of the therapist.

In terms of disturbance from within, the flow of thought may lead clients into a zone of feeling that they did not anticipate; the new feeling jolts them. They come out of the flow and become aware of it. This is a moment of reflexivity. In it, they decide what to do with the disturbance, whether to enter into it or to think about something else, avoiding the feeling. If the experience is spoken about, then they have to decide whether to express the disturbance beneath their verbal expressions or to modulate it, or shift away from it and talk about something else.

Alternatively, the disturbance may result from what the therapist has said or done, which interferes with the client's intention. In their awareness of their self-awareness, they are torn between clinging to the intention guiding their thoughts and directing attention to the therapist. In their minds, the therapist is an expert. His or her words are not to be taken lightly; he or she may know something that the clients do not know. They are inclined to feel that if they follow the therapist's lead, it could be more productive than their own lead. Thus, often clients give way to the therapist. Having complied, should the therapist restore their line of thought, they are relieved. When this happens, it means that by their discretion, they manage to have it both ways: They have shown respect for the therapist, yet have been enabled to come back on track. At other times, the strength of the intention is so great that clients refuse to release it. They may pretend that they did not hear the therapist and keep going. Or they may pretend to listen, while continuing their train of thought silently. Or they may interrupt the therapist, forcing the dialogue back in line.

All this occurs in this way when the relationship with the therapist is comfortable. When it is not comfortable, clients divide their time between following their own lines of thought and managing the relationship with the therapist. The management is complicated. The therapist may be experienced as aggressive, necessitating countermeasures, without giving offense. The therapist may be prejudiced about certain values held dear by the clients, necessitating careful avoidance of those topics. When the relationship is like this, clients work overtime monitoring what they can and cannot say, and how. They try to establish compatibility with the therapist so that they can engage in a worry-free exploration of their experience.

Overall, the analysis of their reports led me to understand that clients are often keenly aware of what they are experiencing in each moment of the therapy. This experience includes their awareness of the relationship with the therapist. They monitor their sense of themselves, of the relationship, and tread their way through the treacherous waters on both fronts, propelled forward by the desire somehow to feel better than they have been feeling.

This study was a large one and gave rise to more than 1800 MUs, and the assignment of more than 3000 MUs to categories (Rennie, 1992). I have found that the constant comparative procedure described earlier produced a management of this large amount of material that facilitated the various writings I have derived from this study. My students, as well, have found the procedure to work well with their studies, regardless of whether they study psychotherapy.

As it happens, the matter of how to approach the task of categorizing in the GTM has, of late, become a matter of rather pressing concern in grounded theory circles. This turn of events has come about because of an emergent difference of opinion between Glaser and Strauss.

THE CURRENT CONTROVERSY OVER THE GROUNDED THEORY METHOD

Following their initiation of the GTM (Glaser and Strauss, 1967), its originators began to see it differently (cf. Glaser, 1978; Strauss, 1987). This growing rift split wide open in the 1990s (cf. Glaser, 1992; Strauss and Corbin, 1990, 1994; see Rennie, 1998b; Corbin, 1998; Rennie, 1998a). It entails two main issues. First, Strauss departed from the original notion that the application of deduction is not involved in the GTM (Strauss, 1987). To demonstrate this, he instituted a procedure described as deductive during which, when encountering something of interest or of significance in the data, the analyst asks what might explain it. In response to this question, hypotheses are created. Additional data, as they unfold, are brought to bear on the hypotheses, leading to judged confirmation of one over the others. The same procedure of question asking, hypothesizing, and testing of hypotheses is used as the analyst proceeds through the overall data. Thus, a more rational, deductive approach to categorizing takes the place of the more empirical, inductive approach to it that is more characteristic of the original way of doing constant comparative analysis.

Another change made by Strauss, together with an associate, Juliet Corbin (e.g., see Strauss and Corbin, 1990), was to insist that in order for a grounded theory analysis to be complete, it must incorporate what they refer to as the *coding paradigm*. This paradigm, or scheme, is a set of "conditions, context, action/interactional strategies and consequences" (Strauss and Corbin, 1990, p. 96) with regard to the phenomenon under study. With this procedure, the initial returns from the application of the constant comparative analysis are to be interpreted within the framework of this paradigm. The effect is to convert every grounded theory analysis into a process formulation, in contrast to the earlier formulation of the method that allowed for the emergence of structural formulations as well.

Alternatively, Glaser has restricted the role of deduction to the activity of theoretical sampling. This means that, in the light of what has emerged as important aspects of the phenomenon as understood in terms of the data sources (e.g., research participants) studied to a given point in the analysis, it is deduced that other kinds of data sources will shed important light on the phenomenon. Correspondingly, he has held to the original, inductive way of engaging in coding, maintaining that the incorporation of deduction in the way Strauss now prescribes could lead to premature closure on the understanding of the phenomenon under study. As for the coding paradigm, Glaser (1992) has argued that this scheme is only one of many sensitizing concepts that may be pertinent to phenomena and that to insist on it alone may force the data. That is, insistence on its use, exclusive of other sensitizing concepts, may threaten the grounding of the analysis.

It will be noticed that in describing our alternative to the way of doing constant comparative analysis, I have made no mention of Strauss' radical new way of doing constant comparative analysis. Nor have I mentioned Strauss and Corbin's coding paradigm. The main reason is that neither innovation fits with our way of doing the constant comparative procedure because it was developed prior to the rift. Thus, it is precisely because the original approach is retained by Glaser that I now find myself agreeing with his concerns about the Strauss–Corbin changes. Thus, I too am concerned that Strauss's more rational approach to categorizing runs the risk of subverting the discovery-oriented intent of the method. And I share Glaser's reservations about the universal applicability of the coding paradigm. I too feel that requiring this application could force the data. Moreover, I feel that these reservations are supported by my observation of what other grounded theorists have done since the emergence of the rift. None of the contemporary manuscripts and publications coming to my attention has demonstrated an uptake of Strauss's deductive way of categorizing, and few users of the GTM have complied with the maxim that the coding paradigm must be applied. Thus, it is my judgment that those considering adopting the GTM will be on safe ground when staying with some form of the original way of doing constant comparison (e.g., see the writings by Charmaz, 1995; Henwood and Pidgeon, 1992; Stern, 1994; and Wilson and Hutchinson, 1996; for commentaries on and variations of the original procedure). When all is said and done, it is adherence to this original way of engaging in the constant comparative procedure, in one way or other, that provides the greatest promise of using the GTM in the discovery-oriented way that was, from the outset—and continues to be—its hallmark.

REFERENCES

Blumer, H. (1969). *Symbolic interactionism*. Englewood Cliffs, NJ: Prentice-Hall.

Bohart, A. C., and K. Tallman. (1996). The active client: Therapy as self-help. *Journal of Humanistic Psychology, 36,* 7–30.

Bohart, A. C., and K. Tallman. (1999). *How clients make therapy work: The process of active self-healing.* Washinton, DC: American Psychological Association.

Charmaz, C. (1995). Grounded theory. In Smith, J., R. Harre, and L. van Langenhove. (Eds.). *Rethinking methods in psychology* (pp. 27–49). London, UK: Sage.

Corbin, J. (1998). Alternative interpretations: Valid or not? *Theory & Psychology, 8,* 121–128.

Elliott, R. (1986). Interpersonal Process Recall (IPR) as a psychotherapy process research method. In Greenberg, L., and W. Pinsof. (Eds.). *The psychotherapy process: A research handbook* (pp. 503–529). New York: Guilford Press.

Fischer, C. T. (1977). Historical relations of psychology as an object science and a subject science: Toward psychology as a human science. *Journal of the History of the Behavioral Sciences, 13,* 369–378.

Gadamer, H. G. (1992). *Truth and method* (2nd rev. ed.). Weinsheimer, J., and D. G. Campbell: (Trans.). New York: Crossroad. [Original work published 1960.]

Giorgi, A. (1970). *Psychology as a human science: A phenomenologically based approach.* New York: Harper & Row.

Glaser, B. G. (1978). *Theoretical sensitivity: Advances in the methodology of grounded theory.* Mill Valley, CA: Sociology Press.

Glaser, B. G. (1992). *Emergence vs. forcing: The basics of grounded theory analysis.* Mill Valley, CA: Sociology Press.

Glaser, B. G., and A. Strauss. (1967). *The discovery of grounded theory: Strategies for qualitative research.* Chicago: Aldine.

Greenberg, L. S., J. C. Watson, and Goldman. R. (1998). Process–experiential therapy of depression. In Greenberg, L. S., J. C. Watson and G. Lietaer. (Eds.). *Handbook of experiential psychotherapy* (pp. 227–248). New York: Guilford.

Henwood, K., and N. Pidgeon. (1992). Qualitative research and psychological theorizing. *British Journal of Psychology, 83,* 97–111.

Husserl, E. (1931). *Ideas: General introduction to pure phenomenology.* Gibson, W. R. B. (Trans.). London, UK: George Allen & Unwin. [Original work published 1913.]

Kagan, N. (1984). Interpersonal Process Recall: Basic methods and recent research. In Larson, D. (Ed.). *Teaching psychological skills* (pp. 229–244). Monterey, CA: Brooks/Cole.

Kvale, S. (2001). The psychoanalytic interview as qualitative research. In Frommer, J., and D. Rennie. (Eds.). *Qualitative psychotherapy research: Methods and methodology* (pp. 9–31). Lengerich, Germany: Pabst.

Madill, A., A. Jordan, and C. Shirley. (2000). Objectivity and reliability in qualitative analysis: Realist, contextualist and radical constructive epistemologies. *British Journal of Psychology, 91,* 1–20.

Rennie, D. L. (1992). Qualitative analysis of the client's experience of psychotherapy: The unfolding of reflexivity. In Toukmanian, S., and D. Rennie. (Eds.). *Psychotherapy process research: Paradigmatic and narrative approaches* (pp. 211–233). Thousand Oaks, CA: Sage.

Rennie, D. L. (1994a). Clients' deference in psychotherapy. *Journal of Counseling Psychology*, *41*, 427–437.

Rennie, D. L. (1994b). Storytelling in psychotherapy: The client's subjective experience. *Psychotherapy, 31*, 234–243.

Rennie, D. L. (1995a). On the rhetorics of social science: Let's not conflate natural science and human science. *Humanistic Psychologist, 23*, 321–332.

Rennie, D. L. (1995b). Strategic choices in a qualitative approach to psychotherapy research. In Hoshmand, L., and J. Martin. (Eds.). *Research as praxis: Lessons from programmatic research in therapeutic practice* (pp. 198–220). New York: Teacher's College Press.

Rennie, D. L. (1998a). From one interpreter to another: Reply to Corbin. *Theory & Psychology, 8*, 129–135.

Rennie, D. L. (1998b). Grounded theory methodology: The pressing need for a coherent logic of justification. *Theory & Psychology, 8*, 101–120.

Rennie, D. L. (1998c). *Person-centred counselling: An experiential approach*. London, UK: Sage.

Rennie, D. L. (1999). Qualitative research: A matter of hermeneutics and the sociology of knowledge. In Kopala, M., and L. Suzuki. (Eds.). *Using qualitative methods in psychology* (pp. 3–19). Thousand Oaks, CA: Sage.

Rennie, D. L. (2000). Grounded theory methodology as methodical hermeneutics: Reconciling realism and relativism. *Theory & Psychology, 10*, 481–502.

Rennie, D. L. (2002). The experience of psychotherapy: Grounded theory studies. In Cain, D. J., and J. Seeman. (Eds.). *Humanistic psychotherapies: Handbook of research and practice* (pp. 117–144). Washington, DC: American Psychological Association.

Rennie, D. L. (2004). Reflexivity and person-centered counseling. *Journal of Humanistic Psychology, 44*, 182–203.

Rennie, D. L., and J. Frommer. (2001). Reflections. In Frommer, J., and D. L. Rennie. (Eds.). *Qualitative psychotherapy research: Methods and methodology* (pp. 183–201). Lengerich, Germany: Pabst.

Rennie, D. L., J. R. Phillips, and G. K. Quartaro. (1988). Grounded theory: A promising approach to conceptualization in psychology? *Canadian Psychology, 29*, 139–150.

Richards, L. (1999). *Using N-Vivo in qualitative research*. London, UK: Sage.

Rosenau, P. (1992). *Post-modernism and the social sciences*. Princeton, NJ: Princeton University Press.

Searle, J. (1983). *Intentionality: An essay in the philosophy of mind*. Cambridge, UK: Cambridge University Press.

Stern, P. A. (1994). Eroding grounded theory. In Morse, J. M. (Ed.). *Critical issues in qualitative research methods* (pp. 212–223). Thousand Oaks, CA: Sage.

Strauss, A. (1987). *Qualitative analysis for social scientists*. Cambridge, UK: Cambridge University Press.

Strauss, A., and J. Corbin. (1990). *Basics of qualitative research: Grounded theory procedures and techniques*. Thousand Oaks, CA: Sage.

Strauss, A., and J. Corbin. (1994). Grounded theory methodology: An overview. In Denzin, N. K., and Y. S. Lincoln. (Eds.). *Handbook of qualitative research* (pp. 273–285). Thousand Oaks, CA: Sage.

Taylor, C. (1971). Interpretation and the sciences of man. *Review of Metaphysics, 25*, 45–51.

Taylor, C. (1989). *Sources of the self: The making of modern identity*. Cambridge, MA: Harvard University Press.

Turner, B. (1981). Some practical aspects of qualitative data analysis: One way of organizing the cognitive process associated with the generation of grounded theory. *Quality and Quantity, 15*, 225–247.

Wilson, H. S., and S. A. Hutchinson. (1996). Methodologic mistakes in grounded theory. *Nursing Research, 45*, 122–124.

Zaner, R. M. (1970). *The way of phenomenology: Criticism as a philosophical discipline*. New York: Pegasus.

BIOGRAPHICAL BACKGROUND

DAVID L. RENNIE, PhD, CPsych, is a Professor of Psychology at York University, Toronto, where he has taught since 1970. He took his first two degrees in psychology at the University of Alberta, in 1959 and 1965. He worked at a number of clinical and counseling positions in Alberta from 1959 to 1967, when he departed for the University of Missouri, Columbia, where he obtained a PhD in clinical psychology in 1971.

At Missouri he conducted research on imative learning as well as the related topic of vicarious reinforcement. Upon arrival at York, his interest shifted to counselor training research and then to research on the client's experience of therapy. It was at the point of the second shift that he abandoned the conventional approach to research in favor of the grounded theory form of qualitative research.

Having been trained as a positivistic, quantitative researcher, the shift to qualitative research required a considerable adjustment. Thus, while applying it, he was also interested in justifying it. This interest took him to the theory of the GTM, or its methodology, and to coherent epistemological underpinnings of it. This work on methodology has become his main focus in recent years.

Throughout the course of his career, he has produced 60 publications, including a book on counseling and two co-edited books on the application of qualitative research methods and methodologies to the study of counseling and psychotherapy. He is a fellow of both the Canadian and American Psychological Associations and is currently president-elect of the humanistic division of the American Psychological Association (APA).

4

PHENOMENOLOGICAL ANALYSIS: IMPRESSION FORMATION DURING A CLINICAL ASSESSMENT INTERVIEW

SCOTT D. CHURCHILL

EDITOR'S INTRODUCTION

This chapter is based on part of Dr. Churchill's dissertation, which addressed how clinical psychologists come to understand a patient/client during the initial interview phase of psychological assessment, prior to the use of any tests. Dr. Churchill uses the term *psychodiagnostic,* not in its too-frequent current meaning of applying a label, but rather in the earlier one of knowing (*gnostic*) through (*dia*) efforts to understand what the deeper person (*psyche*) is like.

Dr. Churchill videotaped two experienced clinical psychologists as they interviewed their respective patients in a psychiatric facility. Then he audio-taped discussions with each psychologist about what the latter was seeing and thinking during the interview. The videotape was accessed as desired. Typescripts of these discussions along with formal assessor self-reports ("protocols") became Dr. Churchill's data, which he analyzed using the empirical phenomenological approach developed in the Psychology Department at Duquesne University. This approach involves systematic reading and rereading to get in touch with how persons (here, the psychologists) are in relation to and participate in the meanings of particular situations (here, their emerging sense of the assessees). When Dr. Churchill speaks of "intentionality," he is referring to humans always being in relation to whatever we are in touch with, not necessarily to purposiveness. When he speaks of "co-constituting," he is referring to humans forming meaning from their perspectives, which is of course the only way humans can comprehend any subject matter. That is, humans and situations together co-form (co-constitute) what is taken up, understood, by human observers.

Readers may find it useful to read the results and illustrations first, to determine what was learned in this study, and then go back to read the method to see how these findings emerged—that is, to see where the method was going. This chapter is two studies in one: first, method with its philosophical grounding, and then the study. Readers will readily see that empirical phenomenological research does not simply involve experiential impressions taken at face value, which is one North American meaning of "phenomenological." Instead, the method involves systematic and demanding reflection.

The findings indicate that assessors were not just trying to "predict" labels or prescribe treatment plans, but rather were attempting to *understand* their clients. Assessors made use of their own experience and lives during this process. Their observations and impressions were important for the next phases of assessment and for immediate planning for treatment within the facility. Churchill's research remains relevant for the recurrent issue of "clinical vs. statistical prediction," correcting several of the usual assumptions in that debate. In addition, assessment practitioners and supervisors likely will find themselves affirming the importance of reflecting on the use of one's own responses to clients and on the process through which impressions evolve. This process fundamentally exceeds inductive and deductive thinking.

BACKGROUND

This study addresses the psychologist's experience while forming impressions of personality during the interview phase of a psychodiagnostic assessment. Although practicing psychologists generally acknowledge that they are themselves "instruments" of assessment, little has been published in the way of clarifying how the psychologist is involved both actively and passively as a perceiving agent during an assessment interview. Empirical research on clinical inference and clinical judgment has focused largely on the processing of information, while dismissing the experience of the diagnostician as extraneous or as nonaccessible to investigation. Although studies of clinical judgment have shown that the computer is a superior processor of data when it comes to the application of actuarial methods, the clinician is, at the same time, acknowledged as probably always being a better collector of information (Grove and Meehl, 1996; Holtzman, 1966; Westen and Weinberger, 2004). Nevertheless, contemporary texts continue to dwell almost exclusively on the task of what to do with the data, while only paying lip service to the fundamental task of the assessor to elicit and perceive the data in the first place. To the extent that the psychologist's own involvement within the assessment process is a "function of covert processes" (Sullivan, 1954, p. 54), it would be helpful if these processes were brought to the clinician's awareness so that they could be used more awarefully and self-critically.

Making conscious experience accessible to investigation is the hallmark of the phenomenological method. The goal of this chapter is to make clear how that method can be applied toward making explicit the implicit or covert functions of consciousness that are lived (and not necessarily known) by the psychologist during a clinical encounter. More generally, the research question is: *How do psychologists form clinical impressions?* The more specific question from the phenomenological perspective is: *What are the "horizons" of perception and cognition that make possible the forming of clinical impressions?* That is, how must the psychologist be standing to see what she sees? (See Keen, 1975, for an illuminating clarification of the notion of perceptual horizons.)

LITERATURE REVIEW: THE COGNITIVE ACTIVITY OF THE CLINICIAN

This literature review consists of a brief sketch of 50 years of research on the psychologist's cognitive activity during an assessment. The idea that clinical impression formation is itself a special form of social cognition has been explored elsewhere (Churchill, 1984b), as was the grounding of social cognition in what phenomenologists call a "primacy of perception." Cognition and perception are treated here not as two distinguishable faculties, but rather as two moments within a figure–ground relationship, in which perceptual experience serves as ground to the cognitive acts that emerge from it. One of the prominent themes in the literature on assessment has been the controversy over *clinical versus statistical models of prediction.* First thematized by Meehl (1954), this distinction continues to serve as a regular basis for discussions in the clinical literature regarding subjective (informal, impressionistic) versus objective (formal, actuarial) approaches to diagnosis (Dawes et al., 1989; Holt, 1962; Sarbin, 1962; Westen and Weinberger, 2004; Wiens, 1991; Wierzbicki, 1993). The issue centers on how psychodiagnostic data are most efficiently processed: intuitively by clinicians or algorithmically, according to the technology of information processing. Researchers from within the statistical tradition, influenced by advances in decision-making technology, have argued that we should replace clinical judgment, a human process that is not fully under-stood in the first place, with a mathematical process that is seemingly more efficient (Arthur, 1966; Grove et al., 2000; Hammond, 1964; Lanyon, 1972). However, it is critically important to note that such opinions relating to data aggregation "have no bearing on whether, or under what circum-stances, clinicians can make reliable and valid observations and inferences" (Westen and Weinberger, 2004, p. 596).

In any comparison of clinical versus statistical methods in which idiographic description—the original meaning of psychodiagnosis (knowing the other's psyche)—is reduced to categorization (labeling) and predic-tion of treatment outcome, the clinician who is sensitive to individual differences may well be at a disadvantage. When we look at the research on clinical versus statistical methods, we find that this indeed has been the case. Studies have compared the two methods with regard to their relative degree of reliability and accuracy in assigning labels (preconceived categorical descriptions) to individuals. In these studies it is presupposed that "accuracy" means the "correct label"; that is, there is no consideration of whether labels are, by nature, adequate to the individual. What such research amounts to, then, is just a comparison of the reliability of two methods of information processing with respect to arriving at a diagnostic category. As might be expected, clinicians relying completely on their own powers of person perception and data combination usually fall short of the achievement of reliability established by statistical methods.

In light of such findings, some have gone so far as to say "the clinician's cognitive task often apparently exceeds the capacity of the human intellect" (Chapman and Chapman, 1967, p. 204). In contrast, Erik Erikson (1958) observed that "there is a core of *disciplined subjectivity* in clinical work which it is neither desirable nor possible altogether to replace with seemingly more objective methods—methods which originate, as it were, in the machine-tooling of other kinds of work" (p. 68). Speaking of the clinical approach, Holt (1971) has acknowledged that there are "informal" processes of observing and listening to the client that do "not generally operate by means of a highly conscious, rational, explicit drawing of inferences" (p. 11). The actual forming of a clinical impression is understood by Holt as a spontaneous event that "typically happens outside the spotlight of our fullest (or *focal*) awareness" (p. 11). In this sense, "informal assessment" might be seen as an example of what Polanyi (1966) refers to as "tacit knowing": Some of the behavioral cues from the assessee, as well as experiential phenomena on the side of the clinician, are "known" to the clinician only to the extent that they tacitly signify something else that does become thematic—namely, the personality of the subject. The informal processes at work during assessment would include everyday modes of person perception such as empathy, intuition, snap judgments, stereotyping, attribution, and projection.

Research on clinical judgment has focused primarily on (1) the relative utility of various kinds of information used for making clinical decisions, (2) the relative efficiency of different methods of processing information, and (3) the relative value of possible decisions regarding treatment. Information processing and decision making have, in effect, been abstracted from the rest of the clinician's experience, resulting in a research tradition that has lost sight of what it was originally seeking: a better understanding of the clinician. Holt (1962) noted long ago that "the objective ideal of completely mechanized assessment will be impossible until computers can be taught to feel, to judge, and to care about people" (p. 12). Notwithstanding decades of research that have established statistical methods as outperforming and thereby setting the standard for clinical judgment, it is nevertheless true that the process of *clinical observation* is distinguishable from the process by which clinicians (or computers) *aggregate data* (see Westen and Weinberger, 2004). Thus a careful study of the clinician's perceptual and cognitive experience should be able to contribute something useful to both the training of clinicians and to our understanding of what it means to be a psychologist.

Speaking a quarter of a century ago, Holt (1971) noted that "as soon as the methods of science are applied to an informal, everyday process, it begins to turn into a discipline" (p. 43). In this chapter, I extend the methods of science to include the "rigorous science" called *phenomenology* by its founder Edmund Husserl (1965). It turns out that much of the research literature on clinical impression formation has centered on the "what" that is perceived (patient attributes) rather than the "how" of the perceiving. The methodological challenge is finding access to this "how." Researchers have complained that the clinician's thinking is too "impressionistic" (Marks et al., 1974) or "complex" (Lanyon, 1972), or that it is too "private, quasi-rational, and non-repeatable" (Hammond, 1966) to be studied empirically. Some have even concluded that the assessor's judgments are a "function of a process they cannot trace" (Hammond, 1966, p. 28). Indeed, Nisbett and Wilson (1977) have argued that the human intellect is incapable of identifying the processes by which it functions (see Churchill, 2000, for a sustained critique of their position). As they see it, self-reports amount to "telling more than we can know." However, even if verbal reports do not reveal so-called *cognitive mechanisms* presumed to underlie experience, this is not to say that they cannot reveal the *style of relationality* of our perceptual experience. Hence, asking psychologists to describe their experience of the process of forming clinical impressions can be a valid mode of access to a better understanding of what Holt and others have referred to as *informal assessment*.

One of the aims of the current study is, indeed, to facilitate a better understanding of how clinicians are present to their clients. Thus, the research question being posed here is: How are clinical impressions grounded in the psychologist's illuminating presence? Practitioners of "collaborative" and "human science" models of assessment (Dana, 1982; Finn, 2005; Fischer, 1985/1994) have advocated using one's own experience in the assessment session both as a source of empathic connection with the client and as a source for reflecting on possible understandings of the client's life world. A better understanding of the perceptual style of the clinician would help psychologists to become better disciplined with respect to their involvement in the "art" of assessment interviewing. This becomes even more important once we recognize that the clinician's art is precisely what a computer alone can never provide: The clinician is the original source of data that statistical methods are so good at aggregating. Lanyon and Goodstein (1971), among others, have argued that research into the clinical art of observation "is essential if we are to understand this critically important process and train others in it" (p. 181). This is as true today as it was 30 years ago.

METHOD

My research interest is how clinicians form and explicate their impressions of an individual's behavior and personality. "When one raises this question there seems to be no escape from claiming some kind of priority to the individual consciousness in which the we-phenomenon takes shape" (Spiegelberg, 1975, p. 237). My methodological question thus became how to facilitate access to the psychologist's consciousness of a very particular "we-phenomenon"—namely, the clinical interview. "Indeed, there is no choice but to put subjectivity into the center of an inquiry into evidence and inference in clinical work" (Erikson, 1958, p. 67). For the purposes of this research, this meant that both the phenomenon of interest (psychodiagnostic seeing) and the situation revealing it (the assessment interview) had to be made accessible for the researcher's analysis.

PRELIMINARY REFLECTION

Before presenting the formal "procedure" of this research, a pause is in order so that the fundamental principle of phenomenology that underlies this work does not become obscured beneath a "matter-of-fact" presentation of the method itself. A phenomenological approach to researching clinical "impression formation" is far from being one that takes for granted the very nature of its subject matter, proceeding directly to a seemingly obvious way of studying this topic as a research phenomenon. Every seeking, as Heidegger (1962) has revealed, is guided beforehand by a preinvestigative sense of that which is sought (p. 191). The upshot is that no genuine inquiry can be a blind or clueless seeking that merely processes data that are present at hand; rather, one is always guided beforehand by prereflective as well as reflective insights into the nature of what is to be formally interrogated. My own first teacher of phenomenological method, Paul Colaizzi, has argued that without an initial personal contact with and reflection on the phenomenon under investigation, all the empirical data and fancy procedures would never add up to a genuine phenomenological investigation of the data (Colaizzi, 1973, 1978, 2001). I therefore pause here to share with the reader this essential preliminary moment within the phenomenological method.

In my own case, it was not a matter of simply identifying a research topic and saying, "Okay, let's take a phenomenological look at how clinicians form impressions of personalities." It began first with my own fascination with what it meant *to be* a psychologist—one who "sees through to" the inner worlds of others. Moreover, I understood that this seeing was not something that took place "inside" my own private world of intuition, but rather something that happened *between* myself and the person I was observing. Indeed, the very use of the term *intuition* is misleading, in that it implies that "inside" view, whereas Kant's original term, *Anschauung*, implied direct perceptual contact (Colaizzi, 2002). My interest in the psychologist's act of seeing others was initially founded in people's reactions when they learned that I was a student of psychology: Their body postures would visibly change as they queried, "Are you analyzing me now?" This precipitated on my part a chain of reflections over a long period regarding the very act of *seeing psychologically*, and, more generally, of what I initially thought of as "psychological presence." Although these reflections were free flowing and rather spontaneous, they turned out to serve as the intellectual context for my eventual analysis of the data that I would collect for my doctoral dissertation. For example, I kept a journal of reflections on "imitative empathy" as a bodily mode of access to the meaning of others' experiences. It comes as no surprise to me now, in retrospect, that a central area of my findings (presented later in the chapter) had to do with an "initial empathic imaging" of the client on the part of the clinician during a diagnostic interview. Did this "finding" simply appear to me (passively) in the data? Or is it not the case that my own personal reflections, prior to conducting my empirical study, served as a "hermeneutic" (interpretive) context for the analyses I would perform later? These and other issues pertaining to reflexivity in interpretive methodologies merit consideration by all researchers (for further discussion see Churchill et al., 1998; Finlay and Gough, 2003; Rao and Churchill, 2004; Walsh, 2003).

PARTICIPANTS

Two psychologists were asked to participate in this research, having met the following criteria: (1) they were licensed PhD clinical psychologists, (2) they were willing to be videotaped interviewing a patient (with the patient's consent), and (3) they understood that the purpose of their interview would be simply to form a psychodiagnostic impression (and not, for example, to provide interventions). (The participants in this study both happened to work in psychiatric hospitals, and both were responsible for the training of interns and medical residents.)

PROCEDURE

Data collection consisted of videotaping assessment interviews and obtaining descriptions of the clinicians' experience during these interviews from two psychologists meeting the criteria described earlier. I then proceeded with a personally modified version of the Duquesne method of protocol analysis (Colaizzi, 1973, 1978; Giorgi, 1970, 1975; see also Colaizzi, 2001, 2002, and Giorgi and Giorgi, 2003a, b, for more recent methodological elaborations) to explore the experiential context of psychodiagnostic seeing. The phenomenological approach to experience can be characterized as an effort to understand the relational stance (or "intentionality") of human beings in specific situations. A phenomenological analysis of experience involves observing and making thematic the ways in which a perceiving subject is "present to" an object such that there emerges a grasp of the object as having a particular meaning. In the current study, the question of how perceptions are co-constituted by the perceiver was taken up in the context of "seeing psychodiagnostically." The assessment interview was chosen as the focus of this research because of its distinctive characteristic of placing the psychologist into direct contact with the client for the sole purpose of forming a clinical impression.

DATA-GENERATING ACTIVITIES

As reported elsewhere (Churchill 1984a, b, 1998), the actual steps for obtaining data consisted of the following activities:

1. Preliminary interview. The purpose of this step was to collect background data to be used in subsequent analyses. The general issues that were raised included how the psychologist sees the function of psychodiagnosis, the role of theory in his assessment of others, and what motivates him to do this kind of work. Such background information was considered to be essential insofar as "the 'sedimented' structure of the individual's experience is the condition for the subsequent interpretation of all new events and activities" (Schutz, 1962, p. xxviii). The data collected at this stage of the research were transcribed and put aside for subsequent collating with the other data.

2. Preassessment protocol. Immediately prior to the assessment, I asked my participants, "How are you going into the assessment? What are the referral questions and what impressions about the client do you already have as you go into the interview?" The purpose of this research step was to discover *prior* to the assessment interview and *prior* to the participant's reflection on the interview, what specific questions and impressions served as "perceptual horizons" of the psychologist's subsequent perception of the client.

3. The interview phase of a psychodiagnostic assessment. This was the concrete research situation itself, lived by the psychologist acting as a research participant, and videotaped for review during subsequent

research interviews. During the assessment, the research participant (the psychologist) encountered his patient and together they went through what, for the psychologist, was a "standard" psychodiagnostic interview—one that was representative of his psychodiagnostic work.

4. Postassessment protocol. Immediately following the assessment interview the psychologist was handed these written instructions:

> Would you please describe, as fully as you can, what you just experienced during the interview phase of your interaction with the client. I am interested in the course of events as they took place *for you* as you moved through the interview, including those momentary experiences and associations that might otherwise not seem directly relevant to assessment as such. I would like for your account to have provided an overview of the entire interview, including your entrance into testing, and detailed accounts of some of the different kinds of experience and activity that you went through. Thank you for your help.

Together with the preassessment interviews, the participant's written responses here became the initial empirical data for this research and thus the basis for further elaboration and clarification of the psychologists' experience.

5. "First Impressions": Reading and posing questions to the protocols. I read and reread the participants' written descriptions to gain a preliminary sense of the content and organization of each description. Through gaining a familiarization with the "whole experience," I began to grasp the contextual significance of individual statements, and developed questions to pose to the participants during follow-up interviews. Moreover, during this step, the researcher begins to become *intuitively present* to the underlying psychological themes within the data. *Such "first impressions" of the significance of the data relative to one's own research interests serve to guide subsequent reflections on the data during formal stages of data analysis.*

6. Follow-up interviews. These interviews were directed toward the elaboration and clarification of the experience to which the data referred. It was the transcripts of these interviews that I later used as primary data for reflection. The interviewing process consisted of a collaborative dialogue between the clinician and myself, during which the former was asked to read aloud from his written statements while I interjected questions to facilitate clarification of issues relevant to my research interests. During these interviews, the videotape of the assessment was at hand to facilitate the participant's recollection of his experience.

7. Collating the data. The purpose of this research step was to assemble a "collated text" out of all the data collected from each participant: the preliminary interviews, the written descriptions of their diagnostic interviews, and my follow-up interviews with each clinician. This step

consisted of juxtaposing statements that spoke to a common theme from different places in the data to form paragraphs of data, and arranging the paragraphs into a somewhat chronological sequence. The end result was a final text of data for each research participant that could be used for my subsequent analyses.

INTENTIONAL ANALYSIS OF THE DATA: THE DEFINITIVE CHARACTERISTIC OF PHENOMENOLOGY

The steps of a phenomenological psychologist's reflection upon self-report data have been described by numerous authors, most notably the originators of the Duquesne "school" of phenomenological research: Colaizzi (1973, 1978, 2001), W. Fischer (1974, 1978, 1985), Giorgi (1975, 1985, 1989), Van Kaam (1966), and von Eckartsberg (1971, 1986, 1998). Elaborations of this tradition of research can be found in Churchill (1998, 2002), Churchill and Wertz (1985, 2001), Fischer and Wertz (1979), Polkinghorne (1989), and Wertz (1983a, b, 1985). What I wish to emphasize here, however, are not so much the "steps" per se, but rather the most oft-neglected yet important characteristics of the researcher's experience *within* these steps—namely, *the researcher's own attunement to intentionality.*

Elsewhere (Churchill, 1998; Churchill and Richer, 2000) I have discussed the meaning of intentionality and of what an "intentional analysis" would consist. To put it most simply, we are looking for the way in which a particular content of consciousness is related to a particular stance or attitude of consciousness. *"What" we see is always a function of "how" we are looking.* To perform an intentional analysis requires that one focus on the "content" of a moment of consciousness (in this case, as reported by a diagnostician) and then, *having made this moment "one's own" through empathy,* to turn one's attention back on this vicariously experienced "presence" in such a way as to be able to "thematize" *how it is that I am standing* (even if only in my imaginative uptake of the subject's experiential description) *such that I see what I see?* Husserl (1973, 1977, 1982), for whom the expression "intentional analysis" meant the same thing as "phenomenological analysis," saw this as an "analysis which pays systematic attention to the parallel aspects of intending act (*noesis*) and intended content (*noema*)" (Spiegelberg, 1982, p. 692). In the case of the current study, the research interest is to understand how the impression of an individual's personality (*noema*) takes shape within the consciousness of a diagnostician (*noesis*).

It is important to note that empirically based phenomenological analysis is not simply a question of collecting verbal reports and accepting them at face value. Nor is it an exercise in projective identification or fusion with the research participant. Rather, it is a question of using one's own powers of empathy and imagination to "feel" one's way or to "image" one's way into the other's experience. "The subject's description functions as a medium through which, as meanings of the subject's experience begin to resonate within the researcher's own experience, the researcher gains access to the world of the subject and at the same time grasps this world as a function of the subject's presence, or intentionality" (Churchill and Wertz, 1985, p. 553). What is important here is that we understand the phenomenological approach to protocol analysis as something far more involving for the researcher than a simple contemplation of words and stories. The words of the research participant open up a world of experience, and it is this world that the researcher directly and vividly intuits through the protocol data. *What is being "looked at" is no longer the raw data, but rather my co-experiencing of the research participant's experience.* The task of the researcher is essentially to imagine the other person's relationship to his or her world of experience. This is what makes the analysis "phenomenological" in the original sense of the word: At the very moment of my descriptive act, I am attuned to what is present to me now in *my* experience:

> Within my own situation that of the patient whom I am questioning makes its appearance and, in this bipolar phenomenon, I learn to know both myself and others. (Merleau–Ponty, 1945/1962, p. 338)

Interestingly, Merleau–Ponty's 1962 comment here is apropos to both my research topic and my research method. Understood phenomenologically, the situation of the psychodiagnostician is not unlike the situation of the phenomenological researcher: In each case it is a matter of finding a way to *access* the other's experience *personally*.

THE FORMULATION OF FINDINGS

Once I had subjected each of the moments of the original protocol to reflective analysis, I was then able to bring together my descriptive "thematizations" of the psychologist's intentional (relational) stance and synthesize them into a culminating description capturing the whole of what was being investigated. In any phenomenological investigation, it is important to make a distinction between *what is being interrogated* (the data) and *what is being sought* (the psychological meaning or significance of the data). Thus while *looking at* the experience of the psychodiagnostician, I was *looking for* the constitutive "style" or "modes" of the psychologist's acts of seeing.

Individual Structural Descriptions (ISDs)

The goal here was to articulate the "intentionality"—that is, the structural relationship between perceiver and perceived—revealed in the moments of the clinician's experience that were described within each paragraph of collated text. The question that I formally posed to the data was: What does this moment of the clinician's experience reveal about his meaning-constituting activity in seeing the client psychodiagnostically? This question placed my focus squarely on the perceiving as distinguishable from but inextricably bound to the perceived. It was precisely the latency of the act of perceiving within the perceived that I was seeking to uncover. My analysis proceeded from "what" was seen to "how" it was seen—that is, to what constituted the "seeing" as such. The work of the structural analysis, then, became an effort on my part to focus on the very act of seeing through which the clinicians were able to understand their clients, but which necessarily remained invisible to them as long as they remained focused (even during the research interviews) on their clients.

The results of this first step of data analysis were articulated as ISDs of each subject's experience. These descriptive findings express both the intentionality of the individual moments of the subject's experience and the contextual interweaving of these moments. (Technically speaking, this part of my research was performed under what Husserl [1970, pp. 327ff] described as the "personalistic attitude" aimed toward bringing individual moments of intentionality thematically into view. "Free variation" was not yet used at this stage, and thus the ISDs reflect certain textures of experience that may or may not be "essential" at the individual level.)

General Structural Description

Having prepared ISDs from both participants' data, I was next faced with the task of bringing all the results together into a statement articulating the general characteristics of psychodiagnostic seeing. The movement from individual to general levels of analysis was carried out by means of the two *essential* steps of phenomenological analysis as defined by Husserl (1973, pp. 340ff): "eidetic reduction" and "free variation in the imagination." It is important to note that any such reference to "steps" in phenomenological research is best grasped as a reference to *shifting moments of reflection* on the part of the researcher. By this I mean that one does not "first" bracket preconceptions, and "then" try to see essential characteristics at the individual level, "followed by" performing free variation to arrive "finally" at general or even universal findings. The fact is that one is constantly shifting between idiographic and general insights, as well as between efforts to "see" the phenomenon directly and efforts to "hold back" when ideas from elsewhere begin to intrude spontaneously. Likewise, "empathic dwelling" with the data, "amplification" of meanings, "hermeneutic" interpretations, and researcher "reflexivity" do not comprise a series of steps within a process, but rather shifting moments in the researcher's experience, and hence they are better thought of as *possibilities of reflective experience* rather than as steps, stages, or levels of analysis.

So what is going on when one engages in the "seeing of essences" by means of "free variation in the imagination?" Here it is a question of altering one's attitude toward the empirical data in such a way that the data are no longer taken to be of interest for their own sake, insofar as they reveal peculiarities at the idiographic level; but, rather, they become of interest as a starting point for an, in principle, *infinite series of variations* by means of which the researcher is able to *see* what Husserl (XXX) calls a "unity of sense" (or *eidos*). The reader should note that the movement from individual to general levels of analysis is *not* simply looking for commonalities among the cases studied idiographically, but is rather *a procedure that enables the researcher to transcend the limitations of the empirical data.* This is accomplished by "*'running through' a plurality of instances—both empirically given and imaginatively conjured—until a unity of sense becomes apparent*" (Husserl, 1973, pp. 340–341). This "unity" is what remains thematically given throughout all the variations displayed before the researcher's consciousness. The reason why this step is so important is that by means of it, the researcher is capable of making statements that apply beyond the scope of the data collected. That is, by means of "free variation in the imagination" the researcher is able to achieve a sense of "external validity" with respect to the findings. To put it another way, without using free variation, the would-be phenomenologist articulates results that can have claim to validity only relative to the experiences sampled (but not to the "universe" of experiences targeted). Thus, in order for the current study to have relevance beyond the two experiences that served as a basis for reflection, I had to spend considerable time pondering each statement made at the individual level, considering whether and how this might be true in any or all cases of forming clinical impressions.

In the end, what is "phenomenological" about the kind of research described here is *not* simply its foundation in individual experience, but rather *its movement from individual to universal possibilities of experience by means of free (or random) variation.* Indeed, it is the *randomness* of any variations produced by the researcher's imagination of the experience under investigation that ensures *external validity* of the study, just as it is the randomness of sampling in experimental research that guarantees generalizability of results.

Concretely, the research question I posed at this point was: What *kinds* of experiential phenomena have been represented in the data and articulated in the ISD? Under the "eidetic reduction," the experiences that formed the basis for the ISDs were no longer of concern to me with respect to their status as actual facts (that is, as representative of concrete experiences), but were transformed in my imagination into possibilities of psychodiagnostic experience lending themselves to "free variations." Concretely, I would read a statement from the ISD, then pause and consider what other ways a psychologist *might* experience the same *kind* of moment during an assessment. By "freely" varying the context of a particular clinical impression from that of my research participants (who were cognitive–behavioral and existential–psychoanalytical in orientation) to other contexts (such as gestalt, family systems, Jungian, or neuropsychological, for example) I was then able to arrive at a way of characterizing the intentionality of psychodiagnostic seeing in ways that could embrace all the variations (in this case, of interpretive frameworks) that I could conjure up at random. At each step along the way in the ISDs, I then articulated my sense of what was the same about the imagined variations and the original empirical example as a general "essential" theme—that is, a theme common to all variations.

After I had reflected on all the statements in the ISDs in this manner, I prepared a general statement articulating the intentional structure of any psychodiagnostic act of seeing. The general structures of seeing that emerged during the final analysis were the psychologist's (1) constitutive projects and interests, (2) modes of attention, and (3) modes of explication. It is worth noting that these three aspects of psychodiagnostic seeing would in fact be general structural categories of any kind of seeing directed toward meaningful impressions. Although I did not "know" this prior to embarking on my research, it turns out that these dimensions would have to be interrogated and explicated to arrive at a structural understanding of any perceptual experience that results in a thematization of the perceptual object. Although the three aspects are themselves universals of seeing, *it is the particular way in which these universals are found to be concretized in psychodiagnostic assessment that makes the results of this research distinctive of psychodiagnosis.* It is important to note that "structures of seeing" represent a different *kind* of structure from the structures of experience revealed in phenomenological investigations of phenomena based on stories of events or "dramas." Hence, the structure of a "cognitive style" (as revealed in the current study) looks a little different from the structure of a "dramatic event" (as revealed, for example, in studies of emotions). See Churchill (1998, pp. 190–193) for a discussion of different ways of articulating "structures."

To communicate a vivid sense of what was revealed at the individual level, the results are formulated here as an illustrated general structural description. The illustrations that follow the general structural statements in the following Results section are, in fact, selections from the ISDs (and ultimately the data) that served as the basis for eidetic reduction and free variation. Thus, the presentation of results follows a *hermeneutic* approach "in which a structure, a system of order, is derived from the instances, and which serves to unify them as parts of a whole" (Dilthey, 1977b, p. 138).

RESULTS

The following outline is included to help orient the reader to the overall structure of the results of this study. For reasons of space, only selections

I. Projects and interests constitutive of psychodiagnostic seeing

A. The motivational context of the psychologist
B. General interest in the "psychological" as a province of meaning
C. Prognostic interests
D. Preconceptions and questions constitutive of a specific interest in the client's self-presentation

II. Psychodiagnostic presence: the attentive regard of the psychologist

A. Consciousness of the client

1. Passive receptivity: apperceptive and empathic modes of presence
2. Active seeking: the psychologist's probing presence
3. Consciousness of rapport: the psychologist's task-facilitating presence

B. Reflexivity in the psychologist's experience

1. Self-monitoring presence
2. Self-consciousness and role awareness
3. Critical reflection

III. The formation of clinical impressions

A. Empathic contemplation and initial imaging
B. Simple explications: apperception and recognition
C. Contemplative explication: typification
D. Contemplative explication: prediction
E. Contemplative explication: integration

from the third area of findings, pertaining to *"modes of explication,"* are presented here. See Churchill (1984a, b, 1998) for presentation of other areas of the findings, including the psychologist's *attentive regard* and *horizons of presence* within the diagnostic interview.

THE FORMATION OF CLINICAL IMPRESSIONS: MODES OF EXPLICATION

Initially and at times throughout the interview, the psychologist allows an impression of the client to form, not as the result of deliberate contemplation, but rather as a spontaneous adumbration of images. The initial imaging of the client under the receptive regard moves rather spontaneously toward making explications about the psychological meaning of what has been perceived, even if these explications are not yet formally integrated into a diagnostic statement. There are simple acts of explication as well as more contemplative acts that synthesize several images, percepts, and/or explications into complex explications, including (but not limited to) categorical judgments using psychological jargon. All modes of explication are revealed to be correlatives of the specific interests, preconceptions, and expectations of the psychologist.

EMPATHIC CONTEMPLATION AND INITIAL IMAGING

The psychologist's first impressions are essentially based on a prereflective experience of the client that is primarily *empathic* in nature. This tendency to feel a sense of the client is preparatory for the psychologist's making explications about the client. The empathic "feeling" of the psychologist "into" the experience of the client is lived prethematically: Only after the encounter does the psychologist look back and recognize a moment of his experience as one in which he was "feeling a sense of" the client's experience or imitating the client's behavior. Such moments of co-experiencing give way to a passive genesis of images, which subsequently become "languaged" as explications about the client. In this way, the physiognomic features that were originally striking to the psychologist are subsequently taken up in acts of explication whereby the sense or meaning of those features becomes thematic. This sense is what is meant by a first impression, but also any impression to the extent that it is grounded in the perceiver's perceptual experience. It is always an explicative act of the psychologist, motivated by psychodiagnostic interests, that constitutes the more subtle empathic experiences as information.

Illustration

Dr. S's understanding of his client found its genesis even prior to his first encounter over the phone. There was already a directing of interest toward the client in Dr. S's listening to the referral agent's description of him as "a seminary student under a lot of stress." It was on the basis of this description that he first directed his attention to the client imaginatively. The initial image was "a very vague, not well-formed image of what the person [was] going to look like." Dr. S imagined his client to be somewhat thin based on his knowledge that the client was a seminary student. Most seminary students, in Dr. S's experience, had been thin. There was, then, a spontaneous awakening of Dr. S's sedimented perceptions that constituted an image of the client according to the kind of images Dr. S associated with the client's type of work. Specifically, the information given about the client evoked an image of his physical appearance, based to some extent on thematic meanings of the client's occupation ("a very ascetic, disciplined, self-depriving mode") and to some extent upon tacit meanings that were vivified through an associative awakening in the form of images ("thin, dark hair, kind of ordinary looking"). In addition to physical appearance, knowledge of the client's occupation created certain expectations with regard to his verbal facility. Prior to the assessment Dr. S stated, "I'm looking forward to an articulate client for a change." Although it later "gets replaced by the reality," this initial imaging serves to bring Dr. S into a relationship with the client—a first attempt to become familiar with the unfamiliar.

A more thematic expectation was established when Dr. S was informed beforehand that the client was hesitant about the assessment interview. Dr. S recalls that when he first encountered the client, his thin, slight, wispy stature "fit with my expectation that he was hesitant ... like [there was] a fragile quality of his appointment, as well as his physical manner; it was very striking." Dr. S's first visual perception of the client was thus integrated with his expectations in an active, contemplative way. This reveals that preconceptions about the client are not only horizons of passive perception, but become part of the structure of the psychologist's active seeking as well. Moreover, Dr. S not only perceived the antsy disposition of the client, but also, for a moment, lived the situation "with" the client in such a way that he was able to feel a sense of his client's hesitancy (namely, "like any minute he would walk out"). Here, Dr. S's feel for the client's antsy stance, as well as his understanding of the possible meaning of hesitancy within a potentially anxiety-provoking situation, became constituents of what I have termed here an *empathic contemplation* of the client's behavior. This impression, grounded in empathy, subsequently functioned as the diagnostician's "evidence" of the hesitancy that had been suggested to him by the referral agent.

SIMPLE EXPLICATIONS

Knowledge that the psychologist has about people in general, either from informal acquaintance or formal training, is a horizon of psychodiagnostic seeing: Past experiences constitute the thematic field of the psychologist's perception of the client. There is a spontaneous, nondeliberate, associative relating of the person currently being seen by the psychologist to persons seen in the past. Understanding the current client involves the awakening of already familiar understandings about similar kinds of people, without which the client would remain unfamiliar. The awakening of these sedimented understandings makes possible *recognition* and *anticipation*, each of which is a part of the structure of psychodiagnostic seeing. Concretely, the psychologist finds himself informed by the different histories he has had with different kinds of people, in a way that is motivated distinctively by the task of psychodiagnosis.

Illustration: Biographical Presence

Dr. S described a need "to know what I am looking at" precisely *in order to* understand his client and thereby perform his duties as a psychologist—that is, to make "an educated guess as to the course this is going to run." To this end, he found himself informed by the "different histories" he had with different kinds of patients. These histories were there for Dr. S as "part of the whole atmosphere" or background against which the client became seen as a particular *kind* of figure: "there's a feeling of 'I've been here before.'" From his description, it seems clear that it is not a matter of Dr. S trying to form cognitive associations *deliberately* in terms of past experiences; rather, in his original perceiving of the client, he *feels* something familiar about the client: "It's there in my perception of him, but I don't think explicitly about all the other people." Moreover, for Dr. S, this horizon of past experiences is functional for him in the context of an assessment interview, in a way that does *not* enter into his perceptual experience of others in everyday circumstances, such as car mechanics or grocery store cashiers. This fact implies that the horizon of past experiences, while essentially latent in any perceptual act, becomes functional when motivated by a particular interest in the current object of perception.

CONTEMPLATIVE EXPLICATION: TYPIFICATION

In synthesizing images of the client into explicative impressions, the psychologist moves from the individual in his or her givenness to an understanding of the general and typical meanings of that givenness. This movement is achieved by seeing concrete events described by the client or observed by the psychologist as examples of general psychological phenomena that are known in advance by the psychologist. Such foreknowledge is a horizon of psychodiagnostic seeing that makes possible explications in which the psychologist recognizes the general meaning "in" the particular event. It is through such generalizations that the psychologist is able to specify his or her comprehension of the client. The specifications of the individual belong to the specific province of meaning referred to by the psychologist as "the psychological." The explicating is a contemplative perceiving that consists of "seeing" the psychological meaning that is inherent in a simple apprehension of the individual. What is distinctive about typification is the contemplative shift from a simple perception of the client's presentations to a specifically psychological explication of general, abstract meanings. The psychologist's reaching beyond the client's self-presentation to grasp psychological meanings can occur either spontaneously, as in simple acts of recognition, or deliberately, as the result of an active interest or striving toward narrative closure.

Illustration

Dr. S's perceptual activity was not a merely passive listening; rather, he saw himself consciously ("in my own mind") "looking for threads"—that is, discerning the essential elements of his client's experience and locating them within his stock of theoretical knowledge. This knowledge provided Dr. S with the universal concepts that generally inform his understanding of individuals—that is, that enable him to "go back to the person and say, 'I think *this* is what's happening.'" When Dr. S reflected on the lived meanings described by the client, this reflection took him into a second-order scientific level of "abstraction," where concrete elements perceived in the client were understood, for example, as "traits"—that is, as instances of behavioral styles that could be referred to in a more general way (for example, "the client is very self-effacing"). In such instances Dr. S was constituting the meaning of the client's lived experience by "seeing" the psychological meaning that was inherent in the client's expression—in effect, by moving from the meaning of the experience for the client to the meaning of the client's experience for the psychologist. Such shifts occurred continuously throughout the interview, in a back-and-forth movement between the two "levels" of understanding:

> He never came out and said to me, "I don't have a mutual relationship." He never came out and said to me, "My self-esteem is lousy." But he did say things like, "I just don't feel like I've accomplished anything in life." I think that you have to break it down. There are times when it's a deliberate act and there are times when it's more implicit. I sometimes found myself deliberately trying to listen to everything that he was saying and seeing where I could push it, in the sense of trying to grasp some theme.... That's different from what happens naturally, in which I'm not striving after it. But I find that, I'll be damned, that happens a lot of times and the interpretations I make will come out of it."

The themes that became part of the framework of Dr. S's understanding of his client were "second order" to the extent that they were "grasped" in *a reaching beyond* what the client was explicitly saying, toward a hypothesis. This could either occur "naturally" (spontaneously) or as the result of a deliberate striving on Dr. S's part. In the latter case, Dr. S was seeking an understanding of the "why" of the client's experience and behavior: "perhaps he's doing this because ...". The "because" implies an interest in relating the expressed experiences of the client to an implicit explanatory framework. Likewise, the other research participant, Dr. C, stated that his primary intent was to understand the client's story—that is, how he saw himself and "where he was at"; and, just as for Dr. S, this involved both listening to what the client expressed and at the same time finding ways of improving on the client's self-description. Although Dr. C really wanted "to see it as [the client] sees it," he ultimately articulated the client's experience as he saw it, according to his own "outline" of what he was looking for. For both participants, then, the interest in the client's self-understanding became subordinated to the psychologist's own "outline" (Dr. C) or "framework" (Dr. S) of understanding.

CONTEMPLATIVE EXPLICATION: PREDICTION

The diagnostic interest is lived by the psychologist as a striving toward the goals of understanding and helping the client. Diagnostic classification is but one variation of understanding. Another kind of reaching beyond what is given by the client is the psychologist's striving for prediction. What the psychologist attempts to see *through* to (*dia*gnosis) is at the same time something that makes possible a seeing *ahead* (*pro*gnosis). Psychodiagnostic seeing is oriented toward that which is knowable (*gnosis*) and posits its understanding of the individual in a knowing way—that is, in a way that can serve to predict behavior. Specifically, the psychologist may be interested in whether the person can be helped through some form of psychological intervention. This interest is directed toward the realm of the possible. Psychodiagnostic seeing appears here as a future-oriented interest grounded in a present-centered perceptual experience. The foreseeing of virtual adumbrations of the individual appears as an essential aspect of the structure of the psychologist's explication of the individual. The fulfillment of this prognostic interest is achieved in moments in which the psychologist imagines how the individual might behave in other settings.

Illustration

In his concentrated listening to the client, Dr. S rarely thought about arriving at a diagnostic label or classification. His listening was in service of subsequently describing what the person was like. However, it was not a matter of merely describing the patient's behaviors and experiences in their contexts, because these themes, for Dr. S, needed to be taken up in light of the treatment issues that the diagnostic assessment was intended to address. Dr. S lived the task of addressing himself to the diagnostic issues as "a sorting out of problems" without necessarily arriving at an official, sophisticated psychiatric label. (The latter would require "fancy footwork"—a stance in which the person is languaged in a "fancy" or jargonized way.) The clinical goals for Dr. S were to understand the person and to suggest appropriate treatment.

An example of Dr. S's prognostic interest was his attempt to determine whether the client and he might work well together in a therapeutic relationship. A variation of this occurred in Dr. C's assessment, during which he was interested in whether his client would be "a candidate for the kind of intensive group psychotherapy program that we run in the day hospital." There was also an interest in the potential benefit of this specific program for the client. Dr. C's assessment was aimed ultimately toward "an idea of the prognosis for the outcome of our day hospital program—not necessarily for therapy in general." In both cases, the psychologists imagined, on the basis of their perceptions of the client during the assessment, how the client might act and respond during a particular therapeutic situation.

CONTEMPLATIVE EXPLICATION: INTEGRATION

As the psychologist's clinical impressions develop, there occurs a *synthesis* of the various profiles of the client. The psychologist does not merely add together separate themes, but comprehends them as "belonging together": *It is in the relation of one theme to another that the psychologist discovers the psychological significance that he or she seeks.* This interrelatedness of various profiles of the client is, moreover, not something that necessarily emerges in a formulaic fashion (that is, following a prescribed sequence of thought processes), but happens more spontaneously in the *play* of what might be referred to as "figure–ground reversals."

One variation of integrative contemplation is the psychologist's active interest in streamlining disparate perceptions and conflicting explications in an effort toward closure—that is, toward forming a clear and definite impression. In the face of this goal, the psychologist finds himself or herself affected by the degree to which such closure has or has not been obtained. The presence of contradictory explications becomes a stress for the psychologist; the resolution of discrepancies becomes a source of satisfaction. Given the psychologist's task to form an integrative impression, ambiguous presentations of the client are sometimes resolved ambivalently through "totalizations."

A configural grasp of profiles, or themes, can be the result of a deliberate striving to establish meaningful connections, or it can be the result of a more sudden, passive genesis of meaning. In either case, psychodiagnostic seeing is lived as an interest in holding together the various impressions around a central integrative explication ("diagnostic impression") that serves to establish a meaningful connection among the themes disclosed during the interview.

Illustration

Transitions during which the client moved from one topic to another were understood by Dr. C as signifying a relationship between the two topics. He saw the death of his client's grandmother in relation to the antecedent presenting complaint about "anxiety attacks," rather than treating it as a separate topic altogether. What stood out as particularly salient and important for Dr. C was something that, at face value, would seem to be quite removed from the presenting complaint. For Dr. C, whatever the client talks about immediately following the presenting complaint is presumed to be very importantly connected with the presenting complaint, especially when there appears to be no face value to the connection: What was important to Dr. C was not the sequence itself, but the relationship established by the sequence. The contiguity thus served to establish a kinship between the two themes. Dr. C's act of seeing can be described here as a gathering of related themes: the root meaning of the word *gather* is "akin to," and in the example just cited, Dr. C's integrating tendency established the "kinship" of two separate themes.

Dr. S also revealed an interest in integrating various themes from throughout the interview. He was not merely accepting information as it came up, but was actively "building" a concrete database by "listening for clues." The integration of themes was, for Dr. S, a higher order explication that brought together other explications into one coherent understanding or "framework." Dr. S experienced this integration in both active and passive modes: "There are times when it's a deliberate act and there are times when it's more implicit. I sometimes found myself deliberately trying ... to grasp some theme ... to generate a hypothesis .... That's different from what happens naturally, in which I'm not striving after it." Spontaneous integration occurs often toward the end of an interview as a result of the cumulative filling out of profiles of the client (i.e., an integrative understanding is suddenly triggered as the profiles "naturally" fall into place).

Immediately after the interview, Dr. S recalled that the client had been relaxed and unhesitant about the interview when they first met in the waiting room. However, looking back later (during a follow-up research interview), Dr. S remembered that in the waiting room the client had been "standing up like any minute he would walk out," which "fit in with my anticipation that he was hesitant." Originally, then, Dr. S sought coherence between the referral agent's information (that the client was hesitant about seeing a psychologist) and what Dr. S had seen in the waiting room. After the interview was over, by which time he had come to like the client, Dr. S "remembers" his perception of the client earlier as having been "not at all anxious and hesitant the way a lot of people are." Confronted with the discrepancy between the two integrations, Dr. S qualified his original statement by saying that "although [the client] had seemed a little antsy in the waiting room, ... once we sat down it changed." Dr. S simply "remembered" what fit in with his final synthesis of impressions. Interestingly, this final impression was congruent with Dr. S's tendency to like self-disclosive clients—a tendency that itself was consistent with Dr. S's own gentle, nondirective personal/professional style.

These excerpts from the full analysis illustrate that, in general, psychodiagnosticians seek to explicate their various perceptions in such a way as to integrate them into a coherent whole. Variations of this integrating tendency cited earlier revealed an interest in avoiding discrepancies by giving more weight to one of the impressions on the basis of the psychologist's own preferences. Dr. S, for example, eventually "streamlined" an originally ambiguous perception so that what remained was a more definite impression. Dr. C admitted that he generally found himself, in the past, prepared to prioritize test data over his own informal impressions in the formulation of his assessment findings (although he was quite pleased in the case at hand to see his perceptions confirmed). Both instances appear as variations of the more general, and essential, integrative tendency of the psychologist seeking to comprehend a relationship among themes that have been gathered during the course of an assessment. The nature of this relationship, stated generally, would be configural and would be formed by the psychologist's interest in holding together the various assessment impressions around a central theme or integrative explication (i.e., a "diagnostic impression") that serves to establish a meaningful connection between the themes.

DISCUSSION

THE PSYCHOLOGIST'S ATTENTIVE REGARD

Modes of attention and modes of explication were presented separately in the original research results (Churchill, 1984b) only for the sake of analytical clarity, for they are inextricably bound together in the intentional act of seeing. Psychodiagnostic knowledge is formed out of the psychologist's various acts of predication whereby the psychologist's experience of the client builds upon images to produce explications that are revelatory of the psychological life of the client. There is plenty of literature on the psychologist's acts of typification, predication, and interpretation, which together comprise the explications arrived at by means of a more deliberate striving. Such "findings" are the intentional correlatives of a regard that "seeks." My results reveal that clinical impressions are also, to a large extent, based upon a spontaneous genesis of images that are the correlatives of an empathic, receptive regard. Such images form the basis or noematic nucleus for all subsequent perceptions and explications that are integrated into the clinical impression. The initial imaging is an essential part of the "act" of assessment even if it is an "informal" (Holt, 1971) procedure that has only a "tacit" presence in the assessment findings.

THE PROBLEM OF DIAGNOSTIC SIMPLIFICATION

The overriding concern of diagnostic assessment is the formulation of a statement descriptive of the client's personality. All of the psychologist's efforts are directed toward this task of *putting into words* the psychologist's understanding of the client. One of the findings was that there is a tendency to resolve ambiguity by giving more weight to some of the data. Which data are given preference was found to be a function of the biases of the psychologist. Dr. C "prioritized" test data over interview data; Dr. S gave preference to appearances that confirmed what he already was thinking about the client. Of interest here, however, are not the reasons why the psychologist gives priority to one kind of data over another, but why the psychologist attempts to resolve ambiguity in the first place. It is here that contingencies of the assessment situation come to bear on psychodiagnostic seeing. In the face of time pressure, or of an uncooperative client, or the desire to please a referral agent or impress a colleague, a psychologist might opt for simplifying a complex matter that would otherwise require more patient contemplation. This simplifying occurs when the psychologist puts into words a diagnostic impression that does not reflect all that has been observed. Rather, such a "languaging" of the client is aimed toward clarity over and above accuracy. In light of this finding, we might call upon assessors to be cognizant of this tendency to resolve ambiguity through simplification (most typically in the form of categorizations and totalizations) in the hope that they might strive harder in their diagnostic formulations to be faithful to *all* the data.

CLINICAL VERSUS STATISTICAL INTEGRATION OF DATA

Studies addressing the "clinical versus statistical" controversy have compared the clinician and the computer and have discovered that computers are more reliable and efficient at processing data because they rely on a mathematical decision-making approach (see, for example, Kleinmuntz, 1968, 1975, 1991). Even if clinicians cannot work as efficiently as computers, the "statistical" side of the controversy argues that clinicians could become more reliable if they would limit themselves to mathematical formulas for the combination of data. There are two problems with this argument: The first is that clinical assessment's purpose is to *understand* (and not simply to classify) the person. The second problem is that such an approach would no longer be true to the human experience of psychodiagnostic seeing as it was revealed by this study. In one of the types of contemplative explications presented in the results—namely, "integration"— it was found that regardless of whether this explication occurred naturally or as the result of a deliberate striving, the integration was experienced as a "sudden gestalt" precipitated by new data. The sudden gestalting of a clinical impression has as its prerequisite the whole of what the psychologist has come to know up to that point about the client. The weight that a new piece of information has in restructuring the relationship of all the other data was found to be constituted by the psychologist. An awakening of constitutive intentional horizons such as past experiences, theoretical background, and expectations was an essential moment in my subjects' formation of clinical impressions.

How can one begin to speak of an "awakening," however, in something that isn't even awake? A computer never has a "hunch"; it never starts to think in one direction, then change its mind. It does not have the power to accept or reject a hypothesis, or to pull back from one direction of insight in favor of another. The implication is that the clinical versus statistical controversy compares apples with oranges. Thematic gestalts cannot be compared with combinations of data, no matter how complex the formulae, because combinations always break down into linear sequences of simple decisions, whereas the sudden "falling into place" of impressions is a higher order of organization. The term *higher* here refers not to the degree of sophistication of a formula for information combination, but to the kind of approach to the data—namely, a human approach. Such an approach supersedes all artificial methods of information processing when two people enter into communication. Research on clinical versus statistical methods of impression formation fails to take into account that psychodiagnostic data originate in word and gesture. (How does a computer respond to silence?) Further research efforts might be better directed toward improving our understanding of human communication processes in real-life clinical encounters.

CLASSIFICATION AND CREATIVITY IN FORMING CLINICAL IMPRESSIONS

One of the more interesting findings of my research is that formal diagnostic classification is not essential to psychodiagnostic seeing. Actually, an empirical study is not needed to reach this conclusion. Formal diagnostic language merely serves classification, which is but a variation of a more general and ultimately essential act—namely, *typification*. In this study, I found that typification involved the psychologists' seeing concrete events as instances of behavioral styles that could be described using more general, even abstract, concepts. Such concepts could include formal diagnostic nosology as well as theories of personality and psychopathology. Seeing the data of the assessment interview in terms of preconceived models and constructs appears to be so taken for granted that some psychologists see these typifying acts as synonymous with clinical thinking. Although explications of the typifying variety will always be a significant part of the psychodiagnostic process, I would place equal emphasis on the integrative explications that establish relations among various assessment data and facilitate a *configural* grasp of diagnostic themes.

Proponents of the clinical approach from within the "personological" school (Dana, 1982; Fischer, 1985, 1994; Korchin, 1976) regard typifications as functional only to the extent that they open dimensions of the individual for further exploration. The goal is to move from typifications toward understandings of others in their uniqueness, and not the reverse. This view is expressed ironically by the oft-cited remark of the distinguished psychiatrist Adolf Meyer: "We understand this case; we don't need any diagnosis" (Korchin, 1976, p. 104). Thus, in addition to learning to recognize diagnostic types and to use actuarial-derived classifications, trainees should be taught to see significance in the configural relations of assessment data. Mechanical processes have a high degree of reliability and have been developed into decision-making technologies for assessment, but "the mathematical equation [has] no flexibility" (Westen and Weinberger, 2004, p. 595). Creative and contemplative explications are part of what is called the "art" of assessment and were revealed to be essential to the cognitive experience of both my subjects. Rather than following prescribed "decision trees" to arrive at personality description, psychologists are capable of experiencing a synthesis of impressions—a "sudden gestalt"— that could occur either spontaneously or as a result of more deliberate contemplation. Such integrative explications are a function of what Dilthey (1924/1977a) has called "the living artistic process of understanding" (p. 57), and it is on the basis of this creative aspect that one can say, "understanding rests on a special personal giftedness" (Dilthey, 1977b, p. 135). The creative synthesis of impressions into an overall picture of the individual plays an essential role in the "clinical" approach to psychodiagnostic seeing. The implication for training would be to place greater emphasis on developing the trainee's own creativity in forming clinical impressions through utilization of all the natural human powers of comprehension—thinking as well as perceiving, remembering, imagining, feeling, and intuiting.

Allport's (1937) remarks pertaining to the role of intuition in the work of the psychologist are relevant here and serve as an appropriate final statement for this research report. He writes,

> It would not have been necessary to discuss at such length the part that intuition plays in the understanding of personality were it not for the fact that the psychologist (of all people) tends to forget about it. The psychologist delights in the use of recording instruments . . . and scales of all kinds. Yet strange to say he discredits the most delicate of all recording instruments—himself. The human mind is the only agency ever devised for registering at once innumerable variables and for revealing the *relations between them*. It is the one and only instrument capable of comprehension. Failing to employ intuition the psychologist unduly limits his resources. Without it he starts with analysis and ends with conceptualization; on the way he sacrifices his chance to understand living people. (Allport, 1937, p. 547)

CONCLUSION

The chief virtue of phenomenological research lies in its capacity for rendering clear, concrete, and comprehensible articulations of experiences that heretofore have been dismissed as "subjective" and thereby "private" and "inaccessible" to empirical analysis. The greatest struggle involved in this tradition of research probably lies in its final stage—namely, the *description* of one's findings. This is not to say that the processes of intuition and analysis do not present the researcher with enormous challenges, especially when the experiences under investigation originate not in one's own experience but in the experience of another. Upon reviewing my own articulations of the data that I originally analyzed more than two decades ago, I was struck by the clumsiness of some of my descriptions presented in the results, even as I also was impressed by moments of clarity.

A critical review of others' research efforts is, perhaps, the best way to proceed in developing one's own approach to doing phenomenological research. It is also the way that phenomenologists approach questions of validity and reliability—namely, by performing one's own analysis of the data while attempting to look at that data from the perspective of the first researcher's questions. During this process one becomes aware of the researcher's presence to the data, and in reading the results of a phenomenological investigation, one begins to resonate with this intentional relationship between the researcher and the data. In the end, phenomenology enables a researcher to enter into the experience of a research participant, just as it invites the reader to enter into both the experience under investigation and the experience of doing research.

REFERENCES

Allport, G. W. (1937). *Personality: A psychological interpretation.* New York: Henry Holt.

Arthur, A. Z. (1966). A decision-making approach to psychological assessment in the clinic. *Journal of Consulting Psychology, 30,* 435–438.

Chapman, L. J., and J. P. Chapman. (1967). Genesis of popular but erroneous psychodiagnostic observations. *Journal of Abnormal Psychology, 72,* 193–204.

Churchill, S. D. (1984a). Forming clinical impressions: A phenomenological study of psychodiagnostic seeing. In Aanstoos, C. M. (Ed.). *West Georgia College Studies in the Social Sciences* (vol. XXIII, pp. 67–84). Carrollton: West Georgia College.

Churchill, S. D. (1984b). *Psychodiagnostic seeing: A phenomenological investigation of the psychologist's experience during the interview phase of a clinical assessment.* Doctoral dissertation, Duquesne University. Ann Arbor, MI: University Microfilms International (8412495).

Churchill, S. D. (1991). Reasons, causes, and motives: Psychology's illusive explanations of behavior. *Theoretical and Philosophical Psychology, 11,* 24–34.

Churchill, S. D. (1998). The intentionality of psychodiagnostic seeing: A phenomenological investigation of clinical impression formation. In Valle, R. (Ed.). *Phenomenological inquiry in psychology: Existential and transpersonal approaches* (pp. 175–207). New York: Plenum.

Churchill, S. D. (2000). "Seeing through" self-deception in verbal reports: Finding methodological virtue in problematic data. *Journal of Phenomenological Psychology, 31,* 44–62.

Churchill, S. D. (2002). Stories of experience and the experience: Narrative psychology, phenomenology, and the postmodern challenge. *Constructivism and the Human Sciences, 7,* 81–93.

Churchill, S. D., J. E. Lowery, O. McNally, and A. Rao. (1998). The question of reliability in interpretive psychological research: A comparison of three phenomenologically based protocol analyses. In Valle, R. (Ed.). *Phenomenological inquiry in psychology: Existential and transpersonal approaches* (pp. 63–85). New York: Plenum.

Churchill, S. D., and P. Richer. (2000). Phenomenology. In Kazdin, A. E. (Ed.). *Encyclopedia of Psychology* (pp. 168–173). London: American Psychological Association and Oxford University Press.

Churchill, S. D., and F. J. Wertz. (1985). An introduction to phenomenological psychology for consumer research: Historical, conceptual, and methodological foundations. In Hirschman, E. C., and M. B. Holbrook. (Eds.). *Advances in consumer research* (vol. XII, pp. 550–555). Provo, UT: Association for Consumer Research.

Churchill, S. D., and F. J. Wertz, (2001). An introduction to phenomenological research in psychology: Historical, conceptual, and methodological foundations. In Schneider, K. J., J. F. T. Bugental, and J. F. Pierson. (Eds.). *Handbook of humanistic psychology: Leading edges in theory, research, and practice* (pp. 247–262). London: Sage Publications.

Colaizzi, P. F. (1973). *Reflection and research in psychology.* Dubuque, IA: Kendall/Hunt.

Colaizzi, P. F. (1978). Psychological research as the phenomenologist views it. In Valle, R. S., and M. King. (Eds.). *Existential–phenomenological alternatives for psychology* (pp. 48–71). New York: Oxford University Press.

Colaizzi, P. F. (2001). A note on "fundamental structures" thirty years later. *Methods: A Journal for Human Science.*

Colaizzi, P. F. (2002). Kant and the problem of "intuition." *Methods: A Journal for Human Science,* 7–47.

Dana, R. H. (1982). *A human science model for personality assessment with projective techniques.* Springfield, IL: Charles C. Thomas.

Dawes, R. M., D. Faust, and P. E. Meehl. (1989). Clinical versus actuarial judgment. *Science, 243,* 1668–1674.

Dilthey, W. (1977a). Ideas concerning a descriptive and analytical psychology (1894). Zaner, R. M. (Trans.). In Dilthey, W. (Ed.). *Descriptive psychology and historical understanding.* The Hague: Martinus Nijhoff. [Original work published 1924.]

Dilthey, W. (1977b). The understanding of other persons and their expressions of life. Heiges, K. L. (Trans.). In Dilthey, W. (Ed.). *Descriptive psychology and historical understanding.* The Hague: Martinus Nijhoff. [Original work published 1927.]

Erikson, E. H. (1958). The nature of clinical evidence. *Daedalus, 87,* 65–87.

Erikson, E. H. (1968). *Identity: Youth and crisis.* New York: Norton.

Finlay, L., and B. Gough. (Eds.). (2003). *Reflexivity: A practical guide for researchers in health and social sciences.* Oxford: Blackwell Science.

Finn, S. E. (2005). How psychological assessment taught me compassion and firmness. *Journal of Personality Assessment, 84,* 29–32.

Fischer, C. T. (1994). *Individualizing psychological assessment* (2nd ed.). Mawah, NJ: Lawrence Erlbaum and Associates. [Original work published 1985.]

Fischer, C. T., and F. J. Wertz. (1979). Empirical phenomenological analyses of being criminally victimized. In Giorgi, A., R. Knowles, and D. Smith. (Eds.). *Duquesne studies in phenomenological psychology* (vol. 3, pp. 135–158). Pittsburgh: Duquesne University Press.

Fischer, W. F. (1978). An empirical–phenomenological investigation of being anxious: An example of the meanings of being emotional. In Valle, R. S., and M. King. (Eds.). *Existential–phenomenological alternatives for psychology* (pp. 166–181). New York: Oxford University Press.

Fischer. (1974).

Fischer, W. F. (1985). Self-deception: An existential–phenomenological investigation into its essential meanings. In Giorgi, A. (Ed.). *Phenomenology and psychological research* (pp. 118–154). Pittsburgh: Duquesne University.

Fischer, W. F. (1994). On the phenomenological mode of researching "being anxious." *Journal of Phenomenological Psychology, 4*, 405–423.

Giorgi, A. (1970). *Psychology as a human science*. New York: Harper & Row.

Giorgi, A. (1975). An application of phenomenological method in psychology. In Giorgi, A., C. Fischer, and E. Murray. (Eds.). *Duquesne studies in phenomenological psychology* (vol. 2, pp. 82–103). Pittsburgh: Duquesne University Press.

Giorgi, A. (1985). Sketch of a psychological phenomenological method. In Giorgi, A. (Ed.). *Phenomenology and psychological research* (pp. 8–22). Pittsburgh: Duquesne University Press.

Giorgi, A. (1989). One type of analysis of descriptive data: Procedures involved in following a scientific phenomenological method. *Methods: A Journal for Human Science*.

Giorgi, A., and B. Giorgi. (2003a). Phenomenology. In Smith, J. A. (Ed.). *Qualitative psychology: A practical guide to research methods* (pp. 25–50). London: Sage Publications.

Giorgi, A., and B. Giorgi. (2003b). The descriptive phenomenological psychological method. In Camic, P., J. E. Rhodes, and L. Yardley. (Eds.). *Qualitative research in psychology* (pp. 243–273). Washington, DC: American Psychological Association.

Grove, W. M., and P. E. Meehl. (1996). Comparative efficiency of informal (subjective, impressionistic) and formal (mechanical, algorithmic) prediction procedures: The clinical–statistical controversy. *Psychology, Public Policy, and Law, 2*, 293–323.

Grove, W. M., D. H. Zald, B. S. Lebow, B. E. Snitz, and C. Nelson. (2000). Clinical versus mechanical prediction: A meta-analysis. *Psychological Assessment, 12*, 19–30.

Hammond, K. R. (1966). Probabilistic functioning and the clinical method. In Megargee, E. I. (Ed.). *Research in clinical assessment*. New York: Harper.

Hammond, K. R., C. J. Hursch, and F. J. Todd. (1964). Analyzing the components of clinical influence. *Psychological Review, 71*, 438–456.

Heidegger, M. (1962). *Being and time*. Macquarrie, J., and E. Robinson. (Trans.). New York: Harper & Row. [Original work published 1927.]

Holt, R. R. (1962). Clinical and statistical prediction: A reformulation and some new data. *Journal of Abnormal and Social Psychology, 56*, 1–12.

Holt, R. R. (1971). *Assessing personality*. New York: Harcourt Brace Jovanovich.

Holtzman, W. H. (1966). Can the computer supplant the clinician? In Megargee, E. I. (Ed.). *Research in clinical assessment*. New York: Harper.

Husserl, E. (1965). Philosophy as rigorous science. Lauer, Q. (Trans.). In Husserl, E. (Ed.). *Phenomenology and the crisis of philosophy* (pp. 71–147). New York: Harper Torchbooks. [Original work published 1911.]

Husserl, E. (1970). The *crisis of European sciences and transcendental Phenomenology*. Evanston, Illinois: Northwestern University Press. [Original work published 1954.]

Husserl, E. (1973). *Experience and judgment*. Churchill, J. S., and I. Ameriks. (Trans.). Evanston: Northwestern University Press. [Original work published 1948.]

Husserl, E. (1977). *Phenomenological psychology*. Scanlon, J. (Trans.). The Hague: Martinus Nijhoff. [Original lecture course given during the summer of 1925.]

Husserl, E. (1982). *Ideas pertaining to a pure phenomenology and a phenomenological philosophy. First book: General introduction to a pure phenomenology*. Kersten, F. (Trans.). Boston: Martinus Nijhoff. [Original work published 1913.]

Keen, E. (1975). *A primer in phenomenological psychology*. New York: Holt, Rinehart & Winston.

Kleinmuntz, B. (1968). The processing of clinical information by man and machine. In Kleinmuntz, B. (Ed.). *Formal representation of human judgment* (pp. 149–186). New York: John Wiley & Sons.

Kleinmuntz, B. (1975). The computer as clinician. *American Psychologist, 30*, 164–175.

Kleinmuntz, B. (1991). Can computers be clinicians? Theory and design of a diagnostic system. In Hersen, M., A. E. Kazdin, and A. S. Bellack. (Eds.). *The clinical psychology handbook* (pp. 506–515). New York: Pergamon Press.

Korchin, S. S. (1976). *Modern clinical psychology: Principles of intervention in the clinic and community*. New York: Basic Books.

Lanyon, R. I. (1972). Technological approach to the improvement of decision making in mental health services. *Journal of Consulting and Clinical Psychology, 39*, 43–48.

Lanyon, R. I., and L. D. Goodstein. (1971). *Personality assessment*. New York: Wiley & Sons.

Marks, P. A., W. Seeman, and D. L. Haller. (1974). *The actuarial use of the MMPI with adolescents and adults*. Baltimore: Williams & Wilkins.

Meehl, P. E. (1954). *Clinical versus statistical prediction: A theoretical analysis and a review of the evidence*. Minneapolis: University of Minnesota Press.

Meehl, P. E. (1960). The cognitive activity of the clinician. *American Psychologist, 15*, 19–27.

Merleau–Ponty, M. (1962). *Phenomenology of perception*. Smith, C. (Trans.). London: Routledge & Kegan Paul. [Original work published 1945.]

Nisbett, R. E., and T. D. Wilson. (1977). Telling more than we can know: Verbal reports on mental processes. *Psychological Review, 84*, 231–259.

Polanyi, M. (1966). *The tacit dimension*. New York: Doubleday.

Polkinghorne, D. E. (1989). Phenomenological research methods. In Valle, R. S., and S. Halling. (Eds.). *Existential–phenomenological perspectives in psychology: Exploring the breadth of human experience* (pp. 41–60). New York: Plenum Press.

Rao, A., and S. D. Churchill. (2004). Experiencing oneself as being-beautiful: A phenomenological study informed by Sartre's ontology. *Qualitative Research in Psychology, 1*, 55–68.

Sarbin, T. R. (1962). The present state of the clinical–statistical prediction problem. *Anthropology and Medicine, 10*, 315–323.

Sarbin, T. R., R. Taft, and D. E. Bailey. (1960). *Clinical inference and cognitive theory*. New York: Holt, Rinehart and Winston.

Schutz, A. (1962). *Collected papers I: The problem of social reality*. The Hague: Martinus Nijhoff.

Spiegelberg, H. (1975). *Doing phenomenology*. The Hague: Martinus Nijhoff.

Spiegelberg, H. (1982). *The phenomenological movement* (3rd ed.). Boston: Martinus Nijhoff.

Sullivan, H. S. (1954). *The psychiatric interview*. New York: Norton.

Tavris, C. (2003). Mind games: Psychological warfare between therapists and scientists. *Chronicle of Higher Education, 49*, B47.

Van Kaam, A. (1966). *Existential foundations of psychology*. Pittsburgh: Duquesne University Press.

von Eckartsberg, R. (1971). On experiential methodology. In Giorgi, A., W. F. Fischer, and R. von Eckartsberg. (Eds.). *Duquesne studies in phenomenological psychology* (vol. 1, pp. 66–79). Pittsburgh: Duquesne University Press.

von Eckartsberg, R. (1986). *Life-world experience: Existential–phenomenological research approaches in psychology*. Washington, DC: Center for Advanced Research in Phenomenology and University Press of America.

von Eckartsberg, R. (1998). Existential–phenomenological research. In Valle, R. (Ed.). *Phenomenological inquiry in psychology: Existential and transpersonal approaches* (pp. 21–61). New York: Plenum.

Walsh, R. (2003). The methods of reflexivity. *TheHumanistic Psychologist, 31*, 51–66.

Wertz, F. J. (1983a). From everyday to psychological description: Analyzing the moments of a qualitative data analysis. *Journal of Phenomenological Psychology, 14*, 197–241.

Wertz, F. J. (1983b). Some constituents of descriptive psychological reflection. *Human Studies, 6*, 35–51.

Wertz, F. J. (1985). Methods and findings in a phenomenological psychological study of a complex life-event: Being criminally victimized. In Giorgi, A. (Ed.). *Phenomenology and psychological research* (pp. 155–216). Pittsburgh: Duquesne University Press.

Westen. Weinberger. (2004).

Wiens, A. N. (1991). Diagnostic interviewing. In Hersen, M., A. E. Kazdin, and A. S. Bellack. (Eds.). *The clinical psychology handbook* (pp. 346–361). New York: Pergamon Press.
Wierzbicki, M. (1993). *Issues in clinical psychology: Subjective versus objective approaches.* Boston: Allyn & Bacon.

BIOGRAPHICAL BACKGROUND

SCOTT D. CHURCHILL, PhD, earned his doctorate in clinical psychology at Duquesne University, where he completed an empirical–phenomenological dissertation on psychodiagnostic seeing. He is a Professor of Psychology at the University of Dallas, where he has taught since 1981. He has served as senior thesis supervisor for two decades, conducted qualitative research workshops, and overseen the research projects of psychology majors. More recently he has been involved in implementing two psychology master's programs with clinical concentrations for which he serves as Graduate Program Director.

He has taught a wide range of classes—from social, developmental, and clinical psychology to qualitative research, projective techniques, film studies, and Daseinsanalysis. His university classes on primate studies and his zoo habitat research at the Dallas Zoo attracted the attention of Jane Goodall, who visited him and his students to help establish a chapter of her Roots & Shoots program in Dallas.

He is an APA Fellow, and has served for many years on APA division executive boards, including as President of the Division of Humanistic Psychology and Secretary–Treasurer of the Society for Theoretical and Philosophical Psychology. He has also served as Editor of *Methods: A Journal for Human Science*, Associate Editor for the two APA division journals, and consulting editor to other journals. In addition, he has been a film critic for local television and a juror at Dallas film festivals for more than 20 years. On a recent sabbatical he presented papers, colloquia, and workshops in Europe, Great Britain, North America, Hawaii, and Australia.

Dr. Churchill's recent publications include entries in the APA's *Encyclopedia of Psychology*, chapters in the *Handbook of Humanistic Psychology* and in Valle's *Phenomenological Inquiry: Existential and Transpersonal Dimensions,* as well as articles in *The Humanistic Psychologist, Constructivism in the Human Sciences, Journal of Phenomenological Psychology, Journal of Theoretical and Philosophical Psychology, The Psychotherapy Patient,* and *Somatics.*

5

DIAGNOSTIC DISCOURSE IN PATIENT–STAFF INTERACTIONS: A CONVERSATION ANALYSIS CLARIFIED BY PARTICIPANT INTERVIEWS

JESSIE GOICOECHEA

EDITOR'S INTRODUCTION

Dr. Goicoechea was aware of the usefulness of psychiatric diagnosis for such purposes as shorthand communication among mental health professionals and for clarity of diagnostic criteria for research on treatment effectiveness. However, she was also aware of the typically unacknowledged impact of this system when used by professionals in their discussions ("discourse") among themselves and with patients. In this study, which took place in a psychiatric hospital, she goes beyond published social and political critiques to look at how actual conversations utilizing diagnostic language shape roles, expectations, understandings, and identities. The critiques come alive, no longer being just philosophical and conceptual. We also see that both staff and patients take up diagnostic talk in diverse ways not noticed in the literature, and we are encouraged to think critically about how "insight into illness" is negotiated.

Goicoechea, like many of our researchers, adapted an established method, conversation analysis, to suit her subject matter best. She added phenomenologically analyzed interviews of all parties to clarify and extend her understandings of how staff and patients participated in diagnostic practice. Earlier, as a doctoral practicum student, she had, in effect, conducted an ethnographical familiarization with the hospital culture. This carefully tailored methodological combination culminated in findings that invite us to reflect on the powerful systemic impact of psychodiagnostic language on its participants.

The chapter's Background section provides a useful feel for some of the philosophical assumptions of phenomenological, hermeneutic, and discourse analysis researchers. Then the chapter provides us with a vivid description of the hospital setting, an illustrated account of the method, and a report of the findings and their implications.

BACKGROUND

The establishment and use of an official diagnostic language have been extremely influential in shaping the mental health field. As Kirk and Kutchins (1992) noted in regard to the *Diagnostic and Statistical Manual of Mental Disorders*, fourth edition (DSM-IV):

> It immediately shaped almost all discussion of diagnosis not only in the United States, but throughout the world. References to it are ubiquitous in the mental health journals, where by 1990 over 2,300 scientific articles explicitly referred to it in the title or abstract. Most clinical discourse and psychiatric research are conducted within its confines. (p. 11)

Although many have argued for the clinical necessity and scientific validity of such a system (e.g., Kendell, 1975; Klerman, 1984; Maxmen,

1985; Wolman, 1978), others have voiced concerns regarding the ways in which mental illness has been socially constructed through the establishment and application of this psychiatric vocabulary (e.g., Caplan, 1995; Kirk and Kutchins, 1992; Szasz, 1974, 1993). Although these debates have attended to the ways in which diagnostic language permeates clinical and scientific discourse *about* mental illness, relatively little has been said regarding how diagnostic language enters directly into conversations between clinicians and patients. Hence, for my doctoral dissertation, I conducted a qualitative study of the ways in which diagnostic language, a language that makes reference to one's status as mentally ill, organizes patient–staff interactions within treatment team meetings on an adult, inpatient unit of a state psychiatric hospital. My research included the following questions: How is diagnostic discourse used to inscribe some identities as therapeutic experts and others as mentally ill patients? How does this discourse shape the patient–staff relationship? How does this discourse promote (or impede) a shared understanding of the patient's difficulties, an understanding that holds compelling meaning for both staff and patients?

In this chapter, I present the study as a whole, but focus mostly on how I used a conversation analysis (Levinson, 1983; Nofsinger, 1991) modified and informed by the following research approaches: discourse analytic (Potter, 2003), phenomenological (Giorgi, 1970, 1985; Wertz, 1985), and hermeneutic (Packer and Addison, 1989; Walsh, 1995). I supplemented a conversation analysis of transcribed treatment team meetings with a thematic analysis of my own interviews with treatment staff and patients. Drawing on these approaches and methods, which value language as constitutive of social reality and are rooted in a philosophical anthropology that allows access to intersubjective meanings, my analysis focused on patient–staff interactions as *those actions occurred*, and on the ways in which the participants *experienced* those actions. By integrating three different sources of data, I gained access to places of convergence and divergence within the participants' experiences.

My results are a structural description that weaves together the findings from the conversation analysis of the team meetings and the thematic analysis of the interviews. This description shows how diagnostic discourse was used by the staff to teach patients to interpret their experience and behavior as being symptomatic of mental illness. Diagnostic discourse was used to promote insight, which is constituted by staff as the patient's acceptance of him or herself as mentally ill. The development of insight was held as one of the main goals of treatment, for it was viewed as ultimately enabling the patient to manage his or her symptoms and to reach stabilization. However, although the patients in this study could name their diagnoses in ways that closely matched their charts and even accepted their diagnoses as accurately representing certain aspects of themselves, they did not necessarily feel understood by the staff. These patients asserted their own understanding of themselves as a way of resisting being categorized, within a struggle over identity and understanding. Whether these patients accepted or rejected the staff's view of them, their identity was at stake. Ultimately, the research results illustrate that diagnostic meaning is locally forged within a context of identity construction and within a struggle for mutual understanding.

In the final section of this chapter I discuss my findings in light of the existing literature on diagnostic terminology in patient–staff interactions. This discussion is not exhaustive, but situates the results of this study theoretically by attending to claims made by labeling theorists and more traditional approaches to psychiatric diagnosis.

A PHENOMENOLOGICAL, HERMENEUTIC, AND DISCOURSE ANALYTICAL APPROACH

A human scientific approach to psychological research develops methods that do justice to its subject matter—namely, human beings and their experiences. Recognizing the importance of allowing the subject matter to speak on its own terms, researchers return to the phenomena of everyday life as they are actually lived, experienced, and enacted. Concretely this means that rather than forcing the subject matter to conform to a preexisting method, the researcher allows the phenomenon of interest to guide her to an appropriate method.

With the introduction of hermeneutics, social constructivist approaches, and postmodern perspectives, the inescapability of interpretation has demanded that qualitative researchers think critically about how their approach prefigures not only their methods, but also their findings. My understanding of a researcher–researched dialectic draws from the Heideggarian notion of the hermeneutic circle: "Whenever something is interpreted as something, the interpretation will be founded essentially upon fore-having, fore-sight, and fore-grasp. An interpretation is never a presuppositionless apprehending of something presented to us" (Heidegger, 1962, pp. 191–192). Within this hermeneutic tradition, unlike perhaps a more Husserlian phenomenological approach, the issue becomes not so much putting aside or out of mind one's assumptions to reach clarity, but being aware of and articulating the way one's assumptions radically inform one's reading of the text.

The research results are not evaluated according to a correspondence theory of truth, but as a new text and an interpretation that is open to more interpretation. As von Eckartsberg states, "It is a process of contextualization and amplification rather than of structural essentialization. Hermeneutic work is open-ended and suggestive, concerned with relational fertility" (1986, p. 134). The research becomes a text that answers the questions for which the study was conducted. When evaluating validity, criteria of coherence, comprehensiveness, consistency, and plausibility are used (Packer and Addison, 1989).

This study also drew from the approaches of discourse analysis and discursive psychology, as the study of how talk is used to perform social actions and the application of these ideas respectively (Potter, 2003). As Potter (2003) discusses, discursive psychology focuses on talk and texts within specific social practices. Its basic theoretical principles include (1) that discourse is the primary medium of human action and that actions are embedded in broader practices; (2) that discourse is locally, institutionally, and rhetorically situated; and (3) that discourse is constructed and constructive, the latter meaning that versions of the world and people's experiential worlds are created and maintained through talk. Given these principles, discourse analytic studies, including those that utilize conversation analysis, typically ask "how" questions. Examples of research topics include the ways psychological terms and notions are used in practical settings, such as what resources are used to construct and identify "delusional" speech in psychiatric practice (Georgaca, 2000), and how the psychoanalytical notion of repression can be understood in conversational terms (Billig, 1999).

As "an *approach* or a stance rather than a method" (McLeod, 2001), discourse analysis allowed me to develop a method unique to this study—one that utilized a conversation analysis clarified by a thematic analysis of participant interviews. As McLeod (2001) "In terms of specifying or recommending procedures for conducting research studies, discourse analysts place most weight on the capacity of the researcher to understand the *idea* of discourse analysis, rather than on his or her willingness to master particular research techniques" (p. 100).

THE RESEARCHER'S PRECONCEPTIONS

The design, method, and results of a study imply the researcher's particular approach to that study. The insight that consciousness is always perspectival has been one of the great contributions of phenomenology to psychology. It is always from a certain perspective that we gain access to things, others, and ourselves. What certain things come to mean for us depends on our personal, existential projects. In that acknowledgment and explication of one's perspective situates and facilitates evaluation of the research, I attempted to document explicitly the thoughts, feelings, and expectations I held prior to this study. Following Walsh's (1995) recommendation, I also provided a reflective account of my assumptions and preconceptions as they evolved during the course of collecting and interpreting the data. I share some of these reflections here, and some of them have been woven into the method section. A fuller account can be found in the dissertation.

My research interest emerged from a number of personal experiences. While I worked as a practicum student on the admission unit of a state psychiatric unit, I witnessed several events that evoked an interest in diagnostic language. During an initial assessment, I asked a woman why she had tried to kill herself. She looked sad and answered, "I'm tired of being a schizoaffective disorder." Ah, despite that the DSM-IV states that the diagnosis refers to the syndrome and not the person who exhibits it (American Psychiatric Associations 1994, p. xxii), some people must feel like they are the diagnosis. Weeks later, I attended a grief and loss group during which a man became upset that he wasn't home to cut the grass. He pleaded with the psychologist, "Can't you take these *charges* off my back, Doc? What did I do to deserve them? What does that word even mean— schizophrenia?" Another time during rounds, a psychiatric nurse said about one patient, "And this one is still pretty delusional." The psychologist turned toward the man and said, "In order to get out of here, you're going to have to start speaking our language." The patient responded, "What do you want of me? A sissy? A god, a dazzling god? Or maybe just a man with a six foot tie?" No one answered his questions. The looks on some of the staff's faces said that his questions were further evidence of his "delusional" state.

As I reflected on these experiences, I thought of Gadamer (1994): ". . . the hermeneutic phenomenon . . . implies the primacy of dialogue and the structure of question and answer. That a historical text is made the object of interpretation means that it puts a question to the interpreter . . . . To understand a text means to understand this question" (pp. 369–370). I wondered if patients feel confused, evaluated, or even condemned by their diagnoses. Szasz's (1974) questions sprang to mind: "What is the difference between a person complaining of pain and calling himself sick? What is the difference between a physician complaining of a person's misbehavior and calling him a mentally sick person?" (p. viii). I also found myself thinking of Foucault's (1965) words: "We have seen by what means—and by what mystification—eighteenth century therapeutics tried to persuade the madman of his madness in order to release him from it" (p. 264), and wondering if something similar goes on today.

METHOD

SITE OF DATA COLLECTION AND ILLUSTRATION
OF THE CONTEXT

This study took place on an adult admission unit of a local state mental hospital, where a summer before conducting the study I had worked as a doctoral practicum student for 12 weeks. The hospital has been open since 1892. At its height, the patient population was around 3500. Today, 16 units large, the patient population is 450 to 500, illustrating the deinstitutionalization that has been occurring since the 1980s.

The hospital grounds, consisting of beautiful, but dilapidated and empty brick buildings and newer, metal buildings, stretch across a landscape of trees and gently rolling hills. Weathered farmhouses where superintendents and their families once resided also sit on the grounds, not far from the medical buildings. Visitors can see patients walking, visiting a snack shop, and working in greenhouses.

I collected data on one of two admission units, both of which are locked and have approximately 40 beds each. Primarily, patients on these units have been court committed for not more than 90 days. Should a patient require longer treatment, he or she is relocated to another unit within the hospital, usually one with fewer restrictions. This is not an infrequent occurrence, as three of the four patients I interviewed in November had been moved to chronic units and were still there when I returned in March.

Entering the locked admission unit, the heavy door shuts quickly. About two yards beyond the door, a painted red line stretches across the floor and part way up the wall on both sides. At waist level, the line ends in signs printed, STOP. NO PATIENTS BEYOND THIS POINT WITHOUT STAFF ESCORT. In that this warning had not been there when I did my practicum, it served as a rather startling introduction to the study on which I was embarking.

The three days I spent gathering data, along with the earlier 12 weeks of practicum, allowed me only to begin to imagine what life away from home was like for the patients behind those walls. Upon arriving, patients confront a profound restriction of everyday personal freedoms, like deciding when to wake up, shower, and eat. Ground cards, which allow patients to leave the unit in the morning, and/or afternoon, along with home visits, are contingent on police clearance and the person's improved functioning.

As I tried to imagine what living in the hospital was like for patients, I also tried to imagine what the treatment staff's experience was like. With a ratio of approximately 40 patients to one psychologist, one psychiatrist, and one social worker, along with several nurses, I realized how busy the clinicians on this unit were. This ratio of patients to staff seemed to limit the time spent in individual interaction with patients. I also was struck by how difficult it can be to work in an involuntary treatment setting, particularly with the challenges such a setting creates for building rapport and a working alliance with patients.

From the perspective of a nondualistic ontology or understanding of human life, things and personhood come to be what they are within a certain social and historical context. In my analysis of the data, I tried to appreciate and make explicit how these contextual elements of the setting provided a ground for and organized patient–staff interactions.

This contextual reflexivity also led to a local analysis of the research project itself (see Walsh, 2003). By attending to the milieu in which the research was conducted and my place as researcher within that context, distinctions emerged that informed my results. For example, during the stage of collecting data, when it seemed that the patients had a difficult time making sense of who I was, I had the impression that within these walls, there are only two groups of people: staff and patients; those who wear badges and those who don't; those who are free to leave and those who are not. This recognition probably foreshadowed the parts of the results that illustrate how diagnostic discourse can emerge from and constitute an inherent difference between normal and abnormal, and an "us" versus "them" way of viewing the world. These contextual elements and my own assumptions and perspective inform the validity and broader applicability of this study's results.

DATA COLLECTION: TREATMENT TEAM MEETINGS AND INTERVIEWS

Data for this study were comprised of three sorts: (1) observation (and audiotaping) of two days of treatment team meetings, (2) individual interviews with four patients (whose treatment team meetings I attended), and (3) individual interviews with four treatment staff members (the psychologist, the psychiatrist, the clinical nurse specialist, and the social worker).

I chose the treatment team meetings as the main context for my study because they were a structured time and place for the treatment staff and patients to discuss *together the* patient's "mental status," his or her progress in treatment, and discharge planning. It is here that the staff formally gives patients a picture of how they are seen in the staff's eyes. The task of the meetings lent itself to my focus on how staff and patients talk to each other, how diagnostic language enters that talk, and ultimately how a mental illness narrative is constructed during the talk.

Collecting information from three sources—team meetings, patient interviews, and staff interviews—provided different access points to the phenomenon, thereby rendering a fuller interpretation of the lived events. With this triangulation of data collection (see Maxwell, 1996), I reduced the risk that my results merely reflect the limitations that gathering information from only one of these areas would pose.

Finally, interviewing as the sole method of data collection would not make sense because the nature of languaged interactions between patients and staff is not something that participants would reflect upon during an interview.

Interview Format

Both staff and patient interviews occurred after the treatment team meetings and on the unit. With both sets of interviews, I attempted to ground my questions in the concrete events of the meetings. I started each interview with some variation of, "What would you say happened in that meeting?" Guided by Kvale's (1983) discussion of qualitative research interviews, I wanted to ask questions that would elicit responses about specific events, times, and actions, to keep the interviews from becoming too abstract, theoretical, or intellectualized. However, many of the staff's responses still seemed as if I was asking about what they intend to accomplish or the *purpose* of treatment team meetings. Perhaps this was because I was asking what happened during an event at which I myself was present, which in our everyday world may not be customary.

After this first question, I asked about specific interactions that I had witnessed during the meetings. For example, I asked the clinical nurse specialist what it was like to converse with a patient she had described as particularly resistant and as lacking in insight. With the staff, the remaining portion of the interviews focused on how they understood or conceptualized certain patients' difficulties, and their sense of a patient's understanding of him- or herself. As the staff members brought up various treatment issues like compliance and insight, I inquired deeper into their understanding of these concepts and the value they assign to them. Finally, I asked each staff person what role diagnosis plays in their work with patients.

The interviews with the patients followed a similar format. After asking specifics about the treatment team meeting, I inquired into their own understanding of their difficulties and the need for psychiatric treatment, including medication. I also attempted to get a sense of how they understood the staff's views of them. Finally, I asked them about their diagnoses—if they knew what they were, how they were told about them, and their own definitions or understanding of their diagnoses.

Participants

To select patient participants, I obtained a list from the psychologist of the 11 patients who would be attending a treatment team meeting during the next two days. This method of selecting patient participants ensured that gender, age, diagnosis, and number of previous hospitalizations were not factors in choosing participants. In that I could not physically identify the listed patients myself, the psychologist either pointed them out to me from a distance, or in a few cases accompanied me to make introductions. These introductions, a seemingly simple aspect of the process, highlighted the question of my identity for the participants. That is, at one point, the psychologist introduced me as "a friend," thus possibly aligning me with staff in that patient's eyes. I was also required to wear an identification badge much like the staff wear. Some patients had difficulty differentiating me from staff. For example, as I explained the nature of my research, one patient asked if he was up for a ground card and another referred to me as "nurse."

Following the treatment team meetings, I chose four patients to interview based on their availability (i.e., without having to pull them from group therapy or a ground pass), and to a lesser degree the diagnostic content of their team meetings. For example, the first patient I interviewed had discussed with the psychologist the nature of her depression, a discussion I thought might prove fruitful to explore further. I chose another patient because during his meeting, he had objected to the staff's implication that he was a "psychopath," another interaction particularly relevant to this study.

Patients

The patient participants consisted of four adults, all with a history of multiple hospitalizations and psychiatric medication. I have given all patients pseudonyms. Irvin was an 18-year-old, single, unemployed African-American man who was diagnosed with major depression, recurrent and borderline personality disorder. Katie was a 36-year-old, single, unemployed white woman who was diagnosed with chronic paranoid schizophrenia. Delmo was a 47-year-old, single, unemployed white man diagnosed with chronic schizophrenia, undifferentiated, and cannabis and alcohol abuse. Sheri was a 53-year-old, married, unemployed white woman diagnosed with bipolar disorder, mixed and personality disorder NOS, with dependent traits.

The Treatment Staff

The psychiatrist had worked at this hospital for 2.5 years following the completion of her residency at a local psychiatric hospital. She also worked night shifts at a local emergency room and did some outpatient work at another local hospital. The social worker had worked at this hospital since 1980, previously as a recreational therapist. The clinical nurse specialist had a master's of science degree in adult, psychiatric nursing. She had worked for 14 years in this hospital and previously worked for five years in a local community hospital. The psychologist had also worked for many years at this hospital and had previously worked at another state hospital before it was shut down.

INTERPRETATION OF THE DATA

The method of interpreting the data that is described in the following sections evolved during the course of the research. Most likely, the following description appears too clean and straightforward, and belies the fumbling I experienced with what at times seemed like an overwhelming stack of data. I have attempted to document some of my wanderings.

Fixing the Object of Inquiry

The first step of interpretation involved "fixing" the interviews and the treatment team meetings. I did this by transcribing the audiotapes into written form. As the hermeneutic philosopher Ricoeur (1979) points out, fixing the data is a fundamental step of interpretation, for social action and speech are fleeting and hence resist systematic inquiry. Although the fixed text preserves "what happened," the action is dislodged from its original spatial and temporal situatedness, and can become a meaningful record for participants who were not originally present. As Ricoeur (1979) states, fixing the discourse "prepares the detachment of the *meaning* of the action from the *event* of the action" (p. 81).

The fixed text now holds meaning that no longer coincides with the agents' intentions at the time of the event. This does not mean that one stops inquiring into a participant's experience of the event, but that one need not confine one's reading of the text to that which was meant by its participants. One is now free to read the text for social meaning. As Ricoeur (1991) states in his essay, "The Hermeneutical Function of Distanciation":

> If we can no longer define hermeneutics in terms of the search for the psychological intentions of another person which are concealed *behind* the text, and if we do not want to reduce interpretation to the dismantling of structures, then what remains to be interpreted? I shall say: to interpret is to explicate the type of being-in-the-world unfolded *in front of* the text. (p. 86)

As each reader approaches the text from his or her own situatedness, the text is always open to new interpretation. Human action as text is "an open work, the meaning of which is 'in suspense'" (p. 86).

A final cautionary note on the step of transcribing the audiotapes is in order: One can lose sight of the temporal unfolding and open endedness of the events as they were lived. Once one "knows the ending," one can forget the fundamental ambiguity that belongs to the horizonal character of lived time (Packer, 1989).

Conversation Analysis of the Treatment Team Meetings

After transcribing the audiotapes, I began a conversation analysis of the treatment team meetings guided primarily by Nofsinger's (1991) text. Conversation analysis draws from speech act theory, the American sociological movement of the 1950s and '60s associated with Erving Goffman, and Harold Garfinkel's ethnomethodology. As conversation analysis holds as its basic premise that speech is not merely the vehicle for knowledge or information, but that social actions and institutions are accomplished in speech, this method provided a useful hermeneutic to guide my reading of the text. As Nofsinger (1991) states, "Conversation is a primary method through which interpersonal relationships are formed, maintained, and dissolved" (p. 3). And as Gale (2000) says, "Utterances are viewed as practical activities that both create and maintain our social selves" (p. 2).

Conversation analysis holds that the meaning of a given utterance "depends overwhelmingly on where it is located in a sequence of actions" (Nofsinger, 1991, p. 50). This view highlights conversation as locally and interactionally managed. As Nofsinger (1991) says, "The participants themselves, during the course of their interaction, determine which people get to speak, in what order they speak, and for how long. The things people are expected to talk about, what they actually say, and how they say it are also worked out among the participants as the conversation progresses" (p. 4). Viewing conversation as locally managed allowed me to turn my attention to the participant concerns that guided the emerging organization and design of the team meetings.

Conversation analysis researchers have developed a wide variety of tools or "sensitizing constructs" (McLeod, 2001, p. 93) by which to make sense of how social realities are constituted through language. These constructs attune the researcher to the *process* of conversation, in addition to the *content*. Heritage (1997) discusses a number of such principles or questions that I found useful in my own analysis: the organization and "rules" of turntaking and how these rules reflect the values and goals of the institution, the patterns within conversation sequences, conversational asymmetries within institutional discourses or relationships, and lexical choice, or how speakers use descriptive terms according to institutional context. Although explicitly interested in the latter—that is, how the speakers used diagnostic terms—I also began to make note of the general format of the treatment team meetings. For example, after inviting the patient into the room and reviewing the treatment goals, a series of question/answer sequences followed in which the staff person generally reserved longer turns and asked questions seeking the patient's agreement.

I also made use of the way Nofsinger (1991) characterizes utterances in terms of three dimensions: action sequences, conversational actions, and extended structures, such as arguments and narratives. I documented this step of my analysis in the left column of the transcripts (see examples later in the chapter). The following gives a brief description of these three dimensions and various types of each:

1. Action sequences: an utterance's position within a sequence of utterances. An utterance's relationship to the surrounding talk, not only in terms of *what* is said, but in terms of its location, is influential in how it will be interpreted by the speakers. Types of action sequences include the following:

   • Adjacency pairs: A sequence of two communicative actions among which the first pair part is typically matched with or calls for one of a relatively few types of second pair parts. For example, there are question–answer adjacency pairs, summons–answer pairs, invite–acceptance/refusal pairs, assessment–agreement/disagreement pairs, and blame–denial/admission pairs. Adjacency pair sequences include presequences (Pre), which serve as a way of checking out a situation before performing some action; first pair part (FPP); second pair part (SPP); and insertion sequences (insert), which consist of an action inserted between the FPP and the SPP. Gale (2000) suggests that adjacency pairs be looked at in terms of the assumptions embedded within a question or response, the method of question construction, and the implication of the question/response situation to the relationship between participants.

2. Conversational actions: The performative function of an utterance; what the speech act does or is meant to accomplish. Types of conversational actions include the following:

- Commissives: speech acts whose function is to commit the speaker to some course of action
- Directives: speech acts whose purpose is to get the recipient to do something
- Assertives: speech acts that serve to display the speaker's belief in the propositional content of the utterance. The talk attempts to describe an object as it appears to the speaker.
- Expressives: how the speaker feels about what he/she is saying
- Alignment: utterances that keep the conversation "on track" and that potentially demonstrate a move toward convergence between two (or more) participants' interpretations. Some forms of alignment are as simple as news marks (e.g., "Oh") or continuers (e.g., "Mhm"). More complex forms of alignment include collaborative completions, when one participant completes another person's statement for him or her, and formulations, which are summaries of another participant's previous talk. Gale (2000) points out that formulations

  > are not necessarily neutral or comprehensive summaries, but can provide an upshot or re-presentation of what was said with changes added. Thus, a formulation displays its speaker's alignment as it exhibits not only what he/she understands of a prior turn, but what is proposed as important to focus on for further talk. (p. 8)

- Repairs: utterances that fix a breakdown in the conversation. Repairs can be initiated by the speaker or the recipient, and generally assist alignment.

3. Extended structures: a series of utterances that constitute a certain pattern of discourse. Types of extended structures include the following:

- Narrative: a series of utterances that tell a story. Speakers orient other participants to the time and place of what is narrated. They also tell the story from a particular perspective, one that is often implicit in the storytelling, but says much about their view of self, world, and others. Narratives often consist of accounts, which are defined by Gale (2000) as "ways that people explain actions .... Accounts can be used as an excuse ... or as a justification claim..., as apologies, requests, and disclaimers" (p. 9).
- Argument: extended structures of utterances that constitute and manage disagreement. Participants can *make* an argument *for* some belief, action, etc.; they can also *have* an argument *over* a given event, interpretation, etc. The basic elements of argument include the following:

  Claims: utterances that state one's position and invite others to agree or disagree

  Grounds: utterances that give the underlying foundation for the claim to be agreed upon

  Warrants: utterances that give the connections between the grounds and claims, or that illustrate what is at stake in the argument

  Rebuttals: utterances that give the circumstances in which an argument may be unreliable

  Backing: utterances that back up the claim or warrant

Analyzing the team meetings in these ways was an initial step and not an end in itself, but provided the foundation for a fuller, narrative account of the patient–staff conversations. For it is the microactions within conversation "that coordinate (either through binding or unraveling) the broader moves of discourse, which lead to the construction of social narratives"(Gale, 2000, p. 1). As Gale (2000) says

> This [method] contradicts the Parsonian view that individuals are the product of a society which dictates activities and functions (and that the ordinary judgments of individuals are irrelevant). Instead, our social institutions are constructed through the managed practices of the participants themselves. (p. 3)

The Delineation of Meaning Units

After identifying the previous conversational moves within the treatment team meetings, I printed out the excerpts of the meetings for each of the four patients I had individually interviewed. Taking one segment at a time, I divided each into meaning units (MUs). I did this by attending to shifts in what the participants were doing in their talk, and with regard to the emergence of diagnostic terminology and its meaning within the conversation. My earlier step of marking the conversational moves in the left margin of the transcripts facilitated this delineation of the text, as it was already a process that focused on the cohesion among the utterances, and on the shifts in conversational actions.

Delineating MUs is an important step in phenomenological research with protocol analysis (Giorgi, 1985; Wertz, 1985) in that it makes the text more manageable while it invites the researcher to begin to shift his or her attention to the *meaning* the events have for the participants.

A Narrative Interpretation of Each Unit

The next step involved articulating what the participants were doing during their talk. To aid this process, first I put it in boldface type any part of the conversation that included diagnostic terms. Attempting to stay close to the participants' own words, I wrote out how they answered each other's concerns and what that implied about their relationship. I also attended to the rhetorical structure of their discourse, to the ways in which diagnostic terminology encourages patients to believe certain things about themselves. This narrative interpretation took its lead from all the previous steps, particularly the identification of the conversational moves.

After a lot of rereading and trimming, I underlined (italicized below) those sections of my own narrative description of their talk that seemed particularly salient to this study. These sections were the ground for a more abstract level of description, as well as for providing concrete examples with which to illustrate the results. By comparing commonalities from across all four analyzed portions of the treatment team meetings, I developed a structural description of how diagnostic discourse constitutes the patient–staff relationship in general.

The following examples utilize the following transcript notations standard to most conversation analysis (see Atkinson and Heritage, 1984):

Symbol	Meaning
[]	At the end and beginning of lines indicate overlapping talk
(1)	Numbers in parentheses represent silence measured to the nearest tenth of a second
end of line=	Latching symbols indicate that there was no hesitation or
=start of line	pause between the utterances
Under	Underlining indicates words that were uttered with vocal emphasis
CAPITAL	Words in uppercase are louder than the surrounding talk
( )	Empty parentheses indicate talk that was inaudible or impossible to interpret
((laughing))	Double parentheses enclose transcriber comments
Wait a min-	A hyphen indicates a sudden cutoff of speech

The following segments are two examples of these procedures:

Repair/First Pair Part/	Social Worker: **Okay, you're all set. 'Kay, Irvin, you**
Question	**came in- Can you tell us why you came into the hospital?**
Second Pair Part/	Irvin: **Anger, depression, irritation, and flippin' out**
Answer	**((staff laughs)) and suicidal thoughts =**
Agreement/Request	Social Worker: **Alright, well those are some of the things that we found from your records and those are the things we wanna work on while you're here.**
Assertive	Irvin: My records suck.
Informative	Social Worker: 'Em 'kay, well I'm gonna tell you what your discharge criteria is, what you have to accomplish in order to be considered for discharge ...

After greeting Irvin, the social worker begins to inform him of his admitting circumstances, but interrupts herself to ask him why he *feels he's been admitted. (She seems to be checking to see if he holds the same view as they do, a view she earlier asserted during her case presentation to the staff: "He states he's very depressed and afraid to be alone due to suicidal feelings. Reports command hallucinations to harm self .... Mental health, he can be impulsive and angry ....") Irvin answers with a quick list: "Anger, depression, irritation, and flippin' out and suicidal thoughts." After the staff briefly chuckles at his term* flippin' out, *the social worker confirms that his own characterization is in line with what his records say and frames his response as the problems needing "work." In accepting his response, she confirms a correspondence between what he has said about himself and what she previously presented to staff. Furthermore, the social worker locates their view of him in his "records," creating anonymity to their view, along with backing it up with a sense of evidence and authority.* Without giving much attention to Irvin's response that his "records suck," she continues to hold the floor by informing him of the conditions of his discharge.

Request	Psychologist: **We want you to continue to go to groups that help you =**
Overlap/	Delmo: **= I'M NOT A PSYCHOPATH!**
Argument; Claim	
Rebuttal	Psychologist: **No one even mentioned the word "psychopath."**
Preface	Delmo: **Well|**
Overlap/Assertive	Psychologist: **|No one mentioned—you didn't hear me say that.** But we want you to go to the groups, the different groups that we have for you, okay? One of which is for you to go to the anger management group, which you'll come, although I have to invite you many times, but you know that we have a group every Wednesday, and we'd like you to come to that group.

The psychologist informs Delmo that the staff wants him to attend groups and he begins to offer justification for this request. *Delmo interrupts to assert loudly and adamantly, "I'm not a psychopath." Delmo interprets the psychologist's statement as implying something offensive and inaccurate about his identity. He interprets the psychologist as implying that he is a psychopath, a diagnosis he finds insulting and inaccurate. The psychologist responds to this outburst by attempting to correct Delmo's perception of the conversation, informing him that "no one even mentioned the word 'psychopath'." When Delmo tries to take a turn, the psychologist interrupts, reiterating that Delmo misperceived him.* The psychologist continues to request Delmo's attendance at groups, particularly the anger management group.

Thematic Analysis

Interviews

To interpret the interviews, I used a modified version of the phenomenological method generally used for protocol analysis as described by Giorgi (1970, 1985). Because my interviews were not descriptions of an event or situation per se, I did not delineate them into MUs. Instead, I used this method to guide me in an analysis of the *themes* implied by the participants' understanding of how diagnosis enters into the therapeutic relationship.

Step 1: With each of the eight interviews, starting first with the four staff interviews, I read through each to gain a sense of the whole. Next, I highlighted diagnostic terms and discussions about diagnoses, noting in the margin key words or phrases. This involved jotting down my impressions of how a patient's diagnosis guides the staff person's perspective and clinical work. I also attended to the terms the staff used to describe mental illness. For the patients, I focused not only on how they understand their diagnoses, but also on their own vocabulary and understanding of why they've been psychiatrically hospitalized. I tried to articulate what place the patients give diagnostic terminology in their own understanding of themselves.

Step 2: Next, I grouped the marginal notations into themes for each of the individual interviews. I did not view every marginal notation as revealing a new theme, but often listed many of the notations as constituents of already existing themes. This step also involved articulating what was prethematic or implicit within the participants' descriptions.

Example of a Theme from My Interview with the Clinical Nurse Specialist

Treatment is constituted as an educational process.

- Patients who "need to be educated about their diagnosis and symptoms ..." attend symptom management group.
- Treatment consists of "repeated sharing of their symptoms.... Then they become more receptive to it if you repeat it enough."
- Therapeutic groups are understood as primarily educational.

- Patients are taught how to interpret their behavior as being symptomatic.

Step 3: I read each of the individual interviews again, with the individual themes at hand, looking for disconfirming information that then led me either to new themes or to a revision. At times, an ambiguity arose that did not necessarily find its way neatly into the themes, and I simply noted it as such.

Step 4: This step involved moving from individual themes to two sets of general themes, one for staff and one for patients. I illustrated each theme with examples from all participants.

Example of a Theme from the Staff Interviews

Patients are understood as having impaired insight.

- When a patient says, "I don't need to be here" (clinical nurse)
- When disagreeing with the diagnosis—e.g., "No, I don't have schizophrenia. I'm not paranoid." (clinical nurse)
- When patients blame others (e.g., the police) for their admission to the hospital (clinical nurse)
- The clinical nurse specialist describes one patient as "pretty resistant ... I knew that there would be a lot of denial there. And that's why I wanted to go with a meeting with kind of clear-cut goals for her. One of them was to increase your level of insight into why you're here."
- Patients "forget the symptoms they had," leading to noncompliance (clinical nurse specialist)
- Team meeting as time to "help reestablish the awareness" (social worker)
- Patients may "know" what mental illness they "have" and yet still lack insight regarding the course of illness and their need for medication (psychiatrist)
- The psychologist constitutes many of the patients as not being able to understand their diagnoses. For example, he says that Sheri "might have some recollection ... some awareness of that diagnosis ... but I don't think so ... and I don't know if that means anything to her."

Example of a Theme from the Patient Interviews

The patients accept certain aspects of their psychiatric diagnoses as accurate descriptions of themselves.

- Sheri: "I think the closest one was the first one [recurrent major depression with suicidal ideation]...." When asked what that diagnosis meant to her, she stated, "That I've been in the hospital with depression a whole bunch of times." Sheri was able to state two more recent diagnoses with technical accuracy, but she didn't agree with either of them: "They changed it ... to um, um manic depression, although I've never had a manic episode in my life that I remember.... And then the third one I got was um, um schizoaffective disorder ... I didn't agree with that either."

- Katie: "I'm paranoid schizophrenic." When asked what that diagnosis meant to her, she gave a descriptive definition: "Paranoid, you're scared, you think someone's after you. You're scared to go out. And schizophrenia is hearing voices and seeing things." She acknowledged that she had experienced such things.
- Irvin: "I was diagnosed with depression and dyslexia.... Hey, that's what I do ... That's what I do. I get depressed all the time."
- Delmo: "Catatonic schizophrenia.... That's like the, uh, Rolls Royce of the mental illnesses. It's really good quality.... Confident, confident that I really had it.... Oh, there's no doubt in my mind."

Step 5: Finally, I looked at similarities and points of tension across the two sets of general themes from the interviews and all the places during the treatment team meetings where diagnostic terminology emerged. This step is documented in Table 5-1. The grouping of themes in this manner facilitated articulating a structural description that incorporates all the findings.

TABLE 5-1

General Themes, Staff	General Themes, Patients	Treatment Team Meetings
Treatment as an educative process	Patients have been taught a language within which to view themselves as mentally ill. Patients accept their diagnoses as accurately describing *some* aspects of themselves. Patients monitor themselves in line with the staff's interests.	Diagnostic terms emerge in conversation with patients during a process of sharing with the patients their view of the problems. A correspondence between the staff's view and patient's view is sought. Patients are required and taught to interpret aspects of their experience as being symptomatic of mental illness.

A Structural Description

This final step involved weaving together the two sets of general themes from the interviews, along with the insights gained from the conversation analysis of the treatment team meetings. While writing this structural description, I frequently returned to the raw data, including the areas in the treatment team meetings beyond the four patient visits, to confirm or disconfirm my interpretations and to include any overlooked data. Following convention within conversation analysis research reports, quotes from the transcripts of the team meetings and the participant interviews are included in the results.

RESULTS: DIAGNOSTIC DISCOURSE IN PATIENT–STAFF INTERACTIONS

The staff use diagnostic terms in conversation with each other to present a clinical portrait of a given patient. This portrait or case presentation is not without a perspective; it is reflective of and configured by what this staff view as "psychiatric." Certain aspects of the person's life world are focused on while others are left out. The description of the person, along with the stated treatment goals, is grounded in an understanding of him or her as "mentally ill." The description is given not only to acquaint the other staff with the patient, but also to provide implicitly a case for why that person warranted involuntary treatment. To facilitate building this case, the term *patient* is peppered throughout the presentation, often in lieu of the person's name. Furthermore, the patient is often identified as being in denial and as refusing to acknowledge the need for treatment. When presenting a patient, the authority and anonymity of the record are invoked; the staff builds their argument within a rhetoric of "evidence."

It is usually only immediately prior to the patient's attendance at the team meeting that formal or specific diagnoses are discussed. Within the context of paperwork and administrative concerns, the diagnosis and explicit goals can sometimes eclipse interest in the patient's recovery and well-being. For example, the psychologist explains that the substance abuse group cannot be listed as one patient's goal because his diagnosis is substance abuse in remission: "It's not a goal because it's in remission.... Now we can invite him to come..., that's different. But as far as the goals are concerned, umm." The staff's operating conceptualization of pathology as located within the individual can also undermine therapeutic concerns. This is illustrated in the community liaison's frustration about the difficulty of including Sheri's husband in treatment. She rhetorically asks the rest of staff, "... can we make him go? We can't do that. ( ) I mean, who is the patient here?"

Once a patient arrives at the meeting, diagnostic terms emerge within the purpose of the treatment team meeting—to share with the patient how he or she is seen in the staff's eyes and to inform the patient of his or her goals. Diagnostic terms emerge within the staff's project to teach patients to interpret certain aspects of their experience and behavior as being symptomatic of mental illness. The staff view this project as promoting insight and maintain that it fosters treatment compliance and, ultimately, symptom management and stabilization. For example, the clinical nurse specialist summarizes one patient's goals: "... that she'll demonstrate less denial of her illness and more a willingness to listen to the explanations of professionals as to why she's here; that she'll comply with recommended treatment and state benefits of doing so." That the patients become subject to the implicit conversational format of these meetings, also serves to establish the staff's authority—the staff make assertions, ask questions, redirect the conversation, and, only at the end, give patients some time to voice their own concerns.

Within their attempt to persuade patients to hold an understanding of themselves that corresponds with the staff's view, the staff use both diagnostic terminology and descriptive terminology. At times, the staff translate their clinical and technical terminology into a language that may be more easily understood and meaningful to patients. For example, when the psychologist is reviewing Katie's progress, he asks her if he is correct in maintaining that she is still "hyperverbal." Assuming that Katie may not understand this specialized term, the recreational therapist clarifies the question by explaining that it means to "talk, talk, talk, talk, talk." Offering further assistance, another recreational therapist gives an example of when she noticed this behavior. Katie begins to disagree, but changes her mind: "It wasn't- oh yeah, I was." This dialogue illustrates how diagnostic meaning is locally forged.

Another example of the shift from diagnostic terminology to every-day language occurs when the psychologist is speaking to the staff about Delmo. He asserts, "Many times when he talks, it's irrelevant, kind of flight of ideas to be exact." Later, in conversation with Delmo, the psychologist begins to inform him of their concern: "... sometimes when we talk with you=". However, before the psychologist can complete his turn, Delmo finishes his sentence for him: "=I don't make sense." The psychologist confirms Delmo's perception: "You don't make sense." To which Delmo eventually responds, "Am I rambling like a brook sometimes?" With some correction, the psychologist again confirms Delmo's perception: "Yeah, sometimes you do babble like a brook." This conversation illustrates the interface of two vocabularies, along with demonstrating Delmo's alignment with staff. He communicates that he is aware of how they see him.

When patients are expected to interpret aspects of their experience and behavior as being symptomatic of mental illness, the patient's own perspective is often constituted as being false. Its own meaning is invalidated and leveled. When the staff's diagnostic perspective is held over and against the patient's, that patient's behavior is not understood as a meaningful and valid response to his or her world or to the immediate interaction with staff. For example, when Delmo's talk is understood as disordered and as nonsensical, its meaning is not inquired into. Furthermore, when "not making sense" is cast as diagnostic of mental illness, making sense becomes the burden of the patient. Rather than attempting to *understand* the patient's speech or behavior, the discourse is focused more on *changing* the patient's views and behavior. This stance is framed by the staff as a way of assigning responsibility and as empowering their patients toward recovery.

Whether these patients accept or reject the staff's view of them and the mental illness narrative offered to them, their identity is at stake. These patients are striving to come to terms with the practices of this community, adopting various attitudes, and attempting to take a stand on the way the staff have positioned them. For example, Irvin seems eager to align himself with the staff's view of him and with their recommended treatment. Delmo, on the other hand, expresses frustration. When he is trying to express that he doesn't like how his medication makes him feel, he backs up his complaint with the assertion that he's "a damn good psychiatrist." Perhaps Delmo feels that he's not being listened to or that he's not being understood as insightful about the way his medication is affecting him. Perhaps he feels that to be taken seriously, his complaint must be grounded in the kind of expert knowledge the staff possess. But instead of responding to Delmo's feelings about his medication, the psychologist argues, "This is where you get to be a problem...." When resistance to the staff's view is understood as a function of one's illness and within a problem discourse, it is not appreciated or explored as part of the patient's struggle over his or her identity.

When the staff set aside their agenda to address and understand a patient's concern, the staff and patient together forge a shared understanding of that patient's difficulties. For example, the psychologist and Sheri reach an understanding of her difficulties that is meaningful to all of them when they allow themselves to be engaged in dialogue with her.

The psychologist begins the meeting with Sheri by giving her encouraging feedback regarding her insight into her difficulties: "... what I mean by that is, uh, beginning to recognize how you are ... when your husband, let's say, when he gets angry and upset with what happens with you.... And I think you're just coming to recognize that there has to be some changes there in order for you to stay out of the hospital." He expands this view of her when he informs her of her goals. Summarizing from the written treatment plan, he states, "One of them is certainly that we want you to express your feelings ... rather than you kind of turn them over in your head.... I think sometimes you get upset, but you don't share it with us.... So, that's one of the goals that we want you to do." The staff have formulated a goal that is grounded in their view of Sheri as "not the type to deal with confrontation well ... and [who] retreats and isolates herself," as the social worker explained to me in her interview.

After the psychologist finishes explaining the treatment plan and begins to involve the rest of the staff in paperwork, Sheri tentatively asserts herself. Despite the psychologist's view, as given in his interview with me that Sheri "doesn't spontaneously talk [during the meetings]," she seeks permission to steer the conversation in a particular direction. Despite how risky it feels to her to speak up in life, as she described in her interview with me, she requests the staff's attention: "Can I ask you something ... uhm, when you were talkin' about my comin' back here, what did you mean by that?" In asking the psychologist for clarification, Sheri calls the staff away from their immediate agenda.

Making implicit reference to Sheri's status as mentally ill, the psychologist responds by predicting that if she were discharged to home, she would "decompensate" or "deteriorate" and thus return to the hospital. He uses these terms to argue that she should instead be discharged to a residential treatment setting. He shares his belief that after some time at home, Sheri and her husband would eventually argue. He states, "He would yell and scream. You would get angry and upset with yourself and it wouldn't be very long before you're talking about hurting yourself... what I think happens Sheri, and you correct me, but I think you get angry and you never speak up, you never assert yourself...." Agreeing with him, Sheri completes his sentence and offers her own conceptualization, "Yeah, I go into a ball and stay there." At this point, Sheri and the psychologist are speaking together about the way she retreats from others to protect herself.

That this shared understanding has been accomplished not by way of imposing a diagnostic label, but in a conversation that takes into account Sheri's own narrative, is consistent with the psychologist's view that being descriptive addresses the patient as an individual. As he says in his interview with me, "Probably if you use the label as a way to communicate to the patient, you are really dehumanizing that individual. You are intellectualizing that person. You don't see the person for who they are.... Sheri is a person to me ... not a diagnosis." Furthermore, helping to "reestablish [the patient's] awareness," as the social worker states in her interview, is the purpose of these meetings, is accomplished not by *informing* Sheri of her diagnosis, but by addressing her concerns and engaging in dialogue *with* her. This last part of their conversation with Sheri holds so much more vitality and concreteness than one of the abstract goals it might fulfill— that she "discuss two symptoms of [her] illness and its relation to interpersonal kinds of difficulties."

DISCUSSION

Research in labeling theory has claimed to look at the ways in which a psychiatric diagnosis, as a tool of social control and through a process of stigmatization, can launch patients "on a career of 'chronic mental illness'" (Scheff, 1975, p. 10; see also Link et al., 1989; Scheff, 1966). However, most of this research has remained quite vague about the actual conversations within which clinicians discuss diagnoses or mental status with patients. Although labeling theorists have maintained that a "built-in 'catch-22' ... is that nonacceptance of the feedback is deemed lack of insight, which is used as another symptom or evidence of mental illness" (Wilson and Plumy, 1984, p. 7), they have not clearly spelled out how such conversations occur. Research into labeling theory has been criticized for having "largely overlooked practices of talk, action, and social interaction. Consequently, even in research arguing most fervently that labeling profoundly affects the lives of individuals, the acts of giving and acquiring labels appear as obscure, disembodied events" (Gill and Maynard, 1995, p. 11; see also Maynard,1988; Raybeck, 1988).

Gill and Maynard (1995) have pointed out how in focusing on "what happens to the targeted individual, rather than on the way in which group members enact practices" (p. 12), labeling theory has ignored systematic inquiry into the local and interactional character of diagnostic events. In Gill and Maynard's (1995) own study, which used conversation analysis to examine how clinicians informed parents and children of developmental disabilities, they found that clinicians used ways of engaging the recipients in the conversation and even in the decision regarding the diagnosis: "By delivering the news as a confirmation of the recipient's views, the clinician incorporate[d] the recipient's perspective within the actual delivery, in effect transferring to them some of the 'authorship' of the news" (p. 16). Gill and Maynard (1995) found that when recipients resisted labels, clinicians used remedial strategies, such as eliciting those aspects of the parents' views that are most consistent with the diagnosis, in an attempt to obtain some agreement. But clinicians also backed down from or modified their own judgments in light of parental response. Clinicians were also found to minimize the positivistic meaning of diagnoses and to depict the label as less of "a pristine, objective reflection of the child's abilities" (p. 26), and more as a tool that can result in desirable or undesirable outcomes.

Gill and Maynard's (1995) focus on local praxis provided support for my own study and an example of how conversation analysis can be applied to similar topics. Similar to Gill and Maynard's 1995 findings, my study showed how diagnostic meaning is locally forged and negotiated, but also how this staff invoked a rhetoric of facts, evidence, and authority to obtain the patients' agreement with their diagnostic views.

Research in labeling theory also has been critiqued for portraying those who receive diagnoses as passive targets (Davis, 1975; Hagan, 1973; Schur, 1971), for not adequately addressing those people who voluntarily request mental health services and seek a diagnostic understanding of their situation (Thoits, 1985; Wilson and Plumy, 1984), and for collapsing subjective experiences of pain and confusion into social deviance (Whitt et al., 1979). In my own study, I have attempted to avoid these assumptions. My method gave me access to the staff's sensitivity to the limitations of imposing a diagnostic discourse, and to how patients descriptively situate their own suffering in terms of problematic life events, accept certain aspects of their experience as diagnostic of mental illness, but also resist being categorized within a struggle to define themselves. My study showed how both "patient" and "clinician" are social positions that are constituted by a community of practice and within a diagnostic discourse.

In reaction to labeling theory, researchers have suggested that accepting one's psychiatric label can improve functioning. Schwartz et al. (1997) found that for inpatients diagnosed with schizophrenia, those with good insight showed more improvement after long-term inpatient treatment. Similarly, Walker and Rossiter (1989) found that among outpatients diagnosed with schizophrenia, those who perceived themselves to be mentally ill had a shorter duration of the most recent hospitalization, a smaller number of previous hospitalizations, and greater compliance with treatment. Influenced by findings of this sort, Will (1980) and Kemp and David (1997) have argued that the promotion of insight into illness ought to be one of the principal goals of treatment.

My interviews with the staff and the conversation analysis of the team meetings revealed that such an approach is operant within this treatment setting. However, rather than studying this approach from a factors-and-outcomes logic, my study investigated *how* clinicians promote insight in actual conversations with patients, and how insight is negotiated in the talk. That is, rather than asking whether insight as a form of cognition impacts a patient's functioning, my qualitative research approached insight discursively. As Potter (2003) states, "Discourse work is not designed to answer questions of the kind, 'What is the influence of X on Y' ... [but] typically asks questions of the form, 'How is X done?' " (p. 78).

By approaching insight discursively and by utilizing participant interviews to clarify the conversation analysis of the treatment team meetings, my findings can offer a critique of the previous label–acceptance or "psychotherapeutic model" (Warner et al., 1989). In my interviews with patients, I found that all of them could name their diagnoses in ways that closely matched their records, and even accepted and agreed with their diagnoses as accurately describing certain aspects of themselves. During the treatment team meetings, they also demonstrate alignment with the staff's diagnostic view, and yet these patients continue to suffer and return for multiple hospitalizations. They report losing hope in treatment, not feeling understood by staff, and assert their own understanding of themselves. They voice ambivalence toward the staff, which emerges within a conflict of wills, agency, expertise, and identity. The patients make an appeal for the staff to appreciate what is at stake for each of them in accepting a mental illness narrative and in complying with treatment. My study encourages critical thinking about this model and suggests that "insight" is most successfully negotiated in *dialogue with* patients. Indeed, despite its tradition within sociology and its emphasis on explicating the discursive structure of social and institutional settings, conversation analysis research can speak directly to the therapeutic implications of the identified practices (McLeod, 2001).

My findings, then, also give empirical support to many therapists' views that imposing a diagnostic perspective on the patient can become an obstacle to the therapeutic relationship. Karon and Van den Bos (1981), psychoanalytically oriented psychologists who have worked with patients diagnosed with schizophrenia, have suggested that contrary to the "psycho-therapeutic" or label–acceptance model, asking the clients to accept an illness identity impedes the therapeutic relationship, the vehicle for change:

> It is true that if you asked him whether he was paranoid or schizophrenic, he would get very angry at you and not accept such words. Why should he? What benefits derive from accepting a "diagnosis?" From his standpoint, the primary consequence of accepting the "diagnosis" would be to legitimize the right of others to make decisions about his life. On the other hand, when a therapist says to him, "What's your problem?" and he says, "I hurt people even though I don't want to," and the therapist offers to deal with that problem, the patient suddenly becomes part of a working alliance. (1981, p. 154)

Yalom (1990) has also maintained that a reliance on diagnosis to guide treatment obscures empathy and genuine listening. He warns against letting diagnostic formulations take precedence in the therapy:

> Beyond these relatively crude determinations, which serve the function of initial triage, further and "finer" diagnostic discriminations not only offer little help to the therapist but often interfere with the formation of relationship.... The standard diagnostic formulation tells the therapist nothing about the unique person he or she is encountering; and there is substantial evidence that diagnostic labels impede and distort listening.... Too often diagnostic categorization is a stimulating intellectual exercise whose sole function is to provide the therapist with a sense of order and mastery. The major task of the maturing therapist is to learn to tolerate uncertainty. (p. 410)

Finally, current psychotherapy research (e.g., Norcross, 2002; Wampold, 2001) clearly identifies the relationship between therapist and client as a critical component of successful outcome. I believe more now than I did at the beginning of my research that addressing patients' lived worlds as the context of problematic (diagnosed) behavior strengthens the therapeutic relationship and maximizes collaborative involvement toward positive change.

At this point, my research into diagnostic discourse in patient–staff interactions suggests that a fruitful follow-up study would be one addressing how treatment teams are influenced by and perpetuate a complex allegiance to caring about patients, following hospital mandates, and utilizing a closed diagnostic system. Such a study would identify points at which all systems could more flexibly serve patients. Outcome studies based on these considerations would be motivating for staff, legislators, hospital directors, and other policy makers.

REFERENCES

American Psychiatric Association. (1994). *Diagnostic and statistical manual of mental disorders* (4th ed.). Washington, DC: Author.

Atkinson, J., and J. Heritage. (Eds.). (1984). *Structures of social action.* Cambridge: Cambridge University Press.

Billig, M. (1999). *Freudian repression: Conversation creating the unconscious.* Cambridge: Cambridge University Press.

Caplan, P. (1995). *They say you're crazy: How the world's most powerful psychiatrists decide who is normal.* Reading, MA: Addison-Wesley.

Davis, N. (1975). *Sociological constructions of deviance: Perspectives and issues in the field.* Dubuque, IA: W. C. Brown.

Foucault, M. (1965). *Madness and civilization: A history of insanity in the age of reason.* New York: Random House.

Gadamer, H.-G. (1994). *Literature and philosophy in dialogue: Essays in German literary theory.* New York: State University of New York Press.

Gale, J. (2000). Patterns of talk: A micro-landscape perspective. *The Qualitative Report, 4,* 1–18.

Georgaca, E. (2000). Reality and discourse: A critical analysis of the category of "delusions." *British Journal of Medical Psychology, 73,* 227–242.

Gill, V., and D. Maynard. (1995). On "labeling" in actual interaction: Delivering and receiving diagnoses of developmental disabilities. *Social Problems, 42,* 11–37.

Giorgi, A. (1970). *Psychology as a human science: A phenomenological based approach.* New York: Harper & Row.

Giorgi, A. (1985). Sketch of a psychological phenomenological method. In: Giorgi, A. (Ed.). *Phenomenology and psycholgoical research* (pp. 8–22). Pittsburgh: Duquesne University Press.

Goicoechea, J. (2002). *The invocation and inscription of mental illness: A phenomenological and hermeneutic study of diagnostic discourse in patient–staff interactions.* Unpublished doctoral dissertation. Duquesne University.

Hagen, J. (1973). Labeling and deviance: A case study in the sociology of the interesting. *Social Problems, 20,* 447–458.

Heidegger, M. (1962). *Being and time.* Macquarrie, J., and E. Robinson. (Trans.). San Francisco: Harper & Row. [Original work published in 1927.]

Heritage, J. (1997). Conversation analysis and institutional talk: Analyzing data. In D. Silverman (Ed.). *Qualitative research: Theory method, and practice,* (pp. 161–182). London: Sage.

Karon, B., and G. Van den Bos. (1981). *Psychotherapy of schizophrenia: The treatment of choice.* New York: Jason Aranson.

Kemp, R., and A. David. (1997). Insight and compliance. In: Blackwell, B. (Ed.). *Chronic mental illness: Treatment compliance and the therapeutic alliance* (vol. 5, pp. 61–84). Singapore: Harwood Academic Publishers.

Kendell, R. (1975). *The role of diagnosis in psychiatry.* Oxford: Blackwell Scientific Publications.

Kirk, S., and H. Kutchins. (1992). *The selling of DSM: The rhetoric of science in psychiatry.* New York: Aldine De Gruyter.

Klerman, G. (1984). The advantages of DSM-III. *American Journal of Psychiatry, 141,* 539–542.

Kvale, S. (1983). The qualitative research interview: A phenomenological and hermeneutical mode of understanding. *Journal of Phenomenological Psychology, 14,* 171–196.

Levinson, S. (1983). *Pragmatics.* Cambridge: Cambridge University Press.

Link, B, F. Cullen, E. Struening, P. Shrout, and B. Dohrenwend. (1989). A modified labeling theory approach to mental disorders: An empirical assessment. *American Sociological Review, 54,* 400–423.

Maxmen, J. (1985). *The new psychiatrist.* New York: New American Library.

Maxwell, J. (1996). *Qualitative research design: An interactive approach.* Thousand Oaks, CA: Sage Publications.

Maynard, D. (1988). Language, interaction, and social problems. *Social Problems, 35,* 311–334.

McLeod, J. (2001). *Qualitative research in counseling and psychotherapy.* London: Sage.

Nofsinger, R. (1991). *Everyday conversation.* Newbury Park: Sage.

Norcross, J. (Ed.). (2002). *Psychotherapy relationships that work: Therapist contributions and responsiveness to patient needs.* New York: Oxford University Press.

Packer, M. (1989). Tracing the hermeneutic circle: Articulating an ontical study of moral conflicts. In Packer, M., and R. Addison. (Eds.). *Entering the circle* (pp. 95–117). New York: State University of New York Press.

Packer, M., and R. Addison. (Eds.). (1989). *Entering the circle.* New York: State University of New York Press.

Potter, J. (2003). Discourse analysis and discursive psychology. In Camic, P., J. Rhodes, and L. Yardley. (Eds.). *Qualitative research in psychology: Expanding perspectives in methodology and design.* (pp. 73–94). Washington, DC: American Psychological Association.

Raybeck, D. (1988). Anthropology and labeling theory: A constructive critique. *Ethos, 16,* 371–397.

Ricoeur, P. (1979). The model of text: Meaningful action considered as text. In Rabinow, P., and W. M. Sullivan. (Eds.). *Interpretive social science: A reader* (pp. 73–101). Berkeley: University of California Press.

Ricoeur, P. (1991). The hermeneutical function of distanciation. In Ricoeur, P. (Ed.). From text to action: Essays in hermeneutics, II (pp. 75–88). Evanston, IL: Northwestern University Press.

Scheff, T. (1966). *Being mentally ill: A sociological theory.* Chicago: Aldine.

Scheff, T. (1975). Schizophrenia as ideology. In Scheff, T. (Ed.). *Labeling madness* (pp. 5–12). Englewood Cliffs, NJ: Prentice-Hall.

Schur, E. (1971). *Labeling deviant behavior: Its sociological implications.* New York: Harper and Row.

Schwartz, R., B. Cohen, and A. Grubaugh. (1997). Does insight affect long-term inpatient treatment outcome in chronic schizophrenia? *Comprehensive Psychiatry, 38,* 283–288.

Szasz, T. (1974). *The myth of mental illness* (rev. ed.). New York: Hoeber-Harper. [First edition published 1961.]

Szasz, T. (1993). *A lexicon of lunacy.* New Brunswick, NJ: Transaction Publishers.

Thoits, P. (1985). Self-labeling processes in mental illness: The role of emotional deviance. *American Journal of Sociology, 91,* 221–249.

von Eckartsberg, R. (1986). *Life-world experience: Existential–phenomenological research approaches in psychology.* Washington, DC: University Press of America.

Walker, E., and J. Rossiter. (1989). Schizophrenic patients' self-perceptions: Legal and clinical implications. *Journal of Psychiatry and Law, 17*, 55–73.

Walsh, R. (1995). The approach of the human science researcher: Implications for the practice of qualitative research. *The Humanistic Psychologist, 23*, 332–344.

Walsh, R. (2003). The methods of reflexivity. *The Humanistic Psychologist, 31*, 51–66.

Wampold, B. (2001). *The great psychotherapy debate: Models, methods, and findings.* Mahwah, NJ: Erlbaum.

Warner, R., D. Taylor, M. Powers, and J. Hyman. (1989). Acceptance of the mental illness label by psychotic patients: Effects on functioning. *American Journal of Orthopsychiatry, 59*, 398–409.

Wertz, F. (1985). Method and findings in a phenomenological psychological study of a complex life-event: Being criminally victimized. In Giorgi, A. (Ed.). *Phenomenology and psychological research* (pp. 155–216). Pittsburgh: Duquesne University Press.

Whitt, H., R. Meile, and L. Larson. (1979). Illness role theory, the labeling perspective and the social meanings of mental illness: An empirical test. *Social Science & Medicine, 13*, 655–666.

Will, O. (1980). Schizophrenia: Psychological treatment. In Kaplan, H. I., A. M. Freedman, and B. J. Sadock. (Eds.). *Comprehensive textbook of psychiatry III: vol. 2.* Baltimore: Williams and Wilkins.

Wilson, H., and S. Plumy. (1984). The rotten apple stigma. *Journal of Psychosocial Nursing, 22*, 7–10.

Wolman, B. (1978). Classification and diagnosis of mental disorders. In Wolman, B. (Ed.). *Clinical diagnosis of mental disorders* (pp. 15–47). New York: Plenum Press.

Yalom, I. (1990). *Existential psychotherapy.* New York: Basic Books.

BIOGRAPHICAL BACKGROUND

JESSIE GOICOECHEA, PhD, received a BA in psychology from the University of Dallas, where the department's commitment to a human science approach and her growing interest in phenomenological and existential philosophies led her to Duquesne University, where she received her MA and PhD in psychology. She completed her predoctoral internship at Clinton-Eaton-Ingham Community Mental Health Center in Lansing, Michigan, which consisted of rotations in a psychiatric hospital and a rural outpatient clinic. Experiences in both settings contributed to her interest in the systems and institutions within which mental illness is socially constructed. In 2003, Goicoechea joined the faculty at Duquesne as assistant professor and director of the psychology clinic, the primary training facility for the graduate students. She enjoys the combination of participating in the students' academic and clinical training, including teaching introductory courses on psychotherapy and assessment, and overseeing the procedural and program development aspects of the clinic to ensure that clients are served well.

Goicoechea also works as a psychotherapist at Persad Center, a community mental health agency that serves the gay, lesbian, bisexual, transgender, and HIV communities. An area of special clinical interest and expertise is domestic violence in same-sex couples. She leads a psychotherapy group for offenders and would like to extend her general research interest in language as constructive of social reality, to look at how the terms *perpetrator* and *victim* are used in treatment discourse. She has co-authored an article that articulates themes of a nondualistic ontology within the sociocultural perspective on learning and that proposes a reconciliation between this perspective and constructivist theories.

PART

II

AFFECTIVE AND COGNITIVE PROCESSES

6

HONOR AND RESPECT: FEMINIST COLLABORATIVE RESEARCH WITH SEXUALLY ABUSED WOMEN

SUSAN L. MORROW

EDITOR'S INTRODUCTION

Feminist qualitative research ranges from studies of content that is of interest to feminists to studies that also embody feminist values in all phases of the study. Dr. Morrow's study exemplifies the latter practices with lively you-are-there accounts of the research process. From the beginning, her participants are co-researchers. She explores cultural/historical contexts of childhood abuses, the research process was repeatedly open to comment from colleagues as well as participant co-researchers, individual constructions of meaning are genuinely respected, and the research process is personally transformative for all the co-researchers, including Dr. Morrow. Themes common to all participants are presented, but without covering over the life experiences they summarize. Power is a subtext, all the clearer for not being made focal.

This chapter illustrates the rigor of bringing together data from multiple sources—interviews, focus groups, journals, and collaborative co-researcher groups. It also illustrates the process of starting with explicit analytical procedures (grounded theory) and then being open to "emergent method"—accommodations in procedures to meet the research phenomenon more fully as the study goes on. We also see how the researcher is involved with the participants, but maintains a separate stance.

Dr. Morrow agreed to write this chapter based on her 1992 dissertation to provide a fuller voice to the article she published in 1995, which contains her findings but was constrained by journal expectations and page restrictions. Here, the research process and the co-researchers' experience come to life.

BACKGROUND

The amount of, just, honor and respect—it's just not like anything I've ever experienced. The research is also ... it rings true. Honor and respect. That's what we all lost when we were abused.

These were the words of Megan, one of the women who had been involved for 16 months in my investigation of the ways women who had been sexually abused as children had survived and coped with their abuse. In this chapter, Megan and others describe their journeys to find their voices, once silenced in childhood and reclaimed as they healed through therapy or through their shared participation in this research.

Initially I conceptualized this research as giving voice to women who had been sexually abused as children. I hoped to unearth the voices buried—as Sarton (1980) wrote—beneath "an underground and secret river," to "reach the source" and "go there, comfort, entreat, and bless the magic throat" (p. 21). "Voice" was my chosen metaphor based on influential feminist writings by Gilligan (1982); Belenky, Clinchy, Goldberger, and Tarule (1986); Brown and Gilligan (1992), and others. These authors suggested that, not only were women's experiences different from those of men, but girls' and women's authentic voices had been silenced as a result of their experiences as marginal members of a patriarchal society.

In addition to a legacy initiated by Gilligan (1982) regarding voice, literature about childhood sexual abuse has also addressed issues of silence and voice. Although women who were sexually abused as children used creative and adaptive strategies, their survival has not been without cost. Secrecy has frequently shrouded sexual abuse, muffling the child's protestations and cries for help. Even as adults, women find disclosure difficult (Bass and Davis, 1988; Briere, 1992; Russell, 1986). Louise Armstrong (1978) and Judy Freespirit (1982) were among the first voices to break the silence about their own and other women's experiences of childhood sexual abuse. More recently, Pipher (2002) has written of the importance of "healing stories." But despite the changing climate that permits the terrible silences to be broken, finding voice still remains an enormous personal, therapeutic, and societal task. In her research on the language used by women to talk about their abuse, Barringer (1992) described the struggle for voice experienced by many survivors:

> Speaking is a profoundly significant act for the survivor of childhood sexual abuse. To speak of her abuse, the survivor must not only defy her perpetrator's threats and the societal taboo, but she must also give up the very protections that have enabled her to survive—the forgetting, the denial, the numbness. She must push against the enormous weight of her isolation and shame. Just as she trained herself, in childhood, to endure in silence, she must now retrain the tongue, the throat, the chest, to release the words that choke her into paralysis. (p. 8)

Of the importance of coming to voice, Barringer (1992) wrote:

> To speak of sexual abuse is an act of courage, an act that defies the authority of the perpetrator. It is an act that violates that most fundamental rule of survival—silence—when survival has been, for many victims, the only goal they have been able to sustain. Speaking about sexual abuse is an act in which the survivor returns to the scenes of her psychic destruction to reclaim herself, for herself. (p. 8)

Silence is not simply a personal matter. Herman (1997) spoke of societal silencing surrounding childhood sexual abuse and other forms of trauma, noting that only rarely in history have issues surrounding trauma been addressed publicly. She wrote, "The ordinary response to atrocities is to banish them from consciousness. Certain violations of the social compact are too terrible to utter aloud: this is the meaning of the word *unspeakable*" (p. 1). Each time trauma has received public attention, it has been in conjunction with a political movement. The second wave of feminism in the United States and Europe made it possible to bring abuse of women and children out of the closet and address issues of prevention and treatment. Yet, noted Herman (1997), those who speak out on behalf of victims are often subject to the same stigma that attaches to victims themselves. Consequently, just as Freud was effectively silenced after he proposed his "seduction theory" (in which he articulated his belief that his hysterical patients were indeed victims of incest), Herman (1997) noted that "history teaches us that this knowledge [about psychological trauma] could also disappear" (p. 32). Counterforces, including attacks on the validity of recovered memories of abuse and legal charges against therapists working with abuse survivors (Pope and Brown, 1996), continue to challenge the progress that has been made during the past years.

Although I originally framed my research process as giving voice to the silenced, the metaphor had problems. Had I retained the "voice" metaphor throughout the project, the metaphor itself might have become reified. Consequently, I set the metaphor aside as I began the study. Upon completing the project, I discovered that the metaphor was indeed apt.

THE CONTEXT FOR THE RESEARCH

My own interest in feminist research originated in my grassroots feminist evolution. A political activist since the Civil Rights Movement in the 1960s, I later took part in peace activities during the Vietnam War and finally was drawn irresistibly to the Women's Liberation Movement in 1972. My emerging feminism informed all my subsequent activities, including my graduate work in counselor education and counseling psychology. Therefore, as I embarked upon academic research, I was influenced by my feminist perspective both to choose a topic that would be relevant to women and to develop a method that would be compatible with feminist principles.

I was already a masters-level psychotherapist at the time I identified my doctoral research interests. I had worked for several years with women survivors of childhood sexual abuse and had heard stories of unimaginable trauma; in addition, I had regularly observed instances of incredible resilience and survival. It was this latter that spurred me to want to learn more about the ways that women had survived and coped with their childhood abuse.

FEMINIST RESEARCH: MUTUALITY AND CONTEXT

In the 1980s, feminist researchers called for more participatory engagement with those who are the "subjects" of investigation (Maguire, 1987; Roberts, 1981; Stanley and Wise, 1983). Continuing through the last decade, feminist researchers have addressed issues of power, privilege, subjectivity, equality, collaboration, and voice (Fine, 1992; Lather, 1991; Maher, 1999; Reinharz, 1992). Critical, feminist, and action researchers have attempted to remedy power imbalances inherent in the research relationship by asking questions about whose agenda is being addressed, who benefits from the research experience, and whose voice is heard when the research is made public. Two key components of feminist research relevant to the current study are *mutuality* and *context*.

Mutuality has as its underpinnings issues of privilege, power, and equality. Central to feminist research is an understanding of power in the lives of those whose lives we investigate as well as between the researcher and the researched (Fine, 1994). Childhood sexual abuse is a horrendous abuse of power. When forced to relive experiences of powerlessness, abuse survivors may become retraumatized. Therefore, addressing issues of power in the research relationship is essential. An empowered relationship between investigator and participant is characterized by the participant's voice being heard as well as her meanings sought and adequately conveyed in the analysis and writing. In addition, such a relationship should result in improving the lives or well-being of participants, often by enhancing their understanding of their experiences within the social context (referred to as ontological authenticity by Guba and Lincoln [1989]). In addition, it may spur them to action (catalytic authenticity).

Context is often lost in the research endeavor. Although this context stripping is most typically the case in laboratory research, even qualitative researchers may ignore the sociopolitical realities of the phenomena we investigate. This is particularly evident in psychological research, in which the focus is frequently on the intrapersonal and intrapsychic rather than on the contextual variables that influence human distress. Feminist research seeks to contextualize the lives and experiences of women and understand their social realities (Reinharz, 1992). In the feminist tradition of looking at the personal as political (i.e., intrapersonal and intrapsychic experiences have sociopolitical underpinnings related to privilege, power, and oppression [McLellan, 1999]), feminist research examines participants' meanings within the sociohistorical–political context.

As I worked to integrate my feminist perspective with the demands of qualitative research situated in counseling psychology, I soon realized that what I was attempting held many contradictions. My qualitative training had been broadly based and permitted a wide range of possibilities. Yet my challenge was to frame this research in such a way that it would be credible to scholars in psychology, a field that was at once situated in a positivist tradition *and* in its early stages of embracing qualitative methods. Early on, I feared that I would be required to sacrifice my feminist goals to produce an acceptable piece of work. But there were surprises in store for me. Some of the paradoxes and contradictions in juggling different perspectives gave way to exciting opportunities for integration and growth.

IS FEMINIST PSYCHOLOGY AN OXYMORON? FEMINIST RESEARCH, QUALITATIVE METHODS, AND PSYCHOLOGY

Kitzinger and Perkins (1993) addressed the contradictions between feminism and psychology, noting that feminism emphasizes political realities, whereas psychology is focused on individualistic phenomena. They noted that many early feminist constructs have been co-opted by the language of psychology and psychotherapy and that once-political terms such as *empowerment* have been watered down to express a subjective internal experience. Indeed, one might think of the juxtaposition of feminism and psychology as an oxymoron.

In another vein, psychology has long yearned to be seen as "real science," modeling itself after the hard sciences. In fact, some departments of psychology are the final bastions of postpositivism, refusing to consider alternative paradigms to the traditional research model. Thus, qualitative researchers sometimes find themselves in hostile company when relating to mainstream psychological scholars.

However, feminist research, qualitative methods, and psychology may not be altogether strange bedfellows. Feminists have been drawn to qualitative methods because those methods lend themselves so well to hearing the stories—the voices—of women and other marginalized groups who have long been silent. In addition, ethnographic and interview-based methods facilitate a relationship with participants, which is important to many feminist investigators (Reinharz, 1992). Feminism has also gained a foothold in psychology, as illustrated by a large and powerful division (Society for the Psychology of Women, Division 35) of the APA. Thus, the synthesis of feminism, psychology, and qualitative research is both timely and credible. Many aspects of qualitative research lend themselves to a feminist approach, including emergent design, self-reflection, and "thick description" (Geertz, 1973; Morrow and Smith, 2000).

EMERGENT DESIGN AND THE EVOLVING
NATURE OF QUALITATIVE RESEARCH

Qualitative research is often characterized by its emergent design, in which the investigator proposes a plan for the study that is flexible based upon findings in the field as well as her or his own evolving thought processes. The investigator is free to adapt data-gathering methods and analytical strategies to the emerging demands of the study. Such a design is particularly appropriate to a feminist perspective that seeks to empower participants in that it permits those participants to have a voice in the process and outcome of the research.

When I originally planned the research described in this chapter, I intended to conduct individual interviews and a focus group of several weeks. As the focus group progressed, it became clear not only that the group process was extremely valuable as a source of data, but that participants became increasingly involved and empowered. At the end of the nine-week group, therefore, I invited any women who wanted to continue as "participant co-researchers" to do so. This process is reflective both of the "emergent design" features characteristic of many qualitative investigations and of a mutual, collaborative, and participatory process of feminist research.

Another example of emergent design in service of feminist goals was when I had repeatedly attempted to impose a particular structure, as recommended by Strauss and Corbin (1990), on the data. Specifically, I attempted to find one overarching core category that would fit all the data, even though my research participants insisted that two overarching categories were essential to capturing their meanings. In the true spirit and flexibility of emergent design, I changed the rules, as it were, allowing my participants' analysis to supersede the original design.

SELF-REFLECTION OR RESEARCHER REFLEXIVITY

Qualitative methods seek to accomplish purposes different from more traditional paradigms. Instead of striving for validity and reliability to arrive at generalizable results, the qualitative investigator uses various strategies for the purpose of understanding and accurately portraying the meanings made by participants of the phenomenon in question. One of these strategies is self-reflection, or researcher reflexivity, which involves self-examination to understand the assumptions and biases that may affect the study. Feminist scholars too use self-reflection as well as self-disclosure when explicating theory or research. It is not uncommon for a feminist researcher to describe herself and the various cultural and experiential variables that affect the lens through which she views her research.

In this investigation, I began with reflexive activities such as keeping a journal of my activities, thoughts, and feelings. I also met regularly with a team of peer researchers who acted as "devil's advocates" to challenge my thinking and point out where my feelings and biases might limit the research. Early in our meetings, I had shared with my research team extensive personal and political writings about my interest in the topic of sexual abuse. However, during the course of the research, I inadvertently retreated to a more postpositivist stance, endeavoring to keep both my personal feelings and my feminist politics out of the way. Two experiences stand out as ways in which my research team facilitated my awareness of my own biases and assumptions.

In the first example, although I regularly kept a journal about my experiences of conducting the research, as I began writing the results of the investigation, my teammates noted that "I" had disappeared. So intent was I on accurately portraying the experiences of the research participants that I had silenced my own voice. With my research team's encouragement, I began to allow my own feelings and experiences to reemerge, guided by my journal entries.

In the second example, I went so far as to attempt to redirect a heavily political discussion during one of the focus groups. One evening Velvia (all names of participants in this chapter are pseudonyms selected by participants) began the discussion by expressing a need to "debrief" from a front-page news item that morning. Women's right to choose abortion had just been severely limited by the state legislature. Velvia, and subsequently the other group members, discussed the subject with intensity while I stewed about how to bring them back to topic. Fortunately, I failed miserably in my attempts, and the resulting videotape was rich with the women's expressions of how their right to control their bodies had been robbed from them as children; they viewed this legislative decision as a recapitulation of that original violation. My peer researchers were astute as I complained about my participants getting "off track," pointing out that my rigidity in trying not to bias the participants with my feminist perspective might silence their voices when they expressed their own political rage.

THICK DESCRIPTION, OR CONTEXTUALIZING PARTICIPANTS' EXPERIENCES

Because psychology has typically focused on the intrapsychic and interpersonal aspects of human experience, psychological research can easily be stripped of context. Geertz (1973) described "thick description" in terms of rich depiction of context in which participants make meaning and in which the research is conducted. Its purpose is to contextualize participant experiences, giving the reader a deeper understanding of the phenomenon under investigation. The feminist scholar attends particularly to historical and political contexts.

Because primary data were gathered in individual interviews and focus groups, this study could easily have emphasized solely the participants' understandings of their intra- and interpersonal experiences surrounding sexual abuse, survival, and coping. To frame the results in context, I explored the historical and societal concomitants of participants' abuse. First, I studied the historical contexts within which the eldest and youngest participants were abused. What resources had been available to Barbara, born in 1920 and abused throughout her infancy, childhood, and teens? To understand the cultural context during this time, I studied popular magazines that had graced coffee tables throughout the United States in the 1920s: *The Ladies' Home Journal* and *The Saturday Evening Post*. The youngest participant, Paula, had been born in 1965; she and her brother had grown up reading their father's *Playboy* magazines. The consequences of my investigations of these media, presented later, were shocking and surprising. I followed these investigations with a discussion with one of the participants about a little girl—a friend's daughter—who was nine years old at the time of the investigation. This child's experience is an example of "theoretical sampling"—investigating outside the parameters of the study to shed additional light on a phenomenon—and helped to contextualize further the experience of sexual abuse and coping.

The second foray into the historical and cultural contexts of survival and coping was an exploration of the psychological, therapeutic, and healing contexts of the adult survivors in the study. I examined the language of participants carefully, searching for the ways in which participants "psychologized" everyday life—that is, how did their language reflect the ways in which survivors have adopted psychological terminology such as *in denial* and *repression* to describe their experiences? The various discourses of healing provided an understanding of the many "survivor cultures" (e.g., 12-step groups and psychotherapy) that influenced participants' constructions of how they had survived and coped, both as children and adults. Thus, this research synthesized emergent design, researcher reflexivity, and thick description, enriching psychological research by embedding it in a historical, cultural, and political context.

METHOD

PARTICIPANTS

Eleven women in a large southwestern metropolitan area were recruited through therapists who specialized in working with adult survivors of child sexual abuse. (Although in many instances a larger sample size is warranted, the multiple data sources and extensive contact with participants described here ensured that I collected sufficient data.) I sent therapists letters explaining the project in detail, along with accompanying letters to be given to appropriate potential participants. Prospective participants called me if they were interested. A particular attraction for participants to participate was a nine-week research support (focus) group that they would attend at no cost. Because I was also a therapist working in the community with survivors of sexual abuse, both therapists and potential participants expressed confidence that the group, although not designed to provide therapy, would be a supportive and potentially therapeutic experience. Of the 11 participants, seven were able to participate in the group. Four women participated only in individual interviews but were unable to attend the group because of work commitments or because they had been recruited after the beginning of the group. Seven women took part in the group, and, of those, four continued later as participant co-researchers.

The women in the study ranged in age from 25 to 72 years. One was African-American; one, West Indian; and the remainder, European American. Two identified as lesbian, one as homosexual or "a woman who loves women" ("A Lesbian is someone from the Isle of Lesbos!"), one bisexual, and seven heterosexual. One was mobility impaired, another experienced multiple physical illnesses and disorders, a third was hard-of-hearing, and the remainder were able bodied. Participants came from a variety of socioeconomic classes, educational backgrounds, and religious or spiritual orientations. All had been in formal healing or recovery processes from one meeting to several years: nine in psychotherapy and six in 12-step programs (some in both).

Prior to the interviews, I attempted to establish an egalitarian relationship and a context of mutuality with each participant. In my recruitment letter, I informed participants I was an abuse survivor as well as a therapist who worked with sexual abuse survivors. From the beginning of the interviews, participants revealed that my survivor status as well as my experience as a therapist helped them to feel safe and facilitated their belief that I would understand them.

PROCEDURE

At the outset, I had planned to conduct individual interviews and an ongoing focus group of approximately eight to ten weeks. In addition, I had planned to invite participants to keep ongoing journals about their experiences in the research project, particularly related to topics we discussed in the focus group. The combination of interviews, focus groups, and journals was intended to provide multiple data sources, or *triangulation* of data, to increase the rigor of the investigation and enrich the data. I also had planned to keep two journals: (1) an analytical journal containing my interpretations of the data, memos about the phenomena under investigation, and emerging themes; and (2) a self-reflective journal. As the project emerged, I added analysis meetings with participants and combined the analytical and self-reflective journals into one document. The data sources are described in more detail later.

Individual Interviews

All but one of the individual interviews were held in my home office, a comfortable environment with a casual ambiance. I met with participants during a warm southwestern autumn beneath an open window through which we listened to birds chirping in a huge mulberry tree. An occasional car drove by on the quiet street, and the sounds of children playing could be heard a block away. One participant, a disabled woman, asked that I interview her at her home. At her request, we met across her kitchen table, where she might feel some degree of safety and distance imposed by the barrier between us. I began each interview following recommendations by Spradley (1979) with informal conversation to establish rapport, followed by explaining the informed consent form and obtaining written and verbal audiotaped consent from the woman to participate.

Although I had originally constructed an interview guide consisting of 12 questions, my first interview changed my plans. I had originally planned to meet for a short time with each interviewee to explain the project, get acquainted, explain and have participants sign the informed consent form, and schedule our longer interview. I had explained this expectation to the first participant, Paula, when we first made telephone contact. However, after we had finished the informed consent process and I pulled out my calendar to schedule our interview appointment, she objected, saying, "I thought we were going to do the interview now. I'm ready to talk!" I consented and, feeling a little panicky, searched for my interview guide. Unable to find it, I finally responded, "Well, uh, er, um. Tell me, as much as you are comfortable sharing with me right now, um, what happened to you when you were sexually abused." This kind of question, both very personal and potentially disturbing for a participant, is not the kind of question with which I would normally begin an interview, but Paula's desire to tell her story and my own personal style (I've been described as an "earth mother" who elicits trust very early in a relationship) converged to make the question both appropriate and effective.

Paula proceeded to tell her story for about an hour before pausing. When she came to a natural ending to her story, I, unable to recall any of the questions on my interview agenda, asked, "How did you survive and cope?" Those two questions became the guiding questions for all the interviews and provided a framework upon which I built, individualizing additional questions for each participant as her narrative unfolded. Generally, the first interview question took about 45 minutes to an hour to answer, the second from 15 to 30 minutes. The longest interview lasted four hours. The interviews were audio-taped. Each interview ended with my helping to reorient the participant to the present, establishing that she felt safe to drive home, and confirming the starting date of the focus group.

During the rapport-building part of the interview, I worked to establish a sense of mutuality by disclosing a bit about myself and my excitement over the project. During the interview, I used selected disclosures of my own experiences to assist participants in feeling they were neither alone nor odd in any way. At times, when a participant disclosed what she considered to be a problematic way of coping, I responded with a positive affirmation about her having found a way to survive in the midst of what must have been an impossible situation. When one participant described vomiting to release her emotional pain, I responded, "Wow, what an incredible coping strategy!" She looked at me in surprise and said in awe, "I never thought of it like that!"

Individual interviews served to give each woman a sense of connection to me and, indirectly, to the other women in the study. They led naturally to our first focus group meeting.

Focus Group

Focus groups are discussion groups with a purpose. Morgan and Krueger (1993) noted that focus groups are particularly useful for investigating the complexity of human behavior and motivations. Focus groups may be used at the beginning of a study to identify questions for subsequent interviews or following interviews to explore phenomena in more depth. They may also be one-shot or ongoing group meetings. I chose to schedule ongoing group meetings after the individual interviews to achieve as much depth as possible as well as to add to the complexity of the data by investigating the collective meaning-making process of the participants. Focus groups were held in a group room of the in-house counselor training center at the university in which I was a graduate student. The room, carpeted and with padded chairs and posters on the walls, was nonetheless somewhat institutional in appearance, with soundproofing panels on the walls and large two-way mirrors. I showed participants the opposite sides of the mirrors, which led to two empty counseling rooms and a room from which one of the two video cameras would record. A second video camera was set up in the group room itself. By using two cameras I hoped to maximize my observation of the facial expressions and body language of participants as well as having a backup in case of technological difficulties. The first session consisted of introductions, after which I identified some of the themes that had emerged from interviews and inquired what the group would like to discuss. The first session became a brainstorming session about words: survival, survivor, coping, victim. I invited participants to keep weekly journals. Subsequent group sessions were determined by the emerging categories of the research.

During the focus group, I used specific strategies to establish mutuality and collaboration. These included a characteristic inherent in feminist groups, which is that groups tend to reduce the hierarchical power of the facilitator. Deliberate strategies included disclosure about my own survival and coping strategies whereby I took the role of more-participant-than-observer on a participant–observer continuum (Adler and Adler, 1987). In addition, I asked participants to identify "research questions" to guide focus group discussions, which they did. A particularly powerful question posed by Kitty, one of the participants, was: "How did we all manage to not kill ourselves?" Other questions generated by participants or my emerging analysis focused on inner children or parts of self, anger, religion, and spirituality, additional ways beside sexual abuse that robbed women of control of their bodies, and other topics.

Participants asked many questions about the research process itself. In fact, they demonstrated such interest in the study as well as reluctance to terminate our meetings as the ninth week drew near that I modified the study design by inviting them to continue as co-analysts of the data. Of the seven women, one felt she needed to take a break from focusing on abuse because of how the research was affecting her emotionally, and two decided not to go on with the group because of busy lives or other commitments. Four chose to continue with the project.

Postfocus Group Participatory Analysis

During the postfocus group analytical phase of the study, my own role became even more participatory and mutual as the four remaining participants took increasing "ownership" of the research. It now became *our* study. We began by viewing group videotapes that I had selected on the basis that all the group members were actively participating. Participant co-researchers, as we began to refer to them, used their own intuitive analytical skills; and I instructed them in some of the basic analytical strategies that I was using. Fairly early during the process, we abandoned the video analysis as I began to share my emerging outline resulting from the analysis and to ask questions of the participants that would yield deeper understanding of certain phenomena. Co-analysts' sense of ownership of the process was further illustrated when they challenged my analytical interpretations and insisted that I revamp my conceptual framework to make it better fit their experiences and the data. Although during this period we all became very close, the co-researchers involved themselves in a different kind of relationship with one another than with me, socializing with and calling one another for support, but limiting their extrameeting contact with me to calls related specifically to data analysis.

Throughout the focus group and analytical sessions, participants and I logged our activities, reflections, and experiences of the research process. Participants kept journals specifically for the research process, while I maintained my self-reflective journal (described later) to address my own subjectivities. Participants also contributed various kinds of other documents to the study.

Journals and Other Documents

All participants kept weekly journals about our focus group discussions. I provided audiotapes for those women who preferred to tape their journals. At times, I asked them to write about or tape-record specific issues we discussed or planned to discuss in the group. Other times, they wrote freely about whatever they wished. In addition, I invited participants to share other documentary evidence with me that related to the research. These documents included old journals, poetry and art, and editorials from one woman's high school newspaper. In keeping with the emergent nature of the study, two strategies involving video were particularly noteworthy. In the first, one group member, Paula, had brought her paintings and sketches from childhood onward to share with the group. During the group, we discussed the contexts for those drawings. After the group's end, Paula stayed, and I videotaped each picture as she told me what it meant to her. Ananda, another artist, wanted to tell her story not of abuse but of healing. During our interview, she showed me, page by page, the contents of four large albums of her pastels as she documented her process of healing from sexual abuse.

Self-reflection

My own experiences were captured in a reflexive journal in which I examined my feelings before and during the investigation. Beginning with asking myself, "Why am I doing this?" I tracked my own process over time to become more aware of my motivations, assumptions, and biases that might affect the research as well as to discharge troubling emotions that emerged as the study progressed. At one point I wrote:

> How am I doing, reviewing the horrors? Okay but unsettled. This is rough stuff. The question comes back and back, "How could people do this to children?" Amazing how much I forgot until I typed this transcript. No wonder I have difficulty recording my reactions or making field notes after these sessions. I am powerfully dissociated. I frequently cannot recall, after an interview or a group, what was discussed, although it comes back (it is not new) when I transcribe it.

An advantage of journal keeping was to accomplish the elusive task of maintaining the position described by Fine (1992) as the activist feminist stance, which is " committed to positioning researchers as self-conscious, critical, and participatory analysts, *engaged with but still distinct from our informants* (p. 220, emphasis mine). The reflexive process enabled me to maintain my stance as researcher while being intensely engaged with participants. Furthermore, my reflections helped me track how my feelings, biases, and assumptions affected the research process.

Historical Analysis

To complement the other data and to understand better the context of sexual abuse in the lives of the participants, I examined magazines from the periods in which the eldest (72 years) and youngest (25 years) participants had been abused. For the eldest participant, I selected popular magazines such as *Ladies Home Journal* and *The Saturday Evening Post* from the years 1920 and 1925. For the youngest, I selected only *Playboy* magazine from 1976, which she said her brother was reading avidly at the time that he sexually abused her. In addition, I examined the language of participants to understand better the discourses of psychology, therapy, and healing that contributed to various "survivor cultures" experienced by sexual abuse survivors.

Transcripts of individual interviews, focus group videotapes, audiotapes and notes from participant co-analysis, participants' journals and other documentary evidence, my own self-reflexive journals, and historical analysis formed the *data corpus*. It was this body of data that provided the raw materials for the data analysis that follows.

DATA ANALYSIS

I used three complementary approaches to analyze the data: (1) grounded theory (Glaser and Strauss, 1967; Strauss and Corbin, 1998), (2) analytical induction (Erickson, 1986), and (3) narrative analysis (Polkinghorne, 1988). Grounded theory, also known as the *constant comparative method*, analyzes data inductively (from the ground up) to develop a *theory*, model, or conceptual framework that is *grounded* in the data. During the grounded theory phase, I first transcribed each interview, making analytical notes or *memos* as I transcribed. I then immersed myself in the data through repeated readings, highlighting MUs (words, phrases, and sentences that related to the research question) and writing codes (short names for the MUs) in the margins of the transcript. Next, I wrote these codes on small Post-It notes, which I arranged at random on large poster boards. Through repeated coding, sorting, and comparisons, I rearranged the codes, gathering them into increasingly more inclusive and abstract categories and themes. I continued to revisit the transcripts as I wrote about the conceptual framework that had emerged through the analysis process, integrating my interpretive commentary with quotes from participants. I began this process soon after the first interview was conducted. My immersion in the data was complete when I was able to identify a theme, then move unfailingly to the correct place in a participant's transcript that would contain a supporting quotation. As I began meeting with the group, I integrated focus group information, along with journals and documents, into the analysis. I knew this analysis was complete when all the existing data were accounted for by the emergent conceptual framework, and additional data did not yield further complexity or depth to the results. This process formed the heart of the data analysis and was supplemented by the other two approaches to provide triangulation by research design.

To enhance the rigor of this investigation, I used analytical induction (Erickson, 1986). Analytical induction, as contrasted with grounded theory's fine-grained analysis, involves a more global process of immersion in the data and searching for overarching themes. This procedure complemented the grounded theory analysis by assisting me to step back from the "trees" so that I could better observe the "forest." Like grounded theory, this approach is largely inductive. I began this process immediately following the first interview by tape-recording my immediate thoughts while they were fresh. At least once a week, but more often daily, I searched for "the finding of the week/day"—a theme or hunch that would be added to the emerging analysis. In addition, Erickson (1984) recommended searching for disconfirming evidence to enhance the rigor of the analysis, which I did by reviewing data as well as by contacting participants for additional information and to clarify discrepant information. The search for disconfirmation is critical, because we humans operate with a confirmatory bias, selecting information to confirm our everyday hypotheses (Mahoney, 1991). An active search for discrepant information helps to combat that tendency. Finally, I constructed research vignettes consisting of a theme statement and a short illustrative story, which helped to test themes against data. These vignettes did not become part of the final writing; rather, I used them to understand better the phenomena described by participants and to test the coherence of the GTM. This approach complemented the first, adding rigor and enriching the final description; however, it did not result in a separate set of results.

Finally, I used narrative analysis to honor the stories of women in the study and to ground the study further historically. In addition to grounded theory and analytical induction as methodological approaches to analyze the transcribed narratives, I also developed specific questions to "ask of the data" to uncover the storied aspects of the narrative. Some of these questions included: What metaphors and patterns of metaphors were contained in the accounts of participants? What story did the survivor tell herself and others about why the abuse happened? What evidence is there for historic self-awareness? How were stories or components of stories used to dramatize? To "do being ordinary?" (Sacks, 1984). Was there a moral to the story? And others. This approach complemented the research vignettes described earlier. As a result, in addition to the grounded theory conceptual model, I wrote three composite stories to illustrate survival and coping strategies that emerged from the overall analysis (found in Morrow, 1992), described by Strauss and Corbin (1998) as the "story line."

I used supplemental strategies to enhance further the rigor of the investigation: a peer research team, an analytical journal, and an audit trail. Throughout the investigation, I met weekly with an interdisciplinary peer research team of three other female doctoral students also working on qualitative projects. We discussed the emerging findings, with team members questioning, playing "devil's advocate," requesting supporting data for the emerging model, and offering feedback. My journal for the project was an ongoing log of meetings with advisors and the research team; observational notes following interviews and focus groups; memos describing "hunches" and insights during the overall data analysis; and emerging codes, categories, and themes. As noted earlier, this journal was soon integrated with my self-reflective journal because reflection often led to analysis and vice versa. An audit trail in total consists of all the materials related to the study, including tapes, notes, transcripts, memos, journals, documents, and poster boards with Post-It notes (Lincoln and Guba, 1985). In addition, I kept a chronological record of the major research events, beginning with my early conceptualization of the study; continuing with its refinement; and including emergent codes and themes, major shifts in conceptualization as the research progressed, and events that stood out as catalysts in the research process. This chronological audit trail appears as an appendix in my dissertation (Morrow, 1992).

RESULTS

The results of this investigation could be presented in many ways. In a more traditionally framed presentation and in keeping with the grounded theory approach described by Strauss and Corbin (1998), I might illustrate—with interpretive comments, quotes, and diagrams—the particular strategies that the participants developed to survive and cope with their sexual abuse. In fact, this particular presentation is provided elsewhere (Morrow and Smith, 1995). In the current chapter, the results are presented in four parts: the first is women's voices—stories of their own journeys about how they survived and coped with being sexually abused. The second form of results focuses briefly on the experience of participants as they engaged with me to make meaning of those journeys. The third form is a story of my own journey through this research project. The final presentation is a reflection about and confirmation of the "voice" metaphor.

THE JOURNEY: STORIES OF SURVIVAL AND COPING TOLD BY WOMEN SURVIVORS OF CHILDHOOD SEXUAL ABUSE

I had expected, when I examined the historical contexts in which research participants had been abused, to find very different social contexts underlying Barbara's abuse in the 1920s and Paula's in the 1970s. What I found shocked and horrified me. I realized that I had expected Barbara's abuse to be an anomaly, unsupported by the popular culture or at least occurring in a vacuum of silence. To the contrary, the popular magazines I examined contained fiction that would raise the ire of many of us today as "Dimity Gay, Grandpa's Little Maid" (Atkey, 1925) sexualized a little girl and made her the prey of Grandpa, who sidled up to Dimity "like the wolf to Red Riding Hood" (p. 3). *Playboy*, in March 1976, set the stage for Paula's abuse. During our interview, Paula had described the relentless manner in which her brother grabbed, pinched, and poked her breasts, buttocks, and nipples. Later, reading the cartoon "Little Annie Fanny" (Kurtzman and Elder, 1976) was a déjà vu experience, in that Annie was fondled, grabbed, suckled, and pinched throughout the cartoon, a model for Paula's abuse.

With the assistance of my participant co-researchers, I identified two overarching themes describing how the participants had survived and coped, both at the time of their abuse and through the years into adulthood. The first theme was finding strategies to keep from being overwhelmed by feelings that participants experienced as threatening or dangerous to themselves; the second was managing helplessness, powerlessness, and lack of control. These strategies are described here and are illustrated with the words of the participants. Not all participants used all these strategies, and the participant co-researchers and I did not give undue weight to strategies used by more participants.

STRATEGIES FOR KEEPING FROM BEING OVERWHELMED BY THREATENING AND DANGEROUS FEELINGS

Megan: Being overwhelmed (by the feelings) would be like being in a car crash, ripping, screaming metal, screaming people, bodies pierced by shards of hot metal, blood, anguish, ongoing, ongoing anguish. It would be worse than just dying. It would be pain and anguish that goes on, and on, and on. Nothing you can ever do would stop it. That's what being overwhelmed by emotions means. Pain that goes on and on and on and never stops.

These images of injury and death, pain and horror described by Megan and the other participants hint at the feelings of the child being sexually abused. From the adult's perspective, it is barely possible to glimpse the child's terror, pain, and rage. Yet many times the women in the study spoke for the children they had been, as in Danu's words, "Icicles pierced the child's heart, while sheets of ice fractured her soul." In the face of such strong and violent emotions, it is little wonder the women in this study were forced to develop strategies to keep from being overwhelmed. The strategies they used helped them to (1) reduce the intensity of their feelings, (2) escape the abuse or the feelings, (3) substitute or distract from feelings, (4) release overwhelming emotions, (5) comfort themselves, (6) not know about all or part of the abuse, and (7) compartmentalize the experience or the feelings associated with it. Each of these strategies is illustrated next.

Participants found ways to *reduce the intensity* of overwhelming feelings by **reframing the abuse** ("He was just a boy"), dulling or numbing them with substances ("I can work for three hours and not have a cigarette, but when we do this stuff [analyze the data], it's a little more intense"), preventing themselves from feeling ("I totally lost touch with any feeling"), and "stuffing" their emotions, as Paula did:

> Paula: I was always real heavy into sports my whole life, and I was always the best. If I wasn't the best, I wouldn't do it. So the thing is that I was the best at everything. ... and I think that's what kept the anger in. It helped me stuff it better.

In addition to reducing the intensity of the feelings, participants found ways to *escape* them by actually trying to avoid the abuse. As Lauren recounted, "I remember him chasing me literally all over the house and out the door and all the way down the street. ... I just wanted to get away from him, as far as I could." Velvia illustrated this by saying, "I kept wanting it to be like it was and I kept asking him, 'Let's just read' ... and I kept trying to make him be like he used to act towards me." Unable to escape physically, some tried to hide themselves, as Lauren disclosed: "I tried to be quieter, more secret and private. I knew it would be safer if no one noticed me." Another way of escaping was to ignore the reality of the abuse:

> Kitty: And all through my whole life I would think this is all a dream and I'm going to wake up and I'll be a baby again. ... and I'll know all this and it's all pretend, and make believe nothing happened around me had anything to do with reality.

Participants also escaped mentally or emotionally (Paula: "Mind, take me outa there!"), sometimes with the assistance of drugs or alcohol, or through art, as Barbara did: "And every time my feet hit the ground, I bounced higher and higher. I had to spiral down to breathe."

In addition to escaping feelings, participants *substituted or distracted* from overwhelming emotions, often using self-induced physical pain to "drown out" the emotional pain:

> Liz: Pain. Physical pain keeps me from feeling my feelings. That's where my anorexia came from .... The physical pain of not eating, I can't feel things when I'm in pain. I can't feel my feelings. Pain is a wonderful coping skill for me.

Paula stated, "I carved a cross in my wrist .... I'd burn myself, and what it would do was, ... the pain came out of my soul and into my arm, and it was gone."

Another way of managing overwhelming feelings was to *release* them through talking (Kitty: "After doing all the talking with everyone, I think I'm okay."), humor (Paula: "I've been a walking apology all my life. ...

'Hello, I'm Paula, and I'm sorry'!"), screaming, vomiting (Liz: "I'll go purge and, uh, I'll feel elated, and better, and I also got rid of some of the feelings as a way of letting go."), or acting out violently:

> Kitty: I'm an ass-kicker. I mean, I was a violent drunk. I'd get myself killed or kill somebody else. I was invincible, and I would kick anybody's ass and it didn't matter whether it was a guy who was eight feet tall. I did not care.

Yet another way for participants to handle unmanageable feelings was to *comfort and nurture* themselves with pets, toys, food, or by developing internal symbols of comfort. One woman found comfort from a song by Libby Roderick (1990)[1]:

> How could anyone ever tell you you were anything less than beautiful?
>
> How could anyone ever tell you you were less than whole?
>
> How could anyone fail to notice that your loving is a miracle?
>
> How deeply you're connected to my soul!

Spiritual comfort was another way many women survived:

> Kitty: The survivor in me is that power, that strength or whatever it is that kept me from dyin', even though I tried to die so hard. And, uh, I'm still not sure where that comes from. I'm pretty sure it's from my precious child, which to me is part of God—that power, that inner strength that was given to me at birth.

Simply *not knowing* was a powerful strategy for some women. It was clear as I listened to their stories that gaps in their memories for specific events coincided with the most frightening parts of their abuse. Velvia reported:

> There are some things that I remember, but only come up to a certain point, and I don't know what happened next. Those pictures stick in my head, to the place where it stops sticks in my head ... and so, I'm not always sure how much happened.

When I asked Lauren, "If you could really identify the major thing that helped you survive what happened, what would it be? She responded immediately: "Not remembering any of it."

The final way participants coped with overwhelming emotions was to *compartmentalize* experiences and feelings to make them more manageable, much as many of us divide up tasks that seem overwhelming. One way of compartmentalizing was, as Paula described, to "disassociate":

> I was sittin' on the bed and it felt like I just flipped up! It—it's like I felt like I was floating and I felt taller, even though I was sitting on the bed. It was like I could only look at the floor, and I couldn't talk. ... and then I kind of (whistles, gestures downward), and I'm back down again and it was like, "Son of a bitch, I think I just disassociated!"

---

[1]From the song, "How could anyone," from the recording "If You See a Dream," (1988). Reprinted with permission of Turtle Island Records, Anchorage, AK.

Another way to compartmentalize was to hide vulnerabilities. Liz said, "I developed and wore this, this mask you couldn't penetrate." Some women compartmentalized parts of themselves:

> Barbara: I killed that little girl (inside) growing up. ... wasn't 13 yet ... I killed her. And I can't resurrect her. So I can't find her. ... just told her she couldn't live anymore. "No place here for you. People are going to continue to hurt you and hurt you and hurt you, so die." And so she did, so nobody can hurt.

In addition to handling overwhelming emotions, the women in this study also found ways to manage their powerlessness in the face of their abuse. These strategies are described next.

STRATEGIES TO MANAGE HELPLESSNESS, POWERLESSNESS, AND LACK OF CONTROL

> Lauren: He stands there. A silhouette at first and then his face and body come into view. He is small but the backlighting intensifies his figure and he seems huge, like a prison guard. He is not always there but it feels like he might as well be. When he's not there, I search the distance for him and he appears. He seems to be standing there for hours. As if he's saying, "You are weak, I am in control."

Lauren's words illustrate the powerlessness experienced by all the women in the study. These women (1) utilized strategies of resistance, (2) reframed the abuse to create an illusion of control or power in their own minds, (3) tried to master the trauma in some way, (4) attempted to control other areas of their lives when they couldn't control the abuse, (5) sought confirmation or evidence of the abuse from others, or (6) rejected power.

Using *strategies of resistance,* some women resisted externally, such as refusing to eat. Rage was an important resistance strategy for many, symbolized by the dragon in Paula's drawings, the symbol for her rage and her power: "Nobody fucks with the dragon." Even as an adult, Kitty resisted:

> Those fuckers aren't gonna get me. I'm not gonna kill myself because that would be the ultimate shame, the ultimate waste, because that's what I mean by them winning. That's when they win. And they're not gonna win. They won't. I won't allow it.

Ananda declared: "Art is never giving up."

Sometimes participants *reframed their experiences to create an illusion of power or control.* Megan believed that "If somehow I could be good enough and do things right enough, my mother wouldn't be like that anymore." By believing she could do something to stop the abuse, she maintained an illusion of power. Many participants adopted caretaking roles to assure themselves that they were in control, such as Paula: "Here I am, bein' nine, ten, y'know, tryin' to save Ma, when it should be the other way around."

Participants also *attempted to master the trauma*. Although they had no control over their abuse, some women identified ways in which they recapitulated that abuse as teens or adults by returning to abusive situations. When Kitty talked about placing herself in abusive relationships, she said, "I knew what was going to happen to me and I allowed it to happen.... If I can create pain that I can feel, and I'm in control, it's different. It's totally different."

Another way that participants managed their lack of control was to *control other areas of life besides the abuse*. Most of the women in the study joked about being "control freaks." Megan attributed her control issues to her lack of control during her abuse: "I couldn't manage the abuse, but I could manage the household." Velvia, sexually abused when she was seven, stopped eating after her abuse:

> From that day forward, I was afraid that I was pregnant, (sobbing) and I thought that I would just wake up pregnant one day. Just no nine-month pregnancy. ... I quit eating food ... I would, a little bit, but I was afraid to eat, and for some reason mostly of cheese. I remember being afraid to eat cheese, thinking every day if I didn't wake up pregnant, I thought, "Okay, if I don't eat cheese today, I will probably not get pregnant."

Even though women knew they had been abused, they *sought confirmation from others*. Velvia told this story:

> We would go by, about a block away from his house. I always remember this. I still remember this street. And every day we'd drive by there I would stare at their house and watch and see it and I couldn't remember if it was real, if it really happened. And, and like I knew it did, but my mom didn't look at the house. Whenever I looked at it—and I would be, between looking at her and looking at the house—I would be waiting for her to say, "That's it, that's the house, that's the one," and she didn't ever say anything. She just drove on by, day after day, week after week, to and from my lessons.

All the women but one described ways in which they sought to have power, almost as a way to make up for that which had been denied them. Liz alone *rejected power* altogether:

> Uh, power in myself makes me feel like—I don't want to be like her, I don't want to be like that. She was very powerful. She was *very* powerful. Power seems scary to me. I'm afraid of power in myself, even.

These stories of ways in which women survived and coped by developing strategies to keep from being overwhelmed by threatening and dangerous feelings, as well as managing helplessness, powerlessness, and lack of control, led them in many different directions. Most developed a strong sense of justice, which led some to become activists. Sometimes the strategies they adopted were highly successful, although at times it appeared those strategies boomeranged and created many problems in their lives. They vacillated between wanting to give up and having hope. Kitty appeared closest to giving up, saying "I can't do this anymore." Lauren wrote about Kitty in her journal after group one night: "Kitty's eyes make my heart ache, and my stomach tightens when I see them. It's like death looking into her eyes. And she says she wants to die." Others, such as Megan, found strength they hadn't known existed: "My will to survive is strong, stronger than I realized." They were motivated to keep healing and growing, such as Lauren: "I don't want to just survive; I want to live." Even Kitty, who expressed the most hopelessness, said:

> I'm really blessed. ... I have hope in my life. God hasn't brought me this far to let me drop on my head. ... There's just a little bit of sunlight coming in. There's a little bit of heaven up there that comes inside of my soul and heals.

MAKING MEANING OF THE JOURNEY:
COLLECTIVE CONSTRUCTIONS OF PARTICIPANTS

All the participants expressed their gratitude at being able to be part of this research, which they considered meaningful and with which they hoped to make a difference. Paula, who participated in an interview and the nine-week focus group, had wanted the opportunity to tell about her abuse because she had looked without success for accounts of girls abused by their brothers. She wanted to contribute so other women could identify with her story. Barbara, an interview-only participant, called me two years after the research was completed to thank me for giving her the opportunity to understand and reach a new level of healing as a participant in the study. But by far the most powerful experiences were those of the participant co-researchers. Velvia said, "This is one of the neatest experiences of my life to date. This is the coolest thing; it's important stuff." Megan captured the experiences of the co-analysts in a particularly powerful way:

> Your interest and invitation to be in the role of participant co-researcher communicated to me that you liked me and respected me. ... As I thought about what was important about it all, I think the thing that was so powerful in terms of empowerment was participating in the grounded theory-generating process. That was the key to the empowerment. It wasn't really the ten weeks. It was really the five of us. I am an individual voice in all other settings. The group provided some support, but was still a collection of individual voices. ... But the participant co-researcher analytic process was a shared voice, a shared paradigm. It provided a system into which my experience fit that I had a part in creating. That creates the experience of being understood.
>
> The amount of, just, honor and respect—it's just not like anything I've ever experienced, Sue. The research is also ... it rings true .... You have done something really extraordinary. It's so much more than a dissertation. ... Honor and respect. That's what we all lost. Reading it was an experience of that. It's touching the place I've been protecting, I think—the place I'm afraid to open up, even to myself. It's the place that believes I'm honorable, worth knowing. It's the place that's protected

by thick spiraling cords coiled like a snake around a core that's truly loved and honored. It's the place that yearns to be told in a voice that resonates with foreverness, "I love you."

A RETURN TO VOICE: THE JOURNEY OF THE RESEARCHER

My own story is that of my experiences as I conducted this research. What is relevant to how this research came into being and evolved are the ways in which I survived and coped with the repeated reminders of my own abuse as I conducted the research. Conducting the interviews and group sessions, I began protecting myself in the ways that I usually do when counseling abuse survivors: I maintained a certain emotional distance from what women were saying, and I promptly forgot their stories of abuse once the interview or group had ended. Over the years in which I have been conducting therapy with abuse survivors, I have had to keep extensive case notes to remember details of the survivors' experiences. Similarly, I depended upon my audiotapes and field notes to recall the experiences of the research participants. I was so well buffered against my own feelings about abuse that I was frequently surprised when the participants asked me how I was feeling.

When I began transcribing and analyzing the data in earnest, I discovered that I had shifted my emphasis from recording information and impressions to searching actively for the constructions of the research participants. As I searched for the meanings of the participants, I experienced deeper levels of empathy than I had allowed myself when I first heard their stories. I was no longer buffered! I wrote these memos during and just after transcribing Liz's interview:

> . . . a plethora of thoughts and feelings as I listen to and type this transcript. My own body reaction is of nausea. I had forgotten much of this abuse since the interview, as is the case with many of the abuse stories I have heard. . . . The predominant feeling is of being overwhelmed that people can do such things to children. I am closer to the story tonight than when I heard it may be because I am defended when I expect to hear abuse stories, but just typing I was not. I don't know.

Despite the strain involved in being immersed in stories of abuse, survival, and coping for more than 17 months, the process of self-reflection became very rewarding. When my peer research team challenged me about the absence of my voice in my early drafts of the manuscript, I realized that I had silenced myself, in part to avoid facing what it might mean to be truly open as an author of this research. Therefore, I reclaimed my own voice as part of the story of this research.

VOICES: REFLECTION AND CONFIRMATION

Letting go of this project was a relief. The hours, days, weeks, and months during which I immersed myself in this work were demanding, sometimes painful, and always challenging. I was sickened as I learned more clearly what cruelties human beings are capable of perpetrating on those less powerful than themselves. I wept as I saw grief, pain, and terror in the eyes of women I grew to love. I wanted to hide the past behind the present and forget that these women I knew had actually been babies and little girls when their bodies, minds, and spirits were violated.

I had originally chosen the metaphor of "voice" to illustrate the work of this research. Not wanting to influence the direction of the research, I had laid the metaphor aside. My reexamination of tapes and transcripts verifies that I did not initiate "voice" talk during the investigation, either in individual or group settings. However, the day I defended my dissertation, Lauren, one of the participant co-researchers, presented me with a framed poem she had written:

A Voice, My Voice

A Voice
Rings loud and strong
Not my voice
That of a man; or should I say boy
Mean, rough
Don't move, Don't tell, Don't cry
He yelled!
Another voice
Quiet, frightened
Smothered with a hand
Still screaming, silent
Help me!
Why can't anyone hear me?
My Voice?
Not a voice at all.
He hurt me more
Each time I cried
The pain lay deep inside
A knife, a strange fire.
I learned not to cry
Not to speak
Shh ... don't bother
Who the hell knows
Where's my mother or father?
Silence became easier
Years pushed memories
Deeper and deeper inside
Left in a room

Echoing darkness
Feelings too, are stored, abandoned
Seemingly left a mystery ...
She came along
No coincidence; I'm sure
Some sort of incest survivors group
Me involved?
Why should I care?
With her pen in hand
Eyes kind and compassionate
I heard a voice
Soft and reassuring
Determined, motivated
A Voice, Her Voice.
After a while
My silence was lifted
Anger, sadness, and pain surfaced
Not his voice; MY VOICE
Louder and stronger.
No more, will I be silent
My tears
Now flow freely
A gift from a woman
Inspiring, moving
A Voice, My Voice
No longer a mystery.
The thought of the noise
What power, how precious
Both yelling and crying
Sadness—reality
More joy—freedom
As you share with others
Your gift, Your voice.
Softly I thank You
  With deep love
  In MY Voice.

HONOR AND RESPECT: REFLECTIONS ON THE STUDY RESULTS

The multiple strategies engaged to gather data for this study and to analyze the data enhanced rigor, yielded richness and depth, and honored the different communication styles of participants as well as their varying interests in the ongoing process of analysis. Because the lens through which I observed and inquired was one that valued strengths and viewed "symptoms" as coping strategies, I believe the results reflect my respect for participants as well as the honesty and mutuality described earlier. In addition, the integration of the various strategies for gathering and analyzing data enabled me to probe deeply the meanings of individual participants while embracing the larger societal context that has spawned abuse and silenced its victims. The centrality of *voice* throughout the study reflects the importance to participants of breaking that silence and underscores the value of eliciting the stories of survivors.

DISCUSSION

Returning to this research many years after its completion has been a remarkable experience. First, I am still in love with it. The design is one I have drawn on repeatedly because of its effectiveness in gathering rich, meaningful data as well as establishing empowering relationships with research participants. I have found it difficult at times to arrange ongoing focus groups because I have conducted research out of state, where it is impossible to meet more than once or twice with a given group of participants. I find that, as people's lives become busier, it is impossible to expect of participants the duration and intensity of participation that was possible when I conducted this study. I do continue to meet with peer research groups and to attempt to contextualize my research by investigating with participants the historical context of their experiences and setting what I learn from them in a sociopolitical context.

The research changed forever how I do therapy with survivors of abuse. I frequently compared Sue the researcher with Sue the therapist and realized that what I had come to know about the research process was changing my approach to therapy. I now listen less for what isn't being said and more for what my clients mean. My focus on positive coping strategies has proved to be exceptionally empowering for clients. I frequently hear clients themselves assess their own behaviors as good coping strategies that are not as effective anymore. In group therapy, they congratulate one another for successes with statements such as, "What a warrior!" The implications of this research for therapists working with abuse survivors are that it is important to step out of the box of traditional psychotherapeutic perspectives on pathology and ground our work in a feminist therapeutic approach (e.g., Brown, 1994).

Most important is what I want to do in the future. In my future research I want to return to the model described in this chapter, doing longer term focus groups and participant co-analysis. In addition, I would like to explore avenues for participant observation that will further contextualize my work. Juxtaposing this chapter with the article I first wrote from the research (Morrow and Smith, 1995) reminds me just how much I silenced my own voice to publish in a prestigious journal, how much I decontextualized the research. I would like to have the courage to reclaim my voice in my writing as I have done in this chapter. I believe we qualitative researchers in psychology are continually confronted with challenges and choices about how we present ourselves and our research. We are confronted with dilemmas of credibility when we are deeply honest with ourselves and our audience. However, the personal rewards of this kind of honesty can be immeasurable, and our research gains richness from our self-reflection. This is no exercise in narcissism. Rather, we are committing ourselves to a process in which the researcher-as-instrument is clearly defined, our assumptions and biases are clearly stated so that the reader may assess our interpretations, and the voices of our participants may be heard clearly and distinctly.

Finally, I want to pursue what it fully means to empower research participants. What are the limits of equality in the participatory process? How might participants have even greater ownership of the research? As Michelle Fine (1992) articulated:

> I have to acknowledge the emergence of a new generation of epistemological dilemmas: What makes this research? When does intervention stop and reflection begin? How do I/we "know" what I/we "know?" What are our grounds for disproof? What are the limits of collaboration? And what are the bases for shared censorship? Herein grows the delicious next generation of feminist research dilemmas/possibilities. (p. 230)

REFERENCES

Adler, P. A., and P. Adler. (1987). *Membership roles in field research.* Newbury Park, CA: Sage.

Armstrong, L. (1978). *Kiss daddy goodnight: A speak-out on incest.* New York: Hawthorne.

Atkey, B. (November 7 1925). Dimity gay, grandpa's little maid. *Saturday Evening Post,* pp. 3–5, 161, 164, 166, 169.

Barringer, C. E. (1992). Breaking silence about childhood sexual abuse: The survivor's voice. *National Women's Studies Association Journal, 4,* 4–22.

Bass, E., and L. Davis. (1988). *The courage to heal: A guide for women survivors of child sexual abuse.* New York: Harper & Row.

Belenky, M. F., B. M. Clinchy, N. R. Goldberger, and J. M. Tarule. (1986). *Women's ways of knowing: The development of self, voice, and mind.* New York: Basic Books.

Briere, J. N. (1992). *Child abuse trauma: Theory and treatment of the lasting effects.* Newbury Park, CA: Sage.

Brown, L. S. (1994). *Subversive dialogues: Theory in feminist therapy.* New York: Basic Books.

Brown, L. M., and C. Gilligan. (1992). *Meeting at the crossroads: Women's psychology and girls' development.* Cambridge, MA: Harvard University Press.

Erickson, F. (1986). Qualitative methods in research on teaching. In Wittrock, M. C. (Ed.). *Handbook of research on teaching* (3rd ed., pp. 119–161). New York: Macmillan.

Fine, M. (1992). *Disruptive voices: The possibilities of feminist research.* Ann Arbor: University of Michigan Press.

Fine, M. (1994). Dis-stance and other stances: Negotiations of power inside feminist research. In Gitlin, A. (Ed.). *Power and method: Political activism and educational research* (pp. 13–35). New York: Routledge.

Freespirit, J. (1982). *Daddy's girl: An incest survivor's story*. Langlois, OR: Diaspora Press.

Geertz, C. (1973). *The interpretation of cultures: Selected essays* (pp. 3–30). New York: Basic Books.

Gilligan, C. (1982). *In a different voice: Psychological theory and women's development.* Cambridge, MA: Harvard University Press.

Glaser, B. G., and A. L. Strauss. (1967). *The discovery of grounded theory: Strategies for qualitative research.* New York: Aldine.

Guba, E. G., and Y. S. Lincoln. (1989). *Fourth generation evaluation.* Newbury Park, CA: Sage.

Herman, J. L. (1997). *Trauma and recovery: The aftermath of violence—from domestic abuse to political terror.* New York: Basic Books.

Kitzinger, C., and R. Perkins. (1993). *Changing our minds: Lesbian feminism and psychology.* New York: New York University Press.

Kurtzman, S., and V. Elder. (1976). Little Annie Fanny. *Playboy, 1 March*, pp. 243–245.

Lather, P. (1991). *Getting smart: Feminist research and pedagogy with/in the postmodern.* New York: Routledge.

Lincoln, Y. S., and E. G. Guba. (1985). *Naturalistic inquiry.* Beverly Hills: Sage.

Maguire, P. (1987). *Doing participatory research: A feminist approach.* Amherst, MA: University of Massachusetts.

Maher, M. (1999). Relationship-based change: A feminist qualitative research case. In Kopala, M., and L. A. Suzuki. (Eds.). *Using qualitative methods in psychology* (pp. 187–198). Thousand Oaks, CA: Sage.

Mahoney, M. J. (1991). *Human change processes: The scientific foundations of psychotherapy.* New York: Basic Books.

McLellan, B. (1999). The prostitution of psychotherapy: A feminist critique. *British Journal of Guidance & Counselling, 27*, 325–337.

Morgan, D. L., and R. A. Krueger. (1993). When to use focus groups and why. In Morgan, D. L. (Ed.). *Successful focus groups: Advancing the state of the art* (pp. 3–19). Newbury Park, CA: Sage.

Morrow, S. L. (1992). *Voices: Constructions of survival and coping by women survivors of child sexual abuse.* Unpublished doctoral dissertation. Tempe: Arizona State University.

Morrow, S. L., and M. L. Smith. (1995). Constructions of survival and coping by women who have survived childhood sexual abuse. *Journal of Counseling Psychology, 42*, 24–33.

Morrow, S. L., and M. L. Smith. (2000). Qualitative research for counseling psychology. In Brown, S. D., and R. W. Lent. (Eds.). *Handbook of counseling psychology* (3rd ed., pp. 199–230). New York: Wiley.

Pipher, M. (2002). Healing wisdom: The universals of human resilience. *Psychotherapy Networker, Jan/Feb*, 59–61.

Polkinghorne, D. E. (1988). *Narrative knowing and the human sciences.* Albany, NY: State University of New York Press.

Pope, K. S., and L. S. Brown. (1996). *Recovered memories of abuse: Assessment, therapy, forensics.* Washington, DC: American Psychological Association.

Reinharz, S. (1992). *Feminist methods in social science research.* New York: Oxford University Press.

Roberts, H. (Ed.). (1981). *Doing feminist research.* London: Routledge & Kegan Paul.

Roderick, L. (Songwriter). (1990). *If you see a dream.* Anchorage: Turtle Island Records.

Russell, D. E. H. (1986). *The secret trauma: Incest in the lives of girls and women.* New York: Basic Books.

Sacks, H. (1984). On doing "being ordinary." In Atkinson, J. M., and J. Heritage. (Eds.). *Structures of social action: Studies in conversation analysis* (pp. 413–429). Cambridge: Cambridge University Press.

Sarton, M. (1980). A voice. In *Halfway to silence*. New York: W. W. Norton.
Spradley, J. P. (1979). *The ethnographic interview*. New York: Holt, Rinehart and Winston.
Stanley, L., and S. Wise. (1983). *Breaking out: Feminist consciousness and feminist research*. London: Routledge & Kegan Paul.
Strauss, A., and J. Corbin. (1990). *Basics of qualitative research: Grounded theory procedures and techniques*. Newbury Park, CA: Sage.
Strauss, A., and J. Corbin. (1998). *Basics of qualitative research: Techniques and procedures for developing grounded theory* (2nd ed.). Thousand Oaks, CA: Sage.

BIOGRAPHICAL BACKGROUND

SUSAN L. MORROW, PhD, is an associate professor and program director of the Counseling Psychology Program at the University of Utah, where she has taught since 1993. Her educational journey was strongly affected by her experiences as an activist in the civil rights, peace, feminist, and lesbian/gay/bisexual (LGB) movements beginning in the 1960s, when she was an undergraduate at Concordia Teachers College and then a Lutheran elementary school teacher. She completed her master of counseling degree at Arizona State University (ASU) and worked as a feminist therapist for many years before returning to ASU for her PhD in counseling psychology, graduating in 1992. During her doctoral program, her feminism, which had pervaded her work as a counselor, strongly influenced her development as a researcher and academician.

While at Utah, she has seen her role as affecting social change within the academic environment through her research, teaching, and clinical supervision. As a feminist multicultural scholar, she has focused her research on survival and coping of women survivors of childhood sexual abuse, academic climate for graduate women students of color, work and career development of LGB people and women with HIV, and feminist therapy. In addition, her scholarship addresses LGB and women's concerns more broadly, recently in the area of religious conflict of people with same-sex attractions and feminist multicultural counseling for social justice. A primary focus of her scholarship is qualitative research methodology, and she is the author of two handbook chapters on qualitative methods as well as guest co-editor with Beth Haverkamp and Joe Ponterotto of a special issue of *Journal of Counseling Psychology* on qualitative research.

Dr. Morrow has been active professionally as coordinator of two national Association for Women in Psychology (AWP) conferences (Phoenix and Salt Lake City), as well as having served as chair of the Section for the Advancement of Women of the Society of Counseling Psychology (American Psychological Association Division 17). Her awards include the APA Counseling Division's Fritz and Linn Kuder Early Career Scientist–Practitioner Award, the AWP Christine Ladd–Franklin Award, and the APA Committee on Women in Psychology Emerging Leader Award.

7

An Empirical, Phenomenological Study: Being Joyful

Brent Robbins

EDITOR'S INTRODUCTION

Dr. Robbins takes us on a scholarly but lively review of the literature on joy, differentiating it from "subjective well-being" and introducing us to the debates about the nature of emotion. He cites not only research literature but the poet William Blake and philosophers such as Jean-Paul Sartre and Quentin Smith.

He makes a case for the necessity of grounding qualitative research in experience, and spells out related philosophical considerations, including the character and role of hermeneutics. He guides us through the usual steps of data analysis in empirical phenomenological research.

As he introduces his own study, Robbins explains that most qualitative researchers rely on participants' remote recall of events, which is dependent on their current state. Hence he introduces an innovation, using an adapted version of Scheier's psychotherapeutic *imagery in movement method*, to put participants in embodied touch with their experiences of being joyful. Specifically, he asked participants to create color drawings to indicate "what it means to be joyful." They verbally conveyed their felt sense of drawing (and of the drawing), and Robbins noted their expressive gestures throughout. Next, each participant role-played a particular story of joy from the past. Following these activities, the participants wrote descriptions of their experience of joy.

From his analysis of these descriptions, Robbins presents 16 themes, each illustrated with data from all participants. I found myself smiling broadly, and gesturing as the participants had, as the themes evoked my own past joyful moments. A general structure then presents all the themes in their interrelations. Robbins closes the chapter with a return to the reviewed literature and a discussion of surprises to him and for our understanding of being joyful.

During the last 30 years, psychology journals have published more than 45,000 articles on depression, yet only 400 on joy (Hall, 1998). As Seligman (1998) has argued, there has been a bias favoring the research of negative emotion in psychology. Positive experiences such as joy are viewed as mere coping mechanisms and negative experiences are believed to be authentic. Yet, if psychology is to have any authority for articulating the "good life," it must take seriously the effort to investigate empirically those human experiences that "lead to well-being, to positive individuals, and to thriving communities" (Seligman and Csikszentmihalyi, 2000). The investigation of the emotion of joy is indispensable if such a mission is to be accomplished; hence, my study on being joyful aims to begin filling a gap in the literature where the emotion of joy has been ignored.

When Martin Seligman became president of the American Psychological Association, he helped launch the "positive psychology" movement (Seligman and Csikszentmihalyi, 2000). Within a few short years, the field witnessed a virtual renaissance of ideas and research on various aspects of human well-being, including the publication of various edited volumes on positive psychology (e.g., Aspinwall and Staudinger, 2002; Keyes and Haidt, 2002; Linley and Joseph, 2004; Lopez and Snyder, 2003; Snyder and Lopez, 2002). The positive psychology movement is built upon the premise that psychology has tended to neglect the study of human well-being in favor of researching human disease. The movement consists of "three pillars": the study of (1) positive subjective experiences, (2) positive individual characteristics (strengths and virtues), and (3) positive institutions and positive communities.

In his interviews with the press, Seligman (1998) has continuously used "joy" as an example of what he means by "positive subjective experiences." But, since the birth of the positive psychology movement, have we come much farther in our understanding of joy? Before we can address this question, we must first ask what "joy" means and whether it differs from what psychologists have called "subjective well-being" (SWB; e.g., Diener, Emmons, Larsen, and Griffin, 1985a; Myers, 1992).

JOY AND SUBJECTIVE WELL-BEING

SWB is a construct that refers to the way people evaluate their lives (Diener, Suh, and Oishi, 1997; Diener and Lucas, 2000). In the measurement of SWB, the instruments account for a person's cognitive assessment of his or her life, the frequencies with which he or she experiences pleasant emotions (e.g., joy), and the frequency with which he or she experiences unpleasant emotions (e.g., sadness, anger; Andrews and Withey, 1976). Although the cognitive and affective components of SWB can be separated (Lucas, Diener, and Suh, 1996), they are highly correlated. Therefore, the SWB construct represents a "higher order" of "happiness," which accounts for both components (Diener and Lucas, 2000; Kozma, 1996). When compared with others, a person with high SWB will tend to report relatively more satisfaction with life, more frequent positive emotions, and less frequent negative emotions (Diener et al., 1997). SWB, in this sense, is a unique measure of happiness because it accounts for undesirable as well as desirable states and because its measurement depends solely upon the participant's own, experience-based self-evaluation. Moreover, SWB is a construct that is exclusively interested in the assessment of a person's affect or mood *over a period of time*, not momentary emotional states (Diener et al., 1997).

In contrast to studies of SWB, the study of joy is concerned with the experience of the momentary, emotional state of joy. Although affective traits may influence affective traits, the study of emotional traits is performed on a different level of analysis than the study of emotional states (Rosenberg, 1998). Indeed, it is conceivable that a person could have relatively low self-reported SWB while still having periodic experiences of joy. Lucas and Diener (1998) found that SWB tends to be predicted by the frequency but not the intensity of a person's affect. Research has tended to support the hypothesis that people who report intense positive emotions also tend to report intense negative emotions (Diener, Larsen, Levine, and Emmons, 1985b; Larsen and Diener, 1987; Schimmack and Diener, 1997). If these findings are accurate, it is possible for a person to score relatively low on a measure of SWB yet still have intense experiences of joy.

Because SWB does contain a measure of the frequency of joy, research on SWB may still offer some insight into the potential structure of joy, and it may also suggest hypotheses for predicting antecendents of joy. Cognition is one variable to consider. Studies suggest it is possible for people to manipulate their own cognitions to intensify or dull their emotional experiences (Gross, 2002; Larsen, Diener, and Cropanzano, 1987). For example, people may be capable, in some circumstances, of interpreting apparently "neutral" events as positive. Researchers have found that participants scoring high in SWB are more likely to interpret ambiguous events in a positive way (Lyubormirsky and Ross, 1999; Seidlitz and Diener, 1993). If these findings were to generalize to experiences of the state of joy, we would expect to find at least some people who experience joy in response to ambiguous events.

McCrae and Costa (1986) found that people who tend to be happy are more likely to use a variety of effective coping mechanisms, including positive reappraisal, spirituality (prayer), problem-focused coping, and seeking help from others. In contrast, unhappy people were more likely to engage in magical thinking, to externalize and/or internalize blame, and to cope through avoidance. Happy people, even when under stress, tend to remain actively engaged in the struggle to cope, whereas unhappy people have a tendency to disengage either through rumination (cognitions of blame, fantasy) or diversion (avoidance). Perhaps, then, we might expect joy to occur when people are actively engaged in the world. Indeed, people with high SWB tend to be extraverted (Diener, Sandvik, Pavot, and Fujita, 1992). Thus, we would expect joy to occur when a person is engaged in the kind of actively engaged behaviors characteristic of the extravert.

Because religious people have high SWB (Ellison, 1991; Myers, 1992; Pollner, 1989), we might expect joy to occur in response to religious events or perhaps even to contain classically religious or spiritual themes. Also, research suggests that people with SWB tend to be more optimistic and to have higher self-esteem compared with people with lower SWB scores (Diener et al., 1992). Consequently, we might expect people to have experiences of joy at times when they feel hope; that is, when they are able to envision a pathway to achieve their goals and when they believe they have the agency to transverse that pathway (Curry, Snyder, Cook, Ruby, and Rehm, 1997; Snyder, Harris, Anderson, Holleran, Irving, and Sigmon et al., 1991). Likewise, we might find that people are more likely to experience joy when they have experiences of pride. Indeed, Parecki (quoted in Lazarus, 1991) has defined high self-esteem as "pride in oneself in which one becomes aware and accepting of one's imperfections while cherishing one's inherent strengths and positive qualities" (p. 441). In experiences of joy, therefore, we would expect to find that the person feels personally affirmed for their positive qualities and/or accepted for their negative qualities.

Joy research may also glean some insight from various theories about the motivational basis for SWB (for a review, see Diener et al., 1997). Although Veenhoven (1991) argues that SWB results from the satisfaction of basic, universal needs, context theories of SWB argue that the antecedents of SWB vary depending on the temporal and/or social context of the person's experience. Context theories of SWB include the adaptation theory, the social comparison theory, and the telic theory. Adaptation theory suggests that SWB changes in relation to a person's past. If a person has become habituated to a positive event, it will no longer influence SWB. However, a person who experiences a positive life-changing event will be more likely to display an increase in SWB. For example, we might expect lottery winners to be happier than others, yet they are not (Brickman, Coates, and Janoff-Bulman, 1978), a finding that implies that lottery winners eventual habituate to the positive experience of their windfall. The social comparison theory argues that SWB is relative to a person's social position in his or her given social–cultural context. For example, Easterlin (1974) argues that differences in SWB are the result of social comparisons within nations, not between nations. Finally, telic theories hold that SWB is a consequence of achieving personal goals and needs. The theory holds, further, that personal goals and needs do not have to be universal to affect SWB and in fact they tend to differ from person to person as a function of their values and desires (Diener, 1984).

The universal need theory and contextual theories of SWB raise questions about the causal antecedents of joy. If Veenhoven's (1991) theory is correct, we would expect people to experience joy mainly in response to the satisfaction of basic, universal human needs. For example, Aube and Senteni (1996) have contended that emotions function to motivate a "need to belong," which in evolutionary terms functions to facilitate adaptive social relations. If so, we would expect joy to erupt mainly in the context of social relationships.

Adaptational theory predicts that joy is most likely to occur for people who are undergoing positive, life-transforming experiences. It predicts, further, that joy should occur less often in response to recurring positive events. In other words, joy should be elicited more often by novel, positive events. Neuroscientific evidence lends some support to the adaptational theory. For example, when participants were shown repeated images of emotional faces, functional magnetic resonance imaging measures found neurological correlates to the decreasing salience of the repetitious stimuli (Feinstein, Goldin, Stein, Brown, and Paulus, 2002). In particular, they found that brain areas responsive to attention became increasingly habituated and sensitized to the pictures.

Based on social comparison theories, we may hypothesize that people are more likely to experience joy when they engage in downward social comparisons and, vice versa, that people are unlikely to experience joy when comparing upward. As we might expect, previous research has found that people who engage in upward comparisons tend to display an increase in negative mood whereas those who engage in downward comparisons tend to have an elevation in mood (Wheeler and Miyake, 1992).

Finally, in conjunction with telic theories of SWB, we would expect people to experience joy only in response to the achievement of goals that reflect their individual values and desires. Carver and Scheier (1990) have argued that positive affect will increase or decrease in relation to the standard rate at which a person is approaching his or her goals. For example, Brunstein (1993) found that SWB was highest for those participants who had both a high commitment to a goal and a sense that they were making progress toward that goal. Likewise, joy may be more intense and/or more frequent in cases when persons make progress toward a goal to which they have committed themselves.

Although these need and contextual theories of SWB and joy are productive for the purpose of generating hypotheses about the causal antecedents of joy, they do not shed much light on the experiential structure of joy. What is it like for a person to experience joy? How does the world (e.g., self, body, others, things, time, space) appear to those who are swept up in joy? If the need and contextual theories do not directly address these questions, one might argue that they do not especially illuminate the *meaning* of joy. As Smith (1986) and Robbins (2003) have argued, philosophy and the sciences have had a tendency to reduce the meanings of emotion to their causal antecedents or, in some cases, to their purposes. Yet, along with arousal, reflection, and expression, experience is an essential component of emotion (Kennedy–Moore and Watson, 1999). When we are in the throws of an emotional episode, whether positive or negative, the meaning of the emotion is revealed to us primarily through our temporally unfolding world and through our relation to others as we engage with things of relative importance to our lives. In our everyday lives, the experience of emotion is the closest to us of all the components of emotion, yet in the psychological research literature, it is the component of emotion that remains the most undeveloped.

THE QUESTION OF THE MEANING OF JOY

If we look to the literature on the structure of positive and negative emotions, we find the literature rife with controversy. Frijda (1999) has defined emotion as composed of five essential aspects: affect, appraisal, action readiness, autonomic arousal, and cognitive changes. On the other hand, Fredrickson (1998) rejects the idea that emotions—positive emotions in particular—have action tendencies. According to Lazarus (1991), the emotion process contains six appraisal components. Three are primary and three are secondary. The primary components include goal relevance, goal congruence or incongruence, and the type of ego involvement. The secondary appraisal components include blame or credit, coping potential, and future expectations (pp. 168–169). Yet Lazarus' model rests on the primary assumption that all emotions are necessarily goal directed. Turner and Ortony (1990) even suggest that emotions need not be positively or negatively valenced. Among those who accept the premise that emotions are valenced, there remains disagreement regarding the nature of positive emotions. For example, Larsen and Diener (1992) contend that positive emotions should be defined by their pleasant valence. However, Lazarus (1991) argues that positive and negative emotions should be distinguished based on the relative goal congruence or goal incongruence of the eliciting event.

In dimensional approaches to the structure of emotion, factor analytical studies have revealed conflicting findings. Although some researchers have concluded that emotions can be described by two independent factors—pleasantness and arousal (Russell, 1980; Russell and Barrett, 1999)—others have contended that negative emotions are best described by the factors of high unpleasantness and arousal (Watson and Tellegen, 1985; Waston, Wiese, Vaidya, and Tellegen, 1999). Diener, Smith, and Fujita (1995) argue that pleasant emotion can be broken down into two types: joy and love. However, de Rivera and colleagues (1989) were able to distinguish between joy, elation, and gladness. Watson (2000), moreover, differentiated between three types of pleasant affect: joviality, self-assuredness, and attention. Although each of these factors are highly correlated (Diener et al., 1995; Fredrickson, 1998; Watson and Clark, 1992), it is not clear how best to define joy in distinction from general positive affect, love, or other similar constructs. To complicate matters, researchers continue an ongoing debate about the unresolved question of the independence of positive and negative emotions (Cacioppo, Gardner, and Berntson, 1999).

Fredrickson (1998, 2000) is an example of one researcher who has taken the initiative to reconceptualize the meaning of positive emotion, including joy. She points out that past approaches to emotion were based on general models of emotion. However, they were largely based on the research of negative emotions and therefore failed to do justice to the structure of positive emotions. In particular, she takes issue with the pervasive assumption that all emotions involve specific action tendencies (Frijda, 1986; Frijda, Kuipers, and Schure, 1989; Lazarus, 1991; Levenson, 1994; Oatley and Jenkins, 1996; Tooby and Cosmides, 1990). Positive emotions such as joy and contentment do not appear to have specific action tendencies (Fredrickson and Levenson, 1998). By disregarding the assumption that emotions elicit action tendencies, Fredrickson (1998) suggests that negative and positive emotions can be distinguished by the varied width of their respective thought–action repertoires. Although negative emotions are characterized by *narrow* repertoires, she suggests that positive emotions *broaden* a person's thought–action repertoire.

Fredrickson (2000) argues that joy shares with other positive emotions the tendency to broaden a person's intentional horizons. Her theory is supported by evidence that joy appears to occur in those who experience themselves in a safe and familiar environment (Izard, 1977), who are involved in an activity with little effort (Ellsworth and Smith, 1988), and, sometimes, in those who perceive themselves to be making progress toward a personal goal (Izard, 1977; Lazarus, 1991). A person who is in a state of joy is not oriented to achieve a particular instrumental task they appraise to be at stake, which is a hallmark of negative emotions such as anger and fear. In joy, rather, the person enters a state of play, an orientation that is open to the many possibilities at hand. Fredrickson (2000) argues that, from an evolutionary perspective, joy and other positive emotions are adaptive because they help the person to build vital physical, intellectual, and social resources. As she notes, "these new resources are durable, and can be drawn on later, long after the instigating experience of joy has been subsided" (p. 5). Research by Isen, Johnson, Mertz, and Robinson (1985) lends support to Fredrickson's "broaden and build model" of positive emotion. Given that positive emotions "broaden and build" a person's thought–action adaptive resources, it makes sense that positive emotions also increase innovative thinking, flexible cognition (Isen and Daubman, 1984), creativity (Isen, Daubman, and Nowicki, 1987), and receptivity (Estrada et al., 1997).

Fredrickson's "broaden and build model" of positive emotions is consistent with the psychoevolutionary model of emotion (Frank, 1988; Plutchik, 1980). Both stress that emotions serve a biologically adaptive function that ultimately serves a biologically rooted, instrumental purpose: survival. However, unlike the psychoevolutionary models of the past, Fredrickson does not assume that a biologically adaptive emotion must have an immediate, instrumental goal. An emotion such as joy can be phenomenologically aimless and without an immediate goal or purpose yet still serve long-term survival functions for the species.

Furthermore, as Fredrickson (2000) notes, the evolutionary model helps to explain why biological mechanisms appear on the scene, but we should not assume that an organism is therefore precluded from using that same biological mechanism for functions that are unrelated to its survival value. Humans adapted to a world in which food was scarce; thus, in our remote past, it was adaptive to eat sweet and fatty foods. Yet in a world in which sweet and fatty foods produce risks to survival, including diseases such as obesity and diabetes, the human desire for "comfort food" no longer serves the function nature intended (Weil, 2000). Likewise, it is highly probable that joy and other positive emotions, although once serving the ends of survival, now serve different purposes.

If we are to address adequately questions about the causal antecedents and functions (purposes) of joy, we must first develop a clearer, empirically grounded, experientially based understanding of the meaning of joy. If we can better define joy, then we are in a better position to assess what causes it and the functions it serves. An empirical–phenomenological approach to emotion provides a sensible approach to clarify what joy means to the people who experience it.

Phenomenological philosophers have paid some attention to joy. Jean-Paul Sartre's (1993) model of emotion made many of the same assumptions criticized by Fredrickson. Like the evolutionary–expressive theory of emotion, Sartre (1993) assumed that positive emotions, like negative emotions, served an instrumental purpose. In particular, he believed they were a form of "bad faith," an attempt to simplify or dedifferentiate a complex situation to cope with it. He concluded that emotions, including joy, are choices we make to avoid responsible action.

Sartre's theory of emotion must be understood in light of his view of the world. For Sartre, life is difficult. Emotion is a move away from responsibility to the extent that it serves the purpose of helping us to escape temporarily the difficulty of living. He assumed that a complex, differentiated life world was more authentic or real than a world experienced as simple and unambiguous. In short, he gave ontological priority to a world perceived to be complex, ambiguous, and difficult. Sartre felt joy to be a way of deluding ourselves into believing the world is good by avoiding a more complex view of the world that would include all the world's misery and pain. Lee (1979) contends, in contrast to Sartre, that the choice of joy does not necessarily imply a person is in "bad faith." The choice of joy, she argues, can also be construed as an "acceptance of the world" rather than a "denial of the world" (p. 70).

The notion that meaning of joy might be an "acceptance of the world" is implicit in William Blake's (1994) poem:

> He who bends to himself a Joy
> Doth the winged life destroy;
> But he who kisses the Joy as it flies
> Lives in Eternity's sunrise (p. 143)

Blake implies that joy is an experience that, like a delicate creature, cannot be captured intact. I interpret Blake to mean that joy resists attempts to pursue it in an instrumental fashion. To the extent that joy becomes the goal, it eludes us. If Blake's wonderful imagery captures a truth about joy, perhaps joy is an emotion that responds, not simply to a broader and more encompassing world, as Fredrickson's theory suggests, but more specifically to a world that is freely accepted *as it is*. If so, then Blake offers us a meaning for joy that stands in sharp contrast to Sartre's. Whereas Sartre understands emotion to serve the function of escape and avoidance, Blake's description suggests that joy is an affirmation of the world, including all its complexities and difficulty. In either case, an empirical–phenomenological investigation of joy might be instructive. If joy presents an oversimplified, "Pollyanna" view of the world, we would expect to find related themes in the data. But, on the other hand, if joy is an affirmation of the world, the data should reflect the affirmative theme instead.

Philosopher Quentin Smith (1986) has suggested that, when understood on their own terms, emotions reveal how the world is important to the experiencing person. In his own analysis of joy, Smith concludes that joy reveals the world as a fulfillment. The world is experienced, according to Smith, as "a plenum, a fullness, a positivity." One's self and the world "has what it needs to be fulfilled." Furthermore, he suggests that the feeling of joy is a sense of fullness in the present: "One is able to 'live in the present' and appreciate the present as a fullness in itself" (p. 152).

Smith's phenomenology of joy is consistent with de Rivera's (1988) analysis of joy. "In joy," writes de Rivera, "the self is realized or actualized. The person experiences his existence as meaningful, as coming closer to the self that he 'really' is" (p. 65). For de Rivera, joy is a feeling of fulfillment that involves the implicit instruction to "let it be." Rather than the willful calculating mentality of instrumental engagement with the world, and contrary to the escape–avoidant coping style of Sartre's "bad faith," the joyful person seems not to reduce things to their mere use–value nor does he or she perceive the world as an undifferentiated positive blob. Rather, he or she relinquishes the willful grasping after ends in a fulfilled presence in the world. Consistent with Buddhist philosophy, which associates grasping and craving with suffering, a nongrasping orientation to the world can lead to experiences of genuine joy (see, for example, Goldstein, 1987).

de Rivera's theory has been supported by a factor analytical study that was able to distinguish the emotions of joy, elation, and gladness (de Rivera, Possell, Varette, and Weiner, 1989). They found that joy, in contrast to elation and gladness, "occurs when there is a mutual meeting between the person and another, in which the other is perceived as unique"; furthermore, joy "functions to affirm the meaningfulness of life" (p. 1016). Elation and gladness, on the other hand, were concerned with particular goals. The former was concerned with unexpected attainment of fantasized goals, whereas the latter was focused on the expected attainment of goals.

The hypothetical qualities of joy outlined here appear to share some similarities to Csikszentmihalyi's (2000) concept of "flow." Like the descriptions of joy by Blake, Smith, and de Rivera, Csikszentmihalyi and

Larson (1984) described "flow" as a feeling of control that, paradoxically, happens when a person has given up trying to be in control. Isomorphic with this paradoxical control via a relinquishing of control is the "autotelic" character of one's task during flow. By calling the task *autotelic*, Csikzentmihalyi means that the task is an end in itself, rather than a means to some other end. The person engaged in the task is intrinsically motivated by the process of the task itself, not necessarily by a reward waiting at the end of the process. Other characteristics of "flow" include a sense of being so concentrated on a task that one feels completely immersed in it (Csikszentmihalyi, 2000), a forgetting of one's self (Csikszentmihalyi and Figurski, 1982), a feeling of transcendence, and a distortion of one's sense of time (Csikszentmihalhyi, 2000). If joy has the kind of non-instrumental character suggested by the literature, it may share some of the characteristics of flow.

I am inclined to understand flow as a subcategory of joy. Flow is fairly specific to largely solitary tasks that typically have pragmatic purposes (e.g., work). What makes flow unique, from my perspective, is that it involves the paradoxical transformation of the meaning of work to that of play. By comparison, an experience of joy does not seem to require such a transformation, nor does joy seem to rule out such a transformation. If Fredrickson's (1988) theory is correct, the experience of joy gives rise to a playful orientation to the world. Such a playful orientation need not arise from a work environment, although it certainly can and seems to do so during the experience of flow. In any case, the empirical–phenomenological study of joy has the benefit of clarifying these finer points, particularly given the fact that Csikszentmihalyi (2000) also derived his theory of flow using a qualitative, phenomenological method of research.

At this point, theories of joy remain speculative. If we can ever hope to understand joy properly, the construct must first be grounded in lived, human experience. Only then will we be in the position to develop more confidently measures to quantify the construct of joy. Based on the literature, we confront the data with some expectations that may or may not come to be confirmed by the data. If the "broaden and build model" is correct, we expect to see themes in the data that reflect a broadening of thought and action and a sense of playfulness. If the structure of joy includes a noninstrumental, "autotelic" orientation in the world, we expect to find themes of joy such as an acceptance of the world and personal feelings of fulfillment, meaning, and mutual meeting with others. Likewise, as in flow, we expect to find themes that reflect the paradox of achieving a sense of autonomy and control precisely when control has been relinquished, when the person has forgotten him- or herself, and when the person is actively immersed in the experiential world. On the other hand, we would not expect to see themes that focus on striving toward personal goals, downward social comparisons, or attempts to escape or avoid difficult, complex circumstances.

PHILOSOPHICAL RESEARCH CONSIDERATIONS

As the majority of researchers on emotion agree, emotion appears to occur, at least initially, at a tacit, preconscious or even "unconscious" level of awareness (e.g., Arnold, 1960; Greenberg and Safran, 1984; Lazarus, 1982; Plutchik, 1980; Watts, 1983). In this sense, emotional experience appears to emerge from an intuitive, "felt sense" prior to explicit conscious awareness (e.g., Gendlin, 1981; Greenberg and Safran, 1987).

The notion that emotion begins at a preverbal lived or "felt sense" accords with my orientation as a scholar–practitioner situated within a phenomenological approach to psychological events. According to Merleau–Ponty (1962), human beings come to know things by first having a hold on them within a given horizon. Phenomena that are ambiguous and indeterminate take on a determinate form in our grasp of them. In turn, the body as a lived body—as an opening onto a world—both shapes and is shaped by things in the world.

Any particular research method or "approach" to given phenomena will always already circumscribe the ways in which the phenomena being researched may show itself. Hence, phenomena being researched will exceed the grasp of any given research method or approach. In this sense, the researcher and the researched can be understood as in a subject–object dialogue. W. Fischer (1974) refers to such a research–researched dialogue as "the dialectical process of research."

What is more, the presuppositions and preconceptions of the researcher exceed the researcher's determinate grasp as well. The method itself, which most often precedes the researcher and which has its own unfolding history and tradition, brings with it the "embedded ideas" (e.g., epistemological presuppositions) from which it arose (Slife and Williams, 1995). Whether the researcher is explicitly aware of them, the method is already tacitly circumscribing how the researched may be approached and thus how it will appear (Berman, 1981; Polanyi, 1958, 1969; Robbins, 1998, 2001). The method as part of the "equipment" of an approach to research never arrives at a phenomenon without also influencing how the phenomenon will appear and be understood (Kuhn, 1962; Robbins, 1998, 2001; Rouse, 1982). At the same time, the phenomenon cannot appear as something to be understood unless it is first approached.

The idea that the researcher is not a passive recorder of external, objective events is an idea that differs from empiricist epistemological perspectives. A hermeneutic–phenomenological approach understands the circularity of researcher/method–researched not as a vicious circle (e.g., the method provides an insurmountable bias that denies any access to the truth of a phenomenon), but as the only way to gain access to a phenomenon. Rather than a barrier, it is an entry point to a "hermeneutic circle" (Heidegger, 1927/1962; Packer and Addison, 1989; Robbins, 2000).

The concept of the "hermeneutic circle" can be found in Heidegger's (1962) early work. Human understanding for Heidegger always arises within the constraints of a "forestructure," "some preliminary understanding of what kind of phenomenon [is being understood], and of what possible things might happen to it" (Packer and Addison, 1989, p. 33). However, the forestructure is not an impediment for research, but rather the very framework that permits the researcher to move forward into his or her interpretation of the phenomenon. If inquiry is a circle, the forestructure is the forward arc of the circle. But to be a complete circle, a hermeneutic circle, the method cannot stop there. The encounter with a phenomenon within that forestructure leads us on a path of return—the reverse arc of the circle—wherein an evaluation of the forestucture itself becomes part of the research. To put it a different way, the indeterminate, ambiguous object under investigation is formed and shaped by the way in which we grasp it. But as the object becomes determinate in our grasping of it, the object acts back upon the method to shape it further to conform better to the contours of the phenomenon. For a method to submit properly to the hermeneutic circle, the researcher must allow the method to remain pliable enough that it can be molded to fit better the phenomenon under investigation.

If method is a matter of good "fit," it is difficult to know in advance how well a method will fit with the phenomenon under investigation. What can be done, however, is the task of explicating the forestructure as much as possible in advance. The literature review portion of this research study is an attempt to describe the process of arriving at a preliminary understanding of the lived experience of being joyful. I also attempted to articulate how current models of emotion had not adequately accounted for the possibility that joy might be a feeling of fulfillment in the present. The task of this section, therefore, is to describe a method or approach that allows joy to become evident as fulfillment as opposed to a means to an instrumental end.

A method that would seem to fit best the study of emotion would be a method that permits the research participants to discover the meaning of emotion as emerging more and more explicitly from an ambiguous felt sense. Phenomenological method seems particularly suited for studying the emotions. Of course, to determine the relative "fit" of the method is something that cannot be fully addressed until the researcher puts the method into practice. In the act of engaging the hermeneutic circle, the researcher must be open enough to be surprised when the phenomenon does not fit so well, and must also be willing to modify the method to fit better the phenomenon as it emerges. This is the essence of the "dialectical" approach to research that defines the practice of hermeneutic–phenomenological research.

METHODS

In searching for a method, at least two steps are necessary. First, one must decide the means by which the data will be collected. Second, one must choose a method of interpretation. When choosing a method of interpretation, I decided to use the "protocol analysis" method, developed by Giorgi (1970, 1971, 1975, 1985a,b) and Fischer (1974, 1985) at Duquesne University. However, with regard to data collection, I decided to use an innovative approach, originally designed for therapy, called *the imagery in movement method* (Schneier, 1989).

Because protocol analysis historically precedes my method of data collection, I chose to organize my methods according to historical rather than procedural chronology. Thus, I will first discuss analysis before describing data collection. My deviation from the standard approach to data collection is based on a mild criticism of protocol analysis. Hence, my utilization of Schneier's (1989) imagery in movement method is unprecedented and was selected as a means to perfect and overcome what I perceive to be shortcomings of protocol analysis for the study of emotion. Schneier's method was originally conceived as a therapeutic technique. Although she suggests the tool might be useful for research, I found it was necessary to modify the method for the purposes of data collection.

METHOD OF DATA ANALYSIS: PROTOCOL ANALYSIS

I chose the method of protocol analysis for a variety of reasons. The first and most obvious reason is because I am trained in protocol analysis. As a doctoral student at Duquesne University, I learned the Giorgi/Fischer method of data analysis, as well as other hermeneutic approaches, in a research course. Second, and more important, during the past three decades protocol analysis has been successfully applied to the study of a variety of emotions, including anxiety (Fischer, 1974, 1991), anger (Fischer, 1998; Frankel, 1985; Stevick, 1984), and boredom (Bargdill, 2000). Finally, and most persuasive for me, is the fact that protocol analysis as a method emerged from a phenomenological approach.

Essentially, protocol analysis involves a rigorous approach to interpreting texts. Although from a hermeneutic standpoint anything can be interpreted like a text, protocol analysis has been specifically designed to analyze written and verbal reports or "protocols." Typically, a uniform request is formulated by the researcher, and that same request is given to all research participants. For example, in his research of self-deception, Fischer (1985) requested that participants describe a situation in which they had tried to deceive themselves. He then asked them to describe how they had come to realize they had been trying to deceive themselves (p. 139). Participants wrote a verbal report, and, when Fischer read the reports, he followed up by interviewing each participant. To be sure that he understood the more ambiguous sections of the protocols, Fischer asked an open-ended question to elicit further information (e.g., could you tell me a little bit more about that?). Once the data are gathered, the reports can be analyzed.

Reading Descriptions

During the initial stage of the analysis, how a protocol is read matters a great deal. Many traditional scientific approaches have advocated that the researcher maintain a detached point of view. Such a detached attitude is thought to assist the researcher in abstracting clarity from ambiguous data. However, as Heidegger (1962) has shown, a detached or "present-at-hand" mode of engagement can also be understood as secondary or privative—and hence a distortion—of genuine participatory engagement in the world (what Heidegger calls a *"ready-to-hand"* engagement; Packer and Addison, 1989). A detached mode of engagement is already a way of approaching the phenomenon, and it is a way that hermeneutics considers to be less desirable than a participatory engagement. Consistent with this hermeneutic–phenomenological attitude, the protocol should be read in such a way that the researcher becomes more or less empathically attuned with the experience of the research participant (Wertz, 1985).

Delineating MUs

Upon a second reading of the protocols, the researcher can take a more professional position and read with the eyes of a psychologist. This step is important because the text as an ambiguity can be given different forms depending upon the lenses through which it is viewed. A psychologist will work within a different frame than those researchers of other human sciences, such as anthropology, sociology, or gender studies. As Romanyshyn (1982) has pointed out, even the heart can be viewed from a multitude of perspectives. Although a psychologist may read the heart metaphorically as a source of feeling, the biologist is inclined to see it as a mere pump.

In this second reading of the protocol, with the eyes of a psychologist, the text is broken down into meaning units or MUs. Because phenomenology is a wholistic approach to studying phenomena, this may appear to be a rather atomistic or elementalistic approach to the data. However, MUs are not to be understood as self-contained elements. They are used to generate general themes in the protocols. These general themes should be understood as "constituents" (Giorgi, 1985a,b). The term *constituent* is derived from phenomenological and gestalt theories of perception. In gestalt theory, a "gestalt" is a structure that is different than the sum of its parts (Arnheim, 1961; Fuller, 1990). In other words, a structure is what it is because of the parts or "constituents" that make it up. At the same time, the structure is not a mere summation of parts, but is co-determined by the parts. Whole and part co-determine one another in a circular relationship.

In the process of moving from individual protocols to the constituents of general themes and finally toward a wholistic structure, delineating MUs is a way of managing the potentially overwhelming complexity of the data. Hence, discriminating meaning units, as Wertz (1985) points out, "insures that all data are carefully treated and accounted for (thus avoiding possible dangers of sloppiness and/or selective bias)" (p. 165).

The process of delineating MUs will slightly differ from researcher to researcher. But as a rule, an MU can be defined "in general as a part of the description whose phrases require each other to stand as a distinguishable moment" (Wertz, 1985, p. 165). Given this definition, MU can vary considerably regarding length. One MU can vary from one word to a string of sentences. For example, in my research on joy, *electric* was a single word that stood as a constituent. On the other hand, there were other times when a string of sentences served as a single constituent:

> There was a sense of goodwill and good spirit that somebody was nice enough and cared enough to leave special things for each of us that each of us would like. My oldest brother, Mike, got an electric train and he liked to figure out gadgets and I liked to play house and I got play dishes and play kitchen utensils. My brother Jim got cowboy toys and he liked to run around and make lots of noise.

It is important, given the variability of length for MUs, that the research not become too preoccupied with discovering a precise delineation of units.

Organization of MUs

Once MUs have been discriminated from the rest of the text, I like to cut out each MU using a pair of scissors. I literally lay the strips of paper on the floor or on my desk and begin to sort them. First, I sort them according to redundancies. Oftentimes, a protocol will contain the same report in various parts of the text. These redundancies can be placed in the same piles and counted as a single MU. I usually keep one that best captures the meaning and discard the rest. Once I've reduced the number of MUs by eliminating redundancies, I make a judgment about the relevance of each MU (Wertz, 1985). Some MUs will not be relevant to the investigation. In my study of joy, for example, there were times when research participants went in to explicit details about their past histories with other people in the story. Although this was sometimes relevant, most often these details were not very important for illuminating the essential structure of the experience of joy.

Once the redundant and irrelevant MUs have been discarded, the process gets a bit more interesting. In light of the protocol as a whole, I begin to sort the MUs according to larger themes. Personally, I prefer to sort themes according to *existentials* such as time, space, body, others, things, and language. Such *existentials* are, per existential–phenomenological anthropology, "givens" of existence that remain invariant for human beings, even as their meaning may change over history and across cultures (Boss, 1979; Heidegger, 1962; Robbins, 1998). All human beings have bodies, are temporal and spatial beings, are social, and encounter things in the world.

In studying emotion, and consistent with Smith's (1986) analysis of emotion, what becomes central for the analysis of joy is *how these existentials are important* within the world of being joyful. In other words, I am concerned with how existence—and, by implication, these existentials as givens of existence—*matter* for people when they are joyful. At times, these themes may not be explicit in the protocols, but can easily be inferred given the context. Temporality, for example, is rarely found to be a direct theme of a participant's narrative account. However, the temporal unfolding of the event is already implied in the very structure of the narrative told by the participant.

Seeing Psychologically

At this point in the project I then take each MU of a protocol and transpose the meaning psychologically. For this process, I am influenced by Romanyshyn's (1982) understanding of the "psychological" as neither fact nor idea, but as relational and nonliteral, as taking place in and making sense of the world, and as a visibility of the world. This is a way of seeing to be differentiated, for example, from the seeing of the natural scientist or philosopher (Robbins, 2000). Joy is disclosed in the protocols, not as intersubjective entities or as physical brain activity, but in the descriptive character of the participant's world. What is most psychological are the metaphors used by the participants to describe their experience. As Romanyshyn (1982) points out, metaphorical reality is the reality disclosed by seeing psychologically, "the way of seeing which opens up a world which matters and which must be understood" (p. 173).

In one protocol, a participant focused on the importance of the color green in her experience. "The green was important to me, important to me at the end," she said, "because of, like, being, like verdance, like, nutritious, life-giving kind of thing." To take the color green as a literal quality of joy would be somewhat absurd. Rather, understood psychologically, I attempted to see with the participant to the meaning of the color green as a metaphorical reality for her. The meaning of green for this participant was its metaphorical character as verdant, nutritious, and lifegiving. Based on this psychological reading of the color green, it was much easier for me to see the relationship of this theme to themes in the other protocols. For example, the other protocols also specified, in different ways, the nurturing, life-affirming, life-sustaining, and youthful quality of joy.

The process of seeing the protocols psychologically is a slow and delicate process that requires patience and reflection on the part of the researcher. Wertz (1983, 1985) has provided some excellent guidelines for this process of moving from "everyday" to psychological description.

Situated Structural Descriptions

When the MUs have been seen psychologically, I then write a "situated structural description" for each protocol (Giorgi, 1985a,b). The situated structural description takes the form of a narrative, written to evoke the world. The description is written in such a way that it maintains the concrete moments and specific situation of the original protocol, but emphasis is placed on the psychological meaning of the situation as it relates to the subject of the study (e.g., being joyful).

Identifying General Themes

Once the situated structural descriptions are completed, it is time to move toward synthesis. By virtue of the researcher's attending to psychological meanings, common themes among various protocols become more apparent. This last step of the analysis has two steps: First, the development of "general themes," and second, a formation of a "general situated structure." The development of general themes is perhaps the most challenging portion of the analysis. It requires a certain talent for empathic imagination and synthetic cognitive insights that are difficult for some people. For the most part, it requires the identification of recurrent themes among the protocols. To do this properly, the researcher must tack back and forth among the situated structures of each protocol.

I find that, at first, common themes are not always obvious. To boost my confidence, I start with the easiest themes to identify: recurrent patterns that are clearly seen in all the protocols. Once these initial themes are identified, I find it becomes easier to discover less obvious patterns. Once several recurrent themes are identified, they are constituents that help give a directionality to the common gestalt of the experience shared by all the participants. It is somewhat like putting together a puzzle. One begins with the easiest pieces, typically the edges, and the rest of the puzzle follows more rapidly once the overall form of the puzzle becomes more apparent.

The main objective in identifying general themes is to discover what is "structurally invariant in the given event of meaning, the phenomenon's unvarying constitution" (Fuller, 1990, p. 32). Or, in the words of Merleau–Ponty (1968), the phenomenological researcher aims to discover the "relationships and structures" that one cannot "suppress or change without the thing ceasing to be itself" (p. 111). In other words, the researcher must ask: What general themes, meanings, or constituents are present in these descriptions of the phenomenon that are essential to the phenomenon? And likewise, the researcher asks: What themes, meanings, or constituents are *not* essential to the phenomenon? The key to this approach is the technique called *imaginative variation*. As Wertz (1985) explains, "imaginative variation" involves "asking all constituents, distinctions, phases, and themes if they could be different or even absent without altering the individual's psychological reality" (p. 176).

In this study, I am concerned with identifying essential constituents of being joyful. When I encounter what appears to be a common theme among the protocols, I imagine what would happen if that theme were absent from the experience of being joyful. Would joy still be possible? If not, I feel relatively confident that I've identified a general theme. If I can imagine being joyful without the presence of that constituent, I discard the constituent by setting it aside. Likewise, if I can imagine the constituent could be different without significantly altering the experience of joy, I slow down and dwell in the constituent. I wonder if the theme I am seeing is not perhaps a minor aspect of a more general theme or if it is an invariant part of the structure after all. For example, when I consider the theme of joy as "life affirming," I feel confident that it is a general theme, because I cannot imagine an experience of joy that is not, in some sense at least, an affirmation of life. However, when I consider that some protocols include the theme of achieving a personal goal, I can imagine an experience of joy that emerges without such an achievement. For example, in aimless play, a person can experience joy without achieving any goal whatsoever.

General Situated Structure

The last step of the analysis is writing the general situated structure. Slowing down and dwelling in the general themes, I find that, quite naturally, the directionality or demand of the general themes moves toward a gestalt or form. Viewing the general themes wholistically, the co-determination of the parts in their relationships to one another tends to have a kind of magnetic force that demands a particular structure.

As Gestalt theory has shown, life world phenomena are dynamic processes that tend toward order (Fuller, 1990). In constructing the general situated structure, I take advantage of the "law of good gestalt" (*Praegnanz*) by permitting the general themes to show me their structural relationship as a tendency toward a certain "necessity." By "necessity," I mean with Fuller (1990) "the urgency with which a meaning presses for balanced fulfillment, in accordance with intrinsic structural demand" (p. 114). In other words, I try to allow the general themes to emerge in their invariant structure as striving toward its own perfection. This is not to say, however, that in the final analysis the gestalt that is formed will *necessarily* be the best gestalt or general structure possible. It simply means that, given the subject–object dialogue, dialectical analysis, and paths through the

hermeneutic circle I've taken during the course of the study, the interpretation of the data should emerge as an internally consistent and
harmonious structural whole. At the same time, the phenomenon will
always exceed the structural grasp I have of it at any given time. For this
reason, the general structure is always *situated* in and emerges from the
concrete experiences of the participants. Hence, it is a general *situated*
structure.

Protocol analysis lends itself to the study of a wide variety of phenomena.
To give only a few examples, protocol analysis has been used to study
phenomena as diverse as suspicion (de Koning, 1979), the experience of
being criminally victimized (Fischer and Wertz, 1979; Wertz, 1985), self-
esteem (Murk, 1983), verbal learning (Giorgi, 1985a,b), thinking in chess
(Aanstoos, 1985), self-deception (W. Fischer, 1985), music representation of
extramusical ideas (Osborne, 1989), and perceptual abnormalities (Richer,
1996). For an excellent introduction to the method of phenomenological
research, I recommend *Phenomenology and Psychological Research* edited
by Amedeo Giorgi (1985a). The book includes a wide variety of studies,
including most of the previously mentioned research. Giorgi's introduction
to the book provides an outline of the method that is very straightforward,
using everyday language.

PARTICIPANTS

The sample used in this research included two women and one man, for
a total of three participants. The ages of the subjects were 26, 27, and 50
years. Two of the subjects have a master's-level education and the third
has a bachelor's degree. All three participants were people who knew and
who felt comfortable with me during the process.

Although three participants might seem to be an unusually small
sample size compared with the size of samples in traditional, quantitative
research, it is typical for qualitative methods to use six or fewer
participants. This is simply because the qualitative approach requires a
kind of analytical depth that most quantitative methods do not. The
depth of analysis using the methods of this study requires a considerable amount of time, and a pool of participants larger than six would
be impractical. Although the small sample size could be criticized for
external validity, because it cannot be easily generalized to a larger
population, the method's richness and depth lends itself to complex
internal consistency that would not be possible with other, quantitative
methods. In seeking a balance between richness and clarity (Merleau–
Ponty, 1962), qualitative methods tend to err on the side of richness and
complexity whereas quantitative studies tend to err on the side of clarity
and simplicity. The collection of more data would surely strengthen
the credibility of the study, but for now, the analysis we have included

does demonstrate the utility of the empirical–phenomenological method, albeit with limitations.

During the process of data collection, the participants remembered experiences of joy. They recounted these experiences in a narrative form from a first-person perspective. Participant 1 recalled her first Christmas memory. She felt an increasing excitement that morning as she walked down the steps with her brothers. When they walked onto the first floor of the house, she discovered the tree lined with presents and her parents waiting. Participant 2 remembered a time when he was playing with his two young cousins in nature. His entry into their world of childhood, combined with the beauty of the valleys and mountains that surrounded him, were important aspects of the experience for him. Participant 3 described a memory of profound excitement at the moment when her horse won a race. She was in early adolescence at the time. The peak of joy was experienced for her as she ran toward the horse and caught a glimpse of blue sky.

METHOD OF DATA COLLECTION: MODIFICATION OF THE IMAGERY IN MOVEMENT METHOD

My criticism of protocol analysis for the study of emotion derives from insights based on the research of "state-dependent memory." Clearly, protocol analysis relies upon the research participant's memory of past events. However, researchers developing and utilizing protocol analysis have not paid heed to the "state of mind" of the research participant at the time of memory "retrieval." Yet research has shown that the retrieval of memories is dependent upon the degree to which a person's state of mind at retrieval coincides with the person's state of mind at the time of the remembered event ("encoding"; Leahy and Harris, 1989, p. 146). Researchers had demonstrated that a person learning material under the influence of a drug will be more likely to remember what he or she learned when again under the influence of that same drug (Eich, De Macoulog, and Ryan, 1994; Goodwin Powell, Bremer, Hoine, and Stein, 1969; Parker, Birnbaum, and Noble, 1976). More significant, Bower (Bower, 1981; Bower, Monteiro, and Gilligan, 1978; Bower and Mayer, 1989) has provided consistent evidence that mood as a state of mind predicts retrieval. For example, when Bower used posthypnotic suggestion to induce happy or sad moods, he found that retrieval was significantly improved when the mood at retrieval coincided with the mood at learning. Also, research by Blaney (1986) has shown that a given mood is far more likely to induce memories congruent with that mood.

Given that memory retrieval is highly dependent upon a person's state of mind and/or mood, protocol analysis' traditional method of data collection is flawed. When studying an emotion using protocol analysis, the research participants are asked to remember and record a past event when they experienced the emotion. However, the participant's mood at the time of recollecting the memory is not guaranteed to be (and is highly unlikely to be) congruent with the mood at the time of the memory. In fact, when a person writes down or types an emotional experience, or even when the experience is recounted in an interview, such modes of engagement are likely to be incongruent with the mood or emotion at the time of the remembered event. I submit, therefore, that the vividness and richness of the description of the emotion is likely to be compromised. Considering that my thesis suggests being joyful is an emotional experience that resides outside the instrumental engagement of typical day-to-day practical activity, I became concerned that the typical data collection process would interfere with the results of the study.

　　I was attracted to Schneier's (1989) imagery in movement method because I believed it would resolve the problem of state-dependent memory for my protocol analysis of joy. The procedure was specifically designed to assist clients in therapy to move more fully into an emotionally engaged experience (p. 312). The method involves a step-by-step process that can be understood as a gradual shift from an intuitive "felt sense" of meaning toward a more fully articulate, explicit, and structural understanding. The technique begins with abstract drawing (image), then proceeds to using role play (movement) to enhance the vividness of an emerging memory, and concludes with a verbal and written description of the experience. Using this approach, I could work with the research participants to assist them in a dynamic movement from an intuitive sense of joy toward the articulation of a vital, lived reexperienc- ing of an emerging memory of being joyful. By the end, I would have both a verbal and written account of the experience. Even better, I would also have three sources of data: the drawings, gestures, and verbal/written protocols. With three sources of data, the data can be triangulated.

　　Triangulation is the combination of several research methods in the study of the same phenomenon. It is a strategy for founding the credibility of qualitative analyses and works as an alternative to traditional criteria for quantitative research, such as reliability and validity. Triangulation can involve a variety of different combinations, including multiple observers, theories, methods, and/or empirical materials. In the case of this study, the use of multiple sources of data constitutes *data triangulation*, and the use of multiple methods can be considered a form of *methodological triangulation*. The credibility of the results is further substantiated when three sources of data are used, because each of the empirical materials should reflect the same structure of the phenomenon, but in different ways. When one source of data is ambiguous, it can be clarified by the other empirical materials, and when all three sources of data demonstrate the same emergent form or structure, the findings are more persuasive.

In summary, the use of the imagery in movement method for data collection, combined with protocol analysis for explicating the general themes and structure of the phenomenon, overcomes the problem of state-dependent memory and gains two more sources of empirical material.

The imagery in movement method, as modified for research data collection, is a five-step process: (1) expression, (2) mapping, (3) role-play, (4) verbal translation, and (5) written protocol. To perform these steps, I required a variety of materials, including paper, magic markers, a tape recorder with an appropriate audiotape, a private room, and a preformatted "summary sheet." Most of these materials can be substituted. Obviously, magic markers can be exchanged for other materials, such as chalk, pastels, or paint. However, it is important that the materials are colored. Although I chose to use audiotape, another researcher might prefer to use video recordings instead.

Expression

Although it may be obvious, it is worth mentioning that all my research participants were informed of the process when they read and signed their informed consent forms. The participants were prepared for the emotional involvement of this process. After I gave the participants the drawing materials, I asked them to create a spontaneous, abstract, color drawing in response to the question: What does it mean to be joyful?

The instruction to draw an abstract picture prevents the person from immediately forming a determinate image in response to the question. An abstract picture becomes an interesting source of data because its geometrical shape, as I've discovered, often reflects the structure of the gestures of the participant during role play as well as the narrative that emerges later in the process. For example, one participant drew a picture using yellow markers that resembled water shooting upward into the sky, like a geyser. In her exploration of the drawing, the metaphor of the geyser became a guiding metaphor, and in her narrative a similar structure emerged in her description of her uplifting exuberance. This same structure was evident even earlier in the process in the form of her gestures. Without being explicitly aware of her gestures, the participant repeatedly lifted open her widespread arms in a way that strongly resembled the structure of the abstract drawing. Finally, the process of drawing an abstract picture with magic markers, as the participants informed me, conveniently evokes for people a playful, youthful mood that is conducive to and congruent with the feeling of joy.

The rather open-ended question, "What does it mean to be joyful?" invites the participant to dwell with the intuitive, general sense of joy before immediately evoking a particular memory. The aim is to have the memory emerge from the feeling rather than the feeling emerge from the memory.

Mapping

During the mapping phase, the participant was invited to explore the body sensations, thoughts, images, and feelings associated with the different colors and shapes of the drawing.

I asked the person to focus on a particular color and/or shape in the drawing that seemed the most vivid to him or her. Then, I asked the person to explore what this shape and/or color evoked for them. In describing the intuitive, felt sense of the drawing, the participants expressed themselves in gesture. When a gestural style began to emerge, I called attention to the gesture and invited the participant to explore its meaning. Through this process, the participants began to discover how the gestures, images, sensations, thoughts, and feelings they were experiencing evoked a particular narrative or story from the past. This whole process was recorded on audiotape, but I also took notes.

Role Play

Once the participant became aware of an emerging narrative, I invited him or her to role-play his or her part in the story. The notion of role play as a therapeutic technique originated in the work of Moreno (1983), the innovator of psychodrama (Blatner, 2000). In psychodrama, as well as in gestalt therapy, role play is often used as a technique for amplifying an emotional experience. Role play is useful for helping the participant, as it is for assisting clients in therapy, to form concrete, richly descriptive, and vibrant descriptions of past experiences as opposed to relying upon abstractions, vague words, and generalizations (Blatner, 2000, p. 156).

Verbal Translation

According to Schneier (1989), the verbal translation phase of the method has the participant responding to a series of questions. These questions are designed "to uncover the symbolic meanings of the drawing and the events in the [role play]" and further questions are put forth "to determine how these symbols relate to one's current life situation" (p. 313). The types of questions used by Schneier are more suited for therapy than research, so I took the liberty of modifying this portion of the method to suit my research project. Rather than asking specific questions, I ask open-ended questions regarding portions of the previous phases that were still unclear for me as the researcher. For example, I said, "I noticed during the role play that you gestured like this [mimicking gesture]. Can you tell me more about that?" or "When you were coloring this orange portion of the drawing [pointing to section], I noticed you kept that color contained in the bottom portion of the drawing. Could you explore that further for me?"

Writing Protocol

During the final phase of the process, I instructed the participants to record their experience of joy on paper. Specifically, I asked the participants to write down, in their words, the bodily sensations, thoughts, images, and feelings that emerged for them during the process. I also instructed them to record metaphors for their experience that seemed most to capture the essence of the feeling of being joyful. Next, I asked them to list what they felt were dominant themes that emerged during the various phases of the process. To conclude, I directed the participant to write a narrative account that best captured the temporal unfolding of the memory (or dominant memory) that emerged for them during the session.

Concluding Notes on Analysis of the Data

When the process of data collection was concluded, I had a diverse and significant quantity of qualitative data to use for my analysis. There was no need to spend considerable time interpreting nonverbal events during the process, because the participant and I had already collaborated in doing so. I simply used the written reports and interpreted them using protocol analysis. However, the strength of the imagery in movement method is that it allowed me to turn to the concrete data of the drawings, audio recordings, and notes whenever (during the process of data analysis) I remained unclear about a portion of the protocols.

FINDINGS

Because I have already spent considerable time explicating the process of moving through the various phases of my method, and for the sake of brevity, I am including as my findings only the general themes and general situated structure of my analysis.

General Themes

1. Center as origin of experience

    Participant 1: "In the center, going up (hand motion is palms inward, moving up from waist in expanding arcs)."
    Participant 2: "... the center, is felt as a tension in the stomach."
    Participant 3: "I started from the middle and arced it out with purple."

2. A movement toward and achievement of fulfillment

    Participant 1: "Full, complete, ecstatic everything and every-body wholeness, a sense of having it all—the be all and end all moment."

Participant 2: "... the world says 'YES!' to where you are at that moment ..."

Participant 3: "But, for that moment, like, everything else fell away."

3. Fulfillment was discovered through an intimate connection with others

Participant 1: "I feel joy when I am together with others ..."

Participant 2: "... a wanting to be closer, y'know, a desire to be closer."

Participant 3: "I loved being a part of the well-being of this great feminine power."

4. A feeling of awe at the experience of being fulfilled

Participant 1: "I really had a sense of awe."

Participant 2: "A good place, but more powerful than you can imagine."

Participant 3: "I was always in awe of her ..."

5. The world is felt as a benevolent power greater than the self

Participant 1: "There was intensity but a peace that the world is a good place and a loving giving hand guided it and created it."

Participant 2: "... the world ... watching over you, somehow in sympathy ... with what you're doing ... that awareness of being cradled."

Participant 3: "... connected me into a power that felt greater and more expansive ..."

6. Joy as a movement up and out

Participant 1: "Its a center and up."

Participant 2: "Coming up through you, um, out into the world."

Participant 3: "Soaring out, up and out."

7. Shift from containment to directed diffusion

Participant 1: "A burst of joy. It's warm. Electric ..."

Participant 2: "... how free, open, and unbound the game had made me feel."

Participant 3: "I decided I didn't want it contained."

8. Experience of a profound feeling of presence in the moment

Participant 1: "... a sense of having it all—the be all and end all moment."

Participant 2: "the world says 'YES!' to where you are at that moment, y'know?"

Participant 3: "... joy of the moment, when all the distractions of the world fell away."

9. Experience of freedom in the moment

Participant 1: "... a sense of having it all—the be all and end all moment."

Participant 2: "You know, like, a freedom."

Participant 3: "I felt open and free."

10. Joy as life affirming and nurturing

Participant 1: "... the world is a good place and a loving, giving hand guided it and created it."

Participant 2: "... that awareness of being cradled. Its okay, 'Yes!' The world is saying 'yes' to you."

Participant 3: "The green was important to me, important to me at the end, because of, like, being, like verdance, like, nutritious, life giving kind of thing."

11. Joy as an experience of youthfulness

Participant 1: "Christmas when I was about two."

Participant 2: "The connection is playing with my cousins."

Participant 3: "... a sense of innocence and purity ..."

12. Joy as openness rather than willfulness

Participant 1: "... it requires an external event to start the elation geyser."

Participant 2: "It cannot be willed. There must first be a sympathy with the world."

Participant 3: "... this is completely spontaneous."

13. Joy as rarity

Participant 1: "... it requires an external event to start the elation geyser."

Participant 2: "Joy does not happen often enough."

Participant 3: "I'll remember happy times or really pleasurable, cool times, and they all seem so tenuous."

14. Joy as emotional intensity and power

Participant 1: "... a numbing intensity."

Participant 2: "Yeah, that kind of power."

Participant 3: "... power, kind of ... And travel ... You know, and some velocity, kind of."

15. Joy as being high

Participant 1: "There is a sense of 'highness.'"
Participant 2: "... playing up above."
Participant 3: "Maybe its, like, higher ... Atmospheric."

16. Joy as lacking an instrumental aim

Participant 1: "There was the element of surprise."
Participant 2: "I gave myself up to the game ..."
Participant 3: "... this is completely spontaneous."

GENERAL SITUATED STRUCTURE

Prior to the peak of joyful experience, the participants felt a sense of awe. Awe was experienced as a veneration and wonder regarding the power of other and world. The presence of the world was felt as a power that was greater than one's self. It was experienced as beyond the control of the self, but also benevolent, evoking a sense of peace, tranquility, and being held.

Joy, as an embodied felt sense, emerged when the participants were centered and from the center of their individual being. Joy, as a powerful, warm feeling, was felt as a movement up and out from the center of being. The existence of the participants, as a world, was felt to be an expansiveness. The movement was felt to be moving toward a feeling of fulfillment that was powerful, intense, and marked by earnest enthusiasm and fervor. Yet, this intensity was tinged with a softness, a feeling of peace, tranquility, and harmony. In moving up and out, joy was a movement toward highness, and it had an elevated and lofty quality. At the same time, this movement was not an emptying out, but a fullness of character. In the intoxicating highness of joy, self, other, and world were all positively affirmed. In being affirmed, the self moved toward the world in its positive fullness. The fullness of self, other, and world met each other.

In joy, the state of fulfillment was realized, in part, through a connection with an other or others. As self, other and world were felt to be connected; there was a loss of the participants' defended boundaries. Rather than a terrifying loss of self, this connectedness was harmonious. When the participants were joyful, self, other, and world were in accordance. The diffusion of self into world and world into self was a self-transcendent state of being wherein the participant fully stood out, affirmatively in existence.

Joy was not experienced as willed, but resulted from an openness to the possibility of a connection to the world out of which joy erupted. The connectedness of joy required a reciprocal openness to the experience by self, other, and world, which, in the right moment, came together in harmonious agreement and affirmation of existence. Joy, in the case of these participants, was not experienced as the result of accomplishing an instrumental aim. Rather, joy was felt to be completely spontaneous and without expectation. Instead of a movement toward an instrumental goal or the achievement of a previously calculated purpose, joy involved an immersion in present activity.

During the peak of joy, everyday, mundane clock time was transformed. At the moment of joy, the participants felt a sense of completeness, and they lived in a world in which, temporarily, their worries of the future and the remembrance of painful past experiences were no longer included in the present moment. Hence, joy was a profound feeling of presence in the moment. This unbounded moment of joy was felt as a freedom. Yet rather than being a freedom to do whatever one pleases, it was a freedom to take up fully one possibility offered by a welcoming and benevolent world that affirmed that choice. Freedom in joy was a freedom to be and a safety in being in the moment.

Joy's movement from awe to fulfilled being was experienced as harmony, completeness, and perfection in which the daily imperfections of life were momentarily forgotten and placed aside. The world took on the character of an undifferentially good place in which there were no impinging complications and nothing was lacking.

Joy is a life-affirming experience. Joy is lived as a nurturing, life-sustaining experience in which one feels fully alive. Self, world, and others appear as fertile ground ripe with possibilities. This verdant quality of joy is experienced as youthful. Joy and youth share a quality of vibrancy and growth, as well as naivete and innocence. Yet for the adult, who lives predominately in the workaday, instrumental world, joy is rare. In remembering experiences of joy, one longs for more.

DISCUSSION

The results of our analysis lend some support to the "broaden and build model" of positive affect. As we expected, the participants described the experience of joy as a broadening of their thought–action repertoire, which they described as a sense of openness. The participants, as expected, described their respective environments as safe and familiar, even to the point of personifying the world as a benevolent power. Participants also described a sense of freedom, which may be analogous to the sense of play predicted by the broaden and build model of positive affect. It is not clear whether the participants experienced themselves as engaged in activities that required little effort. Perhaps effort was so lacking that it was not salient enough to emerge as a theme in the data. Further research on the relationship between effort and joy will be necessary to clarify the relationship between these constructs. The sense of progress toward a personal goal was also not salient in the data. One participant experienced joy as a result of her horse winning a race, which could be construed as the achievement of a personal goal. Yet the other participants did not describe events that could be confidently interpreted as goal related. The lack of a goal-oriented theme may, instead, be reflective of a fundamentally non-instrumental orientation of the participants during the experience of joy.

The data and analysis also appear to support the hypothesis that joy is associated with a noninstrumental orientation to the world. The participants described their experience of joy as one that was not geared toward the attainment of an instrumental aim. In this sense, as in the experience of flow, the participants found themselves engaged in activity that was autotelic, an end in itself. The noninstrumental orientation, as expected, was accompanied by themes of playfulness/freedom, a sense of fulfillment, present centeredness, a feeling of connection with others, and an immersion in the world that was accompanied by a dissolution of the ego or a for-getting of one's self ("directed diffusion"). Also similar to experiences of flow, the participants mentioned what could be described as a feeling of transcendence, captured by various themes, including a felt movement up and out, the sense of freedom, and the sense of being "high." The partic-ipants also experienced what might be called a "distortion in the sense of time." Participants referred to a feeling that the current moment had expanded even, in one case, to include the "infinite," as one participant said. In contrast to research on flow, however, the data did not yield essential themes related to the participants having clear goals, immediate feedback on a task, or a balance between task difficulty and personal ability. The latter themes might mean that flow is a subcategory of joy that designates experiences of joy that emerge during work-related activities. Further research will be necessary to clarify the relationship between flow and joy.

The participants were clear that they felt the world affirmed them in the moment of joy. This theme of acceptance appears to contradict Sartre's characterization of joy as a form of escape or avoidance from the com-plexities and difficulties of living. Nevertheless, the participants did experi-ence a sense of fulfillment that approximated the Sartrean characterization of joy as an appraisal of the world as undifferentially positive. However, in contrast to Sartre's theory of joy, the participants did not appear to be faced with particularly complex or difficult situations. In any case, the data do not appear to provide an unambiguous confirmation of Sartre's theory of joy as "bad faith." The only way to judge that the participants were in "bad faith" would be to judge them according to the assumption that the world is fundamentally complex and difficult. But we have no way of making such a claim. The only claim we can make, tentatively, is that these particular participants felt the world to be a benevolent, fulfilling, and nurturing place, at least for a brief moment. Whether these feelings correspond to the reality of the situation cannot be inferred by the data. Even if there were independent observers during these events, however, it would be difficult to say which perspective would be more accurate. We believe it is important to remember that these substantive evaluations of the world through emotion cannot be verified in any "objective" way without losing the human significance of these phenomena.

Some of the other hypotheses appear to be supported by the data as well. The participants were all actively engaged in "extraverted"-like actions; namely, they were immersed in situations with other people. Whether such "extraversion" occurs in *all* experiences of joy is a question that will require further research and, in particular, would require quantitative methods of approaching the problem. The data also found support for the prediction that joy might include religious/spiritual themes. The feelings of awe, the world personified as a benevolent power, the movement up and out (transcendence), the diffusion of the "ego," the profound feeling of presence in the moment, the life-affirming and nurturing quality of the experience, and the feeling of highness characteristic of "peak experiences" are all common themes found in the literature on religious and spiritual experiences. Research into the relationship between joy and religious experiences would likely be a very fruitful area for future investigation.

The data provide some insight into the applicability of theories of subjective well-being for understanding joy. The participants described what could be construed as a sense of being fulfilled, and one could make tentative inferences about how the fulfillment of certain needs may have led the participants to feel this way. The participants felt an intimate connection with others, which would support the hypothesis that joy and other positive affects result from fulfillment of the "need to belong." Other needs that might have been met include a feeling of freedom and a sense that one has been affirmed as a person. Yet it is not possible to conclude that these "needs" and values were not in fact personal values for these participants rather than universal needs. Such questions cannot be addressed by the type of method we have used in this study. The study, however, does shed some light on how the fulfillment of such needs might appear from a first-person experience. Finally, we did not find any evidence in the data that the participants were engaged in downward social comparisons, and we are inclined to believe that, at best, a social comparison theory of joy has limited predictive power.

The results of our analysis also yielded some unexpected findings. That joy erupted from a feeling of being centered and from the center of one's body was not anticipated. Nor did we anticipate the pervasive theme of youthfulness or the appraisal that joy was a rare experience for these participants. We were also intrigued by the pervasiveness of the theme of freedom in the data. We hope these findings will stimulate more research on these themes. For example, the feeling of "being centered" might be related to the kind of centeredness that practitioners of meditation strive to achieve. Future research might be able to confirm better how a feeling of being centered and the experience of joy might be related products of meditation and other ritualistic practices. The theme of youthfulness raises questions about whether people experience joy less frequently during the course of their life span, and, if not, whether they perceive they do and why. Finally, the theme of freedom raises interesting philosophical questions about the nature of freedom, and we hope to review more of the philosophical literature on liberty (e.g., Isaiah Berlin) to frame better our questions about the relationship of freedom and joy.

Our study clearly has its limits. With only three participants, our sample is hardly representative, and the qualitative methods we are using are not meant to identify relationships among variables or determine cause-and-effect relationships between variables. Future research should perform these analyses on a larger pool of participants. Also, questions about the relationship between joy and the variables identified in our study will require quantitative research. Yet, our study raises questions and stimulates hypotheses that likely would not have been raised without it. Also, our study has a certain ecological validity because participants were describing an actual life experience. The themes in the data emerged spontaneously from the participants' own stories. They were not predetermined categories that we decided in advance, as would be the case with quantitative measures. To perform quantitative research of joy, we will need a measure of joy, and we believe the scale development of a joy measure will be better served if the production of test items are based on open-ended, qualitative research, such as in this study. Finally, we cannot overemphasize that our interpretive framework—the preunderstanding that oriented us in the interpretation of the data—was a necessary basis upon which to enter the analysis, but nevertheless also closes off other potential approaches to the data. Ideally, our data will be subject to public scrutiny and other interpretive frameworks and, as a result, will likely bear fruit in ways that we could not have otherwise dreamed.

REFERENCES

Aanstoos, C. M. (1985). The structure of thinking in chess. In Giorgi, A. (Ed.). *Phenomenology and psychological research* (pp. 86–117). Pittsburgh, PA: Duquesne University Press.

Andrews, F. M., and S. B. Withey. (1976). *Social indicators of well-being: America's perception of life quality.* New York: Plenum Press.

Arnheim, R. (1961). Gestalten—Yesterday and today. In Henle, M. (Ed.). *Documents of gestalt psychology* (pp. 90–96). Berkeley: University of California Press.

Arnold, M. B. (1960). *Emotion and personality* (vols. 1 and 2). New York: Columbia University Press.

Aspinwall, L. G., and U. M. Staudinger. (Eds.). (2002). *A psychology of human strengths: Fundamental questions and future directions for a positive psychology.* Washington, DC: American Psychological Association.

Aube, M., and A. Senteni. (1996). What are emotions for? Commitments management and regulation within animals/animats encounters. In Maes, P., M. Mataric, J. A. Meyer, J. Pollack, and S. W. Wilson. (Eds.). *From animals to animats 4: Proceedings of the Fourth International Conference on Simulation of Adaptive Behavior* (pp. 264–271). Cambridge, MA: The MIT Press/Bradford Books.

Augustine. (1979). *Confessions.* New York: Viking Press.

Bargdill, R. W. (2000). The study of life boredom. *Journal of Phenomenological Psychology, 31,* 188–219.

Berman, M. (1981). *The reenchantment of the world.* Ithaca: Cornell University Press.

Blake, W. (1994). *The works of William Blake.* Herdfordshire: Wordsworth Editions.

Blaney, P. H. (1986). Affect and memory: A review. *Psychological Bulletin, 99,* 229–246.

Blatner, A. (2000). *Foundations of psychodrama* (4th ed.). New York: Springer.

Boss, M. (1979). *Existential foundations of medicine and psychology.* New York: Jason Aronson.

Bower, G. H. (1981). Mood and memory. *American Psychologist, 36,* 129–148.

Bower, G. H., and J. D. Mayer. (1989). In search of mood–dependent retrieval. *Journal of Social Behavior and Personality, 4,* 133–168.

Bower, G. H., K. P. Monteiro, and S. G. Gilligan. (1978). Emotional mood as a context for learning and recall. *Journal of Verbal Learning and Verbal Behavior, 17,* 573–587.

Brickman, P., D. Coates, and R. Janoff–Bulman. (1978). Lottery winners and accident victims: Is happiness relative? *Journal of Personality and Social Psychology, 36,* 917–927.

Brunstein, J. C. (1993). Personal goals and subjective well–being. *Journal of Personality and Social Psychology, 65,* 1061–1070.

Cacioppo, J. J., W. L. Gardner, and G. G. Berntson. (1999). The affect system has parallel and integrative processing components: Form follows function. *Journal of Personality and Social Psychology, 76,* 839–855.

Carver, C. S., and M. F. Scheier. (1990). Origins and functions of positive and negative affect: A control–process view. *Psychological Review, 97,* 19–35.

Csikszentmihalyi, M. (2000). The contribution of flow to positive psychology. In Gillham, J. E. (Ed.). *The science of hope and optimism* (pp. 387–395). Philadelphia: Templeton Foundation Press.

Csikszentmihalyi, M., and T. Figurski. (1982). The experience of self–awareness in everyday life. *Journal of Personality, 50,* 14–26.

Csikszentmihalyi, M., and R. Larson. (1984). *Being adolescent.* New York: Basic Books.

Curry, L. A., C. R. Snyder, D. L. Cook, B. C. Ruby, and M. Rehm. (1997). Role of hope in academic and sport achievement. *Journal of Personality and Social Psychology, 73,* 1257–1267.

de Koning, A. J. J. (1979). The qualitative method of research in the phenomenology of suspicion. In Giorgi, A., R. Knowles, and D. L. Smith. (Eds.). *Duquesne studies in phenomenological psychology,* (Vol. III, pp. 122–134). Pittsburgh, PA: Duquesne University Press.

de Rivera, J. (1988). A structural theory of the emotions. *Psychological issues, 10,* 38–74.

de Rivera, J., L. Possell, J. A. Verette, and B. Weiner. (1989). Distinguishing elation, gladness and joy. *Journal of Personality and Social Psychology, 57,* 1015–1023.

Diener, E. (1984). Subjective well-being. *Psychological Bulletin, 95,* 542–575.

Diener, E., R. A. Emmons, R. J. Larsen, and S. Griffin. (1985a). The Satisfaction With Life Scale. *Journal of Personality Assessment, 49,* 71–75.

Diener, E., R. J. Larsen, S. Levine, and R. A. Emmons. (1985b). Intensity and frequency: Dimensions underlying positive and negative affect. *Journal of Personality and Social Psychology, 48,* 1253–1265.

Diener, E. and R. E. Lucas. (2000). Subjective emotional well-being. In Lewis, M., and J. M. Haviland. (Eds.). *Handbook of emotions* (2nd ed., pp. 325–337). New York: Guilford.

Diener, E., E. Sandvik, W. Pavot, and F. Fujita. (1992). Extraversion and subjective well-being in a U.S. national probability sample. *Journal of Research in Personality, 26,* 205–215.

Diener, E., H. Smith, and F. Fujita. (1995). The personality structure of affect. *Journal of Personality and Social Psychology, 50,* 130–141.

Diener, E., E. Suh, and S. Oishi. (1997). Recent findings on subjective well-being. *Indian Journal of Clinical Psychology, 24,* 25–41. Also available at www.psych.vivo.edu/~ediener/hottopic/paper1.html. Accessed September 1, 2004.

Easterlin, R. A. (1974). Does economic growth improve the human lot? In David, P. A., and M. W. Reder. (Eds.). *Nations and households in economic growth: Essays in honor of Moses Abramovitz.* New York: Academic Press.

Eich, J. E., D. De Macoulog, and L. Ryan. (1994). Mood-dependent memory for events of the personal past. *Journal of Experimental Psychology: General, 123,* 201–215.

Ellison, C. G. (1991). Religious involvement and subjective well-being. *Journal of Health and Social Behavior, 32,* 80–89.

Ellsworth, P. C., and C. A. Smith. (1998). Shades of joy: Patterns of appraisal differentiating pleasant emotions. *Cognition and Emotion, 2,* 301–331.

Estrada, C. A., A. M. Isen, and M. J. Young, (1997). Positive affect facilitates integration of information and decreases anchoring in reasoning among physicians. *Organizational Behavior and Human Decision Processes, 72,* 117–135.

Feinstein, J. S., P. R. Goldin, M. B. Stein, G. G. Brown,and M. P. Paulus. (2002). Habituation of attention networks during emotion processing. *Neuroreport, 13,* 1255–1258.

Fischer, C. T. (1998). Being angry revealed as deceptive protest: An empirical–phenomenological analysis. In Valle, R. (Ed.). *Phenomenological inquiry in psychology: Existential and transpersonal dimensions* (pp. 111–122). New York: Plenum.

Fischer, C. T., and F. J. Wertz. (1979). Empirical phenomenological analyses of being criminally victimized. In Giorgi, A., R. Knowles, and D. L. Smith. (Eds.). *Duquesne studies in phenomenological psychology* (vol. III, pp. 135–158).

Fischer, W. F. (1974). On the phenomenological mode of researching "being-anxious." *Journal of Phenomenological Psychology, 4,* 405–423.

Fischer, W. F. (1985). Self-deception: An empirical–phenomenological inquiry into its essential meanings. In Giorgi, A. (Ed.). *Phenomenology and psychological research.* Pittsburgh, PA: Duquesne University Press.

Fischer, W. F. (1991). The psychology of anxiety: A phenomenological description. *The Humanistic Psychologist, 19,* 289–300.

Frank, R. H. (1988). *Passions within reason: The strategic role of emotions.* New York: Norton.

Frankel, C. A. (1985). The phenomenology of being angry: An empirical study approached from the perspectives of self and other. Doctoral dissertation. Duquesne University. *Dissertation Abstracts International, 46,* 959B.

Fredrickson, B. L. (1998). What good are positive emotions? *Review of General Psychology, 2,* 300–319.

Fredrickson, B. L. (2000). Cultivating positive emotions to optimize health and well-being. *Prevention and Treatment, 3.* Available at: http://journals.apa.org/prevention/volume3. Accessed September 1, 2004.

Fredrickson, B. L., and R. W. Levenson. (1998). Positive emotions speed recovery from the cardiovascular sequelae of negative emotions. *Cognition and Emotion, 12,* 191–220.

Frijda, N. H. (1986). *The emotions.* Cambridge: Cambridge University Press.

Frijda, N. H. (1999). Emotions and hedonic experience. In Kahneman, D., E. Diener, and N. Schwarz. (Eds.). *Well-being: The foundations of hedonic psychology* (pp. 190–210). New York: Russell Sage Foundation.

Frijda, N. H., P. Kuipers, and E. Schure. (1989). Relations among emotion, appraisal and emotional action readiness. *Journal of Personality and Social Psychology, 57,* 212–228.

Fuller, A. R. (1990). *Insight into value: An exploration of the premises of a phenomenological psychology*. Albany: State University of New York Press.

Gendlin, E. T. (1981). *Focusing*. New York: Bantam Books.

Giorgi, A. (1970). *Psychology as a human science*. New York: Harper and Row.

Giorgi, A. (1971). A phenomenological approach to the problem of meaning and serial learning. In Giorgi, A., W. Fischer, and R. von Eckartsberg. (Eds.). *Duquesne studies in phenomenological psychology I*. Pittsburgh, PA: Duquesne University Press.

Giorgi, A. (1975). An application of the phenomenological method in psychology. In Giorgi, A., C. Fischer, and E. Murray. (Eds.). *Duquesne studies in phenomenological psychology II*. Pittsburgh, PA: Duquesne University Press.

Giorgi, A. (Ed.). (1985a). *Phenomenology and psychological research*. Pittsburgh, PA: Duquesne University Press.

Giorgi, A. (1985b). The phenomenological psychology of learning and the verbal learning tradition. In Giorgi, A. (Ed.). *Phenomenology and psychological research* (pp. 23–85). Pittsburgh, PA: Duquesne University Press.

Goldstein, J. (1987). *The experience of insight*. Boston: Shambhala.

Goodwin, D. W., B. Powell, D. Bremer, H. Hoine, and J. Stein. (1969). Alcohol and recall: State dependent effects in man. *Science, 163*, 1358–1360.

Greenberg, L. S., and J. D. Safran. (1984). Integrating affect and cognition: A perspective on the process of therapeutic change. *Cognitive Therapy and Research, 8*, 559–578.

Greenberg, L. S., and J. D. Safran. (1987). *Emotion in psychotherapy*. New York: Guilford.

Gross, J. J. (2002). Emotion regulation: Affective, cognitive, and social consequences. *Psychophysiology, 39*, 281–291.

Hall, T. (1998). Seeking a focus on joy in the field of psychology. *New York Times*, Tuesday, April 28, Section F, p. 7.

Heidegger, M. (1962). *Being and time*. New York: Harper and Row. [Originally published 1927.]

Isen, A. M., and K. A. Daubman. (1984). The influence of affect on categorization. *Journal of Personality and Social Psychology, 20*, 203–253.

Isen, A. M., K. A. Daubman, and G. P. Nowicki. (1987). Positive affect facilitates creative problem solving. *Journal of Personality and Social Psychology, 52*, 1122–1131.

Isen, A. M., M. M. S. Johnson, E. Mertz, and G. F. Robinson. (1985). The influence of positive affect on the unusualness of word associations. *Journal of Personality and Social Psychology, 48*, 1413–1426.

Izard, C. E. (1977). *Human emotions*. New York: Plenum Press.

Kennedy–Moore, E, and J. C. Watson. (1999). *Expressing emotion: Myths, realities, and therapeutic strategies*. New York: Guilford Press.

Keyes, C. L. M, and J. Haidt. (2002). *Flourishing: Positive psychology and the life well-lived*. Washington, DC: American Psychological Association.

Kozma, A. (1996). *Top-down and bottom-up approaches to an understanding of subjective well-being*. Presented at the World Conference on Quality of Life. University of Northern British Columbia. Prince George, Canada.

Kuhn, T. (1962). *The structure of scientific revolutions*. Chicago: University of Chicago Press.

Larsen, R. J., and E. Diener. (1987). Affect intensity as an individual difference characteristic: A review. *Journal of Research in Personality, 21*, 1–39.

Larsen, R. J., and E. Diener. (1992). Promises and problems with the circumplex model of emotion. In Clark, M. S. (Ed.). *Review of personality and social psychology: Emotion* (vol. 13, pp. 25–59). Newbury Park, CA: Sage.

Larsen, R. J., E. Diener, and R. S. Cropanzano. (1987). Cognitive operations associated with individual differences in affect intensity. *Journal of Personality and Social Psychology, 53*, 767–774.

Lazarus, R. S. (1966). *Psychological stress and the coping response*. New York: McGraw–Hill.

Lazarus, R. S. (1982). Thoughts on the relations between emotion and cognition. *American Psychologist, 37*, 1019–1024.

Lazarus, R. S. (1991). *Emotion and adaptation.* New York: Oxford University Press.

Leahy, T. H., and R. J. Harris. (1989). *Human learning* (2nd ed.). Englewood Cliffs, NJ: Prentice-Hall.

Lee, S. H. (1979). "Sense and sensibility": Sartre's theory of the emotions. *Review of Existential Psychology and Psychiatry, 17,* 67–78.

Levenson, R. W. (1994). Human emotions: A functional view. In Ekman, P., and R. Davidson. (Eds.). *The nature of emotion: Fundamental questions* (pp. 123–126). New York: Oxford University Press.

Linley, P. A., and S. Joseph. (Eds.). (2004). *Positive psychology in practice.* Hoboken, NJ: Wiley.

Lopez, S. J., and C. R. Snyder. (Eds.). (2003). *Positive psychological assessment: A handbook of models and measures.* Washington, DC: American Psychological Association.

Lucas, R. E., and E. Diener. (1998). *The importance and frequency of affect.* Working paper. Chicago University of Illinois.

Lucas, R. E., E. Diener, and E. M. Suh. (1996). Discriminant validity of well-being measures. *Journal of Personality and Social Psychology, 71,* 616–628.

Lyubormirsky, S., and L. Ross. (1999). Changes in attractiveness of elected, rejected, and precluded alternatives: A comparison of "happy" and "unhappy" individuals. *Journal of Personality and Social Psychology, 76,* 988–1007.

Marcuse, H. (1966). *Eros and civilization.* Boston: Beacon Press.

McCrae, R. R., and P. T. Costa. (1986). Personality, coping, and coping effectiveness in an adult sample. *Journal of Personality, 54,* 385–405.

Merleau–Ponty, M. (1962). *Phenomenology of perception.* Smith, C. (Trans.). London: Routledge and Kegan Paul.

Merleau–Ponty, M. (1968). *The visible and the invisible.* Lingis, A. (Trans). Lefort, C. (Ed.). Evanston, Il: Northwestern University Press.

Moreno, J. L. (1983). *The theater of spontaneity.* New York: Beacon House. [Originally published 1923.]

Murk, C. J. (1983). Toward a phenomenology of self-esteem. In Giorgi, A., A. Barton, and C. Maes. (Eds.). *Duquesne studies in phenomenological psychology* (vol. IV, pp. 137–150). Pittsburgh, PA: Duquesne University Press.

Myers, D. G. (1992). *The pursuit of happiness: Discovering the pathway to fulfillment, well-being, and enduring personal joy.* New York: Avon.

Oatley, K., and J. M. Jenkins. (1996). *Understanding emotions.* Cambridge: Blackwell.

Osborne, J. W. (1989). A phenomenological investigation of the musical representation of extra-musical ideas. *Journal of Phenomenological Psychology, 20,* 151–175.

Packer, M. J., and R. B. Addison. (1989). Introduction. In Packer, M. J., and R. B. Addison. (Eds.). *Entering the circle: Hermeneutic investigation in psychology.* Albany: State University of New York Press.

Parker, E. S., I. M. Birnbaum, and E. P. Noble. (1976). Alcohol and memory: Storage and state dependency. *Journal of Verbal Learning and Verbal Behavior, 15,* 691–702.

Plutchik, R. (1980). *Emotion: A psychoevolutionary synthesis.* New York: Harper Row.

Polanyi, M. (1958). *Personal knowledge.* Chicago: University of Chicago Press.

Polanyi, M. (1969). *Knowing and being.* In Green, M. (Ed.). Chicago: University of Chicago Press.

Pollner, M. (1989). Divine relations, social relations, and well-being. *Journal of Health and Social Behavior, 30,* 92–104.

Richer, P. (1996). Phenomenological studies of perceptual abnormalities: Methodological considerations. *Methods,* 28–47.

Robbins, B. D. (1998). A reading of Kuhn in light of Heidegger as a response to Hoeller's critique of Giorgi. *Janus Head, 1,* 2–35.

Robbins, B. D. (2000). On the history of rhetoric and psychology. *Janus Head, 3,* 62–76.

Robbins, B. D. (2001). *Scientia media,* incommensurability, and interdisciplinary space. *Janus Head, (Supple.) Winter,* 67–83.

Robbins, B. D. (2003). *Joy and the politics of emotion: Towards a cultural therapeutics via phenomenology and critical theory.* Unpublished doctoral dissertation. Pittsburgh: Duquesne University.

Romanyshyn, R. (1982). *Psychological life: From science to metaphor.* Austin: University of Texas Press.

Rosenberg, E. L. (1998). Levels of analysis and the organization of affect. *Review of General Psychology, 2,* 247–270.

Rouse, J. (1982). Kuhn, Heidegger, and scientific realism. *Man and World, 14,* 269–290

Russell, H. A. (1980). A circumplex model of affect. *Journal of personality and social psychology, 39,* 1161–1178.

Russel, J. A., and L. F. Barrett. (1999). Cone effect, prototypical emotional episodes, and other things called emotion. Dissecting the elephant. *Journal of Personality and Social Psychology, 74,* 805–819.

Sartre, J. P. (1993). *The emotions: Outline of a theory.* Frechtman, B. (Trans.). New York: Carol Publishing Group. [Originally published 1948.]

Schimmack, U., and E. Diener. (1997). Affect intensity: Separating intensity and frequency in repeatedly measured affect. *Journal of Personality and Social Psychology, 73,* 1313–1329.

Schneier, S. (1989). The imagery in movement method: A process tool bridging psychotherapeutic and transpersonal inquiry. In Valle, R. S., and S. Halling. (Eds.). *Existential–phenomenological perspectives in psychology: Exploring the breadth of human experience* (pp. 311–328). New York: Plenum Press.

Seidlitz, L., and E. Diener. (1993). Memory for positive versus negative life events: Theories for the differences between happy and unhappy persons. *Journal of Personality and Social Psychology, 64,* 654–664.

Seligman, M. (1998). Quoted in Hall, T. (1998). Seeking a focus on joy in the field of psychology. *New York Times,* Tuesday, April 28 Section F, p. 7.

Seligman, M. (2003). Foreward: The past and future of positive psychology. In Keyes, C. L. M., and J. Haidt. (Eds.). *Flourishing: Positive psychology and the life well-lived* (pp. xi–xx). Washington, DC: American Psychological Association.

Seligman, M., and M. Csikszentmihalyi. (2000). Positive psychology: An introduction. *American Psychologist, 55,* 5–14.

Slife, B. D., and R. N. Williams. (1995). *What's behind the research? Discovering hidden assumptions in the behavioral sciences.* Thousand Oaks: Sage.

Smith, Q. (1986). *The felt meanings of the world.* West Lafayette, IN: Purdue University Press.

Snyder, C. R., C. Harris, J. R. Anderson, S. A. Holleran, L. M. Irving, S. T. Sigmon, L. Yoshinobu, J. Gibb, C. Langelle, and P. Harney. (1991). The will and the ways: Development and validation of an individual–differences measure of hope. *Journal of Personality and Social Psychology, 60,* 570–585.

Snyder, C. R., and S. J. Lopez. (Eds.). (2002). *Handbook of positive psychology.* Cambridge: Oxford University Press.

Stevick, E. M. (1984). Being angry in the context of an infinite relationship: An epistential phenomenological investigation. Unpublished doctoral desertation, Duquesne University, Pittsburgh, PA.

Tooby, J., and L. Cosmides. (1990). The past explains the present: Emotional adaptations and the structure of ancestral environments. *Ethology and Sociobiology, 11,* 375–424.

Turner, T. J., and A. Ortony. (1990). Basic emotions: Can conflicting criteria converge? *Psychology Review, 99,* 566–571.

Veenhoven, R. (1991). Is happiness relative? *Social Indicators Research, 24,* 1–34.

Watson, D. (2000). *Mood and temperament.* New York: Guilford Press.

Watson, D., and A. Clark. (1992). Affects are separable and inseparable: On the hierarchical arrangement of the negative affects. *Journal of Personality and Social Psychology, 76,* 805–819.

Watson, D., and A. Tellegen. (1985). Toward a consensual structure of mood. *Psychological Bulletin, 98*, 219–235.

Watson, D., D. Wiese, J. Vaidya, and A. Tellegen. (1999). The two general activation systems of affect. Structural findings, evolutionary considerations, and psychobiological evidence. *Journal of Personality and Social Psychology, 76*, 820–838.

Watts, F. (1983). Affective cognition: A sequel to Zajonc and Rachman. *Behaviour Research and Therapy, 21*, 89–90.

Weil, A. (2000). *Eating well for optimum health.* New York: Knopf.

Wertz, F. J. (1983). From "everyday" to psychological description: An analysis of the elements of the moments of a qualitative data analysis. *Journal of Phenomenological Psychology, 14*, 155–216.

Wertz, F. J. (1985). Method and findings in a phenomenological psychological study of a complex life-event: Being criminally victimized. In Giorgi, A. (Ed.). *Phenomenology and psychological research.* Pittsburgh, PA: Duquesne University Press.

Wheeler, L., and K. Miyake. (1992). Social comparison in everyday life. *Journal of Personality and Social Psychology, 62*, 760–773.

BIOGRAPHICAL BACKGROUND

BRENT DEAN ROBBINS, PhD, is Assistant Professor of Psychology at Daemen College in Buffalo, New York. He has a BA in psychology and media communications from Webster University and he graduated from Duquesne University's doctoral program in Clinical Psychology, which is internationally known for its existential–phenomenological approach to research and practice. He completed his predoctoral internship at the University of Pittsburgh Counseling Center and worked for two years as Visiting Assistant Professor of Psychology at Allegheny College in Meadville, PA. Robbins was drawn to Daemen College because he was impressed with the institution's strong emphasis on innovative teaching and, in particular, the school's efforts to nurture interdisciplinary pedagogy and service learning opportunities for students. He also works part-time teaching psychology courses to inmates at Wyoming Correctional Facility in Attica, New York. The program, known as the Consortium of the Niagara Fronter, began in 1975 and now serves 49 inmates. When he is not teaching, Robbins performs psychotherapy and does psychological assessment in private practice.

Robbins is Editor-in-Chief and a founder of *Janus Head: Journal of Interdisciplinary Studies in Literature, Continental Philosophy, Phenomenological Psychology and the Arts*, which is available both in hard copy and on-line (www.janushead.org). The journal, which was founded in 1998, is devoted to maintaining an attitude of respect and openness to the various manifestations of truth in human experience; it strives to foster understanding through meditative thinking, narrative structure, and poetic imagination.

Robbins' research on joy was selected for the 2001 Sidney M. Jourard Award, granted by the APA's Division 32. His work has appeared in a number of peer-reviewed journals, including *Journal of Phenomenological Psychology, American Psychologist, Journal of Theoretical and Philosophical Psychology, Journal of Emotional and Behavioral Disorders, International Journal of Existential Psychology and Psychotherapy, BioMed,* and *Janus Head*; and he has presented his work at more than 25 international conferences and events. He regularly writes book reviews for *Contemporary Psychology, Metapsychology Review,* and *Janus Head.* His research interests include peak experiences such as joy and ecstasy, the self-regulation of emotion, religious and spiritual experience, and existential–humanistic approaches to human suffering, including anxiety, depression, and schizophrenia.

8

CONCEPTUAL ENCOUNTER: THE EXPERIENCE OF ANGER

JOSEPH DE RIVERA

EDITOR'S INTRODUCTION

Dr. de Rivera's method of conceptual encounter can be used for a delimited study, such as a dissertation, or, as in his account in this chapter, in an ongoing dialogue with sought-out and encountered resources. Like other qualitative methods, conceptual encounter begins with actual instances of a phenomenon and seeks to develop a way of describing how the phenomenon is organized (its structure, a sort of map of how its aspects are interrelated and how the experiencing person contributes to the structure). Conceptual encounter, however, purposely moves quickly from the instances to developing abstract concepts that are continuously checked against further instances and against other authors' conceptualizations.

In the case of his continuing study of anger, Dr. de Rivera began with instances of his own anger, and then worked with a series of research partners—graduate students, colleagues, undergraduates. Their own examples of anger "encountered" the conceptualizations offered by Dr. de Rivera. They then gave their impressions of whether Dr. de Rivera's current conceptualization provided an accurate account or required revision.

Unlike many "single-study" research reports, this chapter's report on anger continues an engagement of scholarship from many disciplines and from across areas of scholarship. We note that these continuing encounters are respectful of reported accounts and of others' efforts to conceptualize, and that Dr. de Rivera's conceptualization broadens and becomes more replete with nuances with each encounter. His reports invite a similar attitude on the part of readers; I found myself taking notes to bring back to my own qualitative analyses of becoming angry. I experienced myself as a member of a community of scholars, rather than as someone concerned with being right. All the conceptual encounter studies I have read have been reported in this same spirit.

Many qualitative researchers note that we should be more aware of cultural differences. Dr. de Rivera goes further, both to find anthropological and other studies of anger across diverse cultures, and to explore how people do and do not experience and express anger to preserve culture.

In this chapter, rather than presenting a condensation of the current structure of anger, Dr. de Rivera takes us along his journey of encounters, showing us how he revised his conceptualizations as he encountered new instances of anger and other conceptualizations. I suggest that each reader take a preliminary moment to recall a specific instance of his or her own having become angry, and compare it with Dr. de Rivera's accounts throughout the chapter. I imagine that readers will find themselves recalling still more examples and discovering the richness of conceptual encounter.

Conceptual encounter is a qualitative method for exploring the structure of our experience, the different ways we have of being in the world. Conceptual encounter involves the creation of a conceptualization that may depart from particular accounts from respondents. As in the creation of a work of art or a piece of mathematics, it involves an abstraction that shapes experience and is designed to reveal what may not have been seen before the creation made it evident. For example, although people may experience "a round shape," we may abstract an ideal circle as a locus of points that are equidistant from a center. It may then be clear that a line that touches the circle at only one point (a tangent) must be perpendicular to the radius at that point.

The method has been used to investigate the experience of aloneness (Nisenbaum, 1984) and loneliness (Levin, 1986); anger (de Rivera, 1981); anxiety and panic (Goodman, 1981); closeness (Kreilkamp, 1984); depression (Kane, 1976); joy, elation, and gladness (Lindsay–Hartz, 1981); exaltation (Kahn, 1984); false memory syndrome (de Rivera, 1997); laughter (Funk, 1981); psychological distance (Kreilkamp, 1981); and shame and guilt (Lindsay–Hartz, 1984; Lindsay–Hartz, de Rivera, and Moscolo, 1995). It may be used to compare analogous experiences represented in different languages, as in the comparison of English shame and Japanese *haji* (de Rivera, 1989), and to explore emotions named in other languages, such as the Japanese emotions of *tanoshi*, *urashi*, and *yorokobi* (Ono and de Rivera, 2004).

In this chapter I begin by providing an overview of the method. Then I illustrate how the method was used to conceptualize the experience of anger, and show how the conceptualization can be tested by deliberately having it encounter exceptions. After a brief discussion of the method's limitations and advantages, I present a radical critique of the results of the conceptualization for anger, show how the conceptualization can encounter material from different cultures, and present the current state of the conceptualization.

OVERVIEW OF THE METHOD

Conceptual encounter refers to an encounter between the concept of the investigator and some aspect of human experience, such as getting angry, falling in love, or making a decision. The investigator is trying to comprehend this experience fully—to understand, for example, the way in which our lives are structured when we are angry or in love, to grasp what alternatives are available, and to be able to articulate an abstract description of the general phenomenon that will illuminate our specific experiences and enrich our appreciation of life. But to achieve an abstract conceptualization that really comprehends experience and is not a mere intellectualization, the investigation must be solidly grounded in the concrete experience of actual events. Accordingly, the investigator must deal with specific, concrete examples of anger, love, or whatever is being studied. The investigator may be able to use written accounts and often, such as when he or she is dealing with experiences from other times or cultures, this is the only material available. Usually, however, the investigator will be dealing with the account of a person who has agreed to act as a research partner and who has been asked to describe faithfully an experience in as much detail as possible. Their account may be written, but is usually given in an interview, which may or may not be tape-recorded.

Carefully listening and skillfully questioning, the investigator allows the partner to recall, and to some extent to relive, a concrete experience. *After* this is achieved (perhaps 15 minutes, perhaps an hour or two may have lapsed), the investigator shares with the partner his or her abstract ideas about the essential characteristics of anger, love, or whatever is the general type of experience under discussion. Now the inquiry shifts its focus from the concrete experience of the other to the abstract ideas of the investigator. He or she attempts to get the partner to comprehend these general ideas and asks the partner to what extent they fit the specific reality of his or her concrete experience. Thus, the abstract conceptualization that has been created by the investigator encounters the concrete experience as comprehended by the partner. Is there an enlightening fit between ideas and experienced reality or is something wrong?

THE CONCRETE EXPERIENCE

The topic of inquiry may involve any experience, behavioral pattern, or psychological phenomenon. However, experiences should always be personal, in the sense of being the person's own experience, rather than hearsay, and should be a concrete instance (e.g., "Last night when I was angry at Sally I got hot" rather than "When I'm angry I get hot" or "People get hot when they're angry"). However, the experience may be the person's own experience of someone else's behavior (e.g., "He was so angry he turned red"). At first, the partner's awareness of the experience may be rather sketchy. However, if the investigator quietly listens to the experience and is sincerely interested in finding out exactly how the event was experienced, amazingly detailed accounts may unfold. After this spontaneous account of the experience, the investigator may ask about important details.

Often, the investigator prepares a list of questions about general aspects of the experience and inquires into whatever aspects are not spontaneously mentioned. Thus, if the research partner has not mentioned how he or she experienced time or bodily sensations or psychological space, the investigator may ask how time, the body, or space was experienced, in whatever areas seem to warrant attention.

THE ABSTRACT CONCEPTUALIZATION

The concrete experience of the individual case provides the raw data of the investigation—the "facts" or "existence" or "reality" that the investigator's conceptualization must fit. Hence, the existential details of the individual case are extremely important. However, the investigation would soon be hopelessly mired down in detail were it not balanced by the abstract conceptualization provided by the investigator. This conceptualization is an attempt to capture the essence of the phenomenon by describing how the experience is organized, and explicating its structure and dynamics. Such a description attempts to provide a sort of map or plan of the experience of anger, laughter, distance, or whatever phenomena are under investigation. It describes how the person's experience must be organized if he or she is to become angry, to laugh, to be distant. It describes what changes in experience occur with the anger or laughter, what other organizations were possible, and how the "choice" of the particular configuration that constitutes anger, laughter, or whatever, functions in the overall context of the person's life. Needless to say, a conceptualization that accurately fits experience and that reveals a hitherto unexpected order is almost an artistic creation that can only occur after patient study of numerous instances of the phenomenon.

In this task, the investigator is guided by two quite different demands. First, the conceptualization must be true to experience; it must fit the various concrete experiences of the phenomenon. It must be broad enough to include all instances of the phenomenon, yet narrow enough to exclude related phenomena. Thus, a conceptualization of joy must include all examples of joy, but exclude cases of elation or gladness. Second, the conceptualization must be elegant. That is, it must be relatively simple rather than cumbersome, it must describe different aspects of the phenomenon, and, ideally, it should use concepts that are related to other investigations of interest to the psychologist. It is the tension between these two poles—the dialectical encounter between concrete instances of the phenomenon and abstract, elegant conceptualization—that leads the investigator to create an interesting nontrivial conceptualization. In one sense, to formulate a good conceptualization, the investigator must move away from the concrete data.

That is, he or she cannot simply select some concrete feature that seems important in many of the experiences, or abstract concrete features that different experiences have in common, or articulate some "family resemblance" shared by the experiences. Rather, the investigator must intuit an abstract symbolic form that succeeds in capturing the essential relationships involved in all the concrete individual experiences. Like Michelangelo sculpting, she or he must free the form that lies hidden in the rock.

ADEQUACY OF THE CONCEPTUALIZATION

An adequate conceptualization usually takes a long time to develop. At first the investigator may not be aware of any particular pattern in the different experiences that are examined. Then, a pattern may gradually emerge as he or she sifts through examples of the phenomenon and reads through the literature. Or there may be a sudden grasping of a pattern, such as when the report of a single experience leads to an insight into the essential structure of the phenomenon. An investigation may begin in a hit-or-miss style, with the researcher having a notion about the structure that is conceived in advance and only later checked with the literature, the observations of others, and examined through self-reflection. In such a case, repeated revisions will occur. Regardless of personal style, the formation of a good conceptualization is continually in the making as the researcher moves back and forth between interviews, observations, literature, and reflection, gradually becoming more alert to the nuances and patterns of the phenomenon.

The conceptualization develops through successive insights as it repeatedly encounters the experience of different persons. In one sense it can never be finished, for there is always room for development in science, mathematics, and art. But there is a point when it is finished enough to share with others, a point when a product has been completed and publication is desirable. There are at least three criteria for this point at which a conceptualization may be judged to be complete:

1. It is successful in explicating what has previously only been implicit in the phenomenon. Hence, it reveals the phenomenon in a new light so that a person examining his experience has a better understanding and appreciation of the experience. This is particularly evident when the conceptualization provokes an "ah-ha," such as when a person suddenly gains insight into his experience and realizes something of which he was not previously aware.
2. It replicates in the sense that it fits all the different experiences that different persons have related, and further encounters no longer add anything new or no longer challenge the investigation.

3. The conceptualization is elegant and parsimonious. It uses few but powerful concepts in a precise way, concepts that may be related to the work of other investigators so that the conceptualization becomes a part of a wider sphere of inquiry. Rather than detracting from the precision of the fit between conceptualization and concrete personal experience, this systematic requirement seems to enhance the power of the conceptualization so that it is more apt to capture the essence of an experience. The requirement seems to function in much the same way that requirements of rhyme or meter and a sense of the history of literature seem to stimulate a poet's creativity.

THE ENCOUNTER

Although the excellence of the investigator's work necessarily depends on his or her attaining a thorough acquaintance with the relevant literature and then struggling to achieve creative insights, the development and testing of the conceptualization are ultimately dependent on the nature of the encounter between investigator and research partners. In one sense, this is an intensely personal encounter. Its fruitfulness depends on both persons feeling comfortable with each other *and* the situation so that they can try to be completely open and honest with each other. However, the encounter is clearly structured with a *research* goal. Hence, it is not personal in the sense of two friends sharing an experience, nor is it personal in the sense of a therapeutic encounter. From the very beginning of the investigation, when the investigator asks the other if he or she would be willing to be a research partner, there is an atmosphere of partnership within the structure of objective inquiry. Open communications about very personal experiences have a meaning that is controlled (and often made possible) because of this research context.

After the research partner has shared an experience and the investigator has offered a conceptualization, the two must work together to determine whether the conceptualization fits the experience. Of course, it may be immediately apparent that there is an excellent fit, or that there has been miscommunication and that the conceptualization and experience have little to do with each other. Often, however—and these are the most interesting encounters—some parts of the conceptualization fit but others do not. When these cases are pursued, something new is learned. Either the conceptualization will help the research partner attain a new insight into the nature of the experience so that he or she becomes aware of hitherto ignored aspects of the experience, or the concrete experience will convince the investigator that the conceptualization is in error and must be modified.

AN ILLUSTRATION OF THE METHOD AT WORK:
THE EXPERIENCE OF ANGER

When I began my work on anger I was interested in discovering the essence of anger. What made anger, anger? What was true of all instances of anger and could distinguish these instances from emotions such as fear or depression? We might say that I was primarily interested in the *structure* of anger, and that only later did I become interested in its dynamics, in what preceded its development, and how it could be transformed. A literature review had revealed an interesting distinction between the relationships of anger and fear (Tolman, 1923), and a very interesting early study distinguished between the anger of frustration and the anger of humiliation (Richardson, 1918). I wondered whether I could articulate what was essential to the anger experience.

I began with some facts that were apparent to me (although obviously not apparent to everyone). First, although anger is in some sense "negative," it is not always unpleasant. Although it often felt awful and upsetting, there were times when I enjoyed being angry. It felt good and powerful, and it enabled me to clear the air. Hence, the unpleasant quality often associated with anger could not be an essential aspect of the experience. Second, and regardless of whether the anger is unpleasant or pleasant, it is not always bad in the sense of negatively valued. Although anger is often unproductive, and Fischer's (1998) study of angry outbursts shows how some instances of anger may be regarded as self-deceptive and disempowering, there are times when anger appears to be a good thing to have. Therefore, I could not say that anger was essentially a negative experience.

Yet there was something clearly negative about all anger. What was it? I, or whoever was angry, was directing the anger at something that was negatively evaluated, something that was "bad" or "wrong," and this was an essential aspect of the emotion. At first, I thought it was the destructive character of anger. I have often sworn at people with whom I am angry; others I have wanted to hit, choke, bang their heads against a wall, and so on. I have wished that people would die or fantasized shooting them, and it was clear to me that the "urge to kill" was often present in the anger of many people. Hence, I postulated that anger must evoke a wish to hurt the object of anger. I began with this conceptualization and found that it often fit the experiences of my research partner. To test whether it was always true, I began asking my research partners if any had experiences that contradicted this conceptualization.

One responded with an experience that was a clear exception: She had become angry when her puppy wet the rug, yet did not want to hurt the puppy. She said that she was simply mad that the incident had happened and wished that her rug was not wet. Now an exception to a conceptualization may only be an apparent exception. The person in question may not have really been angry or may have had the desire to hurt the puppy but not let herself experience the desire because she felt such a desire would be wrong. But these alternative explanations did not seem to be valid. The woman had acted angrily in other respects, and she seemed to be capable of admitting her aggressive impulses. Thus, I concluded that my conceptualization needed modification. This particular encounter with a person's experience forced an important revision of the conceptualization.

There is little in common between a wish to kill and a wish that a puppy not wet a rug, at least if we think in terms of common features. However, if we move to a higher level of abstraction, we may see that there is a similar relationship between the person and the object of anger. The angry person wants to change the object of anger, to make it other than it is. There is no Rogerian acceptance here. Rather, the person wants to remove or alter the other, and this seems inherent in all instances of anger. Furthermore, this wish makes an interesting contrast to the wish inherent in fear that seems to involve escape from something that is dangerous, rather than an attempt to change something that might be alterable.

To advance the conceptualization, we may want to relate the wish of anger to the conditions that occasion anger. What are the essential conditions, those that are invariably present, when anger occurs? It is often postulated that frustration is such a condition. For example, Izard (1977) states that anger occurs when one "is either physically or psychologically restrained from doing what one intensely desires to do" (p. 329). However, frustration can, and often does, occur without a person becoming angry. Sometimes people find another way to their goal, change the goal, or become resigned not to get what they want. One can feel frustrated, yet not become angry.

As I listened to accounts of anger and examined my own experiences, I began to realize that all angry persons feel the other *ought* to behave differently. Although the person who is frustrated feels that he or she would *like* things to be different, the angry person acts as though things *should* be different. Sometimes these "oughts," "shoulds," or "rights" are explicitly stated. Thus, one research partner, who realized that an acquaintance was listening through a door to a private conversation, said, "I demanded that she explain to me what gave her the right to do what she did." At other times, oughts are implicit, as in a statement such as, "I was angry at the professor for not taking my study seriously." When a person making such a statement is asked if they simply want the other to behave differently or if they feel the other should behave differently, they respond in terms of shoulds or oughts, rather than desires. One of the characteristics of conceptual encounter is that it aspires to build a system of interconnecting concepts. Therefore, as soon as it became apparent that the concept of ought was implicated in anger, I immediately made a search for what had been written about the concept. Note that this temporarily involves going *away* from the immediate, concrete experience of anger and toward abstract conceptualization.

THE CONCEPT OF OUGHT

I knew that the concept had been explicated by Heider (1958), thus I turned to his analysis for ideas. He points out that the concept of ought implies a force that is suprapersonal. That is, what ought to exist is not just what some person desires, but what is perceived as required by some objective order of affairs. This corresponds to the experience of the angry person who does not simply feel that his or her wishes are being frustrated, but that the other ought to behave differently, that something is wrong with the basic order of existence and needs to be set right. For Heider (1958), what a person desires at a particular moment may be related to what the person likes. What a person believes ought to be in any particular instance is related to what the person values. That is, if a person holds a given value, he or she believes that under certain conditions persons ought to behave in certain ways. Note that this way of construing value (as the basis of what is required to be) is different from conceiving value as determined simply by what a person desires or fears (positive or negative valence) and oughts as simply stemming from the desires of some authority.

Heider (1958) explicated a number of important properties that oughts and values have. First, the concept is related to the concept of *can* (of ability), in that we cannot hold a person responsible, say that he or she ought to do something, if it is impossible for the person to do it. If p ought to do x, then it is implied that p *can* do x. Second, because what ought to be is perceived as stemming from an objective order, oughts (and values) have the same status as beliefs about the nature of reality. Thus, although it is perfectly permissible for another person to have likes and desires that are quite different from our own, sometimes it is as upsetting as if the other person saw red when we saw green. If the person is close to us (and we are not protected by the distance of seeing them as foreign), the mere fact of a value disagreement creates tension in our relationship.

Having noted these characteristics of oughts, we add this to our conceptualization and return to concrete instances of anger. Do we always find that objects of anger are held responsible? That they can (have the ability to) act differently?

I witnessed the angry explosion of a seven-year-old girl at a sled that kept falling down no matter how it was propped up against a wall. Talking with her afterward, I asked why she was angry and she patiently explained that the "darned old thing" would not stay. As she was talking, a grin flitted across her face. I asked her why she had smiled and (after some "do tell me") she stated, "Well, I *told* it to stay up. I know it can't really *do* things but I haven't had a thing I wanted all day long, so I told it to and it should have"—and here she smiled again.

THE CONCEPTS OF UNIT AND RESPONSIBILITY

We may extend Heider's (1958) analysis of ought by noting that oughts imply some form of unity. Thus, a given set of oughts does not apply to everybody, but only to members of one's community. No one feels that a dog ought to be charitable with its bones or that foreigners ought to be loyal Americans. It is precisely the fact that they do not obey our own oughts that makes them foreigners. To the extent that we do feel that others ought to do certain things, we are including them in the community to which we see ourselves as belonging. Of course, such "communities" may include various subsets of humanity. Thus, "property rights," with their related set of oughts and duties, only apply within a national community. Membership in a private club may require the acceptance of a specific set of oughts pertinent only to club members. And the rights of a husband or of a wife (or any couple who are committed to each other) include the right to expect a response to personal needs and, hence, involve values and oughts that only pertain to that particular couple. For this reason I shall call any group whose members recognize a common set of values a *unit*. Thus, a unit may be as small as two persons or as large as the community of human beings.

When others belong in a unit with us, when they recognize the same oughts that we do—share common values—then we may appeal to these oughts if we are in conflict with them. If our analysis is correct, the person who is angry feels that he or she has some influence over the other because the person is experienced in his or her unit, sharing some common values. Otherwise, the other could not be held responsible and could not be perceived as one who ought to act otherwise. One cannot be angry at a person who is not perceived to be responsible for his or her actions—who either *cannot* behave differently (and hence is not subject to the force of ought) or who is in a different unit (is not subject to the same oughts).

It is important to note that as persons develop, they have the *choice* of whether to join a unit—of whether *to belong*. Fingarette (1967) has pointed out that one cannot force a person to be "responsible" (that is, to obey oughts) and that many persons living in our society (e.g., sociopaths) have never really decided to be responsible—to join a community. Although we may act as though the person belongs and our anger presumes this, in fact, only that person can decide whether he or she belongs.

Conversely, as I witnessed other examples of anger it became apparent how often what ought to be is negotiated by the parties in the unit. For example, I observed a one-year-old become angry when his mother began to take him away from a place where he wanted to continue playing. Note that, although we might say that he "wanted" to stay, I believe that the child's anger shows that *he* felt he ought to be allowed to stay. However, the mother had important things to do and was a "no nonsense" mom who simply scooped the child up and refused to grant the legitimacy of his demand to stay. It was fascinating to observe how quickly the anger was aborted.

THE CONCEPTS OF CHALLENGE AND DISTANCE

Having examined the abstract concepts of oughts, units, and responsibility, I returned to specific instances of anger. Although every instance of anger implied that the other ought to change his or her behavior, it seemed clear that this condition was necessary but not sufficient. I now focused on instances when a person did *not* become angry in spite of the fact that an ought was violated, and I asked research partners to find examples. I found that research partners were able to report instances in which they believed the other ought to change his or her behavior and yet no anger occurred.

In some of these instances the persons did not permit themselves to be involved or it became clear that the other was not intentionally violating the ought. In others, the person had enough control over the situation simply to state a request, a reminder, or command that brought the other's behavior in conformity to what ought to be. For example, when a professor (known for her assertive ability) attempted to register at a hotel for which she had reservations, the clerk informed her that he was sorry but that there were no rooms available at the specified price. Rather than becoming angry she simply stated (in a firm voice), "I'm sure you can find one for me" (which the clerk proceeded to do).

Note that when I say she did not become angry, I imply that her *body* was not changed. I do not simply mean that there was no objective physiological response (no increased heart rate, skin temperature, or muscle tension), but that the body was not experienced as transformed. Clearly, an important aspect of anger is that it is embodied, that we are aware of a change in our body. In fact, it is easy to overemphasize the body's arousal. The angry body may be experienced as expanding with aggressive energy, as tense, as on the verge of exploding. However, and this often seems the case in instances of deep anger, the person may simply report being "a little sore." Thus, we must not simply think of the body as a physical object that is separate from its environment. Rather, we must conceive of the body as lived in the time and space we experience, and anger as embodied in the motive structures that relate us to the world. The angered body is experienced as strengthened.

When anger occurred, it was clear that the person always felt *challenged*—that is, the other was perceived as intentionally violating the ought and the angered person was involved yet lacked control. The person was involved in a situation in which the other's behavior defined a reality that contradicted the reality of the angered person. There was a real contest over what ought to be; the contenders occupy the same "reality space" and one must leave.

For example, consider this instance. Two class friends (Dorothy and Peter) were active in a youth organization and both decided to run for regional offices. They talked with each other and agreed that because Dorothy had been more active in the organization and cared about it a lot, she should run for vice-president (the more responsible and prestigious position) and Peter should run for treasurer. However, during the regional convention, Peter stated that people had made him realize that he should run for vice-president and he told Dorothy that if she wanted to run against him that was her decision. He then abruptly walked away. Dorothy stated,

> For a moment I was paralyzed ... fighting tears ... I was deeply hurt .... Soon after Peter came over ... I looked out at him. I told him. I couldn't believe what he did, that our friendship must mean very little to him. ... I very seldom became angry, mainly because anger frightens me. Usually I back down ... this instance I was incapable of backing down when Peter challenged me. I wanted that office and Peter knew how much it meant to me. I knew I was right ... he should never have challenged me.

The concept of challenge implies that the other is a serious contender for the space, and this suggests that an alternative to anger is to perceive the other in such a way that he or she is not a real contender. This may be done in a number of different ways.

The other may be perceived as "not responsible" for his or her action (e.g., drunk, insane, only a child). Because the other *cannot* really control his or her behavior, the behavior does not challenge the ought.

The other way may be regarded as unqualified to be a challenger because of the person's status (e.g., a foreigner, a woman, a member of a different caste). The other does not challenge the ought because his or her position as an outsider does not permit a challenge.

The other may be seen as having a character structure that works against his or her being an adequate member of the group (e.g., as "phony," "disagreeable," or "basically weak"). In this case the other is usually *disliked*, and this sentiment takes the place of anger.

Notice that all these ways of perceiving the other involve increasing a distance between oneself and the other. Instead of a person getting angry, he or she sees the other as different from oneself so that the other cannot present a real challenge. Instead of the emotional force of anger, we have a *structural* change—in effect, a change in psychological space so that a person who may have been close is now distant.

THE FUNCTION OF ANGER

At first, our analysis simply suggested that anger instructed a person to change the object of anger. Then it became clear what this object was—a challenge to what the person believed ought to exist. But implicit in this idea of removing a challenge is the notion that the person *can* remove the challenge; in other words, that the person not only has a belief about what ought to exist but also that he or she has the power to *assert* that belief and to maintain his or her position about what ought to exist. This is not always easy to do. Although both the angry person and the other belong to an identical unit, and hence recognize the same values, the two persons do not necessarily agree on what ought to exist. Just as liking only becomes desiring when the person who likes something also has a need, values become oughts only when a person recognizes that objective conditions require the value to be expressed.

In most contests there is a disagreement over what is recognized as the situation. To one person the salient features of the situation indicate that *x* ought to be done, and to the other person the situation calls for *y*. The contest itself is over what the situation actually requires (and this depends on the meaning of the situation). It is a contest over what reality is like and, hence, what ought to be done. The presence of anger implies that, in this contest, the person continues to assert his or her own position, to *will* what he or she recognizes as existent and, therefore, to determine what ought to be in the face of the other's will to define reality differently. Thus, anger supports a person's position; if it is not present, the person may "fold" and give in to the other's position.

At first, I presumed that anger gave persons the power to assert their position publicly, and often I found that this was so. For example, a woman in public relations work was given a contract to change the image of a firm that was expanding its business. After doing some work on the contract, she had lunch with a member of the firm and happened to express her political views. She noted that the conversation grew strained and realized that she had made a mistake in speaking so openly about her beliefs. The job called for further contacts with the firm, but the other did not call and "could not be reached." This placed the woman in conflict. Clearly a contract had been signed, some work had been done, and she should attempt to collect her fee. On the other hand, her client was in a position from which he could injure her reputation with other clients if he promulgated his judgment of her and, consequently, she hesitated to press him for payment. Because she was angry about the client's condemning her professional ability on account of her politics, and his failing to cancel the contract in a responsible way, she had her lawyer write a letter threatening court action. (She collected half the fee called for by the contract.)

However, I have since found other instances in which persons experienced anger but did not publicly assert their position because they believed it would be ineffectual, inappropriate, or dangerous to do so. For example, a college student received a Valentine's Day card from her father. Enclosed were a check and a note that asked her not to mention the gift to her stepmother. The student was angry because she believed that her father ought not to have her stepmother's permission to send his daughter a check. Although she expressed her feelings to several friends, she did not assert her position with her father. In this, and other similar instances, anger only appeared to maintain a person's private sense of what ought to be. It appeared to give persons the power to maintain their own position, but not to assert their position to the person who challenged this reality. It may be observed that although this created a type of distance between themselves and the challenger, the other was not "distanced" in the sense of being regarded as irresponsible. The difference between these and other types of psychological distance has been delineated by Kreilkamp (1981).

Does the anger really serve to maintain the person's position? It certainly appears that way. Consider what occurs when an ought is violated and the person does not become angry.

A student wrote a paper for a course and felt that she had done a good job. It was returned with a mark of D+. She later reported that rather than becoming angry she had two thoughts in quick succession: "She [the grader] obviously doesn't know what I am talking about" and "The course has a pass/no record option anyway, so nuts to grades." The first thought created distance by considering the reader unintelligent whereas the second thought removed the student from any involvement in doing well in the course and asserting herself. If she had become angry, she might have confronted her professor with the assertion that she ought to get the grade her paper deserved. Without the anger, she did not risk an actual confrontation about the grade. Of course, we do not know whether the student was maturely reacting to an obtuse reader with false grading standards or whether she was avoiding a confrontation out of an insecurity about what the paper was really worth. In either case, in the absence of anger and an actual confrontation, the student was able to maintain her private belief that the paper was good, but the grader's judgment determined social reality.

If we postulate that anger serves to strengthen the will to maintain one's position, how can we account for the fact that the student with the D+ could maintain her private belief that the paper was good without experiencing anger, whereas the student with the note from her father apparently needed the support of her anger to maintain her private belief that her father ought not to have to ask her stepmother for permission? I believe this is because the first student was able to distance herself from her professor and from her commitment to the course. This option was not available to the second student because she wanted to maintain her closeness with her father. If this conjecture is correct, anger may, paradoxically, maintain closeness. This occurs when the unit of shared oughts is maintained by the presence of anger.

TESTING THE CONCEPTUALIZATION WITH FURTHER ENCOUNTERS: HURT AND DEPRESSION

At this point in the exploration, research partners were given the following conceptualization:

> Anger is a way of being in which the angry person's will is strengthened so that he or she can remove a challenge to what he or she asserts ought to exist, thereby preserving the unit between the angry person and the object of anger and the shared values of this unit.

Students in a class on emotions were asked to write short (three- to five-page) papers based on an encounter between this conceptualization and their own personal experience. I pointed out the difference between a sort of mild meeting, during which one sticks to generalities and is satisfied with an easy fit between idea and experience, and an exciting encounter, during which the power of the conceptualization reveals aspects of the experience that were previously unnoticed, or the details of the experience force a modification of the conceptualization. I made it clear that I valued exciting encounters more than mild meetings and that the former occurred when one went into the concrete details of some specific experience and pitted them against the specific terms of the conceptualization.

In one paper, a student gave an experience in which the conditions for anger were met, but she had experienced hurt rather than anger. A close friend should have phoned at a mutually agreed-upon time. When he did not call, he was held responsible, and his not calling was a challenge to the value of responsive friendship, yet she did not experience anger nor create distance. Instead, she felt very hurt.

THE EXPERIENCE OF HURT

The report of such an experience forces us to expand the conceptualization of anger so that we may discriminate the conditions underlying hurt from those underlying anger and show the relationship between these conditions. Clearly there is some sort of close relationship between anger and hurt. Often when a person is subjected to a sudden physical hurt, the person reacts with an outburst of anger. Furthermore, the etymology of the term suggests a connection. Anger stems from the Icelandic *angr* (grief) and is related to the Latin *angro* (anguish). If we were simply to speculate about the relationship, we might conclude that anger was simply an expression of hurt or that hurt was simply a form of inner-directed anger. However, it is clear that anger and hurt *feel* differently; the experiences are quite distinct, and our existential perspective leads us to consider them to be alternative ways of structuring our experience to meet a violation of what ought to be. Rather than speculate, we must carefully describe the experience of hurt and attempt to articulate a conceptualization for the experience that will allow us to relate it systematically to the conceptualization of anger.

How, then, can we describe the structure of hurt? From the examples I have examined, it appears that the person retains a sense of what ought to have happened and a sense that the other is responsible, but the person does not really assert his or her will in an attempt to remove a challenge. Rather, the will collapses and the person *suffers* the hurt. This seems to occur along with a loss of confidence or trust in the other's regard for the self, and a realization that one cannot will the other to love the self. The reaction to the suffering is often to close off, pull in, or tighten up, to deaden the hurt or prevent its future occurrence. The alternative is either to share the hurt or to "choose" to experience anger, with the emotions often shifting back and forth.

During the experience of hurt, the other's response seems to have challenged the very existence of the personal unit and the closeness that would sustain anger. Rather than the person distancing the other, the other seems to have distanced the self—so there is no longer a common ground for anger to occur.

Although we can begin to relate hurt to anger on the basis of this crude sketch, a more accurate analysis of hurt would require a complete conceptual encounter, testing the sketch against the details of a number of concrete experiences. Such an analysis would have to take into account the fact that the experience of hurt must be related to the somewhat different experience of psychological pain. The latter appears to occur when self-boundaries are broken—such as when a person has to separate from a union, or has to recognize some new aspects of the self, or even, at times, when a person must break open the self to experience love. In fact, the intimate connection between pain and the realization of love is shown clearly in the works of writers such as William Blake and D. H. Lawrence. See, for example, Blake's (1991) poem, "The Little Black Boy," or Lawrence's (1979) short story, *Daughters of the Vicar*. Such pain appears to have a somewhat different structure from the "hurt" of rejection that we have been considering.

In any case, for our current purpose of illustrating the method of conceptual encounter, we note how a personal experience provoked by the conceptualization forces a modification in the conceptualization. Examples show that a violation of what ought to exist may result in hurt rather than anger, may remind us that there is an intimate connection between the two, and may challenge us to define hurt and specify when it will exist rather than anger. Tentatively, we propose that as an alternative either to structuring a situation so that there is a challenge to what ought to exist, or to distancing the other, the person may suffer being distanced.

"OBJECTIVE" VIOLATIONS

Let us look at a student's paper with a different sort of challenge to the conceptualization.

> At the beginning of this last module I decided to do well in my organic chemistry lab. ... I accepted it as a challenge, as a task. ... Implied in this task was the assertion: *I do not fail at what I really try to do*. ... I completed four tests moderately successfully. ... The following week I did the next four tests with little trouble. The last test, however, was marred by a minor disaster. This test consisted of slowly adding nitrous acid to a test tube containing an organic compound that was cooled in an ice bath. There were three different compounds in separate test tubes. Two of them behaved nicely. The third (quite comically in retrospect) started foaming madly and started to come out of the top of the test tube. Obviously I had either added the acid too fast or had not cooled it down enough. I tried to cool the test tube down some more by moving it around in the ice bath, but only managed to knock one of the other test tubes over, losing its contents to the ice bath. Then I impulsively removed the troublesome test tube from the ice bath, propping it up against my lab towel. But it managed to fall over and spill its contents on the lab table. At that moment I was feeling my anger. I felt an incredible tension which seemed directed at holding back from shouting innumerable obscenities. I felt that what was happening shouldn't have been happening. I felt a strong desire to smash all of my glassware. I decided not to finish the experiment and started to clean up. While cleaning up I managed to break, unintentionally, two beakers. This didn't relieve my anger, though, because they merely broken, they didn't shatter. It didn't add to my anger either because I didn't care that I broke them.
>
> It is important to note that my anger was not directed at anyone or anything specific. While in the lab it wasn't at myself, not the lab assistants, not the professor, not the students around me, and certainly not at N, N-dimethylaniline (the nasty organic compound that started the whole mess). My desire to smash the glassware wasn't because I was angry with the glassware, but because I desired to destroy something. And against whom or what would have shouting obscenities been directed?
>
> I propose that the statement that anger is felt, "when there is a challenge to what we assert ought to exist," is a specific case of a more general statement, "when there is a violation of what we assert should (or does) exist." ... Should refers to what one sees as the structure of the world and the violation is the interpretation of an act. This act could be caused by an intentional being (who may have a different view of the world) or by the encountering of the view of the world and the real world.

This example poses a different sort of problem for the conceptualization: What happens when the challenge to what the person asserts ought to exist is not issued by an opposing will? In the previous example, it is an impersonal reality that challenges the person's will (although the tendency to personify may be noted in the statement that the test tube "managed to fall over"). There is only an impersonal violation of the reality that should be. Nevertheless, it is important to note that the angered person responds as if he or she were challenged. The person responds with the same disbelief that occurs in examples of personal anger. And although the person realizes the irrationality of the anger, that he or she "should" not really feel anger, and even though he or she controls its expression in various ways, there is still the impulse to deal with a sort of challenge. The person wants to see some other as responsible, to smash something, to somehow restore his or her power to act in the world, and to regain confidence in the world as it should be.

THE EXPERIENCE OF DEPRESSION

We may inquire what happens when a person who is challenged fails either to become angry or to distance. I postulate that when this occurs a person abandons his or her position and becomes *depressed*. This will occur when there are forces that prevent the challenge from being removed and when there are reasons not to exercise the alternative of distancing the challenger. The depression may be seen as analogous to the surrender mechanism that some species use to signal the acceptance of defeat and, hence, to end the fight.

From my perspective depression is not simply a passive reaction to a situation of loss. On the contrary, a conceptual encounter by Kane (1976) has shown that depression may be regarded, like anger, as transforming the person's situation. In fact, we may understand depression as an emotion whose structure is the reverse of the emotion of anger. Whereas anger instructs the person to remove the challenge, the instructional transformation of depression is "remove the self." Just as anger works to strengthen the person's will so that he or she can remove the challenge, depression works against the person's will so he or she *can't* fight against the challenge. Thus, part of the experience of depression is that one cannot do anything about one's situation. The instruction "remove the self" is not necessarily dysfunctional. It prevents distancing from the other. Although the person's position is abandoned, the person's values are preserved. Ordinarily, if a person failed to assert his or her position, the person would be abandoning his or her values. But in depression one *cannot* act; therefore, oughts cannot apply and the failure to act does not mean that the person no longer subscribes to the group's values. Kane (1976) has shown that in many cases of situational depression, the person is caught in a situation in which his or her values require an action that would have unfortunate consequences. When the depression occurs, the person cannot perform the required action, thus preventing the consequences while still preserving the person's commitment to values and group membership.

For example, in one instance a teenager became pregnant and was caught in a situation in which her value for human life required her to have the child in spite of the fact that her young boyfriend could not marry her and that she believed she could not confide in her mother because of her mother's opposition to premarital sex. Although there were moments of anger at the mother—when she was perceived as one who ought to accept sex—the predominant emotion was a mild depression that lasted for about a month as the young woman decided that she *had* to have an abortion. (Note how the depression structured the situation so that she did not really *act* against her values—she experienced *having* to get the abortion rather than wanting to get it.) Thus, her values were maintained in spite of the fact that she acted in a way that seemed to contradict them.

Returning to the emotion of anger, we now see that in both anger and depression there is a challenge to the person's belief in what ought to exist but that in the former the person continues to assert his or her position whereas in depression the person no longer can assert what ought to exist.

Note that our evolving conceptualization rejects the idea that under some objectively determined stimulus conditions a person will necessarily react with anger. There is no situation that is independent of the person. The conceptualization asserts that anger is one structure, one way, that a person may be in the world. It asserts that when a person is in the world in an angry way, the person is necessarily experiencing a challenge to what he or she is asserting ought to exist. There are other ways in which the person could structure the situation. Thus, as we have seen, the person could create a distance between the self and the other, rather than experience a challenge, or could become depressed and fail to assert what ought to exist. But in such other cases, the person would not be angry. The person has a number of degrees of freedom, but there are definite consequences to whatever alternative is selected (or comes into being). If one perceives the other as belonging to one's unit but does not get angry, then one must increase distance (or become depressed). Our freedom involves the recognition of these psychological necessities. Implicit in this way of experiencing one's situation is the "response" of anger, the "instruction" to the person to remove the challenge.

LIMITATIONS AND ADVANTAGES

LIMITATIONS OF THE METHOD

Although conceptual encounter is extremely flexible, it has a number of inherent limitations. First, because the investigation begins with a concept, the method is initially dependent on the existence of a term that names the experience to be studied. Thus, it is unlikely that an American investigator would discover and explicate the experience of sweet dependency denoted by the Japanese term *amae*. Second, the method's emphasis on the search for what is essential to an experience leads it to ignore situational factors that are important to study and understand. For example, anger appears much more likely to occur when a person is overworked, fatigued, tense, or "overstretched," and it often involves aggressive behavior. Interviews may reveal such facts, but the method does not encourage such observations or note how they may be conceptualized. Third, the focus on experiential structures does not lend itself to the description of emotional processes or developmental dynamics. Thus, the investigator is apt to over-look how anger may be replaced by the process of resignation or gradu-ally developed as one person begins to feel dominated by another. These limitations require conceptual encounter to be supplemented with other methods.

ADVANTAGES OVER TRADITIONAL APPROACHES

Because it is focused on both concrete human experience and systematic conceptualization, the method lends itself to rapid hypothesis testing. Although it is primarily designed to contribute to our understanding of the choices that underlie our emotional experience, the results of conceptual encounters provide important suggestions and correctives to the under-standing of more traditional psychology. Thus, the analysis of anger has implications for clinical psychology, social psychology, and emotion theory. Clinical psychology tends to focus on the defensive uses of anger and on anger management programs designed to help those who become violently aggressive. However, our conceptualization reveals anger to be an aspect of interpersonal relationships. This makes it possible to distinguish between a healthy anger that asserts what ought to be in the context of a unit with shared values, and a defensive anger that operates to protect egoistic needs. Thus, it supports Roffman's (2004) contention that anger may be under-stood as a resource rather than as simply something to be managed. It suggests that anger and aggression should be separated, that there are different reasons for dysfunctional anger, and that anger management programs should focus on different aspects of anger. Narcissism is often treated as a uniform entity (Rhodewalt and Morf, 1998). However, our analysis suggests a distinction between the defensive rage expressed by people with low self-esteem (who frequently mistake the behavior of others to be a challenge to the assertion that they ought to be treated with respect) and the aggression of people with an inflated self-esteem (who lack a con-cern with the perspective of others and confuse what they want with what ought to be). The conceptualization may also help us understand why cognitive therapies seem more effective for problems with trait anger (which are probably more apt to involve disturbances of the perception of what ought to be), and behavioral relaxation approaches seem more effective with state anger (which is more apt to involve the assertive component of anger [Del Vecchio and O'Leary, 2004]). In general, the analysis suggests that it may be helpful to distinguish between the anger of people who are bound by what ought to be, and those who are attempt-ing to maintain closeness and reluctant to grant the distance of separation. It also suggests that at times it may be helpful to understand depression as stemming from a situation in which a person cannot allow anger yet must maintain closeness.

Social psychology usually conceives anger to be an emotion with specifiable physiological, expressive, and subjective aspects—a discrete entity caused by a situational appraisal and leading to predictable consequences. Although our conceptualization views anger as a "choice" of how to relate to others, it is possible to use the conceptualization heuristically to create a social psychological model that can be examined experimentally. On the causal end, such a model would predict that anger would be more likely to occur when norms were violated than when a person was simply frustrated, when circumstances discouraged a person from creating distance, and when a person had the power to assert his or her position. On the consequence end, because anger involves the assertion of a position about what ought to be, the model suggests that anger may confer power and status in cultures that value assertiveness (such as our own). Thus, van Kleef, De Dreu, and Manstead (2004) show that people are apt to make concessions to an angry negotiator, and Tiedens (2001) shows that people confer more status to angry than sad political targets. The model suggests that anger will persist until a challenge is removed. We know that anger may have aftereffects, and it has been shown experimentally that people who have been angered are more apt to attribute responsibility in subsequent tort cases.

However, Goldberg, Lerner, and Tetlock (1999) show that this carryover only occurs when a perpetrator is not punished. Our analysis suggests that this is because the unfulfilled desire to remove the challenge to what ought to exist is influencing the subsequent judgments of responsibility. It is important to note that our conceptualization places anger in the context of interpersonal responsibility and suggests the importance of distinguishing the attribution of responsibility that is involved in angrily *blaming* someone for an undesirable outcome, and the angry assertion that one expects the others to accept responsibility for their behavior. The former involves an individualistic expression of what one thinks ought to be (if the other did what he or she ought to have done, things would be better), whereas the latter sees the other as a responsible member of a common unit.

With regard to our understanding of emotions in general, a number of studies have begun to contrast central nervous system differences between anger and other emotions. It has been postulated that there is an approach system that involves activation of the left frontal lobe (with activation lowered in depression), and a withdrawal system that involves activation of the right frontal lobe (and is active in fear). In congruence with our conceptualization of anger as involving a strengthening of will and the assertive removal of a challenge (in contrast to either a depressive submission or a fearful withdrawal), evidence reported by Harmon–Jones and Sigelman (2001) suggests that anger involves activation of the approach system. In a related vein, Lerner and Keltner (2001) have shown that angry people are optimistic and are risk seeking, in contrast to fearful people who are more pessimistic in their risk estimates and are risk aversive in their choices. The advantage of the conceptualization provided by conceptual encounter is that it reveals the relationship between different options so that we may understand how basic processes may be reflected quite differently in different personal and cultural choices.

A CRITIQUE AND ALTERNATIVE CONCEPTUALIZATIONS

Although it is possible to test the usefulness of a conceptualization by using the traditional methods of clinical or social psychology, it may be more fruitful to expose it to philosophical, theoretical, or cultural critiques. As an example, consider the following critique and alternatives. The conceptualization presented earlier treated anger as a universal emotion with invariant properties. However, Lau (1990) has argued that the conceptualization is actually a narrative paradigm that Western culture uses to socialize aggressive impulses.

ANGER AS A NARRATIVE FORM

Lau (1990) argues that children have a variety of preverbal *angriform* reactions such as biting and hitting that are responses to pain, discomfort, and frustration. Societies must control these aggressive responses, and in our culture this is done by socializing children so that the impulses are organized into the emotion we call anger, an emotion that we only permit when there is a challenge to shared values. In this view, what provokes *angriform* reaction is frustration, pain, or discomfort (rather than a challenge to what ought to exist). However, we are socialized so as to not allow ourselves to experience anger unless we can perceive a challenge to an ought.

On the one hand, Lau (1990) grants that our anger at impersonal objects is a strong argument for the ought–challenge structure. As he states (1990), "The components he specifies as necessary to the experience of anger are projected where reflection does not recognize their existence and is a little embarrassed by the projection" (p. 4). However, Lau (1990) takes this ought–challenge form to be a narrative template. For him, assertions, challenges, and oughts are elements of discursive consciousness rather than perception. Experiences of anger do not belong to a naturalistic class as apples or eclipses do, but to a dramatic–historical class such as wars of liberation or championship games. Their form is a narrative form that is created by our culture and is used to manage conflict and aggression between the members of our society. Aggression that does not fit the ought–challenge paradigm is not allowed as anger and appears contranarrative or, at least, not to be emotionally motivated. That is, we feel *we* should not get angry unless there has been a challenge to what ought to exist. Lau (1990) shows that in our accounts of the anger of *other* persons, we often do not use the ought–challenge paradigm. We often describe others as becoming angry because they do not get what they want or are in discomfort. It is only our own anger that is invariably described in terms of challenge to oughts.

Of course, although the observer may only perceive a frustrated wish, the person who is becoming angry may perceive a challenged ought, and even extremely aggressive, poorly socialized men experience their own anger as a response to oughts being challenged. For example, Toch's (1993) accounts of violent men reveal that these explosions are often occasioned by the perceived slights to which the insecure are liable. Yet Lau (1990) points out that when we are frustrated or tense, we may rein in aggressive impulses. Lacking a challenge to oughts, we may inhibit our anger, yet allow gestures, tones of voice, and fantasies that reveal "anger," although they fall short of the fully developed anger experience. It is interesting that in such cases the observer may see "anger" (the rising voice, clenched fist, sharp remark) that the putatively angry persons denies. ("I'm not *really* angry.") In any case, we do not see a fully developed anger response in the sense of an attempt to change the person who is challenging what ought to exist.

Attempting to integrate the positions, Lau (1990) suggests that there may be a prefiguring of ought–challenge anger at a preverbal perceptual–motor level. At this level there would be no discursive oughts or challenges, but there would be a sense of narcissistic entitlement. Given adequate mothering, the infant would have a sense of self as entitled to adequate nurturance and would imagine a world that ought to facilitate its autonomy. However, such an analysis seems based on an essentially Freudian conception of the self as an autonomous being with aggressive impulses. By contrast, we could regard narcissistic entitlements as primitive oughts that are embedded in the early personal relationship between mother and child.

As a result of this dialogue, I now realize that the conceptualization I advanced is a view of anger as essentially interpersonal rather than either intrinsically biological or cultural. Lau's (1990) interesting exposition, together with the fact that feelings of hurt are an alternative to anger, and the fact that anger may be expressed at impersonal reality, suggest that the conceptualization needs to be related to a more comprehensive view of the interpersonal. Hence, I was delighted when I discovered the personalistic philosophy expounded by John Macmurray.

ANGER AS AN EXPRESSION OF DEPENDENCY

Macmurray (1961) suggests that persons qua persons only exist in the context of interpersonal relations. We are born into a dependency relationship with our mothers or mother substitutes and, even as adults, can only survive if others care for us. Every one of these personal relationships is characterized by two motivational strands: a genuine caring for the other and an anxious concern for the self. At any moment in time, and to some extent in our habitual attitudes, one of these motivations is dominant while the other is constrained in a necessary but subordinate position. We begin life with an outward, heterocentric focus, but when it appears that we are betrayed, abandoned, uncared for, our self-concern becomes dominant. As long as our caring for the other is dominant, the ideal outcome we imagine and our perception of actuality form a unitary whole. There is an inevitable discrepancy and tension between the ideal and the actual. However, the two are kept in relationship and the person works for what is ideal while staying in touch with the actual. The mind and body, reason and emotion, are united. What is presented to the world is in harmony with what is felt within; behavior is both spontaneous and rational. By contrast, when we believe we cannot depend on the other, our self-concern becomes dominant and a splitting occurs. Because of our fear for ourselves, we either believe we must primarily look out for ourselves, becoming independent of the untrustworthy other, and searching for control and power, or we believe we must become "good," conforming to what the other wants so that he or she will (in the future) care for us. In the former mode we are pragmatic "realists," using our imaginations to gain power and pay only lip service to "unrealistic" ideals. In the latter mode we are sentimental idealists, and use our imaginations to create a sentimental substitute that serves as an opiate for the pain of reality. It is only when our faith in the other is restored that our unity is regained and we can use our imaginations to make the actual ideal.

What has this to do with anger? When Macmurray (1961) analyzes the development of the child, he points out that the child initially expects the mother to satisfy all his or her needs. The child imagines that this will occur and develops this ideal. It is what the mother ought to do, and if the child has adequate mothering, this ideal will be largely met. However, in order for the child to grow, weaning must occur and the child must learn to do things that had been done for him. Hence, there will be a conflict of wills and, in my own terms, the child's ought will be challenged by the mother's behavior, and anger will occur. However, Macmurray's (1961) analysis goes deeper because he sees that anger is a defense against the threat of personal annihilation. Speaking of the child, he states, "He is refused what experience has given him the right to expect, and his cosmos has returned to chaos" (p. 98). In this particular struggle of wills, the child must lose and do what the mother requires. However, the child may eventually do this out of self-concern—by being either rebelliously independent or conformingly good, or out of a genuine cooperation made possible by faith that the mother really does care for him or her.

Macmurray (1961) can account for certain cultural differences by specifying different defenses that may be used when fear for oneself begins to dominate one's relationships. For example, people who decide they are not really loved will elect to take care of themselves and develop an individualistic culture that will stress the rights of individuals to pursue their own happiness, whereas people who elect to be good so that they will be loved will develop a collectivist culture that will emphasize conformity and the welfare of the group. Although both types of cultures will also have times when people generally care for one another and may experience anger when oughts are challenged, they will handle the anger of children in different ways. More individualistic cultures will allow the experience of anger but defend against its potential violence by insisting that the challenged ought be socially agreed-upon values in the manner suggested by Lau (1990), or by developing ways in which people may be reconciled. Collectivist cultures may deny the experience of anger or only allow its expression in fantasy or in displaced aggression.

Bearing these considerations in mind, I continue the conceptual encounter by examining accounts of anger in "primitive" cultures. Fortunately, there are a number of interesting accounts available. I have included all those with which I am familiar. My question is whether the conceptualization of anger as a response to a challenge to what ought to exist allows us to understand "anger" in other cultures. I begin with cultures that appear most similar.

ENCOUNTERS WITH THE EXPERIENCE OF OTHER CULTURES

First, let us consider the Ifaluk of the South Pacific. In her investigation of the Ifaluk on their Micronesian atoll, Lutz (1988) contrasts a number of types of anger that are named and that correspond roughly to our terms for irritability, annoyance, and helpless frustration. She points out that these are all distinguished from *song* or "justifiable anger." Although the former types are devalued, *song* is taken seriously as a moral assertion. For the Ifaluk there is an explicit rule violation that is pointed at, along with condemnation and a call for the violator to mend his ways. A woman may become *song* if her husband drinks too much and fails to meet his obligations; a man may become *song* when he is hungry and the women of his household have not prepared food. However, the *song* is not accompanied by any physical violence. It is expressed by a refusal to speak to or eat with the offender, speaking impolitely, pouting, or throwing objects (but *not* at the person). A fine may be levied or gossip begun and the object of the *song* is expected to show repentance. Although what ought to be is construed somewhat differently, and although the Ifaluk are clearly less violent, one has the impression that both *song* and anger deal with challenges to oughts. Thus, although American anger is more apt to involve the ought of individual rights and even a sense of narcissistic entitlement, Ifaluk *song* is almost a perfect example of Lau's (1990) ideal ought–challenge anger, without much of a component of preverbal passion. It is anger with a minimum of aggressive energy.

Turning to how anger is experienced by the Taita of Kenya, we note that anger occurs when one person transgresses another's rights (Harris, 1978). This is in accord with our conceptualization. However, the anger itself is not encouraged as a way to remove this challenge to what ought to exist. Rather, it is regarded as a mystical source of inherently dangerous wishes that will cause the illness, or even death, of the transgressor or his livestock. To avoid such disastrous consequences, one of the Taita's central religious acts involves the casting out of anger from the heart so that peace and general well-being can be restored. Harris (1978) notes that rights could not be transgressed without endangering the wrong-doer because the anger that was caused would mystically result in later suffering of the transgressor. Note, however, that although the angry Taita may attempt to remove their anger rather than to use it to assert what ought to be, the anger functions within the society in a way that removes challenges to what ought to exist.

The ought–challenge conceptualization is not as easy to apply when we turn to Briggs' (1970) classic description of the Utku Eskimos in northwestern Canada. She records five terms that refer to aspects of anger and records many instances of the angry behavior of children. However, the Utku culture values warmth, protection, nurturance, and even-tempered persons. They devalue unkindness, bad temper, and aggressiveness, and their devaluation is to the extent that adults do not express anger and deny experiencing it. She cites an Eskimo informant recorded in 1931: "It is generally believed that white men have quite the same minds as small children. Therefore one shall always give way to them. They are easily angered, and when they cannot get their will they are moody and, like children, have the strangest ideas and fancies" (p. 329).

What makes Utku children angry and how do adults manage to avoid anger? Briggs' (1970) descriptions of childhood anger clearly support Macmurray's (1961) description of the emotional turmoil surrounding weaning. It is clear that when small children do not get what they want, they scream. Their will is frustrated and it appears that they experience a violation of what ought to be. Among adults, the major way in which anger is averted appears to have to do with the development of *ayuqnaq*, an attitude/feeling of resignation to the inevitable, to what cannot be helped or is impossible to change, a rational, pragmatic recognition that an unpleasant situation is unavoidable. When whites or children violate oughts, they are viewed as lacking reason. In my terms, they are "distanced" so there is no challenge to what ought to be. In the 17 months Briggs lived with the Inuit, she did not observe a single instance of expression of adult anger.

Of course, this does not mean that no anger was present. Briggs (1970) clearly believes that hostility was experienced in displaced aggression in the form of fantasies, fears, and nightmares. She points out that the Ulku beat their dogs unmercifully with the excuse that it makes them behave, and her Eskimo "father" had extremely violent fantasies that were full of stabbings, whippings, and murders. He usually spoke of these when he felt hopeless in his dealings with whites. Furthermore, Eskimos particularly feared people who *never* lost their temper because such a man could kill if he ever did become angry. And it was believed that "strong thoughts" could kill or cause illness, so that people took care to satisfy the wishes of others so that resentment would not accumulate in the mind.

What may we conclude from our encounter with Briggs' (1970) account of Utku anger? On the one hand, it would seem that Lau (1990) is correct. We do not find instances in which anger is manifested as the removal of challenge to what ought to exist, and the Utku do not appear to manage their aggressive impulses by creating a "justice" narrative in which angry assertions are used to remove their challenges. On the other hand, it does not seem that Utku anger is simply a response to frustration. On the contrary, they are adept at resignation, and the anger that is present appears to occur when oughts are challenged (even if these may be construed as "narcissistic entitlements"). Furthermore, the fits of sullenness, the violent fantasies, and the displaced aggression do not appear as "angriform" responses that have not been organized into what we would call *angry*. Rather, they seem to be aspects of the embodied anger with which we are all too familiar. Hence, it seems to me that it is more parsimonious to say that the conceptualization of ought–challenge anger fits the experience of the Utku, but that the society does not utilize anger as we do. Rather than using anger to assert what ought to be, they cultivate acceptance so that they are not challenged.

An even more unusual way of experiencing transgressions to what ought to be is found in Malaysia. Although all societies appear to have angry children, and at least some outbursts of adult aggression, there are cultures that clearly do not use anger as a means of redressing violated oughts. Just as an individual in our own culture may feel hurt rather than angry, a society may encourage its members to feel hurt and afraid rather than angry when oughts are violated. This appears to be the case among the Chewong and Semoi of peninsular Malaysia. Both peoples strongly value sharing, and the refusal to share or grant a request is a clear violation of what ought to occur. However, rather than perceiving a challenge that leads to anger and an assertive attack or a supernatural infliction of pain, the violated person is afflicted with fear. The wronged person is believed to be in danger of attack by animals, illness, or supernatural beings. Although such a person may seek compensation for this wound and ask the offender to apologize and pay a fine, the emotional response to the violation of the ought is clearly one of unhappiness and fear rather than anger. Although one who is afraid is regarded with approval rather than contempt, how may we explain the fact that the injured party experiences fear rather than anger? Different explanations seem possible. Heelas (1989) suggests that, although it is not just, the moral order may be *justified* by the anticipation of punishment. As Lerner (1980) suggests, we may believe that we live in a fundamentally just world and if something bad happens to someone that person must *be* bad and can expect more bad things to happen. Alternatively, Roseman (1990) suggests that the failure of sharing rends the cosmic network of mutual dependency so that one experiences that something has gone wrong with the world and so one is justifiably afraid. Or it may be that the person may simply be hurt as we may be when we feel unloved. In any case, as in the case of someone who experiences hurt rather than anger, the violation of what ought to be is not perceived as a challenge to one's will and is not experienced as anger.

Rosaldo (1980) suggests that in hunter–gatherer groups (such as the Utku, the Ilongot, and the Chewong and the Semoi), people think of anger as something that will destroy social relations if it is experienced. They fear that anger will lead to killing, so they "forget" anger—set it aside—rather than allow it within the group. It is not safe to hold on to the anger and use it to remove the challenge to what ought to exist, to use it as a motive to restore justice. An example of the "setting aside" of anger is provided in Rosaldo's (1980) account of the Ilongot headhunters in the Philippines. A 19-year-old, evidently angry at the failure of his kinsmen to hold an important ceremony for him, slashed a footbridge that his aunt had to cross so that it would give way under her weight. She noticed the damage in time and was enraged. However, there was nothing the aunt could do to restore justice. The youth was not yet at a stage in life where he was held responsible for such actions and could not understand the indemnatory payments sometimes used between adults. If she asked for an indemnity, would she kill him, her own nephew, if he refused? So an uncle took the youth aside and lectured him on kinship and the aunt had to set her anger aside. By contrast, in more complex tribal groups (such as the Ifaluk or Taita), in which there is a hierarchical command structure or jural system that can check anger and modulate its expression, it is safe to experience anger and publicly express it. In these societies, if anger is not expressed it may work to harm people in hidden witchlike ways.

In reading Rosaldo's (1980) account of the Ilongot, one has the impression that there is a lot of anger, as well as a lot of joy, in these passionate people. (Unlike the Utku, resignation is not cultivated.) Rosaldo (1980) appears to be correct in asserting that often there is no way for the anger to be expressed short of violence. (There are no authorities to mediate disputes or teach "assertiveness training!") My impression is that the anger is a response to a challenge as to what ought to exist. However, there is no way for the anger to be expressed as an assertion about what ought to be. Hence, when it is expressed, it leads to a direct confrontation with a high probability of violent consequences and, consequently, is usually set aside. Just as the Utku appear to display a certain amount of displaced aggression when they beat their dogs, one cannot help wondering if the Ilongot's headhunting may be partially grounded in unexpressed anger. Although traditional headhunting expeditions are organized by older men and give young men prestige and the ability to marry, the violence occurs outside the tribe (whereas the celebrations of victory involve women and children within the tribe). The Ilongot say that they organize a headhunting expedition when their hearts are heavy with envy and greed, and often the expedition follows the deaths of leaders or close kin. The violence is accompanied with a sense of vital energy and joy, and one senses that deep challenges have been removed and what ought to be has been restored.

CURRENT STATE OF THE
CONCEPTUALIZATION

Societies organize personal relationships and make sense of the misfortunes and tragedies of life in very different ways. Does it really make sense to take a conceptualization of anger that is based on the experiences of educated adults socialized in the United States and apply it to the experiences of persons in completely different societies? I believe it does, because in spite of vast societal differences, in spite of the fact that the narratives of different cultures create different realities for different peoples, there is an underlying reality that we hold in common. This reality is that all humans are dependent on others. We all have wishes that may be fulfilled or frustrated and wills that may be asserted or resigned. We all imagine what ought to be and distinguish this from what actually is. We all suffer when there is a discrepancy between what ought to be and what is. We must all must cope with that discrepancy in some way, and often that discrepancy involves the will of an other who could reduce the discrepancy between what ought to be and what is.

I suggest that anger is one way in which we humans attempt to cope with the discrepancy between what is and what ought to be. In my view, anger itself is not a narrative. Rather, anger is an embodied organic whole that involves a perception of a challenge to what ought to exist and an impulse to remove that challenge. Rather than a narrative, it is the stuff of which narratives are made. If our perception changes, if the other apologizes, or if we discover we were mistaken, or we abandon our project, then our anger may completely vanish. Conversely, although we may become resigned, or we may "distance" the other, our anger may be expressed in sulkiness, aggressive fantasy, and "displaced" violence.

Thus, after encountering different cultures, the experience of anger still appears, at least to me, to be a universal aspect of human nature rather than a human invention to manage aggressive impulses (such as the invention of political campaigns to replace civil war). However, it would also appear that anger is not as humanizing as I initially portrayed it. Although it presupposes common values, the oughts asserted by the angry person are often imposed rather than shared. Hence, although to be angry is to be human, the management of anger by the nonviolent assertion of what ought to be is a cultural achievement that we have only begun to realize.

REFERENCES

Blake, W. (1991). *Songs of innocence and experience*. Princeton, N.J.: Princeton University Press.

Briggs, J. (1970). *Never in anger*. Cambridge, MA: Harvard University Press.

Del Vecchio, T., and K. D. O'Leary, (2004). Effectiveness of anger treatments for specific anger problems: A meta-analytic review. *Clinical Psychology Review, 24*, 15–34.

de Rivera, J. H. (1981). The experience of anger. In de Rivera, J. H. (Ed.). *Conceptual encounter: A method for the exploration of human experience*. Lanham, MD: University Press of America.

de Rivera, J. H. (1984). Emotional experience and qualitative methodology. *American Behavioral Scientist, 27*, 677–689.

de Rivera, J. H. (1989). Comparing experiences across cultures: Shame and guilt in America and Japan. *Hiroshima Forum for Psychology, 14*, 13–20.

de Rivera, J. H. (1997). The construction of false memory syndrome (target article). *Psychological Inquiry, 8*, 271–292.

Fingarette, H. (1967). *On responsibility*. New York: Basic Books.

Fischer, C. T. (1998). Being angry revealed as deceptive protest: An empirical–phenomenological analysis. In Valle, R. (Ed.). *Phenomenological inquiry in psychology: Existential and transpersonal dimensions* (pp. 111–122). New York: Plenum.

Funk, J. (1981). Laughter. In De Rivera, J. H. (Ed.). *Conceptual encounter: A method for the exploration of human experience* (pp. 225–271). Lanham, MD: University Press of America.

Goldberg, J. H., J. S. Lerner, and P. E. Tetlock. (1999). Rage and reason: The psychology of the intuitive prosecutor. *European Journal of Social Psychology, 29*, 781–795.

Goodman, S. (1981). The experience of anxiety as differentiated from panic. In de Rivera, J. H. (Ed.). *Conceptual encounter: A method for the exploration of human experience* (pp. 83–161). Lanham, MD: University Press of America.

Harmon–Jones, E., and J. Sigelman, (2001). State anger and prefrontal brain activity: Evidence that insult-related relative left-prefrontal activation is associated with experienced anger and aggression. *Journal of Personality & Social Psychology, 80*, 797–803.

Harris, G. (1978). *Casting out anger: Religion among the Taita of Kenya*. Cambridge: Cambridge University Press.

Heelas, P. (1989). Restoring the justified order: Emotions, injustice, and the role of culture. *Social Justice Research, 3*, 375–386.

Heider, F. (1958). *The psychology of interpersonal relations.* New York: Wiley.

Izard, C. E. (1977). *Human emotions.* New York: Plenum Press.

Kahn, W. A. (1984). The structure of exaltation. *American Behavioral Scientist, 27,* 705–722.

Kane, R. (1976). Two studies on the experience of depression. Unpublished master's thesis. Clark University. Worcester, MA.

Kreilkamp, T. (1981). Psychological distance. In de Rivera, J. H. (Ed.). *Conceptual encounter: A method for the exploration of human experience* (pp. 273–341). Lanham, MD: University Press of America.

Kreilkamp, T. (1984). Psychological closeness. *American Behavioral Scientist, 27,* 771–784.

Lawrence, D. H. (1979). *The complete short stories.* New York: Penguim.

Lau, J. R. (1990). *Emotional experience as narrative compromise and de Rivera's "ought–challenge" formulation of anger.* Unpublished doctoral dissertation. Clark University. Worcester, MA.

Lerner, J. S., and D. Keltner. (2001). Fear, anger, and risk. *Journal of Personality & Social Psychology, 81,* 146–159.

Lerner, M. J. (1980). *The belief in a just world: A fundamental delusion.* NY: Plenum Press.

Levin, M. (1986). *A phenomenological analysis of loneliness.* Unpublished doctoral dissertation, Nova Southeastern University. Fort Lauderdale, FL.

Lindsay–Hartz, J. (1981). Elation, gladness, and joy. In de Rivera, J. H. (Ed.). *Conceptual encounter: A method for the exploration of human experience* (pp. 163–224). Lanham, MD: University Press of America.

Lindsay–Hartz, J. (1984). Contrasting experiences of shame and guilt. *American Behavioral Scientist, 27,* 689–704.

Lindsay–Hartz, J., J. H. de Rivera, and M. F. Mascolo, (1995). Differentiating guilt and shame and their effects on motivation. In Tangney, J., and K. W. Fischer. (Eds.). *Self-conscious emotions: The psychology of shame, guilt, embarrassment, and pride* (pp. 274–300). New York: Guilford Press.

Lutz, C. A. (1988). *Unnatural emotions: Everyday sentiments on a Micronesian atoll and their challenge to western theory.* Chicago: University of Chicago Press.

Macmurray, J. (1961). *Persons in relation.* Atlantic Highlands, NJ: Humanities Press.

Nisenbaum, S. (1984). Ways of being alone in the world. *American Behavioral Scientist, 27,* 785–800.

Ono, K., and J. de Rivera, (2004). *Japanese positive emotions: A conceptual encounter.* Poster session presented at meeting of the American Psychological Association. Honolulu, HI.

Rhodewalt, F., and C. C. Morf. (1998). On self-aggrandizement and anger: A temporal analysis of narcissism and affective reactions to success and failure. *Journal of Personality & Social Psychology, 74,* 672–685.

Richardson, R. F. (1918). *The psychology and pedagogy of anger.* Baltimore, MD: Warwick and York.

Roffman, A. E. (2004). Is anger a thing-to-be-managed? *Psychotherapy: Theory, Research, Practice, Training, 41,* 161–171.

Rosaldo, M. (1980). *Knowledge and passion: Ilongot notions of self and social life.* Cambridge: Cambridge University Press.

Roseman, M. (1990). *Healing sounds: Music and medicine in Temiar life.* Berkeley, CA: University of California Press.

Tiedens, L. Z. (2001). Anger and advancement versus sadness and subjugation: The effect of negative emotion expressions on social status conferral. *Journal of Personality & Social Psychology, 80,* 86–94.

Toch, H. H. (1993). *Violent men: An inquiry into the psychology of violence.* Chicago: Aldine. [originally published 1960.]

Tolman, E. C. (1923). A behavioristic account of the emotions. *Psychology Review, 30,* 217–227.

van Kleef, G. A., C. K. W. De Dreu, and A. S. R. Manstead, (2004). The interpersonal effects of anger and happiness in negotiations. *Journal of Personality & Social Psychology, 86,* 57–76.

BIOGRAPHICAL BACKGROUND

JOSEPH H. DE RIVERA, PhD, is Professor of Psychology at Clark University and Director of its Peace Studies program. As an undergraduate at Yale he began an investigation into the differences between fear and anxiety. Going to graduate school at Stanford, he studied chemistry and physiological psychology with the hope that it would help him distinguish different emotions, but he soon realized that the emotional experience he loved was so rich and varied that the techniques of physiological psychology would not be that helpful. After doing some research on happiness at the Naval School of Aviation Medicine, he returned to Stanford and completed a dissertation on a way to distinguish different emotions as perceptual choices (the latter is published as *A Structural Theory of the Emotions* [Psychological Issues Monograph 40, International Universities Press, 1977]).

Beginning teaching at Dartmouth, his interest in emotional experience was augmented by a desire to understand the nuclear arms race and, with the encouragement of Charles Osgood, he wrote *The Psychological Dimension of Foreign Policy* (Charles E. Merrill, 1968). Moving to NYU, his insistence on the importance of feelings came into dialogue with the behavioristic psychology of Isidor Chein. He became impressed with the early experimental phenomenology of Kurt Lewin and edited *Field Theory as Human Science: Studies of Lewin's Berlin Group* (Eardver Press, 1974).

Accepting a position at Clark University, where he particularly enjoyed talking with Tamara Dembo, he encouraged the qualitative analysis of emotions, working with a number of students and colleagues to develop the method presented in this volume and published as *Conceptual Encounter: A Method for the Exploration of Human Experience* (University Press of America, 1981).

Later, his enthusiasm for emotional experience was dampened when he discovered that patients and therapists could be completely misled by the intensity of the emotional experiences that were involved in the production of false memory syndrome, and, together with Ted Sarbin, he edited *Believed-in Imaginings: The Narrative Construction of Reality* (American Psychological Association, 1998).

He is currently engaged in trying to weave all these threads together, investigating collective emotional climates and political behavior; hoping that the qualitative methods presented in this book may help us understand the emotional experience of our friends, allies, opponents, and enemies; and that we may use our imagination to construct a culture of peace.

9

EMERGENCE OF THE DIALOGAL APPROACH: FORGIVING ANOTHER

STEEN HALLING, MICHAEL LEIFER, AND JAN O. ROWE

EDITOR'S INTRODUCTION

Dr. Halling and his co-authors provide a rich account of the journey through which they developed a dialogal qualitative research approach. Later in the chapter they provide a list of 15 characteristics of a well-functioning dialogal research group. "Dialogal" is derived from "dialogue," and is a shorter form of "dialogical." "Dialogal" refers back to its use by Strasser and Buber. Our authors and others at Seattle University have used this approach to research several phenomena; here they report their research process and findings with regard to forgiving another person, of arriving at foregiveness—the state of having forgiven.

247

Halling et al. emphasize that their approach involves a phenomenological attitude, but does *not* involve a stepwise analysis of text units. Rather, the researchers—in this instance two faculty members and four graduate students in an independent study course—cycled through literature, through all six researchers' reports of their own forgiving, through reports from other people, and through their continuously revised understandings of and questions about forgiving. Their journey included a retreat meeting, dyads reporting back to the group on assignments, all researchers sharing their analysis of a particular description of forgiving, and discussions of such issues as how it is possible to analyze meaning and in what senses had participants described forgiving as spiritual.

The eventual structure of forgiving held surprises and brings critical insights to psychology's literature. For example, it turns out that forgiving can be seen not as a decision or an act, but as a discovery, a shift in perspective toward self and other, and a coming to terms with deeper implications of what it means to be human.

The chapter returns to discuss its epistemological position (how we come to know and how that relates to what we know), and it closes with a discussion of how findings from that position relate to evolving literature on forgiving and forgiveness.

In this chapter we introduce the dialogal research approach. It is not so much a method, in the sense that it entails following predefined steps and procedures, as it is a process of discovery that takes place when a group of researchers sets out to study a particular phenomenon in a profoundly collaborative way.

The method grew out of a research project on forgiveness that included a group of students who were beginning their first year in the master's program in Existential–Phenomenological Therapeutic Psychology at Seattle University and two faculty who taught in the program. The authors of this chapter were members of that research group.

To give a sense of how the method originated and a "feel" for the process, we begin by describing the research we undertook and how it unfolded. Our assumption is that the story format is an effective way to present this method. We want to let the reader know what it was like to participate in a project in which the study of a particular topic gave rise, unexpectedly, to an innovative method. Second, we present the understanding of forgiving another that evolved out of the group discussions. Third, we turn to the distinctive features we have discerned about the process over the years, and provide a list of questions as guidelines for anyone using this method. This is followed by a discussion of the epistemological considerations of the dialogal method. Finally, in the context of evaluating the scope and limitations of our method, we consider ways in which our studies are related to and relevant for mainstream research on forgiveness.

PROCESS AND EVOLUTION OF THE
DIALOGAL METHOD

The original study that gave rise to the dialogal method was conceived in the fall of 1984. At that time, Steen Halling and Jan Rowe, both faculty members in the department of psychology at Seattle University, realized they had a mutual interest in the experience of forgiveness and its implications for one's well-being. They decided to offer an independent study for a small group of graduate students to research this phenomenon.

Halling and Rowe did separate interviews with each student who expressed an interest in working on the project. To their surprise, they wanted the same four students (Michael Leifer was one of them) to be in the group. Because there were no explicit criteria for inclusion, Halling and Rowe had relied on their felt level of comfort with the students and their assessment of the nature of the students' interest in forgiveness. Intuitively they selected students who were mature, genuinely interested in the topic, and who were clear that this would be a research project and not a therapy group. The students had given considerable thought to this topic but they were also open to exploring it anew.

So we were a group of six. Rowe and Halling had knowledge of qualitative research. Each had used qualitative methodology for his/her dissertation and Halling had a strong background in phenomenology. The students, however, were new to phenomenology as a research tradition. At this point we only had two givens: the topic of study would be forgiveness and we would proceed in a genuinely collaborative manner. This commitment to a collaborative process led to the formulation of the dialogal method.

Beginning the process of studying forgiveness was not easy. We did not know each other as a group. The students had only associated with each other in class, and the two faculty members had never collaborated on research. There was also a bit of awkwardness in that Halling was Department Chair and Rowe was relatively new to teaching. In addition, although these faculty were familiar with a variety of phenomenological methods, they were not committed to any of them for this study, leaving us uncertain about how to proceed. Not surprisingly, the initial meetings were characterized by a sense of tentativeness and floundering. To establish some direction, we decided as a group to interview friends and colleagues informally and ask them: "What does forgiveness mean to you?" In addition, Rowe and Halling suggested it would be helpful to read about qualitative methodology so the students could begin learning about this tradition. We also decided to review the literature on forgiveness. We divided the readings among ourselves, wrote extensive summaries of what we had read, and shared them in the group. This allowed us to cover more ground in a shorter time. Writing summaries also required a disciplined attention to the readings, which was helpful when they were discussed and gave us the basis for what eventually became the formal review of the literature. For the sake of this chapter we offer only an abbreviated version of our initial literature review, but with enough detail to give an indication of our point of departure. (The complete review is in Rowe, Halling, Davies, Leifer, Powers, and van Bronkhorst, 1989.)

We discovered that psychology had paid scant attention to the topic of forgiveness, whether in the form of forgiving another, oneself, or of being forgiven. What was available fell into three categories: (1) case studies, (2) theoretical psychological discussions, and (3) experimental studies.

The case studies included Hunter (1978), who in writing from a psychodynamic perspective considers paranoid reactions and forgiveness as two dramatically different responses to psychological injury. Martyn (1977) attempts to integrate psychoanalytical concepts regarding personality structure with theological concepts about forgiveness by considering the situation of an abused child who is in play therapy. In a third study, Close (1970) describes in everyday language how a young woman who had been sexually abused moved toward forgiveness. In this context, he contends that a movement beyond blame and recrimination requires that the injured person look at his or her own responsibility.

There is no doubt that analysis of psychotherapy cases can contribute to our knowledge of issues such as forgiveness. The overall limitation of this literature, however, is that psychotherapists typically approach the situation of a particular client primarily from the point of view of the particular theory to which they are already committed. Furthermore, the struggle with forgiving in therapy may take a different form and direction than in everyday life. For example, in therapy obstacles to forgiveness may be resolved due to the systematic intervention of an attentive and empathetic professional.

The second category, theoretical psychological studies, is a larger one. It included two studies on revenge (Heider, 1958; Searles, 1956), an analysis of forgiveness in families (G. Kunz, unpublished manuscript), a manuscript that integrates the insights of the Essene Code of Conduct (*the Khabouris Manuscript*) with psychosynthesis (E. Stauffer, unpublished manuscript), Smedes' (1984) book *Forgive and Forget* (an interesting mixture of psychological insights, theological assumptions, and anecdotal material), and an article by Pattison (1965) on the failure to forgive. As the category itself suggests, these studies are not based on a systematic examination of people's experience with forgiveness.

Attempts have been made to study forgiveness using traditional research methodology. For example, we looked at two experimental studies. Both investigations (Gahagan and Tedeschi, 1969; Tedeschi, Hiester, and Gahagan, 1969) involve a prisoner's dilemma game situation. Within this experimental context, forgiveness is operationally defined as the giving of a cooperative response by a subject after his or her opponent has made a competitive response to a prior cooperative response. Although a simple change in behavior along this line may be associated with forgiveness, this phenomenon cannot reasonably be defined so narrowly, because the process entails a fundamental shift in attitude. Such a shift can by no means be fully explicated from an observer stance because neither the inner meaning of the act of forgiveness nor the significance of the process is directly visible.

Many of the questions we had while reading the literature (e.g., What is the relationship between forgiveness and the situation one is in at the time of forgiveness?) called for a study that would allow us to learn about how forgiving is experienced in everyday life. Although, as we indicated earlier, psychology has paid more attention to forgiveness since our original study was completed, at the time there had been no systematic study to try to understand such a very fundamental human experience as it is lived out.

As we talked to others and did the reading, we decided to follow the example of Fischer and Wertz (1979) and write descriptions of our personal experiences with forgiveness. Sharing these descriptions was instrumental in breaking down the hierarchy that was intrinsic to the group: student/ teacher and chair/junior faculty member. Sharing our own experiences also gave forgiveness a more immediate and intimate presence. In writing these descriptions, we also became more clearly aware of our preconceptions about this phenomenon. Following Gadamer (1975) and Giorgi (1970), we did not assume that one could be free from assumptions. Rather, we believed that coming to an awareness of one's already existing beliefs would make it possible to examine and question them in light of new evidence. Slowly we were getting to know each other and to understand what was known and not known about forgiveness. And although we were excited about doing something that seemed important and had not been done before, we were still unsure how to tackle a project that seemed so immense.

At this point we decided to go on a day-long retreat to provide ourselves with the time and leisure to be together and to attend to our many concerns and questions. During this day together we decided to focus on forgiving in terms of hurt in a personal relationship (as opposed, for example, to being injured by a stranger). Out of this focus came the question that we would ask of subjects: Can you tell me about a time during an important relationship when something happened such that forgiving the other became an issue? This was an open-ended question that invited the respondents to tell their stories on their own terms, and it did not assume that forgiveness had occurred. As people told us their stories, we asked them to elaborate or clarify what they were telling us insofar as this seemed necessary. We also decided to interview people from a variety of backgrounds and contexts of forgiveness. Interviews would be audio-taped and transcribed, and at least one follow-up interview would be conducted. The purpose of the follow-up interview was threefold: to find out from our respondents how they had been affected by being interviewed, to ask questions that arose from our discussion of the first interview, and to present the respondents with a summary of the initial interview so that they could elaborate on what they had said previously and correct any misunderstanding on our part. All members of the group would be involved in interviewing. There was also a discussion of interview procedures and techniques. Although there was still a great deal of anxiety, particularly among the students, about actually interviewing, we were buoyed by having decided on a direction. More fundamentally, we were heartened by the comfort and trust we were developing with each other. Intuitively we realized that the kind of relationships we developed within the group were critical for our success. In retrospect, this day together was pivotal in the research process.

After the retreat we continued reading qualitative studies to get a "feel" for various ways of analyzing descriptive data. The next step involved playing our taped interviews for each other and discussing issues of interviewing (e.g., How does one interview a person who gives extremely verbose and/or tangential answers?). As a way of looking more closely at the data, we decided that we would each write a narrative summary of the same transcript and compare notes.

When we met together to share our narratives, we found that most of the group had had real difficulties with the assignment. As we discussed these problems, several important questions related to analysis became evident: How do I move from what is said to what is meant? What if I overlook or do not deem important some aspect of the person's experience that is central for him or her? How do I deal with my own strong emotional reactions to certain aspects of people's experience? These concerns had made most members of the group reticent to begin interpreting the people's experience on the basis of one transcript. We discovered, however, through sharing and discussing our hesitancy and concerns, that we could use the group for feedback and to keep us honest, and we could always return to the data to check our analysis. In fact, many of our concerns dissolved as we voiced them, and we felt a new freedom in writing our narratives.

Next, we decided to divide into pairs and continue summarizing the transcripts, attempting to move toward a more interpretive presentation for each interview. The purpose of forming the dyads was to have the person who conducted the interview work with another member of the research team, thus bringing together two distinct perspectives on the interview. Once the summary had been written, the entire research group read and discussed it, looking for themes that were specific to the particular description. The discussion also included questioning members of the dyad who had written the summary.

Having identified themes in the individual stories, we began to compare the narratives to find common themes. Slowly a tentative structure of "forgiving another" became evident. We began writing and critiquing rough drafts of our interpretation, which were skeletal at first. However rough these early formulations were, they gave us the basis for beginning to clarify and integrate our understanding. The process of writing and critiquing involved continually returning to the narratives and transcripts, the literature, and our own experience to refine, revise, expand, and flesh out our interpretation. The ongoing interaction between what we wrote and our dialogue with each other about our growing understanding of forgiving led to our final interpretation.

This process was never linear, but seemed more spiraling in nature. Many of our insights came from moments when something caught someone's attention and the group turned its focus to that issue. For example, at one point while we were analyzing the material from one of the interviews, a member of the group noticed that there appeared to be a discrepancy between what an interviewee believed would be the necessary conditions for forgiving another and what had actually happened. This opened up a discussion in which others remembered a similar discrepancy in their interviews. We talked about how we might account for this finding and returned to the data with new questions to clarify our understanding.

What we discovered was that people initially had specific expectations about what the injuring party would have to do to ameliorate the hurt and anger. It became clear that the meeting of such expectations was not sufficient to bring about forgiveness. What we did find was that the people who were able to forgive had undergone a shift in their own perspective that had allowed them to see the injuring person and event in a different light.

Working in dialogue and comparing personal experiences and the interviews with each other allowed us to come to a rich, collective understanding of the process of forgiving another. The group often held this understanding implicitly before we had fully acknowledged it. For example, on one occasion it became clear that we had been assuming, without articulating them, that there were two levels of meaning in forgiving another: (1) the immediate injury and healing in that regard and (2) coming to terms with deeper implications of what it means to be human. Although the latter meaning was not specified as such in the transcripts, when we returned to the data it was "there." This new understanding gave us the basis for articulating the structure of forgiving in the final analysis.

FORGIVING ANOTHER: OUR FINDINGS[1]

We now turn to the research group's interpretation of forgiving another, identifying the qualities and stages of responding to harm and coping with injury. These "stages" are far from sharply delineated or easily defined. By speaking of stages, we are addressing the fact that specific kinds of experiences seem to be dominant at certain points in the process.

From the descriptions we collected, it was evident that the process begins when one perceives oneself as harmed by another, and comes to a resolution insofar as the process ends in a psychological, if not face-to-face, reconciliation with the one who was perceived as hurtful. There are two basic levels to this process. First, forgiving another is most immediately experienced as interpersonal; it occurs within the context of a relationship involving another who has deeply affected one in a hurtful way. Second, and perhaps more profound, this experience of forgiveness also has qualities that transcend one's relationship with that person and opens one up to oneself and the world in new ways. It is more than a letting go—it is also a new beginning. The specific nature of these qualities, which only become apparent toward the end of the forgiving process, led us to describe the experience as being spiritual as well as interpersonal. It is noteworthy that our research group did not start out with a "religious" or "spiritual" agenda, and that some of the interviewees who did not think of themselves as religious used religious words (e.g., grace) in describing their experience.

The need for forgiveness arises when someone has acted in such a way as to bring about a fundamental disruption to the wholeness and integrity of one's life. Initially, on a deep, almost organic level, there is a tearing of the fabric of one's life, one's world. The injury that involves forgiving another is one that violates the person's sense of self. The unfolding of one's life and identity is impeded and profoundly disrupted. The future, as it was anticipated before the event, is irrevocably changed—a particular future is experienced as lost altogether, destroyed. A more general future, one beyond injury, is simply not there for oneself as a possibility, except insofar as particularly engaging activities or situations take one away, momentarily, from the recollection of the hurtful event. When one does recollect the event, hurt, pain, and loss of future reemerge at the center of one's life. Thus, the injurious event and relationship are somehow central or pivotal to the network of one's identity in such a way that the disruption impinges upon one's only world, one's only meaningful identity as perceived at that time.

In the face of the realization of the hurt, this disruption is profoundly felt. One feels uprooted, off center. Upon hearing from a friend that her lover had been unfaithful, one woman stated, "As [she] talked, my throat became

1. This section is based on Rowe et al. (1989).

dry and restricted. It was suddenly extremely cold in my apartment and I began to shiver. I was stunned and unaware of how to react." Relationships to the world and others at this point are characterized by distance and disease, and most dramatically so with respect to the injuring person. The distance or sense of disease remains in relation to that person even after connections with friends and objects in the familiar world have been reestablished. When, for example, familiar streets no longer seem foreign and forbidding. However, the deeper levels of meaning of the disruption to one's sense of self are typically not yet articulated (or conscious). These will unfold later.

On a lived level, one experiences the injury as a blow inflicted by the other. There is the conviction that the other's behavior was aimed at oneself, that one was the target of the other's demeaning or intentionally unjust and damaging behavior. At the very least, one believes the injury to have been avoidable had the other person been sensitive to and respectful of oneself. One man said, "If she hadn't known how I felt about it, then it wouldn't have made any difference." He believed that she acted in conscious disregard of what mattered to him.

Oftentimes an acknowledgment of responsibility, an apology from the other person, is thought to be necessary for healing: The man just quoted said, "She could acknowledge that her position is costly to me. She could apologize, not for her decision, but for how it affects me. That'd be nice, I would like that." Underlying the wish for an apology is often a wish for the other to be different from the person as experienced. Many times we seem to believe that the situation can only change if the other does.

The ongoing experience of hurt entails a preoccupation with the injury. At the time, one is apt to assume that the other's actions were the simple and sufficient reasons for the hurt and disruption in one's life. Typically it is only later that one starts to look at the deeper implications of the injury in relationship to one's sense of self. The hurtful interaction is remembered as the transition point between a comfortable and familiar sense of the world, and an existence that is disturbing and uprooted. The following is a particularly vivid description of this transition:

> The next morning I felt a slow hideous obsession creeping into [me]. I felt it taking over my life. I felt fear and then the fear turned into a cold terrifying anger ... I cried and screamed at the injustice of it .... It wasn't fair. Why? Why? Why? I asked myself ... what had I done to deserve this? My questions remained unanswered, and I became angrier.

The initial hurt is often accompanied by anger; in other cases, anger becomes an issue later on. However, it is important that anger and blame be allowed to be experienced. Genuine forgiveness cannot take place if one disavows some vital aspect of one's own experience and of the relationship to the other person. In some cases, it may be especially hard for a person to allow anger to emerge—if the other is someone on whom one depends, if one has a habit of blaming oneself, if one believes that it is bad to be angry at someone to whom one is close.

Along with anger, there is frequently a desire for revenge or retribution. These fantasies carry the promise of some sort of partial balancing of an injustice; they provide, however artificially, a future of sorts. Most important, they offer a future in which one is no longer a victim, but the victimizer. The possibility of forgiving the other seems unlikely at this point, and the anger may be perceived as extending indefinitely. One middle-age man seemed to be in this place, "My mother is a stubborn, bigoted, disappointing woman. I don't see how I can forgive." This quote also provides a good example of the perspective that views one's own reaction as simply a function of the behavior of the other person.

If the other person and the relationship are valued, and if one is troubled by one's own obsession with the hurt, thoughts of revenge are apt to become interspersed with a wish for reconciliation. Although thoughts of the other as blameworthy may still predominate, increasingly there are moments of questioning oneself. So we may ask: "Did I misconstrue the intentions of the other? Did I do something to contribute to the problem?" After being wronged, one becomes preoccupied with the other and with the hurt that his or her actions had brought about. During this phase, this preoccupation with the other and with oneself as injured starts to unravel or diminish. One begins to see glimpses of the other in terms apart from the immediate relationship. Preoccupation with the other's wrongdoing begins to be pierced by guesses at explanations for his or her behavior that make it more understandable or acceptable. And there is a dawning awareness that one is somehow helping to keep alive the feelings of discomfort in relation to the other person. Yet exactly how these feelings are kept alive, and therefore how to move toward a resolution, is not clear. One woman wondered:

> I see the obstacle in front of me but I can't seem to move it. How do I forgive her without her showing me she knows how much pain I've experienced? How do I forgive and not forget so I can go on? How do I rid myself of the selfish demand that she acknowledge my pain?

Aside from concerns about restoring the relationship or the growing desire to feel peaceful rather than haunted by what happened, one may also be moved by an inner obligation to forgive. Additionally, there may be a sense of guilt about being angry with the other. But one is unable simply to let go of the hurt and recriminations. At this time in the process, some critical form of healing has not taken place, and there is a moving back and forth such that one might speak of being caught between what seems like irreconcilable opposites: holding on to hurt and anger that create distance, and accepting the relationship as it is currently by somehow letting go of the meaning one has assigned to the hurtful event.

Letting go, then, although consciously preferable or at least an "ought," does not as yet really feel possible. There is a sense of clinging to the hurt and anger, which is to be distinguished from earlier phases of more spontaneous hurt and anger. This clinging appears to have the function, in part at least, of keeping oneself away from the other while staying engaged with what might have been. As distancing implies, mistrust is often a pervasive theme. This phase may be experienced as an impasse and one feels trapped. One man said, "I did not like the anger and rage I felt, but I also did not know how to leave behind the hurt."

To achieve resolution, one may try to forgive, and may even say one has, only to find the old pain, anger, and confusion returning. One woman described:

> I wrote her ... that I [forgave] her ... you see I know that not forgiving her would only destroy myself .... By going through the motions I hoped to feel forgiveness. But I continue to hang on. Perhaps it is because I feel forgiving her would mean I would have to forget what she did to me. I don't want to forget because if I do, it may happen again.

There may also be some awareness that clinging to the hurt and anger may serve to move one away from other experiences such as grief. This grief may concern both the loss of what was and/or could have been, and, on a deeper level, the loss of a particular way of viewing one's self and the world. The latter loss is the deeper metaphorical level of meaning that is not yet entirely clear to the person. One woman, after forgiving her father for years of hurt said: "[I] am left ... with a deep sadness for me, for my dad, for all of us who keep ourselves separate out of hurt and fear." She went on to consider, "The avoidance of this ... sadness may be one reason why [I] resisted forgiving."

During this time there also may be moments when one feels freed from hanging on to the injury. However, these times are fleeting and cannot be willed. One man said:

> My hurt and anger vanished as I thought about [her] ... I felt healed .... This experience was deeply moving, but I would hesitate to call it dramatic. The next day ... I was back to my previous state, and yet I knew that something was possible even though I had no idea how to get "back there."

The resolution, in the form of forgiveness, appears to come to us in an unexpected context, often at an unexpected moment. And yet, as one is surprised by the resolution, it becomes apparent that at some level it was sought—one was willing to forgive and was open to this possibility. It seems that this willingness, even if the person never consciously thought of forgiveness, is crucial for forgiving to occur. In contrast, not imagining how he might forgive his mother, one man said: "I don't see how I can forgive anything. Maybe it's because I'm stubborn or maybe I've talked myself into not being able to back down."

Experientially, however, the moment of forgiveness appears to be the moment of recognition that it has already occurred. Rather than being aware of changing, one realizes that one has changed, one has forgiven the other. Forgiveness comes as a revelation and is often viewed as a gift. One woman reported, "I proceeded to call him and apologize for the letter he was going to receive and in the same breath I said I forgave him. When I said this I was taken by surprise. It had, in a sense, come out of nowhere." It is important to note there may be a series of revelations—that is, one may forgive a number of aspects of a relationship independently, or all the injury may be forgiven at once. This may depend upon whether the injury was a discrete event or a more complicated series of happenings, as well as upon the intensity and significance of the hurt.

Previous thoughts about what conditions make it possible to forgive (e.g., if the other were to apologize) turn out not to fit the reality as experienced. The focus has been on what "the other should do" and less on what one needs to do to overcome the injury. Even when apologies were forthcoming, this did not typically enable people to forgive and, likewise, people forgive even without acknowledgment on the part of the wrongdoers. In a parallel vein, although the immediate experience of the hurt is very conscious, it seems doubtful that there was clarity to the broader, deeper meaning of the injury. One seems long in coming to a realization of what significance the wrongdoing had in terms of one's life as a whole. As previously noted, the focus was on the wounding rather than on the underlying meaning of the injury.

The critical dimension of forgiving is that one experiences a shift in one's understanding of and relationship to the other person, one's self, and the world. The implications of the original situation are cast in a new light: The hurt is no longer merely an injury that another has inflicted and that, therefore, acts as a barrier, but instead becomes appropriated as pain shared with other human beings. In some sense, it is disengaged from the "injuring" person or at least no longer solely referential to that person. One man described this awareness: "[I now felt her] as another human being who was struggling and who basically did not mean me any harm." There is an experience of reclaiming oneself, which at the same time involves a shift into a larger perspective. No longer does one see oneself in a relationship of victim and victimizer: One is freed from the status of being the object of another's actions and so is able to return to oneself. No longer is there only one possible connection with the other person. There are alternatives where before there were none, and this new vision reinstates choice into one's life. A sense of responsibility for one's life and relationships is recovered. After forgiving her father, one woman said:

> My life immediately began to change. After spending almost six years in a profession that I did not enjoy, but had entered to gain my father's approval, I decided to return

to school to study what I loved. By opening my mind to forgiveness, I was able to open my heart, and the transformation affected my life.

After forgiving a family member for sexual abuse, one person stated, "For the first time in my life I feel free." And another person said: "I realize that forgiveness has set me free. Free to continue my life, free to exist without pain and anger, and free to love again." The vision of newness is so compelling, so like a gift of grace, one will not choose other than to move gratefully into it. The future—an immediate sense of being on the verge of new beginnings—is again available where before it wasn't; the past, although neither forgotten nor rationalized away, is no longer a haunting, heavy, and troubling issue.

At the level of lived experience, there is a release of tension, yet this release is one in which one's active participation is acknowledged on some level, although perhaps most clearly in retrospect. Thus, people frequently speak of having been able to let go of anger, hurt, and recriminations. One experiences a restoration of a sense of wholeness and of inner direction and an opening up to perceiving how other people and situations are in their own right, as distinct and separate from one's own needs and desires: "I stopped trying to pigeonhole her into a ready-made mold." One has an attitude of openness to the other. As one person said, "I feel more relaxed and can look her in the eye, where before I couldn't." On a reflective level, one sees the other as having acted in a way human beings do, out of his or her own needs and perceptions. There may even be the recognition that what he or she did is something one has done or could well do: "Forgiving came with acknowledging that we aren't perfect." One understands the other person, and oneself, in a new and fuller way.

The experience of forgiveness is one of radically opening to the world and others, as well as to the person who hurt oneself. There is a sense of arriving home after a long journey and the world is welcoming, so well remembered and yet transformed. One woman wrote: "I knew at last that home was where I was. The past was no longer menacing ... the future was no longer foreboding ... [I] was no longer adrift in a sea of chaos but at the helm in a world that welcomed me. I wept for joy." Others emerge as persons separate from oneself and yet one's connection with them is more tangible than before. There is a clarity about one's relationship to self and others.

There is a sense of relatedness and freedom that did not exist before. It is because of the transforming nature of forgiveness, coupled with the experience that this involves more than one's own will, that we are suggesting there is a spiritual dimension to forgiveness. More specifically, as we have already indicated, forgiveness comes as a gift or as a "revelation," and it involves coming to a deeper sense of connection to oneself and to others, and, in some cases, with something beyond oneself. There is a movement of transcendence—that is, an unanticipated and yet welcomed opening up to the new, and an experience of being freed from burdens and restrictions.

DISTINCTIVE FEATURES OF THE DIALOGAL METHOD

Since completing the study on forgiving another, we have been involved in a number of other studies using the dialogal method, and Steen Halling and Michael Leifer have taught classes in which groups have conducted small research projects in dialogue. Over the years, we have spent much time reflecting on and articulating what is essential to this method and how it differs from other kinds of research. In this section we give a brief outline of the distinctive features of the dialogal method that we have discerned.

The central feature of the dialogal method is that dialogue is at its core. Dialogue, as we have seen, was the basis for every step of the research, such as making decisions about what to do next, sharing tasks, and interpreting the data. As implied earlier, the process is never linear, nor can it readily be divided into discrete steps. Although difficult to capture on paper, a major turning point in our study of forgiving another illustrates how continuous and subtle this process is. After we had read and discussed the literature, shared our own descriptions of forgiving, and completed and discussed the interviews, we were confronted with doing the "real analysis." At that point we realized that we had already done much of the analysis—that is, we had been reflecting on the descriptions from the beginning as a part of our ongoing conversation or dialogue. We only had to continue returning to the data to check and expand our understanding.

The centrality of dialogue became obvious to us after several months of working together. Leifer, a graduate student at the time, decided to try to get a better understanding of the nature of the dialogal process. Toward this end, he became a participant–observer in another research group. He carried out a systematic, empirical study, recording the meetings of the two groups during their first phase.

On the basis of careful reflection on the data, Leifer came to the conclusion that there are three levels of dialogue at work in dialogal research: (1) preliminary, (2) transitional, and (3) fundamental (Halling and Leifer, 1991; Leifer, 1986).

Preliminary dialogue is especially evident during the initial meetings within the group. The discussion centers, to a large extent, around the group members' individual theories and opinions about the phenomenon, and therefore has a tangential and abstract quality to it. This level of dialogue is indispensable as a starting point because it allows for a sharing of preconceptions and a gradual getting to know one another more fully. It is also a way of deciding together how to begin the research.

If the researchers are responsive to the research questions in the sense of addressing and sharing their own experience with the phenomenon, they are drawn into transitional dialogue. This brings the phenomenon into the group in the sense that the researchers enter into the experience in a more immediate and direct way.

The last level of dialogue, fundamental, arises when there is a discussion not only of personal accounts of the phenomenon, but of the descriptions collected from participants as a well. During fundamental dialogue, there is a building on previous themes and an interweaving of these themes as they are further illuminated by the data. It is in an atmosphere of openness to each other and the phenomenon that fundamental dialogue gives rise to a collective understanding of what is being studied. The written articulation of that understanding constitutes the findings of the group.

Since Leifer's (1986) study, we have further articulated the essential characteristics of authentic dialogue (Halling, Kunz, and Rowe, 1994). These are structure, freedom, and trust. Structure provides the backbone for the conversation and is apparent in the dialogal process through (1) the researchers' disciplined attentiveness to a particular phenomenon, (2) the rigor and integrity of their interpreting, and (3) the development and maintenance of a specific direction of inquiry. Freedom infuses the process with a spirit of exploration and discovery, and is evident through the group members' ability to be playful and imaginative with their interpretations. Trust provides the capacity to be genuinely receptive to what is new and different in the others' experiences and expressions, and accounts for respect toward each person's descriptions, interpretations, and stories. Thus, we see that trust and openness have a reciprocal relationship. When structure, freedom, and trust are present and supported in the dialogal process, a foundation of cohesiveness and communal commitment emerges that allows the conversation to deepen and expand among the group members.

Fostering an atmosphere that allows for these elements requires considerable mindfulness and creativity from the researchers. For example, writing our own descriptions helped us identify our preunderstanding and gave us a foundation on which to build the next steps in the research. It also moved "experience" center stage as the essential aspect of the investigative process, helping the researchers to differentiate between experiential description and theoretical generalization. Ultimately, it got us "back to the thing itself" and beyond our preconceptions. This movement helped open up and extend the discussions while creating a sense of group cohesion.

The process-oriented nature of our approach differentiates it both from "mainstream" research and from most phenomenological research. It is also in contrast to other approaches using collaborative research groups, including those described by Reason (1988), as well as the grounded theory approach. Although these collaborative approaches advocate group cooperation and sharing of tasks, the context for this cooperation are specific, predetermined procedures and steps.

In contrast to these collaborative and phenomenological approaches, mainstream psychology rests upon the assumption that "subjective factors," such as the personal history and predilections of researchers, will confound or distort the process of data collection as well as the process of data interpretation. The envisioned solution is to neutralize somehow or cancel out such "subjective" factors. As we know, elaborate methods (e.g., double-blind procedures), often derived from laboratory principles, have been developed to provide guidance for the proper collection of data and the formulation of scientifically valid interpretations.

On what basis, then, would we claim that our method, which apparently involves no standard procedures to reduce personal bias, can lead to valid conclusions? In discussing the meaning of validity in the context of qualitative research, Polkinghorne (1989) has suggested that it involves the question of whether the findings can be trusted and whether they can be used as the basis for actions, such as the planning of further research, planning therapeutic interventions, or developing public policies. It follows from this notion of validity that interpretations should be carefully grounded in the data and should move toward depth of understanding— that is, move beyond the obvious. It seems to us that any approach to research has to address both of these aspects. As we have indicated, direct involvement with the topic under investigation is traditionally regarded as problematic because of the concern about subjective bias. The sophisticated methodological maneuvers that have been developed to prevent the researchers from having a direct impact on the object of study have the consequence of creating a distance between the researcher and the topic. Without the benefit of direct experience, the researchers have additional reasons for doubting the adequacy of the data they are collecting, and so further methodological constraints seem necessary. Also, without an ongoing exploration of subjects' reports, the researchers have to speculate regarding what is going on for the subjects.

For phenomenology generally, ongoing, direct contact is the basis out of which understanding unfolds. This unfolding may be both complex and subtle, and it is to this process that one must look to understand the safeguards that guard against arbitrary interpretations within the dialogal approach. The dialogue within the group simultaneously gives impetus for moving beyond the preconceived theories of its members and for overcoming personal bias. As Kunz (1988) has suggested, the other person, in this case the fellow researcher, challenges each one of us to become aware of and put aside our ready-made assumptions. This movement toward greater openness is also a movement toward deeper understanding. As becomes apparent to many of those who have participated in this approach, the phenomenon being studied becomes a partner in the dialogue, and it also becomes apparent that the researchers are bringing the phenomenon to life. When the members of a research group start to realize that the understanding or interpretation for which they have been searching is not a truth "out there," but a truth that comes alive in their dialogue, there is a noticeable shift in the group. As Gendlin (1973) has written, "If experience appears, it talks back" (p. 294). This shift can be described as a release from a straining to hear and to see. It is an acknowledgment that seeing and hearing are already taking place among the members of the group and the phenomenon. In other words, the researchers do not "construct" the phenomenon even though they obviously approach it from their own perspective. Rather, the phenomenon and the researchers are engaged in a process of co-creation or dialogue. The atmosphere and process in our recent study on despair (Beck, Halling, McNabb, Miller, Rowe and Schulz, 2005), for example, were quite different from those in our initial study of forgiveness (Rowe et al., 1989).

In this regard, we want to focus on one of the critical dimensions of group functioning—namely, the attitude that group members develop toward different perspectives and opinions. As we have indicated, it is the very existence of multiple perspectives that enables the dialogue to move forward. In our experience, tensions arising out of differences of perspective were not disruptive in the groups that functioned well. Rather, the groups were able to utilize these differences constructively. For example, in a group that has a high level of trust, there would be a genuine openness to considering the view of a member who had an interpretation of the data that differed from those of the others. The challenge would be to find some way to explore this divergent interpretation and to consider its possible merit. The final court of appeal, so to speak, would be the question of the extent to which this interpretation fit with the collected descriptions and deepened the researchers' understanding of the phenomenon under study. This, in our view, is fundamentally different from seeking a group consensus arrived at through a process of compromise.

On the basis of such an engagement with the phenomenon and with each other, the researchers can more adequately attend to the presence of distortions or self-deception in their own approach to the issue and in the accounts provided by the subjects they interviewed. Of course, such safeguards do not eliminate the possibility of "subjective bias" or self-deception, for these possibilities are integral to human life.

As we have indicated, this approach to research does not follow a set of predefined steps or procedures to the extent that other methods in psychology do. However, as we have also suggested, there are general stages in the research process as well as characteristics of a well-functioning dialogal group that are observable. A number of these characteristics—the presence of trust, cohesion, careful listening, and creative collaboration—are similar to those found in well-functioning therapy (e.g., Yalom, 1985) or task groups (e.g., Cota, Evas, Dion, Kilik, and Longman, 1995; Dion, 2000). Rather than providing a list of stages or guidelines, we outline some basic questions that might be useful to either group members or observers at various points during the research process. The list is not exhaustive and includes questions relevant for other forms of research. We would also encourage readers to consult Halling and Leifer (1991) for additional information.

1. Are the members of the research group genuinely interested in the topic and in working collaboratively? Are there members of the group who have prior knowledge of phenomenological or qualitative research as well as group process, and, if not, does the group have ready access to a teacher or consultant?

2. Is the group moving toward identification of a particular phenomenon that can be described in experiential terms (e.g., the process of forgiving another) as opposed to a general concept or topic areas such as "forgiveness?"

3. Are the group members taking time to understand each other better as well as each person's relationship to and interest in the topic?

4. Have the group members written descriptions of their own experience of the phenomenon (or of their assumptions about it if they have not had direct experience of it)? Has there been an opportunity for listening to and discussing these descriptions in an atmosphere of acceptance?

5. Is there a development of a basic question that can be used to obtain a description, whether through interviews (preferable in most cases) or written accounts? This question should be written in plain English, be open ended, and yet be focused on the specific phenomenon. Has this question been tested out on "ordinary people?"

6. Have the researchers read and discussed the literature pertinent to the topic?

7. Has there been a thorough discussion of the kinds of people that one should approach to obtain descriptions? Have informed consent forms been prepared?

8. As data are collected (and transcribed) is there an increased emphasis on grounding the discussion of the phenomenon in the data (including the researchers' own description)?

9. Does a collaborative decision process guide the direction of the research? Are the researchers able to tolerate uncertainties and ambiguities along the way or do they rush into making decisions, rather than allowing themselves to discuss issues in depth? In other words, is there a sense of faith in the process?

10. Do the researchers, in spite of whatever conflicts and frustrations exist, seem to respect each other and, overall, enjoy or appreciate the

process of working together, even if some of the meetings are difficult.

11. Are there moments of playfulness or creativity in the group? Are the group members able to resolve conflicts, address these conflicts directly if necessary, and appreciate different points of views? Do the group members carry out the tasks assigned to them and show up on time?

12. Overall, are the researchers willing to reflect on their personal experience as part of the effort to deepen their overall understanding of the phenomenon?

13. As the stories/data are being discussed, is there an emergence of an understanding of the phenomenon that increasingly focuses on its basic themes and structure?

14. As the analysis of the data is being written up, is there a balance between the focus on general themes and structure, and the particular examples from which they are derived? Is there an effective use of examples and quotes to illustrate the overall findings?

15. Does the project end with an acknowledgment not just of the work that was accomplished, but also of the relationships that were developed along the way among the members of the group?

EPISTEMOLOGICAL CONSIDERATIONS

So far we have presented the dialogal method as a discovery and yet this is only part of the story. This discovery was made within the context of a certain tradition in psychology (phenomenology) as well as within a broader philosophical and educational dialogal tradition that is closely connected to phenomenological and existential thought. Most of the researchers went into the project with some familiarity with this dialogal tradition at a theoretical level. And all the researchers were in some way personally attuned to the practice and value of dialogue. In what follows, we provide a brief overview of the work of those dialogal thinkers whose ideas have been most important for us (see also, Halling and Leifer [1991] and Halling et al. [1994]).

The philosopher Karl Jaspers (1957) has very aptly articulated what we regard as the core epistemological assumption of a dialogal perspective: "Conversation, dialogue, is necessary for the truth itself, which by its very nature opens to an individual only in dialogue with another individual" (p. 16). The notion that dialogue is central to the process of understanding and the search for truth is the common thread tying together these dialogal thinkers, whatever their differences may be.

Martin Buber (1958), whose philosophy consistently points to the relational core of all human existence, is widely regarded as one of the most influential proponents of dialogue. In his book *I and Thou* (1958), he outlines the "twofold attitudes" that are fundamental to all of human relationships. The "I–it" relationship is one that is primarily functional, seeing the other in terms of his or her use to us, and the "I–Thou" is one of openness to the other in his or her personhood. Buber (1965) also emphasizes that in genuine dialogue, which presupposes an I–Thou relationship, one is confronted with one's own limitations while having the opportunity to expand and enrich one's relationship to the truth.

Stephan Strasser (1969), in *The Idea of Dialogal Phenomenology*, provides a theoretical framework that extends Husserl's (1913/1962) phenomenological method to include a phenomenology of the world that is social, pluralistic, and inherently dialogal. He outlines what he refers to as the three laws of dialogue:

1. In speaking and listening I must adjust myself to, that is, be responsive to, question, listen carefully to the "you" with whom I hold dialogue.
2. In knowing, evaluating, and striving I must adjust myself or be responsive to the matter that happens to be the object of our dialogue. In other words, discussing the best way to build a bridge requires a different approach than discussing the merits and limitations of democracy.
3. In knowing, evaluating, and striving I must approach the matter under discussion in a way that is formally the same as that of the "you" with whom I am in dialogue. That is, dialogue is fruitful insofar as the participants can agree on similar standards or criteria. If one person evaluates as bridge solely in terms of beauty and the other solely in term of utility, there will not be any dialogue between them (Strasser, 1969, p. 103).

Strasser's ideas about dialogal phenomenology helped in the original articulation of what was lived out and experienced by the researchers' study of forgiving another.

It is the German hermeneutic philosopher Hans–Georg Gadamer (1975) who provides one of the clearest descriptions of what actually happens during process of dialogue when he writes, "We say that we 'conduct' a conversation, but the more fundamental a conversation is, the less its conduct lies within the will of either partner." Furthermore, he suggests "a conversation has a spirit of its own, and that the language used in it bears its own truth within it" (p. 345). This characterization of dialogue fits well with our experience using the dialogal approach to research.

In addition, Gadamer (1975), as well as other hermeneuticists (e.g., Polka, 1986, 1990), has maintained that "truth" (1) should not be construed as either absolute or relative, (2) is not simply the consequence of "method," and, (3) in accord with Jaspers' (1957) position, arises in the context of community. Polka (1986) emphasizes that freedom and responsibility are critical in the practice of dialogue. In our group we found that as trust developed, each member became increasingly free to express his or her point of view, to agree and to disagree, and that a sense of responsibility to the phenomenon and to fellow group members characterized the way in which we worked together.

Another thinker who also questions many accepted dualisms and who has significantly influenced our work on dialogal method is the sociologist and educator Parker Palmer. According to Palmer (1983, 1987), knowledge in contemporary Western culture has been defined to a large extent as that which is objective and analyzable. He contends that the desire for this kind of knowledge is motivated by two passions: curiosity and the desire for control. Palmer (1983) maintains that these passions lead to knowledge that is self-serving rather than committed to the common good. Within this framework, human experience itself is no longer regarded as a reliable source of knowledge.

In contrast, Palmer (1983) argues for a different kind of paradigm, one that originates out of compassion and therefore moves toward "the reunification and reconstruction of our broken selves and worlds" (p. 8). This way of knowing, based on the recognition that the self and the world are intertwined, transcends the dichotomy of objectivity (distant, out there) and subjectivity (private, in here) through "reflective conversations" or dialogue. Reflective conversation—what we have described as a dialogue—refers to ongoing, deliberative discussions between people who are working together and are engaged in a level of understanding that will be beneficial to the community as well as illuminating in a theoretical sense. Out of this dialogue comes knowledge that creates community and is grounded in community. Although dialogal research groups are not communities in the deep sense that Palmer intends, we have found that this statement nonetheless does describe research groups that work well together. That is, a common goal and collaboration are the basis for emerging knowledge and that knowledge, in turn, deepens the sense of common purpose and of companionship.

SCOPE, LIMITATIONS, AND DIALOGUE WITH
MAINSTREAM LITERATURE

We have had a sequence of research groups at Seattle University, studying a variety of topics. There have been two studies that grew out of the project discussed in this chapter. After the study of forgiving another was completed, two new members were added to the group, and the issue of self-forgiveness became the focus for almost a year (Rowe et al., 1989). Several years later, the current authors and five graduate students approached the very difficult topic of self-forgiveness once more, this time reaching a greater clarity of understanding (Bauer, Duffy, Fountain, Halling, Holzer, and Jones et al., 1992). Subsequently, a study of the lives of social activists evolved out of the work on forgiving, and gave rise to two conference presentations (Halling, Leifer, Menuhin–Hauser, Pape, and Rowe, 1992; Halling, Leifer, and Rowe, 1990). Most recently, we (Halling and Rowe) have worked with four graduate students, looking at the experience of hopelessness in everyday life (Beck, Halling, McNabb, Miller, Rowe, and Schulz, 2003) and then at how psychotherapists experience and respond to despair, be it their own or that of their clients, during the therapy hour (Beck et al., forthcoming).

Another faculty member, Georg Kunz, first brought together a research group in 1985. In its first phase, it focused on helping and healing (Kunz, Clingaman, Gonzales, and Soper, 1986, 1987b). During its second phase, humility was the topic under study (Kunz, Clingaman, Hulet, Kortsep, Kugler, and Park, 1987). Although the practice of the first group was explicitly dialogal from the outset, that of the second group became more so over time.

Our studies on forgiveness have been referred to in journal articles and book chapters (e.g., Baures, 1996; Dillon, 2001; Malcolm and Greenberg, 2000; Newberg, d'Aquili, Newberg, and deMarici, 2000; Phillips and Osborne, 1989; Rye and Pargament, 2002; Thomson, 2000) and in doctoral dissertations addressing forgiveness (e.g., Bowman, 2003; Ferch, 1995; Fow, 1988; Milburn, 1992; Rooney, 1989). It is not surprising that we have had the greatest influence on other phenomenological studies (ours was the earliest), such as the dissertations listed here and published studies such as those by Fow (1996) and Ferch (2000). However, it is difficult to assess the extent to which the dialogal method has been influential beyond Seattle University. There are a few examples of the dialogal method being used with doctoral-level students at other institutions (e.g., Thomas, Chambers, Kraus, and Soparkar, 1988) and it is referred to in texts on qualitative research methods (e.g., Cohen and Omery, 1994; Dahlberg, Drew, and Nystr'm, 2001). A recent study on how residents in a predominantly African-American community experienced and benefited from a community-built wellness program was based on the dialogal research approach (Barnard, Dunn, Reddic, Rhodes, Russell, and Tuitt et al., 2004). We would also like to think that the researchers and scholars who have come to our presentations over the years at the annual International Human Science Research Conference have been influenced by our experience with dialogue in the context of research, just as we have benefited from our discussions with them.

Much of the validation of our research has come from phenomenological studies, such as the ones listed here. Because of space limitations, suffice it to say that, overall, the findings in these studies overlap with ours. In addition, when we present our findings at conferences or other public venues, we consistently hear that our portrait of the process moving toward forgiveness and of the nature of forgiveness resonates with the personal experience of those in the audience.

But what about the relationship of our work to that of the researchers who are currently using traditional psychological methods to study this phenomenon? Are there overlapping results? Are there ways in which these divergent approaches to psychological research complement each other? We believe that a dialogue between phenomenological and mainstream researchers can be productive and stimulating, as we try to demonstrate, here. We discuss this dialogue in terms of similarities and differences in findings on a given topic, ways in which the phenomenological research can be a source of questions and hypotheses, and ways in which findings in mainstream research can be further explored through phenomenological studies.

It is clear that currently there is far more research on forgiveness than was the case in the mid 1980s. For example, during the last ten years there have been about 200 dissertations addressing psychological aspects of forgiveness. The number of studies that are experimental or correlational in nature have increased significantly and are based on a conceptually sophisticated understanding of forgiveness (for overviews, see Enright and Fitzgibbons, 2000; and McCullough, Pargament, and Thoresen, 2000).

A number of studies, such as the ones carried out by Enright and colleagues at the University of Wisconsin, are not focused on the experience of forgiveness per se, but are intended to evaluate various methods for helping people who have been injured to move toward forgiveness. The psychoeducational interventions in the studies carried out by those working with Enright are based upon a stage model of forgiveness that has been derived theoretically (Enright and Fitzgibbons, 2000; Enright, and North, 1998). This model is a synthesis of insights found in religious, philosophical, and psychological literature. Freedman's (Freedman and Enright 1996) year-long work with incest survivors is a particularly compelling example of how educational and therapeutic interventions based on this stage model can be effective. At the end of the study, those in the experimental group were significantly less depressed and anxious, and more hopeful and forgiving—as measured by various scales and according to their own reports. Studies of this type provide evidence that various kinds of interventions may be helpful.

The Enright stage model overlaps, in some ways, with our findings and those of another qualitative researcher (Flanigan, 1992). It consists of four phases—uncovering, decision, work, and a deepening—each of which is divided into more precise units (Enright and Fitzgibbons, 2000, p. 68). Examples of agreement include the confronting of anger and admittance of shame during the first phase, empathy and compassion toward the offender during the third, and finding of new purpose and meaning during the fourth. We would also agree with Enright and Fitzgibbons (2000) that "a decision to forgive is only a part of the process" (p. 49), although we would add that such a decision is not essential. There were those in our study who ended up forgiving without thinking explicitly about doing so at an earlier stage, even though they recognized that living with bitterness and anger was destructive to them. However, our studies also support Patton's (1985) assertion that forgiveness is not an act or an attitude, but a discovery. But this view is not necessarily at odds with the practice of using interventions specifically designed to help the injured person become less bitter and see the other more as a fellow human being. Yet we believe it is important, when comparing studies, that one keep in mind differences in method and rationale. Our purpose was to learn how people struggle with issues of forgiveness in everyday life and we turned to interviews to answer this question. We did not intend to come up with a model that would lead to step-by-step interventions to help people forgive. Much later, we published a chapter discussing the implications of our study for in-depth psychotherapy (Rowe and Halling, 1998). Enright and colleagues used a different method (drawing upon existing theories) and a different goal (constructing a system of interventions designed to help people move toward forgiveness).

One of the important issues raised by traditional researchers is whether there is a connection between religious practice and commitment, and a person's capacity for forgiving another. As McCullough and Worthington (1999) have pointed out, forgiveness is both psychological and spiritual in nature, and for Christians forgiveness is typically regarded as an obligation. This is another arena for productive dialogue between phenomenological and mainstream researchers, especially because the relationship between religiosity and forgiveness is not likely to be straightforward. Mullet, Barros, Frongia, Usa, Neto, and Shafgi (2003) found that those with strong religious commitment and practice indicated that they were also committed to forgiving, and this was especially true for those with a religious vocation. However, Wade and Worthington (2003) did not find a direct relationship between self-rated religiosity and readiness to forgive. On the basis of our studies (Bauer et al., 1992; Rowe et al., 1989), we suggest that the following would be fruitful topics to investigate: First, the role of clergy in facilitating or obstructing the movement toward forgiveness. To be told that one should forgive (ready or not), could increase the injured person's sense of shame and unworthiness, whereas empathy and acceptance of one's anger and hurt might be highly beneficial. Second, along the same line, one could ask not just whether a person is committed to forgiveness, but what his or her understanding of forgiveness is. As Patton (1985) has pointed out, some understandings of forgiveness are unhelpful from a psychological point of view, as well as theologically unsound, and thus having forgiveness as a value does not by itself facilitate forgiveness. Third, we found that some of our subjects who were not religious (in any traditional sense) had experiences of forgiveness that had clearly religious or spiritual dimensions (Rowe et al., 1989; see also Halling, 1994). Consequently, one could see whether there is a correlation between the extent to which subjects rate themselves as religious, and the extent to which there appears to be a religious or spiritual dimension to their experiences of forgiveness.

Finally, we want to illustrate how the findings from a mainstream (quantitative) study can be further explored through a qualitative study. Kadiangandu, Mullet, and Vinsonneau (2001) have looked at differences in willingness to forgive among French and Congolese subjects. They found that, overall, the Congolese indicate a greater willingness to forgive and a greater reluctance to seek revenge than the French. They also found that within the Congolese population, there was less variability in responses between men and women, and between those who attended church and those who did not than among the French. They conclude that "forgiveness may be characteristic of collectivistic cultures than of individualistic cultures" (p. 511). A follow-up interview study could compare how the French and the Congolese think about forgiveness, and, perhaps more important, what their own experience with this phenomenon has been. Are there characteristic ways in which responses to certain kinds of psychological injury, for example, differ in these two cultures? Are there differences in cultural support for a person who is thinking of forgiving another? Finally, what is the relationship between the cultural beliefs about forgiveness and what people find in their actual experience as they struggle with injury, revenge, and reconciliation in their daily lives?

CONCLUSION

At this point, we assume that our readers have some sense of the advantages as well as some of the difficulties of the dialogal approach to research. We want to conclude by briefly summarizing both of these aspects as we see them (see also Halling and Leifer, 1991; Halling et al., 1994).

There is no question that there are numerous difficulties in doing dialogal research. Groups are most likely to work well if their members like and respect each other, have some skill collaborating and attending to process, and have a genuine openness to their own experience and that of others. The members of any group should have a basic understanding of phenomenology, and at least some members of each group should have experience with phenomenological research. It is not easy for any group to meet all these conditions. Although careful selection of group members is critical, it is not until the project is under way that one comes to know whether these researchers actually will work well together in a group context.

There is a further difficulty in that the university is not typically a setting in which cooperation and dialogue are encouraged. Most students and many faculty members work alone and have limited experience with cooperative endeavors. In addition, there is little emphasis on an embodied and personal approach to understanding in academic settings. It is our impression that a group of researchers consisting entirely or primarily of men is likely to run into difficulties insofar as men, to a greater extent than women, have incorporated the cultural value of competition, efficiency, and a more cognitive approach to understanding into their lives. We have had positive experiences with groups consisting of faculty and graduate students working closely together, but we have also been fortunate in that the students who ended up joining our groups were committed and thoughtful.

Finally, we would be the first to acknowledge that this approach to research is time-consuming, presents significant logistical problems, and can be quite difficult to use with some topics. In a world in which people are increasingly living frenzied lives, finding mutually convenient meeting times can be extremely difficult. It is also the case that some topics in psychology can be studied more readily by researchers working individually or by using a method that emphasizes predetermined steps rather than one that relies on the direction emerging from a process of dialogue. Our experience using this method in graduate classes in which students do small-scale studies suggests that some topics are especially difficult to manage. For example, students working on topics such as competition or countertransference find that the issue they are studying can become all too powerfully present in the group. On the other hand, we have been gratified that this approach, perhaps partly because we are working with stories, transcends cultures, and is appealing and understandable to students from a variety of backgrounds in terms of ethnicity and nationality (e.g., Japan and Malawi).

In spite of the difficulties that may be involved, we believe that finding ways of entering into dialogue is of great importance. In terms of its social and educational dimensions, we think the collaborative approach has extraordinary value. When groups work well, researchers learn about the importance of cooperation, the spirit and practice of phenomenology, and their own creativity. In contrast, solitary researchers often get stuck precisely because they are working alone and are unable to find a new way to think of the problem, to recognize their limitations or their own preconceptions, or to find the words to express their understanding of the issue. Similarly, researchers who take existing research methods to be authoritative may have few opportunities to think through new ways to approach the topic under investigation or to discuss and receive validation of their doubts about the "fit" of particular procedures.

Dialogal research can certainly also bring frustrations, disappointments, and the anguish that comes from not being able to accept one's own limitations gracefully or those of others. But in a real sense, this method is a profound avenue to experience knowing as a communal activity—an activity that has at its heart respect for the other and the phenomenon under study, and gives rise to knowledge that is shared and that brings us together. It overcomes, in a large measure, the dichotomies between the classroom and the outside world, between research and lived experience, and between research and clinical practice, and for this reason alone it is worth pursuing.

REFERENCES

Bauer, L., J. Duffy, E. Fountain, S. Halling, M. Holzer, E. Jones, M. Leifer, and J. O. Rowe. (1992). Exploring self-forgiveness. *Journal of Religion and Health, 31,* 149–160.

Baures, M. M. (1996). Letting go of bitterness and hate. *Journal of Humanistic Psychology, 36,* 75–91.

Beck, B., S. Halling, M. McNabb, D. Miller, J. O. Rowe, and J. Schulz. (2003). Facing up to hopelessness: A dialogal phenomenological study. *Journal of Religion and Health, 42,* 339–354.

Beck, B., S. Halling, M. McNabb, D. Miller, J. O. Rowe, and J. Schulz. (2005). On navigating despair: Stories from psychotherapists. *Journal of Religion and Health, 44,* 187–205.

Barnard, S., S. Dunn, E. Reddic, K. Rhodes, J. Russell, T. S. Tuitt, B. P. Velde, J. Walden, P. P. Wittman, and K. White. (2004). Wellness in Tillery: A community-built program. *Family & Community Health, 27,* 151–157.

Bowman, I. G. (2003). *Exploring the experience of self-forgiveness in psychotherapy.* Doctoral dissertation. University of Pretoria, South Africa.

Buber, M. (1958). *I and Thou* (2nd ed.). New York: Scribner & Sons.

Buber, M. (1965). Distance and relation. In Friedman, M. (Ed.). *The knowledge of man: Philosophy of the interhuman* (pp. 59–88). New York: Harper and Row.

Close, H. (1970). Forgiveness and responsibility: A case study. *Pastoral Psychology, 21,* 19–26.

Cohen, M. Z., and A. Omery. (1994). Schools of phenomenology: Implications for research. In Merse, S. M. (Ed.). *Critical issues in qualitative research methods.* Thousand Oaks, CA: Sage.

Cota, A. A., C. R. Evas, K. L. Dion, L. Kilik, and R. S. Longman. (1995). The structure of group cohesion. *Personality and Social Psychology Bulletin, 21,* 572–580.

Dahlberg, K., N. Drew, and M. Nystr'm. (2001). *Reflective lifeworld research.* Stockholm: Studentlitteratur.

Dillon, R. S. (2001). Self-forgiveness and self-respect. *Ethics, 112,* 53–83.

Dion, K. L. (2000). Group cohesion: From "field of forces" to mulitdimensional construct. *Group Dynamics, 4,* 7–26.

Enright, R. D., and R. P. Fitzgibbons. (2000). *Helping clients forgive: An empirical guide for resolving anger and restoring hope.* Washington, DC: American Psychological Association.

Enright, R. D., and J. North. (1998). Introducing forgiveness. In Enright, R. D., and J. North. (Eds.). *Exploring forgiveness* (pp. 3–8). Madison, WI: University of Wisconsin Press.

Ferch, S. R. (1995). The experience of touch in love relationships: An interpretation of its significance in forgiveness. Doctoral dissertation. University of Alberta, Edmonton, Canada.

Ferch, S. R. (2000). Meanings of touch and forgiveness: A hermeneutical phenomenological inquiry. *Counseling and Values, 44,* 155–174.

Fischer, C. T., and F. J. Wertz. (1979). Empirical phenomenological analyses of being criminally victimized. In Giorgi, A., R. Knowles, and D. L. Smith. (Eds.). *Duquesne studies in phenomenological psychology* (vol. 3, pp. 135–158). Pittsburgh, PA: Duquesne University Press.

Flanigan, B. (1992). *Forgiving the unforgivable.* New York: Macmillan Publishing.

Fow, N. R. (1988). An empirical–phenomenological investigation of the experience of forgiving another. Doctoral dissertation. University of Pittsburgh, Pittsburgh, PA.

Fow, N. R. (1996). The phenomenology of forgiveness and reconciliation. *Journal of Phenomenological Psychology, 27,* 219–233.

Freedman, S. R., and R. D. Enright. (1996). Forgiveness as an educational goal with incest survivors. *Journal of Consulting and Clinical Psychology, 64,* 983–992.

Gadamer, G. H. (1975). *Truth and method.* New York: Crossroad.

Gahagan, J. P., and J. T. Tedeschi. (1969). Strategy and credibility of promises in the prisoner's dilemma game. *Journal of Conflict Resolutions, 12,* 224–234.

Gendlin, E. T. (1973). Experiential phenomenology. In Natanson, M. (Ed.). *Phenomenology and the social sciences* (pp. 281–322.) Evanston, IL: Northwestern University Press.

Giorgi, A. P. (1970). *Psychology as a human science.* New York: Harper and Row.

Halling, S. (1994). Embracing human fallibility: On forgiving oneself and on forgiving another. *Journal of Religion and Health, 33,* 107–113.

Halling, S., and M. Leifer. (1991). The theory and practice of dialogal research. *Journal of Phenomenological Psychology, 22,* 1–15.

Halling, S., M. Leifer, C. Menuhin–Hauser, K. Pape, and J. O. Rowe. (June 1992). When injustice cannot be ignored: Living as social activists. Paper presented at the 11th International Human Science Research Conference. Oakland University, Rochester, MI.

Halling, S., M. Leifer, and J. O. Rowe. (August 1990). *A preliminary study of the nature of social activism: The tension between struggle and compassion.* Paper presented at the Ninth International Human Science Research Conference. University of Laval, Quebec.

Halling, S., G. Kunz, and J. O. Rowe. (1994). The contributions of dialogal psychology to phenomenological research. *Journal of Humanistic Psychology, 34,* 109–131.

Heider, F. (1958). *The psychology of interpersonal relations.* New York: Wiley.

Hunter, R. C. A. (1978). Forgiveness, retaliation, and paranoid reactions. *Canadian Psychiatric Association Journal, 23,* 167–173.

Husserl, B. (1962). *Ideas: General introduction to pure phenomenology.* New York: Callier (Original work published 1913).

Jaspers, K. (1957). *The great philosophers.* New York: Harcourt, Brace, and World.

Jaspers, K. (1970). *Philosophy.* (vol. II). Chicago, IL: University of Chicago Press.

Kadiangandu, J. K., E. Mullet, G. Vinsonneau. (2001). Forgivingness: A Congo–France comparison. *Journal of Cross-Cultural Psychology, 32,* 505–511.

Kunz, G. (June 1988). Psychology honors the paradoxical: The power of weakness. Paper presented at the Seventh International Human Science Research Conference. Seattle University. Seattle, WA.

Kunz, G., D. Clingaman, J. Gonzales, and P. Soper. (June 1986). Helping and healing in the context of the paradox of power and weakness. Paper presented at the Fifth International Human Science Research Conference. Berkeley, CA.

Kunz, G., D. Clingaman, R. Hulet, R. Kortsep, B. Kugler, and M. S. Park. (June 1987a). A dialogal phenomenological study of humility. Paper presented at the Sixth International Human Science Research Conference, University of Ottawa. Ottawa, Canada.

Kunz, G., D. Clingaman, J. Gonzales, and P. Soper. (1987b). Healing and helping: The paradox of power and weakness. *The Humanistic Psychologist, 15,* 208–214.

Leifer, M. (June 1986). The dialogal approach to phenomenological research. Paper presented at the Fifth International Human Science Research Conference. Berkeley, CA.

Malcolm, M. W., and L. S. Greenberg. (2000). Forgiveness as a process of change in individual psychotherapy. In McCullough, M. E., K. I. Pargament, and C. E. Thoresen. (Eds.). *Forgiveness: Theory, research, and practice* (pp. 179–202). New York: Guilford.

Martyn, D. W. (1977). A child and Adam: A parable of two ages. *Journal of Religion and Health, 16,* 275–287.

McCullough, M. E., K. I. Pargament, and C. E. Thoresen. (Eds.). (2000). *Forgiveness: Theory, research, and practice.* New York: Guilford.

McCullough, M. E., and E. L. Worthington. (1999). Religion and the forgiving personality. *Journal of Personality, 67,* 1141–1165.

Milburn, M. C. (1992). Forgiving another: An empirical phenomenological investigation. Doctoral dissertation. Duquesne University, Pittsburgh, PA.

Mullet, E., J. Barros, L. Frongia, V. Usa, F. Neto, and S. R. Shafgi. (2003). Religious involvement and the forgiving personality. *Journal of Personality, 71,* 1–20.

Newberg, A. B., E. G. d'Aquili, S. K. Newberg, and V. deMarici. (2000). The neuropsychological correlates of forgiveness. In McCullough, M. E., K. I. Pargament, and C. E. Thoresen. (Eds.). *Forgiveness: Theory, research, and practice* (pp. 91–110). New York: Guilford.

Palmer, P. (1983). *To know as we are known.* New York: Harper & Row.

Palmer, P. (1987). Community, conflict, and ways of knowing. *Change. September/October,* 20–25.

Pattison. (1965). On the failure to forgive or be forgiven. *American Journal of Psychotherapy,* 19, 106–115.

Patton, J. (1985). *Is human forgiveness possible?* Nashville: Abingdon Press.

Phillips, L. J., and J. W. Osborne. (1989). Cancer patients' experiences of forgiveness therapy. *Canadian Journal of Counselling, 23,* 236–251.

Polka, B. (1986). *The dialectic of biblical critique: Interpretation and existence.* New York: St. Martin's.

Polka, B. (1990). *Truth & interpretation: An essay in thinking.* New York: St. Martin's.

Polkinghorne, D. (1989). Phenomenological research methods. In Valle, R. S. and S. Halling. (Eds.). *Existential–phenomenological perspectives in psychology.* (pp. 41–60). New York: Plenum.

Reason. (1988).

Rooney, A. J. (1989). Finding forgiveness through psychotherapy: An empirical phenomenological investigation. Doctoral dissertation. Georgia State University, Carrollton, GA.

Rowe, J. O., and S. Halling. (1998). The psychology of forgiveness: Implications for psychotherapy. In Valle, R. S. (Ed.). *Phenomenological inquiry: Existential and transpersonal dimensions* (pp. 227–246). New York: Plenum.

Rowe, J. O., S. Halling, E. Davies, M. Leifer, D. Powers, and J. van Bronkhorst. (1989). The psychology of forgiving another: A dialogal research approach. In Valle, R. S., and S. Halling. (Eds.). *Existential–phenomenological perspectives in psychology* (pp. 233–244). New York: Plenum.

Rye, M. S., and K. I. Pargament. (2002). Forgiveness in romantic relationships in college: Can it heal the wounded heart? *Journal of Clinical Psychology, 58,* 419–441.

Searles, H. (1956). The psychodynamics of vengeance. *Psychiatry, 19,* 31–39.

Smedes, L. (1984). *Forgive and forget.* New York: Harper & Row.

Stauffer, E. *Unconditional love, will and forgiveness.* Unpublished manuscript, Diamonds Springs, CA.

Strasser, S. (1969). *The idea of dialogal phenomenology.* Pittsburgh, PA: Duquesne University Press.

Tedeschi, J. T., D. S. Hiester, and J. P. Gahagan. (1969). Trust and the prisoner's dilemma game. *Journal of Social Psychology, 79,* 43–50.

Thomas, L., K. Chambers, P. Kraus, and B. Soparkar. (June 1988). Levels of meaning in the qualitative analysis: Comparison of the thematic and metaphoric approaches. Paper presented at the Seventh International Human Science Research Conference. Seattle University. Seattle, WA.

Thompson, E. A. (2000). Mothers' experiences of an adult child's HIV/AID diagnosis: Maternal responses to and resolutions of accountability. *Family Relations, 49,* 155–164.

Wade, N. G., and E. L. Worthington. (2003). Overcoming interpersonal offenses: Is forgiveness the only way to deal with unforgiveness? *Journal of Counseling & Development, 81,* 343–353.

Yalom, I. (1985). *The theory and practice of group psychotherapy* (3rd ed.). New York: Basic Books.

BIOGRAPHICAL BACKGROUND

STEEN HALLING, PhD, is a licensed psychologist and Professor of Psychology at Seattle University, Seattle, WA, where he teaches in the master's program in Existential–Phenomenological Psychology as well as in the undergraduate program. The graduate program provides students with a solid foundation for the practice of therapeutic psychology with emphasis on philosophical foundations of psychology, the contributions of the humanities to an understanding of human existence, clinical theory, and supervised experience in community agencies.

Dr. Halling grew up in Denmark and came to Canada at the age of 12. As an undergraduate he studied history and political science at York University in Toronto, Canada, in preparation for teaching high school. After spending a summer working at a maximum security mental hospital, he changed his major to psychology with the goal of becoming a psychotherapist. He received his MA and PhD from Duquesne University. While studying at Duquesne, he also worked in state psychiatric hospitals. In 1972, his interest in teaching was rekindled and he joined the Psychology Department at Seton Hill College, in Greensburg, Pennsylvania, as a full-time instructor.

Since 1976 he has been at Seattle University, where his research and publications have focused on topics such as psychology of forgiveness, phenomenological study of psychopathology, psychology of hopelessness, interpersonal relations, psychology of imagination, the history of phenomenological psychiatry and psychology, and qualitative research methods. For the last 20 years, Dr. Halling has worked closely with Dr. Rowe and small groups of graduate students on phenomenological research studies that have resulted in numerous presentations and publications. He is editor of *the International Human Science Research Conference Newsletter,* and co-editor (with Ronald S. Valle) of *Existential–Phenomenological Perspectives in Psychology* (Plenum, 1989). He has been a visiting professor at Duquesne University and at Pretoria University in South Africa.

MICHAEL G. LEIFER, MA, LMHC, is a counselor in private practice in Redmond, WA. He received his graduate degree from Seattle University and has co-authored articles on dialogal research (1991) and the psychology of forgiveness (1986). Michael Leifer has taught qualitative research methods at Antioch University in Seattle. He was a program coordinator at Seattle Mental Health Institute, where he helped to develop Emerald House, a community-centered treatment program. He was Branch Manager at Family Services for five years and Clinical Supervisor in Seattle for Divorce Lifeline.

JAN O. ROWE, PhD, is Associate Professor of Psychology at Seattle University and Director of the MA program in Existential–Phenomenological Therapeutic Psychology. Her undergraduate work was completed at Georgia State University with a major in psychology and a minor in the humanities. After traveling and working for several years, she returned to Georgia State to pursue a doctorate in counseling psychology with a cognate in clinical psychology. Her intention was to work as a clinician when she graduated. However, her experience teaching as a graduate student led her to apply for a position at Seattle University, when she read about its program with an emphasis on phenomenology and the humanities. She has been there since 1982, teaching and supervising students, primarily at the graduate level.

This has been a good match. The program is designed to train master's-level students to work in the clinical area. The focus is on the therapy relationship, which is grounded in the valuing of human experience as lived. This is seen as central to understanding and working effectively with those who are often marginalized by society, and it is the basis for the program's teaching—both practical and theoretical. To foster this way of knowing, the research of the faculty who teach in the graduate program is phenomenological. In this tradition, Dr. Rowe and her colleague Dr. Halling began working with a group of graduate students in 1984 on a research project studying forgiveness. This led to the articulation of the dialogal method. Since then she has been involved in seven more groups, resulting in 14 presentations and 8 publications.

In addition to her work in academia, Dr. Rowe maintains a small private practice—her original intent. This allows her to continue being involved with her first love and remain current for her students.

10

A THEMATIC ANALYSIS OF WRITTEN ACCOUNTS: THINKING ABOUT THOUGHT

HOWARD R. POLLIO AND MICHAEL J. URSIAK

Editor's Introduction

Method

Results

    Themes Describing Human Thinking

    Interrelationships Among Themes

Discussion

Conclusion

References

Biographical Background

EDITOR'S INTRODUCTION

Drs. Pollio and Ursiak take us on a brief but scholarly review of what thinkers from Plato through Descartes and William James have said about the nature of thinking. Then they report their study of pretheoretical every-day thinking that they conducted to ensure as they say, that "theoretical conceptions retain a sensible connection to those everyday experiences from which they were derived in the first place and to which they must ultimately return." They first asked 84 undergraduates to list three situations in which they found themselves to be thinking, and then to describe in detail one of those instances. They developed categories for the situations, and then, as in all qualitative research, read and reread the descriptions. They developed groups of provisional themes, usually named with participants' own words, and eventually expanded the themes into four, each with subthemes: control (letting go, being controlled), location (in my head, in a different world, in the problem), flow (change, tempo, stuck), and clarity (exactness, focus, confusion). These themes are dynamic and often include affect; they are seen not as independent, but as interrelated—as patterns. The researchers went back to all 84 of the descriptions to check their work against the student reports and found that typically all four themes appeared in a student's description.

It is noteworthy that Drs. Pollio and Ursiak calculated a statistical correlation to determine the relation between frequency of topics listed and those that were described ($P < 0.01$). They also advocate for using qualitative analysis, such as this study, for exploring cortical involvement in thought. This chapter reminds us that qualitative research certainly is not antithetical to natural science endeavors.

The chapter concludes by returning to psychological literature on thinking and daydreaming to compare this study's findings with those of other researchers and philosophers. The authors make William James their "85th participant" and find the four themes in his accounts of thinking. Coming back to Aanstoos' phenomenological study of thinking while playing chess, the authors saw that they had come to similar findings, although of course location was restricted to the chessboard in the Aanstoos research. They also found touch points with the work on daydreaming by Singer and by Klinger, and provided new clarifications. The chapter concludes with a return to Descartes, Hume, and Kant and finds that each emphasized some of the four themes over others.

The history of philosophy provides psychology with many different ways of thinking about thinking. Plato, for example, said it was impossible for us to think with perfect clarity because by our very nature we are able to experience only faint copies of the ideal form of our ideas and concepts. Descartes also struggled with the difference between clear and confusing ideas and, primarily on the basis of God's guarantee, came to conclude that human beings could think "clear and distinct" thoughts only if such thoughts met the criteria of taking up space and/or could be quantified in some way. This issue was an important one for Cartesian philosophy because clear thinking was the defining property of what it meant to be a human being; hence, his famous if enigmatic phrase: "I think; therefore, I am." A further implication to Descartes' position was that mathematics defined the hallmark of good thinking, and rationalist philosophers from Spinoza to Leibnitz all have held this value to a greater or lesser degree. This should come as little surprise since the word *rational* itself derives from a Latin root meaning *to calculate* or *compute*.

Whether thinking moves from confusion to certainty is not the only difference separating philosophical approaches to human thought. Much of the historical controversy between rationalism and its most significant philosophical opponent, empiricism, concerned the issue of where and how knowledge originated: in the world or in the mind of the thinker. When the largely empiricist position of associationism (Hume, Locke, and so forth) considered thinking, it concluded that all ideas originated in the external world and, thus, the structures of mind only mirrored those of the world. Although Kant reported that Hume awakened him from his "dogmatic slumber," Hume was unable to dissuade Kant from describing knowledge in terms of mental categories. Although Kant did agree that knowledge began with experience, thereby casting a sop to Hume's position, he never suggested that knowledge derived from experience, thereby indicating a more basic allegiance to rationalism.

Combined with these distinctions between rational and empirical views of knowledge is a correlated concern: whether the thinker controlled, or was controlled by, the process of thinking. Associationist philosophers, by and large, viewed human thinking as passive, primarily at the mercy of mental tracks laid down by prior interactions between the person and the world. Rationalist philosophers such as Kant, and the present-day cognitive psychologist who is heir to this position, described thinking as something the thinker controls, not something done passively or determined by preexisting chains of mental linkages. To think is always to participate actively in the process and requires the thinker to develop not only rigorous deductions, but also plans, schemas, algorithms, and a host of other mental procedures upon which thinking ultimately depends.

In addition to concerns about whether thinking is an active or passive process, some philosophers also were concerned with its temporal organization. Although every theory recognized that thinking flowed to a greater or lesser degree, only William James (1890) provided that flow with the metaphorical power of a stream. For James, thinking not only flowed, it also flew, hovered, and perched, as some living bird might do. Even though the Jamesian notion of change-in-continuity was taken up by philosophers such as Husserl and Heidegger in terms of a concern with time, its most significant home was, and remains, in literature (Pollio, 1990). Within this domain, the French novelist Marcel Proust described thinking in terms of language: as an orderly, if complex, internal monologue. Other writers, such as James Joyce and William Faulkner, were not satisfied with this description and tried to provide the stream of thought with the edginess and personal signature of individuals in the midst of tales they lived, but were not necessarily able to make sense of or understand.

Despite this embarrassment of riches in literature and philosophy, few psychologists (aside from William James) attempted to describe what thinking was like for the person doing it. In one of the few attempts at providing such a description, Aanstoos (1985) asked chess players to "think aloud" during the course of a match and then analyzed the resulting transcripts through phenomenological methods. As a result of his analysis, Aanstoos (1985) concluded that chess players always think about the game from a specific perspective—that is, they do not consider all possible moves, only those related to their overall understanding of the current game. Within each player's perspective, thinking was described as a process of finding, and of then making clear, a small number of possibilities having the potential of transforming one's current position on the board into a stronger (or winning) one. Possibilities were experienced as questions to oneself designed to clarify the meaning of one's own moves as well as those of the opponent. Each player also tried to picture possible relationships among the various pieces. Such mental pictures had both a temporal (past, present, and future moves) and a spatial aspect (where the pieces are now on the board) that, together, produced an overall pattern of the game for that player.

Aanstoos' (1985) phenomenological research on thinking coincided with a larger movement in psychology in which thinking again become a central topic. One way this new/old emphasis was related to other ongoing work in psychology emerged when the American Psychological Association designated the ten-year period from 1990 to 2000 as the "Decade of the Brain." The expectation here was that newer biological technologies such as PET scans or MRIs would help psychology determine the biological basis of thinking and other cognitive activities. This approach was based on the prediction that cognitive psychology was destined to become cognitive neuroscience, and that the primary task of experimental work in contemporary psychology was to map relationships between brain activity and various mental processes.

What these approaches overlooked was that research of this type could take place only if the psychological descriptions on which it was based were clearly drawn. This understanding led, in part, to the development of a new journal entitled *Phenomenology and Cognitive Science*. As editors Natalie Depraz and Shaun Galligher (2002) wrote in their editorial introduction:

> Phenomenologists who want to understand cognition are now encountering scientists and other philosophers who are studying the very same issues .... At the same time, scientists and non-phenomenological philosophers are encountering phenomenology and the first-person issues that define phenomenological subject matter. All of this interest creates an exciting opportunity for interdisciplinary cooperation and exchange .... It would be unfortunate if this opportunity were not fully exploited to everyone's advantage .... It would also be unfortunate if the issues were investigated by each of these approaches in an isolated manner, working side-by-side, but always remaining one sided. (p. 4)

Other work, deriving both from biology (Varela, Thompson, and Rosch, 1991) and phenomenology (Dreyfus, 1992), also stressed related ideas. What these considerations all point to is that before we can examine relationships between thinking and the brain, we must have an openness to relevant phenomena on both sides; cognitive neuroscientists must think phenomenologically and phenomenologists must think biologically. It will do little good to have beautiful technology if the processes being investigated have not been carefully described from the side of experience. From a phenomenological perspective, this means that research on thinking must provide information on the following two topics: (1) where in everyday life do respondents report that thinking takes place and (2) what meaning do these experiences have for the individuals reporting them.

METHOD

To provide relevant information on both these topics, we asked 84 undergraduate psychology students, each of whom received course credit for participating in the study, to respond to two questions. The first question asked the student "to list three situations in which you experienced yourself to be thinking"; the second, "to pick one of the three situations and describe that situation in as much detail as possible." The reason for asking for more than a single situation in the first question was to encourage the student to think about thinking in as broad a perspective as possible before choosing to write about one of these situations in detail.

After all the essays had been collected, we developed a categorized list of situations to include the various settings in which participants said they experienced themselves to be thinking. Categories were defined by looking at individual answers and grouping together those that seemed similar. For example, one major category, "In Bed," was arrived at by grouping situations described by participants in the following ways: "I think before I go to sleep in bed," "When I wake up in bed in the morning," "before I go to sleep," and so on. Other categories were developed in a similar way; for example, the category "Watching" was defined by the relatively passive situations of watching TV, looking at a movie, and so on.

Once we developed categories, we "thematized" participant essays on the basis of an interpretive approach similar to the one described by Pollio and his associates (Beier and Pollio 1994; Pollio, Henley, and Thompson, 1997; Thomas and Pollio, 2002). In all cases, the process of interpretation entailed a continuous reading and rereading of individual descriptions to pick out thematic meanings. How this process works may be illustrated in terms of the following essay:

> When I sit down at a piano, at first I think about the piece of music I am playing and I pay particular attention to playing the notes that are on the page. As I get more familiar with the piece of music I am playing, I start to think of other things. I think about things that happened to me during the day or maybe things that

happened long ago. As my fingers play one thing my mind thinks about other things and I get lost in my flow of thoughts and I don't realize I am thinking of things other than piano until I stop playing. Then I begin to think about everything that ran through my head as I played piano and I can only remember my last thoughts. I can never remember the original thoughts that lead to these final thoughts.

After reading through this description a number of times, we attempted to specify as many different thematic meanings as possible that were mentioned by the participant. In the current case, the participant began by describing herself as thinking about "the piece of music I am playing" and of "paying particular attention to the notes that are on the page." Once familiar with the music, she started to "think of other things," some of which might have happened "during the day" or "long ago." She also noted getting "lost in a flow of thoughts" as her "fingers play one thing" and her "mind thinks about other things." In addition, she reported being unclear about "thinking of things other than" playing the piano until she stopped playing. Finally, she reported "thinking about everything that ran through" her head while playing, although she was only able to remember the "last thoughts" and not the "original thoughts that lead to these final thoughts."

Next we considered provisional meanings of the themes derived from other essays. For example, the participant noted that "My mind thinks about other things" and "I get lost in my flow of thoughts." These descriptions were grouped together with quotations from other essays in which participants described their thoughts as "going on their own," "not being under my control," "wandering," and so on. The title selected for the more general theme emerging at this stage of analysis was usually a verbatim statement found in one or another protocol: in the current case, "not being in control."

An individual sentence or phrase often concerned more than a single theme. For example, in the preceding case, the participant wrote: "I get lost in my flow of thoughts." This statement might be taken to express two themes in addition to that of not being in control—namely, that the participant experienced a flow to her thoughts and that she experienced herself as "lost" in that flow.

After organizing participant descriptions into potential themes such as control, flow, lost, and so on, the next step was to group themes into a smaller number of more inclusive ones. This was accomplished by defining major themes in terms of similar subthemes. For example, the theme of control was derived from participant statements to the effect that they sometimes "were in control" of their thoughts, that sometimes they "relinquished control" of their thoughts, and that sometimes they experienced their thoughts as "not under my control." After developing a smaller set of more global themes, several essays were selected at random to deterime if, and how well, such emerging themes fit the essays selected. If the thematic structure currently under consideration did not fit the particular essay very well, changes were made in specific themes; if it did fit, no changes were made. This process was continued until all essays could be included within the overall set of themes developed.

RESULTS

Table 10-1 presents a categorized list of situations in which participants described themselves as "thinking about something." The most frequently mentioned situation, "In Bed," refers (as already noted) to cases in which participants wrote that they experienced thinking before going to sleep at night, before getting up in the morning, and so on. The second column, Number of Times Listed, presents the number of times a particular situation was reported. The third column, Number of Times Described, refers to the number of participants who provided written descriptions of that situation. The fourth column, Difference in Rank, presents the difference in rank between values in the second and third columns. For example, "In Class" was listed 20 times and was ranked 4.0 in terms of the number of times it was listed. At the same time, it was discussed only four times and therefore earned a rank of 6.5; hence, the resulting rank difference of –2.5 (in column 4) indicates that it was written about relatively less frequently than it was mentioned. A rank order correlation computed between values in the first two columns, however, did produce a value of $r = 0.82$ ($P < 0.01$), suggesting that situations mentioned by many different participants also were described quite frequently. The most obvious exceptions were those of Studying/Homework and Being Alone, which were mentioned more frequently than they were described and Substance Use and Daydreaming, which were written about each time they were mentioned.

The most frequent situation participants both listed and wrote about was that of In Bed. In these situations, participants described thinking about various life events such as might have happened during the previous day or week, or might be expected to happen during the next day or on the following weekend. The second most frequently listed (and described) situation was When Driving, either to school or on a long trip, such as going home at a school break. A negative difference in rank was found for the next three items: Studying/Homework, In Class, and Taking a Test. Although it makes sense that college students would list these situations frequently, what seems noteworthy is that they chose not to describe them as frequently as they listed them. In fact, if we look at the nine situations described three or more times, we note that only three concern academically related events such as Taking a Test, Being in Class, and School Related. Of the remaining six situations, two clearly involve other people (Dating, Interacting with Other People) and four describe situations in which the person, basically,

TABLE 10-1   Situations in Which People Report Experiencing Thinking

Situation	Number of Times Listed	Number of Times Described	Different in Rank
In bed (before sleep/waking up)	41	20	0.0
When driving	29	8	0.0
Studying/homework	22	2	−10.0
In class	20	4	−2.5
Taking a test	16	3	−3.5
Watching TV, movies, news	13	6	2.0
Taking a shower	12	2	−6.5
Dating, talking to the someone of the opposite sex	11	6	4.5
Walking	11	6	4.5
School related	10	4	3.5
Being alone	8	1	−10.0
Reading/writing	7	2	−1.5
Interacting with other people	6	3	4.5
Making decisions	5	2	1.5
Hobbies (horse riding, piano playing, etc.)	5	2	1.5
Working	5	2	1.5
Eating	4	1	−4.0
Resting	3	1	−1.5
Traumatic event	3	1	−1.5
Praying in church	3	0	−7.0
Being bored/upset	3	2	6.0
Substance use	2	2	10.0
Day dreaming	2	2	10.0
Trying to figure out a problem	2	1	2.5
Going to the toilet	2	0	−3.5
Lying on tanning bed	1	1	6.5
Shopping	1	1	6.5
Looking, thinking about clouds	1	0	1.0
When future is affected	1	0	1.0
Total	249	84	

is alone (In Bed, Walking, Driving, Watching TV). The overall impression conveyed by these results is that thinking is not only, nor even primarily, reported to take place in academic settings, and that it seems to take place both in the presence of other people and when one is alone.

This last observation suggested that it might be interesting to consider the current set of situations in terms of their interpersonal settings. For example, the most frequently mentioned situation (In Bed) describes a setting in which the participant is alone (we believe) and in which there seems to be no specific demand on what he or she is to think about. If we use these two factors to divide the current set of situations, it is possible to code every situation into one of four possible categories: alone/low demand, alone/high demand, with others/low demand, with others/high demand. For the current analysis, a situation was coded as with others even if the participant did not specifically describe interacting with someone else in that situation.

To make sure that we understood the meaning of each situation from the perspective of the participant, only the 84 situations about which students wrote in their essays were considered. When these situations were coded on the basis of the two categories with/not with others and high/low demand, results indicated that the majority of settings (58%) fell in the category alone/low demand; the prototype situation here was In Bed or Taking a Shower. Situations falling into the second most frequently described setting (18%) were those in which the person was alone and was required to think in a relatively demanding way. The prototype situation here was Doing Homework. Both remaining categories—with others/low demand, with others/high demand—produced values of 8% and 15%, respectively. The prototype situations for these latter two categories were Talking with Other People and Trying to Learn Something in Class, respectively. The majority of settings in which thinking was reported to have taken place thus concerned situations in which the person was alone rather than with others (76% versus 24%) and in which there was only a low degree of intellectual demand (67% versus 33%).

THEMES DESCRIBING HUMAN THINKING

Four major themes captured student descriptions of the experience of thinking. Using specific terms found in the essays, we labeled these themes control, location, flow, and clarity (for specific examples, see Table 10-2). The first major theme, control, captures experiences in which participants described themselves as being, or not being, in control of their thoughts. This theme was defined by three subthemes: "I control," "letting go," and "being controlled." For the "I control" subtheme, participants described experiences in terms such as: "I have a sense of control: this is my world and what I think goes." The second subtheme, "letting go," described experiences in which participants characterized themselves as giving up control over their thoughts: "I allow my mind to wander." A third subtheme, "being controlled," describes participant experiences of their thoughts as under the control of some event or situation other than

TABLE 10-2　Examples for Each of the Major Themes

Theme	Description
Theme 1	Control: Letting go, being controlled
I control	I have a sense of control: this is my world and what I think goes.
	I have to grimace [to keep] ... bad thoughts under control.
Letting go	I allow my mind to wander.
	I let my mind wander to various subjects.
Being controlled	I could not seem to get it off my mind.
	It's like my brain has a life of its own.
Theme 2	Location: In my head, in a different world, in the problem
In my head	I played back the entire day in my head.
	Things were racing through my head.
In a different world	My mind is in a totally different world.
	I went back to that time in my mind.
In the problem	I was completely in the problem; I started thinking exactly where I was in the problem and how I was going to get there (to solve the problem); I mentally talk out what exactly I'm doing.
Theme 3	Flow: change, tempo, stuck
Change	It was in a constant state of changing.
	The flow of thoughts.
Tempo	Events of the day are tumbling about [in your mind].
	My mind began to wander.
	All sorts of things were running through my mind.
Stuck	My train of thought got stuck on one idea.
	My mind kept going around and around in circles.
Theme 4	Clarity: exactness, focus, confusion
Exactness	I begin to think of a certain incident in complete detail.
	My thoughts are clear.
Focus	I focus my attention on that specific thought.
	I try to pay attention to that thought.
Confusion	It really confuses me.
	I'm not sure of something.

themselves: "I could not seem to get it off of my mind"; "It's like my brain had a life of its own."

The second major theme concerned participant reports of where they described thinking to take place: "In my head," "in a different world," "in the problem." For the first subtheme, participants wrote about thinking in the following terms: "I played back the entire day in my head." The second subtheme captures participant experiences in which they noted: "My mind is in a totally different world." They sometimes also noted that: "I was in a different time" or "I went back to that time." The third major subtheme was described by students as in the problem: "I started thinking exactly where I was in the problem . . . I mentally talk out exactly what I'm doing." The last part of this description also serves to relocate this particular participant's experience back into his head: "I mentally talk out . . . ." Taking all three subthemes into account suggests that the theme of location was defined both in positive terms—in my head, in the problem, in the problem in my head—and in negative ones—not in the ordinary world, in a different time.

Flow, the third major theme, concerned experiences of change, tempo, and being stuck (not flowing). The subtheme of change specifically described thinking as in a constant state of change. One participant noted, "my thoughts kept changing." The subtheme of tempo captured the experience of a sense of movement. It sometimes was described by relatively straightforward phrases such as "All sorts of things were going through my mind" or by more metaphoric ones such as "my train of thoughts" Finally, experiences of being stuck were expressed by statements such as "My mind kept going around and around in circles" or "I got stuck on one idea."

The fourth major theme, clarity, concerned participant experiences in which they reported being aware of how clear or confused their thoughts were to and for them. This theme also was defined by three subthemes: exactness, focus, and confusion (lack of clarity). Exactness referred to participant experiences of precision or detail—for example: "I thought about that in complete detail." The second subtheme, focus, concerned participant descriptions of the following sort: "I had a clear focus on that" or "I paid careful attention." The third subtheme, confusion, referred to participant experiences in which "My thoughts were all confused at that moment" or "It really confused me."

One additional aspect to the current set of essays concerned the way in which participants described the form of their thoughts—as involving picture-like images, internal monologues, or implicit movements. When two independent judges looked at the 84 complete essays produced by participants, it was possible to code each description into one of four categories: visual, verbal, movement, and unspecified. The category of visual was scored whenever the writer used words such as "I picture it in my mind," "I could see it," and so on. Words and phrases falling in the category of verbal were: "I told myself," "I questioned/answered myself," I talked myself through it." Phrases defining the category of movement were: "My fingers practiced" or "I could feel myself make a great catch." When none of the preceding words or phrases appeared, the essay was coded as unspecified. Of the 84 protocols, 40 fell into the category of unspecified (48%), 20 into the category of visual (24%), 20 into the category of verbal (24%), and 4 into the category of movement (5%). When subjects spontaneously used words other than the specific verb "to think" in describing situations in which they experienced themselves to be thinking, such activity was described in about equal measure as involving visual imagery as some more language-based type of internal monologue.

INTERRELATIONSHIPS AMONG THEMES

Although the themes of flow, control, location, and clarity (and their associated subthemes) provide one way of describing what student essays were about, they fail to capture the patterns of connection that usually occurred between and among themes. For example, one participant described her experience of thinking before going to sleep in the following terms: "When I try to go to sleep I have a million and one confusing things racing through my head and I end up being 'wired' and unable to get to sleep. In order to calm myself I focus on something happy or of being in a happy place."

To capture the pattern of thematic connections in this essay, note that the experience of "confusing things racing through my head" refers to four different subthemes: being controlled, flow, tempo, and clarity. The participant's attempt to focus on "something happy" suggests the additional subthemes of focus and I-control. Thus, even within this relatively brief description, it is possible to find at least one subtheme from each of the four major thematic groups.

Consider a second example: This participant noted that "until I've emptied my thought box and can clear my mind, I am unable to sleep." She further noted that she is "confused by some thoughts that linger in my head for hours" and, to ease her mind, "I rehash daily events and contemplate the next day's expectations." The theme of being controlled appears in her description of thoughts "that linger in my head for hours," the theme of confusion appears in terms of her report of "being confused," the theme of focus appears in terms of her "rehashing the day's events," and the theme of I-control is expressed by the phrase "emptying my thought box." This essay describes an experience of being confused by unwanted thoughts the writer was unable to let go of before going to sleep. She describes an attempt to regain control by focusing on the events of the day, and by trying to rid herself of such unwanted thoughts. The location theme also appears quite frequently: "my thought box," "in my head," "my mind," and so on.

These examples, and many others like them, indicate that participants rarely expressed only one theme in their essays, or even in a single sentence or phrase. Rather, most if not all the themes were interwoven within descriptions of specific events and experiences. Unlike a category-based analysis of text, which requires each category to be independent and

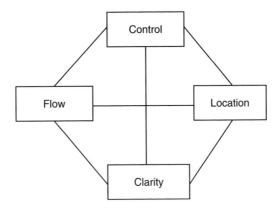

FIGURE 10-1   Pattern of themes describing human experiences of thinking.

mutually exclusive of all others, thematic analysis invariable discovers a complex pattern of interrelationships among themes. For this reason, qualitative researchers sometimes present their findings in the form of a geometric figure such as a triangle or pentagon. For figures of this type, corner angles are used to specify major themes. In addition, lines connecting the various corners are used to indicate relationships between and among themes. What is important to keep in mind, however, is that it is the complete figure (involving both lines and corners) that serves to define the overall thematic meaning of the specific experience in question.

To emphasize the patterned nature of current results, themes have been mapped onto the geometric figure of a diamond (Fig. 10-1). The control theme is located at the apex largely because of the importance assigned to it by most participants. Each of the remaining themes was used to define a different corner of the figure. Lines have been drawn between all pairs of themes, because even a casual reading of the essays revealed clear connections between each theme and all other themes. Examples of such cross-thematic relationships were presented in the two preceding essays in which participants described experiences of confusion combined with those of not being in control of thoughts taking place in their mind (or head). Although not all essays exhibited such obvious intertheme patterns, none was without connections between (or among) the four major themes.

DISCUSSION

William James (1890) left psychology and philosophy with a bit of a problem concerning the specific pattern of relationships obtaining among the topics of thinking, consciousness, and self. Although this problem is nowhere explicitly raised in his classic textbook, it comes up in terms of James' continuing tendency to label the stream of consciousness as the stream of thought, and the stream of thought as the stream of consciousness. Because James is hardly ever unclear or imprecise in how he names things, we are left with the following pair of interrelated questions: Is thinking the same as consciousness? Is consciousness the same as personal existence or self?

James (1890) comes close to providing an answer to these questions when, in his chapter on the consciousness of self, he points out:

> The consciousness of self involves a stream of thought, each part of which, as "I," can (1) remember those which went before, and know the things they knew; and (2) emphasize and care paramountly for certain ones among them as "me," and appropriate to these the rest. The nucleus of the "me" is always the bodily existence felt to be present at the time. Whatever past-feelings resemble this present feeling are deemed to belong to the same me with it .... [The I is] a thought, at each moment different from that of the last moment, but appropriative of the latter, together with all that the latter called its own .... On this basis [we may conclude] that thought is itself the thinker, and psychology need not look beyond. (pp. 400–401).

For James, the thought of the self, as experienced, *is* the self, and psychology and philosophy need not look beyond this fact to relate thinking both to self and to consciousness of self. James (1890) further noted that consciousness of self always involved "the bodily existence felt to be present at the time (p. 401)." In fact, James located such bodily experiences within his head in certain contexts (such as in reasoning or in trying to remember) or between his head and throat in other contexts (such as in making a mental effort or in agreeing or disagreeing with some idea).

If we consider James as the 85th, and last, participant in the current study, we note that he mentioned three of the same themes that were mentioned by all 84 of our previous participants: flow, location, and clarity. What James (1890) also noted was that he was primarily aware of flow and clarity when thinking and consciousness were at issue, and of location and flow when personal existence was at issue. Although he did not specifically use the term *control*, it is also possible to find support for this theme in James' (1890) essay: "[We] care paramountly for certain ones among them as 'me' and appropriate to these the rest." Although James' concerns are primarily theoretical in nature, his description provides many of the same themes found in those of contemporary college students asked to describe what they are aware of when they experience themselves to be thinking.

In addition to providing a thematic structure for experiences of thinking, current results also provide a set of situations in which participants reported that thinking takes place in everyday life. These situations varied from early morning and presleep reveries to more directed attempts at problem solving, such as those that occur in the college classroom. In general, however, thinking was not described primarily in terms of problem-solving tasks, but in terms of more daydream-like contexts such as those that occur in bed or when the thinker had no pressing issues with which to deal. Although it seems unlikely that noncollege-age participants writing about their experiences of thinking would necessarily choose exactly the same set of situations (e.g., thinking about a test), it does seem likely that there would be some overlap in the situations mentioned (e.g., before going to sleep). Even if specific situations varied across different groups of respondents, we should not expect differences in the nature and pattern of themes describing personal experiences of thinking, especially if James' description provides any indication of the experience of noncollege-age individuals. Themes of control, clarity, flow, and location all seem to articulate what is salient whenever someone, anyone, tells us "I was thinking."

Although major themes have been described by a single word, they could also be characterized in terms of contrasting aspects. For example, the theme of control involves a contrast between being controlled and being in control (including the possibility of letting go of control). The theme of clarity, likewise, expresses a contrast—between being confused and being clear. The theme of flow describes a more complex pattern of contrasts— between a fast or slow tempo and/or between experiences of flowing and being stuck. Finally, the theme of location describes a contrast between experiences of being in the world, including that of the problem, or in the head of the person.

Although current themes were not characterized in terms of emotional meanings, each theme could be characterized in such terms. For example, experiences of confusion were sometimes described as frustrating whereas those of clarity (or vividness) were described as satisfying (or pleasing). Although a few participants did write about a "comfortable" tempo to the flow of their thoughts, others spoke about "racing" thoughts that made them decidedly uncomfortable. Participants also wrote about feeling frustrated or angry at being stuck on a single idea, or at not being able to get to the solution of a problem. The theme of control sometimes was described as "hard work" and sometimes as a "feeling of being completely in control ... [which] ... made me feel good."

Comparing current results with those of Aanstoos (1985) reveals that his participants explicitly mentioned three of the four themes in exactly the same words as those used by current respondents: flow, control, and confusion (clarity). What was different between the two analyses concerned the theme of location: For the current set of essays, location referred to "in my head," "in a different world" or "in the problem"; within the context of playing chess, location invariably concerned the unfolding structure of the game. Although participants sometimes did say something like "in my head," thinking was described as taking place primarily in some unique "experiential space," defining the game as it unfolded for the participant. Although themes of control, clarity, and flow were directly comparable with those found in the current study, the theme of location was described by Aanstoos' (1985) participants in terms of experiences relating more directly to the game itself.

Because current results suggest daydreaming as a major activity defining what participants had in mind by the term *thinking*, it seems important to consider them in conjunction with earlier work on this topic by Singer (1975, 1978) and by Klinger (1978). Perhaps the major conclusion to be drawn from Singer's extensive studies of daydreaming is that it is a frequent event and one quite distinct from other, more directed, modes of thinking. Because Singer gathered most of his data on the basis of a self-report inventory, he was able to factor analyze individual items and thereby came to define three different types of daydreaming: positive–vivid, guilty–dysphoric, and distractable–mind wandering. In a different set of studies, this time evaluating randomly cued thought samples, Klinger (1978) came to characterize everyday thinking not in terms of three distinct types, but in terms of three separate factors: operant versus respondent, external versus Internal, and fanciful versus realistic. Within this context, operant was meant to define controlled types of thinking whereas respondent was meant to define less controlled modes of thought.

In relating both prior analyses to those of the current study, the theme of control emerged in many different ways: in the distinction between directed and nondirected thinking made by Singer as well as in the distinction between operant and respondent thinking made by Klinger (1978). The theme of clarity (or confusion) also emerged in both analyses: In terms of the vividness component defining Singer's first type of daydreaming as well as in terms of Klinger's (1978) finding that thoughts rated as nonspecific were also rated as undirected. In terms of location, both sets of studies reported that when the world was experienced as stimulating by their subjects, thoughts were described as in or about the world; when the world was experienced as unstimulating, however, thoughts tended to be located within the person—a distinction captured most specifically in Klinger's (1978) bipolar factor of internal versus external. Although the theme of flow did not emerge quite as directly as those of control, location, and clarity, it did appear in Singer's category of mind wandering. A more obvious place, however, in which a concern for the theme of flow appeared concerns the ways in which both researchers chose to characterize their research: Singer described it as dealing with "the flow of human experience" whereas Klinger (1978) described it as dealing with "normal conscious flow."

As a different way of approaching the current set of results, let us suppose, as is likely the case, that participants know little, if anything, about Descartes, Hume, Kant, or James. What conclusions concerning human thinking might they come to solely on the basis of their own first-person thoughts about thinking? Perhaps one conclusion would be that we, as thinkers, do not always control the nature and content of our thoughts, and that thinking sometimes takes place when we "let go." A second conclusion might be that thinking flows, and it is not in the nature of thought to remain on the same topic for too long. A third conclusion might be that thinking takes place in some domain experientially distinct from other everyday experiences of the world. Finally, participants might conclude that within the unique domain of thinking, some aspects are extremely clear, almost a scene in broad daylight, whereas others are more obscure and elusive, a shadowy object at twilight.

Such reflections should lead us (and our participants) to the conclusion that when we think we both control and are controlled by our thoughts, and that we experience our thoughts as flowing, sometimes in measured cadence and sometimes in more hurried measure. Whatever changes occur in this flow may move our thoughts from confusion to clarity when we are in the clutches of some problem, or may move in no particular direction when we allow them to run freely (as in daydreams or reveries). Regardless of what transpires in any specific case, however, thinking always seems able, as James (1890) noted, to provide the thinker with experiences capable of defining what we come to call "our self." Although thinking is certainly not all there is to what we mean by personal existence, it offers one way in which to experience whatever might be meant whenever the term *I* or *me* is used either in its ordinary or more psychological sense.

Current results also suggest that themes in the world of everyday human thinking described by participants are related relatively directly to prior philosophical and psychological analysis of thinking. Although it is certainly too facile to link specific theorists with specific themes—Descartes with clarity and James with flow, for example—such linkages do serve to specify significant points of emphasis for the theorist in question. To be sure, each theorist also took account of other themes, James was concerned with clarity and location as well as with flow, although each theorist did seem to consider some theme, or subset of themes, as of greater importance than others. What is most significant in the current context, however, is that a return to the pretheoretical world of everyday thinking provides support, not for the correctness of one or another theory of thinking, but for a more complex and patterned experience that exhibits themes considered crucial by most major positions. Going back to the pretheoretical world of everyday life thus serves to ensure that our theoretical conceptions retain a sensible connection to those everyday experiences from which they were derived in the first place and to which they must ultimately return.

An additional possibility suggested by current results would be to make use of phenomenological descriptions in determining the cortical basis of human thought. A useful example of this approach is presented by Russell Epstein (2000), who attempted to define neurological correlates for the phenomenological distinction between the focus and fringe of human thought. Basically, Epstein (2000) identified focus with synchronous firing of different brain regions, and fringe with temporal mechanisms that coordinate the actions of these regions. Whether Epstein is correct in his specific identification of these processes, his attempt to relate phenomenological description to neurological activity would seem to be of greater significance. Here, let us let Epstein (2000) have the final word:

> My claim is that such a mixed investigation tells us something important and interesting about the nature of consciousness. Insofar as consciousness has a structure that can be investigated both phenomenologically and experimentally, and insofar as both approaches reveal a similar structure, consciousness can be investigated in a way that is both scientifically valid and phenomenologically illuminating .... Phenomenology and neuroscience are not separate worlds [and] a mixture of both is necessary if we are ever to arrive at a fully satisfactory understanding of consciousness. (p. 570).

CONCLUSION

Eighty-four college students completed a two-part questionnaire for which they were asked to list three situations in which "they experienced themselves to be thinking" and then to write about one of these situations "in as much detail as possible." On the basis of a textual analysis of participant essays, it was possible to interpret the experiential structure of thinking in terms of four interrelated themes: control, location, flow, and clarity. The theme of control concerned participant experiences of being (or not being) in control of their thoughts, whereas the theme of location concerned participant description of where they experienced thinking to take place: "in my head," "in the problem," "not in the ordinary world." The theme of flow concerned experiences described in terms such as *flowing, being stuck,* and *fast* and *slow*, whereas clarity referred to descriptions of vivid thoughts or of attempts to clarify thoughts originally experienced as unclear or confusing. All four themes were discussed in terms of their relationship to the specific settings in which thought was reported to have taken place, as well as in terms of prior philosophical and psychological analyses of human thinking. Within this latter context, current results make it possible for us not only to relate our themes to the world of everyday life from which they were derived, but also to provide a guide for more biological approaches to the study of thinking. Only if phenomenology is considered in connection with both everyday life and biology will it be possible to attain a clear understanding of human thought as it is experienced (and produced) by the thinker.

REFERENCES

Aanstoos, C. (1985). The structure of thinking in chess. In Giorgi, A. (Ed.). *Phenomenology and psychological research* (pp. 86–117). Pittsburgh: Duquesne University Press.

Beier, B., and H. R. Pollio. (1994). A thematic analysis of the experience of being in a role. *Sociological Spectrum, 14*, 257–272.

Depraz, N., and S. Galligher. (2002). Phenomenology and the cognitive sciences. Editorial Introduction. *Phenomenology and the cognitive sciences, 1*, 1–6.

Dreyfus, H. (1992). *What computers still can't do: A critique of artificial reason.* Cambridge, MIT Press.

Epstein, R. (2000). The neural–cognitive basis of the Jamesian stream of thought. *Consciousness and Cognition, 9*, 550–575.

James, W. (1890). *The principles of psychology.* New York: Holt.

Husserl, E. (1913). *Ideas: General introduction to pure phenomenology.* New York: Collier Books.

Klinger, E. (1978). Modes of normal conscious flow. In Pope, K. S., and J. L. Singer. (Eds.). *The stream of consciousness* (pp. 225–258). New York: Plenum.

Merleau–Ponty, M. (1962). *The phenomenology of perception.* London: Routledge and Kegan, Paul.

Merleau–Ponty, M. (1963). *The structure of behavior.* (Fisher, A. [Trans.].) Boston: Beacon Press. [Originally published 1954.]

Pollio, H. R. (1990). The stream of consciousness since James. In Johnson, M. G., and T. B. Henley. (Eds.). Thompson, C. J. (1987). *Reflections on the principles of psychology.* New Jersey: Lawrence Erlbaum Associates, 271–294.

Pollio, H. R., T. Henley, and C. Thompson. (1997). *The phenomenology of everyday life.* New York: Cambridge University Press.

Singer, J. L. (1975). Navigating the stream of consciousness: Research in daydreaming and related inner experience. *American Psychologis, 30*, 727–738.

Singer, J. L. (1978). Experimental studies of daydreaming and the stream of thought. In Pope, K. S., and J. L. Singer. (Eds.). *The stream of consciousness* (pp. 187–223). New York: Plenum.

Thomas, S. and H. R. Pollio. (2002). *Listening to patients: A phenomenological approach to nursing research and practice.* New York: Springer.

Varela, F. J., E. Thompson, and E. Rosch. (1991). *The embodied mind: Cognitive science and human experience.* Cambridge: MIT Press.

BIOGRAPHICAL BACKGROUND

HOWARD R. POLLIO, PhD, is Alumni Professor of Psychology at the University of Tennessee in Knoxville. He received his bachelor's and master's degrees in psychology from Brooklyn College, and his PhD in experimental psychology from the University of Michigan. His areas of specialization include learning and thinking, college teaching, figurative language, humor, and existential–phenomenological approaches to psychology. He has published more than 120 journal articles, book chapters, and books. He has also directed more than 85 doctoral dissertations, about 50 of which involve qualitative methods. He was the founding editor of the journal *Metaphor and Symbol*. He has been president of the Southeastern Psychological Association and a Phi Beta Kappa national lecturer. He is a

Fellow of two divisions of the APA and has received a number of teaching and research awards.

MICHAEL URSIAK, PhD, received his doctorate in psychology from the University of Tennessee. His bachelor's degree is from Pennsylvania State University, where he majored in both psychology and philosophy. After a few postgraduate years in psychology, Dr. Ursiak returned to graduate school and earned a master's degree in computer science. Currently, he works as a computer consultant in the Washington, DC, area.

LIFE SITUATIONS

11

INTUITIVE INQUIRY: AN EXPLORATION OF EMBODIMENT AMONG CONTEMPORARY FEMALE MYSTICS

VIPASSANA ESBJÖRN–HARGENS AND ROSEMARIE ANDERSON

*Qualitative Research
Methods for Psychologists*

EDITOR'S INTRODUCTION

Dr. Anderson has developed the intuitive inquiry method during the last ten years, and Dr. Esbjörn–Hargens' dissertation, which Dr. Anderson chaired, has contributed to the method's development via both procedural refinement and the content of her study. Dr. Esbjörn–Hargen's illustrations from her research are interspersed in italic font throughout Dr. Anderson's text on the intuitive approach and method.

The method is radically personal, *and* demanding and rigorous. It is suitable for researchers willing to explore their own experience and beliefs systematically, and to open themselves repeatedly to aspects of living that excede our usual materialistic and cognitive orientation. During cycle 1, Dr. Esbjörn–Hargens gave herself over to poetry, music, and related imaginative avenues to prepare for what became her study with 12 women spiritual leaders, teachers, and healers (e.g., Sufi, Tibetan Buddhism, Yoga, Indian Tantra). During cycle 2, in light of theoretical and research texts, she reflected deeply and hermeneutically on her emergingly apparent preunderstandings. During cycle 3, she interviewed the participants and came back to them with her grasp of what they had presented. This cycle provided the study's text for formal analysis. During cycle 4, she transformed and refined interpretive lenses (both ways of looking and what is seen). During the final cycle (cycle 5), Dr. Esbjörn–Hargens integrated what was seen as nondualistic embodiment with theories, research, and other accounts.

With this demanding process of intuitive inquiry, the researcher struggles to put positivistic views at a distance to see what else is there. The researcher is both scientist and artist, is open to reality's being both multiple and in flux, is present to anomalies, cultivates unconscious processes when possible, and in a disciplined manner shifts from intuition to documentation. Many findings surprise the researcher, who is transformed herself during the study. With intuitive inquiry, external validity includes readers' comprehension of findings through a form of sympathetic resonance with descriptions provided, known as *resonance validity*, and the capacity of the study to render added value to the readers' lives, known as *efficacy validity*. The chapter presents this process clearly and evocatively, and concludes with a discussion of future directions for intuitive inquiry.

This study explores the intersection between embodiment and transcendence for contemporary female mystics. It is an inquiry into how women mystics of today make sense of the body. The impulse to understand how the body is experienced and understood by women who have devoted most of their lifetime to prayer, meditation, and spiritual service was felt by the researcher (VE) as a longing to challenge, deepen, and refine my own understanding of spirit and the body, specifically for women with strong spiritual sensibilities such as women in my study. What is the relationship between God and flesh for such women? Is it a relationship of tension, balance, or harmony, and how does it evolve over time? These are some of the questions that guided my investigation.

To the researcher, this research was felt to be a burning in the heart, an urgent desire to connect and bridge the realms of matter and of spirit. For a long time, I considered this longing to be purely personal and spiritual. Now, I understand embodiment and transcendence as the intersection between my personal longing and the cultural and universal impulses of our times. I chose intuitive inquiry as a research method because I felt that the framework Rosemarie Anderson (1998, 2000, 2004) created in intuitive inquiry offers a process of interpretation that simultaneously values embodied and personal perspectives (the "I" of the subjective), behavioral perspectives (the "it" of the objective), and interpersonal and cultural perspectives (the "we" of the intersubjective) in the process of scientific inquiry (Wilber, 2000). My heartfelt desire to understand the territory of body and spirit feels like a response to a cultural need to understand how transcendence fleshes itself out in a human body and to invite others to do the same. My hope is that this research will serve as an exploratory step toward furthering our individual and collective understanding of human embodiment.

What follows in this chapter is a discussion of intuitive inquiry by its developer, Rosemarie Anderson, and a research example by Vipassana Esbjörn–Hargens illustrating the method and printed in italics. Each step of the method is illustrated with a detailed description of a portion of Esbjörn's (2003) dissertation, supervised by Rosemarie Anderson, so that the reader may see intuitive inquiry applied throughout the research process. To the extent possible, the entire chapter and especially the case examples are written in a style of embodied writing, a writing style designed to document embodied experience (Anderson, 2001, 2002a, b).

WHAT IS INTUITIVE INQUIRY?

Intuitive inquiry is a hermeneutic research method that seeks to bridge the gap between art and science. The subtle ways of the heart long claimed as essential to wisdom in indigenous and spiritual traditions worldwide are valued and nourished. From the start, intuitive researchers explore topics that claim their enthusiasm, honor their own life experiences, and invite the research process to transform not only their understanding of the topic, but their own lives. Nurturing their initial understandings through personal and in-depth reflection on the stories, experiences, and accounts of others, new and refined understandings are sought. At every step, compassion softens intellectual discernment, making it whole, warm hearted, and potentially inspiring to others.

Almost always, I (RA) encourage my doctoral students to find research topics that seem to be chasing them. What a researcher feels "called" to study may be a call from the culture at large for change. Therefore, intuitive inquiry both describes current understandings and attempts to discern and envision what the present reveals of future possibilities. As an epistemology of the heart, intuitive inquiry is a search of new understandings through the focused attention of one researcher's passion and compassion for self, others, and the world.

Clearly, intuitive inquiry is *not* for every researcher or every topic. Not every researcher is willing to explore the spontaneous and startling nature of the psyche, as so often happens in the course of an intuitive inquiry. The majority of topics in psychology, and the human sciences generally, do not require such an in-depth, reflective process. Therefore, although certain aspects of intuitive inquiry can be used in any research inquiry and blended with other methods, intuitive inquiry is specifically designed for the study of complex human topics. It is ideally suited for exploring new topics, opening new ways to approach research areas that feel stuck or conflicted, and developing nascent stages of theory construction. I developed intuitive inquiry pragmatically in an effort to support my doctoral students' research on complex topics often characteristic of psychospiritual development, such as "right" body size for women (Coleman, 2000), the healing presence of a psychotherapist (Phelon, 2001), grief and other deep emotions in response to nature (Dufrechou, 2002), true joy in union with God in mystical Christianity (Carlock, 2003), storytelling and compassionate connection (Hoffman, 2003), and the dialectics of embodiment among contemporary female mystics (Esbjörn, 2003) among others. Such topics are more likely to be found in the fields of transpersonal, humanistic, and positive psychology, and their complementary forms in other human sciences. To date, colleagues in graduate programs in humanistic and transpersonal psychology or I have supervised about 25 studies using intuitive inquiry as the primary method or in combination with other qualitative or quantitative research methods.

Initially, intuitive inquiry was a general qualitative approach that incorporated intuitive and compassionate ways of knowing in the selecting of a research topic, data analysis, and presentation of findings (Anderson, 1998). Later, I developed a hermeneutic structure of iterative cycles of interpretation to give more form and clarity to the intuitive process (Anderson, 2000). In its initial development, intuitive inquiry was informed by feminist theory and research (e.g., Nielsen, 1990; Reinharz, 1992), heuristic inquiry (Moustakas, 1990), focusing (Gendlin, 1978), liberation social movements (e.g., Boff, 1993; Gutierrez, 1990), and later by hermeneutics (e.g., Bruns, 1992; Husserl, 1989; Packer and Addison, 1989;

Romanyshyn, 1991). More recently, the phenomenology of the lived body (e.g., Abram, 1996; Levin, 1985; Merleau–Ponty, 1962, 1968) and Gendlin's (1991, 1992, 1997) "thinking beyond patterns" have influenced my understanding of intuitive inquiry. This chapter also incorporates what I have learned from dissertation students who have used intuitive inquiry in recent years. In the discussion, I reflect on possible future directions for intuitive inquiry.

FIVE CYCLES OF HERMENEUTIC INTERPRETATION

Intuitive inquiry is a hermeneutic research process requiring at least five successive cycles of interpretation. During cycle 1, the researcher clarifies the research topic via an imaginative process described later. During cycle 2, intuitive researchers reflect deeply upon their own understanding of the topic in light of a set of texts found in the theoretical or research literature about the topic, and prepare a list of preliminary interpretative lenses. These preliminary cycle 2 lenses describe the researcher's preunderstanding of the research topic prior to the collection of data. During cycle 3, the researcher collects original data and prepares summaries, content analyses, and/or portraits of research participants. During cycle 4, the researcher presents a final set of interpretative lenses that have been transformed in light of personal engagement with data gathered during cycle 3. During cycle 5, the researcher integrates cycle 4 lenses with empirical and theoretical literature reviewed at the start of the study, as is customary in the Discussion section of a research report. See Anderson (2004) for a further explanation of the cycles of intuitive inquiry and suggestions on how to present the cycles in a research report.

By convention in hermeneutics, the hermeneutic circle of interpretation involves a forward and return arc. Cycles 1 and 2 of intuitive inquiry represent the forward arc in which the intuitive researcher clarifies preunderstandings of the topic. Cycles 3, 4, and 5 represent the return arc in a process of transforming preunderstanding via the understandings of others. Each iterative cycle changes, refines, and amplifies the researcher's interpretation of the experience studied. Attention to both objective and subjective data accompanies each cycle.

CYCLE 1: CLARIFYING THE RESEARCH TOPIC

In conventional research, researchers typically choose a research topic depending on the direction of the inquiry in their areas of academic specialization and personal scholarly interest. In intuitive inquiry, however, researchers begin by selecting a text or image that repeatedly attracts or claims the intuitive researcher's attention and relates to his area of interest in a general, and sometimes obscure and unconscious, way. The text or image for engagement and reflection itself may be many things and not just words on a page in the conventional sense. Cycle 1 texts or images may include a photograph, image, symbol, sculpture, screenplay, song, poem, recordings, sacred text or scripture, interview transcript, recorded dreams, or record of a meaningful transformative experience directly related to the topic of study.

Once the art object, image, or text is identified, the intuitive researcher enters cycle 1 interpretation by engaging with the text or image daily and recording both objective and subjective impressions. Researchers spend at least half an hour a day (or approximately an hour every other day) reading, listening, or viewing the identified text. Thoughts, ideas, daydreams, conversations, impressions, visions, and intuitions occurring during sessions, immediately after sessions, and at other times as pertinent are recorded in a noninvasive manner, so to least disrupt the stream of consciousness typically accompanying intuitive insight. Notebooks, hand-held tape recorders, and art supplies should be readily available to support recording of thoughts, images, and impressions. Cycle 1 usually takes place prior to or concurrent with the preparation of a research proposal.

By repeatedly engaging with a potential text in a process of observation, inward reflection, dialogue, and perhaps meditation, impressions and insights converge into a focused research topic. A suitable topic for intuitive inquiry is

1. *Compelling*—For a research topic to sustain the researcher's interest and energy, it should inspire the motivations and intellectual passions of the researcher.
2. *Manageable*—If the researcher is a dissertation student, the topic should be potentially "doable" in one or two years, including time for rest and relaxation, once the research proposal is complete. Personal life events and research logistics can complicate any research endeavor and delay the process, as most researchers know only too well.
3. *Clear*—Good research topics can be expressed easily in one simple declarative sentence. The more a researcher understands a research topic, the simpler the basic statement of the topic becomes.
4. *Focused*—A simple and focused topic with significant implications for human experience is preferable to large, ambiguously defined topics.
5. *Concrete*—The research topic should be directly related to specific behaviors, experiences, or phenomena.
6. *Researchable*—Some topics are too grand or do not (yet) lend themselves to scientific inquiry.
7. *Promising*—A topic is promising when it signifies an experience of something that is still unknown or seems to beg understanding. Because the topics pursued in intuitive inquiry tend to be at the

growing tip of cultural understanding, it is often the case that only the intuitive researcher can evaluate the potential importance of a given topic at the start of the inquiry.

Research Example

During an early stage of cycle 1, a time prior to beginning my formal engagement with a text, I recall one of the first moments when clarity emerged in relation to my topic. I was still uncertain as to what I wanted to study. I began looking at the various ways in which the intuitive inquiry researcher opens oneself to nonrational insights and intuitions, as a way of gathering information about one's topic.

As I drove home late one night, winding my way up a forested mountain road, I prayed out loud. I asked God for my research topic to please be revealed to me. The words flashed in me: "Spirit and body, something about spirit and the body!" In the same moment, I noticed an owl flying closely above my car, winding its way up the narrow mountain road for what seemed to be an inordinately long time. Upon reflection, the owl felt associated with silent wisdom, vision in the dark, and is a symbol of the feminine (e.g., Andrews, 2000; Walker, 1988). I came to understand that encounter as one where the owl was helping to illuminate my topic.

Knowing that my research topic was broadly about spirit and the body, I began to work with two texts that repeatedly drew me. First, I worked with a text called Chöd by Machig Labdrön (Edou, 1996) daily, for 14 days. During that period, each day I spent 30 minutes reading the text aloud. I noted thoughts, images, associations, beliefs, feelings, and sensations that arose within me and recorded them in a notebook. During this first cycle, I also worked with a portion of a poem by William Everson (1978), one that highlighted a different aspect of embodiment. I recorded myself reading Everson's words, and then alternated between reading the poem, and listening to the poem daily, for 14 days. In addition to all the variety of types of responses (thoughts, feelings, sensations, and so forth) outlined with the previous text, during this stage I especially became aware of sensual and sexual feelings that arose with the readings. These were usually intertwined with what might be called a holy longing, an ache that was sometimes felt in my heart or throughout my entire body. These responses were recorded in a notebook. After I completed working with these two texts, I understood my research topic to encompass spirit and the body, transcendence and embodiment, sexuality, and women.

CYCLE 2: DEVELOPING THE PRELIMINARY LENSES

Cycle 2 is an honest and personally revealing process, requiring that the researcher lay bare her values and assumptions about the research topic prior to collecting original data. In so doing, the researcher, and in due course readers, can evaluate the course of change and transformation that follows during cycles 3, 4, and 5. Colleagues who personally contact me about intuitive inquiry often exclaim with a tone of surprise that "It's so honest!"

To disclose and identify the researcher's values and assumptions about the topic, the researcher reengages the topic through a set of texts selected from the theoretical and research literature on the topic. By engaging in a dialectical and reflective process with the selected texts, the researcher clarifies her values and assumptions about the topic and articulates them as stated preliminary lenses. In intuitive inquiry, lenses are both a way of viewing a topic and what is seen through them. We all "wear" lenses all the time, albeit usually unconsciously so, interpreting our lives through our personality histories and habits. This process is not intended to identify and bracket assumptions from influencing the research process so as to set them aside; rather, intuitive inquiry is boldly hermeneutic and subjective in nature. In identifying and articulating cycle 2 lenses, the intuitive researcher consciously places preliminary lenses in full scrutiny and invites their transformation, revision, amplification, deletion, and refinement as cycles of interpretation proceed. Cycle 2 often takes place at the same time the researcher is writing a review of the theoretical and research literature on the topic.

After a period of reflective engagement with the selected texts, the initial phase of developing the interpretative lenses is usually easy and fast, more analogous to brainstorming. At a certain point, the researcher knows that enough is enough. She has read and pondered sufficiently, and quickly prepares a list of possible lenses. The initial list is often rather long because it tends to include everything the researcher feels and thinks about the topic without any attempt to prioritize. Then the researcher reengages with the selected texts on a daily basis to keep the topic elevated in awareness and begins to note consistent patterns or clusters of ideas in her understanding of the topic. Through a process of combining, reorganizing, and identifying emerging patterns, the list usually shortens to a dozen or fewer.

Research Example

During cycle 2 of interpretation, I worked with two additional texts. This cycle lasted six weeks. First, for one month I worked with excerpts from a book by the contemporary mystic, dancer, and teacher of authentic movement, Janet Adler (1995). Daily, I engaged Adler's descriptions of the body and the body in motion in a similar fashion as in cycle 1. I documented my responses in a notebook. I then worked for 14 days with a Sufi song performed by a female singer and performer Zuleikha (undated), the lyrics of which came originally from a poem by the Sufi woman mystic Rabia. This stage included 30-minute sessions over 14 days. Each session consisted of engaging the music (the text in terms of intuitive inquiry) through listening to the song, singing, prayer, and movement. During and after each session, I recorded my responses in a notebook. Throughout cycle 1, my primary intention was to clarify my research topic. During cycle 2, I began to look for emerging themes, values, assumptions—all of which would eventually evolve into my preliminary lenses.

The next phase, generating my preliminary lenses, occurred during the next three months. During the first month of this three-month period, I spent one full day immersing myself in the various notes I had taken thus far, including my notes from both cycles 1 and 2. On this particular day, I sat on the floor of my office loft and spread my notes around me in a circle on the floor. I then read out loud everything I had written, to get a sense of the whole picture up until this point. After spending a few hours engaging the notes I had made to myself, I was ready to generate a preliminary list of lenses about my understanding of this whole vast area we call body. This included my thoughts, feelings, beliefs, values, assumptions, and ideas about the body. I then worked with this list over another few hours, omitting some repetitive ideas, looking for themes, and refining my words. This whole process was quick, because it seemed important at this early stage of the research not to edit myself too closely, nor get tight in my thinking. Although I wanted to refine my ideas, I also wanted to continue to expand them. In working rapidly, I had a better chance of accessing my unconscious, rather than merely my conscious mind.

The following is a list of preliminary lenses that arose out of this second cycle of interpretation:

1. *Inquiring into the tension between spirit and the body enlivens one's felt sense of living as a body.*
2. *Transcendence or disidentification from one's body (or the realization of the body as impermanent) can produce the experience of freedom and liberation.*
3. *I am not the body.*
4. *The body is impermanent.*
5. *Spirit, that which animates our fleshly form, is eternal.*
6. *Spirit transcends flesh; spirit encompasses flesh.*
7. *Part of being human includes fear of the death of this physical form, the body.*
8. *There is a felt sense that, at times, awareness expands beyond the boundaries of my body, although it includes my body.*
9. *Sometimes it feels like spirit, or awareness, is located outside my body, usually behind my head.*
10. *Form, flesh is temporal.*
11. *It is useful (as a spiritual practice) to contemplate death, the eventual end of our physical form.*

12. *Energy animates our physical body.*
13. *Evolution of consciousness includes facing our mortality.*
14. *Physical sensations of energy (kundalini rising) evoke a fear response.*
15. *Energy that animates the body is benign and even has healing capacities.*
16. *Sexuality is body bound.*
17. *Transcendence is preferred over the body realm.*
18. *Awareness exists after death.*
19. *An interconnection exists between body and spirit.*
20. *Women are more embodied than men.*

CYCLE 3: COLLECTING DATA AND PREPARING SUMMARY REPORTS

During this phase, the researcher collects qualitative or quantitative data bearing on the topic. These data may take the form of interviews from participants that meet specific criteria, extant texts that meet specific criteria, or quantitative data directly related to the topic. To solicit or identify texts, the researcher identifies the target population, or target texts, and creates procedures for recruiting a sample of participants, or texts, from that defined population or textural corpus. There is no reason not to include quantitative data when relevant to the research process (e.g., Hoffman, 2003, 2004).

Research Example

The participants for my study were 12 contemporary female spiritual leaders, teachers, and healers who are viewed by their communities as such. The women represent mystical traditions and spiritual paths that include Christianity, Sufism, Tibetan Buddhism, African Spirituality, Yoga, Indian Tantra, Authentic Movement, and Diamond Logos. All of them live in Northern California. Their ages range from 40 to 76 years. One participant is Chinese-American, one is African-American, and the others are European-American.

I interviewed each participant using an in-depth, semistructured protocol. Interviews were 50 minutes to 3 hours long. The interview process spanned a six-month period. I tape-recorded all interviews. I asked participants either to choose a pseudonym to be used during the study or, if they preferred, have me select one for them. Those who chose to use their own name are identified in this study with both a first and last name. Participants who opted to use a pseudonym are identified with a first name only.

My interview questions were as follows:

1. *As a woman deeply embedded in the spiritual life, could you talk about how you experience and give meaning to your body?*
2. *Is there a tradition that informs your perspective? How so?*

3. *How has your experience of sexuality transformed, if at all, throughout your spiritual life?*
4. *Has your physical body changed as you have developed or awakened spiritually? How so?*
5. *Do you experience your sense of "I" or self as having a location, a reference point in or including your body?*
6. *Could you talk about your relationship to death and the body?*

Because the interviews were semistructured and they varied in length, I chose to create a portrait of each woman by editing down the original interview for greater clarity, precision, grammatical accuracy, and sense of flow. The interpretation began, therefore, through the process of deciding what to include and what to leave out from the original transcript. In addition to sending each participant a copy of the entire transcribed interview, I then later sent an edited transcript for review along with a letter. In this letter I asked participants to make changes, omissions, additions, or clarifications to their portrait.

I communicated with all but one participant after the initial interviews. In most cases, during the revision process I went back and forth with participants one or two times before we agreed that their portrait was complete. This collaborative effort resulted in a portrait of each participant, a concise presentation of my empirical data, which in turn served as my cycle 4 interpretive texts.

CYCLE 4: TRANSFORMING AND REFINING LENSES

The researcher then analyzes the texts collected during cycle 3 to modify, refine, reorganize, and expand his understanding of the research topic. The presentation of cycle 4 lenses is the researcher's summary of findings based on his interpretation of cycle 3 data. This cycle invites the researcher to expand and refine preunderstandings by incorporating the experiences of others.

Throughout intuitive inquiry, the most important feature of interpreting data is intuitive breakthroughs, those illuminating moments when the data begin to shape themselves before you. Patterns seem to reveal themselves with each fresh set of information. I usually work with a paper and pencil, drawing small and large circles—representing themes or stray ideas—and shifting the patterns and modifying the relationships and size of the circles, rather like a fluid Venn diagram. I know other researchers who work more acoustically, proprioceptively, or kinesthetically—bringing together sounds, felt senses, or movements that represent features of the experience studied. This interpretative process may go on for several days or weeks, with rest or incubation periods between work sessions.

To identify clearly the degree of change in the researcher's perspective between the lenses of cycles 2 and 4, Esbjörn (2003) developed three categories of presenting her cycle 4 lenses: new, change, and seed lenses. New lenses signify breakthroughs in understanding that were entirely new and unexpected, change lenses signify a significant progression of change from lenses presented during cycle 2, and seed lenses signify lenses that were embedded in the lenses of cycle 2 but became nuanced and developed during the course of the inquiry. I would recommend that future intuitive researchers use this tripart presentation of cycle 4 lenses to spare readers the time and effort necessary to make the in-depth comparisons between the lenses in cycle 2 and cycle 4 themselves.

Research Example

My process of identifying cycle 4 lenses was both long and short. Given that I was often working full-time while conducting this study, I worked with the transcripts over the course of one year—reading each text over and over again, sometimes out loud and other times silently, in different states of consciousness, and at various times of the day. I noted and recorded significant themes, insights, intuitions, dreams, and especially sympathetic resonance with the text. This was the "long" part of the research process in which I noted all sorts of various themes and insights, but keeping at bay or postponing formulating any conclusions. I wanted to allow the themes to gestate in me at an unconscious or semiconscious level for as long as possible. It was not until I began to draft the discussion chapter that my final lenses came into being. When I finally sat down to articulate my cycle 4 lenses, I found that they were already living in me. The task at this point was more a matter of "languaging" what I had been discovering over the course of my engagement with the text, as opposed to creating or generating lenses that were altogether new or unformulated. I spent about one weekend articulating my final lenses, which emerged from me with relative fluidity.

The ways in which my new understandings (cycle 4 lenses) are in relationship to my preliminary ones (cycle 2 lenses) could be understood as falling into three categories: new, change, and seed lenses. First, certain current understandings or lenses appear to be entirely new, not directly in relationship to any of my preliminary lenses. At least on a conscious level, I had not anticipated these findings during cycles 1 and 2. As these insights began to emerge, it often felt like the trickster (Anderson, 2000) was at play with me—catching me off guard, confusing me at times, and presenting to me surprising and unexpected results. I am calling these interpretations new lenses. Second, there are those lenses that came into being through earlier assumptions and understandings being challenged, changed, or transformed throughout the duration of the study. In these cases, there is a direct relationship between certain lenses in cycle 2 and those found in cycle 4—a progression or change can be seen in my thinking. In many ways, it was in these instances that I grew the most, because as my assumptions and beliefs were being challenged and changed, I was transforming through the process. I am calling these interpretations change lenses. *Third, there are those lenses that appear to have their seeds embedded in an earlier cycle 2 lens, or combination of a few lenses. Then, through a process of being expanded, combined, and deepened, those preliminary lenses or rudimentary understandings came into a full, nuanced expression during cycle 4. Because these lenses may be traced back to earlier seeds from cycle 2, I am calling these interpretations* seed lenses.

A summary of cycle 4 lenses, in relationship to each of the three categories previously outlined, is as follows:

New Lenses: Tricksters and Surprise Bring Unexpected Understandings

1. *(a) Childhood experiences, from visions to trauma, serve as catalysts for spiritual sensitivity in the body.*
2. *(b) The body serves as a barometer, where intuition becomes "physicalized."*
3. *(c) Transformation of the body occurs on a cellular level.*
4. *(d) Being embodied is deliberate.*

Change Lenses: Challenged Assumptions Result in a Changed Perspective

Central interpretation: Women who have devoted their lives to God, to a path of spiritual inquiry, tend to go through a process of disidentification and reidentification with the body. This process reveals itself as a dialectic between identification with emptiness and a reidentification with form, taking place over and over, deepening throughout one's lifetime.

1. *(e) Sexuality is integral to embodiment.*
2. *(f) Bringing spirit into matter is purposeful.*

Seed Lenses: Refined and Nuanced Understandings

1. *(g) Spiritual maturation includes an energetic awakening of the body.*
2. *(h) Boundaries—between you and me, world and self—are experienced as permeable.*
3. *(i) Self reference, or awareness of "I," is fluid and flexible and is not fixed in the body.*
4. *(j) The contemplation of death brings into focus the immediacy of life.*
5. *(k) Women are teachers of conscious embodiment.*
6. *(l) Inquiring into the relationship between body and spirit deepens and enlivens one's experience of living as a body.*

A full explanation of the research findings is available in Esbjörn (2003).

CYCLE 5: INTEGRATION OF CYCLE 4 LENSES
AND LITERATURE REVIEW

During cycle 5, the intuitive researcher stands back from the entire research process to date and takes into consideration all aspects of the study anew, as though drawing a larger hermeneutic circle around the hermeneutic circle prescribed by the forward and return arcs of the study. In a conventional empirical study, the researcher always returns to the literature review conducted prior to the study and reevaluates the theoretical and empirical literature in light of her results. The final integrative arc of intuitive inquiry is more demanding still. Not only must researchers reevaluate the literature in light of the results of the study, but they must evaluate how effectively and honestly they undertook the hermeneutic process of intuitive inquiry and to what extent their inquiry fully explored the topic of study. In other words, intuitive researchers must determine what is valuable about the study and what is not, sorting through the assets and liabilities of the forward and return arcs and how these may have affected their final understanding of the research topic. During cycle 5, intuitive researchers must honestly evaluate and tell what they have learned and what they feel is still undisclosed about the topic. The following are two research examples of cycle 5 lenses.

Research Example: A New Lens—Childhood Experiences as Catalysts for Spiritual Sensitivity in the Body

The connection between childhood experiences—of spiritual intuitions and visions, as well as childhood trauma—in relationship to adult spirituality is certainly not a new area of exploration. However, during cycles 1 and 2, I did not consciously reflect on how childhood spiritual experiences or childhood trauma might impact a woman's later relationship to her body. Therefore, I did not include any lenses that explicitly pointed to this area during cycle 2. I did, however, in my interviews ask a brief question about family of origin prior to the start of the formal interview questions.

Generally, the women in this study reported sensitivity to the spiritual realm early in childhood. Half of the women spontaneously reported experiences of childhood trauma that ranged from sexual or violent abuse to neglect. More than half the participants also described childhood intuitions, in the form of spontaneous movements, insights, energetic experiences in the body, and visions. For the women in the study who reported childhood experiences of the divine, most participants also indicated that they did not speak of or fully reflect upon these encounters until later in life.

Yeshe described a vision and powerful shift in consciousness that she experienced as a child and, like many children, it was one that she did not reveal to the adults in her life:

> *I had an experience of my body moving through light blue space, moving through the earth, and the earth was like a white round sphere. I was moving through seven*

*different white spheres of the earth, and it was all made of light. And my body, it was
more like my consciousness, and my body consciousness was moving directly up through
all these spheres of light. I lost ordinary consciousness completely.*

Yeshe also described feeling "the Holy spirit entering me through the
Communion." She also spoke of other divine experiences that were opened in
her young body, through being in church.

Claire grew up Roman Catholic prior to Vatican II, having a deep
impression of the relationship between spirit and flesh through the richly
textural ritual in church services. She described how spirit shaped her thinking
and knowing so that "the other realm was as real as this tangible realm."
Claire described her relationship with angels when she spoke about going
to bed at night. She said that her mom told her if she should fall asleep before
finishing the rosary "the angels would finish it for me. And I absolutely
believed that. The realm of the angels was as real to me as flesh and blood."
Also describing the importance of both ritual in the Catholic Church and her
relationship to Mary, Claire said, "During Lent, we'd walk in and the crucifix
would be covered in a purple cloth, and all the statues would be covered
in purple cloths for the entire time of Lent. We would do Stations of the
Cross." Claire said that Mary was "flesh and blood, and the agony of losing
her son I felt, as a little tiny girl." Claire continued,

> And so within the Catholic context, Mary really was goddess. ... During May,
> we would process and crown Mary with flowers. I would go and pick flowers from my
> garden and weave them together with wire and make these crowns, and then we would
> have these processions. Now, with hindsight, the statues of Mary were representations
> of the goddess; they were the fertility; they were all of that. So having Mary in my life
> was a real gift to me, and it was so important in setting that foundation of the feminine,
> the divine feminine.

Similarly, in their extensive research on the spiritual life of women, Sherry
Anderson and Patricia Hopkins (1991) found:

> As we listened to the women we interviewed for this book describe their childhoods, the
> poetic observation that it is "not in entire forgetfulness and not in utter nakedness" that
> we come into this life began to have the ring of an empirical truth. Most of the women
> we spoke with told us that it was in childhood that they had had their first encounter
> with the divine. And in most cases they described it as a direct connection with
> something inside themselves that they knew to be absolutely real—no matter what their
> parents or peers might say to the contrary.
>   How and when this initial connection—or recollection—occurred, whether it was felt
> in the body as an infusion of energy or light, or took the form of a dialogue with angels,
> the ability to see auras, or an experience in nature, depended on a multitude of factors
> as various as the women themselves. (pp. 24–25)

Describing a natural affinity for inquiring into the body, Cara said, "As a
child, I had many early experiences where I'd naturally be contemplating the
body, and try to see in the body, and wondered about what was in the body, and
why I couldn't just look in the body." Cara also talked about her lived

experience of the body as a young girl. She explained, "As a young child I would love to go on vacation to wooded areas. Scrambling around rocks, I would feel all these various animals and creatures in me, and I'd make up games that involved those. Yoga poses, especially twists and inverted poses, came naturally."

Valerie Vener also reflected on her early relationship to energy and movement felt in her body that seemed to arise out of a deep internal knowing. She said, "I started this lifetime experiencing the body very freely, very aware that I was energy, everything was energy, and that my job was to open as energy in energy." Valerie Vener described spontaneously putting herself in yogic poses as a child to facilitate the movement of energy through her.

Describing spiritual insight experienced through the body, the former Carmelite nun Bernadette Roberts told Anderson and Hopkins (1991) about an event that occurred for her at the age of five. Roberts said, "I was on my way to play with some kids when suddenly I experienced a powerful fusion from within—like the blowing up of a balloon. It was the infusion of an unknown power, energy or presence" (Anderson and Hopkins, 1991, p. 25). As in the case of Bernadette Roberts, and for the women in this study, it is possible that these experiences—of intuitions, visions, energies, movements, and shifts in consciousness—served to catalyze a spiritual sensitivity in these young girls, as well as being expressions of a childhood spirituality.

Childhood trauma—various forms of abuse, neglect, and loss—also impacted the development of many women's spirituality and healing. Arline expressed how this journey of sexual trauma eventually led to many years of healing work and therapy, which ultimately served as her doorway into spirituality. Jessica described how deeply the early trauma she experienced informed much of her later spiritual evolution:

> *I was ill the whole first year of my life and couldn't digest foods. I was put in the hospital at 13 months by a doctor who was not a kind person. He was supposedly the "best pediatrician in the state of Indiana." But this man, really, I think was quite soulless and heartless in his treatment of infants and children. I was tied down. I was force-fed. I was not allowed to see my mother, or any other person in my little life for six weeks. I was abandoned.*

Although many children leave their body or dissociate during painful experiences, Jessica had the opposite experience: "I wasn't one of these children that was full of fantasies and inner experiences that would take me away. I stayed in my body." Jessica said, "The experience of premature separation, psychologically, and then the physical pain—I think those two things happening probably made me more sensitive in terms of the nervous system which I already had." As Jessica suggests, the nervous system may become hypersensitized through wounding or trauma, and this may especially open a person to spiritual experiences as an adult.

A highly sensitive nervous system due to early trauma, or simply a childhood openness to energetic phenomena, appear to be common precursors to energetic and spiritual openings in the body later in life among the women in this study. Some of these women appear to have been aware of spiritual and bodily experiences early in life. These experiences were sources of imagination and spiritual delight. Trauma seems both to open and close spiritual realities, perhaps disrupting the development of a solid self structure and imparting a permeable and porous sense of self that allowed an especially fluid access to spiritual realms.

Research Example: A New Lens—Being Embodied Is Deliberate

This lens was one of the more surprising discoveries in this study, the notion that being embodied is deliberate or intentional. Our will to be alive, to be embodied, may keep us here in our fleshly form. Because this lens was both surprising and unexpected, it is a new lens.

This choice to be embodied, or to turn away from death, is described in a variety of ways by research participants, with shared themes and language. The context through which these experiences of choice occurred came in a variety of forms, including energetic spiritual openings, a psychedelic experience, a childhood dream, and a major illness. The literature in the field that most obviously points to this experience described by a number of women in this study is that of the near-death experience (NDE). Some of the more common features found in the afterlife and NDE literature (e.g., Moody, 1975; Ring, 1984), which are also apparent in these women's stories, describe a movement at death away from one's body, and then a choice point when the person must decide whether to keep going or return to reenter one's body. Out-of-body experiences, however, are not necessarily associated with NDEs, as in the many accounts documented by scholars such as Robert Monroe (1973, 1987), who study out-of-body phenomena extensively. For the women in this study, it seems that part of what happened during these out-of-body experiences, or spiritual openings, was that their consciousness was expanded out beyond the boundaries of the body. A common theme described as part of this experience is that of getting farther and farther away from one's body.

Arline described an experience brought on by taking peyote in the wilderness. Through this encounter she felt she moved out beyond her body to the point that she was barely attached to her physical form. Some participants described being dangled by mere "threads" or "wires." Arline said, "I could feel an extremely fine gossamer thread that was attached to this body." Jessica similarly described a spiritual initiation when she said:

> *I would see electric "wires" going out from my body, into which the energy was funneling. Following the energy out, I knew that there was a critical distance beyond which I could not get back. When the energy was too strong, I wasn't always sure where my boundary was or whether I could hold it, track it well enough, so that I could always*

> get back. I can remember very specifically certain moments when I felt like I knew
> I would die, if I did not stay in my body "enough."

Two women in the study described a similar experience as "teetering on the edge." Jessica said that the two dangers associated with going too far out from her body were psychosis and "death, which I knew would happen if I couldn't stay here enough." She continued, "I can remember those moments when I felt like I was just teetering on the edge of actual, physical death." Rose used the same words to describe what she experienced as she hovered at the edge of life. She said, "Thirty years ago I had a near-death experience and I opened into this incredible space of light. It knocked the pins out of my whole belief system." She said, "I was really teetering on the edge." Precipitated by an intense kundalini opening, Cara described how she felt her soul preparing to leave her body: "Eventually, I felt like I was dying, that I was getting so weak from the force of the energy, and I felt myself preparing to die. I could feel the soul was lifting out of the form, and I realized I really had to find a way to begin to bring a world of form back into apprehension." Virtually every woman who spoke of this phenomenon named a choice point, the moment when they had to make a choice to live or surrender into death.

Arline described her choice point when she said, "There was a moment in which I had the realization that I could just keep on going, and that I could let go of that thread and cause myself to die." She also said that the experience of being so far out of her body was an extremely pleasurable one. Arline described her ultimate decision to remain embodied:

> I then understood the meaning of the will to live. And I stopped myself from going
> higher, farther, more into the light, because I realized it wasn't time for me to let go.
> I started reeling myself back in and becoming less gossamer, less ethereal, less sheer,
> more dense, closer to my body, closer, closer, closer.

Cara talked about the point in her journey when she moved from "boundless vibration" back into solid matter, and how she managed to navigate that process. She described this stage of her journey:

> My consciousness was absorbed and concentrated in a world of vibration, boundless
> vibration. The forms were only loosely there in the foreground. What I did was, I went
> out and I started naming things, and I named myself. I said, "I'm Cara, and this is a
> tree." I remember eating dirt: "This is dirt." I put it into my mouth.

The movement toward density is a common dimension of bringing awareness back into material form. Rose was in the hospital for about a month before her body "made the choice" to stay alive. She said, "Eventually it was my body that made the choice to live. There was something about coming into my body so that it felt like I was in a new body, that somehow this was a second lifetime in this body—just appreciating being alive, being here, and the absolute thread that we all hang from." Arline reflected on just how much "control on the most subtle level" she had over keeping her consciousness embodied.

At the age of 40, Jessica went through a powerful kundalini initiation that at times appeared to endanger her life. She explained, "In the initiation, by necessity, I learned to strengthen my boundaries when the force of the energy was so great that I feared I couldn't stay here, and felt my own life on the line." Jessica described how her intense commitment to her children and her extraordinary will served to keep her alive:

> In those years of initiatory experience, the first and most compelling reason to remain in my body was being the mother of two small boys. I was separated. I knew that I would not leave these children. This was like a command, an inner command. No matter how incredible these experiences are, no matter what they teach me, I will never leave these children, unless I die from this. But I'm not going to allow that to happen. So it was a tremendous experience of will, and I think I came in with that.

Although not necessarily reflecting on the decision to live or die, Patricia spoke of the point when she chose to be embodied. As in Jessica's case, it was her children that gave her a sense of purpose that allowed her to "choose to be here." For Yeshe, it was not in her role as mother (which she is) but as child, when she was faced with the decision to choose or not to choose to be embodied. Through a dream, when she was a young child, Yeshe faced her reluctance to be embodied:

> I had a dream when I was three years old that my spiritual teachers came to me, and it kind of triggered my mind to remember why I came here. My mom said I wouldn't eat before that, and she was worried I was going to starve to death. I would hardly eat anything. I remember waking after this dream and thinking, "Okay, I accept being here, I remember why I'm here." It wasn't so conceptual, but I said, "Okay, I'm going to eat here. I'm going to eat food." And I remember going to the kitchen and eating something. So there's something about the whole eating thing, and being willing to be embodied.

Taking in food appears to have been the symbolic and literal moment of choosing life for Yeshe.

Reflecting back to my cycle 2 lenses, I am struck by how my thinking about matters of embodiment has changed over the course of the three years that I have been cycling and interpreting and changing through the intuitive inquiry research process. Early on during the proposal stage of this research project, I was fairly ambivalent, even reluctant, about embodiment. At that time, I went to an intuitive counselor who said to me, in response to my question regarding having children at some later date in my life, "Having children would really keep you in this world. It would be the one thing, a bridge, that could really get you to stay in this embodied realm." I am coming to understand the ways in which I, too, am choosing to be here, embodied.

A full report of the study's cycle 5 lenses can be found in Esbjörn (2003).

CHALLENGES AND CHARACTERISTICS OF
INTUITIVE INQUIRY

Intuitive inquiry is not easy to do well. Aside from demands of its in-depth scrutiny, intuitive inquiry requires a constructivist and postmodern perspective not easily attained within positivistic sensibilities still widespread in the human sciences. Intuitive researchers must think independently and creatively. The hermeneutic basis and procedures of intuitive inquiry aver a world reality in flux and mutable and, therefore, challenge conventional notions of a static worldview that is separate and distinguishable from the knower. Intentionally, intuitive inquiry invites new visions and possibilities for the future and helps make them possible.

The challenges and characteristics of intuitive inquiry are presented in full in Anderson (2004) and are summarized here:

1. *Being rigorously subjective*—The inchoate nature of intuition tends to resist record keeping, requiring patience, skill, and sometimes sheer force of will to keep records of intuitive impressions and their context. The left-brain skills of documentation and the right-brain skills typical of intuition do not blend easily, requiring the researcher to move adroitly from one to another to suit the task at hand. Some people have no difficulties at all, but most do. Typically, it is easier to slip intuitive insights into rational modes of knowing because this process is familiar in everyday life and occurs without conscious awareness. In contrast, intuitive researchers often protest integrating or switching to linear processes, such as record keeping, when deeply immersed in the surreal dance of intuition. Esbjörn–Hargens describes her experience:

   > Rigorous subjectivity via scrupulous documentation was not an easy task, given that my research spanned three years, during which time I struggled with an illness, often worked full-time, and I bought and moved into my first home. When I began to compile a master list of all of the various intuitions I had gathered for this research over the years, I had the task of sorting through a file full of intuitions scribbled across crumpled napkins, receipts, and bundles of scraps of paper. At times, I felt a little annoyed by this tedious process of recording each and every intuition that seemed relevant to my study, even though I trusted the research process and continued to document everything scrupulously.

   My first formal attempt to encourage documentation was to propose that researchers use a *process grid* (Anderson, 2000). The process grid has not been popular among my students. Sharon Hoffman (2003, 2004) offers some advice. She was unable to use the process grid for documentation, finding that it disrupted her intuitive process. Instead, she set an intention for witnessing and remembering the intuitive process after it had taken place, and recorded the insights, the context, expression, and process *after* the event.

I suspect that documentation will seem inimical to intuition processes from time to time for most researchers and they will need to find idiosyncratic solutions that both allow for documentation *and* their intuitive processes.

2. *Telling the truth no matter what*—An important aspect of rigorous documentation in intuitive inquiry is telling the full truth about the course of the research endeavor, including (1) mistakes made, (2) procedures and plans that did not work, (3) the researcher's apprehensions and puzzlements, (4) the process and content of intuitive interpretation, and (5) what remains unresolved or problematic about the topic or the method.

An intuitive inquiry is also not considered successful unless the reader of the research report understands the researcher's style of intuitive processing and the manner in which intuitions manifested during the course of the interpretative cycles, including the twists, slowdowns, and dead ends, and flow of the unconscious journey. The extended examples given by Vipassana Esbjörn–Hargens in this chapter provide the reader such an in-depth glimpse of her intuitive process.

3. *Avoiding circularity*—The intuitive process itself tends to carry an unfortunate air of certainty. Believing that intuition is more accurate or cogent than other sources of information is seductive and inopportune. Therefore, intuitive researchers must be particularly alert to seeking data likely to contradict their values and assumptions, and openly welcome anomalies in the data. Feelings of confusion and bewilderment are usually good signs that intuitive researchers are encountering what they do not know and yet seek to understand.

In intuitive inquiry, the degree of change between cycle 2 and cycle 4 lenses is at least some measure of the intuitive researcher's willingness to change.

Research Example

My own way of checking that I was avoiding circularity can be seen particularly in two of the three categories of cycle 5 lenses: new and change lenses. These two categories represent interpretations that, by their nature, either challenged my own assumptions (change lenses) or introduced a theme that I had not previously considered (new lenses). An example of this is evident in the change lens that became my central interpretation. Prior to this research I held a belief that suggested a preference for disidentifying from form (the body) to identify more fully with spirit. Throughout a long and sometimes confusing research process, one that included several periods of auspicious bewilderment, those dualistic beliefs were challenged and changed. The result was a fundamentally new understanding that became my central interpretation. This new understanding suggests that nondual embodiment includes both transcendence from the body and a complete embracing of our human form, such that spirit infuses flesh with life just as flesh expresses spirit with texture.

Prior to this study, and even after the interpretive cycles 1, 2, and 3, I also did not consciously consider the possibility that being embodied was a deliberate act. I was aware, however, of distantly related themes such as the importance of contemplating death or that there was value inherent in being embodied. But I would not have imagined that it is in part our will or choice to be here that keeps us alive. Interestingly, in my work as a hospice counselor assisting people in the dying process, I witness this phenomenon frequently—people choosing to stay alive even after they have stopped eating for days or even sometimes several weeks, until they are finally ready to die. Inherent to the hermeneutic process is an understanding that it is my life experience, my embodied subjectivity that allows me to see certain themes such as this one. My interpretations are situated in the context of my particular biology, history, personality, and culture.

4. *Trickstering and auspicious bewilderment*—Contradictory stories and examples are tricksters that deepen the intricacies of any topic of inquiry. Auspicious bewilderment signals renewed understanding. Nuances that do not fit generate new insights. Confusion takes us in an unanticipated direction. Paradox challenges our assumptions and so on. Methodologically, the nature of intuitive inquiry sets the stage for new ideas to happen. They often do. The research project will take longer, require more work, and probably cost more money, and it will also be more complete and useful in the end. Weeks, even months, of feeling auspiciously bewildered—a very different experience than depression, by the way—is not unusual for an intuitive researcher.

   More dangerous to intuitive inquiry is thinking we know what we are doing, being confident that we are on top of it, or having fixed ideas about the findings before we have finished collecting, analyzing, and interpreting the full complement of data. Beware!

5. *Maintaining a postmodern and culturally inclusive perspective*—Intuitive inquiry is a postmodern and culturally inclusive method. Conventional reality is not objectively present, but rather is constructed by the biological, cognitive, and cultural structures and habits we inhabit. Reality does not exist apart from the embodied participation of being a specific human being with a particular

physiology, history, personality, and culture, but is interpretative and intersubjective in the way Ken Wilber (2000) defines intersubjective in his four-quadrant model of human knowing. Human subjectivity is a source of knowing not just solipsistic expression or opinion.

6. *Writing in your own voice*—In intuitive inquiry, researchers are also expected to write compassionately and well. Research reports should convey the distinctive feelings and experiences that the researcher brought to the topic, and to present findings in a manner that allows for sympathetic resonance (Anderson, 1998, 2000, 2002a, b) in the reader as they read. The nature and process of intuitive inquiry begs authenticity. If the authentic voice of the mind, body, and spirit of the inquiry is not revealed in the report, the study is not interpretable and, therefore, is not valid as an intuitive inquiry.

7. *Favoring the particular and the personal*—As has already been said, intuitive inquiry values the researcher's unique experience and interpretations over common patterns that might be observed externally in the experiences of others. Knowledge is always personal, be it individually or culturally wrought.

8. *Imagining the possible*—Intuitive inquiry seeks to find trajectories for new ways of being human in the world by speculating and envisioning possibilities implicit in the data. As explored earlier in this chapter, intuitive inquiry invites researchers to explore topics that require attention by the culture at large and that the intuitive researcher's personal exploration of the topic will see, imagine, or fashion human experience freshly. In this sense, intuitive inquiry is both practical and visionary, allowing research findings to provide new options for the world that is changing and manifesting anew in every moment.

9. *Risking personal change and transformation*—Doing intuitive inquiry can be a whirlwind and overwhelming experience for some. Hermeneutics, generally, and intuitive inquiry, specifically, often feel as though one is chasing a moving target. If you are doing intuitive inquiry well, you are likely to wonder if you are changing or if data are changing before your eyes. From a hermeneutic perspective, both are changing because insight changes what can be seen.

EXTERNAL VALIDITY IN INTUITIVE INQUIRY

For intuitive inquiry, however, external validity is the *value* of the reported findings to the world—or, more specifically, to those who use and receive them. Findings are usually considered valuable if they contribute to understanding a particular topic and related theory. However, the value of an intuitive inquiry, or any study, may be more in its capacity to help readers ask good questions of their own lives or of experiences they wish to understand. Therefore, I propose two new bases to determine external validity for qualitative research: resonance and efficacy validity.

RESONANCE VALIDITY

Resonance validity refers to the capacity of a study and its findings to produce sympathetic resonance in its readers. As a principle, sympathetic resonance is best introduced with an analogy. If I pluck a string on a cello on one side of a room, a string of a cello on the opposite side will begin to vibrate too. Striking a tuning fork will vibrate another some distance away. The resonance communicates and connects directly and immediately without intermediaries, except for the conduits of air and space. The principle of sympathetic resonance suggests that research can function more like poetry in its capacity for immediate apprehension and recognition of an experience spoken by another and yet be true for oneself as well.

Using the principle of sympathetic resonance, research procedures can evaluate the generalizability or transferability of findings by noting consonance, dissonance, or neutrality in response to cycle 4 interpretative lenses across groups and subgroups. Using resonance panels composed of representatives from different groups or subgroups, a kind of mapping of the generalizability or transferability of a research finding is created. A modified sociogram, constructed with concentric circles of resonance, designates subgroups wherein the research findings are immediately apprehended and recognized or reacted to with dissonance or neutrality. Several researchers (Gopfert, 1999; Phelon, 2001, 2004) used resonance panels to evaluate findings in this way, using group interview procedures like those used in focus group research (e.g., Krueger, 1988; Stewart and Shamdasani, 1990).

EFFICACY VALIDITY

Efficacy validity refers to the capacity of a study and its report as a whole to give more value to one's life. Conventionally, a study is considered important for theory if it is replicated in other situations, especially similar situations. However, in the human sciences, I believe that most researchers also value a study if they resonate to the reported findings, and the findings lend their own lives more understanding and meaning. Specifically, when I read a study, I am both researcher and ordinary person trying to make sense of my life. Sometimes, a terrific study gets me thinking in new ways, asking questions of life that I never asked before. Much of good research, especially groundbreaking research, is more about the creative jumps and insights than about constructing theory inductively, one study upon another, like building blocks. Sometimes the most valuable aspect of research is action in the world in terms of new products, services, social movements, or modes of being, as suggested by action research (e.g., Reason, 1994). Therefore, research that inspires, delights, and prods us to insight and action is at least as valuable to the advance of new ideas and discovery in science as the more technical reports that may inevitably follow.

Efficacy validity asks that a reader of a research report change as a result of encountering the findings. The same could be equally said of the researcher and research participants, as I have said earlier. Therefore, a study is high in efficacy validity if (1) the researcher is transformed or gains compassion for self and others during the course of conducting the study, (2) the reader is transformed or gains compassion for self and others in the reading of the research report, (3) the research report is written with such clarity and authenticity that readers feel that they know the researcher personally, (4) the study provides a new vision or possibilities for the future, (5) the researcher or reader is inspired and moves toward action in the world, and (6) the study allows readers to sense possibilities latent in their own life however nascent they may be.

FUTURE DIRECTIONS FOR INTUITIVE INQUIRY

I created intuitive inquiry to "carve" new space or capacity within the scientific enterprise to use intuitive processes. The formative stage of developing intuitive inquiry is complete and I feel rather like a parent watching a child graduate from high school. It is time for me to let go and watch how the method is used and shaped by others. Although intuitive inquiry is only eight years in development, the seeds for intuitive inquiry were sown more than 50 years ago, when I was a gymnast and learned that a net and spotter helped me to risk. I was a better gymnast for the help of the net and the spotters that caught me. In like manner, the five interpretative cycles of intuitive inquiry represent the supportive structure that guides and holds the creative research process of intuitive inquiry. The cycles invite researchers and research participants—and eventually users of the research findings—to inhabit their intuitive ways of knowing confidently and to interpret for themselves the visionary perspectives suggested by the data. Within a positivistic paradigm of current science, doing so is risky business, and researchers need support and encouragement. I developed intuitive inquiry to help fill that need. Each interpretative cycle has a unique purpose and I hope that future intuitive researchers do *not* skip any of the cycles in interests of time and expedience. That said, I trust that intuitive researchers will adapt the method and procedures idiosyncratically to optimize their own intuitive styles, blend the procedures with both qualitative and quantitative methods, expand procedures to new applications, and evolve it further than I have taken intuitive inquiry so far.

In many ways, the development of intuitive inquiry has been an intuitive inquiry in its own right, cycling in and out of my own research entanglements and those of my supervisees—and it is been great, good fun. It has been full of spontaneity, serendipity, and auspicious bewilderment. I never quite knew what would come next—and, frankly, I did not care. Similarly, the spaciousness and permission given by intuitive inquiry invites a discourse in science that positions researchers, together with others, at the leading edge of that which is visionary, inspiring, and new in the realms of ideas and theory.

Specifically, a promising aspect of intuitive inquiry is its capacity to synthesize prior theory and research on a topic and render theoretical integrations in cycles 4 and 5. It is not possible to do intuitive inquiry well without maintaining a big-picture perspective throughout the research process. Therefore, intuitive inquiry encourages theory building because the method does not allow for a reductive perspective. The insistence of the interpretative cycles to stay close to intuitive promptings is not an easy path to travel, because Euro-American culture tends to suppress intuitive processes, especially body-based knowings such as proprioception and kinesthesia. Nonetheless, be brave! This deep listening and witnessing to intuition in research has the capacity to unfold into new ways of theorizing and envisioning that are closer to lived experience than the rationalistic styles that dominate much of world culture and scientific discourse. The iterative cycles of deep listening to and witnessing expand into theoretical formulations over time in a manner akin to Eugene Gendlin's (1991, 1992, 1997) descriptions of "thinking beyond patterns."

In the late 1960s, Abraham Maslow (1968, 1971) recommended that we explore the farther reaches of human experience by studying those individuals who had self-actualized their potential the most. Similarly, intuitive inquiry encourages the actualization of the researchers' capacity to envision creative possibilities that are nascent in what they are gleaning from their research participants. The intuitive researcher is both a scientist *and* an artist.

REFERENCES

Abram, D. (1996). *The spell of the sensuous: Perception and language in a more-than-human world.* New York: Pantheon.

Adler, J. (1995). *Arching backward: The mystical initiation of a contemporary woman.* Rochester, VT: Inner Traditions.

Anderson, R. (1998). Intuitive inquiry: A transpersonal approach. In Braud, W., and R. Anderson. (Eds.). *Transpersonal research methods for the social sciences: Honoring human experience* (pp. 69–94). Thousand Oaks, CA: Sage.

Anderson, R. (2000). Intuitive inquiry: Interpreting objective and subjective data. *ReVision: Journal of Consciousness and Transformation, 22,* 31–39.

Anderson, R. (2001). Embodied writing and reflections on embodiment. *Journal of Transpersonal Psychology, 33,* 83–96.

Anderson, R. (2002a). Embodied writing: Presencing the body in somatic research. Part I: What is embodied writing? *Somatics: Magazine/Journal of the Mind/Body Arts and Sciences, 13,* 40–44.

Anderson, R. (2002b). Embodied writing: Presencing the body in somatic research. Part II: Research applications. *Somatics: Magazine/Journal of the Mind/Body Arts and Sciences, 14,* 40–44.

Anderson, R. (2004). Intuitive inquiry: An epistemology of the heart for scientific inquiry. *The Humanistic Psychologist, 32,* 307–341.

Anderson, S., and P. Hopkins. (1991). *The feminine face of God: The unfolding of the sacred in women.* New York: Bantam Books.

Andrews, T. (2000). *Animal-speak.* St. Paul, MN: Llewellyn.

Boff, L. (1993). *Liberating grace.* Hughes, P. (Trans.). Maryknoll, NY: Orbis.

Bruns, G. L. (1992). *Hermeneutics ancient and modern.* New Haven: Yale University Press.

Carlock, S. E. (2003). *The quest for true joy in union with God in mystical Christianity: An intuitive inquiry study.* Unpublished doctoral dissertation proposal. Institute of Transpersonal Psychology, Palo Alto, CA.

Coleman, B. (2000). Women, weight and embodiment: An intuitive inquiry into women's psycho-spiritual process of healing obesity. *Dissertation Abstracts International, 61,* 1646A. UMI no. 9969177.

Dufrechou, J. P. (2002). Coming home to nature through the body: An intuitive inquiry into experiences of grief, weeping and other deep emotions in response to nature. *Dissertation Abstracts International, 63,* 1549B. UMI no. 3047959.

Edou, J. (1996). *Machig Labdrön and the foundations of Chöd.* Ithaca, NY: Snow Lion.

Esbjörn, V. C. (2003). Spirited flesh: An intuitive inquiry exploring the body in contemporary female mystics. *Dissertation Abstracts International, 64,* 2899B. UMI no. 3095409.

Esbjörn–Hargens, V. (2004). The union of flesh and spirit in women mystics. *The Humanistic Psychologist, 32,* 401–425.

Everson, W. (1978). *The veritable years: 1949–1966.* Santa Barbara, CA: Black Sparrow Press.

Gendlin, E. T. (1978). *Focusing.* New York: Everest House.

Gendlin, E. T. (1991). Thinking beyond patterns: Body, language, and situations. In den Ouden, B., and M. Moen. (Eds.). *The presence of feeling in thought* (pp. 25–151). New York: Peter Lang.

Gendlin, E. T. (1992). The primacy of the body, not the primacy of perception. *Man and World, 25,* 3451–353.

Gendlin, E. T. (1997). *Experiencing and the creation of meaning: A philosophical and psychological approach to the subjective.* Evanston, IL: Northwestern University press. [Originally published 1962.]

Göpfert, C. R. (1999). Student experiences of betrayal in the Zen Buddhist teacher/student relationship. *Dissertation Abstracts International, 60,* 2409B. UMI no. 9934565.

Gutierrez, G. (1990). *A theology of liberation: History, politics, and salvation.* In Indra, C. (Trans.). Eagleson, J. (Eds.). Maryknoll, NY: Orbis.

Hoffman, S. L. (2004). Living stories: An intuitive inquiry into storytelling as a collaborative art form to effect compassionate connection. *Dissertation Abstracts International, 64,* 2150A. UMI no. 3095413.

Hoffman, S. L. (2004). Living stories: Modern storytelling as a call for connection. *The Humanistic Psychologist, 32,* 379–400.

Husserl, E. (1989). *Ideas pertaining to a pure phenomenology and to a phenomenological philosophy. Book 2: Studies in phenomenology of constitution.* Boston: Kluwer. [Originally published 1952.]

Krueger, R. A. (1988). Focus groups: *A practical guide for applied research.* Newbury, CA: Sage.

Levin, D. M. (1985). *The body's recollection of being: Phenomenological psychology and the destruction of nihilism.* London: Routledge and Kegan Paul.

Maslow, A. H. (1968). *Toward a psychology of being* (2nd ed.). Princeton, NJ: Van Nostrand Reinhold.

Maslow, A. H. (1971). *The farther reaches of human nature.* New York: Viking.

Merleau–Ponty, M. (1962). *Phenomenology of perception.* Smith, C. (Trans.). London: Routledge and Keegan Paul. [Originally published in France, 1945.]

Merleau–Ponty, M. (1968). *The visible and the invisible.* Lingis, A. (Trans.). Evanston, IL: Northwestern University Press. [Originally published in France, 1964.]

Monroe, R. (1973). *Journeys out of the body.* Garden City, NY: Anchor Books.

Monroe, R. (1987). *Far journeys.* Garden City, NY: Doubleday.

Moody, R. (1975). *Life after life.* New York: Bantam Books.

Moustakas, C. (1990). *Heuristic research: Design, methodology, and applications.* Newbury Park, CA: Sage.

Nielsen, J. M. (1990). *Feminist research methods: Exemplary readings in the social sciences.* Boulder, CO: Westview.

Packer, M. J., and R. B. Addison. (Eds.). (1989). *Entering the circle: Hermeneutic investigation in psychology.* Albany, NY: State University of New York Press.

Phelon, C. R. (2001). Healing presence: An intuitive inquiry into the presence of the psychotherapist. *Dissertation Abstracts International, 62,* 2074B. UMI No. 3011298.

Phelon, C. R. (2004). Healing presence in the psychotherapist: An intuitive inquiry. *The Humanistic Psychologist, 32,* 342–354.

Reason, P. (1994). *Participation in human inquiry.* London: Sage.

Reinharz, S. (1992). *Feminist methods in social sciences.* New York: Oxford University Press.

Ring, K. (1984). *Heading toward omega: In search of the meaning of the near-death experience.* New York: William Monroe.

Romanyshyn, R. (1991). Complex knowing: Toward a psychological hermeneutics. *The Humanistic Psychologist, 19,* 10–29.

Stewart, D. W., and P. N. Shamdasani. (1990). *Focus groups: Theory and practice.* Newbury Park: Sage.

Walker, B. (1988). *The women's dictionary of symbols and sacred objects.* San Francisco: HarperSanFrancisco.

Wilber, K. (2000). *Integral psychology: Consciousness, spirit, psychology, therapy.* Boston: Shambhala.

Zuleikha. (Undated). Rabia's song. On *Robe of love* [CD]. Boulder, CO: Sounds True.

BIOGRAPHICAL BACKGROUND

Vipassana Esbjörn–Hargens, PhD, is a member of the adjunct faculty at the Institute of Transpersonal Psychology in Palo Alto, CA, and a psychological assistant in private practice and a hospice counselor in Marin county. She spent three years studying Eastern spiritual practices while living in India before attending the University of California at Berkeley, where she received her BA in Art. Her time in Asia and interest in the melding of Eastern and Western philosophy and spirituality resulted in the pursuit of graduate studies in transpersonal psychology. The topic of her chapter, co-authored with Rosemarie Anderson, is based on her dissertation research that used intuitive inquiry to understand the experience of the body for contemporary female mystics.

In her clinical practice, Dr. Esbjörn–Hargens works with individuals seeking to actualize somatic awareness. Her work as a hospice counselor includes assisting people in the final stage of life as it relates to their corporeality. Her clinical practice is also informed by Ken Wilber's integral theory. As a graduate student, she contributed to the formation of Wilber's Integral Institute during its first year of inception. She has co-edited Wilber's most recent book, *The Simple Feeling of Being* (Shambhala, 2004). In a manner that joins her interests in the body, mysticism, and integral theory, her current research explores the integral body.

Dr. Esbjörn–Hargens teaches classes in women's ways of knowing and in intuitive inquiry research at the Institute of Transpersonal Psychology and has been a Board Member for the Association of Transpersonal Psychology. She is a contributing author to *Radical Spirit: Spiritual Writings from the Voices of Tomorrow*, edited by Stephen Dinan (New World Library, 2002) and has published an article based on her dissertation research (Esbjörn–Hargens, 2004).

ROSEMARIE ANDERSON, MDiv, PhD, is a professor at the Institute of Transpersonal Psychology in Palo Alto, CA, and an Episcopal priest in the diocese of El Camino Real. During her graduate training in experimental social psychology at the University of Nebraska–Lincoln in the early 1970s, she initiated and taught the university's first course in the psychology of women—a course that remains on the curriculum to this day. Her interest in feminist studies and women's intuitive ways of knowing in time resulted in the development of a qualitative research method known as *intuitive inquiry*, the topic of her chapter co-authored with Vipassana Esbjörn–Hargens.

After receiving her PhD in 1973, Dr. Anderson settled down into a traditional professorial career at Wake Forest University, NC, until her life was disrupted by an awakening spiritual awareness. Also a lover of travel and exotic places, Dr. Anderson left her successful, youthful career to teach with the University of Maryland, Asian Division. Living in Japan and South Korea, Dr. Anderson studied in monasteries throughout Asia. After her return to the United States, she attended the Graduate Theological Union in Berkeley, CA, to study theology, revel in the eccentricities of Berkeley, and receive an MDiv in 1983. While in discernment for holy orders, she returned to the University of Maryland to serve as a university dean for the university's European Division. She was ordained an Episcopal priest in 1987 and worked for several years as a parish priest and college chaplain.

Since 1992, Dr. Anderson has joined her interests in epistemology and spirituality by teaching, directing doctoral research, and creating research methods at the Institute of Transpersonal Psychology. She has published nearly 100 professional articles, supervised some 50 dissertations and theses, and written two books. Her book *Celtic Oracles* (Random House, 1998) presents her intuitive insights about Celtic mythology. *Transpersonal Research Methods for the Social Sciences: Honoring Human Experience*, co-authored with William Braud, (Sage, 1998) was the first book to advance a transpersonal perspective for research and is considered a classic in the field.

12

AN APPLICATION OF EXPERIENTIAL METHOD IN PSYCHOLOGY: WHAT IS IT LIKE TO BE A STRANGER IN A FOREIGN LAND?

ARNE COLLEN

EDITOR'S INTRODUCTION

Dr. Collen shares his research on experience using procedures he characterizes as methodologically pragmatic, democratically collaborative, and independent of the philosophical foundations presented by most of this volume's authors. In this chapter he shares his reflections on having served as researcher and participant with three separate groups of persons attending his qualitative research seminars held in Burgundy, France. The topic they all explored was the experience of a being in a country in which the participants were foreigners. Comparisons of outcomes allowed exploration of replication in qualitative research. Although tables of themes related to being in a foreign land are presented, the chapter's focus is exploration of the research outcomes of procedural decisions. Throughout, Dr. Collen reminds us of similarities to traditional research design choices and issues, such as convergent and discriminant validity, independence of observations, cross-case analysis, content analysis, meta-analysis, replication, cluster and factor analysis, ipsative and ideographic presentation of data, and within-type and between-type design.

Referring concretely to the activities of his three groups, Dr. Collen also discusses a range of issues of importance to most qualitative researchers, but elsewhere too often not mentioned or mentioned only in passing. These issues include the difficulty of obtaining useful reports for analysis, reports of ongoing experience versus remembered experience, direct versus interpreted experience, multiple accounts by the same participant versus single accounts, multiple researchers versus single researchers, pluses and minuses of bias owned by researchers, manner of posing requests for participant accounts, inclusion of researchers' own accounts versus only those of others, degrees of collaboration among researchers and with participants, and the difficulties of wording experience. I anticipate that as qualitative research expands, we will find ourselves engaged in systematic discussion of just such issues as these raised by Dr. Collen.

The word *experience* refers to one of the main hypothetical constructs in psychology and related fields of study we use extensively to communicate with each other the multitude of events that has happened to us in daily life. The accumulation of events, as we can recall and convey them, we call human experience. We describe it in terms of our feelings, thoughts, reflections, and interpretations of events. In psychology research, we take these descriptions as data, and we call them narratives, memories, self-reports, and recollections. The accumulation of experiences gains a seemingly endless breadth, depth, and richness over our life span. Researchers mine human experience through various forms of disciplined inquiry. This chapter describes and discusses one version of disciplined inquiry to study human experience that makes use of these forms. It has been given the name *experiential method* (Barrell, Medeiros, and Foley, 1990). The approach is a method of research, and it should not be confused with other uses of this phrase in reference to creativity, psychotherapy, and organizational development.

Given the central importance of experience to human nature, it comes as no surprise that many approaches to formalize human inquiry work directly with human experience, according to specified rules and procedures. Taken with those methods presented in other chapters, along with those found in other sources such as Braud and Anderson (1998); Camic, Rhodes, and Yardley (2003); Denzin and Lincoln (1994); McLeod (2001); and Reason and Rowan (1981); the method described in this chapter may serve even further to illustrate the diversity available to and utilized by contemporary researchers of human experience.

It must be clarified that the subject of this chapter is a very limited and modest activity among the many spheres contributing to the study of human experience. This chapter considers neither important philosophical approaches, such as Dewey (1938), Heidegger (1982), and Husserl (1931), nor other research methods for the study of human experience in psychology and allied fields, such as Denzin (1989), Giorgi (1985), and Glaser and Strauss (1967). The purpose of this chapter is to invite your consideration of one specific form of research method called the *experiential method*, as it has been applied to a common human phenomenon—namely, traveling to a place or country that is not one's own. Moreover, this chapter is more about the study of the research method and less about the phenomenon studied, even though I shall cover both during the course of the chapter.

It shall soon become evident that the research occasion provided the opportunity to study the method, and the choice of phenomenon facilitated that study.

The chapter consists of four parts. First, I situate experience as a psychological construct for the experiential method. Second, I describe the form of the method that I used, with particular attention to the steps and decisions I made chiefly for pedagogical reasons to learn about the method. Third, I present the findings of three groups reporting their experiences of the phenomenon designated "being a stranger in a foreign land." And fourth, I discuss the features, shortcomings, strengths, and methodological issues keen to my experience working with the method. Again, primarily my purpose is to present and discuss the method, and secondarily to convey the research findings.

EXPERIENCE AND HUMAN INQUIRY

Essential to our everyday life and applicable to research methodology in psychology, experience has both an active and passive side. An examination of the entries in the dictionary makes this duality clear (Table 12-1).

Experience [L., *experientia*] stems from *experiri* meaning "to try, put to the test." From the 14th to 18th centuries, the idea was an active one, as seen in definitions 1 through 4 in Table 12-1, even though they seem obsolete today. We tend to think of experience in terms of those given in definitions

TABLE 12-1   Denotations of Experience (The compact *Oxford English dictionary* [1994])

1. The action of putting to the test; trial; *obs*

2. A tentative procedure; an operation performed to ascertain or illustrate some truth; an experiment; *obs*

3. Proof by actual trial; practical demonstration; *obs*

4. The actual observation of facts or events, considered as a source of knowledge

5. The fact of being consciously the subject of a state or condition, or of being consciously affected by an event; also an instance of this; a state or condition viewed subjectively; an event by which one is affected

6. A piece of experimental knowledge; a fact, maxim rule, or device drawn from or approved by experience; *obs*

7. What has been experienced; the events that have taken place within the knowledge of an individual, a community, mankind at large, either during a particular period or generally

8. Knowledge resulting from actual observation or from what one has undergone

9. The state of having been occupied in any department of study or practice, in affairs generally, or in the intercourse of life; the extent to which, or the length of time during which one has been so occupied; the aptitudes, skill, judgment, etc., thereby acquired

6 through 9, a more passive and indirect notion compared with the earlier usage. But some derivatives, such as *experiment*, have continued to carry the former emphasis.

The historical development of various contemporary research methods to study human experience springs from a common origin in experience itself. For example, experiential, experimental, and observational types of human inquiry were not as distinguishable methodological tracts in prior centuries, as they are described and applied today. Therefore, some caution is justified, because developing a methodological line of inquiry and calling it the experiential method may be more of a partial return to clarify roots than charting new territory. Given the contributions of numerous others to research methodology during the last 200 years (Collen, 1990), the choice of this name for a human-oriented research method will likely be a cause for confusion as well as skepticism from many researchers and consumers of research.

Two additional points about the central construct are important to mention early in the chapter, because they have a profound influence on all forms of methodology pertinent to human experience. Experience forms the implicit and often taken-for-granted context for the study of the content and structure of human consciousness. Similarly, like a sedimentation process of a flowing river, experience is the residue of what happens to us every day in reference to our stream of consciousness. In contrast to the long-standing Husserlian and Jamesian notions, experience is increasingly discussed in contemporary methodology in terms of story and narrative construction (per ex, Clandinin and Connelly, 1994). Experience is implicitly organized and expressed in spatial–temporal terms (Bruner, 1986). That is, underlying the storytelling and narrative accounts are space–time relations. In the crudest form of organization, we expect an experience to involve a situation and circumstance. Furthermore, it has a beginning, middle, and end. Embellishments of detail upon this skeleton involve descriptions of characters, objects, events, perceptions, thoughts, feelings, viewpoints, and various interpretations of them. The connections and relations among them are seemingly endless. On the side of the construct termed *space*, one takes one's self (the narrator and storyteller) as the point of reference in a first-person account, and experience varies. It varies from an ever deeper inwardness into one's private thoughts and imaginings on the one hand to an unmeasurable outwardness beyond one's self to unseen others and distant lands on the other hand. The complement is the construct of *time*, importantly organized again from the person's point of self-reference. One can go backward as far as one can remember to dwell upon events of the past. Alternatively, one can go forward as far as one prefers to the imagined events of the future.

Regardless of the form that a particular method for human inquiry may take, space–time schemata are central to formulations of disciplined inquiry, especially with regard to research design, data collection, and data analysis (Collen, 1998).

The phrase *experiential method* chosen by James Barrell, Donald Price, and associates is intended to convey their approach to the study of human experience. Greatest details of their method can be found in Barrell and Barrell (1975) and Price and Barrell (1980). Their productivity and application of the experiential method to various human phenomena are evident in their published studies over three decades, and in their experiential descriptions of pain (Barrell and Price, 1975; Price, 1988; Price and Aydede, 2004; Price, Barrell, and Gracely, 1980), emotions (Barrell and Neimeyer, 1975; Lyons and Barrell, 1979; Price and Barrell, 1984; Price et al., 1985), control of time (Barrell and Barrell, 1976); honesty (Barrell and Jourard, 1976), openness (Barrell and Jourard, 1977); stress (Barrell and Price, 1977a, b), motivation (Barrell and Waters, 1980), jealousy (Barrell and Richards, 1982), and performance anxiety (Barrell et al., 1985). More recent examples of their approach to research are to be found in Barrell Foley, and Lueders (1990a), Barrell, Medeiros, and Foley (1990b), and Price and Aydede (2004).

In coming across the body of published work by Barrell, Price, and associates, I began using it and later decided to study its pedagogical and methodological potential in my international summer seminar on human science research methods (Collen, 1995a). Because the purpose of the experiential method is to describe a chosen human phenomenon of experience from first-person reports of those who experienced the phenomenon under study, it fit easily into the seminar work as a means to study, compare, and contrast the experience of participants of the seminar.

RESEARCH CONTEXT

Beginning in 1987, I offered a week-long seminar about various research methods for human inquiry. The seminar involved lecture, discussion, and hands-on research skill-building activities. Participants resided on-site, working as a group six hours per day and individually up to three hours additionally per day with methodology concepts and principles, and methods of human inquiry. Group participatory activities were often complemented by analogous solo assignments later presented to the group. But some solo activities did initiate assignments to be completed after the seminar as part of a longer term educational course or consulting arrangement with me.

In the case of the three seminar events reported in this chapter, they occurred in a renovated country house in the Morvan, a rural national park southeast of Paris, in Burgundy, France. The rustic accommodations and atmosphere of farmland intertwined with forest were very agreeable to an informal, relaxed, and supportive learning environment, in which participants were encouraged to challenge conventional conceptualizations and assumptions about doing research and to think creatively about human-oriented research methods. The seminar was an arena for inquiry to improve research knowledge and skills, explore research interests, and further research projects from home settings. The seminar was the context of the research activity reported in this chapter, and only that group activity designed to bring the participants some familiarity with the experiential method shall be discussed. Although the results of the research activity provided a preliminary study of the phenomenon, to reiterate, my primary aim was pedagogical. Consequently, the results presented in this chapter serve mainly to illustrate various aspects of executing the research method.

CHOICE OF PHENOMENON

It was important to select a phenomenon that would favor quick acquisition of the essentials of the research method, given the brevity of time for didactic group activity. Furthermore, it had to be a phenomenon familiar to all members of the group, and if possible, a phenomenon recently experienced and interesting to them to foster participation and active learning of experiential method. For these reasons, I decided upon the phenomenon I called "being a stranger in a foreign land."

I came to comprehend this phenomenon from my own experience traveling extensively in Europe and the United States. I pondered almost obsessively upon the process of moving from my country to another, and from nation to nation, especially when dramatic and obvious altercations in culture, language, custom, and physical terrain occurred. The dislocation, disorientation, confusion, anxiety, excitement, curiosity, human predicaments, unexpected circumstances, helplessness, frustration, base simplicity, estrangement, new learning, and solitude were some of the many aspects of my experience that came to characterize each personal journey abroad.

Parenthetically, I note that the previous paragraph constitutes my presuppositional statement about the phenomenon. It conveys something of my personal attitude, meanings, and understanding that I brought *a priori* to the study of the phenomenon. The relevance and importance of such a statement are matters for discussion later in the chapter.

Having grown fond of and empathetic to the arrival of the seminar participants to France from distant lands with the beginning of each new seminar, this experience of travel I had coined, "being a stranger in a foreign land," seemed to be a natural and sufficiently common human experience, ready made to apply one or more research methods for pedagogical purposes during the course of the seminar. However, some caution was warranted here, for I had not completed an extensive review of the literature of the phenomenon, and its authenticity could be questioned. The phenomenon was (and still is) meaningful to my experience, and I was curious to know whether this was so for others. It had been repeatedly validated in my personal life and corroborated a number of times in conversation with previous seminar participants and fellow travelers. But one's deep-seated belief coupled with conspiring with others, although a plausible wellspring for phenomena to study, may not in itself be a sufficiently sound scientific basis to accept the authenticity and generalizability of the phenomenon. Certainly thousands of human beings spend their entire lives within a circumscribed and familiar habitat, even though many other thousands traverse to unknown lands. The seminar provided a more public forum to manifest, discuss, and critique the legitimacy of the phenomenon and certain human-oriented research methods, such as the experiential method, to study it.

CHOICE OF RESEARCH METHOD

The importance of the decision connecting the phenomenon to a research method cannot be overemphasized. Ideally, there is a fit between the nature of the phenomenon to be researched and the research method to be applied. The experiential method is intended for the study of the structure and content of human experience and, conversely, human experience is most directly and currently studied via methods developed specifically to study its structure and content. Either way one approaches the decision, the match must result in compatibility. That is, it must contribute to an internal consistency and coherence of the inquiry, most often termed *method validity*. Making the choice of method seems a bit like shooting an arrow to the bull's-eye of the target. It is a matter of accuracy. Does the method enable one to study accurately the phenomenon of interest? Without such accuracy, the findings dim in relevance and importance. Furthermore, under critical scrutiny in the research community, the value of the study usually fades with regard to its overall contribution to the study of the phenomenon.

But note that the researcher may competently execute a research method meeting specific evaluative criteria, such as credibility, reliability, validity, and still miss the mark, because the choice of research method is a somewhat tangential means to the nature of the phenomenon under study. In this case, had I chosen naturalistic observation in its most orthodox form for example, I would have had to make inferences about my participants chiefly from their overt actions at some distance without the benefit of conversing directly with them. Likely I would have had to make many inferences about their thoughts and feelings of being in a strange land that would make it more probable I could miss the mark to know in some depth the phenomenon as others experience it. In the case of the seminar, the findings come to me also indirectly by tapping self-reports of their experience of the phenomenon. Certainly it may be that constructing a methodology from complementary methods would have provided a more comprehensive picture of the phenomenon, and therefore I do not want to dismiss the potential value of naturalistic observation. Given the context and restraints that come with a research study, it is a matter of choosing the research method that will likely yield the richest and most accurate picture of the phenomenon. Again, it is aiming as best as one knows how to hit the bull's-eye of the target.

It must be clear that my inquiry was designed for studying the experiential method as part of the program for three groups taking the seminar, rather than an investigation recruiting persons to study the phenomenon. The challenge for me was to find a phenomenon that had a high potential to maximize the educational value of the seminar for the participants, while simultaneously being one manifest in the experience of the participants and appropriately studied via the experiential method.

To make the phenomenon–method connection, it is critical to stress in human inquiry that the bias tends to be first choose the phenomenon and second choose the research method best suited to study it. The phenomenon becomes the preoccupying concern initially, and secondarily, the researcher selects the research method (or methods) compatible with its study. But in practice, however, methodolatry seems epidemic in human inquiry. Although rarely discussed, the propensity for researchers trained in a particular form of doing research is to study every human phenomenon that interests them by means of their way of doing research.

Despite methodolatrous leanings, I think the play back and forth with possible connections is the more fruitful research strategy than either unidirectional bias. Better also it is, I believe, to allow oneself a course correction early during the process of inquiry, before a large expenditure of resources has occurred, rather than assume the decision of research method is a singular definitive act that, once decided, is a *fait accompli*. Although one may certainly benefit from hindsight, and foresight cannot be assured, a quick decision of method often is a prescription to suffer downstream from repeated unnecessary compromises, awkward rationalizations, and even a neurotic defensiveness about one's research, when it comes time to publish and discuss one's research with peers. Having suspected that a better choice was available, careful study of the choices and pilot research, more often than not, positions the researcher to avoid the ensuing predicament and embark on a sounder, more informative path of study.

Important to mention in passing is the preparatory study of likeness and variation among a number of methods that draw heavily from the phenomenology tradition. Particular attention should be given to compare and contrast the works of Giorgi (1985) and Moustakas (1994) with Barrell et al. (1990a). Barrell, Price, and associates make increasingly clear in their descriptions of the experiential method their interest in and debt to Husserlian phenomenology.

Had I been less interested in studying the experiential method and more serious about an in-depth study of the phenomenon, then auto/ biography (Denzin, 1989; Runyan, 1984), case study (Stake, 1995), ethnography (Fetterman, 1989; Miller, Hengst, and Wang, 2003), focus group research (Greenbaum, 1998), grounded theory (Strauss, 1987; Strauss and Corbin, 1990), hermeneutics (Kvale, 1996; Packer and Addison, 1989), heuristic research (Moustakas, 1990), narrative inquiry (Mishler, 1986; Rubin and Rubin, 1995), and phenomenology (Giorgi, 1985; Giorgi and Giorgi, 2003) represent a plentitude of alternative choices to the experiential method that might make an appropriate and productive connection to the phenomenon, because these forms of human inquiry make extensive use of first-person self-report to study as directly as possible the structure and content of human experience. Unfortunately, the literature of these research methods form research traditions that, until recently, infrequently intersected. Furthermore, the interests of researchers have yet to turn to more meta-analytical and cross-methodological-type syntheses of a specific phenomenon. But I expect comparative research will come. It represents a future focus for advancing human science research methodology, once a sufficiency of empirical studies occupies the subject matter domain of psychology and allied fields.

I suspect a less acceptable practice in coming years is to link the research question and phenomenon under study only to one's favored method. A critical review of method choices should be as important and beneficial as the critical review of research findings pertinent to the focus of inquiry. It is not only what we know already about a phenomenon that is essential to formulate inquiry and advance knowledge, but also what we know about the means used to know what we know that enables us to make sound choices of method and advance research methodology. If we are to improve our understanding of human experience, researchers can ill afford to limit themselves exclusively to one way of doing research.

METHOD

The form of the research method presented by Barrell, Medeiros, Barrell, and Price (1985) provided the means to obtain individual experiential reports of the target phenomenon. At first, I followed what I understood to be their version of the method to generate the data, but I soon found in my seminar that context innovations were required both to apply the method and to make it a training and learning experience for the participants. I have extended substantively their version of it and thereby discovered the value to the inquiry of the collective co-researcher/participant processing of the data generated. There are several steps or phases of the method. I describe them briefly in Procedures.

PARTICIPANTS

Promoted by brochure mailings and announcements in the journals and newsletters of professional associations and societies as the "Human Science Research International Summer Seminar," it attracted a variety of colleagues and their graduate students, mainly from several countries across the European and North American continents.

The number of participants ranged from 5 to 18 persons. The three groups chosen for this report on experiential method had a size of seven, seven, and ten.

The persons in the seminar served simultaneously as both the researchers and the participants. As seminar leader and facilitator, I became a member of all three groups, and I participated in each step of the data collection and processing just as the other members. Thus, the terms co-researcher and co-participant became interchangeable. Parenthetically, the sample sizes stated do not disclose the repeated participation of myself.

TRIGGER QUESTIONS

A trigger question is a prompt posed by the researcher to elicit a self-report from the participant. It is an initial direct question that sets into motion the self-reporting process of data collection. With the experiential method, trigger questions have been used to dialogue with solo participants as well as small groups of participants and/or researchers. I posed one trigger question that was supposed to elicit the phenomenon as directly as possible from a group of participants, asking the group to write down individually on a piece of paper an experience that came to mind in response to the question. Later in the procedure, they were to share their brief narrative reports and discuss them as a group.

In selecting the phenomenon "being a stranger in a foreign land," my presumption was that the participants were not citizens of the country in which the seminar occurred. However, it was not the case for three persons total in two of the participant groups. Consequently, I modified my original trigger question to make the task supposedly more meaningful for all participants. The decision to alter the trigger question had advantages and disadvantages to be discussed later in the chapter.

For group 1, the trigger question was: What is it like to be a stranger in a foreign country? This question was intended to commence the activity, and focus the group immediately and directly on the phenomenon under study.

For groups 2 and 3, the trigger question was: What is it like to experience the Morvan? I assumed this question tapped the phenomenon under study, but the question was clearly a more roundabout means of access to the phenomenon.

PROCEDURES

Each group completed specific steps to generate and process the data. I drew upon previous research, particularly Barrell et al. (1990b), to detail the earlier steps, but freely modified their procedures to innovate and study the method itself. Table 12-2 paraphrases the steps and instructions followed by the three groups. These steps also conveyed to the participants the nature of what is meant by disciplined inquiry (Collen, 1995a, b), for an acceptable human-oriented research method is expected to follow clear rules and procedures in its execution.

Groups 2 and 3 used a variation of the procedure followed by group 1. The essential difference was that groups 2 and 3 were asked to report current and immediate experiences (step 1), and each person wrote an individual synthesis (step 9). Group 1 completed all steps of the activity shown in Table 12-2, group 2 completed steps 1 through 9 and stopped in the middle of step 10, and group 3 completed steps 1 through 9. The idiosyncratic pace of each group in combination with the time allotted for the activity in the seminar program largely determined the extent of completion of the activity. The data of group 1 were collected and processed during the summer of 1991; that of groups 2 and 3, during the summer of 1992.

RESULTS

Each group had its own inquiry process and generated its own findings. True to the autonomous nature of the three groups, the findings were not pooled, but were presented separately. However, some comparisons were made across groups. The research issue concerning the common participant across groups, myself, is taken up later in the section entitled Replication.

Table 12-3 shows the number of experiential reports generated by each person. The experiential reports were subsequently aggregated, integrated, and expressed in terms of a descriptive paragraph that can be termed a *synthesis*.

The total number (T) of experiential reports provided each group with their pool of raw data to be processed. Although the grand total of 85 reports was obtained, the reports of each group formed a separate pool that was processed by each group respectively. Table 12-3 shows T was markedly greater in the first group compared with the second group, despite the equal sample size. However, the number of reports generated per participant was similar in the second and third groups compared with the

TABLE 12-2   Steps and Instructions of Experiential Method Followed by the Three Groups

---

Group 1

1. Present the trigger question. Notice an immediate experience or bring to mind a past one in response to the question.

2. Write down, using first-person present tense, on one piece of paper one experience that answers the trigger question. Describe it as directly as possible. Avoid interpretive, poetic, and historical accounts of the experience.

3. Write down a second experience in response to the question on a second piece of paper following the same instruction. Continue with repetitions of step 2 until a number of these experiential reports are completed. When the group ceases to write further, proceed to the next step.

4. Present verbally and post one experiential report to the group in turn. Continue around the group as many cycles as necessary until all experiential reports are publicly recorded before the group.

5. Study the reports. On a separate piece of paper, write down words and phrases that convey what the reports have in common. When the group ceases to write further, proceed to the next step.

6. Have each person share what is written regarding their words and phrases, and then have the group examine and discuss each experiential report to abstract it. The group task of abstracting is to state a word, a few words, a phrase, or a few phrases intended to capture and represent the content and meaning of the report.

7. As a group, examine the pool of reports as a whole. Discuss the areas in common among the experiential reports. What reports appear to share common meaning in response to the question? What reports appear to share a similar aspect of the experience? Which reports appear to belong together?

8. As a group, aggregate the experiential reports and generate labels for each aggregate.

9. As a group, integrate the aggregates into one paragraph of text, a group description, that represents the pool of experiential reports and their abstracts.

Groups 2 and 3

1. Present the trigger question. Notice an immediate experience or bring to mind a past one in response to the question.

2–8. Same as group 1.

9. Write one paragraph of text that represents the pool of experiential reports and their abstracts.

10. Share the paragraph of text with the group. Post the paragraphs before the group.

11. Discuss the paragraphs and write as a group one paragraph that represents the individual paragraphs, the pool of experiential reports, and their abstracts.

---

first group. Clearly, in quantitative terms, group 1 was more productive in generating their pool of raw data than groups 2 and 3. However, it is important to remember that group 1 received the more direct trigger question to the phenomenon, and groups 2 and 3 received the same (although less direct) prompt to elicit the phenomenon. Furthermore, the instructions

TABLE 12-3   Number of Experiential Reports from Each Participant and Their Distribution among the Three Groups

Group	n	Frequency of Reports	T
1	7	4, 5, 6, 7, 8, 9, 10	49
2	7	1, 2, 2, 3, 3, 3, 4	18
3	10	1, 1, 1, 2, 2, 2, 2, 2, 2, 3	18
Total	24		85

and data processing were biased to yield more reports in group 1, thereby rendering these differences artificial; that is, I think the sizes of the report pools were more illustrative of variations in procedure than a finding linked to the phenomenon studied.

The main results of the data generating and processing of experiential reports are shown in Tables 12-4 through 12-9. The tables convey the number of aggregations created by each group, the results of abstracting their reports, the labels each group chose to represent their aggregations, and the number and content of experiential reports contributing to each aggregation. The raw data are provided in a separate table for each group. When used, abstracting was an intermediate step before aggregation. The groups were not forced to sort each report into only one cluster of reports, and consequently some experiential reports appeared in more than one aggregation.

GROUP 1

The results of group 1 are presented in Table 12-4. Abstracting was not used in this case. The group proceeded directly from their experiential reports to aggregation. There were six aggregations of the experience of "being a stranger in a foreign land." The aggregations are presented in rank order from the one with the greatest number of reports sorted together to the one with the fewest reports, as indicated after each label in Table 12-4. The most prevalent aspect of the experience was labeled "Disconnectedness." The next most common aspect involved various kinds of "Perceptions" of the experience. The third component of the experience centered on "Difficulties with Functioning." The fourth, fifth, and six aspects focused on "Excitement," "Connectedness," and "Threat–Anxiety," respectively. These labels for the aggregations came from group discussion and consensus.

GROUP 2

The results of group 2 are presented in Tables 12-5 and 12-6. There were 18 experiential reports. Reviewing the reports yielded the distinct impression

TABLE 12-4 Experiential Reports, Aggregations, and Their Labels from Group 1, in Response to the Question: What Is It Like to Be a Stranger in a Foreign Land?

I. DISCONNECTEDNESS (n = 16)

1-one of the stones at Stone Henge (England)

1-a Coca Cola in Moscow

1-an Idaho spud being fried at McDonalds' in Munich

1-singing mimi in Russian

1-being Ozawa interpreting Mahler

1-a California white fly being in a red ginger flower in Honolulu

1-being the fingers of a pickpocket

1-a BMW in Los Angeles or an MG in Druisburg

1-being a cowboy in Newark

1-being a behaviorist at Saybrook

1,2-people react to you in different ways (welcome, anger, other)

1-I feel distant and apart from natives because I don't speak the language

1-I do not feel connected because I cannot communicate thoughts and needs

1-less links/connections with life than ordinary life

1-being in a movie in real life than seeing it on the screen

II. DIFFICULTY WITH FUNCTIONING (n = 10)

1,2-people react to you in different ways (welcome, anger, other)

2,6-I assume things won't work as well as at home

2-I do not understand what people say

2-I can't express wishes/thoughts in words

2-I don't know how things function, how to get things (e.g., toilet paper)

2-your own things don't function (e.g., appliance cord)

2,6-to look for equilibrium

1,2-disconnected from adult self, more child-like

2-looking for clues of what to do, because I cannot understand signs

2-flooded with unfamiliar sounds, conversation that's overwhelming

III. EXCITEMENT (n = 9)

3-being a child again, everything is novel

3-live and see different places and situations

3-forget ordinary problems and try to enjoy as much as possible

3-lots of stimuli because find different organizations of life

3-excitement at experiencing something new

3-excitement in prospect of learning about the place

3-to start again

(continues)

TABLE 12-4 (*continued*)

3-excited I'm not just at home

3-energetically depleted from so much social interaction

IV. CONNECTEDNESS (n = 6)

4-I feel lots of connections with fellow man

4-looks like universal connection (i.e., human communication/interactions as home)

4-being between old conceptions and new ones

4-problems in communication with people (written and spoken)

4-feeling completely at home until seeing written language

V. PERCEPTION (n = 12)

5-people think in a different way

5-people and surroundings look different

5-people value you in another way than home

5-hypervision (encompass as much of surroundings as possible)

5-being clumsy and awkward in my movements

5-gratitude for the adventure

5-at the beginning seems to be different, more than it really is

5-different habits of people around that agree/disagree with your behavior

5-being surrounded by a bubble everyone can see but me

5-feeling a different size (larger) than those around me

5-pink rose in a garden of red roses

5-everyone knows something that they are not telling me

VI. THREAT–ANXIETY (n = 5)

2,6-I assume things won't work well as at home

6-I feel more secure, I seek out familiar symbols of civilization

6-scary (to work everything out by myself)

2,6-to look for equilibrium

6-obviously different in feeling exposed when people stare

---

they were less cryptic and more first-hand, present-tense narratives than those produced by group 1. The reports of group 2 were also markedly more mundane and anchored to current situations and circumstances.

The experiential reports (Table 12-5) were examined and discussed as a group to complete the next steps of data processing: (1) abstract the reports, (2) aggregate the reports and abstracts, and (3) to label each aggregation. The results of these three steps are shown in Table 12-6. The aggregations are presented in rank order, similar to Table 12-4 for group 1.

Group 2 clustered their data into seven aggregations: "People, comraderie, group, being together," "Nature, natural landscape," "Person,

TABLE 12-5   Experiential Reports from Group 2 in Response to the Question: What Is It Like to Experience the Morvan?

1. We drove through the countryside and all around are white cows. *Lots* of cows and all white. Very unusual to me. I am fascinated by cows lazily sitting or grazing. So opposite the city.

2. Very clearly I can hear the mooing of cows. Loud, undiluted mooings. To hear such a constant sound is to be stripped of a lot of unnecessary stimulation that fills up my senses.

3. When we were returning from dinner, we saw fireflies. I had always read about fireflies but had never seen one. It was to realize something that had always been in the wings, ready to come on stage and be recognized. Finally I have seen a firefly.

4. Time spent in the morning is a holistic experience that includes nature, comraderie, conversation, and good Burgundy wine in the matrix of scholarly pursuit—an optimum adventure in life.

5. Looking out the farmhouse window at the green mostly highlands of the Morvan, I experience a communion with nature and the peace, contentment, and tranquility reminiscent of past journeys into the countryside.

6. The Morvan beckons to exploration of the area and one's place in the world more deeply. The setting is rural and peaceful in the best sense of the words, excellent for reading and introspection.

7. Yesterday afternoon, I took a walk by myself with my camera. I walked slowly so that I could observe the houses (and hopefully talk with people), the different kinds of trees and flowers. I saw many cows, modern houses, and I was surprised to realize that barns were not barns but also houses, because I saw and heard people in there. And I finally walked in the cemetery. Everywhere it was calm.

8. I observed a cow stopping near the house, a green little two-horse power car. I saw a blond girl with boots walking in the field with her big German shepherd. She was looking to see if everything was OK.

9. I was driving to my son and back through hilly roads in rain, storm, and sunshine, being in the hotel, helping my son to get settled in camping. He forgot his passport, so it meant waiting for the postman and experiencing the adequacy of postal service here. It meant to experience the loneliness of my son and the ways he can be cheered up. He learned to like to eat in restaurants, every time a new restaurant in France. He knows to be with people together in one campsite. Because he is an only child, he knows how to make contacts.

10. The Morvan and to experience it right now is an experience with maps and distances between names and places, and some, to write information. And more close, it is a somewhat hidden, lost village without much life of which I question if I could/would live here. An ongoing question: Do I like to love a house in France? And furthermore, where do I want to live in the coming years?

11. The Morvan means being together with a group of new people working on a subject that is of great interest to me.

12. I took a walk and I saw strange animals. I stopped and, as I thought they were donkeys, I made some hee-haw sound. They looked at me and I was confirmed that they were donkeys. I then made another hee-haw sound. The biggest one walked toward me and the other two followed him. I was surprised and afraid because it was my first experience with donkeys. I didn't know if it could be dangerous. So I kept on my way.

13. Walking around Chateau Chinon, listening to spoken French, wandering in and out of shops, down side streets, looking down at a valley, round a narrow alleyway

(continues)

TABLE 12-5 (*continued*)

14. Pulling into the train station at Autun and drinking beer across the street waiting for a ride to our house

15. Sitting, eating, drinking around a communal table, discussing psychology and life experiences

16. Viewing the graveyard from the vantage point of the fence

17. I walked up the street from the house beyond the graveyard and looked across the valley toward the village. It was peaceful, green, and permanent. It conveyed a sense of long history, as if it was always here before I was born and like this long after I live.

18. I was sitting on the road when a girl about 25 years old came by me on a bicycle. She was riding side saddle and wearing a country, cotton, picnic dress like I've seen in the U.S. American movie *Oklahoma*. She smiled and I did too. She coasted down the hill and no word was exchanged between us. I felt her civil friendliness, as I imagined she felt from me. She disappeared around the corner toward the village.

TABLE 12-6   Abstracts of the Experiential Reports, Aggregations, and Their Labels from Group 2

I. PEOPLE, CAMARADERIE, GROUP, BEING TOGETHER (n = 9)

4-camaraderie, nature, good wine, conversation, scholarly pursuit equals adventure

8-girl with dog walking in field inspecting everything to see all is in order; little two-horse power car

9-hilly roads, rainstorms, sunshine, riding back and forth, hotel, camping, forgot passport, mail service; loneliness; ways to enjoy here

11-being together with group; working subject, great common interest

12-strange animals, beckon them—hee-haw sounds, donkeys follow, surprise and fear, new experience

13-listening, spoken French, wandering, observing, in/out shops and sidestreets

14-into train station, drinking beer, waiting

15-sitting, eating, drinking, communal table discussion life experience

18-local girl, country dress, side saddle, bicycle coasting downhill on country road; no words but smiles exchanged, civil friendliness.

II. NATURE, NATURAL LANDSCAPE (n = 7)

4-camaraderie, nature, good wine, conversation, scholarly pursuit equals adventure

5-communion with nature, peace, content, tranquility; reminiscent of past experiences

6-rural, peaceful, opportunity reading and introspection

9-hilly roads, rainstorms, sunshine, riding back and forth, hotel, camping, forgot passport, mail service; loneliness; ways to enjoy here

(*continues*)

TABLE 12-6 *(continued)*

10-maps and distances between places with some tourist information; hidden, lost village without much life here; where to live?

17-across the valley, green, permanent long history, always there

18-local girl, country dress, side saddle, bicycle coasting downhill on country road; no words but smiles exchanged, civil friendliness

III. PERSON, HUMAN-MADE STRUCTURES (n = 7)

7-walking, surprises, barns were houses, modern houses, calmness

8-girl with dog walking in field inspecting everything to see all is in order; little two-horse power car

9-hilly roads, rainstorms, sunshine, riding back and forth, hotel, camping, forgot passport, mail service; ways to enjoy here

10-maps and distances between places with some tourist information; hidden, lost village without much life here; where to live?

13-listening, spoken French, wandering, observing, in/out shops and sidestreets

14-into train station, drinking beer, waiting

16-viewing graveyard from fence

IV. DIFFERENCES, NONFAMILIAR (n = 7)

1-white cow, sitting, grazing

7-walking, surprises, barns were houses, modern houses, calmness

8-girl with dog walking in field inspecting everything to see all is in order; little two-horse power car

9-hilly roads, rainstorms, sunshine, riding back and forth, hotel, camping, forgot passport, mail service; ways to enjoy here

10-maps and distances between places with some tourist information; hidden, lost village without much life here; where to live?

13-listening, spoken French, wandering, observing, in/out shops and sidestreets

18-local girl, country dress, side saddle, bicycle coasting downhill on country road; no words but smiles exchanged, civil friendliness

V. MOVEMENT (n = 6)

7-walking, surprises, barns were houses, modern houses, calmness

8-girl with dog walking in field inspecting everything to see all is in order; little two-horse power car

9-hilly roads, rainstorms, sunshine, riding back and forth, hotel, camping, forgot passport, mail service; ways to enjoy here

12-strange animals, beckon them—hee-haw sounds, donkeys follow, surprise and fear, new experience

13-listening, spoken French, wandering, observing, in/out shops and sidestreets

18-local girl, country dress, side saddle, bicycle coasting downhill on country road; no words but smiles exchanged, civil friendliness

(continues)

TABLE 12-6 (*continued*)

VI. ANIMALS (n = 5)

1-white cow, sitting, grazing

2-mooing of cows; nature sounds

3-seeing something in my imagination and realizing it with my senses (fireflies)

8-girl with dog walking in field inspecting everything to see all is in order; little two-horse power car

12-strange animals, beckon them—hee-haw sounds, donkeys follow, surprise and fear, new experience

VII. INTROSPECTION (n = 5)

3-seeing something in my imagination and realizing it with my senses (fireflies)

6-rural, peaceful, opportunity reading and introspection

10-maps and distances between places with some tourist information; hidden, lost village without much life here; where to live?

15-sitting, eating, drinking, communal table discussion life experience

17-across the valley, green, permanent long history, always there

human-made structures," "Differences, nonfamiliar," "Movement," "Animals," and "Introspection." The rank order of the aggregations showed a more rectangular distribution, not as marked in descent as those of group 1. Also, compared with group 1, there were many more instances of the same experiential report contributing to more than one aggregate, and finding a clear label to represent each aggregation was more ambiguous and difficult.

GROUP 3

The experiential reports of group 3 are presented in Table 12-7. Group 3 wrote the same number of reports as group 2. Their immediacy was more salient than group 2, and dramatically more so compared with group 1. However, the brevity of reporting fell between those of groups 1 and 2.

As with group 2, group 3 proceeded to abstract and subsequently cluster their reports. The results are shown in Table 12-8. Group 3 clustered their reports as follows: "Personal reflections and feelings," "Weather," "Village life," and "Roads." Although group 3 organized their reports into four aggregations rather than seven (group 2), examination of the content of both groups showed substantial overlap, such as shared references to weather, driving, animal life, landscape, human habitation, and their seminar group. And both groups, to a similar extent, applied their reports to more than one aggregation.

TABLE 12-7   Experiential Reports from Group 3 in Response to the Question: What Is It Like to experience the Morvan?

1. Driving through the Morvan we traveled on brick-colored, one-lane roads that twisted through the trees. We drove as fast as we could and prayed for no oncoming cars.

2. My experience of the Morvan is driving on curvy roads, uncertain of dangers and destination, and experiencing the differences of vegetation and landscape.

3. The wind blows in the afternoon.

4. My first experience of the Morvan was driving through village after village. I found it enchanting and delightful.

5. I walk more briskly in the mornings and my sense of sight and smell is activated by the wet grass and white cows. I am ravenous at meals and sleep deeply.

6. The wind is softly blowing as I sit here on my hard chair in class in the old rehabilitated farmhouse on the hill. I hear the trees shift as the breeze gains force. Now I would like to go lay in the damp grass in the backyard in this Morvan region of France.

7. At eight o'clock in the morning I looked out my window to see a man in T-shirt and shorts and sandals walking out of the bakery with a basket filled with three long loaves of French bread.

8. There is a sense of being at home while not at home. Comfortable, nonthreatening, outdoorsy feeling.

9. The Morvan has been an experience of nature and people living in harmony.

10. It is very green and warm. There is a large, clear lake and sailboats and people and cool water.

11. The snails are large orange slugs without protection and are easily squashed by tires as they cross the road.

12. I hear the rumbling of a small plane overhead. People are shifting in their chairs as they write. I feel content as I notice the simplicity of our task.

13. We slowed down on the narrow one-lane road and drove slowly, half on the grass, so that a man driving a tractor-trailer rig could pass.

14. Stars show in the sky at night.

15. Relaxing in an open unfamiliar natural area, feeling the warmth of the sun and thinking of nothing

16. My experience of walking in the early morning in the Morvan was very enjoyable. I visually experienced the beauty of the surrounding valley, beginning with the village that lay below and the pastures beyond. The sky was clear and the flowers and foliage were beautiful.

17. The midday sun is warm and the breezes cooler, as we struggle to stay awake after meals.

18. I very much enjoyed the ambiance and digestion of the wonderful evening meal. Sampling French and German cuisine while conversing with new people from Saybrook also added to the pleasure of the meal.

GROUP SYNTHESIS

Taking the process of aggregating and labeling one step further, each group attempted to integrate their work. Group 1 did this collectively to produce a one-paragraph description that represented the epitome of

TABLE 12-8   Abstracts of the Experiential Reports, Aggregations, and Their Labels from Group 3

I. PERSONAL REFLECTIONS AND FEELINGS (n = 10)

1-brick colored, one lane, windy roads, going fast, worried about oncoming cars

2-curvy roads, uncertain dangers and destination, differences in vegetation and landscape

4-driving village after village, enchanting, delightful

5-walk briskly mornings, senses activated, white cows, wet grass, ravenous at meals, sleep deeply

6-wind softly blowing, sit hard chair, old rehabilitated farmhouses on hill, trees shift as breeze gains force

8-being at home while not at home

9-nature and people living in harmony

12-(not received—missing data)

15-relaxing, open unfamiliar natural area, feeling warmth of sun, thinking of nothing

18-ambience, digestion of wonderful evening meal

II. WEATHER (n = 8)

3-wind blows afternoon

5-walk briskly mornings, senses activated, white cows, wet grass, ravenous at meals, sleep deeply

6-wind softly blowing, sit hard chair, old rehabilitated farmhouses on hill, trees shift as breeze gains force

10-green and warm, large clear lake, sailboats, people, cool water

14-stars shine sky at night

15-relaxing, open unfamiliar natural area, feeling warmth of sun, thinking of nothing

16-beauty of surrounding valley, village below, pastures beyond, sky clear, flowers and foliage beautiful

17-midday sun warm, breeze cooler, struggle to stay awake

III. VILLAGE LIFE (n = 7)

1-brick colored, one lane, windy roads, going fast, worried about oncoming cars

4-driving village after village, enchanting, delightful

5-walk briskly mornings, senses activated, white cows, wet grass, ravenous at meals, sleep deeply

6-wind softly blowing, sit hard chair, old rehabilitated farmhouses on hill, trees shift as breeze gains force

7-look out window; T-shirt, shorts, sandals, man leaving bakery with basket and three loaves French bread

13-slow down on one-lane road, drive on grass slowly, man in tractor-trailer rig could pass

16-beauty of surrounding valley, village below, pastures beyond, sky clear, flowers and foliage beautiful

---

(continues)

TABLE 12-8 (*continued*)

IV. ROADS (n = 5)

1-brick colored, one lane, windy roads, going fast, worried about oncoming cars

2-curvy roads, uncertain dangers and destination, differences in vegetation and landscape

4-driving village after village, enchanting, delightful

11-large orange snails squashed as cross road

13-slow down on one-lane road, drive on grass slowly, man in tractor-trailer rig could pass

TABLE 12-9   Synthesis and Summaries

Synthesis from Group 1

There are altered perceptions, difficulties with functioning, a sense of disconnectedness, and feelings of anxiety, accompanied by and leading to excitement and feelings of more universal connectedness. This is what it is like to be a stranger in a foreign country.

Summaries from Group 2

1. The unfamiliar contrasts with common experience to create an experience that is descriptive of the Morvan. White cows, barns that are not barns, nice landscape, foreign language, dress and customs *surround* the familiar objects of animals, people, interactions, structures, self-reflection, and the movement within the setting.

2. The Morvan is experienced through observations of animals, persons, human-made structures, and landscapes through movements conducive to contact with nature, people, and nonfamiliar things that bring some introspection. At the same time, the Morvan is also experienced through the togetherness in a group.

3. The provincial French countryside evaded meaningful introspection when I saw the unique and ancient buildings, a landscape like a patchwork quilt, farm animals, and local people who seem to move in slow motion. The camaraderie of the group left an indelible imprint on our souls.

4. The Morvan with its special landscape, animals, buildings, roads, and nonfamiliar features brings me to a deep introspection of how people here live their lives and, even further, of how I can think about my own life and future.

5. The Morvan elicits both personal introspection and group camaraderie. This happens as we move through the areas noticing the nature, animals, structures that are often different from what we either know or expect.

6. To experience the Morvan is to move about human-made structures and interact with unfamiliar people and animals in nature, which provokes introspective thoughts about them and their differences.

7. (Not received—missing data)

their experience of the phenomenon. This synthesis is presented in Table 12-9. Group 2 was asked to write a one- to three-sentence summary to be presented and discussed by the group. These summaries are presented also in Table 12-9. Other events in the seminar precluded group 3 from continuing to process their data beyond their results shown in Table 12-8.

Regarding group 1, the integrations of experiential reports shown in Table 12-9 are not intended to convey every detail of the phenomenon described earlier, because each report often has idiosyncratic features. Rather, the descriptive paragraph represented a meaningful synthesis for group 1—that is, their collective expression of the phenomenon.

In group 2, the paragraphs retained some individualistic views, although a commonness was emerging in the participants' use of the same terminology taken from their abstracts shared earlier. After posting their paragraphs, a group discussion ensued, during which they attempted to integrate their summaries into one group synthesis. They did not accomplish this task in the time allotted within the seminar schedule, but there was general agreement on the terminology used throughout the summaries (Table 12-9). Furthermore, there was the general introspective point of view the experience of the Morvan dramatized: One is a member of a group that is separate from but at the same time within the country setting. The tension and dynamics of this belonging within a social group (seminar), while simultaneously being within and different from the surroundings (Morvan), dominated the discussion. It was this highlight that best represented the epitome of the experience for group 2.

DISCUSSION

In this section I discuss the results of the data-processing experiences of the three groups, the decisions made by the researcher, and select methodological issues with regard to the experiential method. Again, the primary emphasis of this discussion is the learning about the skill building pertinent to the method, rather than the description, explanation, and understanding of the phenomenon, albeit the former is undoubtedly interrelated to the latter. The choice and sequencing of foci that comprise this section of the chapter reflect my personal interest in the method, not any prescriptive approach to research reporting. Furthermore, in the spirit of the method as executed in the seminar, this discussion certainly could have been enhanced by continued collaboration with the seminar participants.

VARIATIONS IN PROCEDURE TO COLLECT AND PROCESS DATA

Given the nature of this book, I thought it *apropos* to begin the discussion with variations in procedure. Does one collect one experiential report from each participant or as many reports as possible from one participant? This choice, or some combination of the two, is a key research design decision with important implications for data processing, because one choice will lead to findings based on (inter-) individual differences, and the other on intraindividual differences. Furthermore, in mixing the two alternatives, it is unlikely one will know the extent to which one or more persons influenced the outcome. To look for commonness among experiential reports either across several participants or within one participant is a choice point in the execution of this method, just as it is for other research methods for human inquiry, whether one labels the method or the design quantitative or qualitative. This basic decision illustrates nicely the ease with which one can generate variations of the method to study human experience. It also shows a pervasive design decision in the collection and processing of data that is typical in psychology research. This decision impacts the manner in which the researcher executes data collecting and processing.

Table 12-10 summarizes five fundamental means for the execution of the experiential method, although this scheme is basic to most research traditions for human inquiry (Collen, 1995a). The personal, or within-type, design features dependence on variability (diversity) within the solo participant who provides all the data—in other words, repeated self-reports. It is also referred to as an ipsative or ideographic-type design. The simple group or between-type design in its most basic form is, also known as a nomothetic-type design. It features dependence on variability (diversity) among a group of persons, each one of which provides one self-report. Mixing these two pure and simple designs involves multiple reports from each member of a group to maximize the efficacy of data collecting and

TABLE 12-10   Five Research Designs for Data Collecting and Processing in Experiential Method

1. *Personal or within*—Synthesize the self-generated experiential reports of a participant to attain the personal synthesis.

2. *Simple group or between*—Synthesize the individually generated experiential report of all participants, without regard to any particular participant's report, to attain the group synthesis.

3. *Complex pooling or mixed type I*—Synthesize the individually generated experiential reports of all participants, without regard to any particular participant's report or reports, to attain the group synthesis.

4. *Parallel pooling or mixed type II*—Synthesize the experiential reports of each participant separately to obtain a personal synthesis for each participant, then meta-synthesize personal syntheses to attain the group synthesis.

5. *Serial pooling or mixed type III*—Synthesize the experiential reports of one participant, then integrate the reports of the next participant into the initial synthesis, embellishing it to arrive at a synthesis of the pair. Following the same process for a third participant, arrive at a synthesis of the triad. Continue in this serial fashion until all participants have been included, thereby attaining the group synthesis.

processing that will enable the researcher to produce an accurate and precise description of the phenomenon.

In the case of my seminar participants, the three groups appeared not to follow the same procedure, even though all routes were aimed to attain a group synthesis. Group 1 appeared to process closest to the pooling procedure, in which the seven participants clustered their experiential reports directly into six aggregations (Table 12-4). The process for groups 2 and 3 was unlike group 1, in that these groups abstracted (summarized) their reports before sorting them into aggregations (Tables 12-6 and 12-8). And, unlike group 1 (Table 12-9), they did not have enough time to attain the group synthesis. However, abstracting (summarizing) may be viewed as one explicit step for groups 2 and 3 that was done implicitly by group 1 in their process of moving from experiential reports to the group synthesis. It would be one area for further inquiry into understanding the method and its versatility to articulate, through group work, various ways in an explicit fashion that groups can derive a group synthesis.

From the findings presented in the tables for the three groups, it has become clear that generating and processing the data consists of at least three levels of abstraction (Table 12-11). The level closest to the personal experience engages the participant to produce his/her own instances of the phenomenon from experience, after which the group process largely dominates. The second level of abstraction unites the group in discussion aimed to abstract, aggregate, and label clusters of reports. The third and most abstract level results in the group synthesis. It becomes somewhat obvious that the less abstract level precedes and greatly determines the content of the more abstract level. All movement toward a more abstract level takes the researcher farther away from the experience itself. In fact, one might claim the very act of experiential reporting produces a text that

TABLE 12-11   Levels of Abstraction in Data Processing Experiential Reports

---

Group 1

  1. Raw data

  2. Abstracts, aggregations, and category labels

  3. Group synthesis

Group 2

  1. Raw data

  2. Abstracts, aggregations, and category labels

  3. Individual summaries

Group 3

  1. Raw data

---

must not be mistaken for the experience itself, but represents the participant's imperfect attempt to communicate the experience. The data processing becomes more theoretical and less empirical as a result. In sum, the process is entirely conceptual, for although the initial instruction may conjure sights, smells, sounds, and other sensorial elements, the participant must be able to find concise wording to articulate them as part of the experiential report. As seen in the raw data (Tables 12-7 and 12-8), it is not necessarily an easy task, and despite instructions to the contrary, the participants freely include associations and metaphors in attempts to capture what presumably linguistic incapability and a limited vocabulary cannot communicate.

Parenthetically, it should be noted that one could ask the participants to abstract their own reports, followed by group work to aggregate and label them. This procedure would be expected in solo processing, and therefore lead to a four-level scheme rather than three levels of abstraction, but it was not done in any variations of the method reported and discussed here. The groups were instructed to abstract, aggregate, and label as a collective activity in one step of the data processing.

The content analysis and synthesis of the qualitative data generated in the forms termed experiential reports may be compared with some procedures for processing quantitative data, such as cluster analysis. There are many conceptual parallelisms between procedures of working with qualitative and quantitative data that polemists of each persuasion conveniently leave out of their presentations. In the case of the experiential method, the divergent process of generating the data is followed by the convergent process of organizing data for subsequent synthesis. To converge, the participants must play with properties and dimensions that join as well as distinguish the experiential reports until each report has been located with those others that form its grouping. Note that in this section I use interchangeably the terms *aggregation*, *cluster*, and *grouping*. Communality is then considered for each aggregation in turn to generate a name label that can meaningfully represent the elements of the grouping. Like a facet of a jewel, each name label is to convey one side that is distinguishable from the other sides, yet all the while be a reflection of the phenomenon.

A parallel procedure is followed with quantitative data processing, particularly cluster analysis and factor analysis. Numerical designations are given to relevant features of the entities to be correlated and aggregated. The features can be weighted in order to sort each entity into one cluster or on each factor, and after numerous iterations to present a scheme of clusters and factors respectively (Grimm and Yarnold, 1995). Like an experiential report, each entity becomes part of one grouping, ideally distinguishable from the others. However, just as the researcher may find a variation in the data processing of the experiential reports—whether to impose the rule that each report may contribute to only one aggregation or each report may contribute to more than one aggregation—in like fashion, the researcher may find it more appropriate to locate each entity in one group (cluster analysis) or allow each to contribute to (load on) each group (factor analysis).

The purpose of comparing and contrasting qualitative data processing in the experiential method with other methods, such as quantitative, is to understand more clearly the basic cognitive processes the human inquirer may utilize to make the data collected interpretable and meaningful. Both qualitative and quantitative data-processing platforms require the researcher to find a name label for communicating each aggregation. In the qualitative case, there is the search for common meaning among the words in the given text of the experiential reports comprising the grouping. In the quantitative case, there is the same search for a name label, but from the weighted loadings that resulted in placement of the entities together. The two means may be viewed as analogous, complementary, and multivariate. They may make use of similar cognitive research skills of data processing.

EXPERIENTIAL REPORTING

One of the most critical requirements for the success of the method is adequate experiential reporting—that is, reports that lend themselves to data processing. The reports must contain the essential aspects of the experience. To promote experiential reporting, Barrell, Price, and associates emphasize the first-person, present-tense writing format when recounting a recent or immediate experience. They also distinguish four kinds of reporting (Price and Barrell, 1980). In contrast to the "in the experience"-type narrative is the interpretive, poetic, and historical types. These latter three forms are to be discouraged in experiential reporting, because they occupy the narrator in levels of thinking and reflection upon the experience, over, outside, and above being with and in the experience itself. It is the purpose of experiential reporting to engage as much as possible in pure description of the experience while one dwells within the reliving of the experience.

Interpretive reporting involves statements on what one thinks about the experience, or what is the meaning of the experience. Poetical (literary) reporting tends to interject statements of simile, metaphor, and free association catalyzed by the experience. Historical reporting tends to mix statements of events leading up to the experience with the event we refer to as the experience. Any exaggerated propensity of the reporter to engage in any one or more of these styles tends to detract from the succinct and direct reporting of the experience. We may think of the three types to be bracketed as most hermeneutic, and the type of interest here, closest to the original and lived experience to comprise the report, as the most phenomenological.

The experiential reports of being a stranger in a foreign country tended to follow the recommended format and style; however, generally, they suffered from another problem—that of brevity. Compression was evident between the attempt to describe the experience and locate its essential aspects. I believe the conflicting tendencies between two research skills—that of generating the report and that of reducing the data—worked against the production of full accounts expected in this application (experiential method), affiliated with the family of self-reporting methods of human inquiry noted earlier in the chapter. I interpret this tendency in experiential reporting to be largely accountable by the seminar activity and, perhaps to some degree, to the inexperience of participants in writing experiential reports. Somewhat cognizant of other materials and methods, such as phenomenology and content analysis, the participants engaged in a didactic and pedagogically oriented exercise to learn about the experiential method. As stated previously, the focus on the phenomenon was the secondary aim of this activity. As instructive as it was for the participants, it yielded truncated reports of lesser value for learning about the method and articulating the phenomenon.

However, engaging those in the data processing who generated the data afforded the advantage of minimizing the distancing commonly evident in research once the data are collected. Typically, data processing is executed by researchers, who are not the participants, and thereby this activity necessitates greater inference than if those closest to and generating the raw data are also those processing it. In the former situation, the researcher is removed from the reality of the phenomenon not only gathering the experience of others, but also working with this material in abstract ways, often far removed from the primary experience itself. When researcher and participant are one and the same person, presumably the researcher is closer to the reality of the phenomenon, because it is his/her experience that is being gathered, abstracted, and synthesized. In this case, the direct experience of the researcher and participants may come into play at any step of data processing to provide an inferential check and guide to the process of reaching the aim of the inquiry. Also, the researcher as participant is the dynamically active consciousness, who lived the experience being processed. In contrast, the researcher who processes only the experience of others is, by the very nature of the activity, removed from the reality of the experience of those others, and thereby the researcher must infer at any point in the process whether the step and aspect of the experience are relevant to the phenomenon generally and his/her own experience specifically. Such checks and guidance are usually more remote when the data of the participant are not that of the researcher. Experiential method exercised, reported, and discussed in this chapter presumes and takes advantage of the common identity of research and participant. Of course, this feature is both a blessing and a curse and is discussed in Researcher Bias.

Finally, it would have been better to engage in experiential reporting early during the seminar, rather than at the start of the learning module studying the method, to allow more time for all three participant groups to process the data to completion. As shown in the tables, only one of three groups reached a group synthesis. I believe this study of the phenomenon would have been of greater value to have three syntheses, instead of one synthesis only, to know more fully the phenomenon as all groups experienced it, and to critique more informatively the final result this method generates. Such cross-group comparisons and discussions would lead to efforts at qualitatively oriented cross-case analysis (Miles and Huberman, 1994), and eventually qualitatively oriented meta-analysis that discerns the common base and diversity within a body of research studies by many investigators studying the same phenomenon (Collen, 1995a).

ASSUMPTIONS ABOUT THE METHOD AND THE PARTICIPANTS

The experiential reports generated by the group served as the raw data processed to describe the phenomenon "being a stranger in a foreign land." Even though more than one report was generated by all but four of the participants, it was assumed that each report could stand on its own, so to speak, as a separate and distinct presentation of an experience of the phenomenon. This assumption is known conventionally as the *independence of observations* in reference to quantitative data-processing procedures, but also may apply equally well to qualitative data processing. In short, for each group of participants, each report constituted a qualitative datum and recognizable contribution to the pool of experiential reports.

The idea of independence of observations may be questioned of course. The fact that each person wrote multiple reports subjects the research to the possible criticism that the act of writing one report determined in some way the writing of subsequent reports. As stated earlier, the participants were not experienced experiential reporters and the brevity of the descriptions, most notably in group 1, stood out. But if the participants followed instructions, such independence may be justified, because the disciplined human participant can effectively "start over" with each writing and hold in abeyance (bracket) what has been stated in previous reports. Be this as it may, exercising such skills is more safely assumed with training and practice than naive presumption. To the positive, practice writing experiential reports may favor their usability in research. Similar arguments in favor of research training may be advanced regarding other research skills required for data collection and processing. Given their interest in joining a seminar focused on research methods, it was further assumed that the participants possessed the capacity to abstract and aggregate data, generate name labels, and synthesize reports.

The research skill levels of both researcher and participants should not be confused with the manifestations of the phenomenon to be reported, because they involve a somewhat different set of assumptions. In common with other research methods that rely on self-reporting, it was assumed that the participants had experienced the phenomenon, understood the instruction to conjure appropriate instances to write, wrote instances of the phenomenon (rather than another phenomenon), and had the linguistic facility to write informative descriptions that could be data processed.

To the extent the assumptions stated are not met in this inquiry, and any other inquiry of this kind, certainly calls into question the validity of the research, as well the credibility and confidence one might have in receiving a research report claiming to describe and account for the phenomenon.

An examination of the experiential reports, shown in Tables 12-4, 12-5, and 12-7, revealed limited success in upholding these assumptions. Perhaps group 2 (Table 12-5) came closest to the kind of fuller and more usable reporting sought with the experiential method. Despite the paucity of data, various facets of the phenomenon were aggregated and acknowledged by each group to be relevant to the phenomenon at each stage of data processing. Such checks and corroborations may serve to counter tendencies for researchers to act in ways that jeopardize the validity of their research when findings begin to emerge that may not meet expectations. I can only speculate that having the co-researchers who generated the data also be the ones who processed the data lent more authenticity to the findings through their continued engagement with the phenomenon throughout data processing. The nature of collaborative team research, characteristic of all three groups, may also have compensated for the shortfalls in detail of the experiential reports. Nevertheless, I would recommend more substantive detail in experiential reporting than demonstrated in this study.

AUTHENTICITY OF REPORTING EXPERIENCE

It was taken as given that each experiential report was sufficiently rich in content to reveal one or more aspects of the phenomenon. This given enabled the groups to carry out the subsequent steps of data processing. The "assumption of authenticity" refers to the relevance and meaningfulness of the self-reports of the phenomenon. Without such an assumption, there is not an empirical foundation upon which to construct the aggregations and group synthesis. The discussion in the previous sections relates importantly to this assumption.

VARIATIONS IN THE USE OF A TRIGGER QUESTION

The form of the trigger question in this study differed in one subtle respect from those used by Barrell, Price, and associates. The difference was in the exclusion of the phrase "in the experience of" after the predicate in the trigger question. Specifically, I used the form "what is it like to be a stranger ... ?" where they would have likely preferred "what is it like to be in the experience of being a stranger ...?" The former directs attention within one's awareness directly to the focal phenomenon, that is to say, to *be once again that stranger*, whereas the latter places the inquirer within the focus of inquiry that implicitly informs the participant of separateness from the phenomenon. That is to say, you are not a stranger, now step into a time when you were the stranger. It also invites the participant to interject reflections upon matters likely tangential to the phenomenon itself, such as being witness to and in the act of experiencing and experiential reporting. My propensity is to prefer the most direct instruction. In the spirit of the method, any innovation that places the participant in touch as directly as possible with the phenomenon to be reported, I assume, enhances the chances that the experiential report will capture more of the lived experience of the phenomenon and contain less tangential text. The subtlety may seem a scholastic and semantic triviality to some in this case, but in my experience doing research using a range of methods for human inquiry, the choice of words and phrases to instruct articulate participants manifesting the phenomenon does influence what is reported. Relevant to this issue is the distinction noted previously regarding such an instruction as "describe in as much detail as you can what happened," in contrast to the instruction "describe what you think it means, about what happened." My point, however, is not to separate the subject from the experience; it is to favor conditions in inquiry that allow the phenomenological aspects of the experience to come into the foreground, while the hermeneutic aspects remain in the background. This bias is the preference of researchers when using the experiential method, but in my view this bias does not preclude increasingly more complex undertakings with the method that might include hermeneutic aspects as well.

Paradoxically, while intending to bring the person to relive intimately the experience, whether the stress is on "being a stranger" or on "being in the experience," the instruction encourages a kind of introspection, in that the participant's awareness is enhanced that one is separate from the experience. One is ordinarily neither a stranger to oneself, nor an inhabitant of unfamiliar territory. In this form of human inquiry, the participant partakes in "being a stranger"—an act that can easily be perceived as a residual entity to dwell upon and recount. Certainly one can argue that being the reflective and articulate participant one is, the act of entering into and reliving the experience is not the original experience itself—only one's memory of it. And more important, one is witness to this reliving while in the act of reexperiencing. It may help our understanding of this form of inquiry to dimensionalize one's relation to the experience in a series of gradations. At one extreme, one is a viewer (spectator, witness) moving into the experience in which one sees onself as a stranger in a foreign land. At the other extreme, one is the stranger in the foreign land, immersed and contained entirely in it. One can move back and forth between these two extremes, the director of one's movie in which one plays its central actor. This activity, akin to an application of imaginative variation developed as a research skill in phenomenological research methods, encourages an objectification of awareness to notice and select from that experience what to include in the experiential report.

Regarding variations in the trigger question across the three groups, one does wonder whether it had any bearing on the execution of the method. The trigger question of group 1 was biased in that it placed the participant as the stranger in the foreign land and communicated the dichotomy of self and other. The participant is the stranger and the context is the foreign land. One might argue that the question biased the research toward findings to corroborate the implicit dichotomy communicated in the question. The trigger question of group 2 communicated the same dichotomy or bias, but asked the participant to situate him/herself in context, which was already the case, having the seminar in a country other than the citizenship of the participants. But this question did not set up a self-referenced relationship as it did for group 1. However, it implicitly presumes that the second question manifested the first question. In other words, I had assumed both questions were equivalent forms of the same general question to tap the phenomenon studied. Yet there was no logical and necessary reason for equivalence. It is possible each trigger question solicited self-reports of a tangential phenomenon. The two forms of the question illustrate a common problem researchers face in posing questions to provoke self-reporting. Does one ask directly or does one approach the phenomenon more circumstantially, which minimizes bias to influence the participant to provide the researcher with a confirmation of the researcher's conception of the phenomenon studied. Generally, we want to avoid such self-fulfillment in scientific inquiry, especially if it leads to disgenuine, artificial, ideologically based, and distorted findings.

OBJECTIFICATION AND SCIENTIFIC INQUIRY

Use of trigger questions in the experiential method encourages an objectification of the entities that come to personal awareness. Furthermore, there is self-awareness about what one is attending to and selecting from experience to comprise the experiential report. This self-awareness enables one to experience movement along a dimension between the objectification to the subjectification of the experience. At one end of the dimension, objectification seems akin to scientific thinking, in that the treatment of selected entities of consciousness are named and described in the fashion of objects perceived externally in the environment, even though one knows all the while they are parts of our experience. At the other end of the dimension, subjectification engages rather than distances one from that which occupies consciousness. Regardless of where one is along this dimension, scientific inquiry requires a careful and methodical description of what one experiences, whether one prefers to conceptualize the phenomenon in objective or subjective terms. In fact, one may favor not to dimensionalize as such, but to focus on the task of articulating, in linguistic terms, as precisely as possible to capture the essence and meaning of the experience for purposes of recording and communicating to others. In a large part, this activity is what science is all about, regardless of the propensity of a researcher to think in terms of the object and subject of study. Consequently, a methodological procedure that brings the researcher into the most direct and least disturbing contact with the phenomenon is often the preferred one, because there is always one's interpretation of what one has observed overlaid upon one's recording of what happened, which in turn overlays recollections of raw experience. In short, what one thinks about the meaning of the phenomenon and what the phenomenon means to its observer must be held from and not be confused with the essential qualities that comprise the experience.

The distinction between the direct and indirect aspects of one's experience often is a subtle one, but is critically important, as I understand the issue. It lines the border of a methodological gray zone between phenomenology and hermeneutics. The more the awareness of the researcher shifts from focus on the phenomenon as a pure manifestation of consciousness to inclusion of reflections upon that experience, the more likely the acts of self-observation and description become suffused with interpretations of the experience itself, hence a movement away from the primary experience to one layered and imbued with interpretive material that followed the experience. Unquestionably, one's experience becomes such, as one dwells upon the course of daily events and what they mean. Requesting a self-report of an experience of being a stranger in a foreign land, or whatever the experience may be in experiential research, one has to contend with this mix of raw experience and one's interpretations of it. The issue certainly represents a central one generating variations of mixed methodology from phenomenology to hermeneutics.

RESEARCHER BIAS

In the previous section on Choice of Phenomenon I provided a brief narrative description I termed my presuppositional statement. It sensitized me to my prior experiences and knowledge of the phenomenon. It confronted me with the challenge to suspend (bracket) that which I consciously bring to the inquiry should it become evident such would interfere and bias the process of inquiry. All the while, I had to remain open to new experiences and knowledge of the phenomenon contributed by the seminar participants. My heightened awareness of my experiences of being a stranger in a foreign land, it seemed, had to be checked, even though they always remained available to me. In fact, as a participant researcher and group facilitator, I had contributed my experiential reports to the pool of reports. The participants and I constantly compared through the steps of processing our reports. Our previous experiences always could potentially influence and bias the processing. In giving importance to particular experiential reports, the participants (as co-researchers) and I brought bias to the process. We had to embrace our personal bias as we proceeded through the data processing. As part of the skill building in becoming efficacious researchers, we sought a balance between recognizing one's experience and bias and admitting to evidence the experiences of others. In the end, what became paramount was not to privilege and exclude prejudicially any tangential report in this kind of research method, but to ensure clear representation in the final synthesis of all essential features of the phenomenon.

Researcher bias is a lean or propensity of the researcher to view or favor something affiliated with the inquiry at hand. It typically is tied to *a priori* experience and knowledge of the phenomenon, participant, research process, and theory about the phenomenon. It can be both advantageous and disadvantageous to inquiry. In its favor, bias may bring some familiarity with the phenomenon and acquired skill to discriminate relevant from irrelevant data. With the experiential method, it facilitates communication between researcher and participants that establishes a common language and enables the data processing. Bias makes available preliminary conceptual categories, metaphors, and hypotheses useful to inquiry. In its disfavor, bias tends to accentuate some aspects of the phenomenon and diminish other aspects of equal or even greater importance in the experiential reports and essential descriptions in anticipation of the group synthesis. Bias can select what one wants to see during the processing of the data. Perhaps worst of all, it can obstruct, even retard, the process of inquiry, when the particular participants become too ideological in the group work.

Although theoretical discussions help articulate the issues, I believe the researcher must find a balance between the two extremes on the matter of bias. The researcher must exercise skill and discretion in minimizing the disadvantages while maximizing the advantages. This requires practice, patience, and skill. Perfecting this balance is a research strategy that illustrates what I term the *minmax principle in human inquiry* (Collen, 1995a).

In common with other approaches to human science research, the experiential method is more competently conducted when the researcher confronts and embraces bias rather than fully brackets, denies, ignores, or rationalizes it away under the guise of probable unimportance

(Collen, 1997). It seems clear that this concern preoccupied Husserl (1931, 1970) and the phenomenology movement (Spiegelberg, 1960) sufficiently to place a high priority on articulating what has become known as the "natural attitude" in phenomenological research. The concern for researcher bias has been given a central place in training those who would conduct forms of human inquiry. This is as true for phenomenology as it is for the experimental method. To bracket one's attitude (that is, temporarily suspend one's *a priori* beliefs, presuppositions, interpretations, and knowledge), while reducing the data to the essentials of the experience, has relevance to the experiential method, although it does not appear as crucial to data reduction as it does in phenomenology. Again, note the balance discussed previously. Nevertheless, given the priority in training to minimize researcher bias, both the bracketing and the presuppositional statement represent two examples of the kinds of methodological skills researchers may use to address the disadvantageous side of bias in human inquiry.

In the case of the experiential method, the presuppositional statement is an option. It is an innovation when added to the experiential method. It is not part of the method as conceived and executed by Barrell, Price, and associates. It may help the researcher to become aware of his or her assumptions, attitudes, beliefs, and expectations about the phenomenon to be studied. It may assist the researcher in gaining clarity of focus in preparation to pursuing an inquiry. At the same time, the researcher must have the restraint not to allow greater cognizance of his/her experience, knowledge, and understanding of the phenomenon to direct this pursuit simply reinforcing the *status quo*. This soft underbelly of vulnerability is by no means unique to the experiential method, but is inherent in all forms of inquiry across the sciences, because the researcher is a human being who is always susceptible to and at the effect of his/her own experience.

Having used the presuppositional statement in my case to study what it is like to be a stranger in a foreign land, I was able to refer to it after the data processing to check whether the findings (1) merely reaffirmed my prior understanding of the phenomenon and (2) were biased in some way that recommended greater caution in accepting the findings. It may be instructive to point out that my presuppositional statement noted previously shared two aggregation labels (excitement and anxiety) generated by group 1 (Table 12-4) and a close similarity with a third (estrangement–disconnectedness), yet apparently little if any communality with those aggregations of group 2 (Table 12-6) and group 3 (Table 12-8), even though I participated in all three groups. The commonness lent some confirmation to my prior experience of and reflections about the phenomenon. But it also left me wondering whether my facilitating role in the first group was more influential than expected, compared with the other two groups. Moreover, the comparing and contrasting provided me with information to evaluate my bias.

REPLICATION

Each group may be taken as a replication of the study of the phenomenon. However, a number of differences distinguishing the groups discussed earlier, for example the form of the trigger question, suggest that one cannot state the replications are exact. However, it need not be a problem with the method. To the contrary, it can be an asset. Variations are important, even when exact replication is attempted, for they provide opportunity to reaffirm what is known and to capture manifestations of the phenomenon to be known in broader contexts. In other words, whenever possible, we want to foster generalizability to a greater range of persons, circumstances, situations, and occasions in which the phenomenon appears.

Given changes in available resources, participants, and research setting, it is very idealistic to expect exact replication. Even in applications of well-known and established methods, such as experimental, observational, and survey research, the point is not exact replication, but reproduction of closely similar findings under similar conditions, such that an inference (generalization) may be justified. Yet the serendipitous nature of variations that occur in any event by mere execution of the study again and again make for one of the more exhilarating aspects of working with experiential and other methods for human inquiry.

In the case of studying what it is like to be a stranger in a foreign land, the pool of experiential reports and aggregation labels provides a richer and more encompassing description of the phenomenon, without undue redundancy, than the results of any one group standing alone. The coverage across the three groups yields the fuller picture. Although more detailed data were preferred, groups 1 and 2 demonstrated the diversity of the phenomenon could be observed through replication. Thus, one might conclude that the replications enabled the researcher to attain a deepened and more comprehensive understanding of the phenomenon with each visitation through the research process.

Another, although complementary, perspective is to state that successive replications made it possible to find multiple facets of the phenomenon, while simultaneously gaining greater confidence in the core description of the phenomenon.

Whatever words one prefers to convey the aim of replications, it is to obtain an informative three-dimensional, essential description in which the researcher can communicate the center, breadth, and depth of the phenomenon. As much may be said about other methods for human inquiry, such as hermeneutic, phenomenological, and the constant comparative method leading to grounded theory. In my view, this replication effect is a distinct advantage for the human science researcher, just as it is a requisite for progress in other sciences that do not make human beings the focus of inquiry.

Examination of the output of groups 2 and 3 revealed they did not completely replicate each other (Tables 12-6 and 12-8). Interestingly, such an expectation may not be held to be a penultimate criterion in this form of research, although highly desired. The matter may be more akin to an interest in convergent and discriminant validity among the three groups. Are the results characteristic of the same phenomenon? Merely clear variations of it? Overlapping through differing manifestations of it across distinct subgroups of participants? Or all of these? In other words, replication of aggregations and the labels participants use to communicate them surely provide some corroboration across groups about the experience of being a stranger in a foreign land. But perhaps more informative is the complementary aspects of the phenomenon that may be revealed as the compilation of results comes across the groups. The richer picture from multiple groups, over one group only, informs us of shades and nuances of this basic human experience that may permit more stability of a basic finding, and more generalizability than one might risk from the findings of one group alone.

In general, multiple groups in the experiential method provide the consistency (reliability) we might come to expect, as well as a kind of validity (accuracy) through the repeated and expanding attainment of the more complete and comprehensive description of the phenomenon.

INDIVIDUAL VERSUS GROUP WORK

The manner in which I have implemented the experiential method has been through group work. A reading of the research by Barrell, Price, and associates suggests a range of possibilities—from the researcher collecting and processing individual experiential reports from participants to a group of co-researchers who are also the participants (again, much like I have done). Perhaps a modal example is Barrell et al. (1990a) on the experience of stress. Thirty participants wrote an experience of stress as a first-person, present-tense account, after which they read their individual descriptions to identify those aspects of the experience they believed are always present when stressed. The procedure then shifted from individual to group work. Given their essential aspects identified, they discussed their experiences as a group to come to a consensus on what aspects of their reports seemed to epitomize the experience.

My overall impression is that Barrell, Price, and associates seem to prefer the more collaborative mode, in which researchers as participants first generate their reports individually, then, second, collectively share, discuss, and synthesize their experiential reports. It is to the credit of the method that it lends itself to a range of variations with regard to the roles and extent of participation by researchers and participants.

PARTICIPATORY EXPERIENTIAL METHOD

The ideas that participants can serve as researchers and researchers become participants in the same inquiry are not new to human science research methodology (Collen, 1995a, b; Reason and Rowan, 1981). Expansions in the roles and responsibilities in areas of decision making (e.g., research questions, research design, research plan, data collection, and data processing) give rise to the more participatory forms of a given method. More genuine collaboration, partnership, shared responsibility, and democratization of power occur when the researchers allow participants to engage more fully in the inquiry as they do, specifically as researchers.

The definition of participation may be applied to experiential method in four basic forms. The traditional form of self-reporting, research interviewing, and data processing is *researcher centered.* Researchers provide instructions and participants generate experiential reports. The researcher collects, processes, interprets, and synthesizes them. This form of the method corresponds to the standard formats (Kvale, 1996; Mishler, 1986). Typically, research interviews are tape-recorded for later transcription. The transcripts provide the records for data processing.

When the researcher and participant dialogue heavily in experiential and related kinds of human inquiry, the traditional format shifts to an exchange that includes mutual feedback. The form of research is a more authentically interpersonal and participatory inquiry; yet, as before, the resultant transcript serves only the researcher. The second form of experiential method can have the researcher contribute experiential reports, but relaxes control over processing, interpreting, and synthesizing. The participants can be invited to comment not only on the instructions, procedures, and other aspects of the method, but also on their data generated. This invited commentary, which is regulated and largely controlled by the researcher, ensures critical feedback that helps the researcher to keep the inquiry on course and assess the internal validity of the inquiry. This form of inquiry, modified from the traditional form, I term *participant feedback.*

In the third form of method, the participant has an opportunity to examine the transcript and, with the researcher, provide clarifications and additions to it before processing the data. Furthermore, the participant begins to have more responsibility for deciding the nature and course of inquiry. I would characterize this third form of the method as *participant centered.*

Finally, in the most participatory form of inquiry, the researcher and participant serve in all capacities as co-researchers and co-participants to engage together in all phases of self-reporting, transcript review, and subsequent data processing. True collaboration, shared responsibility, and

TABLE 12-12 Eight Forms of Experiential Method Based on Participation and Social Dynamics between Researcher and Participant

Participation	Social Dynamic	
	Dyadic	Pluralistic
Researcher Centered	R decides and questions; P answers	R decides and questions; Ps answer
Participant Feedback	R decides and questions; P answers and comments	R decides and questions; Ps answer and comment
Participant Centered	R decides; R and P question, answer, and comment	R decides; R and Ps question, answer, and comment
Fully Collaborative	R and P decide, question, answer, and comment	R and Ps decide, question answer, and comment

P, participant; R, researcher.

democratization of power of the interpersonal relationship between researcher and participant are expected. This form may be termed *fully collaborative*.

Eight forms of inquiry are summarized in Table 12-12. Half the forms comprise dyadic relationships between one researcher and one participant for research purposes. Half the forms comprise collective relationships among one or more researchers and a small group of participants (e.g., 4 to 12 persons). Prototypical at one extreme is a method adhering to individual research interviewing; at the other extreme are group-oriented methods, such as focus groups and participatory action research.

Both the second and third forms of the experiential method characterized the research reported in this chapter. I was markedly restricted by the activities of the seminar program; had I been able to engage my participants in selection of the phenomenon and to allow the groups to decide the rate and extent of completion of their process of inquiry, the work of this chapter would have been more fully the participatory experiential method.

Before moving to conclude the chapter, two qualifying points are important to discuss with regard to the forms and extent of participation in experiential and related methods. First, the articulation of the four kinds of participation (Table 12-12) is rather arbitrary. There are other similar renditions (e.g., Heron, 1981). One could describe various forms of a given method, depending on the features of the interpersonal relationship among the researchers and participants one chooses to emphasize. The key point here is the dimension of participation; it must be examined, defined, and described in each application of the research method. Second, I have mixed in the text of my previous paragraph a singularity, in contrast to a plurality, of persons comprising the inquiry. By this dimension one can double the number of forms of the method—that is, whether one chooses to interact with each participant separately or interact with a group of participants collectively. From solo to collective inquiry, individual work is most clearly understood in classical research interviewing, and group work in focus group research. The crux of this second point is the social dynamics that must also be examined, defined, and described in each application of experiential method.

CONCLUSION

This chapter presents and discusses one form of the experiential research method for human inquiry. No claim is made that the form developed here is any more or less suitable to human inquiry than other forms (e.g., Barrell, Price, and associates). To the contrary, one theme of the chapter has been the diversification of forms among researchers to suit their styles and contexts of inquiry. This quality about the method prognosticates a healthy future.

Unquestionably, the experiential research method is a member of a family of methods stemming largely from the influence of phenomenology on human science research, especially in the latter half of the 20th century. There is acknowledgment of this influence, more recently (e.g., Price and Aydede, 2004). However, as far as I can determine, the experiential method does not follow phenomenological orthodoxy for the study of consciousness in the psychological sciences, such as is shown in the work of Giorgi and Giorgi (2003). It would appear that the experiential method of Barrell, Price, and associates does have some affinity with such research traditions as phenomenology, hermeneutics, thematic analysis, and content analysis, but its practitioners have freely innovated the course of inquiry to such an extent that it would be a difficult argument to convince staunch phenomenologists, hermeneuticists, and content analysts that the forms of experiential method discussed and utilized in this chapter, as well as those experiential research reports referenced in this chapter, are clear derivatives of these research traditions. My strong impression is that the innovations come from the confluence of phenomenology and hermeneutics with other continental North American influences, most notably methodological pragmatism and democratic collectivism. As such, the experiential method seems to be an outstanding example of one emergent and potentially fruitful method for human science research that does not require extensive and involved training by participants and researchers in such research traditions as phenomenology and hermeneutics. In sum, the philosophical and theoretical foundations of the method remain obscure.

Through the empirical example of what it is like to be a stranger in a foreign land, one form of the experiential method has been demonstrated. But like any research method for human inquiry, there are strengths and weaknesses a researcher must face as a practitioner of the method. The composition of the trigger question, training of the participants, quality of the experiential reports, researcher and participant biases, and the research context of data collection are chief considerations in this case. Furthermore, the empirical study of the method and the published research literature also help to accentuate variations of the method available to researchers. The distribution and definition of roles and responsibilities among researchers and participants, coupled with individual and group work at each stage of inquiry, foster various forms of the method. Finally, the empirical examples discussed in this chapter and study of the research literature anchor the experiential method in relation to other members of its family of human science research methods.

In its current state of development, the experiential research method does have its place among contemporary approaches to human inquiry that relies on descriptions of experience. Commensurate with many other human science research methods, the aims of the experiential method are to (1) obtain self-reports that capture in first-person present-tense one or more aspects of the phenomenon; (2) find structure, organization, and meaning in human experience; and (3) deepen the understandings of both researchers and participants engaged in the inquiry. More important, what the variations of the method covered in this chapter seem to show is that the method can fulfill the aim to articulate and establish a public and collective understanding of a phenomenon for a group of persons who manifest the phenomenon.

The experiential method would appear to have great potential for a range of applications in which individuals and groups work directly with self-reports of experience. The research method may be one means to bring disciplined inquiry more directly into clinical, peace and conflict, and psychotherapeutic settings that rely on empathetic mutual understanding. In the workplace of human organizations, the method may be a useful application of disciplined inquiry as part of a larger process to foster a collective understanding and to preface organizational change. These potentials represent important directions for exploring what the experiential method may do to further our efforts to aid and improve our world. However, currently, practitioners of the method cannot make direct claims to explain phenomenon, construct theory, test hypotheses, evaluate treatments and practices, and ameliorate the human condition. In its current state of development as a form of human inquiry, the method stands as preparatory and descriptive to these substantive aims.

ACKNOWLEDGMENT

It is with great appreciation that I thank the seminar participants, who worked with me to generate and process the protocols presented in this chapter, and who shall remain anonymous.

REFERENCES

Barrell, J., and J. Barrell. (1975). A self-directed approach for a science of human experience. *Journal of Phenomenological Psychology*, *6*, 63–73.

Barrell, J., and J. Barrell. (1976). How we can control time: An experiential model. *Journal of Pastoral Counseling*, *11*, 42–53.

Barrell, J., K. Foley, and P. Lueders. (1990a). Discovering lived meanings of stress: An experiential study. *Methods, Winter*, 19–30.

Barrell, J., and S. Jourard. (1976). Being honest with persons we like. *Journal of Individual Psychology*, *32*, 185–193.

Barrell, J., and S. Jourard. (1977). Opening up to others. *Human Behavior*, *6*, 30.

Barrell, J., D. Medeiros, J. Barrell, and D. Price. (1985). The causes and treatment of performance anxiety. An experiential approach. *Journal of Humanistic Psychology*, *25*, 106–122.

Barrell, J., D. Medeiros, and K. Foley. (1990b). *Experiential method: Exploring the human experience*. Acton, MA: Copley Publishing Group.

Barrell, J., and R. Neimeyer. (1975). A mathematical formula for the psychological control of suffering. *Journal of Pastorial Counseling*, *10*, 60–67.

Barrell, J., and D. Price. (1975). The perception of first and second pain as a function of psychological set. *Perception and Psychophysics*, *17*, 163–166.

Barrell, J., and D. Price. (1977a). Stress: Confronting and avoiding. *Brain-Mind Bulletin*, *3*, 1–2.

Barrell, J., and D. Price (1977b). Two experiential orientations toward a stressful situation and their related somatic and visceral responses. *Psychophysiology*, *14*, 517–521.

Barrell, J., and A. Richards. (1982). Overcoming jealousy: An experiential analysis of common factors. *Personnel and Guidance Journal*, *61*, 40–47.

Barrell, J., and J. Waters. (1980). *Consumer motivations—analytical report*. Values and lifestyles program report no. 13. Middlefield, CA: Stanford Research Institute.

Braud, W., and R. Anderson. (1998). *Transpersonal research methods for the social sciences: Honoring human experience*. Thousand Oaks, CA: Sage.

Bruner, E. (1986). Experience and its expressions. In Turner, V., and E. Bruner. (Eds.). *The anthropology of experience* (pp. 3–30). Chicago: University of Illinois Press.

Camic, P., J. Rhodes, and L. Yardley. (Eds.). (2003). *Qualitative research in psychology: Expanding perspectives in methodology and design*. Washington, DC: American Psychological Association.

Clandinin, D., and F. Connelly. (1994). Personal experience methods. In Denzin, N., and Y. Lincoln. (Eds.). *Handbook of qualitative research* (pp. 413–427). Thousand Oaks, CA: Sage.

Collen, A. (1990). Advancing human science. *Saybrook Review*, *8*, 1–38.

Collen, A. (1995a). *Human science research methods, theory, and thinking: Seminar supplement*. Walnut Creek, CA: HSR Seminars.

Collen, A. (1995b). The foundation of science. *Foundation of Science Quarterly*, *1*, 14–18.

Collen, A. (1997). Human science research: An important focus for the next century. In Kocuinas, R. (Ed.). *Proceedings of the international conference humanistic psychology towards the XXI century* (pp. 6–14). Vilnius, Lithuania: Lithuanian Association of Humanistic Psychology.

Collen, A. (1998). Design of a life: Sustainability and the inquirer/researcher alias designer in an evolving world system. *World Futures, 51*, 223–238.

Denzin, N. (1989). *Interpretive biography.* Newbury Park, CA: Sage.

Denzin, N., and Y. Lincoln. (Eds.). (1994). *Handbook of qualitative research.* Thousand Oaks, CA: Sage.

Dewey, J. (1938). *Experience and education.* New York: Collier.

Eisner, E. (1988). The primacy of experience and the politics of method. *Educational Researcher, 17*, 15–20.

Fetterman, D. (1989). *Ethnography: Step by step.* Newbury Park, CA: Sage.

Giorgi, A. (Ed.). (1985). *Phenomenology and psychological research.* Pittsburgh: Duquesne University Press.

Giorgi, A., and B. Giorgi. (2003). The descriptive phenomenological psychological method. In Camic, P., J. Rhodes, and L. Yardley. (Eds.). *Qualitative research in psychology: Expanding perspectives in methodology and design* (pp. 243–273). Washington, DC: American Psychological Association.

Glaser, B., and A. Strauss. (1967). *The discovery of grounded theory: Strategies for qualitative research.* Chicago: Aldine.

Greenbaum, T. (1998). *The handbook for focus group research* (2nd ed.). Thousand Oaks, CA: Sage.

Grimm, L., and P. Yarnold. (Eds.). (1995). *Reading and understanding multivariate analysis.* Washington, DC: American Psychological Association.

Heidegger, M. (1982). *The basic problems of phenomenology.* Hofstadter, A. (Trans.). Bloomington: Indiana University Press.

Heron, J. (1981). Experiential research methodology. In Reason, P., and J. Rowan. (Eds.). *Human inquiry: A sourcebook of new paradigm research* (pp. 153–166). New York: John Wiley and Sons.

Husserl, E. (1931). *Ideas: General introduction to pure phenomenology.* Gibson, W. (Trans.). New York: Collier-MacMillan.

Husserl, E. (1970). *The crisis of European sciences and transcendental phenomenology.* Carr, D. (Trans.). Evanston, IL: Northwestern University Press.

Kvale, S. (1996). *InterViews: An introduction to qualitative research interviewing.* Thousand Oaks, CA: Sage.

Lyons, J., and J. Barrell. (1979). *People: An introduction to psychology.* New York: Harper and Row.

McLeod, J. (2001). *Qualitative research in counseling and psychotherapy.* Thousand Oaks, CA: Sage.

Miles, M., and A. Huberman. (1994). *Qualitative data analysis* (2nd ed.) Thousand Oaks, CA: Sage.

Miller, P., J. Hengst, and S. Wang. (2003). Ethnographic methods: Applications from developmental cultural psychology. In Camic, P., J. Rhodes, and L. Yardley. (Eds.). *Qualitative research in psychology: Expanding perspectives in methodology and design* (pp. 219–242). Washington, DC: American Psychological Association.

Mishler, E. (1986). *Research interviewing: Context and narrative.* Cambridge, MA: Harvard University Press.

Moustakas, C. (1990). *Heuristic research: Design, methodology, and applications.* Newbury Park, CA: Sage.

Moustakas, C. (1994). *Phenomenological research methods.* Thousand Oaks, CA: Sage.

Packer, M., and R. Addison. (Eds.). (1989). *Entering the circle: Hermeneutic investigation in psychology.* New York: State University of New York Press.

Price, D. (1988). *Psychological and neural mechanisms of pain.* New York: Raven Press.

Price, D., and M. Aydede. (2004). The experimental use of introspection in the scientific study of pain and its integration with third-person methodologies: The experiential–phenomenological approach. Available at *http://web.clas.ufl.edu/users/maydede/pain.jcs.pdf*. Accessed October 12, 2004.

Price, D., and J. Barrell. (1980). An experiential approach with quantitative methods: A research paradigm. *Journal of Humanistic Psychology*, 3, 75–95.

Price, D., and J. Barrell. (1984). Some general laws of human emotion: Interrelationships between intensities of desire, expectation and emotional feeling. *Journal of Personality*, 52, 389–409.

Price, D., J. Barrell. and J., Barrell. (1985). A quantitative–experiential analysis of human emotions. *Motivation and Emotion*, 9, 19–38.

Price, D., J. Barrell, and R. Gracely. (1980). A psychophysical analysis of experiential factors that selectively influence the affective dimensions of pain. *Pain*, 8, 137–149.

Reason, P., and J. Rowan. (Eds.). (1981). *Human inquiry: A sourcebook of new paradigm research*. New York: John Wiley and Sons.

Rubin, H., and I. Rubin. (1995). *Qualitative interviewing: The art of hearing data*. Thousand Oaks, CA: Sage.

Runyan, W. (1984). *Life histories and psychobiography: Explorations in theory and method*. New York: Oxford University Press.

Spiegelberg, H. (1960). *The phenomenological movement*. Hague: Nijhoff.

Stake, R. (1995). *The art of case study research*. Thousand Oaks, CA: Sage.

Strauss, A. (1987). *Qualitative analysis for social scientists*. New York: Cambridge University Press.

Strauss, A., and J. Corbin. (1990). *Basics of qualitative research: Grounded theory procedures and techniques*. Newbury Park, CA: Sage.

(1994). *The compact Oxford English dictionary* (2nd ed.). Oxford: Oxford University Press.

BIOGRAPHICAL BACKGROUND

ARNE COLLEN, PhD, is a member of the Executive Faculty and Professor of Psychology, Human Science, and Organizational Systems at Saybrook Graduate School and Research Center in San Francisco, California. He also has a Research and Teaching Adjunct Faculty appointment at Alliant University in both the California School of Professional Psychology and the College of Organizational Studies. Over three decades with an affiliation at these two academic institutions, he has sustained long-term interests in human-oriented research methods and applications of cybernetic and systemic ideas to research methodology for human inquiry. One example is his well-known Human Science Research Summer Seminar, which has helped many professional researchers, academicians, and their students to obtain greater familiarity with several human-oriented approaches to human inquiry. It is from his seminar that he makes his contribution to this book.

After completion of his doctorate in experimental psychology at the main campus of Ohio State University in 1971, he spent three decades studying, teaching, and using a range of human-oriented research traditions involving compatible as well as disparate theoretical and empirical activities, nomothetic and ipsative research designs, qualitative and quantitative data collection and processing procedures, and simple to complex constructions of methodology. His current professional activities involve supervising and training graduate-level research, developing several forms of research methodology for human inquiry, publishing, providing research workshops and seminars, and research consulting.

With his incorporation of cybernetic and systemic ideas into his pedagogy applied to the research process, he has contributed a perspective and approach to human praxis and inquiry that is intended to foster systemic change in individuals, collaborative research teams, and human organizations. An exemplary instance of his approach is his book *Systemic Change through Praxis and Inquiry* (2004). Drawing from several philosophical and methodological streams prominent in the continental United States, his work thrives on a transdisciplinary, pragmatic, and generalist approach to human inquiry. He is known for his devotion to advancing forms of human inquiry that cross paradigmatic boundaries to reveal "do-able" and productive mixed methodologies. He remains an active contributor to several professional associations and their affiliated publications in human-oriented research methodology.

13

Focus Groups and Related Rapid Assessment Methods: Identifying Psychoeducational HIV/AIDS Interventions in Botswana

Lisa Levers

EDITOR'S INTRODUCTION

Focus groups have a long history in market research. They engage people of similar interests or backgrounds in the discussion of a specific research issue. The facilitator introduces the topic and format, and encourages discussion. This method allows for probing, revisiting, and clarifying emerging understandings and concerns. Focus groups produce inexpensive, rapid, flexible, depthful comprehensions that are particularly well suited for guiding community services.

Dr. Levers typically combines three qualitative approaches for rapid assessment research: participant observation, key informant interviews, and multiple focus groups. In the first half of this chapter, Dr. Levers overviews the history of focus groups and what the major contributors to the method have said about it. Her presentation is conversational and easy to follow as she introduces the nitty-gritty of the approach. She then briefly describes three studies with which she was directly involved to give us a sense of the range of content that can be addressed meaningfully through rapid assessment methods (RAMs). I attended a conference at which Dr. Levers' graduate students presented their findings from one of the three studies; they showed slides from a museum-sponsored exhibit about America's history of lynching southern black people, and then presented their findings from interviews with Pittsburgh's elder African-American community leaders, and from focus groups of Pittsburgh African-American representatives who had attended the exhibit. We conference attendees were deeply moved and reflective as the students shared what their study had revealed about the continuing impact of historical lynching on our African-American residents. With regard to these three studies, Dr. Levers presents the topics rather than the findings, the others being the impact of violence and privation on Namibian children and vicarious trauma experienced by child protection workers in Pennsylvania. Dr. Levers then returns to research procedures to discuss planning, institutional review boards (IRBs), format (protocol), conducting the group, and analyzing data.

In the second half of her chapter, Dr. Levers takes us through the procedures and findings of her research with safari workers and administrators in Botswana as they explore together to find ways to educate citizens about HIV/AIDS. We see that she immersed herself in the local culture (including living in a tent for a couple of weeks to be available to talk with all participants), revised plans repeatedly out of respect for participants' well-being, was confident all along that her RAMs would be of help in coping with the AIDS pandemic, and developed a practical table of findings for the safari companies to use as they go about contending with the pandemic.

The focus group had its earliest origins in the social sciences; however, marketing and advertising researchers soon embraced it, and the focus group became increasingly more identified with these fields. It has been over the course of only about the last 15 to 20 years that the utility of focus groups has been realized more fully in the social sciences. Acceptance of the focus group as an effective method has evolved slowly, but in spite of this gradual shift, focus groups have remained relatively underutilized in the fields of psychology and counseling.

As a method of research, the focus group has multiple applications and can be used alone or in combination with other research strategies. There are many applications for focus groups in psychology and counseling that have the potential for rendering relevant data relating to a range of human phenomena. For this reason, and because this book is aimed at preservice training in these fields, I have elected to discuss the use of focus groups within a psychosocial and cultural context. Many of the examples used in this chapter draw from my fieldwork in southern Africa, especially in Botswana and especially concerning the HIV/AIDS pandemic.

The first part of this chapter offers an introduction to the focus group as a qualitative research method. The second part of this chapter provides a sample of one specific application, relating to an HIV/AIDS intervention and illustrating how the focus group can be used as a qualitative research strategy in this context. The chapter concludes with a discussion of helpful tools to get started in using focus groups as a qualitative research strategy.

INTRODUCTION TO FOCUS GROUPS

Focus groups have been used for research purposes, at first ostensibly with some degree of trepidation, then with increasingly greater assurance, throughout most of the 20th and into the 21st centuries. This section provides a brief historical overview, defines the method, elaborates the utility of focus groups, offers examples of how focus groups have been used, and describes the elements of using a focus group approach.

BRIEF OVERVIEW OF THE ORIGINS OF THE FOCUS GROUP

The use of focus groups as a research strategy evolved from promising but reticent beginnings. Morgan (1998b) has collapsed the evolution of focus groups into three periods: The earliest use of focus groups was found largely in the social sciences, prior to and during WWII. The next use of focus groups was located primarily in the field of marketing, during and after WWII, and becoming more robust in the 1980s as the method was refined. And, most recently, focus groups have been used again in the social sciences, as well as in other fields. Morgan (1997) has cited Bogardus' (1926) description of group interviews as one of the earliest publications relating to focus groups. During WWII, military psychologists and civilian consultants extended the use of focus groups to examine the effectiveness of radio broadcasts intended to improve the morale of soldiers. This research ignited an interest in the use of focus groups by social scientists at that time and resulted in several publications (e.g., Merton, Fiske, and Kendall, 1990; Merton and Kendall, 1946). However, this early interest by social scientists waned, and the use of focus groups shifted to and continued to develop in the arena of marketing research, where it remains a dominant research strategy.

It was not until the 1980s that interest in focus groups began to reemerge in the social sciences (Berg, 2001). The focus group has been used increasingly more often throughout the past two decades by psychologists, counselors, anthropologists, sociologists, educators, and other social scientists. For the interested reader, Berg (2001), Morgan (1997; 1998b), and Krueger (1994) have provided detailed accounts of the historical origins of the focus group.

DEFINING THE FOCUS GROUP AS A QUALITATIVE METHOD

The focus group approach to research lends itself well to use as a qualitative method insofar as it assists in obtaining in-depth understandings of perceptions, opinions, and the ways in which people make meaning of a variety of aspects of their lives. Edmunds (1999) has stated, "A focus group brings together eight to ten qualified people for a face-to-face discussion of a particular topic (p. 1)." Dawson, Manderson, and Tallo (1993) have provided the following simple but useful definition:

> A focus group is a group discussion that gathers together people from similar backgrounds or experiences to discuss a specific topic of interest to the researcher. The group of participants is guided by a moderator (or group facilitator), who introduces topics for discussion and helps the group to participate in a lively and natural discussion amongst themselves. (p. 6)

Krueger (1994) has defined focus groups as "carefully planned discussion designed to obtain perceptions in a defined area of interest in a permissive, nonthreatening environment" (p. 18).

Based upon an extensive review of on-line databases, Morgan (1997) has identified three categorical uses for focus groups in contemporary social science research:

> First, they are used as a *self-contained* method in studies in which they serve as the principal source of data. Second, they are used as a *supplementary* source of data in studies that rely on some other primary method such as a survey. Third, they are used in *multimethod* studies that combine two or more means of gathering data in which no one primary method determines the use of the others. (p. 2).

To elaborate on what Morgan has described as the third use, the multimethod study, focus groups more recently have been used in combination with other qualitative methods in a specific set of strategies referred to as *rapid assessment methods* (or RAMs) or the *rapid assessment process* (RAP; Beebe, 2001; Kumar, 1993; Levers, 2003; USAID, 1996). Increasingly, the need for a relatively rapid turnover of research results has marked a distinct pathway in the ethnographic arena (Handwerker, 2001). Although the RAM or RAP has been used frequently for assessment purposes in the international development community, the use also has been extended with increasing frequency to community-based services and matters of psychosocial and cultural concern.

As an example, during the past several years, I have designed a number of studies using the RAM framework. These investigations have ranged from explorations of racism (Levers, Mosely, Conte, Darr, Moore, and Shafer et al., 2002) and issues of diversity and inclusion (Levers, Mosely, Pickett, Angelone, Bigante, and Gruber et al., 2003) in one part of the United States, to children affected by violence (Levers, 2002) and by the HIV/AIDS pandemic (Levers, 2003) in southern Africa. In an ongoing examination of the contextual factors and cultural issues associated with the spread of HIV/AIDS in southern Africa, I have continued to use RAMs and other participatory methods to capture the voices of important cultural brokers like village elders, village chiefs, and traditional healers.

According to one publication, some of the strengths of RAMs are their rapidity, relative low cost, and flexibility, as well as their effectiveness at "... providing in-depth understanding of complex socio-economic systems or processes" (USAID, 1996, p. 2). The efficacious use of the focus group—whether self-contained, supplementary, or as part of a multimethod study, such as in the case of RAM or RAP—is now widely recognized within the social sciences for its valuable contributions.

UTILITY OF THE FOCUS GROUP APPROACH

A consideration of the utility of the focus group approach leads directly to the nature of a specific study's research problem and its ensuing questions. The research problem leads the decision-making process in choosing the best methodological framework. Methodology should never determine the nature of the problem or the question. Focus groups can be very useful in "getting at" a better understanding of certain opinions, perceptions, and attitudes that might otherwise be obscured in other types of investigations. The focus group format easily facilitates clarification of issues and allows for further probing for additional data or for nuances of information already derived. This research method, in some ways, is similar to individual or key informant interviews, but it differs with respect to the synergistic effect of group dynamics. The researcher relies upon group interaction, which has been stimulated by protocol questions that are integrally related to the topic of the research. Focus group participants "play off" one another's responses, and the insightful group facilitator can use this dynamic to acquire deeper levels of information.

PURPOSES OF FOCUS GROUPS

Researchers need to know *why* they have chosen a particular method and to be aware of its advantages and disadvantages. Berg (2001, pp. 126–127) has identified seven advantages of using the focus group as a research strategy:

1. The focus group is highly flexible.
2. The focus group permits observation of interactions.
3. The focus group allows researchers to access substantive content of verbally expressed views, opinions, experiences, and attitudes.
4. The focus group can produce speedy results.
5. The focus group can sample from large populations at a fairly low cost.
6. The focus group can be used to assess transient populations.
7. The focus group places participants on a more even footing with each other and the investigator.

Sometimes disadvantages outweigh the advantages of using a focus group approach. Edmunds (1999, p. 7) has described seven circumstances under which focus groups should *not* be used:

1. To make a final decision
2. To explore extremely sensitive or personal topics.
3. To answer "How many?" or "How much?"
4. To conduct research for an audience that does not understand the purpose of qualitative research.
5. To evaluate a ... [program] ... to which revisions will not be made despite the results of the study.
6. To save money or time required for quantitative research.
7. To set prices for a product or service.

Some in the research arena remain biased against qualitative methods in general, and this bias carries over to particular methods, including focus groups. Although most reasonable people see the usefulness of a balanced perspective about the contributions of both quantitative and qualitative methods, some biases have endured over time (Williams and Katz, 2001). Morgan (1998a) has identified myths that continue to linger and thereby have inhibited the use of focus groups, even in research scenarios for which the focus group would be the best fit. These myths are the following:

- Focus groups are low cost and quick.
- Focus groups require professional moderators.
- Focus groups require special facilities.
- Focus groups must consist of strangers.
- Focus groups will not work for sensitive topics.
- Focus groups produce conformity.
- Focus groups must be validated by other methods.
- Focus groups predict how people will behave.

Morgan (1998a) has further highlighted several beliefs about focus groups that he says *should be encouraged.* These beliefs are the following:

- Skepticism about all research methods is intellectually healthy.
- High-quality moderating is crucial to focus groups.
- Teamwork produces the best focus groups.
- The research team can always learn from the participants.
- There are many possible ways to do focus groups.

The astute reader may have noticed a seeming contradiction between Edmunds' (1999) advice not "to explore extremely sensitive or personal topics" and what Morgan (1998a) has identified as a myth: that "focus groups will not work for sensitive topics." Actually, these assertions are not as contradictory as they are paradoxical. In trying to illuminate ways in which to approach conducting a focus group, it must be emphasized that qualitative research is not a *cookbook* enterprise, and there are no exact *recipes* for conducting a focus group. The manner in which a focus group is run is highly dependent upon the nature of what is under investigation. The paradox here becomes more apparent, then, when we realize that Edmunds' academic background is in marketing, whereas Morgan is a sociologist. By virtue of what each of these researchers may be investigating, respectively, and how each may need to interpret results differently for differing sets of research objectives, we can see that in one type of focus group, such as for marketing purposes, the "sensitive and personal" should be avoided. Whereas, in another, such as for developing a better under-standing of perceptions about a sensitive phenomenon (for example, the use of condoms in HIV/AIDS prevention efforts), the "sensitive topic" is indeed at the very heart of the focus group inquiry.

USING FOCUS GROUPS IN THE FIELD

In an ideal world, the researcher goes into a focus group with solid theoretical and contextual understandings of the topic under examination. A thorough literature review has been conducted and then integrated and synthesized with knowledge derived from the field. However, given the constraints of the real world in which we live, even for academic researchers, the ideal is not always possible, especially when doing field research. Often when social scientists are working in the field, rapid assessments are required for the most immediate development of results. Sometimes emerging challenges and unforeseen limitations threaten to compromise the integrity of the research design, and it becomes necessary for the researcher to make on-the-spot decisions of a compensatory nature.

The location and context of a focus group may influence how the researcher first shapes the group format. For example, the protocol for asking questions may be more or less structured, and the questions may be more or less opened or closed, depending on the location and context of the group. Group members may feel more or less free to disclose information, depending on influences often beyond the scope of the investigation. Any contextual changes or fluctuations may necessitate spontaneous or last-minute alterations, or reshaping of the group format. Any of these nuances in variation may affect the degree to which the researcher is able to "get at" the essence of the issue. Any well-planned research framework takes these types of potential limitations—the reality of "in-the-field" constraints or the reality of human nature—into account during the research design phase.

"GETTING AT" DIFFICULT-TO-OBTAIN DATA

Qualitative research strategies often are used to obtain phenomenological and existential information about the human condition that, by the very nature of the data, would be difficult or nearly impossible to acquire through quantitatively oriented or conventional statistical means. The focus group is one option for *getting at* such difficult-to-obtain data. Using multiple research strategies—that is, methodological triangulation—not only enhances the trustworthiness of the study, it is also a highly efficacious way to *get at* important contextual factors and cultural issues. I offer an example drawn from my current HIV/AIDS work in Botswana.

Much of the anti-AIDS activity on the African continent has been based on Western medical and social service models and has not included the cultural wisdom of the elders, village chiefs, local educators, traditional healers, and spiritual leaders of indigenous religious groups. Even in the 21st century, business continues to be conducted as if medical and social service systems can be extracted surgically from an industrial context and transplanted into a developing context. For example, four of the most common theories of behavioral change cited in the HIV prevention literature (AIDSCAP, 1999) focus on the individual and rely on personal intention as the key predictor of desired change, failing to take environmental and social factors into account. Although efficacious in a Western context, the individualist dimensions of these theoretical frameworks can pose numerous problems when transplanted into a collectivist cultural ethos with a more fatalistic worldview. This is not to suggest a rigid "either/or" proposition in the other direction, which presents its own slippery slope; rather, I raise the possibility of an "and/both" approach to emphasize the essential importance of cultural awareness and sensitivity in designing culturally appropriate psychoeducational interventions. Although well intentioned, Western donor organizations, for the most part, have failed to perceive, understand, appreciate, and engage the cosmological, ontological, and epistemological differences that separate Western and African medical and cultural understandings of the AIDS pandemic. These are paradigmatic differences of great significance, and successful solutions to the current crisis can be attained only through a careful examination of these differences.

As an example, UNAIDS (2000) reports that there has been a dearth of research that actually examines the impact of involving indigenous healers in HIV/AIDS prevention and care activities in sub-Saharan Africa. Yet the services of indigenous healers are sought routinely throughout Africa, and it is estimated that at least 80% of the indigenous African people seek treatment from local healers throughout most of Africa (UNAIDS, 2000). If this is the case, these important cultural brokers should be invited to the decision-making table (Devos, 2004; Levers, in press), and research endeavors should be aimed at understanding the nuances of traditional practices. Such research relies upon the ability to *get at* sensitive data, for which RAMs, including focus groups, can be highly useful.

EXAMPLES OF STUDIES USING FOCUS GROUPS

Drawing from my own research and that of a doctoral student, I provide three examples of research projects using focus groups. The first represents an example of Morgan's (1997) supplementary use of focus groups, the second an example of the multimethod use of focus groups, and the third an example of the self-contained use of focus groups. The descriptions are brief and are intended to highlight the *context* for using the research strategy and not the *content* of the studies.

Children Affected by Trauma in Namibia

This was a study that I completed (Levers, 2002) with teachers at rural and remote schools in northern Namibia on the effects of violence, poverty, and privation on young children's development. The northern part of Namibia is the country's poorest area, where black Namibians were forced to relocate prior to Namibia's independence from the Republic of South Africa in 1990. It is also the part of Namibia that borders with Angola and still experiences border skirmishes. I primarily was interested in children's school-based experiences and how the effects of the region's disadvantages play out in terms of children's trauma and resilience.

The original research design called for key informant interviews with children. I had all the appropriate human subject approvals, and I had been assured that the older children were "past" the trauma and were conversant in English (I am not competent in the local languages). To make a long story short, on the first day of scheduled research I discovered that the children and I could not speak to one another in English. Through a translator, I learned that the children were very anxious, and some were traumatized by the border conflicts still occurring there. In fact, after briefly posing questions to one of the youths, I saw that he and some of the other children had become very agitated. No research project is worth the risk of retraumatizing children by asking them for their narratives, so I scrapped my research on the spot, after making sure that the children had recovered sufficiently from the preliminary questions.

Although what I have described here is one of the hazards of field research and required making immediate decisions, it also served as an inspiration for creativity and spontaneity. I spent a sleepless night redesigning my study, and ended up interviewing teachers about their perceptions of children's school-based experiences. I was able to collect very rich data from the teachers individually, deriving important information about the teachers, the children, the area, the systems, and the resilience of all the people involved. However, at several junctures I had unique opportunities also to conduct focus groups with the teachers. Although these focus groups rendered some additional information, they were a supplementary source of data that relied, here, largely upon the primary method of key informant interviews.

Racism in America

This was a "hands-on" research project that I designed (Levers et al., 2002) specifically for the doctoral students in my qualitative research methods course at Duquesne University. I asked the students to consider the experiences of race-related transgenerational trauma in African-American families within the larger democratic context of US society. I happened to be teaching the course at the same time that the Without Sanctuary exhibit (www.musarium.com/withoutsanctuary/main.html) was showing at the Andy Warhol Museum in Pittsburgh, where Duquesne University is located. This photo exhibit first opened in New York City, but not without contention within the African-American community. Its second venue was the Warhol Museum. In spite of controversial aspects, with its focus on the early 20th century practice by Anglo-Americans of lynching African-Americans, the images shown in the exhibit presented a powerful opportunity for local community dialogue about racism in America in general, and the effects of institutional racism in the Pittsburgh area in particular.

The museum was a wonderful partner in my pedagogical pursuits, and readily agreed to have a special showing. Because I was new to the University, a knowledgeable colleague assisted me in identifying and purposefully selecting mostly elderly leaders from the early civil rights movement (circa 1960s) in Pittsburgh. The students and I invited them to the special showing so that we all could view the exhibit together. After the viewing, we went to a space that the museum had prepared for us, where we held a focus group that examined the participants' experiences of racism. I had arranged for the focus group to be professionally videotaped, and the product was powerful beyond what my own words can ever express. I used the video as a tool to teach my students about conducting a focus group; they then analyzed the group discussion. Following this, each student was assigned to interview one of the focus group participants to learn how to conduct a key informant interview and to analyze the data thereby rendered. We were invited to give a keynote presentation on the project at a national qualitative research conference, and this turned out to be a powerful learning experience for students, professor, and attendees.

Vicarious Trauma Experienced by Child Protection Workers

One of my doctoral students completed her dissertation research (Jankoski, 2001) on the vicarious trauma or secondary victimization experienced by workers in the state's child protective system. Having previously worked in the system herself, and later working with the system as a consultant, she was very knowledgeable about the system. She also had speculations and numerous questions about the emotional effects on the workers of their daily professional dealings with abused children.

Because of her familiarity with the system, the investigator knew the key administrators to whom she might appeal for *entré* into the system as a researcher. She proposed conducting focus groups. The state system welcomed her, but as important, potential participants *wanted* to be included in the study. In fact, all my best mentoring efforts to "protect" this student from conducting excessive research proved fruitless. I had proposed a "purposefully selected" number of counties in which she would conduct the research; but, once she began conducting focus groups, county officials started to contact her to request that she visit their respective local offices to conduct focus groups. For a variety of defensible reasons, we altered her research design and expanded the study to meet the system's requests for greater participation. After she had conducted focus groups in nearly one third of the counties in the state, and the data had reached saturation, I insisted that she close off interviews.

Jankoski's (2001) investigation was not comprised exclusively of focus groups; it included some key informant interviews as well. However, these were incidental, and the main source for data remained the focus groups. She conducted 24 focus groups, thereby meeting with a total of 270 child protection workers in groups. An additional 30 workers participated in key informant interviews only, and 35 of the 270 focus group participants also participated in key informant interviews. Although using only focus groups in this study would have been adequate, the researcher elected to increase the trustworthiness of the investigation by augmenting the results of the focus groups with the results of the key informant interviews. A total of 300 participants was unusually large for a qualitative study, as was the number of focus groups, especially for a doctoral dissertation. However, the researcher's passion for the subject, as well as the enthusiasm of the child protection system for a better understanding of the phenomenon of vicarious trauma, led to the researcher's desire to conduct as thorough an investigation as possible.

ELEMENTS OF THE FOCUS GROUP PROCEDURE

PLANNING THE FOCUS GROUP

Making preliminary decisions about all aspects of the focus group is an obvious important early step in the planning process. An essential first step is ensuring that the research design has undergone a human subject review. The protocol for the focus group must be developed, and the size and composition of the group must be determined.

Human Subject Review

Every institution in the United States that accepts federal funds and that is involved in the conduct of research with people either has its own IRB or, in the case of small institutions, has access to the IRB of a larger "sister" organization. Approval must be granted before data collection can begin.

Protocol

The following protocol is the one that I devised for the Without Sanctuary focus group described in the previous section. I include it here as one example of a protocol and to emphasize the importance of considering many issues prior to going into the focus group.

Protocol for the Without Sanctuary Focus Group

I. Participant induction

    A. Explanation of the framework for the study

    B. Specific purposes of the study

    C. Risks of the study for participants

    D. Benefits of the study for participants and for society

    E. Voluntary status and ability to withdraw at any time

    F. Explanation of informed consent

    G. Addressing any questions or concerns

    H. Explanation of how confidentiality will be maintained and data secured

    I. Signature of informed consent forms

II. Group probes (Probes are questions that are designed to begin an exploration and to stimulate rich narrative responses that may go beyond the boundaries of how the question itself was formulated or posed.)

    A. What was your initial response to seeing *Without Sanctuary?*

    B. What do the images of the lynchings and other associated acts of terror bring to mind for you?

    C. How aware were you, before seeing the exhibit, of the historical legacy of racism in America? What conversations have taken place in your families? Have these kinds of conversations been possible with members of other races? What barriers exist that have prevented more communication about racism?

    D. How has the democratic system worked or not worked in your lifetime?

    E. How might successful culturally sensitive community dialogue about racism in Pittsburgh be facilitated?

    F. What could be a culturally appropriate system for community dialogue?

    G. What could be culturally appropriate public educational strategies?

    H. What needs to happen in our community?

III. Participant debriefing

    A. Addressing participants' concerns or affective responses to the group

    B. Facilitating questions about the group or the study

    C. Asking for any additional input

    D. Offering service information if requested by a participant

    E. Seeking permission for eventual input on accuracy of written transcript and interpretations

The sequencing of protocol procedures may differ from focus group to focus group, depending upon the nature and sensitivity of the research topic as well as the personal style of the group moderator. One researcher may choose to conduct the participant induction individually and prior to the time of the scheduled focus group, whereas another researcher may decide to use the participant induction as a part of the group process. In the previous example of the Without Sanctuary protocol, the probes were not used *verbatim*, but rather were indicated as potential prompts to stimulate discussion or to elaborate comments further. In this case, the participants had been given a copy of the protocol, along with other information about the project prior to the group, so that they would be familiar with the general line of inquiry.

The questions posed for this particular focus group arose from how I conceptualized the study. Another researcher investigating the same subject might have elected to operate from a different theoretical perspective, thereby making a different set of decisions than I made. In the latter case, the questions or probes posed to the group might look very different from those posed to the Without Sanctuary group.

Participant debriefing may be more or less urgent, again depending upon the nature of the research and its potential for raising the anxiety or discomfort level of the participants. The key intention that underlies the incorporation of participant induction and participant debriefing steps in the protocol is one of ethical conduct—that is, *researcher responsibility*. The researcher must take the responsibility to ensure that participants understand the nature of the study and what is being requested of them. The researcher also must take the responsibility to ensure that the emotional equilibrium of all participants is restored, especially in the face of group dynamics or content that may arouse anxiety or other feelings of discomfort.

Size and Composition

The literature about the size of focus groups presents varying opinions. For example, Edmunds (1999) has said that the ideal size should be eight to ten participants, and Morgan (1998a) has said that the typical group size is six to ten; however, some investigators have used slightly larger focus groups. For more complex issues, Berg (2001) and Krueger (1994) have recommended that the size of the group be smaller, suggesting no more than about seven participants. Perhaps the issue of exact size is far less important than knowing when to use a smaller group and when to use a larger group. The decision about size, then, depends upon the nature of the information being sought, the type and number of questions being posed, and the composition of the group.

Group composition differs, depending upon the nature of the study. Usually, participants are chosen for a focus group because they have some special knowledge or experience related to the subject of the investigation, or because they are stakeholders in the phenomenon being examined. However, depending upon the study, there may be an occasion for choosing a highly heterogeneous group. Morgan (1998a) has provided a detailed discussion of group size and composition, and Krueger and King (1998) offer an excellent discussion on the participatory aspect of focus groups and involving members of the community.

CONDUCTING THE FOCUS GROUP

In addition to a well-designed protocol, the next singular important aspect is the skill level of the group facilitator or moderator. The facilitator should have good listening and communication skills, and possess at least basic group facilitation skills and some experience in conducting groups. As is the case in leading any group, moderating a focus group depends somewhat on personal style. Krueger (1998c) has offered the following guiding principles of moderating:

1. Be interested in the participants—show positive regard.
2. Be a moderator, not a participant.
3. Be ready to hear unpleasant views.
4. Be ready to accept that you cannot necessarily moderate all groups.
5. Be ready to use your unique talents.

Another element to consider is the degree to which the focus group is structured. Morgan (1998a) has pointed out that more structure emphasizes the researcher's focus, whereas less structure emphasizes the interests of the group. The goals of the investigation, along with the facilitator's personal style, usually determine the degree of structure.

After explaining the study and attending to participant concerns, the facilitator is ready to begin posing questions. Focus group questions are open ended. Probing depends, to a large extent, upon the degree of structure. In a more structured focus group, the moderator tends to pose questions sequentially, moving from one question to the next only after sensing that the question has been answered in full. In a less structured focus group, there may be fewer formalized questions, and the moderator may tend to use probes that follow particular lines of participant response. Regardless of structure, Krueger (1998b) points to the importance of posing questions in a conversational manner, using clear and concise language that is appropriate for the intended audience.

ANALYZING THE FOCUS GROUP

Krueger (1998a) has stated: "Analysis begins with careful listening" (p. 3). Krueger (1998a) has also insightfully remarked that analysis is ". . . a fluid process rather than a series of isolated tasks" (p. 41). One mistake often made by researchers who are new to the qualitative research paradigm or to the focus group approach is to view analysis as a discreet stage; they then tend to become anxious about what they perceive as the "formal" analysis, which usually is conceived as a highly prescriptive treatment of a tape or its transcription. This anxiety occurs when the researcher has not been thinking about analysis from the onset—as part of a fluid process.

Qualitative analysis is complex; but, like all research, the results from focus groups are evidence based. It is in sifting through the evidence that the researcher looks for patterns and themes. Krueger (1998a) places levels of interpretation on a continuum, from raw data to description to interpretation to recommendation. Furthermore, he has described the four options for analyzing focus group data as ranging from transcript-based analysis, tape-based analysis, and note-based analysis, to memory-based analysis. He has identified the first option (transcript-based analysis) as the most time intensive and the most rigorous and has identified the last option (memory-based analysis) as the least time intensive and the least rigorous. Identifying the range of options in this manner assists the researcher in making some of the important decisions about the analytical protocol.

For most graduate students pursuing a master's thesis or a doctoral dissertation, the fourth option, in all likelihood, is not an option. The other three options may be used singularly or in combination. Full transcriptions of focus groups are very labor intensive in terms of their preparation for use, coding, and manipulation for analysis; a full transcript may or may not be necessary, depending upon the nature of the research. If full transcription is not absolutely necessary to the project, a videotape of the group that can be viewed and reviewed serves as a "text" that can be "read" and "coded" in ways similar to a transcript (Foucault, 1973; Gilman, 1985; Levers, 2001).

ILLUSTRATION: USING FOCUS GROUPS TO DESIGN HIV/AIDS INTERVENTIONS

I recently found myself cast in a unique research role. While working on my established research agenda examining contextual factors and cultural issues associated with the spread of HIV/AIDS in Botswana, located in southern Africa, and providing ongoing pro bono consultation services to a counseling center in northern Botswana, a safari camp there requested my assistance. And so it was that I lived in a tent for 18 days at a camp at the edge of the Okavango Delta, conducting focus groups as part of a larger research strategy to suggest to camp administrators an avenue for designing culturally relevant HIV/AIDS educational and prevention interventions for the camp workers. [The safari companies have numerous camps for tourists throughout the Okavango Delta, a pristine inland delta and wetlands swamp with incredible mazes of waterways and amazing wildlife. The larger camps have corporate headquarter camps in or near Maun, the one larger town at the edge of the Delta; I stayed at one of these headquarter camps. The camp is large, and many employees are trained there before being placed at smaller camps out in the Delta.] I offer my report here, as I delivered it to the camp's administrators, but slightly edited for this chapter.

INTRODUCTION TO THE REPORT

More than 70% of all persons in the world living with HIV/AIDS in 2000 were located in sub-Saharan Africa (UNAIDS, 2001). The HIV/AIDS pandemic has devastated the countries in the southern region of Africa (African Development Forum, 2000). Of these countries,

Botswana has been struck hard and is reported to have one of the highest prevalence rates of HIV/AIDS in the world. (At the time of this report, Botswana had the highest rate; the most recent United Nations report [UNAIDS, 2004] indicated that Swaziland has surpassed Botswana as having the highest prevalence rate.) The pandemic has affected Botswana's economy in significant ways. Tourism is one of the country's major industries, and the safari companies are high-stake contributors to this aspect of the economy. The industry employs mostly persons within the highest risk age groups, and many of the most talented young people involved in tourism have died or are dying. I was already in dialogue with workers and administrators associated with the tourism industry in the Okavango Delta area of north-central Botswana. Some of the largest safari companies are not able to provide useful HIV/AIDS-related programming to their workers, even though they recognize the need. One administrator reported that he had taped STD/AIDS documentaries on his home VCR to show at staff meetings. However, he expressed frustration to me that the televised programs were beyond the level of the less-educated staff members, that the shows "do not go deep enough on the important information," and that the videos are not culturally relevant. I was invited by several safari companies to conduct research that would assist in developing culturally appropriate interventions aimed at the specific needs of tourism workers in the face of the HIV/AIDS pandemic. The manpower concerns are evident, but all the company owners and managers with whom I spoke were profoundly concerned about their workers at the most human level.

RAMs were used in consultation with the administrators to assess staff training needs and to determine the appropriate cultural considerations for such training. The RAMs used for this inquiry included participant observation and key informant interviews, along with the focus groups that were planned as the major source of data collection. Focus groups were conducted with camp operations, housekeeping, and grounds staff. Two separate focus groups were conducted, each lasting for approximately two hours, and involved a total of 22 staff members. The data for each group were recorded separately and then analyzed for thematic content. In addition, nine key informant interviews were conducted, and they served to elaborate and clarify the data collected during the focus groups. As principal researcher, my participant observation required my residency at the camp. I lived in a tent at the camp for 18 days, enabling management and staff to interact freely with me.

In addition to the use of the previously specified RAMs, I used a technique to which I have referred in other studies (e.g., Levers, 2002) as using *cultural experts* to enhance the trustworthiness of the study. Cultural experts are indigenous members of the culture who are knowledgeable about the phenomenon being investigated and who can provide feedback to the researcher about the accuracy of the researcher's perceptions regarding cultural and phenomenon-specific issues. I originally developed this technique as a way to build cultural checks into studies in which I was the sole principal investigator. In the case of a research design using RAMs, Beebe (2001) has asserted that the RAP requires a team of at least two researchers. As the sole outside consultant on this project, I wanted to construct a research team to comply with this reasonable principle. I engaged the assistance of the administrator, who previously had told me about videotaping STD/AIDS programs for his staff. This administrator is an educated Motswana man who has extensive knowledge about his own culture, about the tourism/safari industry, and about the HIV/AIDS pandemic. He and I had developed a trusting and respectful relationship in which we felt comfortable having candid conversations about cultural and pandemic-related matters. We engaged in regular, intense dialogue before, during, and after the study.

The information resulting from the focus groups, and reinforced in the individual interviews is reported here in four sections. Aggregate results are then reported by theme, followed by a discussion of the results. Recommendations, based on the results, were submitted for consideration by camp management.

FOCUS GROUP 1

The first focus group was held early in the morning at the safari camp. This time frame was determined to be the most convenient time for operations staff, because it was shortly after workers arrived, but would not interfere significantly with duties, breaks, travel, and so forth.

GROUP CONSTITUTION AND PROTOCOL

Nine male and two female adult operations staff members participated. The Motswana camp manager, who was trusted by the employees, assisted me in handling language issues related to informed consent, and staff members attested that participation in the focus group was completely voluntary. The protocol for the group was introduced and explained. Participants initially were quiet, but after I explained my purpose for being in Maun and the purpose for the camp asking me to facilitate the group, the participants seemed comfortable and at ease. Conversation flowed easily, with most, but not all, participants responding to questions and offering comments. Not atypical for focus groups, several participants were much more verbal than the others. Although I did not require a translator, as all the participants were competent in the English language, sometimes the idiomatic nuance of an indigenous language word or phrase needed to be translated for me, and this was always done collectively by the participants.

ACCURATE INFORMATION

Clearly participants understood the factual information relating to safe sex practices and the use of condoms. However, they were helpful in assisting me to understand some of the cultural barriers that led some Batswana to refuse to consider the use of condoms.

One complex question related to the handling of body fluids prior to intercourse and specifically during foreplay, but before putting on a condom. We discussed practical aspects of this question, along with the issue of the amount of body fluid necessary for infection; but because I was not able to provide an absolute, accurate, scientific answer, I promised to get additional information to send back to them, which I did.

CULTURALLY RELEVANT TRAINING

The staff members suggested that culturally relevant training should include drama, video, or film. They made the point that actions and pictures are more powerful than words. One staff member said, "The people can see better than be told." Another staff member suggested that a film or video could show the stages of the illness and that this could be a powerful tool for raising awareness. Several staff members became enthusiastic about this, explaining that the programs with which they are most familiar tend to show a fit and healthy person who has contracted HIV. They emphasized that if an example is used showing the progression of the disease from early to late stages, the example would be more powerful in convincing viewers of the consequences of AIDS.

The staff members discussed the cultural ramifications of the stigma associated with HIV/AIDS and suggested that "people should be trained to better accept the sickness of those in the family and in the village." Some of the cultural issues that were identified included (1) people with any illness, but especially HIV/AIDS, are not accepted and are considered bad luck; (2) the workers have heard that in the Republic of South Africa some people with AIDS have been killed as a result of the stigma; (3) many African men believe that because there was nothing like AIDS in the past, their forefathers did not have to contend with it—the implication being that "if the ancestors do not have to deal with it, why should we?"; (4) people need to believe, first, that AIDS exists, before any intervention will be efficacious; and (5) the possibility of *thokolosi* was raised and discussed. (*Thokolosi* is a part of the indigenous traditional belief systems throughout various countries in sub-Saharan Africa. The *thokolosi* is believed to be a disembodied spirit, often thought to be sent by *dingaka* [traditional doctors] for the purpose of magic or sorcery.) On the last point, all the staff members agreed that the *thokolosi* exists, but that they have never actually witnessed the phenomenon. They asked whether the *thokolosi* could infect victims with HIV (just the week before, the local Maun newspaper, the *Ngami Times*, ran a story about a woman who had reported that she had been raped by a *thokolosi*). I answered that if *thokolosi* are real, a real *thokolosi* could not transmit HIV/AIDS, because there is no biophysical embodiment to transmit it. Conversely, I tried to explain the phenomenon that some people might experience as *thokolosi* that is actually hysteria conversion. A woman with a trauma history, for example, might experience *Mowa* (the Setswana word for trance state) as a reaction to the threat of sexual abuse and really believe that she experienced a *thokolosi* as a way of not having to deal with the reality of what occurred or the identity of the perpetrator (for example, if the perpetrator is her father or brother). I explained that in such a case, when the perceived *thokolosi* is actually a human being, then HIV certainly could be transmitted from one partner to another.

On the question of whether a staff training program could be effective, the staff members were enthusiastic about selected staff being trained as paraprofessional HIV/AIDS counselors who could then be looked to by other staff members for accurate information, advice, and counseling. They emphasized that this is an extremely sensitive issue and that the persons selected must be those who can be trusted—trusted both in terms of being perceived to have acquired an authoritative knowledge base about HIV/AIDS and of being able to keep confidential information.

The staff members stated that "there are many . . . companies [other than their own safari company]" and suggested that the management of all the safari companies in Botswana should be trained as well. They said that AIDS patients should be treated by management like other patients and not be stigmatized by their HIV/AIDS status. One staff member stated that "Management has tricks to quickly get rid of staff [who have AIDS]," and most of the participants expressed the belief that management should be trained to be more sympathetic. In places where management is not sympathetic, it is difficult for workers to come forward honestly about HIV/AIDS status. One person stated that "people are not paid well [at the safari companies]," and so this issue—risking job loss by coming forward—becomes even more compounded.

PSYCHOSOCIAL/CULTURAL ISSUES

The group raised several relevant psychosocial and cultural issues:

Hopelessness—There was a strong concern on the part of some of the staff members that the pandemic had become so extreme, there may be no way of changing its progression. This sentiment was echoed numerous times, relative to the pandemic, as a reflection of cultural fatalism.

Gender and sexual exploitation—The sex work industry (prostitution) has helped the disease to spread, and this is of special concern in relationship to single mothers "who have been left behind by the men." Participants viewed this as a serious problem locally. There also was agreement that the strong influence that African men have on the women contributes to HIV/AIDS as well as to other psychosocial and cultural problems.

Effects of awareness campaigns on children—One participant expressed concern for a son and brother, both eight years of age, who had been traumatized by the realism of a school assembly program aimed at making the children aware of HIV/AIDS. Later the same day, the boys then watched *Remokge* ("*We are Together*") on BTV and became very frightened. The staff member questioned whether such a tactic was appropriate for the age level and the developmental stage of the children.

Poverty—There was profound agreement that the issue of poverty underlies and exacerbates all other problems locally. A lively discussion of the overwhelming effects of poverty on HIV/AIDS and other problems concluded the focus group.

FOCUS GROUP 2

The second focus group was held early in the middle of the afternoon at the safari camp. This time frame was determined to be the most convenient time for the housekeeping and grounds staff, because it was shortly after the workers arrived for the late day shift, but would not interfere significantly with duties, breaks, travel, and so forth.

GROUP CONSTITUTION AND PROTOCOL

Nine female and two male adult housekeeping and grounds staff members participated. The Motswana camp manager, who was trusted by the employees, assisted me in handling language issues related to informed consent, and staff members attested that participation in the focus group was completely voluntary. As before, the protocol for the group was introduced and explained. Participants initially were quiet and seemed somewhat apprehensive, but after I explained my purpose for being in Maun and the purpose for the camp asking me to facilitate the group, the participants slowly became responsive, taking a bit more time to become comfortable than the first focus group. Although the discussion was hesitant at first, the conversation flowed more easily as the staff adjusted to me, with most, but not all, participants responding to questions and offering comments. Again, not atypical for focus groups, several participants were much more verbal than the others. As with the first focus group, although I did not require a translator, because all the participants were competent in the English language, sometimes the idiomatic nuance of an indigenous language word or phrase needed to be translated for me, and this was always done collectively by the participants.

ACCURATE INFORMATION

The general attitude in this group was that HIV/AIDS is a "scary situation." Some members questioned the efficacy of condom use "because they are not 100% effective." There was also a strong fear of being tested for HIV status among most of the staff. One very articulate participant was highly knowledgeable about the testing process and accurately described the ease of the process, but the other staff members expressed fearful attitudes that seemed to arise from a lack of accurate information. One participant volunteered that the immediate response to an HIV-positive test result would be to "hang myself." There was no understanding of the notion or frequency of false positives in the testing process, or even of misreporting.

One of the participants stated that "There is a big problem with the culture—most parents do not talk to children about sex." Discussion focused around the lack of accurate information in the home and how this then extends to the community and to Tswana society at large. In fact, the self-admonishment emerged that "There is no open talk about sex." One staff member complained that 18-year-olds are given condoms in school, but that there is little open and honest talk about sexuality—no talk about how to use the condom properly and no talk about prevention or alternative options to condom use. There was consensus that "Parents need to be involved." One participant said that Tswana culture needs to "... give people permission to talk." A concern also was expressed about the absence of accurate information regarding STDs, rape, incest, and their links to the HIV/AIDS pandemic.

The point was made that Maun is a hot spot for tourism, which brings a steady influx of people into the area, thereby setting the stage for a variety of types of sexual exploitation in the general vicinity. Group participants asserted that "community people must be taught about the killer." However, most staff members believed that there is *not* a high rate of rape in Maun or in the Okavango Delta, even though local statistics would indicate otherwise.

Finally, there seemed to be unanimous agreement on one issue related specifically to this camp. The staff members stated that condoms should be kept in multiple public places at the camp. Because the condoms are kept in the reception area, many staff members are reluctant to take them; they would like them to be kept in places where they can take them as needed, but not be seen by others.

The staff members concurred with the first focus group that culturally relevant training should include film or video. Some felt that effective training programs should target younger workers first, and that the programs should be fun and lively and include activities. The participants in this group also agreed that training some of the staff members would be effective. Most of the participants said that they would feel comfortable going to a trained staff member for information about HIV/AIDS.

PSYCHOSOCIAL/CULTURAL ISSUES

Several psychosocial and cultural issues were raised by the group:

Alcohol use—People drink alcohol and then do not use condoms. Alcohol is readily available; even if a person does not have much money, home brew or traditional beer can be bought cheaply everywhere. This was perceived not so much as a problem, but rather as a reality of life.

Boswagadi—Taboos exist concerning death and mourning. When the spouse dies, the widow becomes "tainted," and certain cleansing rituals must be completed prior to engaging in normal daily activities. In the case of some tribal customs, the brother-in-law may take on spousal duties. If he becomes ill, for example, or if rituals are ignored or taboos are otherwise violated, the resulting condition is known in the culture as *Boswagadi*. It is thought to be a cause of severe and lethal illness, and many AIDS deaths are attributed to *Boswagadi*.

Botho—One staff member raised the issue of *Botho* and its implication in the spread of HIV/AIDS. *Botho* implies the cultural transmission to Batswana children of polite manners and respectful conduct, especially toward elders. Under usual circumstances, this serves as a positive and efficacious cultural value. However, the premise here was that some adult men are abusing the concept of *Botho* to exploit very young girls for sexual purposes. It is quite powerful for a *Motswana* adult to say to a child, *"Ga ono botho!"* (you have bad botho); and because of the cultural strength of *Botho*, some young girls feel that they may not say "no" to adult men, and they therefore submit to this culturally coerced sexual abuse. There was agreement that such submission "... is a big problem in the culture ... [that] blocks [anti-AIDS efforts] in every way." Obviously when young girls are socialized to be submissive, the problem extends to adulthood, and as young women they have never learned to be assertive.

Gender and sexual exploitation—The participants noted in many ways and at several junctures in the conversation that sex workers have proliferated in the Maun area. The participants cited the sex work industry (prostitution) as being a large factor in the spread of HIV/AIDS. They targeted mothers who "sell" their daughters for money or household resources. They also discussed the instances of step-fathers sexually abusing their step-daughters.

Traditional healers—Some participants mentioned the traditional practice of scarification, which entails the *Dingaka* (traditional healers) making small cuts into the flesh and usually inserting herbs into the cuts. Participants identified as problematic the *Dingaka* who use the same razor blades from person to person.

MULTIPLE FOCUS GROUPS

After analyzing the data and considering the variation in themes, as well as the overlap in themes, it became obvious that within the context of this study, conducting more than one focus group was important. The differing group composition and dynamics allowed for a richer variance of data. The variation in data further illuminated previous themes and identified new ones.

KEY INFORMANT INTERVIEWS

Several individual interviews were conducted with relevant management members prior to the focus groups to assist me in understanding the magnitude of the problem. Several key informant interviews also were conducted after the focus groups, with both management and staff. In total, nine interviews were conducted; these included five management members and four staff members. The purpose for conducting the key informant interviews was to delineate the parameters of the problem, to understand contextual issues better, and to elaborate upon and clarify the results of the focus groups. No new findings emerged from the interviews; rather, the information served to reinforce and triangulate the data that arose from the focus groups, thus establishing a higher level of trustworthiness regarding the findings of the study. For this reason, and because of the private nature of the personal interviews as well as the relatively small number of employees involved in the study, I elected not to report the individual interview data separately. To preserve confidentiality, the results of the interviews were aggregated with the results of the focus groups.

PARTICIPANT OBSERVATION IMPRESSIONS

My residential presence for an extended period allowed me an under-standing of day-to-day "camp life," which assisted me greatly throughout this consultation. My tent was centrally located, but a bit to the side, so that many staff members felt comfortable stopping by to talk. I easily became a part of the daily routine. My general impressions were that staff members have reasonable autonomy and feel comfortable expressing ideas and concerns to management, especially regarding the topics associated with HIV/AIDS. Participant observations helped me to facilitate group discussion in a sensitive manner and served to clarify and support the data that emerged from focus groups and interviews. Participant observations further assisted in refining analysis of the data. Living on-site ensured exposure to cultural experts, with whom I was able to discuss analyses and interpretations and from whom I was able to obtain immediate critical feedback.

RESULTS AND DISCUSSION

Based on the RAM findings, three major themes emerged through collapsing or subsuming the information divulged in the groups and inter-views. These themes were accurate information, culturally relevant training, and psychosocial and cultural issues. The themes are significant in that they were generated by key stakeholders, especially staff. This information is reported in Table 13-1.

The results of this consultative study suggest the need for *accurate* and *user-friendly* information about HIV/AIDS. Both management and staff expressed a high level of enthusiasm for designing HIV/AIDS-related training for camp employees. The data clearly imply the importance of such training being grounded in an appropriate cultural context. The following section delineates suggestions for consideration by the camp management in implementing such training.

RECOMMENDATIONS

The camp management is interested in providing staff training relative to HIV/AIDS and has requested that recommendations be made regarding such training. Camp staff are eager to receive such training and are par-ticularly enthusiastic about having selected staff receive paraprofessional HIV/AIDS peer–counselor training. Staff assert that they would consult trained peer staff members for information and advice, if those selected are peers who can be trusted easily. Staff also feel that it is important for management to receive management-level training associated with

TABLE 13-1 Themes

Theme	Thematic Content
Accurate information	Access to accurate information regarding HIV/AIDS is necessary and vital. Although many in the community have access to accurate information relating to safe sex practices, there are cultural barriers that lead some Batswana, especially males, to refuse to use condoms. One area of confusion involves accurate information about safe handling of body fluids during foreplay and before putting on the condom.
	Some Batswana question the efficacy of condom use because they are not 100% effective. There seems to be a lack of accurate information about testing for HIV/AIDS that has led to fear about being tested. For cultural reasons, parents typically do not speak with their children about sexual matters. This tendency seems to be nested within the society at large, so that young people move into young adulthood without much accurate information related to sexuality, which of course extends to issues related to HIV/AIDS, STDs, rape, and incest. Because Maun is a center for tourism, thus bringing an influx of people into the area and thereby setting the stage for a variety of types of sexual exploitation, there is a need for community-based awareness, sensitization, and educational programming that emphasizes problems associated with tourism, especially in relationship to sexual abuse. Staff appreciate that camp management wants to provide accurate information, but they wish that this attitude would extend to increased privacy with regard to where condoms are placed. They would like to have condoms placed in multiple sites rather than only in the reception area, so that they can obtain the condoms discreetly.
Culturally relevant training	The staff view film or video as the most effective way of providing accurate information about HIV/AIDS. The issue of stigma must be addressed educationally. Stigma is characterized by associated cultural factors and must be addressed in culturally specific ways. Participants were enthusiastic about selected staff members being trained as paraprofessional HIV/AIDS counselors. Nearly all participants stated that they would feel comfortable seeking information and advice from trained peers. Participants believe that the management of safari companies should receive training as well, especially regarding the treatment of staff having AIDS as no different than staff having other illnesses.
Psychosocial/cultural issues	*Hopelessness*—pandemic so extreme, no way to change progression; *Alcohol use*—when people drink, no use of condoms; prevalent and easy access to traditional beer; *poverty*—underlies all other problems locally
	Gender—sex work industry has helped spread AIDS. Sex workers have proliferated in Maun. Single mothers may become sex workers. Problem locally—mothers who "sell" daughters for money or resources; incestual abuse of female children; control Motswana man has over woman, submissiveness of women
	Children—AIDS awareness campaigns that are not age appropriate, strategies that scare—even traumatize—younger children)
	Traditional practices—*Dingaka* who use unclean razor blades; *Boswagadi* (belief that widow is tainted and cause of severe illness); *Botho* (the practice of socializing Batswana children in the virtues of polite manners and respectful conduct, because it may be implicated in the spread of HIV/AIDS when it is misused by adult males to exploit the cultural submissiveness of young girls for sexual purposes)

TABLE 13-2   Recommendations

Need	Recommendation
Training	General staff training; purposefully selected staff to be trained as paraprofessional HIV/AIDS peer counselors; management training
Cultural relevancy	Aspects of Tswana culture, as well as other local cultures, must be considered in the design of all levels of training; training must be developed to be "user friendly"
Camp condoms	Condoms are currently available only at Reception; staff strongly urge management to place condoms at multiple sites where they can be taken discreetly

HIV/AIDS as well. This suggests three types of training: general staff training, selected peer–counselor training, and management training. It is imperative that all levels of training be designed in ways that are culturally sensitive, culturally relevant, and culturally specific. Table 13-2 presents the major recommendations for consideration by camp management.

The management team of the camp was highly receptive to the report. They invited me to meet with them for a discussion about implementation. Representative participation led to widespread acceptance of the changes that were the easiest to initiate. Although the points in Table 13-2 may seem obvious to readers, it was not obvious within the context of the study, nor would solutions likely have been accepted in the absence of interviews and focus groups.

DISCUSSION OF THE ILLUSTRATION

I am hopeful that the previous straightforward and relatively short reporting of two focus groups serves as an instructional example. There are many facets of the research process represented here that could be discussed; however, I would like to focus briefly on only three in this discussion: the importance of culture, researcher openness to discovery, and researcher decision making.

IMPORTANCE OF CULTURE

Culture was at the heart of this small study, and it was important that, as the principal investigator, I had at least a basic understanding of the role played by culture in this context. Botswana is a country of multiple African and tribal cultures, with multiple cultural overlays and tensions within cultures, such as modern versus traditional, urban versus rural, postcolonial sensibilities in the face of remnants of colonialism, and a return to Afrocentric religious tenets in the face of formal or mainstream religions.

Resources for and access to many modern social and health care services tend to be relatively centralized in the capital and other larger cities, and less available in the more rural and remote areas. The location of this study was in a more remote area of the country, and most of the participants came from rural villages where beliefs and practices remain traditional.

African traditional beliefs and practices, including medical practices, are embedded in African cosmology. Unlike the Cartesian premise of modern Western science, but like other indigenous worldviews, mind and body are not separated; therefore, there can be no separation of that which is scientific from that which is spiritual or existential. Contextual influences relating to the worldview of a particular culture are embedded in that culture and remain important to how members of the culture make meaning of their lives. Although this is a premise open for interpretation, it may well be the most salient part of the explanation for most Western misunderstandings of indigenous knowledge systems in general, and for the failure of so many programs aimed at mitigating the spread of HIV/AIDS in southern Africa specifically.

Understanding the context for these traditional beliefs and practices was essential in this study, especially as particular issues arose. For example, constructs such as *thokolosi* and *boswagadi* do not seem nearly so "strange" or "exotic" when I understand that they represent inherent African ethnomedical conceptualizations of illness and the cause of disease. Rather than attempting to categorize and evaluate, because I had at least baseline knowledge about the cultural context, I was able to understand how these constructs make sense to the participants as they attempt to make meaning of something that seems strange and exotic to them—HIV/AIDS.

OPENNESS TO DISCOVERY

During the process of conducting any type of qualitative research, it is imperative that the investigator maintains a stance of being nonjudgmental with regard to the culture, phenomenon, or individuals being examined. It is this openness that leads the researcher to discovery. Using the example just presented, it was important that I remained open to the existence of *thokolosi* and *boswagadi*, as well as to how these constructs help individuals in the culture to make meaning about HIV/AIDS within the parameters of the culture. By remaining open, rather than judgmental, I was able to probe for nuances within the focus groups and to discover meanings that could help me in better understanding these beliefs. With a greater knowledge about such cultural constructs, I became better positioned for considering how to construct culturally relevant instruction. Obviously, I am not advocating for an instructional module that necessarily teaches or promotes belief in these constructs; but rather, knowing of their existence and how intricately woven they are into the tapestry of local cultures, I believe that instruction can be calibrated to take indigenous understandings into consideration.

RESEARCHER DECISION MAKING

Throughout the process of conceptualizing, designing, conducting, and analyzing research, the researcher is called upon to make numerous decisions. I needed to make a rather simple decision at the beginning of the study. I would have preferred slightly smaller groups. This means that either I could have facilitated two groups with fewer members, or I could have broken the two groups of eleven participants into three or four focus groups. Of course the camp management was eager to see the least amount of interference with camp work by the research activities, but I was given the flexibility. I was interested in having the maximum number of people involved while using the least amount of time. When I considered all the factors, I decided that even though most of the literature says that number of participants should be up to ten, I wanted to follow my sense of "natural occurrence." There were eleven workers each in the operations and in the housekeeping and ground departments, and I ultimately decided that it was important to keep the participants in their natural groupings.

A decision that I had to make during one of the focus groups was a bit more difficult. A question was posed to me, and I was not sure of the answer. I had to make a decision about how to best respond. I could have sidestepped the question by saying that I was asking the questions and they were providing the answers. I could have asked them: What do you think? I could have saved face by giving them what I thought was the answer, even though I had looked into the matter previously and saw that it was a bit more complicated and needed further research. I elected to allow myself to be questioned, and I elected to report honestly that I did not have all the answers, that the matter was complex, and that I needed to obtain the most accurate information possible before rendering an answer. Another researcher might have made a different decision based on a different, but also justifiable, rationale.

The point here is that there are many junctures in the research process that require (1) more than a rudimentary understanding of local culture, (2) openness to discovery, and, (3) the need for the researcher to make decisions—sometimes with time for informed consideration, and at other times immediate and on-the-spot. There is usually no one *right way* to proceed in conducting focus groups. Rather, every step of the qualitative research process depends upon the context of the research and the investigator's theoretical framework.

CONCLUSION

I recall sitting in my university office with a young doctoral student who had approached me about advising her dissertation research. She explained to me her interest in getting at a particular mental health training issue (Stinchfield, 2004), but from a grassroots and consumer perspective. She then hesitantly presented her rationale for thinking that the use of focus groups might be a reasonable strategy for obtaining the information that she desired. Her reticence stemmed from her fear that perhaps no faculty member would see the merit in her idea. However, I was intellectually intrigued by her proposal. I was delighted to support this student's work (Stinchfield, 2003), because her ideas and the rationale were robust, and because I think that more human service-related research needs to be hands on and grounded in the real world. This was precisely what she was proposing, and this is precisely the possibility opened up by the use of focus groups.

This chapter was intended as a *hands-on* introduction to the *real-world* use of focus groups, especially in psychology and counseling. I am hopeful that this chapter also served to open up possibilities for thinking about this methodology in new and different ways. The final *hands-on* contribution here is the following *real-world* tools section.

TOOLS FOR USING FOCUS GROUPS IN QUALITATIVE RESEARCH

An extremely useful tool for anyone interested in focus groups, is Sage's six-volume *Focus Group Kit* (Morgan and Krueger, 1998). This "kit" is a boxed set of user-friendly paperback books with many helpful annotations. The volumes are, respectively, (1) *The Focus Group Guidebook* (Morgan, 1998b), (2) *Planning Focus Groups* (Morgan, 1998a), (3) *Developing Questions for Focus Groups* (Krueger, 1998b), (4) *Moderating Focus Groups* (Krueger, 1998c), (5) *Involving Community Members in Focus Groups* (Krueger and King, 1998), and (6) *Analyzing and Reporting Focus Group Results* (Krueger, 1998a). The contents of the kit offer a wealth of information and are appropriate for use by a student who is new to the research arena, as well as by the experienced qualitative researcher. Numerous other print resources, in addition to the six volumes in the *Focus Group Kit*, are listed in the reference section at the end of this chapter.

There are many electronic resources available online, but several stand out. Six Sigma (2004) has a website with links to a number of short articles. The articles are more oriented toward the business sector and not the social sciences; however, the articles are practical, get straight to the point, and offer baseline information about focus groups. Lewis (2000) reviews the literature regarding the use of focus groups in qualitative inquiries. Finally, a manual (Dawson, Manderson, and Tallo, 1993) for training moderators to conduct focus groups can be found on-line.

REFERENCES

African Development Forum (2000). *Theme 1 ADF Document: HIV/AIDS and economic development in sub-Saharan Africa.*

AIDS Control and Prevention (AIDSCAP) Program. (1999). *Behavior change—a summary of four major theories.* Arlington, VA: Family Health International, Behavioral Research Unit. Also available at www.fhi.org/en/aids/aidscap/aidspubs/behres/bcr4theo.html (March 2003). [Family Health International, funded by the United States Agency for International Development.]

Beebe, J. (2001). *Rapid assessment process: An introduction.* Walnut Creek, CA: Altamira Press.

Berg, B. L. (2001). *Qualitative research methods for the social sciences* (4th ed.). Boston: Allyn and Bacon.

Bogardus, E. S. (1926). The group interview. *Journal of Applied Sociology, 10,* 372–382.

Dawson, S., L. Manderson, and V. L. Tallo. (1993). *A manual for the use of focus groups: Methods for social research in disease.* Boston, MA: International Nutrition Foundation for Developing Countries (INFDC). Also available at www.unu.edu/unupress/food2/UIN03E/uin03e00.htm#Contents (April 2004).

Devos, S. (July 9, 2004). Botswana mixes old and new ways in AIDS war. *MSNBC International News Online.* Available at www.msnbc.msn.com/id/5403208/.

Edmunds, H. (1999). *The focus group research handbook.* Chicago: NTC Business Books.

Foucault, M. (1973). *The order of things: An archaeology of the human sciences.* New York: Vintage.

Gilman, S.L. (1985). *Difference and pathology: Stereotypes of sexuality, race and madness.* Ithaca, NY: Cornell University Press.

Handwerker, W. P. (2001). *Quick ethnography.* Walnut Creek, CA: Altamira Press.

Jankoski, J. (2002). *The impact of vicarious trauma on the child welfare worker.* Unpublished doctoral dissertation. Duquesne University, Pittsburgh, PA.

Krueger, R. A. (1994). *Focus groups: A practical guide for applied research* (2nd ed.). Thousand Oaks, CA: Sage.

Krueger, R. A. (1998a). *Analyzing and reporting focus group results.* Thousand Oaks, CA: Sage.

Krueger, R. A. (1998b). *Developing questions for focus groups.* Thousand Oaks, CA: Sage.

Krueger, R. A. (1998c). *Moderating focus groups.* Thousand Oaks, CA: Sage.

Krueger, R. A., and J. A. King. (1998). *Involving community members in focus groups.* Thousand Oaks, CA: Sage.

Kumar, K. (1993). An overview of rapid appraisal methods in development settings. In Kumar, K. (Ed.). *Rapid appraisal methods* (pp. 8–22). Washington, DC: World Bank Regional and Sectoral Studies.

Levers, L. L. (2001). Representations of psychiatric disability in fifty years of Hollywood film: An ethnographic content analysis. *Theory and Science Pedagogy, 2.* Available at http://theoryandscience.icaap.org/content/vol002.002/lopezlevers.html.

Levers, L. L. (2002). Northern Namibian teachers on the effects of violence, poverty, and privation on young children's development: School-based countermeasures. *Journal of Children and Poverty, 8,* 101–140.

Levers, L. L. (2003). *The consultative workshop as a qualitative method of inquiry: The case of teachers and counselors working with AIDS orphans in Botswana.* Presented at the

15th Ethnographic and Qualitative Research 2003 Annual Conference. Published in conference monograph. Also Available at www.education.duq.edu/institutes/PDF/ papers2003/Levers1.pdf.

Levers, L. L. (in press). An ethnographic analysis of traditional healing in southern Africa: Indigenous knowledge, crosscultural implications, and HIV/AIDS. *One people, multiple dreams of a different world.* Conference monograph. Jinja, Uganda: Mpambo Press.

Levers, L. L., E. Mosely, C. Conte, J. Darr, H. Moore, D. Shafer, C. Snyder, T. Stinchfield, F. Williams, and A. Wood. (June 2002). *Experiences of racism and transgenerational trauma in one African American Community: Portraiture of historical-stirrings-within-a-democratic-context in response to witnessing "Without Sanctuary."* Presented at the 14th Ethnographic and Qualitative Research 2002 Annual Conference, June, Pittsburgh, PA. Conference monograph. Aso available at www.education.duq.edu/institutes/PDF/ papers2002/Leversetal.pdf.

Levers, L. L., E. Mosley, B. Pickett, L. Angelone, T. Bigante, L. Gruber, R. Hoffman, E. Kitchens–Stephens, S. Rosenblatt, J. E. Schoenfelder, T. Tinsley, and S. Tracy. (2003). *Views on diversity and inclusion in Pittsburgh: A community-based rapid appraisal.* Presented at the 15th Ethnographic and Qualitative Research 2003 Annual Conference, June, Pittsburgh, PA. Conference monograph. Also available at www.education.duq.edu/ institutes/PDF/papers2003/Levers2.pdf.

Lewis, M. (2000). Focus group interviews in qualitative research: A review of the literature. *Action Research E-Reports, 2.* Available at www.fhs.usyd.edu.au/arow/arer/ 002.htm.

Merton, R. K., M. Fiske, and P. L. Kendall. (1990). *The focused interview* (2nd ed.). New York: Free Press. [Originally Published 1956.]

Merton, R. K., and P. L. Kendall. (1946). The focused interview. *American Journal of Sociology, 51,* 541–557.

Morgan, D. L. (1997). *Focus groups as qualitative research* (2nd ed.). Qualitative research methods series, vol. 16. Thousand Oaks, CA: Sage.

Morgan, D. L. (1998a). *Planning focus groups.* Thousand Oaks, CA: Sage.

Morgan, D. L. (1998b). *The focus group guidebook.* Thousand Oaks, CA: Sage.

Morgan, D. L., and R. A. Krueger. (1998). *The focus group kit.* Thousand Oaks, CA: Sage.

Six Sigma. (2004). Available at www.isixsigma.com/vc/focus_groups/.

Stinchfield, T. A. (2003). *Family-based mental health therapists' perceptions of the competencies specific to home-based therapy.* Unpublished doctoral dissertation. Duquesne University, Pittsburgh, PA.

Stinchfield, T. A. (2004). *Clinical competencies specific to family-based therapy. Counselor Education and Supervision, 43,* 286–300.

UNAIDS (United Nations Programme on HIV/AIDS). (2000). *Collaboration with traditional healers in HIV/AIDS prevention and care in sub-Saharan Africa: A literature review.* Geneva, Switzerland: Joint United Nations Programme on HIV/AIDS.

UNAIDS (United Nations Programme on HIV/AIDS). (2001). *Report on the global HIV/AIDS epidemic.* Geneva, Switzerland: Author.

UNAIDS (United Nations Programme on HIV/AIDS). (2004). *2004 Report on the global HIV/AIDS epidemic.* Geneva, Switzerland: Author.

United States Agency for International Development (USAID). (1996). *Performance monitoring and evaluation: Using rapid appraisal methods.* Washington, DC: USAID Center for Development Information and Evaluation. Also available at www.dec.org/evals.html. Accessed December 8, 2001.

Williams, A., and L. Katz. (2001). The use of focus group methodology in education: Some theoretical and practical considerations. *International Electronic Journal for Leadership in Learning, 5*(3). Also available at www.ucalgary.ca/~iejll/volume5/katz.html.

BIOGRAPHICAL BACKGROUND

LISA LOPEZ LEVERS, PhD, LPCC, NCC, CRC, is an Associate Professor of Counselor Education and Supervision at Duquesne University. Before arriving at Duquesne in 2000, she chaired the Counseling and Human Development Department at the University of Rochester (1996–2000), worked as an Associate Professor of Counselor Education at the University of New Orleans (1994–1996), and coordinated the Rehabilitation Counselor Education Program at Ohio University (1989–1994). Prior to becoming an academician, she worked for 15 years in the community mental health system, with a clinical emphasis on trauma, the impact of violence on children, and psychiatric rehabilitation.

Dr. Levers obtained her PhD in Counselor Education and Human Development, as well as her MEd in Rehabilitation Counseling and BA in English Literature at Kent State University. When she completed her doctoral dissertation in 1988, qualitative research was not widely accepted in the field of counselor education. Her examination of the depiction of psychiatric disability in Hollywood films was the first qualitative study permitted in her department.

Dr. Levers has directed 18 dissertations, nearly all using qualitative research methods. Her publications include qualitative investigations of the portrayal of mental illness in film, the effects of trauma on children, and the connections between African indigenous healing and culturally relevant counseling. She has held many consultancies related to counseling, supervision, training, and rehabilitation; and she has been awarded grants to conduct research, develop systems of care, and provide counselor training in diverse contexts within the United States, in southern African countries, in Russia, and in Spain.

Dr. Levers received a Fulbright (2003–2004) and lived for one year in Gaborone, the capital of Botswana, located in southern Africa. As a Fulbright Scholar, she taught at the University of Botswana and conducted her research, an examination of contextual factors and cultural issues associated with HIV/AIDS in southern Africa. She has become active in advocating for children who have been orphaned or are otherwise affected by the HIV/AIDS pandemic in the southern African region.

Questions
and Responses

Although most of the following issues are addressed in previous chapters, the queries included here are frequently presented by persons first exploring qualitative research. Although I intend the responses to be representative of what other qualitative researchers would say, I imagine that colleagues from different backgrounds than mine would respond somewhat differently in many instances.

What is the relevance of qualitative research? Is it just to get engaged with something of personal interest?

No, definitely not, although one should be interested in the subject matter, or the research won't go very far. However, qualitative research goes way beyond personal amusement, to show what a phenomenon or situation is like, how it evolves, and how that matters for individuals in that situation. For example, my studies of becoming angry help readers to recognize signs of their own that they are moving toward becoming angry, and to recognize points at which they can continue their previous course and not become angry. We can see the deleterious impact of blaming others, on both self and others. We can compare these studies with those on resentment, frustration, hostility, and others, to see what the essential differences and similarities might be. Qualitative research is uniquely suited for discerning humans' participation in what happens to them. Findings are useful for theory, social policy, counseling and psychotherapy, and for personal reflection.

Are questionnaire summaries qualitative research?

Not if the respondents are limited to specified response options (multiple choice) or to short answers that lead to measurement of answers. Just because data are not in quantitative form does not mean that their use constitutes research, qualitative or otherwise. However, of course requests for descriptions of actual situations, or recordings of actual situations, can provide data for qualitative analysis.

Why do you encourage familiarity with traditional research methods? Why do so many conventions of traditional research appear in this volume?

Because qualitative research *is* research. What sets qualitative research apart from experimental traditions is its subject matter, which requires shifts in philosophical assumptions and methods of analysis, but a continuation of traditional rigor and of insistence on public grounding of findings.

Why do qualitative researchers use so many esoteric terms, like *discourse, deconstruct, reflexive,* **and so on? Why don't they just use ordinary terms?**

I agree that sometimes the language seems a bit clubby—badges of being in a particular special group—and when that is the case, the language does not serve to communicate with other people. However, the terms have come into being when our usual social science vocabulary fails us— that is, when it cannot express new perspectives and ways of knowing and their truths and limitations. I am all for trying to communicate effectively among different approaches, and this book is part of that effort. With regard to this book, I suggest that if a chapter's introductory sections seem esoteric that you read the research report first, and then go back to the introduction; I think that you will then find the language was well calculated to evoke particular ways of looking at data. This book's glossary may also help.

Are "data," "participant reports," "participant descriptions," "text," and "protocols" all the same thing?

Mostly. "Data" and "text" can also include outsider observations, transcriptions of conversation, existing records, and any quantitative measures used along with these forms. I prefer not to refer to participant reports as "protocols" for two reasons. First, the term often is confused with etiquette and ceremonial tradition; and second, researchers have often loosely referred to "protocol analysis," although what we analyze is not that record for itself but rather the lived situation to which the description provides access.

I see that qualitative research requires creativity; one can't just "run" subjects, tally outcomes, and crunch that data through a statistical research program. But doesn't all research, including experimental research, require creativity?

Yes, productive research of any sort involves creatively imagining what designs would be most fruitful, the circumstances in which findings might differ, the implications of findings for received understandings of the subject matter, and imagining the most evocative ways of conveying findings, implications, and suggestions for further study.

In the text, some authors refer to "experiential *or* phenomenological." Are they not the same? I gather "phenomenal" differs somehow from "phenomenological?"

Experience typically refers to what people report directly about how they found themselves affected. *Phenomenal* similarly refers to self-reports about how an object or situation appeared. Phenomenological psychology researchers, however, use *phenomenological* to refer to the study of (*ology*) phenomenal accounts to grasp what they imply about lived relations to the object or situation; about assumptions, meanings, past and future as well as present; and the relations of discerned aspects of a phenomenon to each other and to the overall understanding.

Why do you say *"empirical* phenomenology?"

To differentiate psychological research from philosophical reflection. As psychologists, we are interested in concrete events and specific situations, and in making observations or self-reports (empirical data) available to other researchers. Phenomenological philosophers typically are more interested in reflecting on how things appear to humans to identify the basic (ontological) character of human knowing.

Is there a difference between "method" and "methodology?" I see both terms used.

Methodology is the study of or science of (*ology*) method. So, properly, it should be used when one is discussing the rationale for a particular method, perhaps its philosophical grounding or its current variations. This term gained usage as qualitative researchers used it as a heading for discussion for their nonexperimental assumptions and method. However, by now many researchers use the term interchangeably with *method*— description of participants, data-gathering procedures, and procedures for data analysis.

Is qualitative research dependent on language in that both its data and findings are mostly descriptions? Does reliance on language limit discovery?

Yes and yes. But experimental research too relies on language, including the language of numbers. I think we gain more understanding when we are willing to struggle through language freshly—inventing words, using metaphors—rather than relying on existing words and categories. I am not in agreement with theorists who believe that language totally structures thought or totally limits discovery.

Are some people better suited than others to conduct qualitative research?

Yes, just as some people are better at any research than others are. For all forms of research, success is maximized by enthusiasm about the topic and the research process, confidence from earlier projects that the work will be worthwhile, willingness to repeatedly regroup, acceptance that one will have to struggle to be articulate about one's shifting understandings and approaches, patience with setbacks, openness and flexibility, readiness to give up earlier beliefs, welcoming of serendipitous events, enjoyment of discipline and rigor, respect for procedure while realizing that it is a human-made convention, and, finally, appreciation that one is part of a wonderful (wonder-full) undertaking, to which one is contributing.

However, persons who prefer technical work are especially handicapped in undertaking qualitative research. In all forms of research, there are many phases that involve primarily technical work, sometimes undertaken by specialists or assistants. Just as some psychologists prefer test administration and subsequent classification to collaborative and individualized psychological assessment, so some psychologists prefer the technical aspects of carrying out a project to pursuing broader research.

People who are generally better suited to conduct qualitative research regard events holistically, can place themselves easily in others' situations, are intrigued by the challenge to find the best word or create the best phrase to fit data, and are imaginative and enjoy innovative effort. These researchers often draw on familiarity with the arts and humanities, and on cultural and historical variation.

Are qualitative research computer programs useful?

Sure. Many researchers find them helpful. However, of course, they cannot design research projects, interpret data for you, or craft a statement of findings. They function as specialized word processors offering technical assistance with such tasks as reorganizing text, collating text to which you have assigned various codes that you have developed, cutting and pasting text, and achieving frequency counts of various terms.

With regard to qualitative research, are "procedure" and "method" the same?

No, just as they are not the same in experimental research. For both research approaches, *method* refers to the general means of acquiring and analyzing data—for example, an ABAB study of reinforcing verbalizations, a correlational study of SAT scores and graduation rates, a discourse analysis of psychotherapy dialogue, or an empirical phenomenological study of becoming angry. For both research approaches, *procedure* refers to the many steps that are taken along the way: acquiring subjects/participants, deciding on any equipment, means of obtaining data and preparing them for analysis, conducting statistical or qualitative analyses, and presenting findings.

In qualitative research, the researcher's presence to the data seems to be critical to the findings. Surely you don't assume that all analysts would come up with the same understandings?

No, of course not. But variation is not necessarily a deficiency of method. Assuming serious researchers, the humanly inevitable differences in what is noted, grasped, and represented bespeak the complexity and ambiguity of human phenomena. Somewhat similar to experimental researchers, we gradually come to agreements on some aspects of a phenomenon and continue to study others until substantive consensus is reached.

But is qualitative research scientific?

Yes. Historically, science has differed from other fields of study by insisting that its data be available to the senses (versus philosophical reflections), its methods be repeatable by other investigators, and its conclusions be open to inspection in relation to the data on which they are based. Qualitative research meets these values. But because its subject matter is lived worlds and lived interactions, its empirical data are reports of those realms rather than measurements before and after interventions. Those reports are public, as are methods of study and findings.

Is "hard science" a proper comparative term with qualitative research?

No. The term originated in experimental psychology's relying on "hard data"—data that could be seen and manipulated—data that presumably were real, in contrast to the so-called "soft" impressions of clinicians, philosophers, and theologians. However, today it is generally acknowledged that *hard data* often are actually indirect—largely derived from theoretical constructs that guided development of artificial situations that produced responses that could be transformed into measures. The data often are not so "hard," and the term is no longer informative.

I think the term *hard science* also has implied that such science is hard to do, like often-cited rocket science or brain surgery. By now, readers of qualitative research recognize that it too is challenging and demanding, as are experimental research studies that fall short of rocket science and brain surgery. Anyway, qualitative research, like categorical research, uses empirical data—in this case, self-reports of situations or descriptions of observations. These data can be shared, similar to the data of experimental/ statistical research. Both research approaches must meet rigorous standards.

I still do not see how qualitative research can be scientific when it is so subjective. How do you account for this?

Qualitative research is not merely subjective, merely one person's point of view, or biased toward a particular outcome. If any of these characterizations fits a qualitative study, then that study was not competently conducted. Subjectivity sets humans apart from the objects of natural science, and makes qualitative study possible. Subjectivity is our access to shared meaning, not a liability. Please note that human science is empirical, checkable, and rigorous, but not in the laboratory tradition.

But qualitative research is always interpretive, right?

Right. So is all human perception. Interpretation at many levels is also part of all science, although experimental/statistical research attempts to minimize it in its procedures. In contrast, qualitative research, having a different subject matter, explores interpretation as it occurs in everyday life, and systematically uses interpretation in that exploration.

With regard to subjectivity being in a sense both the subject matter and the means of understanding in qualitative research, is not subjectivity also involved in experimental research in selection of variables, formulation of hypotheses, and making sense of statistical findings?

Yes, of course. But in both research approaches we wish to avoid personal bias—uncorrected assumptions, often unacknowledged—that may predetermine outcomes.

I've heard psychologists say that qualitative research is based on postmodern ideas that all knowledge is relative and just subjective. How would you respond?

I say that all knowledge is relative, in that what we know depends on our questions, our frameworks, our prior knowledge, our methods, our times, and other contexts. Knowledge based on experimental research is similarly relative to its methods, frameworks, and so on. Qualitative research *does* explicitly rely on personal experience as access to its subject matter, but its findings are not *merely* subjective. They hold up coherently under inspection by others. Qualitative research findings are based on data that can be shared (transcriptions, tapes, and so forth), and specified procedures for gathering data and specified steps for analysis of data. Other researchers can check their understandings of data against those of earlier researchers. And, of course, all research advances through recognition of limitations of earlier work, through new insights upon examination of earlier work, and through undertaking new study.

Are not participant reports, like a description of being told that your child is autistic, composed in light of one's personality, vocabulary, interests, frame, and conceptual memory?

Yes. And yet we find that despite these limitations, reliance on verbal reports from different participants is nevertheless productive.

How do I explain to my chemist neighbor how a study with only half a dozen subjects can be scientific?

First, quickly but unapologetically acknowledge that such a study is not a science in the tradition of the natural sciences, but is a sister science, one whose methods have had to take into account that humans besides being physical and biological are at once conscious, unaware, meaning making, affective, future oriented, and so on. To grasp those aspects in their complex unity, our human–science accounts describe rather than measure. Tell your neighbor he or she will be relieved to know that we do not generalize from our small studies, but rather check against other studies, always revising the findings or qualifying the contexts in which they hold. You might explain further that, unlike statistical studies, the findings of qualitative studies must hold for all participants. Still further, you might explain that dealing rigorously with qualitative data developing careful but evocative descriptions is frustrating and demanding, and that one's personal acuity and descriptive skill are always subject to examination by colleagues, much more so than with categorical/statistical researchers.

Finally, you might say that your neighbor is right in that our small-scale, intense studies are more akin to the research of field journalists and cultural anthropologists. Still, we share with all science that our data are empirical and that they—our methods and procedures and findings—are subject to examination.

Why not make up a story that combines what participants have described or what you have observed, without the pretense of being scientific?

Some journalists do just that, explicitly, as composites, often very effectively. Psychologists who write self-help books often informally use a similar method. However, qualitative research is not scientific pretense, but rather the project of developing systematic methods and findings that help all of us to understand human experience, action, and options better.

With regard to presenting findings, what is the difference between representing and evoking?

Representing refers to characterizing the studied phenomenon, describing its necessary aspects, re-presenting them to readers vividly yet in terms of common features. *Evocation* refers to writing so that the findings become alive for the reader, in part reverberating with his or her own related experience. Representing and evoking are difficult tasks, but are regularly accomplished.

Many qualitative research reports are written in first person, saying "I" or "we" rather than "the investigators." Is there a reason for this?

Definitely. Qualitative researchers want to own that the work is done, inevitably, from their perspectives. Using first person pretty much says that. But in addition, the APA publication manual recommends writing in first person, in part to encourage active voice, which is briefer and more to the point than passive voice. "We did thus and so" is more direct than "Thus and so was carried out."

I can see the desirability of qualitative research, but why does it seem to ignore physiology?

Because physiologists have developed research methods that are appropriate to investigating humans' physiology; likewise, neurologists regarding our neurology, and so forth. Much qualitative research does include bodily experience. Still, the task of qualitative research is to access and describe human experience and perceptions in ways that are appropriate to the human order, rather in ways that were developed to explore the other orders of nature. In that advances are being made rapidly in both forms of science (human science and experimental science), with neither being as defensive as in the past, I imagine that an upsurge in integrative work is not far away.

There is so much diversity across these qualitative methods. Are there standard ways of categorizing them?

The major methods that have been established for several decades include grounded theory, ethnographical, empirical–phenomenological, and discourse analysis. As illustrated in this volume, there are many procedures that researchers have developed aside from these classic approaches, yet all share an interest in how people take up particular kinds of situations, both living and affecting them. Research examples are studies of how traumatized Iraq veterans take up civilian life, how severely retarded persons deal with being lost, and how twice-divorced persons regard nonsexual marital intimacy.

Today, as qualitative research is coming into its own in American universities, many researchers modify or combine published procedures to suit their subject matter best, and others develop their own procedures. Both approaches are illustrated in this volume's chapters. Although I imagine that other researchers might characterize contemporary qualitative research in different ways, I think of it as fitting with three broad enterprises:

1. *Ethnographical*—descriptions of a culture or subgroup through direct observation and interaction, either as a study in itself or as familiarization before conducting research within that culture or subgroup.
2. *First-person reports*—descriptive analyses of how people experience, constitute, and influence particular situations.
3. *Interactional*—descriptive analyses of dyadic, group, or cultural interactions that contribute to the participants' situation.

What I refer to as *interactional research* includes discourse analysis and the kind of action research that introduces changes in the participants' situation to see what difference that might make. An example could be how persons already in a treatment program take up changes in that program. Often these changes are introduced during ongoing program evaluation. Typically both experiential/phenomenal and behavioral data are obtained.

How does one get from data to understandings? I can see by quickly reviewing the chapters that authors describe procedures, but how does one use those procedures to interpret the data?

Experimental research from several perspectives seems to indicate that what we call *intuition* is rapid access to previous learning. I think that such learning includes bodily knowledge. Of course there is no manual to teach one how to form understanding, but I believe that the process is similar to those in everyday life when we understand a poem, respond to unspoken requests, and so on. In qualitative analysis, however, we must ultimately show in our data how another person could find the ground for our understandings.

Am I correct that there are very few reviews of qualitative psychological research on a single topic? Why is that so?

Yes, that observation is correct, largely because qualitative research, particularly within psychology, is still in its early stage. We have not yet accumulated many sizeable bodies of research in particular areas. A major exception is the programmatic qualitative research being conducted at Sheffield University in England, and in North America by Arthur Bohart at Saybrook Institute, Robert Elliot at Toledo University, Leslie Greenberg at York University, Larry Leitner at Miami University, David Rennie at York University, William Stiles at Miami University, and many others. These systematic studies also often use both statistical and qualitative methods.

However, most qualitative research is conducted as masters' theses, and doctoral dissertations students typically choose topics that are of idiosyncratic interest. Moreover, students often are under the misapprehension that they will contribute more by choosing a topic that has not already been researched qualitatively. Instead, students often would do better to choose a research topic in the same way others traditionally have chosen topics: reviewing literature in an area of interest to identify what is not yet understood and then design a study with a variation of focus or extend a study into broader groups of people or situations.

Once qualitative research has become better known through meaningful contributions, then governments and foundations will be willing to fund large-scale qualitative research. The time-intensive character of qualitative research makes it difficult for individuals to undertake such projects.

Is there some reason that there are no action research studies in this volume?

Well, I think that although they are not named as such, the chapters by Levers and by Morrow are indeed action research. In both we find examples of participants being affected by being participants, and there are clear policy and counseling implications of each study. Goicoechea's study is certainly action research in that it shows us the effects of using the DSM in one setting; implications are clear. I looked for a research project in which interventions were taken with the participants during the study (to research the effects of that action), but I did not find what I was looking for. Nevertheless, many of this book's chapters carry implications for social or professional practice.

Isn't all research time intensive?

Yes. Research reports of both traditional and qualitative research are deceptively streamlined. In actuality, studies do not proceed in a linear, clean-cut manner. Literature reviews are demanding, formulating and refining the research design require careful planning, negotiating with team members or faculty committees typically is more complicated than one anticipates, and meeting IRB requirements takes more preparation than one initially imagines. Much rethinking and accommodating occurs along the way: piloting and repiloting, finding more participants/subjects, revising in light of new literature, discovering that one has misunderstood an aspect of earlier literature, losing data or report text in computer mishaps, and so on. Developing "results and discussion" is not as linearly deductive as textbooks and research reports imply. Typically, much reflective meandering and muddling precedes the clarity of final reports.

Qualitative research is even more time intensive than traditional psychology research in that data cannot be mechanically processed by statistical programs. Instead, our data are texts that require reading and rereading and rereading, interpretation and reinterpretation, repetitive refinement and correction of understandings, documentation of one's reflective and reflexive steps, and creative storying of one's findings to best evoke the study's subject matter for readers. My dissertation, which included several experiments, was 60-some pages; dissertations in my department at Duquesne University typically run 400 to 600 pages.

Given the extra time intensity and personal involvement of qualitative research, why would one choose this approach over experimental study?

One certainly should not choose this approach to avoid having to learn traditional research design and statistical analysis! Both approaches are demanding, and both can be exciting and rewarding. One chooses a qualitative approach when it is the appropriate course—when the subject matter is uniquely human, involving people experiencing and behaving in accordance with their constructs of situations.

Is it a problem that descriptions obtained from participants in a particular setting will reflect the orientation of that setting? For example, if members of

a support group for pregnant teenagers are asked to write a description of feeling rejected by their parents, wouldn't certain staff jargon and group-think find their way into the descriptions?

Yes, inevitably we humans absorb our environments in various ways. And we express ourselves largely in learned ways. Sometimes researchers decide to select participants from a broad range of settings; other times researchers acknowledge whatever is known about how a particular context may have been taken up. What is striking, however, is that despite the inevitability of context, qualitative analysis leads to commonalities of experience beyond particular contexts.

Do requests for descriptions of particular phenomena, for example, awaiting biopsy results, or an incident of crying or of being jealous, result in extreme or exaggerated examples?

In my experience, surprisingly at first, that rarely happens. Participants typically become caught up in the task of recalling and conveying all the relevant detail of a particular example. Finding the essential commonalities across descriptions seems to obviate the potential problem.

If necessary themes or factors are identified, isn't that a deterministic explanation?

No, not if by "deterministic" you mean predetermined, independent of the participant's situation, perceptions, goals, and so on. The world can be understood as orderly; indeed, humans seek order. A full analytical description *accounts for* a phenomenon by saying what it is. But describing patterns of human "experi-action" does not imply that there are forces or other things that cause them. On the other hand, these statements do not deny that we are also affected by our learning history, genes, biological state, and so on, nor that we often are unaware of our full motives. The account, however, is in terms of the human realm, of a phenomenon as it is lived.

With regard to analyzing discursive data, how do I know when I've truly found a theme?

There is no single external standard like a statistical probability level to indicate when you are there. And there are no "the" themes to be discovered. Still, reading across data from participants, themes readily occur to you. Then you language (find expression for) each theme as faithfully to the data as you can. Develop language geared to that data rather than to theories and jargon. Check to be sure you can illustrate each theme with examples from every one of your participants. Along the way, you may discern subthemes or refine a theme in light of a subsequently named theme. At some point, you will know that although someone else might rename or otherwise amend your characterizations, you have presented a coherent grasp of your subject matter, one that describes what evolved as its essential

QUALITATIVE RESEARCH METHODS FOR PSYCHOLOGISTS

aspects and presents them holistically (in relation to each other). This task is not unlike undertaking to write an evocative description of Western Pennsylvania's late autumn trees as experienced driving along the turnpike, except that you're trying to describe your own perceptions, rather than what you find in other people's description of an event or situation. In either case, you know when you have evoked the essential features and their relations, even though you know that someone else might do so differently, and indeed that you might do so differently later yourself.

A related question: How do I know when I have adequately completed my analysis of data? It seems as though it could go on forever, like writing a perfect poem.

You are correct, in that our findings are always subject to revision, in that sense they are never finished. But just as you know when you have sincerely written an essay to your satisfaction (not perfect, but satisfying, and with no known deficits), so too you know when you have done your subject matter reasonable justice. That is, you have resolved apparent contradictions, accounted for all text in each participant's report, provided examples from each account for each component of your findings, have checked to see that your stated method matches what you wound up doing during analyses, have responded to colleagues' comments about fit of findings with data and about clarity of presentation, and have your own solid sense of the cohesiveness of your representation of your findings. An additional criterion for many researchers for having reached a "for now" stopping place is having systematically thought through the findings' implications for previous research and theory. Often we find that our data tell us still more as we reread with particular questions in mind.

In the 1960s the British pediatrician and psychoanalyst Donald Winnicott, especially in his radio program, reassured new mothers that trying to be a perfect parent often interfered with effective parenting. He spoke positively of "good enough" caretaking. Harper (2003) recommends a similar attitude, by the same term, with regard to discourse analysis, citing Scheper–Hughes' precedent with regard to ethnography.

Does the "good enough" criterion for regarding analysis as being completed, at least for now, apply to experimental research?

Yes, in a way. But please be clear that this term describes a principle more than a criterion, and that it is not demeaning as in the lightly derisive phrase "good enough for government standards." In traditional research, the principle holds more for research design than for analysis. All researchers wish they could include more participants/subjects, build in even more controls and contexts, include more variables that likely would be relevant to competing ways of understanding findings, and so on.

But practical issues such as cost, time, and other constraints require designs that are not comprehensive yet are expected to provide critical data. Unlike qualitative researchers, who seemingly can return endlessly to their data with each new insight to reflect on how their overall understanding is affected, there is a limited series of statistical procedures that categorical researchers can conduct to get the most from their measurements. For all research, a "good enough" closing of the research design and discussion of findings includes specification of limitations and suggestions for further research.

Some participant reports seem much richer than others and I find myself drawing from them more than from others. Is that okay?

Yes, of course, as long as you do not impose participant's experience on that of your other participants. Typically rich descriptions alert us to what then becomes plainly implicit in other accounts. Often one person's account includes a phrase or metaphor that wonderfully expresses what we have been trying to say.

Is it legitimate to make use of informal instances of one's topic rather than relying exclusively on data acquired from formal participants?

Sure. The researcher can use instances encountered in life, novels, and so on, for insight. And insight often arises when one is not directly studying reports—for example, a just-right phrase occurs while driving to work. A semiformal source of material for reflection: I advise students to acquire more reports than can be formally analyzed within their time constraints, and use them as "adjunctive reports." These can be read against emerging findings to check for inclusiveness. And as just mentioned, sometimes it is among the adjunctive reports that a particular phrase, sequence, or metaphor arises that seems to speak for all the reports. However, everything in the findings must be evident in all the formal reports.

I have read a lot about "bracketing" one's assumptions prior to data analysis—that is, putting them aside. Is that really possible?

Yes and no. Spelling out one's anticipations allows one to be surprised at and note exceptions. The practice helps us to avoid conscientiously using theoretical constructs as templates, and to attend to our data in their own right. However, our life experience and concerns also sensitize us to nuances in the data. Either way, we cannot totally set aside who we are as we go about our analyses.

We often discover our assumptions while struggling with data, sometimes tossing them aside to see better what is there without them. For example, in one phase of the Fischer and Wertz (1979) analysis of crime victims' accounts, we five researchers became aware that we had assumed that some crimes, like having one's home burgled, had more of an impact than kinds like kids letting the air out of one's car tires. Gradually the data taught us that we were wrong. On the other hand, it was only as I wrote a draft of one form of our findings that I realized that my background as a political science undergraduate major had come into play (I consistently characterized victims as "citizens"). We later agreed that my orientation helped us to attune to various aspects of the disrupted social order. But we also then revised some of my loaded language.

You speak of struggling. Some research reports make the process seem pretty straightforward, just following the described steps. Can you speak to that?

I think that all qualitative research involves a struggle to comprehend what else is being said within the data, and then to find ways that most faithfully, clearly, and holistically represent what we found across participants' descriptions. Sometimes I have thought that the struggle is similar to that of people in couples therapy, during which new understandings often are hard won and later undone and reexplored, when opinions are argued for beyond credibility and then give way to revised stances, when genuine progress is celebrated, when participants become more patient, when (after a while) implicit understandings are sufficient for some purposes, and when eventually the parties have resolved critical issues but are still open to further learning.

Yes, research reports typically present method as though it were a map, and then a description of the arrived-at destination, but they do not include an account of the ups and downs and arounds of the journey. The map shows what the essential steps were for the researchers, but not where they actually went. I encourage researchers to keep a record of incidents of getting lost, misstepping, and so on, to help readers to understand more of the journey in relation to the ending.

You mentioned "one form of findings." Can there be more than one form of findings?

Sure. Sometimes we write for different groups. In the victimization study we wrote forms that would best help legislators to see the significance of our findings, forms that were useful for victims and perpetrators, and forms that were meant mostly for researchers on victimization. For example, in one form we presented each main finding in bold print followed by illustrative quotations from multiple victims in another font. Some forms were more abstract than others. Individual accounts that preserved only what we had found to be essential across accounts are also a form of finding.

Each form spoke to different interests. From our perspective, there was no univocal truth about victimization, but rather a "palpable" order that we accessed and expressed in different ways, all the while being true to our victims' accounts.

There is so much attention in most qualitative research literature on documentation of steps, cross-referencing sources of ideas, and coding, but this volume does not seem to be overly concerned about those procedures. Why is that?

Coding can be essential to some studies, such as those on psychotherapy and discourse analysis. However, at this point in the development of qualitative methods I think that the proof is in the "convincingness" of the findings, rather than in proof through steps; the proof is in the pudding, not in proof that the recipe was followed. Much of our earlier emphasis on documenting the evolution of findings was defensive—proving to researchers who follow natural science methods that we were being empirical and rigorous. Those earlier efforts surely did help us to be systematic, which we continue to be. It remains important to record steps of analysis carefully so that another person can adopt your frame and pathways to see if similar findings would emerge. But extensive documentation for later readers to show how you personally came to your understandings no longer seems to be necessary.

Beyond whatever system you use to get your evolving understandings onto paper and indexed to your data, there *are* several areas to keep notes about: (1) questions, ideas, and so on to share with your advisor or co-researchers; (2) illustrations of how you carried out procedural steps; and (3) surprises, which you can use to illustrate how the data changed your initial impressions. It is important to record these surprises, discovered assumptions, and so on, because they quickly disappear as you become increasingly familiar with the data.

Some qualitative publications include measures of agreement among raters. Is that necessary?

When multiple researchers are involved, they usually develop conversational means of coming to agreement. However, when extended research involves qualitatively developed categories, researchers often use statistical measures of consistency to check on the clarity of their categories, and later to communicate with readers the levels of agreement for different terms. These measures often are used when tracking the outcomes of psychotherapy in light of various process aspects of the therapy. But I agree with your implication, that today we do not automatically seek rater agreement to prove to readers that a study is valid.

In my report of my study, should I disclose my personal history as part of my access to my study?

Usually, to some degree. However, I've seen too many vivid and dramatic accounts of one's own victimization, mental illness, and so on, usually in dissertations, that wind up detracting from the study. Find a balance between dramatic confession or announcement and hiding your involvement. It is appropriate to say explicitly that you have a longstanding personal interest in a topic that preceded your academic interest, or some such statement. The goals of sharing one's interest are to identify it as part of one's access to the subject matter, to remind one's self to check one's assumptions carefully, and to invite readers to wonder how your background might influence what you saw.

Are qualitative researchers required to retain and make available their data— the texts that they analyzed?

All researchers have an ethical obligation to make their data available for inspection by others. Like other researchers, qualitative researchers are inclined to want to retain their texts for their own later reinspection. At Duquesne University, our dissertation appendixes include the reports provided by all participants. Making texts available encourages collaboration among researchers.

Should there be a manual on how to be reflexive?

Not one like a manual on dance steps. I think there will be more material on training exercises through which people can learn to use themselves as part of the method—use themselves "awarefully" to understand possible meanings of text. In the meantime, the many excerpts illustrating research findings can serve as examples of how one can go from text to themes. Also see Finlay and Gough's (2003) collection of researchers' accounts of reflexivity in their research, and Wertz's (1985) description of how he analyzed a crime victim's report.

Positivism seems to be giving way to understanding knowledge as necessarily partially construed, indeed partially constructed, by scholars and researchers. Are there other epistemological shifts in the offing?

Despite significant shifts, positivism is still the stance taken by many experimental researchers even if that stance is mostly implicit. But I feel sure that other major shifts will occur after hermeneutic approaches are widely and explicitly practiced across most research, although I have no idea what those approaches would be. In the meantime, we have much to learn about reflexivity, insight, openness, and about expression of and integration of what they lead us to.

REFERENCES

Finlay, L., and B. Gough. (Eds.). (2003). *Reflexivity: A practical guide for researchers in health and social sciences*. Oxford: Blackwell.

Fischer, C. T., and F. J. Wertz. (1979). Empirical phenomenological analyses of being criminally victimized. In Giorgi, A., R. Knowles, and D. Smith. (Eds.). *Duquesne studies in phenomenological psychology* (vol. 3, pp. 135–158). Pittsburgh: Duquesne University Press. [Republished in 2002. Huberman, M., and M. B. Miles. (Eds.). (2002). *The qualitative researcher's companion* (pp. 275–304). Thousand Oaks: Sage.]

Harper, D. (2003). Developing a critically reflexive position using discourse analysis. In Finlay, L. and B. Gough (Eds.). *Reflexivity: A practical guide for researchers in health and social sciences* (pp. 78–92). Oxford: Blackwell.

Wertz, F. W. (1985). Method and findings in a phenomenological psychological study of a complex life-event: Being criminally victimized. In Giorgi, A. (Ed.). *Phenomenology and psychological research* (pp. 155–216). Pittsburgh: Duquesne University Press.

GLOSSARY

This list is not comprehensive, but it does include many specialized terms that often appear in discussions of qualitative research. Some of these terms do not occur in this volume, but the reader may encounter them while reading more broadly. Reading through this vocabulary may orient newcomers to a philosophical framework for qualitative research. Concepts are presented with their broadly accepted meanings and often pertain to all science, and then may be followed by meanings within a qualitative research framework. My background in empirical phenomenological research probably shows up; researchers from other qualitative orientations probably would make other distinctions here and there.

action research, (1) Research undertaken to assist in development of social policy; (2) qualitative research that is prepared to intervene during a study to explore the effect of that intervention. This occurs most often during the evaluation of social programs to determine whether a change in the program will result in a change in outcome.

actuality, A term I have used to emphasize that we behave and perceive in terms of personal and social reality; what is actual for us as we go about being *active* in our lives. The term contrasts with the notion of an independently existing reality that is posed by philosophical realism.

agency, The capacity to initiate action, exert power, have an effect; a characteristic of being human that has been side-stepped by traditional research, which has studied the determinants of behavior

alternative hypothesis, In experimental research design, a formal (testable or tested) hypothesis posed to check the researchers' hypothesis that the independent variables used in the research account for outcomes. That is, if the major hypotheses prove to be statistically significant, there is a tested or potential check of whether other variables might also account for the outcome. Qualitative researchers can similarly systematically ask themselves if different meanings might be found in their data, and if there are examples not in their data set that might modify their impressions. The latter query is called *imaginative variation* in phenomenological research.

authentic, (1) Trustworthy; presenting essential characteristics of a studied instance of an action/experience/ situation; in other words, faithful to an original instance of what is being studied; (2) true to one's experience, belief, or feeling

bracket, To identify, and attempt for the moment to put aside, one's assumptions about what one is researching to allow fresh perception; derived from Husserl's *epoché*. For psychologists, our bracketing is closer to Heidegger's hermeneutic instruction to come to know our grasp of subject matter so that we can continually revise that grasp in light of new instances and insights. We recognize that we could never totally suspend our assumptions or preunderstandings, and instead continually revise our understanding.

case study, A thorough study of a particular instance. In categorical research, the purpose is to explain its development or classify its parts. In qualitative research, the purpose is to understand the intrinsic aspects of what is studied. Both approaches to case study are either for treatment planning in clinical or educational settings, and/or to appreciate better other similar instances.

cause, An event or condition that invariably precedes another event or condition that is its effect. Today, experimental researchers usually look at patterns of events rather than addressing single causes. Qualitative researchers also generally look for patterns, but regard them holistically, rather than as patterns of independent variables.

comprehension, Depthful, inclusive (comprehensive) grasping of a subject matter's nature, significance, meaning. In qualitative research, the term highlights that research findings are not about a truth unrelated to the inquirer, but are inherently related to his or her active grasping and forming of the findings. The term also implies that the study's findings/descriptions hold together holistically.

constitute, To form, to compose, to be inherent to the being of something. *Constitutive* is the adjectival form.

constructivism, Contemporary notion that individuals and cultures contribute to what they see as real for them. Individuals construct personal meanings and options, in league with biological, physical, environmental, biographical, and cultural givens. We co-author our lives; we participate in what happens to us. Psychological theories and notions of science are also constructed, rather than discovered.

conversation analysis, Qualitative study of actual conversations to describe the ways in which order is achieved. Psathas (1995) recommends the more accurate term "analysis of talk-in-interaction."

correspondence theory, The philosophical position that research findings match an independently existing reality. Qualitative researchers of course require that their descriptive findings correspond with their data and with other available instances of the phenomenon, but they acknowledge that humans can understand events only in human, perspectival ways, that there is no way we can know what exists independent of our questions, interests, situations, and methods of study.

critique, (both a noun and verb) Especially in postmodern, human science contexts, a critique is likely to examine underlying assumptions and their impact. Although a critique probably will discern negative aspects, it is not synonymous with destructive criticism. Scholarly critique, in any context, reports both shortcomings and contributions of the examined practice or document.

data, Material serving as the basis of analysis. The term is plural when referring to multiple instances of information, and singular when referring to a single piece of information or to information in general (in Latin, *datum*). In psychology research, the term is usually plural. In Latin, *data* refers to *something given*. But in qualitative research, it is more appropriate to think of data as what we *take* from our area of interest to study, shaping it in that taking. This latter point also holds with regard to our term, *findings*. Qualitative researchers often refer to data as "text" in that it typically is in the form of verbal descriptions or records.

deconstruction, Examination of how something has been constructed, especially social conventions and ideological constructs. (1) When identified with the philosopher Jacques Derrida, deconstruction claims that languaged interpretation is a system in which signs refer to other signs and never to something in itself. Hence the characterization of deconstructionism as only offering negative critiques and claiming that everything is only relative. (2) In more popular usage, deconstruction often refers only to examining the assumptions, historical context, and power interests that led to social institutions and practices. Examples include the philosopher/historian Jacque Foucault's analyses of sexuality and psychiatrist Thomas Szasz's analyses of "mental illness."

In this usage, analyses can be followed by efforts to construct alternatives.

discourse, (1) Formal expression of thought on a subject; (2) discussion among practitioners or scholars sharing an interest. *Conversation* usually is regarded as a less formal or specialized verbal exchange on social topics.

discourse analysis, Coding of discourse in terms of speech, language, and behavior, and subsequent identification of interactive patterns of establishing and/or maintaining influence and status

discursive, Proceeding via discussion and argument; often intended as in contrast to statistical reasoning or categorical placement

dualism, (1) Belief that mind and matter are totally separate but can interact; a position typically associated with René Descartes (d. 1650). Some contemporary psychologists do view all psychological matters as a function of biological processes, but many view psychological matters as being at-once physical, neurobiological, cognitive, affective, and behavioral. (2) Belief that humans and reality are separate, that reality is separate from our ways of knowing it.

empirical, Based on direct, first-hand observation of data available to other observers. The term came into being to contrast with reflection based on philosophy, imagination, introspection, and so on. Note that contrary to popular usage within psychology based on the natural sciences, experimentation is not the only means of being empirical.

epistemology, An area of philosophy that investigates the nature, grounds, and limits of human knowledge. Mainstream psychology for the most part has ignored philosophical matters and has assumed that measurability is adequate grounds for knowledge. (And if something can't be measured, it doesn't "count" as psychology!)

ethnography, Originally a branch of anthropology having to do with systematic observation and description of cultures. Today many qualitative researchers from many disciplines practice ethnography either to become familiar with a setting prior to researching some aspect within it, or to study interactions within a particular group or setting (e.g., subway culture or fourth grade playground culture).

experiaction, A term crafted by Rolf Von Eckartsberg (1971) to note that experience and behavior are not separate; we experience as we act and may act as we experience

explication, A spelling out of implications; here, of qualitative research findings

generalize, To claim that findings apply to situations or samples other than those researched. Both experimental and qualitative researchers assume that their findings will be useful in broader samples than those studied. But qualitative researchers typically do not set generalizability as a goal of a study, partly because we work with such small samples, and we anticipate that humans' perception and action will transform at least somewhat with their situations. Knowing that we cannot control the way humans might take up meanings on other occasions, we speak less of generalizability and more of identifying variations in our findings depending on participants' circumstances. Qualitative researchers, however, report findings that hold for all their participants, rather than relying on statistical significance. For both research approaches, sturdiness of findings across sampling is an empirical matter.

grounded theory, One of the earliest and most practiced approaches to qualitative research. Researchers *grounded* themselves in the everyday life world to study a real-life topic, like being bullied in school. Using a detailed system for recording and coding data from several sources, they looked for a core component in the data around which a data-based theory could be described. Grounded theory's enduring success is at least partially related to its disciplined documentation of the sources for all insights, and its inclusion of at least one mainstream instrument that produced statistics—the language understood by mainstream psychologists.

hegemony, (pronounced he-**jem**-oh-nee) The state of a particular theory or philosophy having ruling authority, dominating all others. In North American psychology, positivism's early hegemony is still evident in most university departments, journals, and grant agencies. However, human–science and humanistic psychology, constructivism, collaborative psychological assessment practices, and qualitative research are now well represented in many mainstream settings and publications, and have their own journals and books.

hermeneutics, An ancient and contemporary tradition of interpreting the meaning of a text, particularly exploring its relevance for current times or interests. This interpretation has never been a mechanical translating from one to language into another. Historically the text was one of class proportion, such as the Bible or Shakespeare's plays, or, later, Freud's works. Today, texts can be any recordings of events—photographs, conversation, newspaper accounts, or descriptions of an event written for researchers. Hermeneutic readings in the social sciences usually are for the purpose of identifying essential, invariant aspects of a phenomenon—that is, aspects without which it would not be that phenomenon. Hermeneutic readers self-consciously try to put aside their assumptions beforehand, and when they are discovered while reading a text, so as to read freshly. But they acknowledge that language, culture, history, and personal interest are all nevertheless part of reading any text. Most hermeneutic interpretation involves the "hermeneutic circle": continuous reformulating of a general grasp of a text in light of each evolving understanding of some aspect of the text, as well reformulating each aspect in light of the evolving general comprehension, and each aspect in light of reunderstood aspects. The "circle" is not so much circular, however, as flowing, diverting, rejoining—a process we all have engaged in when trying to comprehend complex subject matter.

holistic, (adjective) Attitude toward humans that they are more than the sum of their parts, that the entire person should be addressed as a whole, rather than being described or treated in terms of one aspect or even several aspects. Some social scientists include situations as lived by a person in a holistic view. See *structure*. Humanistic psychology has argued most strongly for this position.

In biology, *vitalism* is a similar notion that life is not totally explained by physics and chemistry, that it is partially self-determining.

humanistic psychology, Part of the 1960s "third force" movement in North America, that together with existentialism and phenomenology offered an alternative to the first two "forces"—psychoanalysis and behaviorism. Not directly related to Renaissance humanism, although it shares with it concern for well-being, values, and dignity. It has emphasized the person (the human), and aspects of being human that have been bypassed by positivistic psychology, such as spirituality, agency, responsibility, existential meaning, and positive personal and social growth. Likewise, humanistic psychology has challenged psychology's medical model emphasis on disease and deficit to include attention to positive, constructive, healthy aspects of being human.

human–science psychology, An approach to psychological matters that takes into account that humans are more than objects of nature. Beyond being material beings, we are conscious, reflexive, spiritual, and so on. Hence, human–science psychology, along with similar disciplines, has developed research and practice methods and philosophical foundations that are appropriate for people and that can seek to understand human phenomena that often are excluded by natural science psychology. Human–science psychology of course acknowledges that humans are also physical and biological, and that natural science methods are appropriate for studying those aspects. This human-oriented approach is appreciative of statistical methods that can accommodate massive data, and physical and biological data. The term *human science* was proposed by philosopher Wilhem Dilthey in the 19th century in Germany to argue against psychology exclusively adopting the methods of the emerging natural sciences. He argued for developing a discipline to *understand* psychological phenomena rather than only to *explain* them. Amedeo Giorgi initiated a phenomenologically grounded human–science psychology in the United States.

inscribe, To mark or impress deeply and enduringly in individuals' and cultures' memory, practices, and/or in ongoing meaning, often without explicit intention

interpretation, (1) a translation, an explanation; (2) within the context of qualitative research, a presentation of a grasping or construal of psychological meaning; a representation of that descriptive grasp; not an explanation in terms of causes or a translation into a preexisting theory

IRB, Institutional review board. In the United States, a board required by federal mandate to review all research proposals involving human subjects. The goal is to protect subjects' well-being, in part by protecting confidentiality and ensuring informed consent. "Institutions" include any bodies such as universities or agencies that receive federal funds. Typically, the different components of an institution, such as School of Education, College of Liberal Arts, and so on, appoint representatives to the board.

iterative, An adjective referring to revising findings systematically in light of going through a research step yet again. Each revised version is referred to as an *iteration*. Iterative analysis is closely related to hermeneutic interpretation. [Do not confuse with the word "reiterate," which simply means to say the same thing again.]

lived, Experienced, taken up in our (usually daily) lives, as in "lived body," "lived world," "lived context." Describable through reflexivity and reflection (see definitions). Necessarily holistic. Not accessible via experimental methods, which must name parts of the lived phenomenon and manipulate or measure them, thereby losing their lived character.

local, Refers to the particular research locale, participants, and context, usually to emphasize that findings apply to that community and are not necessarily generalizable. This emphasis on the specific participants and their context also bypasses a search for universal underlying causes, attending instead to interaction in its own right. Within qualitative research this distinction is not meant as a criticism but rather to emphasize that qualitative research typically addresses lived meaning—how people take up and deal with events in their ongoing lives—and those meanings vary with circumstances. For both experimental and qualitative research, how common the findings are is an empirical matter to be determined by further study. For both approaches, further study refines, corrects, confirms, and identifies variations.

materialism, Philosophical position that matter is the ultimate reality. Although scholars seem not to take this position explicitly today, some seem to do so implicitly by holding that only measurable "things" are real or valid (if you cannot count it, it does not count).

meaning, The significance drawn from data; what the researcher conveys, shows, or indicates that data imply. For qualitative research, most often the meaning is in terms of the life world—the lived world of individuals or communities—or in terms of patterns of people negotiating meanings through speech and action.

meaning unit, A segment of data (text, protocol) that the researcher has marked as a unit for study, usually because the preceding and following text seem to address something with different significance. Most researchers find that they cannot deal with an entire text as a whole and still bear in mind all of its segments. Marking off segments allows the researcher to return to each unit to check for its inclusion in the interpretive presentation. Different researchers will choose to mark off different segments; there is no *the* correct way to demarcate; the purpose is to chunk text into workable units for the particular researcher.

ontology, Within philosophy, a division of metaphysics, that addresses the fundamental nature of reality, generally in terms of cosmology (the nature of the universe), ontology, and epistemology. Ontology addresses the nature of what exists, of being and of beings. For example, are humans totally and exclusively material? Do they function according to a God's plan? Are they conscious or is consciousness just a shadow (epiphenomenon) of extraneously caused action?

operationalism, Defining variables according to the procedures used to distinguish them in research or test construction; sometimes referred to as *procedural definition.* For example, "hunger" in laboratory mice might be defined in terms of hours since they were last fed. Slippage can occur when we regard the variable as being real in nature, as when IQ scores are seen as measures of "natural intelligence" rather than as of a theoretical (and very useful) construct.

paradigm, A philosophical framework, both explicit and implicit, within which a discipline develops theories, undertakes research, and teaches. Some philosophers of science argue that paradigms do not respond to confrontation with counter paradigms, but rather a differing paradigm emerges as dominant as the times change and younger professionals make their contributions. The dominant research paradigm in North American psychology is that of 19th century natural science and 20th century positivism.

participants, (1) All the persons who are involved in a research project, including researchers, assistants, and people providing data; (2) the term that the APA's publication manual uses to designate the persons who are being studied or who provide descriptions for our analysis. The term was meant to acknowledge that human subjects are more than merely objects. The manual reserves the earlier term "subject" for animals that are subjected to our treatment and measurement but presumably do not participate. The APA usage is ironic in that our traditional research methods do not take into account participants' more-than-object character. Especially with regard to qualitative research, I regard the persons providing our data, who we also sometimes refer to as *respondents*, as being subjects with perspectives and who initiate action (as in the subject of a sentence who acts on an object of the sentence). Canadian psychologists generally follow APA's style manual, but the United Kingdom continues to refer to humans as subjects.

perform, To accomplish, to bring to completion, to act a part; often in postmodern contexts, to bring into being and to act out one's self

phenomenology, (1) The study of (ology) phenomena (things as they appear, in contrast to noumena—things in themselves). The generally recognized founder, the philosopher Edmund Husserl (d. 1938), was interested in studying human consciousness to learn how we constitute what appears within consciousness. Phenomenological psychology in research contexts is referred to as existential or empirical phenomenology to differentiate it from the philosophy on which it is based. Phenomenological psychology studies particular phenomena to describe their essential aspects in their interrelation (the structural whole). Note: Phenomen*a* is plural; phenomen*on* is singular. (2) In the United States, in mainstream psychological contexts *phenomenological* simply means "having to do with experience." This usage is more akin to the formal term, *phenomenal*, which refers to lived experience without systematic study of it. Sometimes loosely used to refer to "the world of," as in "the world of the quarterback." (3) In medical literature, the external appearance of a disease in contrast to its etiology

philosophy, (1) The basic concepts and principles of a branch of knowledge, and their continuous reflective study with the goal of revision or extension; (2) the use of any of the branches of philosophy (metaphysics, logic, ontology, aesthetics, ethics, epistemology) in examining a discipline's content

positive psychology, A 21st century call for psychology to shift from an emphasis on pathologies and their causes to include the study of and promotion of positive experience, well-being, strengths, and virtues. Historically associated with humanistic psychology, and recently championed by Martin Seligman, first in his presidential address to the APA. (The term is unrelated to *positivism*.)

positivism, A 19th century attitude that full assurance and confidence (being positive, assured) could be placed in sensory (positive) data, especially in contrast to metaphysical or theological philosophy. *Logical positivism*, also known as *logical empiricism*, is a 20th century formulation that added formal logic to positivism's emphasis on directly observable data as the indispensable, essential features of science. Nonpositivistic approaches work with empirical data but also respect reflection, experience, and other nonphysical data. Although not often taught as the explicit philosophy underlying psychology as we enter the 21st century, it remains the foundation of experimental psychology. It is not related to contemporary positive psychology, which emphasizes growth and well-being.

postmodern, The worldview following the modern (20th century) view, which grew out of an 18th century enlightenment view that celebrated rationality. The so-called modern view celebrated rationality, productivity, and functionality, all served by a belief in our ability through science to access and manipulate a world whose basic nature was directly knowable through objective observation. Modernism was practiced on a large scale, producing sleek buildings, airplanes, and research programs. The postmodern period, in which psychology lags behind architecture, literature, and various other fields, is said to thrive in the last quarter of the 20th century and into the present. The postmodern approach acknowledges the achievements of rationalism and of traditional science, but also acknowledges that history, culture, and values inevitably are part of our efforts to make sense of our world. Humans can only comprehend in human ways, and must comprehend to be in touch with their particular worlds; hence, our understandings are always "local," in terms of our own situations. Qualitative research efforts grew within many disciplines and from various philosophical starting points, but generally within a postmodern perspective. (Note the irrationality of the term *postmodern*. In a literal sense, "modern" means contemporary, and we cannot in the present be past the contemporary. The apparent confusion disappears when we think of the particular 20th century period that we refer to as "modern.")

poststructural, Character of approaches to meaning that reject the structuralist position that there are invariant patterns and specific, clear meanings and independent laws governing social matters. Poststructuralists put the person back into study by including how people co-constitute their situations. *Poststructural* is a philosophical stance, whereas *postmodern* is a larger cultural movement, in which architecture, literature, and other fields participate.

privilege, (verb) To grant special status and rights to a group

protocol, A record of behavior or a self-report that has not been interpreted. Examples include a filmed interaction of children playing a game, and a written description by a research subject of a particular situation he or she has lived through. In other words, the data that we analyze. I prefer to speak of "data analysis," rather than of "protocol analysis," because some psychologists confuse the latter term with analysis in accordance with a particular protocol—rules for etiquette, or details of a treatment or experimental procedure.

psychology, (1) Historically and etymologically, the study of the psyche—soul or mind, (2) in the heyday of behaviorism and logical positivism, the prediction and control of behavior; (3) in the last three or so decades, the study of mental states and processes as well as of behavior, and the professional practices based on that study; (4) increasingly, also the study of and applied use of persons' lived situations and worlds.

qualiquantive, Transformation of response data, usually from interviews or questionnaires, into measurements. I coined this term to emphasize that these transformations have moved from potential for qualitative inquiry into being quantitative. That transformation may well be worthwhile, but it has lost its claim to being qualitative.

qualitative psychological research, Empirical research that investigates the quality—the distinctive, essential characteristics—of experience and action as lived by persons. Its findings are narrative descriptions, rather than experimentally and/or mathematically derived statements of causality or quantitative relationship. The latter research is appropriate for exploring aspects of human life that are directly related to our biological, neurological, physical nature, and to efforts to gather and evaluate massive categorical data.

qualitative research, A reflective, interpretive, descriptive, and usually reflexive effort to *understand and describe* actual instances of human action and experience from the perspective of the participants' living of a situation. Some qualitative research seeks to identify and describe people's interactive ways of gaining or maintaining influence. The term *qualitative* came into general use to contrast this research endeavor to the long-established quantitative methods that psychology adapted from the natural sciences. Indeed, qualitative research is intended to study human events in terms of how they are lived, which is not possible via experimental methods alone. Both endeavors are empirical in that observable events or reports serve as data (which qualitative researchers sometimes call *text*), and interested persons can read the steps that were taken to come to the study's findings and try them out for themselves. There are many, usually overlapping, approaches and procedures that are used in qualitative research, as illustrated in this volume.

realism, The notion that objects or relations that we perceive are independent of us, that perceiving is unrelated to culture, history, context, or the nature of human consciousness. Measurement and statistical analysis traditionally have been regarded as pure ways of accessing this presumably universal and independent

reality. Contrast this notion to those of *postmodern and relational* understandings of knowledge.

reflection, Careful, calm thinking; cognitive reconsideration

reflexivity, Turning back on one's self; critically viewing one's own part in coming to an understanding or in having taken an action. A form of circumspection but often including an affective aspect rather than purely cognitive introspection or rational reflection. (Do not confuse with another meaning of *reflexive*—to react habitually or without thinking.)

relational knowledge, Understandings that acknowledge that humans are not just objects whose actions are determined by external factors, but rather always perceive, experience, understand, and act in terms of their goals, history, values, situation, and so on. In other words, humans cannot *not* relate to the world, and do so through its perceived implications for their situations.

representation, Portrayal of meanings found in research participants' accounts or actions; an effort to re-present for others the essential aspects of those reports or actions; researchers' efforts to give authentic voice to their findings

research, Systematic investigation, involving searching and re-searching; collecting and interpreting information to develop understandings, theories, and applications

research design, Planning how a research project will be carried out; design includes selection of subjects/participants, specifying procedures (means of developing and analyzing data), and of optimizing the chances that the data and analysis will provide meaningful answers to the researchers' questions (and similarly will best contribute to evolving knowledge). In experimental research, design includes ensuring that there will be adequate entries for productive statistical analysis. In qualitative research, design includes taking care to ensure that findings are particular to the phenomenon being studied.

rigor, Conducting research with strict adherence to specified procedures, including careful reflection on the impact of those procedures while following them; also, systematically checking the presentation of conclusions/interpretations for fit with the data; the opposite of being facile, lax, or complacent in carrying out research. (The term does not carry the meaning that can apply in other contexts—inflexibility or precise even when data do not justify precision.)

science, Systematic methods of developing knowledge or understandings based on collection and analysis of direct observations (empirical data). Replications of procedures and findings by additional research projects, along with variations, build a body of knowledge or understanding for a discipline. Natural science stresses specialized knowledge; human science stresses understandings.

serendipity, The circumstance of making accidental discoveries, often while trying to get somewhere else. B. F. Skinner (d. 1990) in particular wrote about the importance of serendipitous findings, which gave them credibility despite their not being part of the prevailing logical/deductive paradigm for psychology.

standpoint, The place the researcher is standing to gather and comprehend persons' experience/action/reports.

The term was introduced by feminist psychology qualitative researchers, who spelled out their practices that differed from mainstream psychology research, which had been presumed to be value free. Standpoint research explicitly owns the researchers' personal history with a topic and their concern for women's situations. Standpoint research typically has practiced most consistently the principle that qualitative researchers should specify their initial assumptions, modifications in assumptions made in the face of data, and confirmed assumptions.

structuralism, (1) Historically, a psychological school of thought that analyzed mental contents into elementary constituents via both introspection and experiment. Historically, German functional psychology provided an alternative school, analyzing mental processes rather than content. In the United States, functional psychologists were interested in the usefulness (functions) of these processes. These historical undertakings are not generally alluded to in contemporary literature. (2) A contemporary social science approach in which a phenomenon is understood in terms of the overall structures it is part of—political, cultural, economic, and so on, and in which basic structures underlying external phenomena are studied. The French linguist Ferdinand de Saussure (early 20th century) regarded words as having been given meaning only through interactions within the overall structure of a language. The social anthropologist Claude Lévi–Strauss later outlined the ways society reflects underlying systems (structures) of language that determine social behavior.

The French social and literary critic Roland Barthes in the latter part of the 20th century regarded the meaning of any text as determined by the interactions of its signs; external reference played no role. See *poststrucural*.

structure, Especially for empirical phenomenological research, all the identified aspects (sometimes called constituents) of an experience, action, or situation (all of which imply one another) that are presented in relation to one another. In that all aspects are essential for the phenomenon to be what it is, no aspect is more core, critical, or essential than the others to comprehending the phenomenon. However, a particular aspect may be a practical key for accessing a relation to another phenomenon or for arguing for changing social policy, and so on. A structural description or account is a relational comprehension rather than one that explains particular aspects as functions of other "determinants." A structural description is written in narrative form and could be composed in many ways by different authors. This notion of structure should not be confused with physical structures, like molecular models, or the steel girders that serve as the skeleton of a building. Nor should it be confused with structuralism.

subject, In earlier usage, the person or animal that is the source of data in an experiment. Now in accordance with the APA's style manual, this term is reserved for animals, and the term *participant* is used for human sources of data. (See discussion of *participant*, and *subjective*.)

subjective, (1) Within psychology's natural science tradition, an unwanted intrusion of personal bias that compromises the validity of findings; (2) within a human science tradition, the involvement of the stance of humans, which necessarily includes our subject nature—beings who experience, are conscious, plan, react, are always in lived contexts, and so on; in short, our subjectivity. Qualitative researchers study our subjective experience via our own subjectivity, but like all scientists eschew personal bias.

text, A written record that is examined, interpreted, explicated, or deconstructed. Typically the data of qualitative research are texts in this sense, but texts may also be film, international events, and so on. Still, when research is empirical, a record for others to examine is provided.

theory, A system of underlying psychological principles said to account for behavior or experience. Some features usually have been verified via empirical demonstration of some relationships posited by the theory. Theory both guides and is revised by study.

thick description, Descriptions that richly include experience prior to theorizing. The sociologist Clifford Geertz contributed this term in the 1970s, emphasizing the complexity and depth of description that includes contextual touch points.

triangulation, The research practice of gathering multiple kinds of data within one study. For example, a study might include descriptions from high school students of being bullied, an ethnographic summary of the school's atmosphere, and personality tests of bullied students. This practice was first named by researchers conducting grounded theory studies, which typically included three kinds of data (hence *tri*). (There is no relationship between this term and the one identifying a pattern of one person socially setting two others against each other.)

truth, Accuracy, factualness, honesty. When spelled with a capital T, *Truth,* the implication is that a claim is made as to facts about real things and events, independent of an observer.

validity, Traditionally, the successful measurement by an instrument of what it was intended to measure. Validity has been determined by significant statistical relation to another instrument, for example, another psychological test of intelligence. For qualitative research, validity refers to the fit between a descriptive representation and instances of what was described. For example, does an overall description of reports on being criminally victimized fit victims' reports? The fit is not determined by statistical significance, but by reader agreement, which occurs not just intellectually but through resonance with readers' impressions of full texts or illustrations (as well as with any personal experience with the topic being studied). Just as traditional validity is an empirical matter of degree, so also readers of qualitative findings may include suggestions for more felicitous wording, refining characterizations of the participants' or researchers' contexts, and the like. For all approaches to research, even better fit between findings and life (validity) develops with refinements in continued studies.

warrant, Assurance of the reliability and authenticity of research findings; may include vetting (reviewing and approving) by providers of data (participants), and by extended samples, colleagues, and other readers; also a verb: the acts taken to ensure reliability and authenticity.

REFERENCES

Psathas, G. (1995). *Conversation analysis: The study of talk-in-interaction.* Thousand Oaks, CA: Sage.

Von Eckartsberg, R. (1971). On experiential methodology. In Giorgi, A., W. F. Fischer, and R. Von Eckartsberg. (Eds.). *Duquesne studies in phenomenological psychology* (pp. 66–79). Pittsburgh: Duquesne University Press.

INDEX